NOTES AND INDEX

NOTES AND INDEX

TO
SIR HERBERT GRIERSON'S
EDITION OF THE LETTERS
OF SIR WALTER SCOTT

BY

JAMES C. CORSON
Honorary Librarian of Abbotsford

OXFORD
AT THE CLARENDON PRESS
1979

Oxford University Press, Walton Street, Oxford OX2 6DP

OXFORD LONDON GLASGOW
NEW YORK TORONTO MELBOURNE WELLINGTON
KUALA LUMPUR SINGAPORE JAKARTA HONG KONG TOKYO
DELHI BOMBAY CALCUTTA MADRAS KARACHI
NAIROBI DAR ES SALAAM CAPE TOWN

Published in the United States by
Oxford University Press, New York

© *Oxford University Press 1979*

British Library Cataloguing in Publication Data
Scott, *Sir* Walter, *bart*
  The letters of Sir Walter Scott
  Notes and index
  I. Corson, James C II. Grierson, *Sir* Herbert
  826'.7 PR5334 77–30289
  ISBN 0–19–812718–9

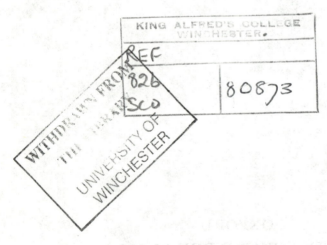
Printed in Great Britain
at the University Press, Oxford
by Eric Buckley
Printer to the University

To
Patricia Maxwell-Scott
of Abbotsford
and her sister Jean
great-great-great-granddaughters
of
Sir Walter Scott

PREFACE

SIR HERBERT GRIERSON's edition of the letters of Sir Walter Scott, though published over forty years ago, still remains the standard work on the subject and is not likely to be superseded for many years to come. It is hoped that the present work, however inadequate, will fill a long-felt need for an index without which the value of Grierson's edition has been greatly impaired.

It was my original intention to compile an index only but it was found that no index could be satisfactory until the parent work had been re-edited. Thus the present work is in two parts: firstly, a section consisting of notes correcting and supplementing Grierson's annotations; and, secondly, a very full index which is not merely a finding list but is so minutely detailed and arranged as to form an epitome of the whole work, with thumb-nail biographies of the persons mentioned. It has not been found possible to identify all the minor persons or supply the biographical details which might be expected. I should be grateful to readers with special knowledge of any of these persons if they would assist in correcting my errors of omission and commission.

Although I have been given the exclusive right to print and publish Scott's letters from the original unpublished manuscripts, I have made no attempt, apart from a few exceptional cases, to correct Grierson's text. This must be left for a new and complete edition. Meanwhile the National Library of Scotland has undertaken a Survey of the letters of Sir Walter Scott, scattered throughout the world, under the charge of Mr Alan Bell, Assistant Keeper of Manuscripts. It is to be hoped that this Survey will eventually form the basis of a new edition.

My grateful thanks are due, in the first place, to the public spirit of the Oxford University Press for undertaking the publication of this work; and to the British Academy for a very generous grant towards the cost of production. To Mr W. E. K. Anderson, Headmaster of Shrewsbury School and editor of the definitive edition of Scott's *Journal*, I am under many obligations. He not only encouraged me in my labours but also paved the way towards publication and undertook the exacting task of reading the proofs. Edinburgh University Court granted leave of absence to Miss Jean R. Guild of the University Library to consult manuscripts in the National Library of Scotland. The information she collected was of great value to me. For this and for other help rendered over many years I am deeply indebted to her. It is also a pleasant duty to record my thanks to Mr Alan Bell, already mentioned, for answering innumerable queries put to him. He had the uncanny knack of always giving me the exact information I required although my questions might not always be clearly expressed. For permission to quote from the manuscript diary of John Smith (whose firm built large portions of Abbotsford) I am indebted to the owner of the copyright, Mr Gordon M. L. Smith, his great-grandson, of Diss, Norfolk.

J. C. C.

December 1978

CONTENTS

CONTRACTIONS

(a) GENERAL

In the Notes (but not in the Index) '*SL*' is used as an abbreviation for 'Scott letters', i.e. Grierson's edition. In the Index (but not in the Notes) 'S.' is used for 'Sir Walter Scott'. The only others which may not be self-explanatory are:

NLS: National Library of Scotland

W.S.: Writer to the Signet (that is, the highest class of solicitor in Scotland)

(b) WORKS CITED

ALC: Catalogue of the Library at Abbotsford. [By George Huntly Gordon. Bannatyne and Maitland Clubs.] Edinburgh [and Glasgow], 1838.

Anderson, *Silences*: Silences that speak; records of Edinburgh's ancient churches and burial grounds . . . By William Pitcairn Anderson. Edinburgh, 1931.

Ann. Reg.: The annual register . . . of 1758 (–) London, 1762–

Archibald Constable: Archibald Constable and his literary correspondents. A memorial by his son Thomas Constable. 3 vols. Edinburgh, 1873.

Bibl.: A bibliography of Sir Walter Scott . . . 1797–1940. By James C. Corson. Edinburgh, 1943. (Repr. New York, 1968.)

Blackwood: Blackwood's Edinburgh Magazine. Vol. 1– Edinburgh, 1817–

Brown: The epitaphs and monumental inscriptions in Greyfriars churchyard, Edinburgh. By James Brown. Edinburgh, 1867.

Buchan, *Peeblesshire*: A history of Peeblesshire. Ed. by James Walter Buchan (and Henry Paton). 3 vols. Glasgow, 1925–7.

Burke: A general and heraldic dictionary of the peerage and baronetage of the United Kingdom. By John Burke [and, later, Sir John Bernard Burke and others]. London. Various eds.

Burke LG: A genealogical and heraldic dictionary of the landed gentry of Great Britain & Ireland. By Sir J. Bernard Burke. London. Various eds.

Chisholm: Sir Walter Scott as a judge; his decisions in the Sheriff Court of Selkirk. By John Chisholm. Edinburgh, 1918.

Clan Donald: The clan Donald. By Angus J. Macdonald and A. Macdonald. 3 vols. Inverness, 1896–1904.

DAB: Dictionary of American biography . . . Ed. by Allen Johnson. 23 vols. London and New York [1929–73].

Dibdin, *Annals*: The annals of the Edinburgh stage. By James C. Dibdin. Edinburgh, 1888.

DNB: Dictionary of national biography. [Ed. by Sir Leslie Stephen and others.] 63 vols. London, 1885–1900. And reissues.

Edin. Ann. Reg.: The Edinburgh Annual Register for 1808(–25). 18 vols. (in 23). Edinburgh, 1810–27.

ER: The Edinburgh Review. Vol. 1– Edinburgh, 1803–

Fasti: Fasti ecclesiæ Scoticanæ: the succession of ministers in the Church of Scotland from the Reformation. By Hew Scott. New ed. 7 vols. Edinburgh, 1915–28.

FL: Familiar letters of Sir Walter Scott. [Ed. by David Douglas.] 2 vols. Edinburgh, 1894.

GEC: The complete peerage of England, Scotland, Ireland, Great Britain and the United Kingdom, extant, extinct or dormant. By G. E. C[ockayne]. New ed. . . . by Vicary Gibbs. 13 vols. London, 1910–59.

GEC Baronetage: Complete baronetage. Ed. by G. E. C[ockayne]. 5 vols. (and index). Exeter, 1900–9.

Grant: The Faculty of Advocates in Scotland, 1532–1943 . . . Ed. by Sir Francis J. Grant. [Scottish Record Soc.] Edinburgh, 1944.

Grove: Grove's dictionary of music and musicians. [By Sir George Grove.] 5th ed., ed. by Eric Blom. 9 vols. (and supplementary vol.). London, 1954–61.

Heber letters: The Heber letters, 1783–1832. [Ed. by] R. H. Cholmondeley. London, 1950.

Herd: Ancient and modern Scottish songs. . . Collected [by David Herd] from memory, tradition and ancient authors. 2nd ed. 2 vols. Edinburgh, 1776.

Heywood: The proverbs of John Heywood . . . 1546. Ed. with notes and introduction by Julian Sharman. London, 1874.

Hogg, *Jacobite relics*: The Jacobite relics of Scotland; being the songs, airs and legends . . . Collected . . . by James Hogg. 2 ser. Edinburgh, 1819–21.

Hughes, *Letters*: Letters and recollections of Sir Walter Scott. By Mrs. Hughes (of Uffington). Ed. by Horace G. Hutchinson. London, 1904.

Johnson: The Scots musical museum . . . Consisting of six hundred Scots songs . . . by James Johnson. 6 vols. Edinburgh, (1787–1803.) New ed. by William Stenhouse. 4 vols. Edinburgh, 1853.

Journal: The journal of Sir Walter Scott. Ed. by W. E. K. Anderson. Oxford, 1972.

K. S. M. Scott: Scott, 1118–1923; being a collection of "Scott" pedigrees . . . Compiled and arranged by Keith S. M. Scott. London, 1923.

Kelly: A complete collection of Scotish proverbs . . . By James Kelly. London, 1721.

L'Estrange, *Fables*: Fables of Æsop and other eminent mythologists . . . By Sir Roger L'Estrange. 2nd ed. London, 1694.

Letters to their old governess: Letters, hitherto unpublished, written by members of Sir Walter Scott's family to their old governess [Margaret Millar]. Ed. . . . by the Warden of Wadham College, Oxford [Patrick A. Wright-Henderson]. London, 1905.

Lockhart: Memoirs of the life of Sir Walter Scott, Bart. [Preface signed by J. G. Lockhart.] 2nd ed. 10 vols. Edinburgh, 1839.

Macintosh, *Gaelic proverbs*: Macintosh's collection of Gaelic proverbs, and familiar phrases; Englished a-new [by Alexander Campbell]. Edinburgh, 1819.

Mackenzie, *History of the Mackenzies*: History of the Clan Mackenzie. By Alexander Mackenzie. Inverness, 1879.

Maturin Corr.: The correspondence of Sir Walter Scott and Charles Robert Maturin. [Preface signed by Fannie E. Ratchford and Wm. H. McCarthy, Jr.] Austin, Texas, 1937.

Minstrelsy (ed. Henderson): Minstrelsy of the Scottish Border. With notes and introduction by Sir Walter Scott. Revised and ed. by T. F. Henderson. 4 vols. Edinburgh, 1902. (Repr. with same pagination, Edinburgh, 1932, and Detroit, Michigan, 1968.)

Moore's *Memoirs*: Memoirs, journal, and correspondence of Thomas Moore, ed. by Lord John Russell. 8 vols. London, 1853–6.

MPW: The miscellaneous prose works of Sir Walter Scott, Bart. [Ed. by J. G. Lockhart.] 28 vols. Edinburgh, 1834–6.

N. & Q.: Notes and Queries. Vol. 1– London, 1850–

O'Byrne: A naval biographical dictionary. By William R. O'Byrne. London, 1849.

Oliphant, *William Blackwood*: Annals of a publishing house: William Blackwood and his sons . . . By Mrs [Margaret] Oliphant. Vols. 1–2. Edinburgh, 1897.

Partington, *Letter-books*: The private letter-books of Sir Walter Scott . . . Ed. by Wilfred Partington. London, 1930.

Partington, *Post-bag*: Sir Walter's post-bag . . . Written & selected by Wilfred Partington. London, 1932.

QR: The Quarterly Review. Vol. 1– London, 1809–

Ramsay, *Proverbs*: A collection of Scots proverbs. By Allan Ramsay. Edinburgh, 1737.

Ray: A collection of English proverbs . . . By John Ray. 2nd ed. Cambridge, 1678.

Refutation: Refutation of the mistatements and calumnies contained in Mr Lockhart's Life of Sir Walter Scott, Bart. respecting the Messrs Ballantyne. By the trustees and son of the late Mr James Ballantyne. London, 1838.

Reply to Mr Lockhart's pamphlet: Reply to Mr Lockhart's pamphlet, entitled, "The Ballantyne-humbug handled". By the authors of a "Refutation . . ." London, 1839.

Ruff: A bibliography of the poetical works of Sir Walter Scott, 1796–1832. By William Ruff. [Edinburgh Bibliographical Soc. Trans. Vol. 1, pt. 2–3.] Edinburgh, 1937–8.

CONTRACTIONS

St. Cuthbert's: Monumental inscriptions in St. Cuthbert's churchyard, Edinburgh (older portion). Comp. by John Smith. Ed. by Sir James Balfour Paul. [Scottish Record Soc. 47.] Edinburgh, 1915.

Scots Peerage: The Scots peerage, founded on Wood's edition of Sir Robert Douglas's Peerage of Scotland . . . Ed. by Sir James Balfour Paul. 9 vols. Edinburgh, 1904–14.

Scott's *Dryden*: The works of John Dryden . . . Illustrated with notes . . . and a life of the author, by Walter Scott, Esq. 18 vols. Edinburgh, 1808.

Scott's *Swift.*: The works of Jonathan Swift, D.D. . . . With notes, and a life of the author, by Sir Walter Scott, Bart. 2nd ed. 19 vols. Edinburgh, 1824.

Sederunt Books: Sederunt books of the Trustees of James Ballantyne & Company, Edinburgh, 1826–34, 1841. NLS MS. 112–14.

Sharpe's Letters: Letters from and to Charles Kirkpatrick Sharpe, Esq. Ed. by Alexander Allardyce. 2 vols. Edinburgh, 1888.

Shine: The Quarterly Review under Gifford: identification of contributors, 1809–1824. By Hill Shine and Helen Chadwick Shine. Chapel Hill, 1949.

Skene, *Memories*: The Skene papers. Memories of Sir Walter Scott by James Skene. Ed. by Basil Thomson. London, 1909.

Smiles, *John Murray*: A publisher and his friends. Memoir and correspondence of the late John Murray . . . [By] Samuel Smiles. 2 vols. London, 1891.

Spec. Soc.: The history of the Speculative Society, 1764–1904. Edinburgh, 1905.

Stuart, *Gleanings*: Gleanings from an old portfolio, containing some correspondence between Lady Louisa Stuart and her sister Caroline . . . Ed. by Mrs. Godfrey Clark. 3 vols. Edinburgh, 1895–8.

Stuart, *Letters*: Letters of Lady Louisa Stuart to Miss Louisa Clinton. Ed. by Hon. James A. Home. 2 ser. Edinburgh, 1901–3.

Stuart, *Selections*: Lady Louisa Stuart. Selections from her manuscripts. Ed. by Hon. James A. Home. Edinburgh, 1899.

Symington, *Some unpublished letters*: Some unpublished letters of Sir Walter Scott from the collection in the Brotherton Library. Comp. by J. Alexander Symington. Oxford, 1932.

Tancred, *Annals*: The annals of a Border Club (The Jedforest) . . . By George Tancred of Weens. Jedburgh, 1899.

Tancred, *Rulewater*: Rulewater and its people . . . By George Tancred of Weens. Edinburgh, 1907.

Taylor, *Memoir of Robert Surtees*: A memoir of Robert Surtees . . . By George Taylor. A new ed., with additions, by James Raine. [Surtees Soc. Publ.] Durham, 1852.

xiv

Trayner, *Latin maxims*: Latin phrases and maxims collected from the institutional and other writers on Scotch law, by John Trayner, Lord Trayner. Edinburgh, 1861. (And later eds.)

Trust Disposition: Trust Disposition Messrs James Ballantyne & Company, and the individual partners. NLS MS. 112.

White: Sir Walter Scott's novels on the stage. By Henry Adelbert White. [Yale Studies in English, 76.] New Haven, 1927.

NOTES

NOTES

(1) The obvious way of indicating the position on a page of the words being annotated would be to give the page and line, but it would be tedious for a reader to count the lines, and to guess them would be difficult. I have adopted, therefore, a different method. Each page is divided into six imaginary strips lettered a–f, so that a reference may read: VII. 320 (c). A strip of cardboard with lines dividing it into six strips, and lettered, forms a useful guide; but it has been found in practice that, without this, it is easy to judge the position by remembering that strips a–c occupy the upper half and strips d–f occupy the lower half of the page.

(2) For references within the same volume, the form used is, e.g.: See above, p. 60 or See below, p. 320. For references to other volumes the form is, e.g.: See *SL* iv. 20.*

(3) Wherever relevant, sources cited are printed and manuscript works known to be used by Scott or, at least, to have been accessible to him. This rule explains why modern, and perhaps better, sources have not normally been cited.

(4) For contractions used, see pp. xi–xv.

* While proof-reading it was found that this rule has not always been followed, but as the meaning is clear no changes have been made.

NOTES

VOLUME I

1 *n.* 2] The song was published in Cook, *New love-poems by Sir Walter Scott*, Oxford, 1932, pp. 3–4.

4 *n.* 1] The complete text of *The false knight* is given in Cook, *New love-poems by Sir Walter Scott*, Oxford, 1932, pp. 12–16.

7 (b) To Jessie] This letter, though here dated 1787, cannot be earlier than 1792. The three songs which Scott quotes are all in Ritson, *Ancient songs*, 1790 [1792]. Ritson printed all three from MSS. Even if Scott had got one from a broadside, the fact that these three songs come almost together in Ritson is proof that Scott took all three from him. It would seem that Scott was wooing Jessie after he had become an Advocate.

8 (a) When the nightingale sings] *A song on his mistress*, st. [1], in Ritson, *Ancient songs*, 1790 [1792], pp. 30–1.

8 (c) For her love in sleep I slake] Based on *A love song*, lines 80–3 and 1–3, in Ritson, *Ancient songs*, 1790 [1792], pp. 26–9. See also my note to *SL* ii. 264 (f).

8 (d) I have enclosed an entire ballad] This is *A song on an inconstant mistress* and is printed in Cook, *New love-poems of Sir Walter Scott*, Oxford, 1932, pp. 24–5. Scott has modernized the version in Ritson, *Ancient songs*, 1790 [1792], pp 72–4.

12 *n.* 1] The quotation is from *Lockhart*, i. 228 *n.* I do not know why Shortreed attributed the squib to Huoy. It was written by W. J. [i.e. William Jerdan]. It is called *Jeddart races; a new song* and contains the lines: 'They rode in *threes* as they were wont / To do at James' fair / The outside legs had each a boot / The *three* had but a pair.'

13 (f) your letter] Not in Walpole Coll. in NLS.

13 *n.* 1] James Ramsay, who was a fellow apprentice with Scott, became a W.S. and died in 1798.

14 (a–b) *nec tam aversus . . .*] Virgil, *Aeneid*, I. 568.

16 *n.* 2] There were new eds. in 1788 and 1789. Perhaps Scott's letter should be dated 1789 instead of 1790. James Ballantyne printed an ed. in 1812.

17 *n.* 1] In line 1, for '1790–91' read '1789–90.' Robert Ainslie did not attend Stewart's class the same session as Scott.

19 (d) *perfervidum ingenium Scotorum*] 'The very ardent temper of the Scots.' Scott attributes the Latin phrase to Scottish lawyers. See *The Heart of Mid-Lothian*, chap. 1, and *The Bride of Lammermoor*, note to chap. 4.

19 *n.* 1] The passage Scott cites is in Robert Lindsay of Pitscottie's *The history of Scotland*, etc., 3rd ed., 8vo Edinburgh, 1778, p. 181.

20 (b) his sister's death] Sarah Irving, daughter of George Irving of Newton, died at Edinburgh, 1 Aug. 1791. (*Scots Mag.* liii. 415.)

20 (b–c) still streams always run deepest] Ramsay, *Proverbs*, p. 57: 'Smooth waters run deep.'

20 *n.* 2] This note follows *Lockhart*, i. 248, but Edie, I think, is John James Edmonstone. 'Fergusson' should be 'Ferguson.'

20 *n.* 3] Ferguson, I think, is 'poor ******.' (The six stars represent the six letters of 'Linton.') The reference to Linton on p. 21 (though a year later) may be to the same subject.

21 (b) Hamilton] Scott seems to have confused Glenlee at Hamilton in Lanarkshire with Sir William Miller's Glenlee in Kirkcudbrightshire. The latter was noted for its oaks.

21 (d–e) brothers of Mr. Walker] David and Thomas Walker.

21 *n.* 1] James Russell (1754–1836).

21 *n.* 4] For 'Fergusson' read 'Ferguson.'

3

22 (b) Walter Fire-the-Braes, or rather Willie wi' the Bolt-foot] Walter Scott, 9th Laird of Sinton (16th cent.) was, according to Scott, called 'Watty Burn the Braes' (Scott's MS. pedigree of the Scotts of Sinton, printed in Sir William Fraser, *The Scotts of Buccleuch*, Edinburgh, 1878, i. 563). His younger brother, William, 1st Laird of Harden (died in 1561), was called 'Willy with the Bolt Foot' (ibid.). Arthur Elliot of Thorleshope in Liddesdale was called 'Fire-the-Braes' (*The lay of the last minstrel*, Canto VI, st. VIII).

23 (b) flourishing like a green bay-tree] *Bible, Psalm* 37: 36. The version with 'flourishing' occurs in the *Book of Common Prayer of the Church of England.*

23 (b) *noctes cænæque deum*] Horace, *Satires*, II. vi. 65.

23 *n.* 1] Ramsay's letter is of 30 Nov. 1796 (NLS MS. 3874, ff. 12–13).

24 (b) Duke of Hexham] Surtees wrote to Scott 28 Feb. 1807 (Taylor, *Memoir of Robert Surtees*, p. 43): 'The present chief [of Beaufort] is a lunatic, and conceives himself to be Duke of Hexham by patent from James III.'

25 (d) my *chère adorable*] Williamina Belsches.

25 *n.* 1] Amend this note. Hamilton established his claim in 1799 to the peerage, dormant since the death of the 5th Baron in 1777.

26 (d) To Patrick Murray] The reference to Valenciennes (p. 28) shows that 1793 is the correct year. Lockhart's account of the long Highland tour, which he assigns to 1793 (accepted by Grierson and Edgar Johnson), must be wrongly dated, as the contents of this letter show.

27 (a–b) the Merse] i.e. Berwickshire in which Murray's home of Simprim was situated.

27 (f) *Alas, Sir! the players be gone*] Scott is probably thinking of Buckingham's *The rehearsal*, V. 1: 'Sir, the players are gone.'

28 *n.* 2] For 'Sheriff' read 'Sheriff Substitute.'

28 *n.* 3] It has been said that Scott in the *Minstrelsy* (ed. Henderson, ii. 71) confuses Thomas Elliot, Reidheugh [*sic*],

with John Elliot, surgeon, Cleuchhead. (See M. R. Dobie in *Edinburgh Bibl. Soc. Trans.* ii. 68 *n.* 3.) Scott is correct. John Elliot was 'of Redheugh,' though he lived at Cleuchhead, and Thomas Elliot, with no territorial designation, lived at Redheugh.

29 (c) weightier matters of the law] *Bible, Matthew* 23: 23.

29 *n.* 1] Quotation from Scott ends at 'ruined chapel.' From 'If the country-people' down to '27th March 1803' is from a note by Lockhart in the *Minstrelsy*, and the concluding quotation marks should be after '1803', not after '*Albion*.' Finlay's letter is in NLS (MS. 3874, ff. 211–12).

30 (a) To Patrick Murray] Date of letter is 16 Apr. The original ALS was sold at Sotheby's, 29 Nov. 1971, in Lot 170.

30 *n.* 1] Amend this note. In *Lockhart* (i. 304–6) 'end of April' should be 'beginning of April.' Trouble began on Monday, 7 April, when *The royal martyr* was played and continued through the week till it culminated on Saturday 12 April. See also the *Scots Mag.* lvi. 233–5. There is a lengthy MS. on this subject in NLS (MS. 1567, ff. 1–18) from which we learn that Scott was counsel for Donald Maclean (mentioned in *Lockhart*, i. 306) who was sued for £500 damages and £100 expenses by Joseph Mason, carpenter in Bradford and student of medicine at Edinburgh. Walter Scott, W.S., acted as agent.

31 (f) Dogberry] Shakespeare, *Much ado about nothing*, III. 3.

32 *n.* 2] Invermay was also called Indermay.

32 *n.* 3] The word 'disseyffer' is used in her letter of 3 June. It is not used elsewhere. In line 2, for '*Humphrey*' read '*Humphry*.'

33 (d) volunteer corps] Royal Edinburgh Volunteers. See *A view of the establishment of the Royal Edinburgh Volunteers; with an alphabetical list of the corps, June 15th, 1795*, 8vo Edinburgh, 1795.

33 (d) Fullartons Legion] Officially The Northern Legion, commanded by Col. William Fullarton, and numbered at this time 101st Regt of Foot. (*Edinburgh Almanack for 1795*, p. 176.) The

Scots Mag. for Aug. 1794, lvi. 509, said the reports of insubordination were 'without foundation.'

34 (a) perceive from the date] Though queried by the editor (*SL* ix. 450 *n.* 2) this is a common expression. (See Index under Date.) Scott also uses it in *The Heart of Mid-Lothian*, chap. 44.

34 *n.* 1] Watt and Downie were originally charged together but they were tried separately. Scott attended the last day of Watt's trial on 3 Sept. The previous days were 14, 15, 22 and 27 Aug.

35 (a–b) *Stook . . .* Burk] See trials of Robert Watt and David Downie in Howell's *State trials*, xxiii. 1167–1404 and xxiv. 1–200 respectively. Stocks or Stoke and Burke or Burk or Burt are merely mentioned. Neither appeared as witnesses. Stoke was a student and there is no evidence in the reports that he 'supplied the money.' The name Stocks (in any of its forms) does not appear in the MS. register of students at Edinburgh Univ.

35 (f) our heroe John] In *SL* xii. 61 *n.* it is stated that Scott's brother John was abroad, 1791–6. This letter shows that he was home in 1794.

36 (b–c) the *Rock*] Gibraltar.

36 (c) Miss R.— Jean Anne . . . Acky] Janet Rutherford, her sister; Jean and Anne Russell of Ashiestiel, her nieces; and, presumably, her nephew Alexander Pringle Russell, the youngest child, born 28 Nov. 1792.

36 (c) tho least not last] Scott may mean 'tho the last not least' or 'tho the youngest not the last.'

36 (d) the coll:] Colonel William Russell of Ashiestiel.

38 (a) how bleak & bare] *Now Spring begins her smiling round,* st. [6], lines 3–4. In Ramsay, *Tea-table miscellany,* where the song is called *Ode. To Mrs A. R.*; also in *Herd,* i. 186.

38 (e) Manners] Messrs Manners and Miller, Edinburgh booksellers.

39 *n.* 1] This is Dr John Jamieson, not to be confused with Robert Jamieson, the ballad collector.

42 (b) "Who is that upon the pony . . ."] From a caricature on Littleton, 1741.

See *Lockhart,* i. 321 *n.* and Boswell's *Johnson,* ed. Hill-Powell, v. 285.

42 (c) my uncle's at Lisburn] Thomas Irving, M.D., lived at Lisburn.

42 (e) "dwindle, peak, and pine"] Shakespeare, *Macbeth,* I. 3.

42 (e) Pharaoh's lean kine] *Bible, Genesis* 41: 19–20.

44 (e) To William Erskine] Scott's address to London was not a mistake. When Scott wrote, Erskine was in London as the reference to London ('Devil's drawing room') on p. 47 shows.

45 (c) Lieut. Drummond] John Patrick Drummond. (*A military history of Perthshire, 1660–1902,* ed. by the Marchioness of Tullibardine [afterwards Duchess of Atholl], Perth, 1908, p. 175.)

45 (d) at John Ramsay's] i.e. at Ochtertyre.

45 *n.* 1] The Advertisement says the treatise might be entitled 'The importance of a Man to himself.' Printed by Scott in his ed. of *Swift,* 2nd ed., xiii. 168–81.

47 (a) married to a relation of mine] Grierson failed to establish the relationship either in his *Sir Walter Scott, Bart.,* p. 34 *n.* or in his article in *Blackwood,* Vol. 241, p. 172. Christian Scott (1732–1808) was the great-granddaughter of James Scott of Thirlestane whose brother Walter was 1st Laird of Raeburn. Scott's father and Christian Scott, therefore, were third cousins.

47 (c) "If it were na my heart's light, I wad die"] Lady Grizel Baillie, *Were na my heart light, I wad die.* In Ramsay, *Tea-table miscellany,* and in *Johnson,* Vol. 2 (1788), No. 121.

47 (c) Fountainhall] Sir John Lauder of Fountainhall's *The decisions of the Lords of Council and Session . . . 1678 to . . . 1712.*

47 (c) with Goose upon Kant] Georg Friedrich Daniel Goess, *Systematische Darstellung der Kantischen Vernunftkritik,* 8vo Nürnberg, 1794.

47 (d) hay! Billy! hay!] 'Hay! [then a name] hay!' was a common expression in songs. Billy was the popular name at this time for William Pitt.

47 (d) Devil's drawing room] Smollett, *Roderick Random,* chap. 18.

47 (e) Keep thy fingers from plackets]
Shakespeare, *King Lear*, III. 4.

47 *n.* 1] For 'George Cranston' read
'George Cranstoun'; for 'Monroe' read
'Monro'; for 'Miss Cranston' read 'Miss
Cranstoun.' Before 'Alexander' delete
'G.'. For 'Bernauerin' read 'Ber-
nauerinn.'

48 (a) trotting over four Inch Bridges]
Shakespeare, *King Lear*, III. 4.

48 *n.* 1] A longer extract from Walker's
letter of 5 Nov. is in Partington, *Post-
bag*, pp. 1–2.

49 *n.*] Scott's letter is addressed to Sir
George Stuart Mackenzie, 7th Bart. of
Coul and the year is 1824. 'Your
interesting vindication' is *A letter to Sir
Walter Scott, Baronet, P.R.S.E. &c. con-
taining observations on the vitrified forts*, 8vo
Edinburgh, 1824. Mackenzie's pamph-
let was a reply to John Macculloch's
The Highlands and Western Isles of Scotland,
4 vols., 8vo Edinburgh, 1824, in which,
Vol. 1, pp. 287–301, there is a chapter
on 'Vitrified forts.'

51 (b) Nelly to Macgriegar] Presumably
Walker's servants.

52 (a) No. 47] No. 47 Princes Street
was the town house of the Erskines.
Edinburgh & Leith Directory, 1796, p. 41.

52 (f) this felonious Sheriff] Campbell
Colquhoun was Sheriff of Perth, 1793–
1807.

53 (b) evil for Man to be alone] *Bible*,
Genesis 2: 18.

53 (f) "presumed to lift his surly eye"]
James Thomson, *Tancred and Sigis-
munda*, IV. 1.

54 (a) slough of Despond] Bunyan, *The
pilgrim's progress*.

54 (d) Ballads] The copy of *The chase,
and William and Helen*, presented by
Scott to Mary Erskine, is now in the
Lockwood Memorial Library in the
State University of New York at
Buffalo. It is inscribed: 'Mrs Campbell
from her sincere and most respectful
humble servant the Translator.'

55 (a) Mundell] *The chase, and William
and Helen* was printed by Mundell &
Son, Royal Bank Close, Edinburgh.

55 (d) gentle Shepherds] Roger Aytoun,
W.S., and presumably his younger

brother Patrick. Patrick Aytoun was in
Fraser's class at the High School, 1779–
80, 1780–1 and in Adam's class, 1781–2
and 1782–3, along with Scott and at the
University along with Scott, 1783–4.
Patie and Roger are characters in
Allan Ramsay's *Gentle shepherd*.

56 (a) what regards M—] M should be
W (for Williamina).

56 (d) Down busy devil down] Otway,
Venice preserved, IV. 2: 'Down, busy
devil!' Dick, who is always quoting
plays, in Murphy's *The apprentice*, I. 1,
says: 'Down, busy devil, down! down!'
Scott may be quoting Murphy rather
than Otway.

56 *n.* 1] Delete this note. For 'graer'
read 'graie.' Scott is quoting *Johnie of
Breadislee*, st. 25, line 2. In *Minstrelsy*
(ed. Henderson), iii. 146.

57 *n.* 1] The work got would more likely
be Schiller's *Trauerspiele*, Mannheim,
1786. It contains *Fiesko*.

58 (d) Falnash] The Laidlaws. Mrs
Laidlaw of Falnash was Jessie Scott of
Skelfhill whom Scott admired according
to Robert Shortreed. (*Cornhill Mag.*
Sept. 1932, p. 278; *Trans. Hawick Arch.
Soc.* 1932, p. 60.)

64 (c) Porte] Did Scott write 'Porte'
instead of 'Ports'?

64 (e) Linton] Adam Ferguson was a
Captain in the Edinburgh Royal Highland Volunteers. *Edinburgh Almanack*,
1800, p. 210.

64 (f) Clerk] William Clerk was 2nd
Lieut. in Mid-Lothian Royal Volunteer
Artillery. *Edinburgh Almanack*, 1800,
p. 210.

66 (b) The Salary is £250 pr. ann:]
Lockhart (ii. 45) says it was £300.
Actually it was only £200 till it was
raised to £300 in 1806. Cf. also *SL* i.
176.

66 (b) The only Gentleman] By a
process of elimination this must be Wil-
liam Elliot (afterwards William Elliot-
Lockhart of Borthwickbrae), Advocate.
At this time he was Lt.-Col. of the
Roxburgh & Selkirk Fencible Cavalry.

67 (f) my Brother] John.

67 *n.* 2] Bird and Brown were both
minor canons of Carlisle Cathedral.

73 (d) Wellcome, business] Sir William Blackstone, *The lawyer's farewell to his Muse*, lines 81–2. In Dodsley, *A collection of poems, by several hands*, London, 1770, iv. 227; and *The English anthology* [ed. by J. Ritson], London, 1794, ii. 135.

75 (a) Miss R.] Janet Rutherford, Scott's aunt.

75 (d) "Can any good thing come out of Nazareth"] *Bible, John* 1: 46.

76 (c) The Erl-King] First printed in the *Scots Mag.* Vol. 64 (Jan. 1802), p. 72, where it is signed E. F. An editorial note states that it was written before Lewis's version, a mistake as Scott's letter shows.

78 (d) letter from Lord Downshire] Dated 29 Oct. and sent on to Scott by Charlotte on 4 Nov. Grierson's *Sir Walter Scott, Bart.*, p. 58.

80 (c–d) Mr. Russell] See my note to *SL* xii. 65 (c).

81 (b) not good for Man to be alone.] *Bible, Genesis* 2: 18.

82 *n.* 1] For note on illustration of the seal, see *SL* xii. 73 *n.* 2.

86 (a) the little Carpenter] I have failed to trace the name of this person who was a Frenchman and Chief of the Five Nations with the nickname 'The Little Carpenter.' He must have been a popular figure, for in Foote's *The liar* (1762), I. 2, Young Wilding says: 'To me we owe the friendship of the Five Nations, and I had the first honour of smoking the pipe of peace with the Little Carpenter.' There was a chapbook called *The Little Carpenter's garland.*

86 (d) as little like the original as Hercules to me] Shakespeare, *Hamlet*, I. 2: 'no more like my father, / Than I to Hercules.'

88 *n.* 1] For '10th October' read '17th October.' An extract from Downshire's letter is in Partington, *Post-bag*, pp. 4–5.

89 (c) a foreign fleet . . . Russians] For reports of the Russian fleet in Leith roads, see the *Edinburgh Advertiser*, 1798, 2 Oct., p. 213 and 16 Oct., p. 254.

89 *n.* 1] At this time Daniel was a Lieut. in the 2nd Batt. of the 5th (or Northumberland) Regt of Foot and was probably with his regiment at or near Stilton.

90 (a) Setons Business] Scott's mother was investing money with Seton on heritable security through Sir William Forbes & Co.'s Bank. See below, p. 219.

92 (e) Adam] Adam, afterwards Sir Adam, Ferguson.

92 *n.* 1] A Mr and Mrs Bink from Edinburgh visited Abbotsford, 26 May 1836. (Visitors' Book; MS. at Abbotsford.)

93 (d) The ghost story . . . [and] a Border Ballad] *Glenfinlas* and *The Eve of Saint John*, both written in 1798, and not in 1799 as Lockhart says, probably misled by this letter.

93 *n.* 1] Scott's spelling Suwarrow was the current spelling in Britain.

94 (b) Eris mihi magnus Apollo] Virgil, *Eclogues*, III. 104.

95 (a) Pringle's] Mark Pringle of Clifton and Haining (1754–1812), who was M.P. for Selkirkshire at this time.

95 *n.*] In line 4, for 'Lenthill' read 'Linthill.' If Riddell had been living at Linthill in 1819 he would have gone to Abbotsford by Midlem and Lindean. He went over Bowden Moor because he was living at Camieston.

96 *n.* 1] A Joseph Gillon of Elliesland married in Edinburgh, 23 Mar. 1808, Miss Baker, daughter of the late Dr James Fowler Baker, physician, Charlestown. (*Scots Mag.* lxx. 315.) I have been unable to prove that this is the same man.

98 (b) To unknown correspondent] Richard Scougall is given in *SL* xii. 487. The correspondence is in NLS MS. 872, ff. 125–6.

98 (b) extraordinary process] 'Two gentlemen [names not given] were yesterday fined for riding on Horseback upon the Links of Leith.' *Edinburgh Advertiser*, 30 May 1800. See also *Edinburgh Evening Courant*, 31 May 1800.

98 (b–c) Mr. Mowbray] Almost certainly John Mowbray, W.S., who married Elizabeth Scougall, sister of Richard Scougall to whom this letter is addressed.

99 (a) I have written to my uncle] i.e. to Robert Scott at Rosebank, Kelso. The letter is not in *SL*.

99 (a) Adml.] Admiral Sir Archibald Collingwood Dickson of Sydenham House, Kelso.

99 (b) Baird] James Baird, Deputy Solicitor in Court of Exchequer. He died the following year on 24 May.

99 *n*. 1] For 'Montague' read 'Montagu.' It is scarcely accurate to say that the persons mentioned were 'fellow soldiers with Scott.' The Duke of Buccleuch was Col. of 2nd Regt of Royal Edinburgh Volunteer Infantry; the Earl of Dalkeith was Col. of, and Lord Montagu Captain in, 4th (or Dumfriesshire) Regt of North British Militia.

102 (c) Brydones old sword] Stoddart in his *Local scenery* (1801), ii. 263, said the descendants of Sir Andrew Brydone, Town Clerk of Selkirk, who fought at Flodden, had 'till lately' his broadsword. In 1882 W. H. Brydone of Selkirk exhibited to the Berwickshire Naturalists' Club an Andrew Ferrara which he said was borne by his ancestor at Flodden. See *Hist. of the Berwickshire Nat. Club*, Vol. 10, p. 62.

103 (a) Old Charter from James 5th] Scott quoted this in Vol. 1, pp. 241-5 of 1st ed. of the *Minstrelsy* (Henderson's ed., iii. 391-5).

103 (c) recoverd of the Small pox] She had recovered from the inoculation against smallpox. See *SL* xii. 173.

103 *n*. 1. The Battle of Corrichie] Printed in Evans's edition, *Old ballads* (1777), ii. 88–91, where it is said the author was 'Forbes, a schoolmaster, at Mary Culter.'

104 *n*.] Currie would read *Glenfinlas* in Lewis's *Tales of Wonder* which, though dated 1801, was issued in 1800 and reviewed in the *British Critic* for Dec. 1800. In last line, for 'Cleveland Road' read 'Cleveland-Row.'

105 (a) *Hawick Arch. Soc.*] Add: *Trans.* 1921, pp. 22–3.

105 (c) the late Act] 39 Geo. III, c. 49 [13 June 1799]: 'An act to extend the bail to be given in cases of criminal information in that part of Great Britain called Scotland.'

106 (a) old Charters] Of James V. See above, p. 103.

106 (b–c) Mr. Pringle . . .] Without knowing the case involved I cannot identify all the names in this paragraph. Andrew Plummer of Middlested died in 1799. His wife was Mary, daughter of James Pringle of Bowland, W.S., and granddaughter of James Pringle of Torwoodlee. James Pringle, W.S., was dead; so that the Pringle mentioned may be James Pringle of Torwoodlee.

106 (d) *secundum bonum et aequum*] According to what is good and equitable. A Scots law phrase. See Trayner, *Latin maxims*.

106 (e) Willie Scott] Son of Scott's uncle Thomas Scott who, at this time, was tenant in Woollee. Delete [?]. The *Queen* was an East Indiaman which sailed from Torbay on 3 May 1800 and arrived at St. Salvadore on 1 July. On 9 July it caught fire and 80 lives were lost. See *Edinburgh Advertiser*, 17 Oct. 1800, pp. 249 and 254.

106 (e) Weights & measures] See above, p. 102.

107 *n*. 1] Grierson is unjust to Scott in saying he was wrong on the point of law. This case arose in 1800 and it was not till 1807 (as Chisholm, op. cit., p. 114, points out) that the Court of Session ruled that it was competent for a Sheriff to try a case for scandal.

108 *n*. 1] The 'earlier letter from Scott' (line 10) was later discovered and printed in *SL* xii. 167–70.

109 (b) Earl of Westmoreland's escape] *The Earle of Westmorland* is in Percy's MS. from which it was printed in Child's *Ballads*. Scott had asked for a copy (*SL* xii. 169).

110 (e) To George Ellis] For rest of letter, see *SL* xii. 175–8.

110 *n*. 1] In last line, for '*Sir Tristram*' read '*Sir Tristrem*.'

111 *n*.] 'Otterbourne' is James Ellis's spelling. Many letters to George Ellis were later discovered and are printed in *SL* xii.

112 (a) To George Ellis] For rest of letter, see *SL* xii. 178–81.

112 (b) as Falstaff says] Shakespeare, *II Henry IV*, III. 2.

112 (d) Sir Otuel] In the Auchinleck MS. It was analysed by Ellis in his *Specimens of early English metrical romances* (1805), ii. 313-55.

113 (c) battle on the Liddle] Carwanolow. See *SL* xii. 213, 213 *n*.

114 (c) To George Ellis] For rest of letter, see *SL* xii. 181–3.

115 (a) Major Sturgeon] In Foote's *The Mayor of Garratt*.

115 (a) like the hart] *Bible, Psalms* 42: 1.

115 (a) your *grande opus*] *Specimens of the early English poets*. See below, p. 116.

115 (a) as iron sharpeneth iron] *Bible, Proverbs* 27: 17.

116 *n.* 1] In line 1, the title should be *Specimens of the early English poets* (1801). (Corrected in *SL* xii. 487.) In line 4, 'Deputy Chief Register' should be 'Deputy Clerk Register.'

117 (c) LASWADE] Read 'LASSWADE.'

117 (d) To George Ellis] For rest of letter, see *SL* xii. 184–5.

117 *n.* 2 at least one other letter] There were at least five other letters—21 Aug., 8 Sept., 24 Sept., 9 Oct., 22 Oct. See *SL* xii. 186–204.

118 (a) "Que diable vouloit-il faire dans cette galère?"] Molière, *Les fourberies de Scapin*, II. 11. Also quoted in *SL* vii. 234; *MPW* xvii. 185; and in *Waverley*, chap. 56. Cf. also *SL* iv. 472.

118 (a) His brother] Robert Leyden who turned out not so 'fine' as Scott here thinks.

118 (b) transcript of *Merlin*] In the Auchinleck MS.

118 *n.*] The 'letter of the 9th' (line 4) is in *SL* xii. 196–9.

119 *n.*] Versions of the ballad containing the lines 'He was a hedge unto his friends; / a heckle to his foes, Lady' are in Child's *Ballads*. Constable printed the ballad in the *Edinburgh Mag.* Vol. 2 (*Scots Mag.* Vol. 81), Feb. 1818, p. 131.

120 (b) "care little for these things"] Cf. 'Gallio cared for none of those things.' *Bible, Acts* 18: 17.

120 (e) Sinbads mountain of Adamant] Scott is at fault here. The mountain of adamant is not in the *Story of Sindbad* but in the *Story of the third Calendar*, a section of the *Story of the three Calendars* in the *Arabian Nights* (Weber, *Tales of the East*, i. 52).

120 *n.*] Delete the last sentence which is an absurd comment. On 'three foot abreast,' cf. *SL* ii. 96.

121 (c) the story of the Bear & Fiddle] i.e. it breaks off in the middle. Butler, *Hudibras*, Argument of the first canto, line 6.

121 (e–f) Miss Elliot transmitted them to me thro' Somerville] Scott's letter of 26 Jan. 1801 to Rev. Dr Somerville of Jedburgh; Jane Elliot's letter of 2 Feb. 1801 to Dr Somerville; and Scott's letter of *c.* 5 Feb. 1801 to Dr Somerville are all printed in *Review of English Studies*, N.S. Vol. 14, Feb. 1963, pp. 61–5, from the originals in Somerville College, Oxford. The information which Scott was passing on to Currie was obtained from this correspondence.

121 *n.* 1] For 'Sir Gilbert Elliot, first Earl of Minto' read 'Sir Gilbert Elliot, 2nd Bart.'

123 (b) To George Ellis] For rest of letter, see *SL* xii. 204–10, where it is correctly dated 7 Dec.

123 (c) Solomon's architects] *Bible, I Kings* 6: 7.

123 (c) Babel] *Bible, Genesis* 11: 4–9.

123 *n.* 1] Lockhart's date is correct. Ellis wrote on 14 Dec. 1801 (NLS MS. 873, ff. 30–1) in reply to Scott's 'kind and long letter of the 7th.' The quotation in this note comes from a letter of 14 Jan. 1802 (NLS MS. 873, ff. 34–5) in reply to Scott's letter of 8 Jan., below, p. 125.

123 *n.* 2] Scott was moving from 10 South Castle Street to 2 North Castle Street which became 39 Castle Street in 1811.

124 (b) Castle Spectre] By M. G. Lewis.

124 (b) Bluebeard] This is probably *Blue Beard; or, female curiosity*, by George Colman, the Younger, acted at Drury Lane and published in 1798.

124 (b) *Plays of the Passions*] By Joanna Baillie.

124 (c) *The Complaynt*] *The complaynt of Scotland*, which John Leyden was editing.

124 (c) William Dundas] Commissioner on the Affairs of India (Board of Control), 1797–1803.

125 (a) To George Ellis] For rest of letter, see *SL* xii. 212–15. Ellis replied on 14 Jan. (NLS MS. 873, ff. 34–5).

125 *n.* 1] The paragraph on Bothwell Castle has no connection with Scott's visit to Hamilton. For *'Secret History of the Court'* read *'The authentic records of the Court of England.'*

126 (c) beautiful french translation] See below, p. 134.

126 *n.*] For 'sixth Earl' read 'fifth Earl.' On 4 Jan. 1802, when Scott was at Hamilton Palace, Lady Anne showed him a MS., *The speech of Logan a Negro Indian to Lord Dunmore then Governor of Virginia in Novr. 1773.*

127 (b) Murray] Andrew Murray, shoemaker. See Index.

127 (b) Princess of Jutland] Sapinelle in Count Anthony Hamilton's *Les quatre Facardins.* (*Œuvres complètes*, nouv. éd., Paris, 1805, ii. 331.)

129 (b) If I can keep my two poets from disputing . . .] Le Sage, *Gil Blas*, Bk viii, chap. 9.

129 (d) your Ladyships letter] Of 28 Jan. 1802 (NLS MS. 3874, ff. 124–5). In it she says: 'My Sister & I will most likely stay as long as the *Duke of York* pleases as we shall attend my Brother 'till his regt. is disbanded.'

130 (b) Lord John] Lord John Campbell, afterwards (1839) 7th Duke of Argyll.

130 (d) with Jaques to rail . . .] Shakespeare, *As you like it*, II. 5.

130 *n.* 2] For *'Humphrey'* read *'Humphry.'* Tabitha's letter is dated 2 Apr. For 'replied' read 'had written.' For the 'jowls' see above, p. 130. In her letter of 28 Jan. (NLS MS. 3874, ff. 124–5) Lady Anne wrote of Scott's *Fiesco* (see above, p. 126) and of Campbell's *Stanzas on painting.*

130 *n.* 3] In line 3, for '1801' read '1803.' The 4to pamphlet, printed by Ballantyne, was simply called *Poems.*

131 (f) Lady Susan's task] Campbell had given preference to painting over music (above, p. 127). In her letter of 28 Jan. 1802 (NLS MS. 3874, f. 124) Lady Anne wrote: 'Susan desires me to say that she is *furious* at the preference the Bard has given to Painting over Music, & that unless he writes something equally beautiful (more so it could not be) upon her favourite Muse she

shall be tempted to blot him from her present good opinion.'

132 (e) To George Ellis] For rest of letter, see *SL* xii. 215–16.

133 (a–b) the elephants] See above, p. 113 *n.* 1.

134 (e) the pamphlets] See above, p. 132.

134 (d) french translation of the *Entail*] *La substitution, fable traduite de l'anglois.* Scott printed it in his preface to his ed. of *The Castle of Otranto* (1811), pp. xl–xliii. See also *SL* ii. 498.

134 (e) the *bequest* which . . . the Wren made] *Robin Red-breast.* In *Herd*, ii. 166–7. Though the wren is mentioned, it is the robin that makes the bequest.

136 (f) your Brother *The Douglas*] She had two brothers. As Lord Archibald is already mentioned, 'The Douglas' must mean Alexander who became 10th Duke.

137 (b) To George Ellis] In *SL* xii. 216 *n.* 2, Grierson refers to the rest of this letter as 'hardly worth reprinting.' It is not, therefore, included in *SL*.

138 *n.* 1] Delete two last sentences. Ellis was referring to Tom, not to Daniel. See *SL* xii. 220. Scott's first request for help for Daniel was on 4 May 1804 (*SL* xii. 246).

139 (b) "What beauties does Flora disclose."] The first line of *Tweedside*, by Robert Crawford, first printed in Ramsay's *Tea-table miscellany.* Scott refers to the two Flowers of Yarrow in a note to Introd. to Canto II of *Marmion.*

139 (c) a portrait . . . at Hamilton] Why the portrait should be at Hamilton Palace is explained by an anecdote of Henry Mackenzie: 'She was the reigning beauty of the time, and so much a favorite with the then Duke of Hamilton that he had her picture painted, which is one of the Hamilton collection, and, it was confidently said, wished to marry her. Why he did not, I never learned.' See *Anecdotes*, ed. Thompson, p. 79.

139 *n.* 3] The authority for John is the marriage contract. See Sir William Fraser, *The Scotts of Buccleuch*, i. lxx.

140 (a) To R. Cleator] This should be Will. Cleator. (NLS MS. 3874, f. 132.)

140 n. 1] In line 3, for 'Liddesdale' read 'Lidderdale.'

142 (c) To R. Cleator] The initial should be W.

143 (e–f) Mr. Liddesdale] Read 'Lidderdale.'

145 (a) *kindly* gallows of Elibank] For a curious explanation of 'kindly' see Scott's note to 'kind gallows of Crieff' in *Waverley*, chap. 18.

145 n.] The reference to 'the late Mr. Headly' (lines 2–3) is to Henry Headley's *Select beauties of ancient English poetry*, 1787. Headley died in 1788.

146 (c) "An old rude tale . . ."] *Love*, st. [6], lines 3–4. Scott printed a version under the title *Fragment* in the *English minstrelsy*, ii. 131–9, in which the couplet appears in st. [10]. For a full account of this poem, see *The complete poetical works of Samuel Taylor Coleridge*, ed. by E. H. Coleridge, i. 330–5.

146 (e) Sir Philip Sydney] See Sir Philip Sidney, *Defense of poesy*. Also quoted in *SL* ii. 264 and *MPW* vi. 210.

147 (c) "Drowsy bench and babbling hall"] William Blackstone, *The lawyer's farewell to his Muse* (1744), line 87. For sources, see above, p. 73(d).

147 n. 1] In line 2, for '15th of July' read '12 Aug.'. (Corrected in *SL* xii. 265 n. 1.) This letter, which is here quoted, is in NLS (MS. 865, ff. 19–20).

148 (a) preserved in the Advocates Library] In the Auchinleck MS.

148 (a) end of the 12th Century] Scott means 13th century. He gives date of his death as 1292 in *SL* xii. 241.

149 (a) Welch Dicty.] William Owen Pughe, *A dictionary of the Welsh language*, 2 vols., London, 1803. Scott's name does not appear among the subscribers.

149 n. 1] Delete and substitute: *Cadyow Castle* in *Minstrelsy* (ed. Henderson), iv. 178.

150 (b) a vile Election] Parliament was dissolved on 28 June and a General Election was held in July.

151 (e) *Three Sisters*] M. G. Lewis's *Oberon's henchman; or, the legend of the three sisters*, printed in his *Romantic tales*, London, 1808.

153 (a) tale of the Corbies] *The twa corbies*. Scott printed Sharpe's version in his *Minstrelsy* (ed. Henderson), ii. 415–18. See also Henderson's note. The couplet beginning 'God send every gentleman' is the conclusion of *The three ravens*, printed by Scott, ibid., from Ritson's *Ancient songs*, 1790 [1792], pp. 155–9.

153 (c) Blackhouse . . . Lord William Douglas] Cf. the conflicting statements in the *Minstrelsy* (ed. Henderson), iii. 1 and *Castle Dangerous*, chap. 9.

153 (e) Mary Hamilton] Scott printed this, under the title *The Queen's Marie*, in the 2nd ed. of *Minstrelsy*, with acknowledgement to C. K. Sharpe. It took the place of *Lament of the Queen's Marie* of the 1st ed.

153 (f) Lady Dismal] Sharpe printed this in his *A ballad book* [1823], pp. 12–16. Scott later referred to it in his 1830 'Introductory remarks on popular poetry' in the *Minstrelsy* (ed. Henderson), i. 13–14.

153 (f) "*Lady Anne* . . ."] In 2nd ed. of *Minstrelsy* (ed. Henderson), iii. 19–23, with acknowledgement to C. K. Sharpe.

155 (c) Tam o' Shanter] In her letter of 10 July she had said of Burns: 'South of the Tweed he has few warmer admirers than myself; and yet I say to you . . . that I would rather have written The Eve of St John, and Glenfinlas than any thing of his, even the Tam o' Shanter, which I consider his *chef d'œuvre*.' (*Letters of Anna Seward*, vi. 36.)

156 (b) "like musick sweetest at the close"] Shakespeare, *King Richard II*, II. 1: 'music at the close . . . is sweetest.'

156 n. 1] Sharpe's letter of 27 Aug. is in *Sharpe's Letters*, i. 138–9.

157 n. 1–2] These two quotations are from *Sharpe's Letters*, i. 139.

158 (a) Alexr. Scott] Rev. Alexander Scott of Beechwood (1781–1834). See Index.

158 (b) To the editor of the "Scots Magazine"] This is a magazine article and does not belong to Scott's private correspondence. It should be printed only in his miscellaneous prose works. Similar errors, on Grierson's part, will be found in *SL* vi. 494, viii. 417, x. 166, 278.

158 (e) "rocked and craddled, and dandled"] Scott is probably quoting Burke. See *SL* vii. 281, 281 *n.*

160 (a) To Charles Kirkpatrick Sharpe] Sharpe's letter, to which this is a reply, is in *Sharpe's Letters*, i. 142–5.

160 (d) Glenriddell] Sharpe in his letter of 12 Oct. (*Sharpe's Letters*, i. 143) said it had been ascribed to Clapperton who denied the authorship and who said it was written by Riddell. A copy of the *Bedesman* was presented to Edinburgh University Library in 1794 by Robert Riddell and this gift suggests that he was the author.

160 *n.* 1] The mistake 'vol. iv' is copied from *Sharpe's Letters*, i. 143. They were printed in Vol. 3 as Scott says.

160 *n.* 2] The correct title is: *The bedesman on Nidsyde*, London, Printed for S. Hooper, No. 112 High Holborn 1790. Contents are: Pp. 3–14. *Legendary fragments. The Bedesman on Nidsyde.* Pp. [15–16] *T'e Mort o' Lauch.*

161 (c) Lagg's elegy] *An elegy in memory of that valiant champion Sir Robert Grierson of Lag. Or, The Prince of Darkness . . . who died, Dec. 23d, 1733,* etc. See *Sharpe's Letters*, i. 142; Alexander Fergusson, *The Laird of Lag*, Edinburgh, 1886, pp. 153–73.

161 (d) print in the Minstrelsy] Sharpe, oddly enough, did not recognize it and asked what it was (*Sharpe's Letters*, i. 145). Scott gave an account of it in his *Journal*, 1 Mar. 1826. His drawing has disappeared but I have a copy of it made by James Skene of Rubislaw.

161 (e) houses & churches . . . geese & turkies] This is a paraphrase of the line in the ballad, *The Dragon of Wantley*, st. 4, line 5: 'For houses and churches were to him geese and turkies'. (*Percy's Reliques.*)

162 (e) Both Miss Sewards favours] Between the date of this letter and his previous letter of 16 Aug. (above, p. 154) I can find only one letter from her (NLS MS. 3874, f. 180, dated 26 Aug.).

163 *n.* 1] In her letter of 26 Aug. (Partington, *Post-bag*, pp. 14–15) she quotes Scott as having said in a previous letter 'That recreant Knight Mackenzie is a *Subscriber* to my 3rd Vol. which will soon see the light.' Scott's letter, from which this is quoted, is not in *SL*.

164 (a) Woodhousilee] Read 'Woodhouselee.'

165 (b) Fame is the *spur*] *Lycidas*, line 70.

165 (e) heaping coals of fire] *Bible Proverbs* 25: 22; *Romans* 12: 20.

165 *n.* 1] In her letter of 26 Aug. See Partington, *Post-bag*, p. 14.

166 (c) your very obliging favour] His letter of 15 July, cited above, p. 147 *n.*

166 *n.* 1] Owen's letter was forwarded to Scott by George Chalmers. (Letter from Owen to Chalmers of same date in Edin. Univ. Lib. La. II. 474.) Owen's letter to Chalmers concerned the first meeting on 15 Jan. of the Celtic Society of which Scott and Leyden are given as corresponding members.

168 (c) dialogue betwixt Tristrem & Gwalchmai] In his letter of 12 Aug. 1802 (quoted above, p. 147 *n.*) Owen said he would send it when it had been returned by a friend to whom he had lent it. In a letter of 10 Jan. 1803 (NLS MS. 865, ff. 21–2) Owen said it had not yet been returned. Scott received it, however, in time to print it as Appendix II in *Sir Tristrem* (1804), pp. xxiii, xcix–ciii.

168 (c) your Dicty.] See my note to *SL* i. 149 (a).

169 (d) Tushilaw lines] This, I think, is *The dowie dens o' Yarrow*.

169 (e) speedily good *Tyrrel*] Shakespeare does not say this but the meaning is implied in *King Richard III*, IV. 2.

169 (e) Sir — Menzies] Sir Robert Menzies, 5th Bart., a large landowner in Perthshire. Rannoch Lodge was one of his seats. His son, later Sir Neil Menzies, was an Advocate and would be known to Scott though Scott did not know his father's Christian name.

170 (b) George] William Laidlaw's brother.

170 (d) Montero cap like Corporal Trim's] Sterne, *Tristram Shandy*, Bk VI, chap. 24.

170 (e) verses respecting the Devils wooing] Laidlaw, in his letter of 3 Jan. 1803 (NLS MS. 3874, ff. 192–3), quoted portions of a ballad from the singing of Walter Grieve. The lines quoted show that he was referring to the ballad, *The daemon-lover*, first printed in 3rd ed.

of the *Minstrelsy* (ed. Henderson, iii. 246–52). William Motherwell in his *Minstrelsy*, Glasgow, 1827, pp. 92–8, printed a version with comments on Laidlaw's 'improvements' on his 'naked original.'

171 (a) Lady Dalkeith] She had sent the version of *Tamlane* and an account of Gilpin Horner which she had received from Beattie in Dec. 1802. (*Trans. Hawick Arch. Soc.* 1973, p. 15.) Scott's reply is not in *SL* but it is printed in *FL* i. 22–3.

171 (c) We sleep in rosebuds] This is st. 35 of *The Young Tamlane* in *Minstrelsy* (ed. Henderson), ii. 396.

171 (d) To William Laidlaw] From the contents this letter should be dated 6 Oct. 1802. Scott will be at Selkirk for Head Court on Friday, 8 Oct. and at Whitebanklee on 9–10 Oct. The letter cannot have been written at Whitebanklee (p. 173).

172 (b–c) *Dundee . . . Glen Lyon*] Scott seems to be referring to *Bonny Baby Livingston* which Jamieson printed from the recitation of Mrs Brown of Falkland. (*Popular ballads*, ii. 135–43.) The names Dundee and Glenlyon both occur in the ballad.

172 (c) Laminton] This is *The Laird of Laminton* in *Minstrelsy*, 1st ed., i. 216–19. Scott rejected it in 2nd ed. and substituted *Katharine Janfarie*. James Maidment in his *A north countrie garland*, Edinburgh, 1824, pp. 34–9, printed *Catharine Jaffery* which, he says, is printed for the first time. It is another version of Scott's *The Laird of Laminton*, to which Maidment makes no reference although he refers to *Katharine Janfarie* in the *Minstrelsy*.

172 *n.* 1] Laidlaw's letter is dated 11 Sept. 1802 (NLS MS. 877, f. 12). The *Companion to Armstrong's map of Peebles or Tweedale* was published at Edinburgh in 1775. Tushielaw belonged to the Scotts till Michael Anderson bought it in 1688. As the ballad would belong to a date prior to 1688 the woman would be right in saying the ballad referred to a Scott of Tushielaw. See Craig-Brown, *Selkirkshire*, i. 334.

174 (a) To G. Ellis] For rest of letter, see *SL* xii. 232–3.

174 (b) *inflammatory* branches of study] Sheridan, *The rivals*, I. 2.

174 (d) "I could be a guide . . ."] *Hobbie Noble*, st. 11, lines 3–4. *Minstrelsy* (ed. Henderson), ii. 121.

174 (e) Ainslie's map] John Ainslie produced a map of Selkirkshire, 21 June 1773, 2nd ed., 1801.

176 (b) increase the appointments of the Sheriffs] See my note to *SL* i. 66 (b).

177 (a) Ld. W. Bentinck] Lord William Henry Cavendish Bentinck, 2nd son of 3rd Duke of Portland, was appointed Governor of Madras in 1803.

179 (d) good friends in Piccadilly] The Dumergues and Nicolsons, early friends of the Carpenters.

179 (e) To Anna Seward] March cannot be right. Scott was in London in April and May and the letter was begun in London but not finished till he was back at Ashiestiel. The date is probably 25 May. For points referred to, see her letter of 19 Mar. quoted above, p. 164 *n.*

180 (c) Mr. Billsbury] Rev. Dewhurst Bilsborrow. An emergency meeting of Lodge St David, Edinburgh, No. 36, was called at Scott's request on 23 Mar. 1802 to elect 'Dewhurst Bilsborrow of Dalby House.' See *N. & Q.*, 11th ser. Vol. 6 (14 Sept. 1912), p. 210. Anna Seward's correspondence with Scott had just commenced and it was probably at her request that Scott introduced Bilsborrow to his Lodge. See also *Letters of Anna Seward*, vi. 52–6.

181 (b) Heber . . . Oxford] Richard Heber took Scott to Oxford on 26 Apr. (*Heber letters*, p. 142.)

181 (e) a truant to the Classic page] Thomas Warton, *Verses on Sir Joshua Reynolds's painted window at New College*, line 8. More fully quoted in *SL* viii. 435.

182 *n.* 1] Delete this note, which is inapplicable. On Leyden's sailing for India, see *SL* xii. 232.

185 (a) To George Ellis] For rest of letter, see *SL* xii. 234–6.

185 *n.* 1] In line 1, delete '(having missed Leyden).' Scott did not miss him. The rest of the note requires modification in light of the letters which turned up late and are in *SL* xii.

186 (a) like Dives] *Bible, Luke* 16: 26.

186 (a–b) best of all possible worlds]
Voltaire, *Candide*, chap. 1: 'dans ce
meilleur des mondes possible.' (*Œuvres
complètes*, tome 44 (1785), p. 224.)

187 (a) Hohenlinden & Lochiel] See
above, p. 130, *n.* 3 and my note.

187 (d) roast potatoes at a Volcano]
Expression also used *SL* xi. 410. Gold-
smith has 'fry beef steaks at a volcano'
(*The good-natur'd man*, Act. IV).

188 (b) To Anna Seward] This is the
beginning of the letter continued on
p. 192 and should be dated, therefore,
10 July 1803.

188 (f) "pomp and circumstance of
war"] Shakespeare, *Othello*, III. 3.

189 (d) your sagacious critic] In her
letter of 20 June 1803 (NLS MS. 865,
ff. 25–8) Anna Seward had referred to
a criticism in the *Literary Journal* of a
line in Darwin: 'And the vast surface
kindles as it rolls.' The critic, she wrote,
'expresses his surprise that so polished
a Poet as Darwin should take his verb'
[i.e. kindles] 'from the common term
used for rabbits bringing forth their
young.'

190 (a) To George Ellis] For rest of
letter, see *SL* xii. 236–7, where it is
dated '[June 1803].'

190 *n.* 1] Ellis's reply of 24 July is in
NLS (MS. 873, ff. 52–3). In line 7,
'Ellis, replying' refers to Ellis's letter of
10 Sept. (NLS MS. 873, ff. 54–5), but
the letter in which Ellis says 'for I am
convinced' is not that of 10 Sept. but
of 24 July.

192 (d) To Anna Seward] This is a
continuation of the letter above, pp.
188–9. This is proved by Anna's reply
in *Letters of Anna Seward*, vi. 91–100.

195 (a) None are unwilling] Sir William
Jones, *Fête champêtre*, st. [4] lines 3–4.
Scott printed the poem in his *English
minstrelsy* (1810), i. 262.

195 *n.*] Delete the whole of this note
which, except for the last sentence,
has no bearing on the subject of Scott's
letter. Scott is claiming exemption from
the Army of Reserve, created by Act of
Parliament passed on 6 July. The
'inclosed summons' (first line of Scott's
letter) is also in Edinburgh Corporation
Museum.

196 (d) like Launcelot Gobbo's]
Shakespeare, *Merchant of Venice*, II. 2.

196 *n.* 2] The quotation is from *DNB*.

199 (a) *Fabliaux*] By Le Grand d'Aussy,
publ. with notes by George Ellis, 2 vols.,
London, 1796–1800.

199 (d) To Joseph Ritson] Scott is
replying to Ritson's letter of 2 July
1803, printed in full in *The Letters of
Joseph Ritson*, London, 1833, ii. 337–41,
and, incompletely, in Partington,
Letter-books, pp. 219–20.

199 *n.* 1] Delete this note. Scott's
translation was of *Recollection des mer-
veilleuses advenues en nostre temps*, by
Georges Chastellain (1403–75), contained in *Faictz et dictz de feu maistre
Jehan Molinet*, 2° Paris, 1531. The
French text was printed with Scott's
translation in Joseph Ritson's *Ancient
songs and ballads*, 8vo London, 1829, i.
144–69. A few months after sending the
translation to Ritson Scott quoted two
lines in his review of Godwin's *Chaucer*
in *ER* Jan. 1804 (*MPW* xvii. 76–7) and
in a letter to Lady Louisa Stuart (*SL* i.
391 and see my note there). For another
translation done at this time for Ritson,
see Index under Leicester (Simon de
Montfort, *Earl of*). Grierson's note is
partly corrected in *SL* xii. 487.

200 (a) The stanza commencing . . .]
The lines in the French and English
versions in Ritson (cited in preceding note) are numbered and Scott's
references can be easily found '"Le
grant Duc de Virtu"' should be '"Le
grant duc de Vertu."' Scott adopted
the personification interpretation.

200 (d) Killiecrankie verse] See my
Bibl. No. 2189.

200 *n.* 1] For source of letter, see my
note to *SL* i. 199 (d).

200 *n.* 2] Kennedy's poem is also in
Johnson, Vol. 2 (1788), No. 102, p. 105.

201 (a) Richards song] In his letter of
2 July 1803 Ritson had said: 'You will
have the goodness to remember
"Richard's song".' (*Letters of Joseph
Ritson*, London, 1833, ii. 340–1.)
Nothing further is known of this
projected translation as Ritson died
twelve days after Scott had written.
There is a translation of *Song by Richard
the First, written during his imprisonment*

in the Tenebreuse, or Black Tower, in Evans, *Old ballads*, new ed., London, 1810, iv. 231–3. This might be Scott's translation.

201 (a–d) Dukes copy of Leader Haughs] Scott is here referring to Ritson's letter of 2 July 1803 in which he discusses *Leader Haughs*. The Duke is the Duke of Roxburghe. Burns is Nicol Burne. Hume is Alexander Home. Ritson accepted Burne as the author of the poem. Douglas is doubtful. There were two of this name at this time— Rev. Dr Robert Douglas of Galashiels and Dr Christopher Douglas of Kelso. He is more likely to be the latter who married a daughter of Home of Bassendean and the reference in the letter to a Hume (or Home) strengthens the identification with him. Ritson's letter is in *The letters of Joseph Ritson*, London, 1833, ii. 337–41. Partington prints the letter in the *Letter-books*, pp. 219–20, but he cuts out all references to Leader Haugh, which makes his concluding paragraph meaningless.

201 (d) your king Arthur] *The life of King Arthur* was not published till 1825. In a letter to Scott, 8 July 1803, Ritson says: 'Longman and Rees will have nothing to do with my *Life* . . . they appear to me a couple of fools.' Partington, *Letter-books*, p. 220.

202 (c) Robin Hood & the Pedlar] Ritson had asked for it in letters to Scott, 10 Apr. 1802 and 2 July 1803. (*Letters of Joseph Ritson*, London, 1833, ii. 220, 341.)

202 (f) Geo. Wallace] His works, referred to by Scott, are: *Thoughts on the origin of feudal tenures and the descent of ancient peerages in Scotland*, Edinburgh, 1783; and *Prospects from hills in Fife*, 2nd ed., Edinburgh, 1800. The latter is in verse.

203 (b) To George Ellis] For rest of letter, see *SL* xii. 239–41 and for corrections to this part see *SL* xii. 242, *n*. 3.

203 (d) Italian policy of locking the lady in a stable] The policy of Italian husbands locking up their wives is often referred to in literature, but Scott is here probably alluding to Ellis's *Specimens of the early English poets* (1801), iii. 71: 'I am no Italian lover, / That will mew thee in a jail.' Scott often paid

similar oblique compliments to show that he had read his correspondent's publication.

203 *n*. 1] Ellis's letter of 10 Sept. is in *Lockhart*, ii. 147–50.

204 (b–c) "In Yorkshire near fair Rotheram"] Line 1 of st. [5] of *The dragon of Wantley.*

204 (c) not fail to inquire] For Ellis's reply on the Dragon of Wantley, see *SL* xii. 242 *n*. 1.

204 (d) To George Ellis] For rest of letter, see *SL* xii. 241–2. The date, 14 Oct., seems to be too early. The volunteers went into quarters at Musselburgh on Friday 28 Oct. (*Edinburgh Advertiser*, 28 Oct. 1803, p. 276). 14 Oct. would be exactly a fortnight before, but Scott says (p. 205) 'Friday se'ennight', suggesting that he was writing about 20 Oct.

204 *n*. 1] There is a better text in D'Urfey, *Wit and mirth*, Vol. 3 (1719), pp. 10–15.

205 *n*. 1] In line 1, for 'R. Ellis' read 'G. Ellis.'

206 (b) author of the "Unnatural Combat,"] Philip Massinger.

206 (c) two fierce Forest greyhounds] Ryno and Fillan. See *SL* i. 199.

207 *n*. 1] The complete letter (last line) from Carlyon to Polwhele, Edinburgh, 1 Sept. 1803, is in *Letters of Sir Walter Scott addressed to the Rev. R. Polwhele*, 8vo London, 1832, pp. 1–6.

208 *n*.] *Local Attachment* (second last line) was quoted in 13th ed. of *The lay* (1812), p. 325. Polwhele, though very proud of this, was annoyed that Scott quoted an early, and inferior, version, See the *Gentleman's Mag.* Vol. 90, N.S. Vol. 13, Pt. 2 (Aug. 1820), pp. 122–4.

211 (a) a large folio] The date should probably be 1554. *Le premier livre du nouveau Tristan, Prince de Leonnais, Chevalier de la Table Ronde, et d'Yseulte, Princesse d'Yrlande, Reyne de Cornouaille. Fait Francoys par Ian Maguin, dit l'Angevin.* 2° Paris, 1554.

211 (f) Gibbon] See *The decline and fall*, new ed. (1802), Vol. 6, p. 388 and note.

211 (f) Tressan] Louis Elisabeth de la Vergne, comte de Tressan, *Corps*

d'extraits de romans de chevalerie, 4 tom. 12mo Paris, 1782.

214 (c) To George Ellis] The date cannot be later than 16 Mar. as Ellis received it on 19 Mar. See *SL* xii. 243, where the rest of the letter is printed.

214 (d) uncastrated copies] The line in Fytte 2, st. ciii, omitted in most copies, was restored in 2nd ed.

215 (a–b) Hornchild . . . Ritson] Ritson's *Ancient Engleish metrical romanceës*, ii. 91–155 and notes, iii. 264–320.

216 (a) Mr. Douce's fragments] See above, p. 210 and below, p. 221.

219 (a) To Mrs. Scott] The suggested date 1804 is impossible as William Keith died on 22 Oct. 1803; and, in any case, Scott was in Edinburgh on 14 Apr. 1804 (previous page) and could have discussed the matter with his mother then. The 'bairns' in the plural in the postscript shows that the letter was written after the birth of Walter on 28 Oct. 1801. The date, therefore, is either 1802 or 1803.

219 (c) Mr. Fergusson] James Fergusson, W.S., who managed (or mismanaged) the estate of Walter Scott, W.S.

219 (c) my fathers Trustees] For their names, see *SL* vii. 460 *n.*

220 (a) To George Ellis] For other portions of letter, see *SL* xii. 244–6.

220 (a) little pieces of business] Arranging for his removal to Ashiestiel.

221 (d) fragments] See above, pp. 210, 216.

221 (d) the copy of Sir Tristrem now sent] Douce did not acknowledge the gift till 29 Dec. 1807. See my note to *SL* ii. 15 (d).

222 (a) To George Ellis] The first paragraph belongs to a letter of 16 May 1804 (*SL* xii. 247–50) and the second paragraph to a letter of 4 May 1804 (*SL* xii. 244–6).

222 (b) *Long sheep* and *short sheep*] See *The Black Dwarf*, chap. 1.

222 *n.* 1] In view of the amalgamating and misdating of the two letters, this note requires to be amended. For first line substitute: 'Writing on 20 May, Ellis,'. In lines 2 and 6 for 'Tristram' read 'Tristrem.' Ellis reviewed it in *ER* for July 1804 (Vol. 4, pp. 427–43).

223 (c) I will also advertise] A long advertisement, describing Rosebank, may be found, for example, in the *Edinburgh Advertiser*, 13 July 1804.

223 (c) with Romeo's apothecary] Shakespeare, *Romeo and Juliet*, V. 1.

223 (e) To George Ellis] This letter is made up of fragments of letters of 18 June and 21 Aug. (See *SL* xii. 258 *n.*, 263.) For rest of letter of 18 June, see *SL* xii. 258–62.

224 (b) about thirty acres] Should be 'about twenty acres.'

224 (d) Laird of the Cairn and the Scaur] Burns, *The whistle*, st. [4], line 1: 'the lord of the Cairn and the Skarr.' The Cairn and the Scar, or Skarr, are two small rivers in Dumfriesshire. Scott punned on these names, making them represent stones and bare, rocky hillsides. For other references, see Index under Burns, *The whistle*.

224 (d) To George Ellis] This fragment, which should be dated 21 Aug., belongs to the letter printed below, pp. 226–7. (See *SL* xii. 262 *n.*) The rest of the letter is in *SL* xii. 262–4.

226 (d) Sir I. P. & his tenant] Sir James Pringle of Stichill, Bart. and his tenant David Murray. See *Chisholm*, pp. 116–19.

226 (e) To George Ellis] The part dated by Lockhart 1 Aug., given above, pp. 224–5, belongs to this letter of 21 Aug. (*SL* xii. 262 *n.*). For rest of letter, see *SL* xii. 262–4.

226 (e) some attempts . . . but they did not succeed] Presumably referring to drawings by J. J. Masquerier. See *SL* xii. 378–80.

227 (b) galled my kibes] Shakespeare, *Hamlet*, V. 1.

227 (b) a very good amanuensis] Henry Weber.

227 (d) Hesperides] In Greek mythology, nymphs who guarded golden apples in a garden protected by a dragon. See also *SL* xi. 248.

228 (a) To unknown correspondent] He is Andrew Scott, the Bowden poet. See *Border Mag.* Vol. 37 (Sept. 1932), p. 149.

228 (e) Nelson] The only information I can find about him is that given by Scott in his *Journal*, 10 Mar. 1826.

229 (a) to touch Irving] Scott did not review his work in *ER*.

229 (a) man of the leaden mace] Shakespeare, *Julius Caesar*, IV. 3: 'O murd'rous slumber! / Lay'st thou thy leaden mace.' Does Scott mean that Irving's books send his readers to sleep?

229 (d) To George Ellis] This portion and the portion below, pp. 230–1, belong to a letter of 23 Nov. for the rest of which, see *SL* xii. 264–6.

229 (e) Hassan's tapestry] *The Story of Prince Ahmed and the Fairy Pari Banou* in *The Arabian Nights*. (Weber, *Tales of the East*, i. 432.)

229 n. 1] For '*Scotch*' read '*Scotish*.'

230 (b) To George Ellis] This fragment belongs to a letter of 23 Nov. See my note to *SL* i. 229 (d).

230 (d) fable of the boys and frogs] See L'Estrange, *Fables*, Fable 398. Author not given. The application of this fable to literature may have been suggested to Scott by Addison in the *Spectator*, No. 23, 27 Mar. 1711.

230 (d) kiss the rod] Shakespeare, *Richard II*, V. 1; *Two gentlemen of Verona*, I. 2.

230 n. 1] Young was reviewed very unfavourably in the *ER* Vol. 1 (Jan. 1803), pp. 450–60 and Vol. 5 (Oct. 1804), pp. 97–103.

231 (a) I declined taking any copy-money] The publishers, however, presented Grose's *Antiquities of Scotland*, 2 vols., 4to London, 1789 and *Antiquities of Ireland*, 2 vols., 4to London, 1791.

231 (b) To George Ellis] For rest of letter, see *SL* xii. 266–8. On the date, see my note to *SL* xii. 266 (d).

231 (c) Beaumont and Fletcher] The ed. which Scott annotated in the margin was *The dramatick works of Beaumont and Fletcher*, 10 vols., 8vo London, 1778. On title-page of Vol. 1 is Scott's signature and 'Duplicate' and on the half-title John Ballantyne has written: 'This Copy, which is filled with critical MS. Notes of the celebrated author of the Lady of the Lake, was exchanged by Mr Walter Scott with Mr Ballantyne, his publisher in Edinburgh, for a Copy

of Ballantyne's new edition on the 13th March 1812. Witness John Ballantyne.' I acquired this copy from a London bookseller in 1955.

233 (a) To George Ellis] Cancel. The complete letter is given in *SL* xii. 270–4.

234 n. 1] The opening sentence is ambiguous.

235 (b) "Queen Eleanor was a sick woman"] *Queen Eleanor's confession*, line 1. In Percy's *Reliques*.

236 (a) Sir John Sinclair] The plan of the 'cockeneys expedition', if seriously contemplated, was not carried out. Sinclair's *The code of health and longevity* was published in 4 vols. in 1807.

236 (b) "& verie pithie comedie . . ."] An interlude, *c.* 1568, by William Wager, with title: *A very mery and pythie commedie called The longer thou livest, the more foole thou art.*

236 (c) Ah silly I more silly than my Sheep] Ambrose Philips, *The second pastoral*, line 67.

238 (c) tale of the Fenwick] *Fair 'Mabel' of Wallington* in Ritson's *The Northumberland garland*, Newcastle, 1793. Sir John Fenwick appears in this song. Also in the collected ed., *Northern garlands*, London, 1810, and in John Bell's *Rhymes of northern bards*, Newcastle upon Tyne, 1812.

238 (d) Thomas the Rhymer] Child printed in his *Ballads* the version she sent to Scott.

239 n. 1] Amend this note. Scott's cousin, John Rutherford, son of Professor Daniel Rutherford, was lost on the *Earl of Abergavenny* (not the *Lady Jane Dundas*). The ship sailed from Portsmouth on 1 Feb. 1805 and was lost on the Shambles on 5 Feb. when the Captain (John Wordsworth), the Chief Officer and 60 of the crew perished. (Charles Hardy, *A register of ships employed in . . . East India Company . . . 1760 to 1810*, 12mo London, 1811, p. 241.) Another victim was James Hamilton Dundas, uncle of John Hamilton Dundas of 15th Hussars (q.v. *SL* ix. 132 n., 136, 145, 177).

240 (c–d) expelled . . . the Fiend . . . I must sweep & garnish the empty tenement] *Bible*, *Matthew* 12: 43–4; *Luke* 11: 24–5.

241 (b) For many a place] The concluding four lines of *Leader Haughs and Yarrow*, by Nicol Burne. In Ramsay, *Tea-table miscellany*. In spite of what Scott says, st. [8] begins: 'In Burn-mill-bog and Whitslaid Shaws.'

242 (a) To Miss Seward] The letter of 7 Mar., which Scott is here answering, is in *Letters of Anna Seward*, vi. 207–14. In it she wrote: 'Will you forgive me if I confess, that your dwarfology has less charms to me than the other rich creations of your fancy.' Scott is replying to this criticism.

242 (e) a ballad on a broomstick] Stella said of Swift that he 'could write finely upon a broomstick.' See Delany's *Observations upon Lord Orrery's remarks* (1754), p. 58. For variation of this anecdote, see extract from Thomas Sheridan's *The life of . . . Swift* (1785) in *The Oxford book of literary anecdotes*, ed. James Sutherland.

243 (c) tinkers . . . make two holes in patching one] This is a proverb. It is introduced by Swift in his *Polite conversation* (Scott's *Swift*, 2nd ed., ix. 428).

245 (d) a good name] *Bible, Proverbs* 22:1.

248 (b) I have imagined a very superb work] Scott seems to have stolen the idea from Thomas Campbell. Campbell had written on 27 Mar. 1805, telling him of his proposed 'collection of the best specimens of English poetry' (Beattie, *Life and letters of Thomas Campbell*, ii. 41). For further correspondence, see ibid., ii. 52, 55–7, 66, 89–92. Scott's plan was given up (below, p. 259) but Campbell fulfilled his project.

248 (b) Johnson's . . . Bell's . . . Anderson's] Samuel Johnson, *The works of the English poets. With prefaces . . . by S. Johnson*, 68 vols., 8vo London, 1779–81; John Bell, *Bell's British poets*, 109 vols., 8vo London, 1777–82; Robert Anderson, *A complete edition of the poets of Great Britain*, 14 vols., 8vo London, 1795.

248 (e) necessity has no law] *Kelly*, p. 266; Ramsay, *Proverbs*, p. 50.

248 n. 1] Delete '1807 or.'

249 (b) To James Skene] The date must be about 25 Apr. Scott would receive Forster's letter of 21 Apr. about 24 Apr.

('yesterday'). Skene was at Ashiestiel on 21 Apr. (below, p. 250) and must have left before Forster's letter came. (The PM 26 Apr. on p. 251 must be the London PM, i.e. date of arrival.) E. Forster's letter of 21 Apr. 1805, relating to the engraving and publishing of some of Skene's drawings, is in Skene's *Memories*, pp. 22–3.

250 (a) Congreve's edition] William Congreve, the dramatist. There were eds. of 1717, 1735, 1762.

251 (d) "Sleep you, or wake you?"] These, or similar, words occur in ballads; e.g. *Minstrelsy* (ed. Henderson), ii. 65, 102.

251 n. 1] Ellis had not written since 9 Jan., though Scott had written on 6 Feb. (*SL* xii. 270). Ellis replied to this letter of 26 May on 4 June (NLS MS. 873, ff. 74–5), cited below, p. 253 n., and Scott wrote another letter on 20 July (*SL* xii. 274–7) to which Ellis replied on 28 Aug. (NLS MS. 873, ff. 76–7).

252 (d) seventeenth century] This should be sixteenth century. Arbuthnot died in 1585.

253 n. 1] For a long extract from Ellis's letter see *Lockhart*, ii. 219–22.

254 (a) Viscount of Dundee] Canto IV, st. II: 'Fell by the side of great Dundee.'

254 (b) Hutson] There is a mezzotint by John Young from a painting by Douglas of Tom Hudson [*sic*] at the age of 67.

254 (c) Park] George Park.

255 (e) Mr. Greenough] George Bellas Greenough. See Skene, *Memories*, pp. 24–5.

255 n. 2] Lockhart's misdated letter, 18 Aug. 1805, is in *Lockhart*, ii. 260–1. The bulk of that letter comes from a letter of 11 Aug. 1806, printed in *SL* i. 314–15.

256 n. 2] Delete this note. The recipient could not possibly be Scott of Raeburn: (1) The recipient is beginning his career, but William Scott, Younger of Raeburn, had been in the East Indies since 1794 and had returned permanently to Scotland in 1805 (NLS MS. 2889, f. 143); (2) The recipient's father is dead, but old Raeburn lived till 1830. He may be the William Scott

who wrote to Scott in 1827 from Singapore (NLS MS. 3905, f. 174).

257 (f) Curver] This must be a misreading of Currie. William Currie (1781–1831) was the tenant in Howford in 1805.

258 (e) To George Ellis] This is part of a letter of 17 Oct., below, pp. 261–4, both parts from *Lockhart*, and completed from original in *SL* xii. 277–9.

258 (f) agog about the Chronicles] Ellis in his letter of 28 Aug. (cited above, p. 251 *n.*) had suggested this. It looks as if Ellis had spoken to Rees before the latter's visit to Scott on 1 Oct.

259 (b) Benedictines] Replying to Ellis, cited above, p. 251 *n.*

259 (d) I am interrupted] The text from this point to the end belongs to a letter of 20 July printed in *SL* xii. 277.

259 (d) like the Count of Artois] In *Sir Eglamour of Artoys*, analysed by Ellis in his *Specimens of early English romances* (1805), iii. 257–81.

259 (e–f) Don Quixote to Pentalopin] Pentalopin should be Pentapolin. Cervantes, *Don Quixote*, Pt I, Bk III, chap. 4. (Lockhart's ed., 1822, i. 187.)

260 (b) Chronicles of England] In his review of Johnes's Froissart in *ER* for Jan. 1805 Scott had written: 'A uniform edition of our chronicles . . . might surely be expected' (*MPW* xix. 113).

260 (e) trippingly off the tongue] Shakespeare, *Hamlet*, III. 2: 'trippingly on the tongue.'

260 *n.* 1] In line 3, for '*Helvellyn*' read '*Hellvellyn.*'

260 *n.* 2] For 'White' read 'Whyte.'

261 (a) The lay] 2nd ed., published in Oct. (*Ruff*, No. 27).

261 (a) Dugi] Grierson says (above, p. 260 *n.* 1): 'What error Dugi was I have not discovered.' 'Dugi' was a misprint for 'Dirge.'

261 (d) To George Ellis] For complete letter, see above, pp. 258–9 and *SL* xii. 277–9.

262 (b) Robert Jamieson] One might think from this passage that Jamieson had copied the MS. in Lincoln Cathedral. But Jamieson, in the 'Advertisement' to his *Popular ballads* (1806), i.

xi–xii, tells us he was unable to visit Lincoln and obtained the transcript from the Rev. William Gray of Lincoln. Jamieson, however, printed his text from a Cambridge MS., noting variations in the Lincoln MS. (See ibid., ii. 3.) The stanza which Scott quotes is not from the Lincoln MS. as his text implies, but from the Cambridge MS. It is second fytte, st. 2. The Lincoln version was later printed by Laing in his *Select remains*. Scott also quoted the stanza in his *Essay on romance* (*MPW* vi. 159).

262 (d) If poor Ritson] The note to this stanza in Jamieson's *Popular ballads*, ii. 27, is: 'How would Mr Ritson, if he were alive, like True Thomas's definition of a profession which he knew so well?' As Scott superintended Jamieson's book through the press, one suspects that Scott added the note.

262 *n.* 1] This note requires to be rewritten. Scott did not have 'a fresh proof of his and Percy's view.' Scott, like Percy, came round to Ritson's point of view. The quotation from Scott's *Introductory remarks* (written, it should be noted, in 1830) is partial and misleading and the whole passage should have been quoted. See *Minstrelsy* (ed. Henderson), i. 30–1.

263 (b) Robert of Sicily] *Robert of Cysille* was analysed by Ellis in his *Specimens of early English romances* (1805), iii. 142–52.

263 (c) a poem called Sir Amadis] 'Amadis' should be 'Amadas.' The poem was printed by Weber in his *Metrical romances* (1810), iii. 241–75.

263 (d) Bibliothèque Bleue] *La bibliothèque bleue, entièrement refondue*, etc. 3 tom. 12mo Liége, 1787.

263 (d) merry tale of hunting a hare] *The hunting of the hare* was included by Henry Weber in his *Metrical romances* (1810), iii. 277–90. For a brief account of the poem, see Scott's article *Romance* (*MPW* vi. 144–5). It is a different poem from *The song of the hunting of the hare* quoted by Scott in his *Journal*, 16 June 1826.

263 *n.* 1] In line 1, for 'Wynne' read 'Wynn.'

264 (a) a burlesque sermon] Scott used this in Chap. 5 of his continuation of Strutt's *Queenhoo-Hall* (1808), reprinted

in *Waverley*, Appendix II to General Introduction (1829). The complete text is in *Miscellany of the Abbotsford Club*, Vol. 1, Edinburgh, 1837, pp. 61–3. In *Redgauntlet*, Narrative, chap. 17, Scott refers to the time when 'Mother Eve eat the pippin without paring.'

264 (c) Any word lately from Jamaica?] See *SL* xii. 279 *n.* 1.

264 (d) To George Ellis] The correct date of this letter is 29 Nov. 1805 (*SL* xii. 279 *n.* 2). For rest of letter, see *SL* xii. 279–80.

265 (d) Master Little] Thomas Moore, the poet.

265 (d) *virginibus puerisque*] Horace, *Odes*, III. i. 4.

266 (d) *Cælum non animum*] Cælum non animum mutant qui trans mare currunt (Those who cross the sea change only the climate, not their characters). Horace, *Epistles*, I. xi. 27.

266 *n.* 1] Crowe was never Professor of Poetry at Oxford as Scott says.

268 (c) To Charles Erskine] The date must be Dec.: (1) Charles was born on 23 Dec., making Nov. too early for Scott's words 'She is still holding out'; (2) 'We got all well to town' shows the letter is after 11 Nov.

268 (d) Gownlock] Scott's letter of 'Thursday' [19 Sept. 1805] to George Rodger, Procurator-Fiscal, which had fixed Gownlock's trial for 9 Oct., is in Selkirk Public Library.

268 *n.* 1] Scott finally decided not to write on Nelson. See below, pp. 282–3, 310 *n.* He also declined to write on Nelson at the request of Warren Hastings. See *SL* xii. 382–4, 382 *n.*

269 (a) Shorthope's] Thomas Macmillan of Shorthope near Selkirk had a house at Musselburgh which he called Shorthope House. His daughter Marion married, June 1812, Walter Scott of Wauchope.

269 (e–f) The tragedy] *The House of Aspen*.

270 (a) a sight of the . . . you] The dots are in the Abbotsford Copy where the transcriber has a pencilled note: 'This was a private paper' (NLS MS. 851, ff. 279–80). Longman & Co.'s letter of 11 Nov. (NLS MS. 3875, ff. 118–19) makes no mention of any private paper.

270 (a) 4th volume of Turners history] Vol. 4 and last of Sharon Turner's *History of the Anglo-Saxons*. Vol. 1 had appeared in 1799.

270 (b) Censure] *Censura literaria*, by Sir Egerton Brydges. (*SL* xii. 487.)

270 (c) To Miss Nicolson] Odd that Grierson should print from the Abbotsford Copies when the original is in Edinburgh Univ. Library (Laing III. 582[2]).

270 (d) "learning is better than house or land"] A popular rhyming proverb: 'Learning is better than house or land: / When house and land are gone and spent / Then learning is most excellent.' Quoted by Foote, *Taste* (1752), Act I, by Garrick in his Prologue to Goldsmith's *She stoops to conquer* (1773) and Charlotte Smith, *The banished man* (1794), ii. 219. Also quoted in the *Journal*, 3 Mar. 1826 and parodied in *Guy Mannering*, chap. 35.

270 (e) whose sudden marriage] See below, p. 290 *n.*

270 *n.* 1] This note should have appeared at p. 68. Delete sentence beginning 'We shall hear'. She has already been mentioned above, pp. 68, 73, 74, 80, 81, 82, 87, 90.

272 (c) Park . . . Gownlock] See above, p. 268.

272 (d) the running noose] Erskine was married to Barbara Pott on 24 Jan.

272 *n.* 1] On Macpherson's work, see *SL* xii. 281 and my note.

273 (d) Alexander Mundell] When in London Scott wrote to Mundell on 7 Feb. on the same subject. The letter, which is not in *SL*, is printed in the *Border Mag.* Vol. 21 (Feb. 1916), p. 34, from the original in the Bodleian Library.

273 (e) Pitt's death] Pitt was already dead, having died on 23 Jan.

274 (a) and (e) Fox . . . Windham . . . Grenville] In Feb. Lord Grenville became Prime Minister with Fox as Foreign Secretary and Windham as Secretary for War and Colonies.

274 (d) profane and unprofitable art of poem-making] John Leyden tells us that when John Wilson was appointed schoolmaster at Greenock he was

required to renounce 'the profane and unprofitable art of poem-making'. (Leyden, *Scotish descriptive poems*, Edinburgh, 1803, p. 8.) Scott quoted this in a note to *The Battle of Philiphaugh* which first appeared in 2nd ed. of *Minstrelsy*, 1803 (ed. Henderson, ii. 213 *n.* 2). See also *SL* viii. 39, 499 and *Waverley*, chap. 13.

275 (b) To Charles Erskine] Scott is here congratulating him on his marriage on 24 Jan. to Barbara Pott, only daughter of late George Pott of Todrig.

276 (d) a good name] *Bible, Ecclesiastes* 7: 1: 'A good name is better than precious ointment.'

277 (a) late commander in chief] Lord Moira, afterwards Marquess of Hastings.

278 (a) now at Abbotsford] The letter is now in NLS (MS. 865, ff. 60–1).

280 (e) "Even when the rage of battle . . ."] Smollett, *Tears of Scotland*, st. [5], lines 5–6.

280 (f) To Charles Kirkpatrick Sharpe] The date, I think, should be Monday, 4 May 1807: (1) Scott stayed in Bury Street in 1807 but not in 1806; (2) Sharpe was in London in 1807 but there is no evidence that he was there in 1806; (3) Lady Douglas was in London in 1807 (*SL* xii. 110) but there is no evidence that she was there in 1806.

280 (f) Tale of the Bard of Caithness] From Scott's comments this seems to be *The Fiend with mantle grey*, which appeared later in the year in Sharpe's *Metrical legends*. I do not know why Scott gives the poem this title.

281 (d) To George Ellis] Saturday was 1 Mar. in 1806. For rest of letter, see *SL* xii. 280–1, where it is dated '[*probably March* 1806].'

281 (e) Bladud] See *SL* xii. 280 *n.* 3.

282 (b) his nephew] Lord Melville's nephew, Robert Dundas, Lord Chief Baron.

282 (e) To George Thomson] This letter should probably be dated early June as Thomson replied on 12 June (below, p. 310 *n.*).

283 (f) strangers within our gates] *Bible, Exodus* 20: 10.

284 (b) Bishop of London] Scott is undoubtedly referring to Dr Porteus's objection to the frontispiece to Hoppner's *Tales*. See also *SL* ii. 45.

284 (b) Ovid's Instructions to his Mistress] Scott's *Dryden*, xii. 259–61.

285 (a) your card . . . to Jeffrey] i.e. concerning Ellis's wish to review David Macpherson's *Annals of commerce*. See above, p. 272 *n.*

285 (c) claimed his acquaintance . . .] A reminiscence of Goldsmith's *Deserted village*, line 154: 'claim'd kindred there, and had his claims allow'd.'

285 (e) Prince of the Black Isles] *Story of the young King of the Black Isles* in *Story of the fisherman* in *Arabian Nights* (Weber, *Tales of the East*, i. 27–32).

285 *n.* 1] Delete 'Presumably.'

286 *n.* 1] Anna Seward's letters of 7 Mar. and 17 Apr. 1805 are respectively in *Letters of Anna Seward*, vi. 207–14, 214–18, and her letter of 26 Mar. 1806 is in Partington, *Letter-books*, pp. 256–8. The MS. of *Address to the River Tweed* (not printed) is in NLS (MS. 3875, f. 75) and is dated 17 Apr. 1805.

289 (a) the lion lies down with the Kid] *Bible, Isaiah* 11: 6: 'the leopard shall lie down with the kid.'

289 *n.* 1] Tony Lumpkin does not fit. Scott is using 'Tonies' in the generic sense.

290 (c) I have written a long letter] The only previous letter in *SL* is dated 6 Mar. 1803 (above, pp. 175–9).

291 (c) "pursuing fortunes slippery ball"] Burns, *Farewell to the mason-lodge, at Tarbolton*, st. [1], line 6: 'Pursuing Fortune's sliddery ba'.'

293 (b) Mrs. Lozd] Apparently a misreading for Mrs Lloyd. See Index.

293 (b) the price of the M.S.] See above, p. 263 *n.*

294 (b) Hamiltons fragment] The fragment supplied by Robert Hamilton, Advocate. See *Minstrelsy* (ed. Henderson), i. 215.

294 (d) Diary of Bannatyne] Richard Bannatyne, *Journal of the transactions in Scotland . . . 1570, 1571, 1572, 1573,*

8vo Edinburgh, 1806. *ALC* gives Sir J. G. Dalyell as editor.

294 (d) James the Sext] Laing edited *Historie and life of King James the Sext*, Edinburgh, 1804. This was incomplete but Laing never found time to finish it. Thomas Thomson, instead of completing it, re-edited the whole work for the Bannatyne Club in 1825. See also my note to *SL* vii. 87 (d).

294 (e) monument dug up] Popularly known as the 'Liberalis Stone.' Much has been written about it, but the most authoritative is in *Royal Commission on the Ancient Monuments of Scotland, Selkirkshire*, Edinburgh, 1957, No. 174, pp. 110–13 and figs. 102 and 132. Cf. Scott's *Minstrelsy* (ed. Henderson), iii. 174.

295 (d) To George Thomson] This letter was written after the middle of July and after the letter on p. 310 which is wrongly dated.

296 (c) the heart as hard as a nether millstone] *Bible*, *Job* 41: 24.

296 *n.* 1] 'When the heathen trumpets clang' is the opening line of *The monks of Bangor's march*. In line 2, delete 'probably', and see my note to *SL* i. 327 (a).

296 *n.* 2] Date is probably 1809. First announcement of James's courtship is 19 Aug. 1808 (*SL* ii. 82). The next (*SL* i. 492) is probably autumn 1808 and before 11 Nov., as Scott is still at Ashiestiel. By 13 Dec. 1808 (*SL* ii. 135) James is definitely getting married. Unless the engagement was broken off immediately after 13 Dec. Scott's letter must be 1809.

297 (a) To Robert Surtees] This letter belongs to the Christmas vacation 1806/7, probably early Jan. 1807 before Scott returned to Edinburgh. The ed. of *Minstrelsy* is 3rd, advertised on 19 Dec. 1806. Jamieson's *Ballads* was published in Oct. 1806.

297 (c) Hobbie Noble] Scott retained 'Earl of Whitfield' in all eds. of the *Minstrelsy*. In 1st ed. (i. 170) he had a note: '*Earl of Whitfield*—The Editor does not know who is here meant.' This note was retained in 2nd to 4th eds. but in the 5th ed., 1810 (i. 249), he added: 'It should perhaps be Ralph Whitfield.'

297 *n.* 1] Amend this note. The earliest letter is the one at p. 341 below.

298 *n.* 1] *Lord Ewrie* was first printed in the *Minstrelsy*, 4th ed. (1810), i. 131–5 (Henderson's ed., i. 363–7). It was a forgery by Surtees.

299 (a) "With a hey and a lily gay . . ."] *The cruel brother; or, the bride's testament.* In Jamieson, *Popular ballads*, i. 66. The burden is 2nd and 4th lines of each stanza: 'With a heigh-ho! and a lily gay, / As the primose spreads so sweetly.'

299 (b) Select Ballads] Correct title is *Popular ballads*.

299 (d) To Lady Dalkeith] This letter, I think, should be dated 1807: (1) Hogg, in his letter of Mar. 1806, refers to a farm, but the subject of Scott's letter here is valuation of sheep land; (2) Parliament was dissolved on 27 Apr. 1807 and Scott's reference to Lord Dalkeith's campaign (p. 300) seems to refer to electioneering which followed that dissolution.

300 (e) To Lady Dalkeith] Note 2 on p. 299, with deletion of first sentence, should be transferred to this letter.

301 (f) To Lady Abercorn] She had written on 5 June (NLS MS. 3875, f. 183), but it is doubtful if Scott had received it by the time he writes this letter.

302 (d) "the drowsy bench . . ."] Blackstone. See my note to *SL* i. 147 (c).

302 *n.*] In line 8, for 'Duddingstone' read 'Duddingston.' The words 'generally refers' in line 14 are misleading. In the 12 vols. Scott calls him the 'Marquis of Carrabas' only twice (*SL* iii. 294, 303). Grierson goes further in *SL* iii. 303 *n.* 1, where he says Scott 'always gives him this addition.'

303 (b) two little things for Welch tunes] *The monks of Bangor's march* and *On Ettrick Forest's mountains dun* for George Thomson's *A select collection of original Welsh airs.*

303 (c) some of the ballads] *Ballads and lyrical pieces*, Edinburgh, 1806.

304 (b) To Lady Abercorn] Date is probably 28 June, for Lady Abercorn, on receiving the squibs, replied immediately on 4 July (NLS MS. 3875, f. 203).

304 (c) a trifling song . . . [and] another ballad] *Health to Lord Melville* and *The lawyer and the Archbishop of Canterbury* (*Ruff*, Nos. 50 and 187).

304 (d–e) as the Duchess . . . accepts of the half dozen of acorns] Cervantes, *Don Quixote*, Pt II, chaps. 52, 57 (Lockhart's ed., 1822, v. 105, 107, 109, 148).

305 (d) my throat as Falstaff says] Shakespeare, *II Henry IV*, I. 2.

305 (f) your letter from Pulo Penang] This was sent to Richard Heber, who did not return it. It is printed in *Heber letters*, pp. 203–8.

306 (b) to Heber . . . to Constable] Leyden's letter to Heber of 24 Oct. 1805 is in *Heber letters*, pp. 200–1 and his letter of 23 Oct. 1805 to Constable is in *Archibald Constable*, i. 203–8.

306 (e) Osen] Aeson, Jason's father.

307 (a) The Cottage] Lasswade Cottage.

307 (c) large of limb and bone] *Sir Cauline*, Pt I, st. [17], line 2: 'And large of limb and bone.' In Percy's *Reliques*. Given as a quotation in *SL* vii. 120.

307 (e) Knight of the Crocodile] Charles Carpenter. In his letter Leyden had told Scott of the experiences of Mr and Mrs Carpenter with a crocodile. See *Heber letters*, p. 204.

307 (e) only five months old] Charles was six and a half months old.

308 (a) Minstrelsy and . . . Sir Tristrem] 3rd ed. of former and 2nd ed. of latter came out in 1806.

308 (e) un petit lavement] Molière, *Monsieur de Pourceagnac*, I. 11.

309 (a) Specimens] Both works were called *Specimens*. Scott is contrasting the English metrical romances with the former English poets.

309 (a) to flourish like a green bay tree] See above, p. 23 and my note.

310 (a) To George Thomson] This letter belongs to the beginning of July before the Courts rose. See also my note to *SL* i. 295 (d). The letter is in Hadden, *George Thomson*, pp. 155–6, where three stanzas of the Morlachian fragment are given. These verses are part of *The lamentation of the faithful wife of Asan Aga*, which Scott translated from

Goethe. See my *Bibl.*, Nos. 721, 744, 2185, 2335.

310 (c) the enclosed squib] Grierson suggests (p. 311 *n*. 2) that it may be *Miseries of human life*. He does not say that he cribbed the idea from Andrew Lang (Hadden, op. cit., p. 155). The squib is either *Health to Lord Melville* or *The Lawyer and the Archbishop of Canterbury*.

311 (a) he died last week] Daniel died on 25 July. (*Edinburgh Advertiser*, 1806 (29 July), p. 71; *Scots Mag.* Vol. 68 (Aug. 1806), p. 647.) This letter, like so many, was probably written in instalments so that 'last week' was correct at the time of writing though the letter was not finished till 6 Aug.

311 (b) eastern Magician] Prince Hussein. See my note to *SL* i. 229 (e).

311 (d) We are eight miles] Scott's distances are not very accurate. He was about five miles from Galashiels and Selkirk; Laidlaw of Peel was close by and the Pringles lived at the Yair about two miles away.

311 *n*. 2] The *Miseries* was written by Rev. James Beresford. Scott had 3rd ed., 1807, in 2 vols. Delete the last line and see my note to *SL* i. 310 (c).

312 (f) their seat in the Highlands] Dunira in Perthshire.

313 (a) my projected romance] *The Lady of the Lake*. See above, p. 303.

313 (a) Princess of Wales] Inquiry into charges of adultery made by Lady Douglas.

313 (f) hiterto] Read 'hitherto.'

314 (a) To James Skene] The date of this letter is confirmed by the report in the *Edinburgh Advertiser* of 12 Aug. 1806 of a violent thunderstorm which raged from 5 p.m. on Saturday, 9 Aug. till 2 a.m. on Sunday, 10 Aug.

314 (b) James] I think this may be James Stewart, the groom at Mertoun. See *SL* ii. 512.

314 (d) execution being done on Cawdor] Shakespeare, *Macbeth*, I. 4: 'Is execution done on Cawdor?'

315 (e) parcel of quills] Cf. above, p. 312.

316 (a) The state of our own weather] See my note to *SL* i. 314 (a).

316 (c) Ogilvie of Chesters] Thomas Elliot Ogilvie (1751–1831). On Ogilvie and the damage sustained by the flood, see Tancred, *Annals*, p. 337.

316 (d) Minto House] 'Lord Minto's house at *Minto*, has likewise experienced considerable injury from the overflowing of a rivulet near the house.' *Edinburgh Advertiser*, 1806 (12 Aug.), p. 102, c. 4.

317 (a) Mr. Fox's death] Charles James Fox, not Judge Fox of three lines above.

317 (c) to please Mr. Pitt] His approbation of *The lay*. See *Lockhart*, ii. 225–6.

317 *n*. 1] Amend. Complaints had been made of the conduct of Mr Justice Fox at the Assizes of Donegal and Fermanagh in 1803. Several petitions were presented to Parliament in 1804, but the House of Lords stopped further proceedings against him on 19 June 1806.

318 (a) three original letters] I cannot find these in either 1st or 2nd ed. of Scott's *Dryden*.

318 (a) Duke of Dorset's papers] See *SL* i. 350, ii. 179 and 394 and my note at last reference.

318 (c) vile weather or it] Read 'vile weather for it.'

318 *n*. 1] This is a very odd note. Scott's spelling was always erratic and he spelt Thomas Thomson as Thompson and George Thomson as Thompson and so on.

319 *n*. 1] Anna Seward's letters of 20 June and 23 Sept. are in *Letters of Anna Seward*, vi. 276–81 and 314–18. In line 10, for 'at Abbotsford' read 'in NLS.'

319 *n*. 2] For '20th July' read '25th July.'

322 (b) "that if they do not prefer Scotland . . ."] 'A Scotchman must be a very sturdy moralist, who does not love *Scotland* better than truth: he will always love it better than inquiry.' (*Johnson's Journey to the Western Islands of Scotland and Boswell's Journal of a tour*, ed. by R. W. Chapman, Oxford Univ. Press, 1970, p. 108.) Boswell regretted that he had not had the chance to persuade Johnson 'to omit or soften his assertion.' (Ibid., p. 229 *n*.)

322 (d) The Highland Society] It is odd that Scott, writing in 1806, should say the Society 'have lately set about investigating' and yet make no mention of their *Report*, drawn up by Henry Mackenzie, and published in 1805. This *Report* had been reviewed by Scott in *ER* Vol. 6 (July 1805), pp. 429–62.

323 (f) his first word received] Read 'his first work received'.

325 (f) To Constable & Co.] The original is now in NLS (MS. 742, f. 10). Slingsby's letter of 29 Sept. 1806 is referred to, but not printed, in *Archibald Constable*, iii. 6 *n*. Constable & Co. replied on 2 Oct. and the complete letter is in ibid. iii. 6 *n*. Scott's letter to Slingsby is not in *SL*. Slingsby's letter, cited in the footnote, is his *second* letter to Constable. On Ritson's share in this publication see *Archibald Constable*, iii. 6 *n*. and H. A. Burd, *Joseph Ritson*, Urbana, 1916, pp. 109–10. The MS. used by Scott was sold at the sale of the Duke of Newcastle's Library at Sotheby's in Feb. 1938.

325 (f) Sir W. Slingsby] The original MS., now in NLS (MS. 742, f. 10) has 'Sir H. Slingsby.'

326 (c–d) There are some papers] In the 2nd ed. of *Sir Tristrem* (1806) there was added a 'Postcript' to the introduction which begins: 'In removing and arranging some ancient papers, lodged in the offices of the Clerks of Session, the following genealogical memoir was discovered.'

327 (a) To George Thomson] Hadden in his *George Thomson*, p. 157, says Thomson noted the song to 'The Sheriff's fancy' was *On Ettrick Forest's mountains dun*.

327 *n*. 1] In line 3, '1809' should be '1818.' This note is partly repeated in *SL* vi. 29 *n*., where the correct date is given.

328 (b) Hogg] *The mountain bard*, published in 1807 and dedicated to Scott.

328 (f) My predecessor] George Home.

328 (f) Lord ——] Probably Lord John Campbell, afterwards 7th Duke of Argyll. He was, at this time, M.P. for Argyllshire and could give Scott a frank.

329 (a) *Diary illustrative*] Add reference: iii. 297–9.

329 *n.* 1] It is printed in *FL* i. 56–61.

330 (e) the first Earl of Buccleuch formed a Legion] Walter Scott, 1st Earl of Buccleuch, served for three periods between 1627 and 1633 in Holland with a Scots regiment raised by himself.

331 (a) Sir William Scott] The MS. of *Description of the Sheriffdom of Roxburgh*, by Sir William Scott of Harden and Andrew Ker of Sunlaws, dated 27 Dec. 1649, was among the Macfarlane MSS. in the Advocates' Library when Scott wrote. It was printed by the Scottish History Society in *Geographical collections . . . made by Walter Macfarlane*, 3 vols., Edinburgh, 1906–8, iii. 135–8. The passage, however, cited by Scott is not contained in this, but in another MS. headed *Information concerning Teviotdale*, which has no author or date. It was printed, ibid., iii. 156–62, the passage cited being at p. 160.

331 (e) beat their own swords . . . into ploughshares] *Bible: Isaiah* 2: 4 and *Micah* 4: 3.

332 (d) In England now the Duchess dwells] Walter Scott of Satchells, *True history* (Hawick, 1894), 'Wats Bellanden,' p. 65.

333 (b) Satchells] Walter Scott of Satchells, *True history* (Hawick, 1894), 'Post'ral,' p. 96.

333 (c) "name & port of gentlemen"] Shakespeare, *II King Henry VI*, IV. 1.

333 (d–e) seven Lairds of the Forest] See *SL* ix. 244.

335 (a) "no longer pipe no longer dance"] *Kelly*, p. 257.

335 (b) Lady D.] Lady Dalkeith gave birth on 25 Nov. to Walter Francis, afterwards 5th Duke of Buccleuch.

335 (d) I will write] This letter to the Duchess of Gordon is not in NLS and is not known to be extant.

335 (e) Smythe] Scott at this time wrote to Smyth about Jamieson's *Ballads* and called him 'the Reverend.' This letter is not in *SL* but Smyth's reply of 12 Dec. 1806, in which he points out Scott's error, is in Partington, *Letterbooks*, pp. 220–1.

335 *n.* 1] The date is about Sept. and the letter should have come before the letter to Constable (p. 325) which is dated 7 Oct. and by which time the *Ballads* had been published.

335 *n.* 2] It was announced in the *Scots Mag.* for May 1806 (Vol. 68, p. 365) that, as Jamieson was abroad, the publication would be superintended by Scott.

336 (a) Dr. Jamieson] John Jamieson.

336 (b) Mr. Millar] I do not know if William Miller visited Ashiestiel. Scott wrote to him on 31 Oct. (letter not known to be extant) and Miller acknowledged it from London on 3 Nov. (NLS MS. 865, ff. 76–7) and wrote about Dryden and the Dorset papers.

336 (d) To Robert Sym] 1805 would be a likelier date than 1806. This letter was printed in full in *Chambers's Jour.* 6th ser. Vol. 8 (Oct. 1905), p. 695, in an article by M. B. M. quoting extensively from Sym's critique. By the time this letter had appeared in *SL*, Sym's MS., Scott's replies and this letter had passed (1931) into the possession of NLS (MS. 667).

336 *n.* 1] See G. A. M. Wood, *Sir Walter Scott and Sir Ralph Sadler*, in *Studies in Scottish Literature*, Vol. 7, pp. 11–20, 147–58, 229–37, Vol. 8, pp. 253–64.

337 (c) get me a *kiver*] Smollett, *Humphry Clinker*; Win. Jenkins to Mrs Mary Jones, 3 June, 18 July and 4 Oct.

337 *n.* 1] The Governor of the Channel Islands was General Sir George Don, uncle of Scott's friend, Sir Alexander Don of Newton Don. Grierson gives no source for the long quotation. It is copied from *FL* i. 63 *n.* In line 1, for 'Fergusson' read 'Ferguson.'

338 (b) Maconochie] Allan Maconochie who became Lord Meadowbank in 1796.

339 (c–d) Edmonstounes health] John James Edmonstone, in spite of this melancholy account of bodily and mental illness, was Sheriff of Bute till 1818 and lived till 1840.

340 (b) "Critical Review,"] Jamieson's *Ballads* was reviewed in the *Critical Review*, 3rd ser. Vol. 9, No. 3 (Nov. 1806), pp. 303–13.

341 (a) Noodle in Tom Thumb] In Fielding's play, *Tom Thumb*.

341 (c) battle of Belrinnes] Scott is referring to Jamieson's *The Battle of Glenlivet* in his *Popular ballads*, ii. 144–5, which is a modern English, and much curtailed, version of the early Scots version of *The Battell of Balrinnes* in Sir John G. Dalyell's *Scotish poems, of the sixteenth century*, Edinburgh, 1801, ii. 347–56.

341 *n.* 1] Surtees's letter, dated 8 Dec. 1806, is in Taylor, *Memoir of Robert Surtees*, pp. 26–30. The suggestion at the end of the note that Surtees's letter 'led to the tale of *Waverley*' is untenable in view of its dating. *Waverley* had been begun more than a year before Surtees wrote. See also *SL* ii. 37.

342 (a) I will certainly insert it] Scott inserted *The death of Featherstonhaugh* in the 4th ed. of the *Minstrelsy* (1810), i. 233–8 (ed. Henderson, ii. 110–14).

343 (c) "Good Night of Lord Derwentwater."] This ballad, beginning 'Farewell to pleasant Dilston Hall,' was a forgery by Surtees. It was printed by Hogg in his *Jacobite relics*, 2nd ser. (1821), pp. 30–1, and in Taylor's *Memoir of Robert Surtees*, pp. 253–5.

343 (d) a stale copy] Read 'a stall copy.'

343 (d) "Mackintosh was a soldier brave . . ."] This is the first stanza of a ballad usually called *On the first Rebellion*, printed by Ritson in *The Northumberland garlands*, 1793, and his *Northern garland*, 1810. Also in John Bell's *Rhymes of northern bards*, Newcastle upon Tyne, 1812, pp. 223–4, and in Hogg's *Jacobite relics*, ii. 102–3. See also *SL* i. 238 (c–d).

343 (f) Bulmer] See note to *Marmion*, Canto IV, st. xxii.

344 (d) To George Home] The month is almost certainly Feb., the month in which the 3rd ed. of *The lay* was published. The lines on p. 138 to which Scott refers were the same in the 2nd ed.

344 *n.* 1] See note to *Marmion*, Canto V, st. xxv. The quotation from Pitscottie there differs slightly from the version given in this letter. Pitscottie says the one man who escaped was Richard Lawson. The 'poem or tale', which Scott mentions, may be *Flodden-Field* (Herd, i. 45–9) in which the Provost is given as the sole survivor. Surtees had, in his letter of 8 Dec.

1806, referred to this story of Plotock. See Taylor, *Memoir of Robert Surtees*, p. 28.

344 *n.* 2] The difficulties did not arise out of the new Judicature Act but were due to Home's obstinacy in declining to avail himself of the Superannuation Act.

345 (a) To Miss Seward] This letter is dated 18 Jan. in *Letters of Anna Seward*, vi. 326.

345 (e) Lord Melville's family his nephew & son] Robert Dundas of Arniston, Lord Chief Baron, is the nephew. The son is Robert Dundas, afterwards 2nd Viscount.

345 *n.* 1] Her letter of 23 Sept. is in *Letters of Anna Seward*, vi. 314–18.

346 (b) with Agrippa . . .] Bible, Acts 26: 28.

346 (c) I am aware of the connection] Anna Seward had referred to Hoare's translation in her letter (*Letters of Anna Seward*, vi. 317–18).

346 (d) price is renderd . . . extravagant by the number of engravings] Anna Seward replied on 29 Jan. 1807: 'I think entirely with you concerning the foppery of the press . . . Those who feel poetry will always feel the engravings a disadvantage to it.' (*Letters of Anna Seward*, vi. 328.)

348 (a) To James Longman] This must be an error for Thomas Norton Longman.

348 (b) my new work] *Marmion*.

350 (f) Dorset papers] See *SL* i. 318, ii. 179 and 394 and my note at the last reference.

351 (a) a new Bill] This became 'An Act concerning the administration of justice in Scotland, and concerning appeals to the House of Lords', 48 Geo. III. c. 151, 4 July 1808. On Scott's speech to the Faculty of Advocates on the bill, see *SL* ii. 180.

351 (b) a new Edition of the Minstrel] Scott means the *Minstrelsy*, 3rd ed., published at the end of 1806 (*Ruff*, No. 14). Three new ballads were added (the 'few additional verses' of Scott's letter).

351 *n.* 2] Scott could not be answering Lady Abercorn's letter of 10 Feb. She

had written on 27 Dec. 1806 (NLS MS. 3875, ff. 261-2).

351 *n.* 3] The dedication is undated, but the 'memoir' (in the form of a letter to Scott) is dated 'Mitchell-Slack, Nov. 1806.' Edith Batho does not record a 2nd ed., but the 3rd ed., 1821, has the date changed to 'Sept. 27, 1807.' Batho, *The Ettrick Shepherd*, pp. 186-7.

352 (b) stocking a small farm] Edith Batho, *The Ettrick Shepherd*, p. 59, says: 'in 1807 . . . he joined with a friend, Adam Brydon of Aberlosk . . . and took the farm of Locherben in Yarrow.' Locherben is not in Yarrow. It is in Dumfriesshire, about 10 miles E. of Penpont.

352 *n.* 2] In line 3, delete 'had.' Hastings did not lose his arm till he was in action in Zealand about July and Aug. 1807.

353 (a) "Knights Squires and Steeds shall enter on the Stage."] Pope, *Essay on criticism*, line 282. Pope was quoting from the continuation of *Don Quixote*, but that Scott is quoting Pope is shown by his quotation on the title-page of *Halidon Hill*.

353 (b) Alas that Scottish Maid] John Leyden, *Ode on visiting Flodden*, st. IV, lines 1-4. In Scott's *Minstrelsy* (ed. Henderson), iii. 415.

353 (b-c) But we may say with Francis I] 'Tout est perdu fors l'honneur.' Said by Francis I after his defeat at Pavia, 1525. See Scott's *Dryden*, ix. 43.

353 (c) Mr. White] Rev. Henry White.

353 (e) 'twere pity of my life] Shakespeare, *A midsummer night's dream*, III. 1.

354 (a) the very latchets . . .] *Bible, Mark* 1: 7; *Luke* 3: 16.

354 (b) "in these days were giants in the land"] *Bible, Genesis* 6: 4: 'There were giants in the earth in those days.'

354 (b) tribute to . . . Garrick] *Monody on the death of David Garrick, Esq.* Printed in the *Scots Mag.* Vol. 41 (Feb. 1779), p. 103, and in her *Poetical works* (1810), ii. 15-17.

354 (f) To Robert Surtees] Scott is answering his letter of 12 Feb. 1807, printed in Taylor, *Memoir of Robert Surtees*, pp. 33-8.

356 *n.* 1] Delete and substitute: James Hogg's *The mountain bard*.

357 (c) Nunnery at Lindisfarne] Scott admitted this was 'altogether fictitious' in the 1st ed. of *Marmion*, note to Canto II, st. xix.

357 (f) Kennedy's *Praelium Gillicrankiense*] Correct title is: *Prælium Gillicrankianum*. See my note to *SL* i. 200 *n.* 2.

358 (a) *Souvenirs de Chastelain*] See my note to *SL* i. 199 *n.*

358 (a) write out the song] *Musgrave's lamentation*. See above, p. 298, 298 *n.*

358 (b) The Dialogue between Jenny Cameron and her Maid] Surtees, in his letter of 12 Feb. 1807 (Taylor, *Memoir of Robert Surtees*, p. 37), had offered this rhyming dialogue. Scott later acquired a copy, probably from Surtees.

358 (c) "The oak, the ash . . ."] This is usually called *The Northern lass's lamentation*. There was a black letter copy in the Roxburghe Collection. Printed in Evans's *Old ballads* (1810), i. 115-19. Quoted in *Rob Roy*, chap. 4.

359 (c) pleasant news of Mrs. Erskine] She gave birth to a daughter at Melrose on 24 Mar. (*Scots Mag.* Vol. 69 (Apr. 1807), p. 316.)

359 *n.* 1] The reader might think that these were Scott's colleagues in 1807. Hume did not become a Principal Clerk till 1811 and Dundas till 1817.

359 *n.* 2] Surtees's letter is in Taylor, *Memoir of Robert Surtees*, pp. 42-7.

360 (a) illness of a particular friend] Colin Mackenzie.

360 (c) address to Collingwood] The lines to which Scott is referring are: 'And fare thee well, George Collingwood, / Since fate has put us down— / If thou and I have lost our lives, / Our king has lost his crown.'

360 (e) stocking his little farm] Locherben. See my note to *SL* i. 352 (b).

361 (a) To Lady Abercorn] Delete date '[1807]' at top. The date '15 May [1807]' is given at end.

361 (e) Liverpool] Liverpool should be Loughborough.

361 (f) Lord Melville . . . Election business] Parliament was dissolved on

27 Apr. and the new Parliament met on 22 June.

363 (d) To James Ballantyne] Date must be about Oct. Scott did not send Cantos I–II to Lady Abercorn till Sept. (below, p. 381) and had finished Canto III by 12 Nov. (below, p. 395). In *Lockhart* (iii. 12–13) this letter is in the narrative for about May and this dating has misled Grierson.

364 *n.* 1] The two issues are amalgamated in this note. There was an ordinary quarto in 2 vols. and a large paper quarto in 3 vols.

365 (e) send you this letter] Letter 53 in Sadler, *State papers*, ii. 110–25.

365 (f) Mr. Lodge] *Illustrations of British history . . . by Edmund Lodge*, 3 vols., 4to London, 1791.

366 (f) Queen Auragua] *Queen Orraca*, by Southey. See above, p. 361, 361 *n.*

369 (b) Old Man of the Sea] *Story of Sindbad the Sailor* in *The Arabian Nights* (Weber, *Tales of the East*, i. 81).

369 (c) Dugald Stuart & Tom Campbell] Dugald Stewart was appointed writer of the *Edinburgh Gazette*, a sinecure of £300 a year, and Campbell received a pension of £200 a year.

370 (d) just recovering from confinement] Birth of the second Walter, 23 June.

370 (f) Your line . . . has fallen in pleasant places] *Bible, Psalms* 16: 6.

371 (c) some unpleasant business] Tom's embezzlement of Lord Abercorn's funds.

371 (c) "I'll be a guide worth any two . . ."] *Hobbie Noble*, st. [11], lines 3–4. In Scott's *Minstrelsy* (ed. Henderson), ii. 121.

371 *n.* 1] The ballads in the list, too long to be copied here, should be checked with those listed in my Index under Ballads and Songs.

372 (c) To Miss Smith] Date is 4 Aug. 1807.

372 *n.* 1] Delete second sentence. Scott wrote *Lines to Miss Smith*, to be recited by her on her benefit night, Saturday, 8 Aug. Dibdin, *Annals*, p. 251, says they arrived too late. The verses were printed in *The Forget-Me-Not* for 1834 (publ. 1833), with the correct date 1807 and Scott's *Poetical works*, misdated 1817.

373 *n.* 1] In line 3 for '26th August' read '24th August' (NLS MS. 865, ff. 97–9).

374 (d) yeoman's service] Shakespeare, *Hamlet*, V. 2.

374 (f) my harp has been hung on the willows] *Bible, Psalms* 137: 2.

375 (a) some verses . . . to the young Roscius] *Address to the young Roscius*, included in Anna Seward's *Poetical works* (1810), iii. 382–5.

375 (c–d) Epic or narrative poem] *Gertrude of Wyoming*, published in 1809.

377 (f) moving accidents by flood and field] Shakespeare, *Othello*, I. 3.

379 (d) tale of the fox] See L'Estrange, *Fables*, Fable 7. *A lion, an ass, &c. a hunting.* By Æsop.

379 (e) a pig in a poke] *Kelly*, p. 221; Ramsay, *Proverbs*, p. 33; Ray, p. 189.

380 (c) his name is up] St. [5], lines 3–4 of *The mock serenade* in Cervantes's *Don Quixote* (tr. by Motteux), Pt II, chap. 44 (Lockhart's ed., 1822, V. 12). Also quoted in *SL* iv. 345, vi. 143, xi. 60.

380 (d) Beatties] Read 'Bettys.' (Correction in *SL* xii. 487.)

381 (b) Mr. Wright] Thomas Guthrie Wright, W.S., Lord Abercorn's law agent in Scotland.

381 (e) a shooting hut of Lord Somerville's] The Pavilion, near Abbotsford. Illustrated, *MPW* Vol. 20, frontispiece.

382 (b) "To throw off her gallant shoes . . ."] *Bonny Lizie Baillie*, st. [4]. Scott quotes from this song several times in his letters. There are various versions, but the one which he seems consistently to quote is in Charles Wilson's *St. Cecilia*, Edinburgh, 1779, pp. 57–8. The stanza quoted here varies considerably with the ones in *Herd* and *Johnson*.

383 (d) To Henry Mackenzie] For rest of letter, printed from original, see *SL* xii. 390–1.

384 (e) "I'll rather dwell in my necessity"] Shakespeare, *The Merchant of Venice*, I. 3.

385 (f) pleasure to receive any token] Southey had written on 27 Sept. saying he was sending *Palmerin of England*. (*Lockhart*, iii. 25.)

385 *n.* 2] The letter 'which came between' is dated 4 Oct. and is in Partington, *Letter-books*, pp. 73–5.

386 (a) *à la Tressan*] See above, p. 211 and my note.

386 *n.*] Amend line 3. Scott did not send a copy to the Princess till later. See my next note. The third last line refers to Wordsworth's *In the Pass of Killicranky*, line 11: 'O for a single hour of that Dundee.'

387 (d) If you wish to oblige her R. H.] Scott sent the verses in 1808 and Mrs Hayman wrote: 'I am commanded to thank you much for *Queen Orraca*.' (Partington, *Letter-books*, p. 9.)

387 (e) your brother] Henry Herbert Southey.

387 (f) Frere's] Southey quoted part of Frere's translation in an appendix to his *Chronicle of the Cid*.

388 (c) the old proverb] *Ray*, p. 210.

390 (b) I am thinking of publishing a small edition of the Morte Arthur] By following the references in my Index, which are arranged chronologically, it will be seen that Scott immediately abandoned the project in favour of Southey in 1807. In the 1810 and 1812 references Southey has transferred the task to Scott. There are no further references; but we know that Scott abandoned the plan and that Southey published his *Byrth, lyf and actes of Kyng Arthur* in 1817.

390 (d) song of Lord Clifford's minstrel] *Song at the feast of Brougham Castle*.

390 (d) *caviare . . . to the multitude*] Shakespeare, *Hamlet*, II. 2: 'caviare to the general'.

391 (a) To Lady Louisa Stuart] From the contents the date must be mid Dec. Lady Louisa's letter, which Scott is answering, is in *FL* i. 85–6, but it is undated.

391 (a) ingratitude much worse than that of witchcraft] This is not Biblical (as Scott says in *SL* ii. 20). He probably got the maxim from Smollett's *Peregrine Pickle*, chap. 14 (see *SL* xii. 165 *n.* 3)

or from a chapbook, *A pious warning against ingratitude, worse than the sin of witchcraft*, n.p., n.d. See also *SL* iv. 3 and *n.*

391 (d) Chapelain] Douglas (*FL* i. 87 *n.* 2) suggested this should be 'Chastelain or Molinet', citing Scott's review of Godwin's *Chaucer* in *ER* for 1804 (*MPW* xvii. 76–7). In the review Scott quoted two lines of verse and said they were from Molinet. Douglas failed to note that the author was Georges Chastellain, the Abbotsford transcriber having misread Scott's long 's' for a 'p.' Although Scott gives Chastellain correctly in this letter, he repeated the error of 1804 in his note to the Introd. to Canto V of *Marmion* (1st ed., p. lxxx and uncorrected in subsequent eds.). For Chastellain, see my note to *SL* i. 199 *n.*

391 *n.* 1] This note is based on Douglas's note in *FL* i. 85 and the error 'fourth Earl' for 'third Earl' has been copied.

391 *n.* 2] The date, 20th Dec., is impossible as Scott says in the letter that he is going to Mertoun for Christmas and then to Glasgow. Colquhoun was installed on 29 Dec. (MS. Minutes of Senatus, Glasgow Univ.)

392 (a) Monsieur] Count d'Artois, afterwards Charles X of France, 1824–30. By the Abbey Scott means the Palace of Holyrood House.

392 *n.* 1] Mrs Hughes, in her *Letters*, pp. 18, 19, says she first met Scott in 1806. The date is given as 1806 below, p. 402 *n.*

393 (c) I have also one with some ornaments] The original drawings were by James Skene. Mrs Hayman sent the Princess's thanks in a letter of 22 Feb. 1808, in Partington, *Letter-books*, pp. 8–9, where it is wrongly dated 1807.

393 *n.*] In line 2, for "Spirits blasted thee" read 'Spirit's blasted tree.' (Corrected in *SL* xii. 487.) The author was George Warrington. Mrs Hughes in her *Letters*, pp. 18–19, explains that the 'doleful song' is Fitz-Eustace's song in *Marmion*, Canto III. (Noted *SL* xii. 487.) See also below, p. 403.

394 (a) Wynne] Charles Watkin Williams Wynn.

394 (b) To Lady Abercorn] Scott is answering her letter of 3 Oct. (NLS MS. 3876, ff. 107–8).

394 (d) R. Dundas] Robert Dundas, afterwards 2nd Viscount Melville.

394 (e) The chief Baron] Robert Dundas of Arniston.

394 (f) whom the King delighteth to honour] *Bible, Esther* 6: 6, 7, 9, 11.

395 (f) Ladies Maria & Harriet] Lady Maria was 3rd daughter and Lady Harriot Margaret was eldest daughter of 1st Marquess of Abercorn.

396 (b) To Miss Seward] In this letter (p. 398) Scott says he showed Copleston's pamphlet to Jeffrey 'this morning.' If the date assigned to the letter (23 Nov.) is correct, the copy must have been a different one from that received from Mrs. Hughes (below, p. 402). Perhaps this letter should be given a later date.

396 n. 1] Delete this note. Scott's reference to Lady Manners shows that he is referring not to Erskine, Lord Chancellor of England, but to Sir Thomas Manners Sutton who had just been appointed Lord Chancellor of Ireland and created Baron Manners.

397 (d) Laird of Kiers Butler] This anecdote does not relate to the Rebellion of 1715 but to the abortive Jacobite rising of 1708. Stirling of Keir and others were tried for treason on 22 Nov. 1708. Scott tells the story in *Tales of a grandfather*, chap. 62 (*MPW* xxv. 154).

397 (e) Lady Lucas] See Index under De Grey.

397 (f) reviewing my poor Shepherd] Hogg's *Mountain bard* was reviewed in the *Critical Review*, 3rd ser. Vol. 12 (Nov. 1807), pp. 237–44. Douglas (*FL* i. 83 n.) says this was by Anna Seward.

398 (b) in poetry never] Scott repeated this statement in the following year (*SL* iv. 156) but he broke the rule later and reviewed the poetry of Campbell, Croker, Southey and Byron.

398 (c) a clever little Pamphlet] *Advice to a young reviewer*, by Rev. Edward Copleston.

398 (f) Ariosto breaking the potters dishes] See *Orlando furioso in English*

heroical verse by Sr John Harington, 2° London, 1634, pp. 420–1.

400 (f) "and yet come of a noble Græme!"] *The Battle of Loudon Hill*, st. 10, line 4, in *Minstrelsy* (ed. Henderson), ii. 266.

400 (f) beastly covenanters] This is not Scott's real opinion. He writes this to please Southey.

401 (c) If . . . you can cast a job] Ballantyne had already printed *Madoc* in 1805 and later printed *Kehama* and *Roderick*.

402 (a) To Mrs. Hughes] There is a facsimile in Hughes, *Letters*, between p. 22 and p. 23. It shows slight variations from the Abbotsford Copy from which Grierson prints.

402 n. 1] In line 5, '1806' should be '1807' according to p. 392 n. above. In lines 5–6, for 'lady-in-waiting to Queen Caroline' read 'sub-governess to Princess Charlotte.' Mrs Hughes's letter cannot be dated 22 Dec. if Scott is replying to it on 15 Dec. In line 4 from foot, 'Coppleston' should be 'Copleston.'

403 (a) elegant Welch tale] *The spirit's blasted tree*, by George Warrington. See above, p. 393.

404 n. 1] For 'Millar' read 'Miller.'

405 (c) The offices have been held by the same person] Sir James Colquhoun of Luss had been Sheriff of Dunbarton, 1775–1805, and Principal Clerk, 1779–1805. Scott refers to this again, below, p. 406 and *SL* ii. 452 and *SL* iii. 336, 345. When Cosmo Innes became a Principal Clerk in 1852 he had to resign as Sheriff of Elgin.

410 (c) Marshall & Coy] James Marshall, cabinet-maker, in partnership with William Hogg. The firm occupied the first storey (i.e. the first floor above ground level) of Paul's Work and James Ballantyne & Co. occupied the second storey. (*Trust Disposition*, NLS MS. 112, f. 54.)

410 (d) House in Foulis close] John Ballantyne's house. (*Edinburgh Directory* 1807.)

410 (d) Otranto] Though not issued till 1811, the text of Scott's ed. of Walpole's *Castle of Otranto* is printed on paper

watermarked 1801. The introd. has 1809 and 1810 watermarks but it looks as if the text had been printed as early as 1807.

411 (f) Shakespeare] Ballantyne printed Shakespeare's *Works*, 8 vols., for Longman in 1807.

411 (f) Mrs. Bruces loan] She is given as Mary Bruce and Miss Bruce in *Reply to Mr Lockhart's pamphlet*, Appendix, pp. 15, 17. 'Mrs' is apparently a courtesy title.

412 (c) a wild sort of an introduction] This became *The inferno of Altisidora*, published in 1811 in the *Edin. Ann. Reg. for 1809*, II. ii. 582–9. The fragments were: *The poacher*, 'Oh say not, my love' and *The vision of Triermain*, imitations respectively of Crabbe, Moore and Scott. The episode of Altisidora occurs in *Don Quixote*, Pt II, chap. 70. (Lockhart's ed., 1822, v. 286.)

412 (e) anticipation] Read 'imitation.'

413 (d) Shakespeare] See my note to *SL* vi. 120 (f).

414 (e) the Georgics] The *British Georgics*, by Rev. James Grahame, published by John Ballantyne & Co. in 1809.

415 (a) you are about to lose Somers] All 13 vols. (1809–15) have Ballantyne's imprint, but this does not necessarily mean that Ballantyne printed them all.

416 n. 2] For '*King James*' read '*James the First*.'

417 (a) Sandie's distress] Alexander Ballantyne's eldest child, James John, born 14 Sept. 1808, died 11 July 1812.

417 (b) Kemble] The Theatre Royal reopened on 27 July with John Kemble as Hamlet.

417 (d) James & Erskine have . . . thrown cold water] Scott had asked their opinion. See *SL* iii. 112.

417 (d) make a bolt or a shaft of it] *Ray*, p. 230.

417 (e) Cato] By Joseph Addison.

417 (f) Necessity . . . has no law] *Kelly*, p. 266; Ramsay, *Proverbs*, p. 50.

418 (c) Canto I] This was probably destroyed, for by 16 Oct. this canto had

not been completed. See *SL* iii. 175 177.

418 (c) *Monday*] Monday was 10 Aug.

419 (a) £150 for the Lay] This is the bill to Stirling which proved to be £158. 12. 10 (p. 420). It is difficult to explain this. Scott had to pay for presentation copies and Stirling, a bookseller, may have dispatched them to Scott's friends, but the sum seems far too large. If surplus stock was being bought up, Ballantyne or Constable should have paid for it, not Scott.

420 n. 1] In last line, for '1st or 2nd October' read '30 Sept.'

421 (a) *hid* Bertrams face] *Rokeby*, Canto I, st. vi, line 2.

421 (b) *Host & lost*] *Rokeby*, Canto I, st. xi, lines 9–10.

421 (c) Scholey] Robert Scholey, London, was joint publisher of Weber's *Tales of the East*, and Vol. 1 of *Edin. Ann. Reg.*

422 (a) Jedburgh] 'tuesday for two days' should be 'Monday for two days.' See *SL* iii. 162.

422 (e) Register] Constable's name does not appear on the title-page of the *Edin. Ann. Reg.* till 1816.

422 n. 1] For 'a second from Jedburgh on the same day' read 'a second from Jedburgh on the following day, Wednesday, 7 Oct.'

423 (d) Brewster & Singers] James Ferguson, *Ferguson's astronomy . . . With notes, and supplementary chapters by D. Brewster*, 2 vols. and plates, 8vo and 4to Edinburgh, 1811; William Singer, *General view of the agriculture . . . of Dumfries*, 8vo Edinburgh, 1812.

423 (e) that which is at press] As 2nd ed. of *Rokeby* came out in Apr. and the 3rd ed. consisted of sheets of 2nd (*Ruff*, No. 123) this must be the 4th.

425 (a) Constable will I think come into the Register] See my note to *SL* i. 422 (e).

425 (d) fac-simile of old poems] William Walter's *Certaine worthie manuscript poems of great antiquitie, reserved long in the studie of a Norfolke gentleman*, etc. Imprinted at London for R.D. 1597. The colophon has: Edinburgh: Reprinted by James Ballantyne & Co.

1812. Only 25 copies were reprinted, price 15/- Sq. 12mo. Pp. [80].

428 (b) Hartstongue] He visited Scott at Abbotsford (*Ode to desolation*, p. [vii]). He was still in Edinburgh in August and visited Roslin when he wrote a poem *On visiting Roslin, August 1813*, printed in *Ode to desolation*, pp. 32–5. The *Edinburgh Evening Courant* of 12 Aug. announced his departure from Edinburgh.

432 (b) To John Ballantyne] The date is 30 July which was a Friday. The part on p. 433 beginning 'As the Marquis does not set off' is a postscript (written on a smaller sheet of paper) and forms part of the same letter (NLS MS. 863, ff. 19–22). Delete, therefore, '[*Nat. Lib. Scot.*]' on p. 433.

435 (a) *Sunday*] Sunday was 1 Aug.

435 *n.* 1] Delete this note, which contains several errors. Scott left Abbotsford for Drumlanrig on Monday, 26 July (above, p. 429). He proposed to leave Drumlanrig on Wednesday, 4 Aug. (above, p. 434), i.e. after being ten days there, corresponding to the 'ten days residence' about which he told Hartstonge (*SL* iii. 318). He then went to Keswick and spent one day with Southey (*SL* iii. 318). He was at Penrith on Tuesday, 10 Aug. (*SL* i. 435–6) and at Brough on the same day (*SL* iii. 315) and at Carlisle on Friday, 13 Aug. (*SL* i. 436, iii. 318), hoping to be at Abbotsford on Saturday, 14 Aug. (*SL* iii. 315). There is nothing in the correspondence to warrant the statement that Scott interrupted his journey by returning to Abbotsford; yet, except for the one-day visit to Southey, there is no record of what Scott was doing between 4 and 10 Aug. Although Grierson rejects Lockhart's statement in this note, he accepts it in *SL* iii. 303 *n.*

436 (c) *friday night*] 13 Aug.

437 (f) Gale] Gale & Co., London, were part publishers of *The vision of Don Roderick*, 2nd ed., 1811, and, as Gale, Curtis and Fenner, of *The Bridal of Triermain*, 1st–3rd eds., 1813, and Swift's *Works*, 1814.

442 (d) Abbotsford *Saturday*] Saturday was 21 Aug.

447 (d) the Dukes books are to be sold] John Ballantyne auctioned a portion of the Library of the 3rd Duke of Roxburghe in Lauder's Ball-Room, Kelso, on 16 Sept. and subsequent days. (*Edinburgh Advertiser*, 7 Sept. 1813.) Ballantyne issued a catalogue, printed at the 'Mail' Office, Kelso.

447 (e) the green paint] See below, p. 450.

447 (e) I wrote fully to James] On 27 Sept. See *SL* iv. 274–5, where the letter is wrongly dated 1816.

447 *n.* 1] In line 1, delete 'Vol. III, p. 355' which is no longer applicable.

450 (b) the paint] See above, p. 447.

450 (f) Messrs C. & D.] Cadell & Davies had no share in *The Lord of the Isles*, which was published by Constable and by Longman.

450 *n.* 1] Delete this note which is not applicable.

451 *n.* 1] Delete first sentence. Kaeside was bought in Nov. 1815. Scott is unlikely to be referring to Kaeside at this time for he had 'a very capricious person to deal with' (*SL* iii. 286) who is Nicol Milne and not John Moss.

453 (c) Lady of the Lake] 10th ed., which came out about June. See my note to *SL* iii. 382 (e).

453 (c–d) Jamiesons copy money . . . Webers] Payment to Robert Jamieson and Henry Weber for editing *Illustrations of northern antiquities*.

453 (e) Memoirs of Charles I] *Memoirs of the reign of King Charles the First*, by Sir Philip Warwick [ed. by Scott], Edinburgh, 1813.

454 (e) Burns Bowl] On this, or another bowl, see Sir John Carr, *Caledonian sketches*, London, 1809, p. 199; *Edin. Ann. Reg. for 1817*, x. i. 356–7; and Tancred, *Annals*, p. 253.

454 (f) portion of W.] This is the earliest reference in *SL* to *Waverley*. Edgar Johnson in his *Sir Walter Scott: the Great Unknown*, Vol. 1, p. 436, and Vol. 1, Notes, p. xlvi, No. 90, refers to a Scott letter of Jan. 1814 to John Ballantyne, sending a portion of the MS. Johnson cites 'Hepburn Millar, MS (Perth)' as his authority. The owner of this letter tells me that it is now regarded as a forgery by 'Antique' Smith.

457 (d) Weber's bill] Copymoney for share in editing *Northern antiquities*. See above, p. 453.

458 (f) *Monday morning*] Monday was 26 Sept.

459 (b) like the crane in the fable] See L'Estrange, *Fables*, p. 7. Scott is here unusually severe on Ballantyne.

460 (e) advertize the register] *Edin. Ann. Reg.* Vol. 5 (for 1812).

460 (e) extracts from my journal] *Extracts from a journal kept during a coasting voyage through the Scottish islands* in *Edin. Ann. Reg. for 1812*, v. ii. 431–46. Here, as elsewhere, Scott was indifferent to chronology. These extracts should have appeared in the vol. for 1814, not for 1812.

460 (f) Walkers Dicty. of rhymes] John Walker, *Rhyming dictionary*, 2nd ed., 2 vols., 12mo London, 1806.

464 (e) To John Ballantyne] Two extracts from this letter, given as separate letters, appear in *SL* iii. 506–7. They should be cancelled and *SL* iii, n. 2 should be transferred to the complete letter here.

464 (f) Kelso expectation] Read 'Kelso expedition' (NLS MS. 863, f. 67).

465 n. 2] Delete and substitute: *Letters on the history of Scotland*. See *SL* iii. 509, iv. 69, 277–8, 279–80, 294.

466 (f) To John Ballantyne] The letter should be dated Saturday 8 Oct. 1814. Scott says (p. 467) 'I shall write to Mr. Innes' which he did on Sunday 9 Oct. (p. 464).

467 (a) "touch pot, touch penny"] *Ray*, p. 351. Used in *Nigel*, chap. 16.

467 (f) Twill be wearing awa, John] Parody of *The land o' the leal*, by Lady Nairne, st. [1], lines 1–2.

467 n. 1] For '1814' read '1815.'

468 (c) To John Ballantyne] The contents, the tone, and the reference to Constable as Goodman Puff all suggest that this letter belongs to autumn of 1816. Cf. below, p. 496.

469 n. 1] Delete and substitute: "goodman Puff of Barson." Shakespeare, *II Henry IV*, V. 3. (Correction in *SL* xii. 487.) See also below, p. 496.

470 n. 3] For 'February' read 'March.'

470 n. 4] Delete. Scott is correct. 'Sound as a roach' was a common phrase. Used, e.g., by Smollett in *Peregrine Pickle*, chap. 18; in Maria Edgeworth, *The two guardians*, III. 1.

472 (c) *Monday*] Monday was the 24th —rather a long time before the PM of 27th.

472 (d) To John] Date is probably 9 Nov. 1814. See my note to *SL* i. 516 (a).

472 (e) on the Parlt. Close] i.e. Sir William Forbes & Co., Bankers, Parliament Square.

474 (c) To James Ballantyne] Date is Monday, 31 Oct.

474 (d) *Nullum numen deest . . .*] Juvenal, *Satires*, X. 365: 'Nullum numen habes, si sit prudentia.'

475 (a) To John Ballantyne] Date is Sunday, 30 Oct.

477 (a) Merit if thou art blessed with riches] George Pickering, *Written underneath an engraving of Apollo rewarding Merit with riches*. (*Poetry, fugitive and original; by the late Thomas Bedingfeld, Esq. and Mr. George Pickering*, 8vo Newcastle, 1815, p. 119.) The complete poem is: 'O Merit, as thou'rt blest with riches, / For God's sake buy a pair of breeches, / And give them to thy naked brother, / For one good turn deserves another.'

477 (c) Major Scott] Scott's brother John had lent £1,200 to James Ballantyne & Co. (*Reply to Mr Lockhart's pamphlet*, pp. 32–3.)

477 (c) about the neck of my conscience] A variation of Shakespeare, *The Merchant of Venice*, II. 2: 'my conscience, hanging about the neck of my heart.'

478 n. 1] The fact that the copy at Abbotsford is the gift of George IV is no proof that Scott did not buy a copy in 1815. It was his custom to dispose of duplicates.

479 (c) the two Mr. Bruces] Thomas Bruce, W.S., and his younger brother Robert, Advocate.

481 (a–b) Triermain] The 5th ed. did not come out till 1817.

481 (c–d) Book of St. Albans] By Lady Juliana Berners. This is Haslewood's reprint of 1810.

482 (a) farces] Ballantyne printed Mrs Inchbald's *A collection of farces*, 7 vols., 1809 and (in part) her *The modern theatre*, 10 vols., 1811. If Scott is referring to these works, Longman is taking a long time to pay for the printing.

483 (b) Mr Forester] Robert Forrester, Treasurer of the Bank of Scotland.

484 *n.* 1] According to John Scott's *Journal of a tour to Waterloo*, p. 281, they arrived at Abbotsford on Tuesday, 26 Sept.

486 (d) *Sunday* Abbotsford] Sunday was 8 Oct.

487 *n.* 2] Add: Shakespeare, *Twelfth Night*, II. 3.

488 (a) To John] Scott's words 'I shall budge on the 12th' indicate that he is writing in November. The letter to his wife with PM 11 Nov. (*SL* xii. 153–4) may be the one here mentioned. If so, date of letter would be 8 Nov.

488 (b) out of Egypt] See a Bible concordance.

488 (c) books from France] Scott's letter to Murray is not in *SL*. Scott, however, had received the books by 20 Nov. (*SL* iv. 128).

488 (d) Abbotrule] Ballantyne sold books from Abbotrule on 19 Jan. 1816. His visit, here referred to, was probably in connection with this sale.

489 (b) Southeys accot. of the battle] In *QR* for July 1815, published about Nov. or Dec. (*Shine*, No. 352). *Paul* did not come out till Feb. 1816.

489 (d) Sasse] A leaf advertising Richard Sasse's print was inserted in copies of *The Field of Waterloo*. (*Ruff*, No. 147.)

490 (b) Boydells Shakespeare] *The dramatic works of Shakspeare*. Revised by G. Steevens. [Ed. by Josiah Boydell.] 9 vols. 2° London, 1802.

491 (b) *friday*] Friday was 27 Oct.

491 (b) To John Ballantyne] The date is Saturday, 21 Oct.: (1) Scott announces bill for £100 after he had written about Tom's bill for £200

(below, p. 494, where the letter is Friday, 20 Oct.); (2) he sent poetry for *Register* 'yesterday' i.e. 20 Oct. (below, p. 494).

492 (a) To James Ballantyne] There is a transcript of this letter, made before it was mutilated, in NLS (MS. 6080). The missing part in line 10 reads: 'No woman thinks a man quite serious unless his attachment to her has shewn that her power can make quite a fool of him. Observe that tho I exhort you heartily to go mad in white sattin if you have a mind yet I bar John's theatrical privilege of going mad as a confidant in white linen. The state of the presses will by no means admit of your being both mad together. Meanwhile employ your frenzy to some purpose—write, run, ride, visit; and be neither surprised nor dismayed should the fair lady exert a little authority and keep you in a gentle suspense. The time of courtship is the short despotism of a woman's life and there are few who do not less or more avail themselves of it.' The reference to 'white sattin' is to Sheridan's *The critic*, III. 1.

492 (e) To John Ballantyne] This letter must precede the letter of 4 Nov. to Cadell (*SL* iv. 116) and date, therefore, is probably late Oct.

493 (b) Mosses land] Kaeside which Scott bought from John Moss.

493 (d) result of his wooing] Miss Christina Hogarth.

494 (b) To John] Date is 20 Oct. (Friday): (1) Mrs Clephane has arrived. Cf. *SL* iv. 105, 106; (2) poetry for *Register* sent today is the 'yesterday' of letter of 21 Oct. (above, p. 491); (3) Tom has drawn on Scott for £200, but next day, i.e. 21 Oct., he has received £100 towards it (above, p. 491).

495 (a) To John] The date must be 18 Apr. 1816, which was a Thursday. On 18 Apr. Scott wrote to Constable on the same subjects (*SL* iv. 215–16).

495 (b) Thoms. of Reading] James Ballantyne reprinted, without date, *Thomas of Reading; or, the sixe worthie yeomen of the West . . .* By T[homas] D[eloney], 4to London, 1632. This was announced as a new publication for Dec. 1817 in the *Edinburgh Mag.* Vol. 1,

p. 477. Also announced as an 1817 publication in *Edin. Ann. Reg.* x. ii. 267.

495 (c) copy with my corrections] Now in British Museum. See *SL* iv. 215 *n.*

495 (d–e) like Falstaff] Shakespeare, *Merry wives of Windsor*, II. 2.

495 (e) Waverley 4th Edition] The MS. (NLS MS. 863, f. 121) has '4th' but this must be an error for '6th.'

496 (c) Goodman Puff] See *SL* i. 469 *n.* and amendment to it.

496 (c) And he may crack . . .] *The maltman*, st. [3], lines 3–4. In Ramsay, *Tea-table miscellany*; *Herd*, ii. 70; *Johnson*, Vol. 5 [1797], No. 433.

496 (e) Thomsons] William Thomson, cabinet-maker, 48 Fountainbridge. (*Post-Office Directory*, 1816, p. 265.)

497 (b) To John] This cancels Lockhart's version in *SL* iv. 222–3. Transfer *SL*. iv. 223 *n.* to here.

498 *n.* 1] No need to cite Lockhart. 29 Apr. in 1816 was a Monday.

499 (e) To James Ballantyne] Date should be 1817 as reference (p. 501) to Glasgow shows. See *Lockhart*, v. 234. (Corrected in *SL* xii. 487.)

501 (c) half a loaf] *Ray*, p. 171.

501 (d) To Longman . . .] This must refer to Scott's introduction to *The Border antiquities*, published by Longman. The reference to 'the highlands' is obscure.

502 (c) To John Ballantyne] The date cannot be Aug. 1816 as Ballantyne was on the Continent at that time. The date is early July 1813, before Scott went to Abbotsford and later in the month to Drumlanrig. The '15th Augt. to retire my Jedburgh acceptance' refers to 1813. See above, pp. 435, 436–7. The reference to Winstanley also relates to 1813. See *SL* iii. 296.

502 (f) Consider weel gude man] Parody of *Maggie's tocher*, st. [5], lines 1–4. In Ramsay, *Tea-table miscellany*; *Herd*, ii. 78; *Johnson*, Vol. 3 (1790), No. 230. The last line is: 'Is Sandy Wilson's mare.'

503 (d) To John Ballantyne] Date cannot be Aug. 1816 as Ballantyne was in Paris at that time. The date, I think, is 1814. Cf. below, p. 516, where the letter should be dated 1814 and *SL* iii. 527 where the letter is dated 18 Dec. 1814.

503 *n.* 1] Delete this note which is no longer applicable.

504 *n.* 1] John was in Paris in July and Aug.

506 (e) 3d part of Vol. iv] *Tales of my Landlord*, 1st ser.

506 (e) The £400 History Bill] Scott's contribution, *History of Europe, 1814*, in *Edin. Ann. Reg.* Vol. 7 (publ. 1816). See *SL* iv. 266. £400 was the sum offered to Lockhart when he took over this part of the *Register* (*SL* vi. 244, 244 *n.*, 262).

507 (c) To John] Date is probably 1 Jan. 1817. Scott says he is returning on Friday, i.e. 3 Jan. (In *SL* iv. 366 he says he returned on Saturday but the day may have been changed.) He is bringing Nos. 1–3 of the *Sale-Room*. Cf. beginning of letter of 26 Dec., below, p. 513. The Wednesday between 26 Dec. and 3 Jan. is 1 Jan. Add source of letter: NLS MS. 863, f. 187.

507 (d) Kerr [?]] Read 'Skene.' In next line, for 'plans' read 'places.' Scott is suggesting that Skene should make drawings and that these original drawings should be bound up with the set for the Prince Regent just as Skene's drawings had been inserted in Princess Caroline's copy of *Marmion* (*SL* ii. 25).

508 (e) consult you about the tales] *Tales of my Landlord* was published on 1 Dec. but Blackwood was able to send two copies to Ballantyne on 22 Nov. (Oliphant, *William Blackwood*, i. 76.)

509 (c) Je suis ennuyé de lui et ses petites affaires] Said of the Marquess of Tulliebardine. See *SL* iv. 321.

512 (c) come to Edinburgh which will be tomorrow] Scott is writing on Sunday, 10 Nov., and as Scott is to be in Edinburgh on 11 Nov. Ballantyne could not get this letter with PM 12 Nov. till after Scott had arrived.

512 (d) To John Ballantyne] From Abbotsford. Date is about 22 Dec. 1816.

512 (e) a trumpery thing] *Verses . . . to the Grand Duke Nicholas of Russia . . . 19th December 1816*. (*Ruff*, No. 153.) Scott must have sent a MS. of this before it was printed; otherwise there

would have been no need to say 'Give no copies.'

512 (f) Giffords Johnson] *The works of Ben Jonson, in nine volumes, with notes critical and explanatory by W. Gifford, Esq.* 8vo London, 1816.

513 *n.* 2] In this letter Scott is referring to Bailey's assistance for *The sale-room.* He wrote to Bailey, 4 Jan. 1817. See *SL* iv. 357.

514 (b) Register] *History of Europe, 1815,* for *Edin. Ann. Reg.* Vol. 8, publ. 1817.

514 (d) To John] Date is 3 May which was a Saturday.

515 (d) To John] Date is almost certainly 8 May.

516 (a) To John] This letter belongs to 1814 and is probably 15 Nov. In the letter above, p. 472, the first paragraph must refer to £300 due to Rev. Dr Douglas and in the second paragraph Erskine is to be repaid. The Wednesday of the letter is probably 9 Nov. Scott is now in Edinburgh, writing on *Tuesday*, the day the sums are due. Cf. *SL* iii. 527 where Scott asks Richardson on 18 Dec. 1814 to discount in London two bills of £300.

516 *n.* 2] For '505' read '506.'

517 (d) Mr. Tournerelle] This should be Turnerelli.

517 (e) busts of Pitt Lord Melville] These are no longer at Abbotsford.

517 (e) Rundell & Bridges] Rundell, Bridge, and Rundell, silversmiths, London. The firm is mentioned in *Chronicles of the Canongate,* chap. 1.

518 (b) To John] The date is more likely to be Jan. 1818 when the 'stipulated copies' of *Rob Roy* had been exhausted and when Matthews was acting in Edinburgh.

520 (c) To James Ballantyne] Date is 6 Oct. Scott wrote on 30 Sept. for Vol. 1 and Vol. 2, sheet A (*SL* iv. 532) and the Monday after that was 6 Oct.

521 (a) Guy Mannering & Waverly] i.e. 4th ed. of former and 7th ed. of latter.

521 (b) To John Ballantyne] *Rob Roy* was advertised in June 1817. This letter, therefore, probably belongs to the beginning of that month.

522 (b) a novel] *Women,* by Maturin.

522 (d) Waverley . . . G. M.] 7th ed. of *Waverley* and 4th ed. of *Guy Mannering,* both published in 1817.

522 (d) St Catherines] Home of Sir William Rae on south side of Edinburgh, at that time outside the city boundaries.

523 (b) Jock] Probably John Stevenson, clerk to John Ballantyne and later a bookseller.

524 (a) To John] The date is Friday, 17 Oct. 1817. Cf. *SL* i. 522, iv. 335.

524 (a) Tony Lumkin] Goldsmith, *She stoops to conquer,* I. 2. It is not Tony, but the Fourth Fellow, who says this. Scott made the same mistake in *SL* v. 159, 348, vi. 176, vii. 379, viii. 247, x. 97, *St Ronan's Well,* chap. 1, and *MPW* iii. 67, xx. 255. Tom Moore made the same mistake in *A curious fact.*

524 (c) G. M. & Wy] 4th ed. of *Guy Mannering* and 7th ed. of *Waverley,* both published in 1817.

525 (a) the Cremona] The horse mentioned on previous page.

525 (d) the Travels] The projected 'New travels on the Continent,' never written, as Scott did not go abroad.

525 (e) To John] The year is 1818. *Rob Roy,* 4th ed., was published in Feb. 1818. Scott referred to the cabinet, for which he paid £21, in a letter to Willie Scott of Maxpoffle of 11 Apr. 1818 (not in *SL* but in NLS MS. 2889, ff. 156–7). The reference to the busts *also* confirms the year. (See above, p. 517.)

526 (a) package of busts] From Turnerelli. See above, p. 517.

526 (c) Douglas ring] See *Lockhart,* x. 108. The ring is in the octagonal showcase in the Library at Abbotsford.

527 (c) To John] Date is Monday, 6 Jan. 1817: (1) Scott's letter to Clarke Whitfeld (*SL* iv. 352–3) can be dated 6 Jan.; (2) the review of Byron was completed and sent off on 10 Jan. (*SL* iv. 366). Delete the two dates 1818/19 and 1818.

527 (c) drawing by Wilson] This is probably the sketch by William Wilson referred to in *SL* iii. 528.

529 (a) Sir Tristram] A new ed. of *Sir Tristrem* came out in 1819.

529 (b) Ye ken that Maggie winna sleep] Burns, *The auld farmer's new-year morning salutation to his auld mare Maggie,* st. [13], lines 5–6.

VOLUME II

1 (a) To Lady Minto] Wednesday, 17 Feb., was a Fast Day. The date of this letter, therefore, is 16 Feb. The reference to Carpenter corresponds to the reference below, p. 17.

1 (d) "stolen waters" or "bread eaten in secret"] *Bible, Proverbs* 9: 17.

1 (e) To C. K. Sharpe] Date cannot be 1 Jan. as suggested below, p. 2 *n.* The first Thursday of 1808 was 7 Jan. Scott's letter to Lady Louisa Stuart (below, p. 3) makes it clear that he has not seen her for some time and has not previously discussed Sharpe's book. The invitation to Sharpe must come after 19 Jan. and when Lady Louisa had come to Edinburgh from Bothwell. By 3 Mar. she had left Edinburgh (below, p. 27). Date, therefore, is probably 26 Jan.

2 (b) To John Ballantyne] Scott sent proofs of Introd. to Canto I to Lady Abercorn on Wednesday, 11 Feb. 1807 (*SL* i. 350). The Saturday before that was 7 Feb. which is probably the date of this letter.

2 *n.* 1] Delete the sentence beginning 'The letters *A.D.*'

3 (a) To J. W. Adam] Adam had written on 28 Dec. 1807 (NLS MS. 3876, ff. 146–7) asking for information about his ancestor, John Adam, a Scot, who was killed at Flodden.

4 (a) Hawthornden] Scott is referring to the place, which Lady Louisa might visit when staying at Dalkeith House, not to Drummond's *History of Scotland,* as stated in *SL* xii. 487.

4 (e) the Queen's Assembly] On 18 Jan. This confirms that dating of letter is correct.

4 *n.* 1] This is an exact quotation and should be in inverted commas. Miss de Lally was governess in the family of Lord Lansdowne *c.* 1818–20 and is probably the same person. See *Maria Edgeworth: letters from England, 1813–1844,* ed. by Christina Colvin, Oxford, 1971, pp. 93–4, 229.

5 (c) To Archibald Constable] Date is probably beginning of Oct. 1808, for on 12 Oct. Scott asks again for the *Examiner* (below, p. 112).

5 (c) The volumes of Swift] This is the ed. by John Nichols. There were several issues and it is impossible to say which ed. Constable sent.

8 (a) Genl. Kerr] General Walter Ker of Littledean, unsuccessful claimant to Roxburghe peerage.

8 (c) Brydone's broadsword] See my note to *SL* i. 102 (c).

8 (d) the inclosed to Mr. Polwhele] This letter is not in *SL.*

9 (d) Lord Melville] The opening sentence refers to Scott's clerkship. What follows relates to the Royal Commission.

9 *n.* 1] Delete the reference to 'Sadler letters.' Scott is not referring to that work but to the Appendix (pp. 183–256), which follows the 'letters' (pp. 83–182) of his ed. of Dryden, Vol. 18 (not Vol. 17, as Scott says).

10 (a) Lord Eldon] Lord Grenville's bill to reorganize the courts of justice in Scotland (*SL* i. 351, 370) was dropped with the fall of the ministry in Mar. 1807. Lord Eldon, who became Chancellor in Portland's ministry, reintroduced the bill which was passed 4 July 1808 as 48 Geo. III, c. 151.

11 (c) Lord Hamilton's renown] The Address to the King in the House of Commons, 21 Jan. 1808, was moved by Lord Hamilton in his maiden speech. It was reported in the *Scots Mag.* Vol. 70 (Feb. 1808), pp. 134–5.

11 (d) royal family] The Portuguese royal family. See *Edin. Ann. Reg. for 1808,* I. ii. 1–2.

11 (e) as McBeth to horrors] Shakespeare, *Macbeth,* V. 5: 'I have supp'd full of horrors.'

11 *n.* 1] For 'daughter of the Earl of Morton' read 'granddaughter of 14th

Earl of Morton' and for 'a year after' read 'in the same year as.'

12 (c) "Good faith . . ."] Shakespeare, *II Henry IV*, IV. 3. Cf. *SL* vii. 419.

13 (c) To Charles Carpenter] This letter dated 8 Feb. should be compared with the letter dated 16 Feb. (below, p. 17). The opening of the letter of 8 Feb. implies that it comes *after* the letter of 16 Feb. and the references to Pringle (p. 13 and pp. 18–19) imply that it comes *before* that of 16 Feb. It is difficult to reconcile these inconsistencies even allowing for the fact that Scott often wrote letters in instalments.

13 *n.* 1] Alexander Pringle Russell died in Jan. 1818.

15 (b) Smith & Jenyns] The only firm, with a name like this, that I can find is Smith, Jennins & Co., wine merchants, 5 St. Paul's Yard, Ludgate Street, London. (*Johnstone's London commercial guide*, 1817, col. 434.) On Smith, see my note to *SL* x. 38 (b–c).

15 (d) To Francis Douce] Scott is replying to Douce's letter from the British Museum, 29 Dec. 1807. Scott had presented an uncastrated copy of *Sir Tristrem* to Douce in 1804 (*SL* i. 221) and this was Douce's belated acknowledgement of the gift.

16 (b) The late Duke of Argyle had a jester] Scott alluded to the Duke's jester in a note to chap. 9 of *Waverley* but he suppressed the names.

16 (c) *roguish* clowns of Shakespeare] *As you like it*, II. 2. 'roguish' is probably a misreading of 'roynish.'

17 (a) the president] Sir Ilay Campbell.

19 (d–e) seizure of the Danish fleet] The Battle of Copenhagen, Sept. 1807.

20 (b) worse than the sin of witchcraft] See my note to *SL* i. 391 (a).

20 (c) Fugitives] Surtees sent the *English fugitives* with a letter of 17 Sept. 1807. See Taylor, *Memoir of Robert Surtees*, p. 63.

21 (c) Sleepest thou . . .] This is varied from the ballads as is shown by Scott's letter to Ellis, 26 May 1805. See *SL* i. 251 and my note.

21 (d) a swinging epistle] This letter of 1 July 1807 is in *SL* xii. 290–5. Scott

refers to it in a letter to Heber of 18 Nov. 1807 (*SL* xii. 297).

22 (b) "So wonder on till time makes all things plain"] Beaumont and Fletcher, *The little French lawyer*, II. 2: 'And wonder on, till time makes all this plain'; a version of Shakespeare, *A midsummer night's dream*, V. 1: 'But wonder on, till truth makes all things plain.'

22 (b) "the hobby-horse is *not* forgot"] Shakespeare, *Love's labour's lost*, III. 1.

22 (c) Douce, whose lucubrations] His *Illustrations of Shakespeare*. See above, p. 15.

22 (c) *caviare* to the multitude] Shakespeare, *Hamlet*, II. 2.

23 (c) Mr. Dent] His bill (36 Geo. III, c. 124) for licensing dogs, came into force on 19 May 1796. It was repealed by 43 Geo. III, c. 161, sect. 84.

23 (d) the ladder by which] This metaphor seems to be a confused rendering of Lieut. Bowling's ladder in Smollett's *Roderick Random*, chap. 41. Cf. *SL* vii. 317, xii. 353 *n.* A similar metaphor is used in *The Bride of Lammermoor*, chap. 25.

23 (e) open locks / whoever knocks] Shakespear, *Macbeth*, IV. 1.

24 (a) "floating like foam on the wave tempest"] For 'wave tempest' read 'wartempest.' See *Madoc*, Pt II, sect. XVIII (1st ed., p. 359).

24 (c) Simeon & Levi] Simeon was a contemporary clergyman (*n.* 1) but I have not traced a Levi. Scott, having written Simeon, probably could not resist punning on Simeon and Levi, Jacob's sons. See *Bible*, *Genesis* 49: 5: 'Simeon and Levi are brethren, instruments of cruelty are in their habitations.'

24 (d) letters from a spy] Sir Robert Constable. See *SL* i. 365.

24 (d) I have written to Wordsworth] This letter is not in *SL*. Wordsworth's reply of 14 May is quoted below, p. 54 *n.*

24 (d–e) his *siege is finished* as Vertot said] Alluding to the anecdote of the Abbé Vertot who refused to revise his *History of the Knights of Malta* in the light of

new material. 'Je n'en ai plus besoin, mon siège est fait.'

24 *n.* 2] Wordsworth's poem is *The white doe of Rylstone*. See below, p. 54 *n.*

25 (b–c) fortunate addition to it] Birth of Southey's daughter Emma who lived only a year.

25 (f) "theres magic in the web on't"] Shakespeare, *Othello*, III. 4.

26 (a) the proposed appointment] As Secretary to the Commission on the Scottish Law Courts. Lord M. is Lord Melville. The Chancellor is Lord Eldon. The bill is 'An Act concerning the Administration of Justice in Scotland,' passed in July of this year. The Lord Advocate is Archibald Campbell Colquhoun.

26 (e) Lord C] Lord Castlereagh.

26 (e) Gathering my brows] Burns, *Tam o' Shanter*, lines 11–12.

27 (a) To Mrs. Pringle] Her letter (NLS MS. 3876, ff. 196–7) is addressed from 55 George's Square [Edinburgh] and is dated 25 Feb. 1808. Scott would receive it the same day and his reply should be dated 25 Feb. which was a Thursday. *Lockhart* (iii. 58–9) prints an extract from Mrs Pringle's letter, attributing it wrongly to Mr Pringle.

27 (a) A great French critic] Boileau.

28 (e) Mrs. Scott has quite recovered] Lady Louisa, in an undated letter, had referred to Mrs Scott's 'nervous attack.' (Stuart, *Gleanings*, iii. 201.)

28 (f) We have Miss Baillie here] She stayed over a month. From her neighbour in Hampstead, Edward Coxe, she brought a *Sonnet* on Scott and Joanna Baillie as a gift. From Edinburgh she wrote to Coxe conveying Scott's appreciation and, as a result of this, Coxe wrote to Scott on 8 Apr. sending a copy of his *Miscellaneous poetry* in which he wrote this *Sonnet* and also another poem, *On reading Marmion*. The latter poem was printed in Joanna Baillie's *A collection of poems*, London, 1823, p. 115.

30 (e) To Lady Abercorn] This is in reply to her undated letter, partly printed in Partington, *Letter-books*, pp. 136–7.

31 (a) Whigs . . . in arms against *Marmion*] Because, in the introductory

epistle to Canto I, Scott had put Pitt before Fox.

32 (a) bricks without clay] Bricks without straw. Scott's error or the transcriber's?

33 (a) silver cup] This is in a show-case in the Drawing-Room at Abbotsford.

33 *n.* 2] Delete. Mrs Dundas was not the wife of the Chief Baron of Exchequer, but wife of Robert Dundas, afterwards 2nd Viscount Melville. At this time he was President of the Board of Control and Scott wanted his patronage for an Indian appointment.

34 (b) "Hugh Scott"] He was 4th Mate of *Thames*, 1798–1801; 2nd Mate of *Brunswick* 1802–3; 1st Mate of *Brunswick* 1804–5 (captured off Point de Galle, 11 July 1805); and 1st Mate of *Thames* 1806–8. The *Thames* arrived home on 2 Jan. 1808—this date coinciding with Scott's 'two months unsuccessful solicitation.' I do not know what success Scott had with David Scott's House but Hugh Scott was not reappointed to H.E.I.C.S. till 26 Oct. 1810 when he was given command of *Ceres*. Hardy, *A register of ships*, pp. 193, 219, 233, 255 and Appendix, p. 143.

34 (f) a rivulet of text] Sheridan, *The school for scandal*, I. 1.

35 (d) silver cup] See my note to *SL* ii. 33 (a).

36 (b) "Spanish Vengeance"] See *Sharpe's Letters*, i. 322–3.

36 (d) I have marked one or two things] A selection of Scott's comments is given in *Sharpe's Letters*, i. 29–30.

36 (e) your letter of 29th February] In Abbotsford Coll. in NLS (MS. 870, f. 15).

36 (f) the Bishop of Durham's letter] This, with the letter referred to below, p. 53, were printed in *Sadler*, ii. 202–7, 'transcribed from the Lansdowne MS. by Richard [*sic*] Surtees, Esq. of Mainsforth,' with a note by Surtees.

37 (b) Lansdowne papers] They had been purchased the previous year (1807) by Parliament for the British Museum. A catalogue was issued, 1812–19.

37 (c) "He, that wandering knight so fair"] Shakespeare, *I King Henry IV*,

I. 2. See eds. of the play by R. P. Cowl and A. E. Morgan (1930) p. 12, and by John Dover Wilson (1946) p. 119.

37 (c) hanging my harp on the willows] *Bible, Psalms* 137: 2.

37 (f) the creation of your letter] Scott, in alluding to the embryo *The Lady of the Lake* and to Surtees's letter, supplies additional proof that Surtees's letter was not the impulse which led to *Waverley*. See *SL* i. 341 and my note.

39 (a) "caviare for the multitude"] Shakespeare, *Hamlet*, II. 2.

39 (d) hiding your talent in a napkin] A combination of two Bible quotations: *Matthew* 25: 25 and *Luke* 19: 20.

39 (d) "there's magic in the web on't"] Shakespeare, *Othello*, III. 4.

39 (e–f) the artist who made the little sketch] C. K. Sharpe according to Stuart, *Gleanings*, iii. 204. The text of *Ugly Meg* is printed ibid. iii. 205–8.

39 n. 1] Lady Louisa's letter is also in Stuart, *Gleanings*, iii. 208–11.

41 (e) as Lady Dalkeith has sent for the book] *Lockhart*, iii. 60, cites Scott's letter to Lord Montagu (not in *SL*) and Montagu's reply, to which Scott is here alluding.

42 (c) For never spell by fairy laid . . .] Thomas Parnell, *A fairy tale, in the antient English stile*, st. [29], lines 4–6. For 'fairy' read 'faerie' and for 'bounds' read 'length.' In Lewis's *Tales of wonder* (1801) ii. 275, the poem is called *Edwin of the Green*.

42 (d) as you are going to town before me] Scott did not go to London in 1808.

42 (e) our friend in Albemarle Street] William Miller. John Murray did not move to Albemarle Street till Miller retired.

42 n. 1] Delete this note and see above, p. 39 n.

43 (a) I have several translations by myself . . . from the German] See *SL* xii. 53.

43 (e) 8vo Marmion & Lay] These would be 2nd ed. of *Marmion*, 1808, and 6th ed. of the *Lay*, 1807.

44 (d) Park & young Hunter] In 1809 Constable opened a London house under the name of Constable, Hunter, Park and Hunter. 'Young Hunter' was Charles, younger brother of Alexander Gibson Hunter, already Constable's partner. Park was John Park who died at London, 13 Nov. 1809, aged 26. The London house was closed on 1 Jan. 1811.

44 n. 1] This title is a mixture of the title-page and the editor's own description.

45 (d) To John Murray] This letter should be dated 16 Apr. 1806: (1) the print of Hoppner's *Tales* relates to 1806 (see *SL* i. 284 (b)); (2) Campbell's magazine was projected in 1806. See Campbell's letter to John Murray, 3 Mar. 1806 in Smiles, *John Murray*, i. 324–5.

45 (d) *cancelled* print] Dr Porteus, Bishop of London, objected to the frontispiece in Hoppner's *Oriental tales* and it was cancelled. See also *SL* i. 284.

46 (d) I have been anxiously expecting a reply] Mrs Siddons's reply of 15 Apr. 1808 is printed in part in Partington, *Post-bag*, p. 34. Scott had apparently not yet received it.

46 n. 1] In line 9, for 'Lord P. Murray' read 'Sir Patrick Murray.' (See *Edin. Ann. Reg.* II. ii. 385.) It was advertised in the newspapers of 29 Dec. 1809 that candidates for the management should send their proposals to 'Mr. Home, Signet Office.' (Dibdin, *Annals*, p. 254.) At this time John Home, W.S., was Substitute Keeper of the Signet. In line 16, for 'brother' read 'uncle' (not 'nephew' as stated in *SL* xii. 487). Lord Dartmouth (line 16) was Lord Chamberlain. (Corrected in *SL* xii. 487.)

47 (b) the Provost] Donald Smith. He was succeeded later in the year by William Coulter.

47 (e) Young] Scott wrote to him, but his first letter is not known to be extant. A second letter dated 15 May 1808 is printed in *A memoir of Charles Mayne Young . . . By Julian Charles Young*, London, 1871, pp. 54–5.

47 (f) a favour of De Monfort] An allusion to Joanna Baillie's *De Monfort*.

50 (f) "wooed and married and a'"] *Woo'd and married and a'*. In Herd, ii.

115; and in *Johnson*, Vol. 1 (1787), No. 10.

51 (c) Portuguese History] His *History of Portugal*, which he worked on for about 40 years, was never finished.

51 (c) Jeffrey] For Jeffrey's letter on the review and Lockhart's commentary on it, see *Lockhart*, iii. 50–5.

52 (a) teaching "the young idea how to shoot"] James Thomson, *The seasons, Spring*, line 1150.

52 (b) Mr. Whalley] Rev. Thomas Sedgwick Whalley received the Hon. D.D. from Edinburgh University later in the year. It looks as if Scott had put in a word for him.

52 (c) as Johnson said *get rich by degrees*] Dr John Fleeman, an authority on Johnson, tells me that these words are wrongly attributed to him.

52 n.] Amend the reference to Arbuthnot. He gave assistance, not in connection with the Commission, but later in 1811–12 with his Clerkship of Session.

53 (a) To Robert Surtees] *FL* i. 104 dates this letter 18 Apr. Scott was in Edinburgh (presumably on Register House duty) from 3 to 11 Apr. and perhaps longer. Jeffrey, according to *Lockhart* (iii. 51), dined at Castle Street on a Tuesday. Tuesdays in Apr. which would fit are 5, 12, 19. As Scott says (p. 54) that Jeffrey showed him the review 'yesterday', the letter is probably Wednesday 13 Apr. *Marmion* for Marriott had been sent by 11 Apr. (p. 44) and Scott mentions this here (pp. 53–4). The letter, in any case, should come before the one to Anna Seward at p. 49.

53 (a) Bishop's two letters] See above, p. 36.

53 (c) Cotton MSS.] Joseph Planta, *A catalogue of the manuscripts in the Cottonian Library, deposited in the British Museum*, 2° [London] 1802.

54 n. 1] The complete text of Wordsworth's letter has since been printed in *The letters of William and Dorothy Wordsworth: the middle years . . .*, ed. by Ernest de Selincourt, Oxford, 1937, Vol. 1, pp. 458e–458f. Delete last sentence of note and see below, p. 161 n. 1.

55 (a) Harleian Miscellany] In the 2nd ed. the tract on Story is in Vol. 3 (1809), pp. 100–8. It is the same as it is in Somers, Vol. 1, pp. 477–87. See also *The state papers and letters of Sir Ralph Sadler*, ii. 113 n.

56 (b) Venetians before they were Christians] A Venetian proverb: 'Pria Veneziani, poi Christiane.' Scott later adapted this as 'We were Scotsmen before we were bibliomaniacs' (*MPW* xxi. 223).

56 (d) To Joanna Baillie] This letter cannot belong to Apr. Joanna returned the *House of Aspen* with her letter of 4 Apr. (below, p. 58 n.; NLS MS. 3877, ff. 3–4). The Saturday before that date is 29 Mar., which is the latest date for the letter. It might, however, be some other Saturday in Mar.

56 n. 1] In line 4, for 'more than half a century' read 'a quarter of a century.'

57 (a) printed by Ballantyne] Ballantyne was the printer of this ed.

57 (e) Tragedy of Tragedies] Alluding to amended title of Fielding's *Tom Thumb*.

59 (c) Ld. Blandford [?]]Delete query. This is Lord Blandford, eldest son of 4th Duke of Marlborough, and later 5th Duke. For Scott's allusion, see the *Scots Mag.* Vol. 53 (1791), pp. 94–5, 178–84, 234–8, 505.

59 (c) D. of Gloucester who wrote Billets Doux] Line 60 of Goldsmith's *The haunch of venison* is: 'And nobody with me at sea but myself.' In Everyman's Lib. the editor, Austin Dobson, has a footnote: 'A textual quotation from the love-letters of Henry Frederick, Duke of Cumberland, to Lady Grosvenor.' In the same ed. of Goldsmith, p. 240, there is a footnote on the Duke of Gloucester's marriage to Lady Waldegrave which led to the Royal Marriage Act of 1772. Scott seems to have confused Gloucester and Cumberland.

60 (a) throw stones . . .] *Ray*, p. 11: 'He that hath a body made of glass must not throw stones at another.'

60 n. 2. Burns's election songs] *Buy braw troggin, an excellent new song* and *The election: a new song*.

61 (e) letter from Mr. Lowes] This letter is not in Walpole Coll. in NLS.

62 (b) Wallis] John Wallis, *The natural history and antiquities of Northumberland*, 1769.

63 (b) The Fox] See suggestion in *SL* xii. 487. Scott, I think, is being metaphorical.

63 (d) expect moss troopers] Read 'expert moss troopers.'

64 (c) "a crow to pluck . . ."] Heywood, p. 122.

64 (e) "bonny bush aboon Traquair"] William Crawford, *The bush aboon Traquair*, st. [1], line 7. In Ramsay, *Tea-table miscellany*.

65 (a) To C. K. Sharpe] The date cannot be 1808 for Anne was too young at that time to sing ballads. The reference to ballads shows that the letter belongs to 1825 (as the next letter does). See *Sharpe's Letters*, ii. 325.

65 (c) The tale of (Piren) Reed] This is *The death of Parcy Reed*. It was not included in the *Minstrelsy*. See Index under Ballads and Songs. *The death of Parcy Reed*.

65 (e) To C. K. Sharpe] This letter belongs to 1825. May 15 was a Sunday in 1825 and Chantrey was in Edinburgh in May 1825. The letter, too, is related to the preceding letter which should be dated 1825. See my note to it.

66 (a) Schetky's prints] The work is: *Illustrations of Walter Scott's Lay of the last minstrel; consisting of twelve views . . . by John C. Schetky*, 4to London, 1808. Another ed. was published in 1810. Two letters from Scott to Schetky dealing with this publication, of 14 Aug. 1808 and 7 Jan. 1808 [PM 1809], are printed in *Ninety years of work and play . . . of J. C. Schetky*, Edinburgh, 1877, pp. 61–3 and 66–7. Neither letter is in *SL*.

67 (b) The Chief Baron] Robert Dundas of Arniston.

67 (b) worthy Advocate Currie] George Currie. The epithet 'worthy' was probably prompted by Scott's discomfiture when his decision against Currie's servant was reversed at the Circuit Court in 1805. See *Chisholm*, pp. 27–8.

67 (d) I was honoured with your letter] Of 27 Apr. (NLS MS. 3877, ff. 31–2) with which she had sent Thomas Att-

wood's letter. He composed music for 'Where shall the lover rest' and 'O young Lochinvar' in *Marmion*. Scott's letter to him is not known to be extant.

67 (e) the original Gaelic air] See *SL* i. 393, and my note.

68 (d) loss of a relation] This may be Miss Hayman's mother who had been dangerously ill at Chester. (Mrs Hughes's letter of 27 Apr.; NLS MS. 3877, f. 32.)

68 (e) George's dexterity] William Laidlaw's brother.

69 (c) the lovely little boy] The infant son of 4th Earl of Aberdeen.

70 (c) if she says I read over *Marmion* to her] R. P. Gillies in his *Recollections of Sir Walter Scott*, p. 137, says that at the Duchess of Gordon's dinner and evening parties 'he was occasionally . . . prevailed on to read aloud some portions of his new poem.'

70 n. 1] In line 2, for '*Miscellanies*, vol. iv.' read '*MPW* xx.'

72 n. 1] The 'eldest son,' in line 5, is Edward Stanley of Cross Hall (q.v. in Index).

73 (d) My poverty and not my will] Shakespeare, *Romeo and Juliet*, V. 1.

73 (e) an author should take care of his literary character . . .] Scott is thinking of David who says of his honour to Bob Acres in Sheridan's *The rivals*, IV. 1: 'I would be very careful of it; and I think, in return, my honour couldn't do less than to be very careful of me.'

73 (f) Jeremy in *Love for Love*] Congreve, *Love for love*, II. 1. Jeremy does admit having 'appetites' but it is Sir Sampson Legend who says: 'nothing under an emperor should be born with appetites.'

74 (a) Thompson . . . a few letters] At this stage Scott had definitely decided on a new edition of James Thomson's *Works* with a life containing 'a number of original letters hitherto unknown to the public.' This was announced in the *Scots Mag*. Vol. 70 (July 1808), p. 519.

74 (f) To Thomas Scott] Date is Oct. 1808. Cf. contents with letters, below, pp. 92–3 and 99–100.

75 (a) approaching military preferment] Commission in Manx Fencibles. See *SL* vii. 398 and my note.

76 (b) grave of all the Capulets] Scott is misquoting Burke, *Letter to Matthew Smith* (Prior's *Memoir of Edmund Burke*, p. 33): 'the tomb of all the Capulets.' He uses the same quotation, also with 'grave,' in his *Life of Dryden* (*MPW* i. 372–3).

77 (e) obliged to announce it prematurely] It was announced in the *Scots Mag.* Vol. 70 (July 1808), p. 519, i.e. after Scott wrote this letter. This magazine usually had the earliest information of Scott's projects. I have not found an earlier announcement.

81 (d) To Rev. R. Polwhele] The date 1808 is impossible. Scott had not been in London in that year and the *QR* had not yet been founded. Correct date is 1809. The words 'in London for these some months past' refer to the visit of Apr. to June of that year.

82 (d) The power of beauty I remember yet . . .] *Cymon and Iphigenia*, lines 2–3. In Scott's *Dryden*, xi. 454.

84 (c) all she has to know . . .] Matthew Prior, *An English padlock*, lines 59, 61: '. . . an empty show, / Powder, and Pocket-Glass, and Beau.' Scott's quotation approximates more nearly to a song called *The English padlock*, made up of lines, with alterations, from Prior's poem. See the *Vocal Mag.*, London, 1781, p. 60.

84 (e) Faulklands . . . Julia] Two characters in Sheridan's *The rivals*.

85 (d) We can go next day to Glasgow] i.e. on 13 Sept. But the visit must have been at the end of the month for Scott is still at Ashiestiel on the 18th (below, p. 90) and we learn from the *Journals and correspondence of Miss Berry*, ii. 371, 372, that Scott dined at Bothwell Castle on 29 and 30 Sept. Scott refers to the visit to Glasgow in a letter to Tom (*SL* vii. 423).

85 (e) To Robert Surtees] The date is 1807. (Corrected in *SL* xii. 487.) Scott is answering Surtees's letter of 22 Aug. 1807 (Taylor, *Memoir of Robert Surtees*, pp. 60–3).

86 (b) the story of the wounded man] See *Tales of a grandfather*, chap. 71 (*MPW* xxv. 381).

86 (d) farm at the head of Nithsdale] Locherben. See my note to *SL* i. 352 (b).

86 (f) The Sheep-book] *The shepherd's guide*, Edinburgh, 1807.

87 (b) voyage à St. Cloud] Néel, *Voyage de Paris à Saint-Cloud, par mer; et retour de Saint-Cloud à Paris, par terre.* In Gronier, *Voyages imaginaires*, Tom 30, Amsterdam, 1788, pp. 303–409.

88 (f) Elliston, Bannister Cooke] A comma should have been inserted after 'Bannister.' They are Robert William Elliston, John Bannister and George Frederick Cooke. See Dibdin, *Annals*, pp. 253–4.

89 (b) some English visitors] The Morritts.

89 (c–d) I wrote a tragedy] *The House of Aspen*.

90 (a) your fair correspondent] Mrs Sterndale (above, p. 88).

91 (a) Pitscottie calls "a blink of the Sun or a whip of a whirlwind"] Robert Lindsay of Pitscottie, *The history of Scotland*, etc., 3rd ed., 8vo Edinburgh, 1778, p. 173.

91 (c) [*sic*]] This should be transferred to the next line after 'Touchwood.'

91 (c) "poor thing, but mine own"] Shakespeare, *As you like it*, V. 4.

92 (a) Was twisting of collars] *The song of Thrym; or, the recovery of the hammer*, lines 20–1; 'For his dogs he was twisting collars of gold, / And trimming the manes of his coursers bold' (William Herbert, *Select Icelandic poetry*, London, 1804, p. 2). Scott reviewed Herbert in *ER* and quoted these lines (*MPW* xvii. 107). Scott varied the lines in *SL* ii. 514 and *SL* xii. 302.

92 (c) Bryant] Jacob Bryant (1715–1804), antiquary. See *Letters of J. B. S. Morritt*, p. vi.

92 (e) Author of the Poor Mans Sabbath] John Struthers.

92 (f) I address this scrawl . . .] This is repeated below at top of p. 221.

93 (b) Weber's Romances] *Metrical romances of the 13th, 14th and 15th centuries*, 3 vols., Edinburgh, 1810.

93 n. 1] Amend this note. For 'Coleman' read 'Colman.' Delete 'obsequious', an epithet which does not apply to Canton.

95 (c) Sotheby's *Orestes*] It was dedicated to Lord Abercorn in 1802. The dedication was rather nonsensical.

95 (d) pomp and circumstance] A reminiscence of Shakespeare, *Othello*, III. 3.

96 (a) "three yards abreast"] Scott here attributes this phrase to his hind. But he had quoted Currie on this in the *Minstrelsy*. See *SL* i. 119 *n.*

97 (b) coin buttress and point of vantage] A reminiscence of Shakespeare, *Macbeth*, I. 6: 'no jutty, frieze, buttress, / Nor coigne of vantage.'

97 *n.* 2] The form Vanora is given by Scott in Note XXI to his ed. of Richard Franck's *Northern memoirs*, 8vo Edinburgh, 1821, p. 369. There he gives the name as 'Vanora, Guenever, or Ganore.'

98 *n.* 1] For 'Note 3B' read 'note to Canto V, st. ix.' The text of *The felon sow* in *Rokeby* follows the Rokeby MS. more closely than the text in Thomas Evans, *Old ballads*, new ed., 1810, iii. 270–81. The reference in this note to *Rookhope Ryde* should have formed a separate note to 'Raid of *Rokeby*' on p. 99.

99 (e) "grave of all the Capulets"] See above, p. 76 and my note.

100 (a) he neglected his sheep . . .] A paraphrase of the first line of Sir Gilbert Elliot's poem, *My sheep I neglected —I lost my sheep-hook*, first printed anonymously in *Herd*, i. 174.

100 (c) Sylvester Daggerwoods] George Colman's play *New hay at the old market* (later called *Sylvester Daggerwood*) was a satire on the enlarged London theatres to which Scott here no doubt alludes.

100 (d) Rock . . . an infamous fellow] The obituary of Rock in the *Scots Mag.* Vol. 77 (Dec. 1815), p. 959, was a most glowing panegyric of him as a man, actor and manager.

106 (f) a trial review] This presumably should be 'a rival review.'

108 (b) the Roses] George Rose and his sons Sir George Rose and William Stewart Rose. Only the last is listed as a contributor in *Shine*.

109 (a) "screw your courage . . ."] Shakespeare, *Macbeth*, I. 7.

109 (c) To James Ballantyne] The preface is dated 1 Apr. 1808. This letter, therefore, is more likely to be Spring 1808. Scott had had Strutt's papers since Nov. 1806. See *Archibald Constable*, i. 354.

110 (d) Several of his fellow students] These are named below, pp. 132–3.

111 (d) The meat we are to dine upon] Not Robin Hood but *Adam Bell, Clym of the Clough, and William of Cloudesly*, Pt III, st. [7], lines 3–4. In Percy's *Reliques*. Cf. *The Bride of Lammermoor*, chap. 8: 'does the deer that is to make the pasty run yet on foot, as the ballad has it?'

111 (e) To Archibald Constable] Date is 12 Oct. We know from Miss Berry's *Journals* (ii. 372) that Scott was at Minto on 7 Oct. The only Tuesdays between that date and the 20th were 12th and 19th. The 19th is too near the 20th. The date, therefore, is the 12th.

111 (f) Thomson or Murray] Thomas Thomson and John Archibald Murray, both Whigs like the Minto family.

112 (b) the Examiner] See above, p. 5.

113 (b) Thomson] This seems to imply that Scott has now abandoned his project for an ed. of Thomson. But cf. *SL* xii. 304.

113 *n.* 2] See also my note to *SL* xii. 398 (c–d).

115 (d) To Joanna Baillie] Scott is answering her letter of 22 Oct. 1808 (NLS MS. 3877, ff. 158–61) in which she says she has heard that Scott is going to dedicate a poem on the Battle of Bannockburn to Jeffrey and reports on the growing preference of the public for *Marmion*.

115 (e) "From the chase on the mountain . . ."] This is the first line of a song with that title, by Maclaren. In R. A. Smith, *The Scotish minstrel*, Vol. 4, p. 49, to the tune 'Macgregor a Ruara,' with the music. Also in *Johnson*, new ed., 1853, iv. 170–1, with the music in Vol. 2 (1788), No. 173.

116 (a) no larger than a *midges wing*] A variation of the Scottish proverb: 'The mother of mischief is no more than a midgewing.' *Kelly*, p. 310. See also *SL* v. 84.

117 (e) roar you as an it were] Shakespeare, *A midsummer night's dream*, I. 2.

118 (b) like Robinson Crusoe] Defoe, *Robinson Crusoe*, Everyman Lib., p. 40.

118 (b) Serbonian whirlpool called *Job*] Scott is thinking of 'that Serbonian bog, / . . . / Where armies whole have sunk' (Milton, *Paradise lost*, Bk II, lines 592–4). The allusion to *Job* is not clear unless it is a pun with a lower case 'j'.

118 (f) The Cid] Robert Southey's *Chronicle of the Cid*, London, 1808. The translations by Frere, in the Appendix, were from a MS. in Frere's possession.

119 (a) To John Murray] Below, p. 123, there is another letter to Murray with same date. There can be no doubt that Smiles split one letter into two to separate subjects as he did elsewhere. See, for example, the letter above, p. 114, which Smiles prints in two portions in reversed order. (Smiles, *John Murray*, i. 99–100, 86–7.)

119 (c) most convenient for a shooting-seat] Scott adopted his own suggestion, for at Abbotsford we find a number of volumes, of the type here described, lettered on the spine 'Cottage Library.'

119 (d) Harrison's series] *The Novelist's Magazine*, published by Harrison & Co., London.

120 (b) "Chaou Kiou Choau . . ."] *Hau Kiou Choaan*, 4 vols., 16mo London, 1761. This was the first work ed. by Bishop Percy. Title varies.

120 (c) To George Ellis] I cannot understand why this is printed from Smiles (*John Murray*, i. 100–2) when the text in *Lockhart* (iii. 127–32) is fuller. Smiles obviously was abridging from *Lockhart*. For a selection from the rest of the letter, see *SL* xii. 303–5.

121 (b) "We foresee a speedy revolution . . ."] The passage occurs in *ER* Vol. 10 (July 1807), p. 421: 'We can see, as well as Mr Cobbett, the seeds of a revolution in the present aspect and temper of the nation.' The passage occurs in a review of Cobbett's *Political Register*.

121 (e) balm in Gilead] *Bible, Jeremiah* 8: 22.

122 (a) "remember your swashing

blow"] Shakespeare, *Romeo and Juliet*, I. 1.

122 (c) "Are not Abana . . ."] *Bible, II Kings* 5: 12.

122 *n*. 1] The reference should be *I Henry IV*, II. 3.

123 (d) To John Murray] A portion of the letter above, p. 119.

126 (b) article on Cevallos' Report] Jeffrey's article was in Vol. 13 (Oct. 1808), pp. 215–34. The 'Report' of Don Pedro Cevallos, dated 1 Sept. 1808, was printed in the *Scots Mag.* Vol. 70 (Nov. 1808), pp. 854–7; (Dec. 1808), pp. 929–35.

127 (b) To George Ellis] Grierson, in printing here from *Lockhart* (iii. 142–6), omits Scott's opening words in which he explains to Ellis that 'the rough scroll' is of his letter to Gifford [of 25 Oct.], 'this being one of the very few epistles of which I thought it will be as well to retain a copy.' For other portions of the letter, see *SL* xii. 305–7.

129 (d) a *prospectus*] It was published on 9 Dec. (*Refutation*, p. 75.) See also below, p. 140.

130 (a) He has flourished like a green bay tree] See *SL* i. 23 and my note.

131 (d) that Bear his partner] Alexander Gibson Hunter.

131 (e) "the whirligig of time . . ."] Shakespeare, *Twelfth Night*, V. 1.

131 *n*. 1] For 'I. 1' read 'II. 1.'

132 (a) To Lady Abercorn] The date is 1 Dec. Scott refers to St Andrew's Day as 'yesterday.'

132 (c) Lady Jane Montagu [?]] Delete the query. She was eldest daughter of 5th Duke of Manchester and Lady Susan, daughter of 4th Duke of Gordon. She died unmarried in 1815.

132 (f) Lord Desart [?] . . . Mr Fazackerly] Delete the query. 'Desart' is correct. See *SL* xii. 298. John Nicholas Fazakerly appears as a student in 1807 in the MS. records of Edinburgh University where the name is spelt 'Fazakerley.'

133 (a) a pretty Lady] Lydia Elizabeth Hoare, only daughter of Henry Hoare of Mitcham Grove. She had married

Sir Thomas Dyke Acland on 7 Apr. of this year.

133 (a) Mr. Price] Robert Price, afterwards Sir Robert Price, 2nd Bart. He is recorded in the University MS. records as attending the classes of Ethics and Physics.

134 (a) "fight dog, fight bear"] *Ray*, p. 244; *Kelly*, p. 315; Ramsay, *Proverbs*, p. 19. Also used in *Waverley*, chap. 71.

134 (b) To George Ellis] For other parts of this letter, see *SL* xii. 308–9.

134 (d) The two Mackenzies] Henry Mackenzie and one of his sons. See below, p. 136.

135 (b) his partner, a sort of Whig run mad] Alexander Gibson Hunter.

135 (f) Oh for True Thomas . . .] An allusion to *Lord Soulis* by John Leyden in *Minstrelsy* (ed. Henderson), iv. 218–58.

136 (a) Lord Soulis's cauldron] See preceding note.

136 (a) To John Murray] Scott is answering Murray's letter of 19 Nov. (Smiles, *John Murray*, i. 116–18).

136 (b–c) reviews of Burns . . .] The books Scott is proposing are: 1. Cromek's *Reliques of Robert Burns* [*Shine*, No. 2]; 2. Southey's *Chronicle of the Cid* [*Shine*, No. 13]; 3. Alexander Murray's *Life of James Bruce*; 4. Abiel Holmes's *American annals* [*Shine*, No. 55]; 5. John Philpot Curran's *Speeches* [*Shine*, No. 9]; 6. Hector Macneill's *The pastoral or lyric Muse of Scotland*. (Macneill had written on 4 Dec. to Scott asking him for his criticism.); 7. M. G. Lewis's *Romantic tales*; 8. Mrs Anne Grant's *Memoirs of an American lady*.

137 (b) Constables migration] For his London branch, see above, p. 44.

137 (d) To George Ellis] Grierson prints from *Lockhart*, iii. 150–1. But the date, 15 Dec. 1808, which Lockhart gives, is the date of the Declaration, *not* of the letter. For other portions, see *SL* xii. 310, where Grierson repeats the wrong date. Correct date, I think, should be 19 Dec.

137 (e) royal declaration] Written by Canning. It is printed in *Edin. Ann. Reg.* I. i. ci–ciii.

137 *n.* 1] Grierson here fails to note Scott's errors. In the 'Biographical memoir of Sir Ralph Sadler,' written by Scott, he says (i. xi): 'the women with their distaffs, and the very stones in the street' and a footnote refers to Vol. 2, p. 559 [*sic* for 560]. But at this reference Otterborn, while referring to 'the stones in the strete', says nothing about 'the women with their distaffs.' The correct reference to the text in *Sadler* is i. 70, where Sir George Douglas (*not* Otterborn) says: 'there is not so little a boy but will hurl stones against it, and the wives will handle their distaffs.' Scott used this passage in *The Monastery*, chap. 36.

138 (a) engaging] See *SL* xii. 309 *n.* 2.

138 *n.* 1] For two letters on this subject from Jeffrey to Macvey Napier, see *Selections from the correspondence of the late Macvey Napier*, priv. pr. London, 1877, pp. 423–5.

140 (a) Keppel] See Thomas Keppel, *The life of Augustus, Viscount Keppel*, 2 vols., London, 1842, i. 288.

140 (b) like Pistol] Shakespeare, *King Henry V*, III. 6.

140 (d) the Prospectus] It was printed in Vol. 1, pp. v–xii. As I have not seen the 1808 version I cannot say if any alterations were made. See also above, p. 129.

141 (c) A female servant] See *SL* vii. 424 *n.* 2.

141 (e) To C. K. Sharpe] For Sharpe's reply of 9 Jan. 1809, see my note to *SL* ii. 148 (a).

141 (f) The inimitable virago] For Sharpe's reply on Queen Bess, see my note to *SL* ii. 148 (a).

141 *n.* 1] It is in the ante-room to the Armoury at Abbotsford.

142 (e) Macneill] He was not reviewed in *QR*. See above, p. 136 and below, pp. 156, 157, 166, 173.

142 (e–f) as good play for nothing] *Ray*, p. 190. Ramsay, *Proverbs*, p. 12, has: 'Better sit idle than work for nought.'

143 (a) like the ghosts in King Richard] Shakespeare, *Richard III*, V. 3.

143 (c) Cumberland] For his review, see *SL* ii. 123 (f).

143 (d) enclosed prospectus] See above, pp. 129, 140.

144 (a) Another person] Robert Southey.

144 (a) your humble comdumble, as Swift says] *Journal to Stella*, Letter X (*Works*, ed. Scott, 2nd ed. ii. 95). Also in *A complete collection of genteel and ingenious conversation* (ibid. ix. 435).

145 (b) Nicols] John Nichols.

146 (d) Cumberlands attempt] See above, p. 123.

147 *n.* 1] There is an extract from Clarke's letter of 22 May, with P.S. 27 May, 1808, in Partington, *Post-bag*, pp. 35–6. The original MS. is in NLS (MS. 3877, ff. 63–4).

147 *n.* 2] For '*Four Scenes*' read '*Four Songs.*'

148 (a) To C. K. Sharpe] This is a reply to Sharpe's letter from Hoddam, 9 Jan. 1809 (misdated 1808). Two extracts are given in Partington, *Letter-books*, p. 11, and *Post-bag*, p. 33. In the former Sharpe refers to *QR* and Moore and in the latter to the drawing of Queen Elizabeth.

148 (c) The letters you mention] Letters of David Hume to Matthew Sharpe of Hoddam. See below, p. 156. They were printed in *Edin. Ann. Reg. for 1809*, II. ii. 552–4.

148 (d) chamber in the wall] *Bible, II Kings* 4: 10.

148 (d) the Cabbin is convenient] Ben Jonson, *Every man in his humour*, I. 4.

149 *n.*] For '*Peregrine Pickle*' read '*Peregrine Pickle*, chap. 62.'

151 (a) a little chamber in the wall] *Bible, II Kings* 4: 10.

151 (a) Thalaba is in parturition] The second ed. was being printed by James Ballantyne & Co.

151 (d) Coleridge's intended paper] *The Friend.* See below, p. 342.

153 (d) Mr. Wharton] Richard Wharton, M.P. for Durham. Scott's letter to him is not in *SL*. See also below, p. 158 *n.*

154 (a) my edition of Swift] Morritt, in his letter of 15 Dec. 1808, had given his views on Swift. See extract in Partington, *Post-bag*, p. 40.

154 (a) Mr. Stanly] James Stanley, Mrs Morritt's brother.

154 (b) To Constable & Co.] Now in NLS (MS. 742, ff. 27–8).

156 (a) your letters of David Hume] See above, p. 148 and my note.

156 (b) what Cadwallader says] Foote, *The author*, I. 2.

156 (c) "casting many a Northward look"] Shakespeare, *II King Henry IV*, II. 3: 'Threw many a northward look.'

157 (a) the proof sheet] Of his review of Cromek's *Burns*.

157 (b) a whisky-frisky article on Sir John] Review of Sir John Carr's *Caledonian sketches.*

157 (d) I expect McNeil] The review Scott wanted C. K. Sharpe to write (above, p. 142). See also below, pp. 156, 166, 173.

158 (a) Sir John's Review] The whisky-frisky article above, p. 157.

158 (e) I received your letter] Of 27 Jan. A small extract is in Partington, *Post-bag*, p. 45.

159 (b) I love a drum and a soldier as heartily as ever Uncle Toby did] This is not a quotation but it sums up Toby's character. He refers only once to the drum: 'when I was a school-boy, I could not hear a drum beat, but my heart beat with it.' (Sterne, *Tristram Shandy*, Bk VI, chap. 32.) See also below, p. 264.

159 *n.* 1] Also quoted in *Waverley*, chap. 19.

160 (a) "*a la stoccata*," as Mercutio says] Shakespeare, *Romeo and Juliet*, III. 1.

160 (b) Coleridge's paper] *The Friend.*

160 (c) I hear very high things from Gifford of your article] 'Account of the Baptist Missionary Society' for *QR* Vol. 1, No. 1, Feb. 1809.

160 (e) *coute qui coute*] Read '*coute que coute.*'

161 (a) the Nortons] See above, pp. 24, 24 *n.*, 54–5, 54 *n.*

161 *n.* 3] This is an odd place to put this long and inaccurate note on the

Ballantynes. John Ballantyne's house was not called Harmony Hall and *The Lady of the Lake* was not the first book published by him.

162 (a) the harvest . . .] *Bible, Luke* 10: 2.

162 (b) To Mrs. Clephane] Marianne Maclean, daughter of Lachlan Maclean, 7th of Torloisk and Margaret Smith, married Major William Douglas Clephane of Carslogie who added Maclean to his name when his wife succeeded to Torloisk in 1799. He became a Lieut.-Col. 20th Foot in 1795 and a Major-General in 1801 when he was a Captain in 3rd Foot Guards. Four children are recorded: (1) Margaret, born 21 May 1793 at Kirkness (*Scots Mag.* Vol. 55, p. 257); (2) a son who died an infant at Kirkness, 26 Nov. 1795 (ibid., Vol. 57, p. 750); (3) Anna Jane, born 12 Nov. 1798 (ibid., Vol. 60, p. 791); (4) Williamina, born 1803, probably in Dec. and, therefore, posthumously (ibid., Vol. 65, p. 883).

162 (b) The air] This is the Gaelic air to which Scott set Fitz-Eustace's Song ('Where shall the lover rest') in *Marmion*, Canto III, st. x. See *SL* i. 393 and my note.

163 (e) To John Murray] Part of this letter is repeated under 1810, below, p. 297.

163 (f) Douglas] See note to *SL* xii. 308 (e).

164 (a) my list of novels] For a projected edition of novels to be edited by Scott. For other references, see Index under Projected Works, under 1808–9.

164 (e) like Aesops Waggon] This fable is by Avianus, not Aesop. See L'Estrange, *Fables*, No. 246.

165 *n.* 1] Delete. The work cited is not an authority on this subject.

166 (a) Your critique] Of Macneill's *The pastoral or lyric Muse of Scotland*. See above, pp. 142, 156, 157 and below, p. 173.

168 (a) Secret History] John Murray, however, did not accept a share and it was published by John Ballantyne and Longman.

169 (a) *portcullis* copies] This plan was never carried out. Eventually, instead of a wooden block to print on the title-pages of his own works, he had a metal stamp which was used on the bindings to indicate ownership.

169 (c) Johnes] See *SL* iii. 81 *n.*

169 *n.* 1] For 'Earl' read 'Marquess.'

170 (a) to my brother] Major John Scott, who had just arrived in London with his regiment.

170 *n.* 1] Delete and substitute: John Derricke's *The image of Irelande*, London, 1581. In Scott's ed. of Somers's *Tracts*, i. 558–621.

171 (a) Wordsworth] Neither *We are seven* nor *Glen Almain* was included.

171 (d) more flax on his spindle] Heywood, p. 128: 'More tow on their distaves than they can well spinne.'

172 (e) "life to the last enjoy'd"] Churchill, *The candidate*, line 152.

172 *n.* 1] In 1949 Percy R. Stevenson erected a tombstone over Camp's grave in the garden of 39 Castle Street. See also *SL* x. 398–9.

173 (a) a letter from Gifford] Gifford's letter of 20 Feb. (NLS MS. 3878, ff. 25–6) was by no means as encouraging as Scott here makes out. Sharpe's review never appeared.

173 (d) "Mantle made Amiss"] *The boy and the mantle*, st. [12]. In Percy's *Reliques*.

174 (a) the article on "Spain"] Vol. 1, No. 1, Art. 1, *Affaires d'Espagne* which Shine (No. 1) attributes to George Ellis and George Canning.

174 *n.* 1] In line 4, for 'Daldon [?]' read 'Dalden.'

176 (c) the new poem] Campbell's *Gertrude of Wyoming*, which Scott reviewed in second number of the *QR*.

177 (c) To William Miller or John Murray] The letter is to Miller (below, p. 179). The year 1809 is confirmed by Scott's letter to Heber of 10 Mar. (*SL* xii. 310–11) on Paton's sale, and by references to Mrs Clarke and the Judicature Act.

177 (d) your old plays] *Ancient British drama*, 3 vols., London, 1810.

177 (d) Derricks plates] Though the text was printed in Vol. 1 of Somers's

Tracts (see above, p. 170, 170 *n.* 1), the plates had to be issued along with Vol. 2. For a full discussion of these plates see my note to *SL* ii. 300 (b).

177 *n.* 1] Delete this note which is not applicable. Scott's letter has nothing to do with Sadler.

178 (a) Patons sale] George Paton, the antiquary, had died in 1807 and his books were sold in 1809. A copy of *Catalogue of the library of Mr George Paton*, 8vo Edinburgh, 1809, is (or was) in the Signet Library.

178 (a) 1715 & 1745] The latter were not required. Somers's *Tracts* stops at 1726.

178 *n.* 1] See Davidson Cook's *Murray's mysterious contributor* in *Nineteenth Century*, Vol. 101 (Apr. 1927), pp. 605–13, and note on it in my *Bibl.* No. 2688.

179 (b) to Mr. Miller ... to Mr. Gifford and to Heber] Letter to Miller is above, p. 177. The letter to Gifford is not known to be extant. The letter to Heber is in *SL* xii. 310–11.

179 (d) To Lady Abercorn] Date is 1807. Also in *FL* i. 132–3 where it is also wrongly dated. The date 1807 is determined by: (1) Charlotte's transcripts, 1806–7; (2) Dorset papers; (3) Scott left Edinburgh on Sunday, 15 Mar. 1807; (4) the Judicature Act was being debated in 1807; (5) *Courier*. Scott's speech was on 28 Feb. 1807. On Charlotte's transcripts, see *SL* ii. 396, i. 350, vi. 253 *n.* On Dorset papers, see *SL* i. 318, 350, ii. 394 and my note at last reference. Scott visited Knowle (*SL* ii. 216) perhaps to see them.

179 *n.* 1] Not necessarily Richardson. Greenfield used also his mother's name Rutherfurd and his son adopted the name Rutherfurd.

180 (a) the *Courier*] I have not had access to the *Courier*, but Scott's speech can be found in *Substance of the speeches delivered by some members of the Faculty of Advocates*, Edinburgh, 1807, pp. 32–48.

180 (d) by Mrs. Clephane] Mrs Maclean Clephane of Torloisk. See above, p. 162 and my note.

181 (d) his partner] Alexander Gibson Hunter.

181 *n.* 1] The copy of *Needwood Forest* which Scott received was not the Lichfield 1776 one but Derby 1808. The *Commendatory Verses*, said to be by the two Darwins and Anna Seward, were all by the elder Darwin. See *Letters of Anna Seward*, iii. 154.

183 (c) Mr. G.] William Greenfield. He adopted his mother's name Rutherfurd.

183 *n.* 1] The review appeared in the second, not the first number. *Shine* (No. 30) gives John Ireland and William Gifford as the reviewers.

184 (d) privy to the transaction, and] For 'and' read 'as'.

186 *n.* 1] For a brief biography of White, see Boswell's *Johnson*, ed. Hill-Powell, iv. 547.

188 (b) To Miss Millar] This letter was printed by A. M. Williams (apparently from the original MS.) in *Scottish Country Life*, Vol. 17 (Nov. 1930), p. 340, where it is dated 15 Apr. (which was a Saturday).

189 (a–b) D. of G's article] Read 'D. of Y.'s article'; i.e. on the Duke of York. The same mistake 'D. of G.' occurs in *SL* v. 394.

189 (e) the Macleans' song] Margaret Clephane's literal translation from the Gaelic was expanded by Scott into his *War-song*.

191 (a) To Mrs. Hughes] Date must be 1807. Scott stayed in Bury Street in 1807, but not in 1809.

191 (e) the tale of Lady's Rock] i.e. *The family legend*. Thomas Holcroft wrote a drama on the same subject. See article, *The Lady of the Rock* in the *Lit. Gaz.* 1824 (20 Mar.), pp. 189–90. This is one of a series of articles which read like the work of Margaret Clephane.

191 *n.* 1] This is Canto III, st. 2 of *The lay*.

192 (b) "commodity of good names"] Shakespeare, *I Henry IV*, I. 2.

192 (d) To Miss White] As this letter deals exclusively with *Marmion* (with the single exception of the reference to the Bishop), 1809 is too late. Lydia White was in Edinburgh from about Nov. 1807 till June 1808. Scott did not visit London in 1808 and Lydia's 'house' must refer to her Edinburgh

one. Letter probably belongs to mid Apr., 1808, after Jeffrey's review appeared and before she went to Ashiestiel later in the month.

193 (b–c) Spencer . . . his Lordship's personal civility] i.e. when Scott was appointed Principal Clerk. See *SL* i. 276, 278, 279.

193 (e) To Lady Louisa Stuart] This letter was probably written on Sunday, 11 June.

193 *n.* 1] In line 2, for 'Barry' read 'Berry.' Scott breakfasted with her on 7 June when *The family legend* was read. Mrs Cholmley and two of her daughters were present. See *Extracts of the journals and correspondence of Miss Berry,* ii. 381.

194 (d) Miscellanies] This is probably Swift's *Miscellanies in prose and verse,* 8vo London, 1711.

195 (b) The Censura] The *Censura Literaria,* edited by Sir Samuel Brydges, was begun in 1805 and ended this year.

196 (e) Mrs. Maclean] Scott means Mrs Clephane.

196 *n.* 1] Scott could not be referring to an article which had not yet been published. He is referring to Art. 17 in No. 1 of *QR,* Feb. 1809.

196 *n.* 2] For 'Mrs. Maclean's help' read 'Mrs. Clephane's help.'

197 (d–e) this confounded visitor of yours] Charles Danvers. (*FL* i. 135 *n.*)

199 (e) To Rev. E. Berwick] Written between 13 and 26 July, i.e. after the Courts rose on 12 July and in time for Berwick to reply on 30 July (*SL* iii. 56 *n.*).

199 *n.* 1] For '1810' read '1809.' For review of *Apollonius* see below, pp. 322 *n.,* 385 *n.,* 386–7 and *SL* xii. 417.

200 (f) Burrell] This should be Barrett.

200 *n.* 1] For 'Barnett' read 'Barrett.'

201 (a) Tisdal] Here and eight lines below 'Tisdal' should be 'Tindal.'

201 (c–d) Dr. Delany . . . consanguinity] See Lady Louisa's letter in Partington, *Post-bag,* pp. 79–80.

201 (e) The Legion Club] Swift's nickname for the Irish Parliament.

For the poem, see Scott's *Swift,* 2nd ed., xii. 456–66.

202 *n.* 1] The paper on Methodism was 'On the evangelical sects,' but it did not appear till Dec. 1810 in Vol. 4, No. 8 for Nov. 1810, pp. 480–514. (*Shine,* No. 127.)

203 (a) Lord of the Lake and the Cairn] This is a variation of 'Laird of the Cairn and the Scaur.' See *SL* i. 224 and my note.

203 (c) our expedition] The disastrous Walcheren Expedition of this year. See below, pp. 211 and 241 and my note at latter reference.

203 (c) *wise behind the hand*] Ramsay, *Proverbs,* p. 44. Also used in *SL* vi. 302 and *MPW* v. 21.

203 (d) the Harleian and Somers] The 2nd ed. of *The Harleian miscellany* had begun publication in 1808 and publication ran almost concurrently with *Somers.* The *Harleian* was being edited by Thomas Park, a much more competent editor than Southey could have been.

203 (e) Eclogue] Southey's *The alderman's funeral; an English eclogue* appeared in *Edin. Ann. Reg. for 1808,* I. ii, Poetry, pp. i–iv (publ. 1810).

204 *n.* 1] For 'Note 52' read 'note to Canto V, st. ix' and see my note to *SL* ii. 98 *n.* 1.

205 (a) terrier puppy] For letter from William Dunlop, 5 July 1809, which accompanied the dog, see *FL* i. 248 *n.* 1.

205 (c) I am just favoured with yours.] Letter of 13 July cited below, p. 206 *n.*

205 (f) Sir George Beaumont] Southey's letter to him is in Knight, *Memorials of Coleorton,* ii. 75–7, and is dated 17 July. He had time to receive Scott's letter of 16 July before writing.

205 (f) Kehama] *The curse of Kehama* was printed by James Ballantyne who also printed other works by Southey.

206 (d) immense London stages] Scott was opposed to large theatres. See Index under Theatres.

207 (a) ballad of Lady Louisa Stuart] *Ugly Meg.* See above, pp. 39–41, 39 *n.,* 42, and below, p. 209.

207 (a) the Minstrelsy] The *English*

minstrelsy, ed. by Scott, 2 vols., Edinburgh, 1810.

207 (e) Weber] This relates to work being done by him on Gordon's *A genealogical history of the Earldom of Sutherland*, issued in 1813.

207 *n.* 1] Elizabeth was daughter of 19th Earl. In 1803 Earl Gower succeeded as 2nd Marquess of Stafford and became 1st Duke of Sutherland in 1833. Scott met Lady Stafford in London in 1806.

208 *n.* 1] One letter turned up later (*SL* vii. 215). See also below, p. 481 *n.*

209 (d) tale of Walter of Harden's wedding] *Ugly Meg*. See above, p. 207 and my references there.

210 (a) as Johnson said] 'A man may write at any time, if he will set himself *doggedly* to it.' Boswell, *The journal of a tour to the Hebrides*, 16 Aug. and cf. 25 Aug. See Boswell's *Johnson*, ed. Hill-Powell, v. 40, 110.

210 *n.* 1] The article on Austrian state papers was in *second* number of *QR*. According to *Shine* (No. 35) it was written by Sharon Turner with help from Canning and possibly from George Ellis. Bishop Warburton's *Letters* was reviewed by Jeffrey in *ER* for Jan. 1809 and by Thomas Dunham Whitaker in *QR* for Nov. 1809 (*Shine*, No. 61).

211 (c) proffered service is of an evil savour] 'Merx ultronea putret' is regarded as a proverb. Morritt probably would not have understood the Scottish equivalent: 'Boden gear stinks' (Ramsay, *Proverbs*, p. 13).

211 (e) our expedition] Walcheren Expedition of this year. See above, p. 203 and below, p. 241 and my note to latter.

212 (b) I have written] On same day, above, p. 209.

212 (c) pirates ditty] Almost certainly Southey's *The Inchcape Rock*. See below, pp. 226 *n.*, 227.

212 *n.* 1] Scott's letter should be dated Sunday, 6 Aug. Grierson, in his *Sir Walter Scott, Bart.*, p. 101, changes the date to 10 Aug. without giving any reason.

213 (a) I have written to Ellis by this post] This letter is in *SL* xii. 311–12.

213 (c) acted as a flapper] Swift, *Gulliver's travels, Pt III. A voyage to Laputa.* (*Works*, ed. Scott, 2nd ed., xi. 202.)

213 (e) Ellis was doing something about Spanish affairs] *QR* for Aug. 1809, Art. 11. (*Shine*, No. 46.) The number was published late Aug. or early Sept.

213 (f) your ancient Seneschal] Walton. See Knight, *Memorials of Coleorton*, ii. 76.

214 (a) Sindbad's Old Man of the Sea] See my note to *SL* i. 369 (b).

214 *n.* 2] See *Lockhart*, iii. 193, and Grierson's *Sir Walter Scott, Bart.*, pp. 100–1.

215 (c) two long epistles] As the letter above, p. 179, dated 1809, should be 1807, the only recent letter is that of 1 Dec. 1808 (above, p. 132). Scott refers again to these missing letters (below, p. 240).

217 *n.* 1] The 'fragment' (line 3) belongs to the letter of 18 Sept. 1808, above, pp. 92–3.

219 (c) "fause Sir John"] Sir John Sinclair. For explanation, see *FL* i. 144 *n.* The epithet 'fause' is taken from the ballad, *May Colvin*.

219 *n.* 1] In line 8 from foot, for 'courage of the Macleans' read 'courage of the Maclean.' Mackenzie's epilogue was printed in the *Scots Mag.* Vol. 72 (Feb. 1810), pp. 126–7.

220 (b) [Carrs] rooms] This should be Corri's rooms. The building in Leith Walk at the top of Broughton Street changed its name many times. From 1809 to 1811 Siddons occupied it as the New Theatre Royal. In 1811 he returned to Shakespeare Square.

220 (e) Prince Housseins tapestry] See my note to *SL* i. 229 (e).

221 (a) this scrawl . . .] See my note to p. 217 *n.* 1, above.

221 (c) Lady Charlotte Rawdon] She was a daughter of 1st Earl of Moira and at this time Berwick was domestic chaplain to the 2nd Earl.

221 (d) letters from the late Lady Moira] Lady Moira who died in 1808 was the wife of the 1st Earl.

222 (d) Whitsted] This should be Whitshed.

223 (c) In a letter of Lord Orrery] Of 4 Dec. 1742 (Swift's *Works*, ed. Scott, 2nd ed., xix. 257–61). 'Dean Swift' should be 'Deane Swift.'

223 (d) "jolly boys of St. Patrick the Cauvan Demons"] Probably an allusion to *The Yahoo's overthrow*, line 1: 'Jolly boys of St Kevan's, St Patrick's, Donore.' (Swift's *Works*, ed. Scott, 2nd ed., xii. 441.)

223 *n.* 1] For 'Drapiers'' re'ad 'Drapier's.'

224 (b) Mr. Robert Dundas] Appointed, 15 Apr. 1809, Chief Secretary to Lord Lieutenant of Ireland, in room of Sir Arthur Wellesley. (*Edin. Ann. Reg. for 1809*, II. ii. 112.) He held this post for only a few months. See below, pp. 275–6.

224 *n.* 1] It first appeared in 4th ed., 1810. It was also printed in *Edin. Ann. Reg. for 1808*, II. ii, Poetry, pp. xiv–xxi (publ. 1810).

225 (b) the Upholsterer in the farce] Quidnunc in Murphy's *The Upholsterer*.

225 (e) I snap at your offer] See below, p. 307 and my note.

225 (e) beggars must not be chusers] *Heywood*, p. 50; *Ray*, p. 99; Ramsay, *Proverbs*, p. 11, and cf. *Kelly*, p. 152. Also used in *SL* ii. 231, 243, iv. 422, vi. 28, viii. 480, ix. 431, xi. 281.

225 (f) wrote . . . to my mistresses eyebrow] Shakespeare, *As you like it*, II. 7.

225 *n.* 1] The work was reviewed in *QR* for Oct. 1813. *Shine* (No. 261) gives John Wilson Croker as possible author with references to *SL* ii. 225, 236–7.

226 (b–c) [A mad world]] The MS. (NLS MS. 144, No. 4) is damaged at this point and it is doubtful if 'my' is correct. I do not think that filling out the text from the title of Middleton's play is justified for there is no Friar John in the play. There is a Friar John in Rabelais who very frequently uses the words 'my masters' and I think Scott may be quoting him.

226 (c) Touchstones chorus] Not Touchstone, but the Fool in Shakespeare's *King Lear*, III. 2, or the Clown in *Twelfth Night*, V. 1.

226 (d) To Miss Clephane] To Margaret.

226 *n.* 1] In lines 6 and 7, 'Mare Stella' should be 'Maris Stella.'

227 (c) Ave Maria Stella] This should be 'Ave Maris Stella.' It is John Leyden's *Portuguese hymn to the Virgin Mary*, "*the Star of the Sea*." Scott inserted it in his *English minstrelsy*, Vol. 2, pp. 144–7.

227 (d) the *air* of Montroses lines] Preserved in Mrs Hope-Scott's MS. Music Book at Abbotsford.

227 *n.* 1] For '1810' read '*for 1810* (publ. 1812), III. ii. lxxxiv–lxxxvi.' Southey's name does not appear as author.

228 *n.* 1] In line 2, for 'Fergusson' read 'Ferguson.'

228 *n.* 2] There is a long account of Glenbervie's projected ed. in the *Eclectic Rev.* Vol. 5, Pt 2 (Oct. 1809), p. 975.

229 (b) Knight of Acre] Sir William Sidney Smith (1764–1840). He successfully defended Acre and forced Napoleon to retreat.

229 (c) the Lady whose arm was broken] In *Tales of a grandfather*, chap. 19, Scott calls her Catherine Douglas, without indicating to which branch of the Douglases she belonged.

229 (d) The Douglas that perished at Chatham] See Scott's *Swift*, 2nd ed., ix. 258 and Scott's note there. Addison in the *Spectator*, No. 72, 23 May 1711, referred to 'the famous captain mentioned in my lord Clarendon, who was burnt in his ship because he would not quit it without orders.'

229 (d) Douglas . . . mentioned in Carletons Memoirs] The reference is to Scott's ed. (1808), p. 64. The officer who retrieved the standard was Sir Robert Douglas.

229 (e) "here's room for meditation"] Nicholas Rowe, *The fair penitent*, Act V. Also quoted in *MPW* xvii. 348.

230 (b) The Coronach of Maclean] In a note to Canto III, st. 15 of *The Lady of the Lake* Scott printed the *Coronach on Sir Lauchlan, Chief of Maclean*, which he said was 'literally translated from the Gaelic.' I suspect that this translation was made by Margaret Clephane. See above, p. 226 *n.*

231 (a) Beggars should not be chusers] See above, p. 225.

231 (b–c) lands of mist and snow] Coleridge, *The ancient mariner*, Pt 2, st. [12], line 4 or Pt 5, st. [25], line 2.

231 (c) the Weird Sisters] Shakespeare, *Macbeth*, I. 3.

231 (d) poet laureate . . . *sic evitabile fulmen*] The poet laureate was Henry James Pye. For the Latin phrase, see *SL* vii. 130 and *n*. 2.

231 *n*. 1] Scott contributed these three poems to Vol. 2, but he also contributed *The resolve* and *Hunting song* in Vol. 1.

232 (b) Mr. Berwick] See my note to *SL* ii. 221 (c).

232 (c) "Go to Berwick"] An old and popular Scottish tune.

233 (b) Lord Hastings] See *Ivanhoe*, chap. 14.

233 (b) your honoured Mother (whose letters . . .] See my note to *SL* ii. 221 (d).

233 (c) birth . . . lamented young Chief] Scott is referring to the birth of Lord John Douglas Scott, her third son, born 13 July 1809. The 'lamented young Chief' is Lord George Henry Scott who died 11 Mar. 1808.

234 (a) His mother and her husband] Carrie Lamb who married Mitchell in Selkirk.

234 (e) the Major] Scott's brother, Major John Scott, who had returned from London (which he left on 17 Apr.) to Edinburgh. See above, p. 188.

234 (f) Daniels education] Scott means William, Daniel's son.

234 *n*. 1] See also *N. & Q.* Vol. 181, pp. 102–4, which has some statements which must be accepted with reservations. He is not mentioned by name in *SL* till we reach 1828. In the *Journal*, 1 July 1826, he is called William Mitchell. This suggests that he was known by the name of his mother's husband (which would avoid awkward questions) until he was ready to go to Canada, when concealment was no longer necessary.

235 (d) what Swift said of Whig and Tory] Scott may have been thinking

of the *Examiner*, No. 43 (Scott's *Swift*, 2nd ed., iii. 507–14).

236 (b) "appalld the guilty and made mad the free"] Shakespeare, *Hamlet*, II. 2: 'Make mad the guilty, and appal the free.'

236 *n*. 2] Scott is not referring to Southey's article in the first number but to his article in the third number. The article on Lord Valentia's travels, also in the third number, was by Southey.

237 (a) Mrs. Montagues *Letters*] See above, p. 225 and my note.

237 (b) Genl. Murray] Afterwards Sir John Murray, 8th Bart. of Clermont.

237 (d) Miss Edgeworths *Tales*] Reviewed in third number of *QR* by Henry John Stephen (*Shine*, No. 42).

238 (a) his lady's sudden decease] She died on 3 Sept.

238 (b) unfeeling speech of a border chief] Walter Scott ('Old Wat') of Harden (died 1629) who said 'The lands of Gilmanscleuch are well worth a dead son,' when he got a charter for the lands after one of his sons was killed in a fray. See Scott's *Minstrelsy* (ed. Henderson), ii. 16.

238 *n*.] Scott was in Edinburgh for one day (28 Aug.) and set off on his tour on 29 Aug. He was back at Ashiestiel by 10 Sept. without having returned to Edinburgh. See *SL* vii. 429, 430. On dating of letters in second paragraph, see above, p. 212 *n*. On Byron's satire, see Grierson's *Sir Walter Scott, Bart.*, pp. 100–1.

239 (e–f) Montrose] The substance of this paragraph was repeated in the 1830 introd. to *The Lady of the Lake*. Montrose's *Lines* were very much in Scott's mind at this time, for Margaret Clephane contributed an air for them. See above, p. 227 and below, pp. 261, 263.

240 (a) a drunken man] James Balfour. Robert Chambers gives some account of him under the heading 'Singing Jamie B—r' in his *Traditions of Edinburgh* (1825), ii. 101–5.

240 (b) of my two letters] See my note to *SL* ii. 215 (c).

241 (a) Huntly] George Gordon, Marquess of Huntly (later 5th and last

Duke of Gordon). In the disastrous Walcheren Expedition in 1809 his task had been to land, with 5,000 men, on the island of Cadsand. See *Edin. Ann. Reg. for 1809*, II. i. 663.

241 (b) Duke of Montrose's seat] Buchanan Castle, west Stirlingshire, now a hotel.

241 (c) "all plaided and plumed . . ."] Thomas Campbell, *Lochiel's warning*, line 51.

241 n. 1] Sarah Wait, a servant where Gordon lodged and described as 'an abandoned woman,' prosecuted the Duke for 'an indecent assault.' The case was tried by Lord Ellenborough and a special jury. 'The jury instantly brought in a verdict for the defendant.' (*Edin. Ann. Reg. for 1809*, II. ii. 308–9.)

242 n. 1] In second line, delete 'probably.'

243 (b) beggars must not be chusers] See above, p. 225.

243 (c) "Too late I staid"] The opening words of *To * * * * * ***, the second of Spencer's poems printed in *English minstrelsy*, ii. 179–80.

244 (e) I long to see the book] If this refers to his *Poems*, it was not published till 1811.

244 n. 1] For 'Sackersen' read 'Sackerson.'

245 (c) Norton's Address] Thomas Norton's *To the Quenes maiesties poore decayued Subiectes of the North Countrey, drawen into rebellion*, etc., London, 1569.

245 (c) Percy's ballad] *The Rising in the North*.

245 n. 1] Tilty and Thaxted are in Essex, but Hadham is in Hertfordshire.

246 (b) Mary Bateman] Of Campfield, near Leeds. Described as a sorceress, she was tried at York in March 1809 for the murder by poisoning in May 1807 of Sarah (or Rebecca) Perigo, of Bramley, and condemned to death. See *Edin. Ann. Reg.* I. ii. 214–16, II. ii. 31, 88.

246 (b) I can give you the very freshest tidings of the Bar-Guest] In the 4th ed. of the *Minstrelsy*, 1810 (i. civ), Scott added a footnote: 'He has made

his appearance in this very year (1809) in . . . York, if the vulgar may be credited' (Henderson's ed., i. 151 n.).

246 (d) Brown Man] This dwarf was mentioned in the introd. to *The Cout of Keeldar* in the 1st ed. of the *Minstrelsy*. Nothing was added in subsequent eds. For other references, see Scott's note to *The Black Dwarf*, chap. 1, and motto to chap. 3.

247 (a) Them Dhu, or Black-knee] This seems to be a misreading for Ghlune Dhu. See 1829 introd. to *Rob Roy*.

247 (d) Your letter] Ellis's letter (NLS MS. 870, f. 16) is undated but '23 Sept. 1809' has been noted in pencil.

248 (b) Robert Dundas] Who became 2nd Viscount Melville. The Earl of Liverpool became War Secretary in Perceval's cabinet, Oct. 1809.

248 (d) the Doctor] The nickname of Henry Addington, Viscount Sidmouth.

249 (c–d) Wellesley] It was Perceval who formed the new ministry which Wellesley did not join till Dec. when he became Foreign Secretary.

249 n. 1] The article on Sir John Moore is in the *third* number of *QR*. Moore's letter of 24 Sept. is in Partington, *Letterbooks*, pp. 14–15.

251 (a) To Samuel Rogers] Rogers's letter of 22 Sept. is in NLS (MS. 3878, f. 147).

251 n. 1] *To * * * on the death of her sister* appeared in the *English minstrelsy*, ii. 238–9, but the poem *On a voice that had been lost* was not included. In lines 3–4, delete 'Sir' and for 'later Viscount Macduff' read 'later 4th Earl of Fife.'

252 (a) like Hamlet] Shakespeare, *Hamlet*, II. 2: 'forgone all custom of exercises.'

252 (c) To The Rev. E. Berwick] This is a reply to Berwick's letter of 26 Sept., cited in *SL* iii. 57 n. 2.

252 (d) Miss Dupasse] The two lines of verse quoted are in Scott's *Dryden*, xv. 211. Scott in his note makes no reference to Miss Du Pas. Horace Walpole, in his note in *Memoirs of Count Grammont*, says the verses refer to Elizabeth Bagot, Dorset's wife. For Miss Du Pas's marriage with 2nd

Viscount Allen, see Scott's *Swift*, 2nd ed., vii. 276 *n*. The bravoes who beat Dryden were hired by Rochester (Scott's *Dryden*, xv. 201).

253 (b) *unrighteous mammon*] *Bible, Luke* 16: 11.

253 (d) the theatre which is temporary] The Circus in Leith Walk renamed the New Theatre Royal. See Dibdin, *Annals*, pp. 258–9.

254 *n*. 1] There is an extract from her letter in Partington, *Post-bag*, p. 50.

255 (c) when I immediately wrote] i.e. on 11 Oct., above, p. 252.

255 (d) Walker] Joseph Cooper Walker. There is a long letter from Scott to Walker, 29 July 1809, discussing problems connected with his ed. of Swift, in *The Athenæum*, 1893 (1 Apr.), pp. 408–9. The letter is not in *SL*.

255 (e) green Erin by the Caledonian Desert of Hills] Southey in *Madoc* calls Ireland 'Green Erin' and Wales 'Land of Hills.' If Scott is thinking of Southey his 'Desert' is less appropriate than 'Land.'

255 (e–f) *Chamber in the Wall*] *Bible, II Kings* 4: 10.

256 (a) as Slender says] See above, p. 244 *n*.

256 (c) To James Moore] On same subject as former letter of 3 Oct., above, p. 249.

257 (c) Freling . . . Coxe] Francis (afterwards Sir Francis) Freeling and Edward Coxe were friends and neighbours at Hampstead. Scott became acquainted with Coxe through Joanna Baillie and, as the letters show, he took advantage of Freeling's franking on many occasions.

257 (d) Venice preserved] By Thomas Otway.

258 (c) our Lord Provost] William Coulter, Lord Provost, 1808–10. See my note to *SL* ii. 336 (a).

258 (f) copy of verses] Probably *The heathcock*. See below, p. 289.

259 (d) a governess] Miss Margaret Millar.

259 *n*. 1] In third line, delete 'probably.'

260 (a) How much I have reapd . . .] *Bible, Matthew* 25: 24.

260 (b) I would willingly attempt a prologue] The prologue was written by Scott and the epilogue by Henry Mackenzie.

261 (c) lovely isle] Read 'lonely isle.'

261 (f) like that of Leontes in the Winter's Tale] Act I, sc. 2.

261 (f) Robert Dundas] Afterwards 2nd Viscount Melville. He was in Scott's class at the High School.

263 (a) To Miss Clephane] Margaret.

263 (b) lines from Coeur de Lions lament] They are given in Margaret's letter of 1 Sept. 1809 (NLS MS. 3878, ff. 130–1) and begin: 'Ne'er will the Knight whom woe oppress / Prate forth his story of distress.'

264 (b) like uncle Toby] See my note to *SL* ii. 159 (b).

264 (d) Col. Douglas] Col. Robert Douglas of Strathendry. His daughter Anna Maria married in 1817 Andrew Clephane, Margaret Clephane's uncle. His son David Douglas was raised to the Bench in 1813 as Lord Reston.

264 (f) The song which Campbell gave you] In her letter of 1 Sept. 1809 (NLS MS. 3878, f. 130) she says: 'Mr Campbell gave us an English song which he says is as old as Henry the Second's time.' She does not say which Campbell nor does she give title or words. The song, however, is in Mrs Hope-Scott's MS. Music Book at Abbotsford (Vol. 1, pp. 101–2). It begins: 'Blow blow thou northern wind' and a note says: 'Mr. Campbell author of the pleasures of Hope from whom this song was got believed it to be as old as Henry the 2d's time.' The song, which is in Ritson, *Ancient songs*, 1790 [1792], pp. 26–9, is called *A love song*, and begins 'Blow northerne wynd.' See also my note to *SL* i. 8 (c).

264 (f) as Sir Philip Sidney says] In his *Defense of poesy*. See also *SL* i. 146.

265 (c) *Marmion*] 5th ed., 1810, printed not by Ballantyne but by J. M'Creery, London.

266 (b) To Archibald Constable] The date is Monday, 6 Nov. 1809.

267 (c) ragged regiment] That Scott is thinking of Falstaff is shown by his quotation below, p. 355.

267 (c) Paull] James Paull, M.P., committed suicide in London on 15 Apr. 1808. (*Edin. Ann. Reg. for 1808*, I. ii. 75, 247.)

268 (d) Wellesley] He became, nevertheless, Foreign Secretary in Dec.

269 (d) *Lochhart*] iii. 206–9.

270 (a) Buchanan] Buchanan Castle.

270 (c) Compte de Grammonts art *d'eterniser sa vie*] See 'Epistle to the Count de Grammont' in Count Anthony Hamilton's *Memoirs of the Count de Grammont*.

270 (c) Bon Acres] A misreading for Bob Acres in Sheridan's *Rivals*. But it is David, not Acres, who says of honour: 'I would be very careful of it; and I think, in return, my honour couldn't do less than be very careful of me.' (Act IV, sc. 1.) Cf. *SL* ii. 73 (e).

270 n. 1] The girl, in line 8 from foot, is Frances Waddington who became Baroness Bunsen.

271 (a) two bars] Swift uses this phrase (*Works*, ed. Scott, 2nd ed., ii. 387, xv. 329) and it is used by Sterne, *Tristram Shandy*, Bk ix, chap. 17.

271 (c) Stella] Scott is referring to Berwick's portrait (*SL* iv. 317). It was not engraved for Scott's *Swift*. Scott later acquired a portrait. See *SL* iv. 317 and my note.

271 (d) Delany's defence] Scott has mixed up the titles. The works are: *Remarks on the life and writings of . . . Swift*, by John, Earl of Orrery, 8vo London, 1752; *Observations upon Lord Orrery's Remarks on . . . Swift*, by J. R. [i.e. Patrick Delany], 8vo London, 1754. Scott may have been able to borrow a copy of Delany's work but he apparently did not acquire one till 1812. See *SL* iii. 121 n.

271 (e) To George Thomson] Thomson's letter of 14 Nov. is quoted in Haddon's *George Thomson*, p. 158.

272 (c) "commerce"] A popular card game. See also *SL* iii. 112, 241, vi. 197.

272 n. 3] Adam died on 18 Dec.

273 (a) "But it grows dark . . ."] Scott varied this in *Kenilworth*, chap. 1.

273 (b) To Archibald Constable] The date is more likely to be late 1810. Scott had not, apparently, read Anna Seward's letters by Mar. 1810 (below, p. 315). The letters were edited anonymously by Rev. Robert Morehead and published in 6 vols. by Constable in 1811.

274 (e) Lord Clarendon] In NLS there are three letters from him about this time; 19 Oct., 3 Nov. and 25 Nov. (MS. 3878, ff. 178, 185–6, 213–14) mainly on Scott's poetry. In the last he thanks Scott for the opening stanzas of *The Lady of the Lake*.

274 n. 2] For 'Periodical Criticism, vol. iv., 1835' read '*MPW* xx. 226–9.'

275 (a) Clifford] Henry Clifford was a well-known barrister and was brother of Arthur Clifford who collaborated with Scott in producing Sadler's *State papers*. See *A poetical epistle to Henry Clifford, Esq. on the late disturbances in Covent Garden Theatre*, Edinburgh, 1810. The poem was anonymous but its author was Anthony Clifford, Henry Clifford's brother.

275 (f) your Viceroy] The Viceroy is the Lord Lieutenant of Ireland who, at this time, was the 4th Duke of Richmond and Lennox. He married in 1789 Charlotte, daughter of the 4th Duke of Gordon. The Duchess of Gordon, to whom Scott refers, was the Lord Lieutenant's mother-in-law.

276 (e) the verses] By Sydney Owenson, afterwards Lady Morgan. See below, p. 284.

277 (a) To James Ballantyne] Date is about middle of May.

277 (d) To James Dusautoy] The date is 6 May 1811. Scott is replying to Dusautoy's letter of 20 Apr. 1811.

278 (f) the words of Solomon] *Bible*, *Proverbs* 4: 7: 'get wisdom, and with all thy getting get understanding.'

280 (a–b) To Archibald Constable] "Lithgow" is William Lithgow's *Siege of Newcastle* (Edinburgh, 1645) and the second work, *The gushing teares of Godly sorrow* (Edinburgh, 1640) is also by Lithgow. Constable is apparently asking for a loan for J. T. Brockett. (See *SL* vi. 289 and n. 1.) This would suggest 1818 for the date but the tone of the letter suggests 1810.

280 (d) To Archibald Constable]
The letter refers to 5th ed. of *Marmion*,
advertised 16 May 1810 (*Ruff*, No. 65).
It should presumably be dated earlier
than the letters on same subject above,
pp. 265, 271, that is, about Sept.–Oct.
1809.

281 (a) To James Ballantyne] Date is
May 1810 and after 11 May by which
time Scott was in Edinburgh.

281 (d) To the Duchess of Buccleuch]
Cancel this letter here as it is printed
under its correct date 1813 in *SL* iii.
238–9. (Error noted in *SL* xii. 487.)

281 *n.* 1] *O'Connor's child* appeared in the
1st ed., 1809.

282 (e) To Robert Southey] The date
is about Sept. 1810 when the Clephanes
were at Ashiestiel.

283 (d) Why not have a squadron of
frigates] This was Southey's own view.
He had written to his brother Tom,
25 Nov. 1809; 'There ought to be four
flying squadrons of 5,000 men, each
ready to land.'

283 *n.* 1] Scott's article, *Of the living
poets of Great Britain*, is in I. ii. 417–43.

283 *n.* 2] For 'The Clephanes. Miss
Clephane' read 'Margaret and Anna
Jane Clephane. The former.' For
'Noels song' read 'Hoel's song.' See
Madoc, Pt II, sect. XII (1st ed., pp.
295–6).

284 *n.* 1] Lady Abercorn's letter,
dated 12 Jan., is in Partington, *Letter-
books*, pp. 137–9.

285 (a) want of candour of a certain
author] Apart from Cumberland,
Scott had reviewed Cromek, Southey,
Barrett, Carr, Campbell and Croker.
He must be referring to Sir John Carr,
but I do not know to which book Scott
is referring.

285 (c) fable of the bundle of arrows]
See L'Estrange, *Fables*, No. 62: *A
father and his sons. By Aesop.*

286 (f) according to promise, to make
"a knight of love . . ."] The quotation
from Dryden (*The flower and the leaf* in
Works, ed. Scott, xi. 371) had been
used by Lady Abercorn in 1808
(NLS MS. 3879, f. 147 and Partington,
Letter-books, p. 136). Scott's 'according
to promise' suggests that he had agreed
to follow her advice.

287 *n.* 1] See *SL* xii. 487.

288 (a) their name here is Legion]
Bible, Mark 5: 9.

288 (c) *in forma pauperis*] As a pauper.
A Scots law phrase. See Trayner,
Latin maxims.

288 (d) Benlora I like least] Benlora was
played by Alexander Archer.

288 (e) Maclean . . . is playd] By
Thompson. Forename not known.

289 (d) To Henry Mackenzie] Jan. 29
was a Monday. Date of letter is Wednesday, 24 Jan.

289 *n.* 2] Delete 'doubtless.'

290 (c) to propagate reports] See
below, p. 293.

290 (e) whole pit box and Gallery as
Mr. Bayes has it] Buckingham, *The
rehearsal*, I. 1.

293 (c) Our Lord president] Robert
Blair.

294 (b) *make his hand keep his head* as we
border folks say] *Græme and Bewick*, st.
25, lines 3–4: 'Sae my father's blessing
I'll never earn, / Till he see how my
arm can guard my head.' (*Minstrelsy*,
ed. Henderson, iii. 83.)

294 (c) A friend of mine] James Ballantyne.

296 (c) Argyle] Argyll was played by
Daniel Terry.

296 (d–e)] The words 'Mrs. President'
down to 'draught' are supplied from
FL i. 168.

297 (a) To John Murray] Cancel.
This letter is correctly given under 10
Feb. 1809 in *SL* ii. 163–4.

298 (a–b) greatly disappointment
[*sic*]] On cancelled visit to Ashiestiel
see above, pp. 220, 259.

298 (c) To Robert Surtees] The text
here is from the Abbotsford Copies
although there is a reference to the
'original', p. 300, *n.* 1. Scott wrote
before he received Surtees's letter of
5 Mar. (Taylor, *Memoir of Robert
Surtees*, pp. 96–8). The *Minstrelsy* was
ready by 2 Mar. (below, p. 307) but
not when Scott wrote (p. 299). Date of
letter, therefore, is probably Feb.

299 (a) Sir somebody Lawson] Sir
John Lawson, 5th Bart. of Brough.

299 (b) "I whip the top . . ."] Cervantes, *Don Quixote*, Pt II, chaps. 43 and 67 (Lockhart's ed., 1822, iv. 278, v. 264).

299 (b) "Brown Man of the Muirs"] See my note to *SL* ii. 246 (d).

299 (f) the ugly hieroglyphic below] This drawing appears in Taylor, *Memoir of Robert Surtees*, p. 95.

300 (b) The prints] John Derrick, *The image of Irelande . . . anno 1578*, 12mo and 4to London, 1581. Pt II consists of 12 plates. By the 'only copy' Scott means the copy in the Advocates' Library. (See his letter to Joseph Cooper Walker, 29 July 1809, in the *Athenæum*, 1893 (1 Apr.), pp. 408–9, but not in *SL*; and see his note in Somers's *Tracts*, i. 584.) Scott was wrong in saying the copy was unique. Furthermore it lacked plates I, III, VI and VIII. These plates, which are not in *Somers*, Scott could have got from a complete copy in the Drummond Coll. in Edinburgh Univ. Lib. The University copy was reproduced in facsimile by John Small in 1883. The original prints were woodcuts with Gothic lettering under each. These had to be re-engraved for Scott's edition, possibly on copper, and although carefully copied they have lost the character of the old woodcuts. The lettering had been given in Vol. 1 but Scott intended to have it also engraved on the plates (see above, p. 177), but this plan was not carried out.

300 (c) To Joanna Baillie] This letter, written 19–20 Feb., should have come before the letter to Sophia Baillie, 20 Feb., above, p. 297. The text is from *ER*, Vol. 216 (Oct. 1912), pp. 363–5.

300 (f) like the rocks in the desart] *Bible, Numbers* 20: 11.

300 n. 1] See my note to *SL* ii. 298 (c).

301 (a) like Sir Hugh Evans] Shakespeare, *Merry wives of Windsor*, III. 1.

301 (b) "If you could not do it . . ."] Scott tells the same story in his 1831 introd. to *Rob Roy*.

302 (b) flat and unprofitable] Shakespeare, *Hamlet*, I. 2.

302 (c) Johnson applies to sacred poems] See Johnson's essays on Cowley, Denham, Waller and Watts in his *Lives of the poets*.

302 n. 1] For '7th' read '4th.' (NLS MS. 3879, ff. 13–14.)

303 (d) Lancelots dog Crab] Shakespeare, *Two gentlemen of Verona*, II. 3. Lancelot should be Launce.

303 (e) I inclose a few lines] i.e. the letter above, pp. 297–8.

304 (d) To Archibald Constable] This letter belongs to the end of March. Scott had not received *Caledonia* by 13 Mar. (below, p. 309). Constable wrote to Chalmers on 5 Apr. that he had received the work 'about a week ago,' i.e. end of Mar. (*Archibald Constable*, i. 433–4).

304 (d) Mr. Jollie of Carlisles MS.] The Glenriddell MS. See *Minstrelsy* (ed. Henderson), i. 167.

305 (a) eat the bread of idleness] *Bible, Proverbs* 31: 27.

305 (b) like Davy to Bob Acres] In Sheridan's *The rivals*. See my notes to *SL* ii. 73 (e), 270 (c).

306 (a) my heel vulnerable] Allusion to Achilles' heel.

306 (b) If I fail] Shakespeare, *Macbeth*, I. 7.

306 (c) Up with the bonnie blue bonnet] Hogg, *Donald Macdonald*, st. [6], lines 11–12, with 'kilt' for 'Durk'. Scott would have read the poem in Hogg's *Mountain bard* (1807).

306 (e) The *feloun sow*] See above, pp. 98 and 204.

306 n. 1] *The goblin groom* was written by Robert Orde Fenwick and published in 1809. I do not know why Morritt should call it a 'bloody satire.' It is quite a harmless poem.

307 (c) because you would not pay your literary subscription] Morritt had offered a translation from Metastasio (above, p. 225), but he wrote in Nov., withdrawing his offer (Partington, *Post-bag*, p. 51).

307 (f) Lady Hood is so far from you] Lady Hood had a new residence in Grosvenor Street which Morritt thought 'the very Antipodes' from his own house in Portland Place. (Letter of 21 Feb. in NLS MS. 3879, f. 28.)

308 (c) Sir Tristrem] The 3rd ed. of *Sir Tristrem* was issued by Constable

& Co. in 1811, and it was printed by Ballantyne—signs of reconciliation.

309 (d) the fine print] This is probably Charles Turner's large mezzotint of Raeburn's 1808 portrait of Scott in Constable's possession. The print is dated 18 Jan. 1810. The copper plate from which it was printed is in my Scott Collection.

310 (a) Christalline la curieuse] Cristalline in Count Anthony Hamilton's *Les quatre Facardins*, in *Œuvres complètes*, nouv. éd., Paris, 1805, where at p. 407 of tome 2 she is called 'Cristalline la curieuse.'

311 (a) silent under your commands] In her letter of 12 Jan. Lady Abercorn had said: 'If you have any sheets of your *Lady of the Lake* send them to me' (Partington, *Letter-books*, p. 139).

312 (b) as Hamlet says *indifferent honest*] Shakespeare, *Hamlet*, III. 1.

312 (d) wild Irish girl] Sydney Owenson, afterwards Lady Morgan. See above, pp. 166, 284.

312 (f) break their heads on another Catholic question] The claims for Catholic emancipation were revived in Feb. when Gratton presented a petition to Parliament. Lengthy debates followed.

312 (f) the flowers] Which Charlotte had sent. See above, pp. 238–9, 276 and below, p. 327.

312 (f) the Chancellors commands] Lord Eldon's.

314 (a) You are a sharp observer] Shakespeare, *Julius Caesar*, I. 2.

314 n. 1] The first paragraph belongs to p. 313. The second paragraph refers to index figure above at 'Miss H.'

315 (a) literary correspondence] See my note to *SL* ii. 273 (b).

315 (c) flat but not unprofitable] A reminiscence of Shakespeare, *Hamlet*, I. 2: 'flat, and unprofitable.'

315 (f) Mrs. Baillies kind token] The gift from Mrs Matthew Baillie. See above, pp. 297, 310.

316 (c) I hope you got the Sadler] In his letter of 14 Dec. 1811 Surtees says he never received it. Taylor, *Memoir of Robert Surtees*, p. 117.

316 (c) A Sir Somebody Lawson] Sir John Lawson. See my note to *SL* ii. 299 (a).

316 (d) Spellman on sacrilege] A reference to Sir Henry Spelman's *The history and fate of sacrilege*, London, 1698.

316 n. 1] Delete the whole of this note and see my note to *SL* i. 199 n.

317 (a) Your Northumbrian Duerguar] In a note to Canto IV, st. XIII of *The Lady of the Lake* Scott quotes a 'Northumbrian legend, with which I was lately favoured by my learned and kind friend, Mr Surtees of Mainsforth.' The passage, then quoted, comes from Surtees's letter to Scott of 9 Nov. 1809. (Taylor, *Memoir of Robert Surtees*, pp. 81–2.)

317 (d) the decayed Aristocrat] Sir Thomas Conyers, Bart. He died on 15 Apr. following. See Taylor, *Memoir of Robert Surtees*, pp. 100–7.

317 (e) the Lambton worm . . . Laidley worm] Surtees had told Scott the story in a letter of 9 Nov. 1809 (Taylor, *Memoir of Robert Surtees*, pp. 82–5). For an account of the former worm, see William Henderson, *Notes on folklore of the northern counties of England*, London, 1879, pp. 287–92, and for the latter, see ibid., pp. 292–5. See also *The Laidley worm of Spindleston Heugh*, in Thomas Evans, *Old ballads*, new ed., London, 1810, iv. 241–8, and elsewhere.

317 (e) serpent slain by our first Scottish Somerville] A stone depicting the incident is above the doorway of Linton Church, Roxburghshire. Cf. *SL* xii. 242, 242 n.

318 (b) the wolf] The last wolf to be killed in Scotland is said to have been killed in 1743.

319 (a) no one can both eat his cake and have his cake] *Heywood*, p. 162; *Ray*, p. 130.

319 (d) Mrs. Siddons (the elder) in Jane de Montfort] On Tuesday, 27 Mar.

320 (f) If I was as tedious] Shakespeare, *Much ado about nothing*, III. 5.

321 (a) two rival sets of illustrations] (1) *The Lady of the Lake . . . Illustrated with engravings from paintings by Richard Cooke*. London, Longman . . . Miller,

and J. Ballantyne & Co., Edinburgh, 1811; (2) *The Lady of the Lake . . . Illustrated with engravings from the designs of Richd. Westall, Esq., R.A.* London, John Sharpe, 1811.

322 *n.* 1] Berwick's ed. was reviewed in *QR* for May 1810 by Thomas Fanshaw Middleton (*Shine*, No. 95). The reference to Scott's apology is below, pp. 386–7.

323 (a) Illustrated copy of the Lay] This copy sent to Berwick is now in the University of Idaho Library, Moscow, U.S.A. It is the 8th ed., 4to, with Schetky's engravings.

323 (c) Dublin Bank] See Scott's *Swift*, 2nd ed., vi. 290–313.

326 (a) Chief Baron] Robert Dundas of Arniston.

326 (a) seventy-five . . . forty years] George Home was probably about seventy at this time and he had been Principal Clerk for only twenty-nine years.

326 (d) I detest the Whigs] This, like so many other misunderstood statements of Scott, is addressed to Lady Abercorn as a stout Tory. Scott had more Whigs than Tories among his friends.

328 (b–c) To James Ballantyne] Date is May 1810 and after 11 May by which time Scott was in Edinburgh.

331 (a) Lord of Tyndale] Earl of Dalkeith. Lord Tindale was one of his father's English titles. He had been summoned to the House of Lords as Baron Tynedale of Tynedale, co. Northumberland 11 Apr. 1807. (*Ann. Reg.* 1807, p. 86.)

332 (c) offer of a harbour for Sophia] Sophia stayed with Joanna Baillie in 1815 (*SL* iv. 59). *Lockhart* (iii. 183–4) wrongly says this visit was in 1809, perhaps remembering vaguely this reference in 1810.

332 (f) miracle of Moses's rod] *Bible, Numbers* 20: 11.

334 (d) weighd in the balance & found wanting] *Bible, Daniel* 5: 27.

334 (e) to you & to your honour I commit her] Otway, *Venice preserved*, II. 3 (repeated III. 1). See also *SL* vi. 180.

335 (d) Delete query in date. It is definitely 1810.

335 (e) To Thomas Scott] For rest of letter, see *SL* vii. 437–9.

336 (a) Bailie Coulter] For an account of his elaborate funeral, see *Edin. Ann. Reg.* III. ii. 55–8. Coulter died on 14 Apr. and was buried in Greyfriars' Churchyard on 21 Apr.

336 (d) "Tanneguy du Châtel, où es-tu?"] Tait in his ed. of the *Journal*, under 12 June 1826, cites J. A. de Thou, *Histoire universelle* (1740), ii. 839.

336 *n.* 1] In last line, for '1631' read '1731' and for 'in Note E in' read 'in note to chap. 11 of.'

337 (a) Johnson's collection] Scott is at fault here. There are two songs on the wren (Nos. 406 and 483) but neither relates to the Manx custom of burial.

337 (b) To Miss Clephane] To Margaret.

337 (c–d) like Lady Macbeth's sea of blood] Shakespeare, *Macbeth*, II. 2. But it is Macbeth who says: 'Will all great Neptune's ocean wash this blood / Clean from my hand?'

340 (d) Don Pelayo] This is *Roderick, the last of the Goths*, not published till 1814.

341 (d) when a school-boy] The Edinburgh High School records show that Scott borrowed *The world displayed* from the school library. (Steven, *History of the High School*, p. 132.)

342 *n.* 2] In second line, delete 'may have'. Henry Southey took his M.D. degree at Edinburgh in 1806 and Scott was known to him at that time (*SL* i. 293).

343 (a) To J. B. S. Morritt] Scott is replying to his letter of 17 May (NLS MS. 3879, ff. 108–9) in which he expresses disappointment that Brian does not play a major part in the denouement; and writes of Lady Hood and of politics.

343 (e) your pamphlet] *Advice to the Whigs . . . By an Englishman.*

343 (f) Library table] The desk was made by Messrs Gillow, cabinet manufacturers, Oxford Street, London. This desk, which arrived in Aug.

(*SL* ii. 369), is in the Study at Abbotsford.

344 (a) his local habitation and his name] Shakespeare, *A midsummer night's dream*, V. 1.

344 (e) the mob of Westminster] Scott alluded to this in *The Lady of the Lake*. See *SL* xii. 325 and *n.* 2.

345 (b) To Thomas Scott] Cancel this extract. The complete letter is in *SL* vii. 439–41.

345 *n.* 1] Delete this note which is not applicable. In his letter of 17 May Morritt said he had begun a ballad based on a story he got from Rose. 'It will be finished abt the year of Grace 1850 if it goes on at the same rate.' (NLS MS. 3879, f. 109 b.)

345 *n.* 3] In second last line, delete 'aristocratic.'

346 (b) To George Ellis] The date of this letter could not be May–June as the review did not appear till mid July. Actually the date is 23 Dec. as it is part of a letter of that date in *SL* xii. 326–7.

347 (b) "Achilles' wrath . . ."] Pope's translation of *The Iliad*, Bk I, lines 1–6. Variations show, as usual, that Scott was quoting from memory.

348 (b) "false gallop" of verse] Shakespeare, *As you like it*, III. 2.

348 (c) To Mrs. Scott] The date cannot be 5 June as (1) 5 June was a Tuesday; (2) Scott at the end of the letter speaks of 5 June as something in the future. The letter should be dated 'Wednesday 9 May.' Scott has written the letter at Melrose (probably at Charles Erskine's) on his way from Ashiestiel to Edinburgh 'au plus vite' for the opening of the summer session on 12 May.

348 *n.* 2] Delete this note, which is of no value, and substitute: Lord Egremont was half-brother of Harriet Bruhl, Mrs Scott of Harden.

349 (f) saddling of a foal] 'Lang or ye saddle a foal.' (Ramsay, *Proverbs*, p. 43.) See also *SL* iii. 341.

350 (a) to assist him in his object] He was a candidate for St George's Chapel, Edinburgh.

350 (a) "more an ancient Roman . . ."] Shakespeare, *Hamlet*, V. 2.

350 (c) The adventure of the Duke of Cumberland] For an account of the attempt to assassinate him on 31 May 1810, see *Edin. Ann. Reg. for 1810*, III. ii. 78–86. The assassin was Joseph Seillis. Neale was Christopher Neale, a page to the Duke.

351 (a) the gentleman whom you mention] Henderson. See below, pp. 406, 420, 524.

351 *n.* 1] The rumour persisted for, on 5 Mar. 1813, White, editor of the *Independent Whig*, was tried for a libel, charging the Duke with the murder of Seillis. He was found guilty. See *Scots Mag.* lxxv. 232, 390.

352 (b) Meadows flower] Joanna Baillie, *The family legend*, III. 3.

352 (e) To Thomas Scott] For rest of letter, see *SL* vii. 441–2.

353 (b) To Thomas Scott] Cancel and see *SL* vii. 443–4.

353 *n.* 1] This is from one of the probationary odes for the laureateship supposed to be written by well-known Tories. It is *Number XIII. Irregular ode, By the Rt. Hon. Harry Dundas, Esq., Treasurer of the Navy, &c. &c. &c.* St. III, lines 13–14 read: 'Thoo Laird o' Graham! by manie a cheil ador'd, / Who boasts his native fillabeg restor'd.'

354 (a) To Lady Abercorn] Scott is answering her letter of 18 July [*sic* for June]. (NLS MS. 3879, ff. 147–8.)

355 (b) Lady Castlereagh's letters] Letters of Swift. See above, pp. 324, 326–7 and below, pp. 386, 417.

355 (c–d) Salaries of £1100] Actually under the Act salary was fixed at £1,000 with £100 compensation. Later £200 extra was got from Exchequer. See below pp. 434, 438 and *SL* vii. 459.

355 (e) rejecting the civic triumph] When Parliament was prorogued on 21 June Sir Francis Burdett was automatically released from the Tower. A procession had been arranged to conduct him to his house, but Burdett departed from the Tower in secret. See *Edin. Ann. Reg.* III. i. 510–13.

355 (f) "march through Coventry"] Shakespeare, *I Henry IV*, IV. 2.

355 (f) wild Macraws] *Little wat ye wha's coming*, st. [5], line 4: 'A' the wild

McCraws' coming.' In *Herd*, i. 118; and in *Johnson*, Vol. 6 (1803), No. 572. This Jacobite song was originally called *The Chevalier's muster-roll, 1715*. Three lines from the song are quoted in *Waverley*, chap. 30.

355 (f) Johnson] See Boswell's *Journal of a tour to the Hebrides*, under 1 Sept. Boswell said of the Macraas that 'it was much the same as being with a tribe of Indians', to which Johnson retorted: 'Yes, Sir; but not so terrifying.' Boswell quoted the line: 'And aw the brave McCraas are coming', substituting 'brave' for 'wild.' See previous note.

356 (b) To Thomas Scott] Cancel this extract. The complete letter is in *SL* vii. 444–5 where it is dated 26 Aug. 1810.

356 n. 2] Cancel and substitute: See *SL* iii. 389 n. 1.

357 (d) "per varios casus"] Virgil, *Aeneid*, I. 204.

357 (e) every London citizen] Cf. 'Moab is my washpot; over Edom will I cast out my shoe.' *Bible, Psalms* 60: 8. See also *SL* vii. 249.

358 (a) bestowing all this tediousness] See above, p. 320.

359 n. 3] He had succeeded his grandfather the previous year (1809).

361 (f) bestowed enough of my tediousness] See above, p. 320.

362 (a) green pebbles from the shore of St Columbus] See below, p. 402 and my note.

362 (d) To George Ellis] Date is Friday, 27 July 1810.

363 (a) silver collar] See *SL* xi. 10 n.

363 (d) seven old castles] See above, pp. 358–9.

366 (e) a young English Scotchman] William Alexander Mackinnon. See above, p. 359 and n.

367 (a) on the 24th] Writing on the same day to Morritt (see next letter) he says (p. 369) 'about the 20th.' There are no dated letters for the period from which the exact date could be determined.

368 (d) Lyson] This should be Lysons. Samuel Lysons was Keeper of the Records in the Tower of London.

368 n. 1] Delete this note and substitute: Don Quixote. Scott uses Motteux's translation 'Figure' here and in *SL* ix. 79. But Motteux also uses 'Countenance' and Scott uses it in *SL* viii. 60.

369 (b) Byrons shipwreck] Four (not two) of the crew were left behind and were seen 'helping one another over a hideous track of rocks.' (*The narrative of the Honourable John Byron . . . containing an account of the great distresses . . . on the coasts of Patagonia*, etc., 12mo London, 1788, pp. 71–2.)

369 (b) Gillows table] See above, pp. 343–4.

369 (c–d) our Hebridean syrens & their Lady Mother] The Maclean Clephanes of Torloisk.

369 n. 1] Delete this note which cites the wrong work.

370 (a) To Robert Leyden] That Scott bore no ill-will is shown by his letter of sympathy to him when John Leyden died. This letter of 22 Dec. 1811 (not in *SL*) is in James Wilson's *Hawick and its old memories*, Edinburgh, 1858, pp. 166–8.

370 n. 2] The omission of Lord John is corrected in *SL* xii. 487. This long paragraph to prove that the date is 1810 is unnecessary. Scott's reference to Lady Rosslyn, who died on 8 Aug. 1810, is sufficient evidence of date.

371 (f) Lady Roslin] See *SL* xii. 113, 113 n.

371 n. 1] Delete 'Presumably.'

372 (c) To Archibald Constable] The date must be 1811. The printing of *Swift* was transferred about Oct. 1810 from Ballantyne to Ramsay, who printed Vol. 7 (and perhaps Vol. 6) to the end, Vol. 18, and finally Vol. 1 (*SL* i. 415 n.). If Ramsay started with Vol. 7 (or 6) in Oct. 1810, Scott could not be sending Vol. 13 in Aug. 1810.

373 (a) To Robert Southey] Date is 20 Sept., which was a Thursday.

373 (c) "wear his heart upon his sleeve . . ."] Shakespeare, *Othello*, I. 1.

373 n. 1] The letter which appeared in the *Courier* for 15 Sept. 1810 gave passages from *The lay* and *Marmion* with parallel passages from other poets, which, the writer suggests,

Scott imitated. Coleridge's letter, denying the authorship of the letter, appeared, in a paraphrased form, in the *Courier* for 20 Sept. See also below, p. 416 *n.*

374 (a) Ethwald] The lines in the *Courier* were from Joanna Baillie's *Ethwald*, Pt I, Act I, sc. 4: 'His spearmen onward move in dusky lines / Like the brown reeds that skirt the winter pool.' This play was published in the second series of *Plays on the passions* in 1802 so that Scott is wrong in saying it was published after *The lay.*

374 (b) my Greta excursion] Scott had told Morritt in May that he hoped to visit Rokeby. See above, pp. 342, 344.

374 *n.* 1] 'Detector' was the Rev. Henry Joseph Thomas Drury. He was the author of *Arundines Cami* in which the Latin version of the lines in *Marmion* appear.

375 (a) To Clarke Whitfeld] Scott is replying to his letter of 29 July 1810 (NLS MS. 3879, ff. 151-2). His settings, referred to in this letter, are: *Huntsman rest, thy chase is done*, etc., 2° London, Messrs Phipps & Co., n.d.; *Lay of the imprisoned huntsman*, etc., 2° London, Messrs Phipps & Co., n.d.; *The minstrel's tale, or Alice Brand . . . respectfully dedicated to Mrs Walter Scott*, etc., 2° London, Messrs Phipps & Co., n.d.

375 (b) from a single voice] This refers to Whitfeld's apology for setting the *Coronach* for a single voice. (NLS MS. 3879, f. 151.)

375 (c) M'Gregor a ruagh ruagh] See my note to *SL* ii. 115 (e) and below, pp. 488, 488 *n.*

375 *n.* 2] Delete this note, which is now unnecessary.

376 (a–b) a flapper] Swift's *Gulliver's travels*. See my note to *SL* ii. 213 (c).

376 (b) your elegant verses] In his letter he had written two sheets of verse beginning: 'Could'st thou, great Bard, my feeble Muse inspire / With smallest spark of thy Promethean fire.' (NLS MS. 3879, f. 152.)

379 (a) To Miss Clephane] To Margaret. Scott went to Edinburgh on 11 Oct. to do Register House duty and left on Saturday, 27 Oct. The Thursday of this letter, therefore, is 25 Oct.

379 (d) despatches hear] Read 'despatches bear'.

379 *n.* 1] Delete. This is Cannon Hall, Yorkshire, home of the Stanhopes, friends of the Maclean Clephanes. See *SL* iii. 302.

380 (a) To J. B. S. Morritt] This letter cannot be 3 Oct. for Scott is replying to Morritt's letter of 29 Oct. (NLS MS. 3879, ff. 245-6). It should be dated 3 Nov.

380 (b–c) Condemnd to Hopes delusive mine] Samuel Johnson, *On the death of Mr. Robert Levet*, st. [1].

380 (c) Mrs Cholmly] Mrs Francis Cholmeley of Brandsby, Yorkshire. Morritt, in his letter of 11 Feb. 1811 (NLS MS. 3880, ff. 36–7), confirmed her identity to Scott's satisfaction but not to ours. Her identity, however, is established by a letter of Lady Louisa Stuart (Stuart, *Letters*, i. 403).

380 (f) Carron Hall] Read 'Cannon Hall.' See my note to *SL* ii. 379 *n.*

380 *n.* 1] For 'another friend' read 'Mrs Cholmeley.'

381 (e) Clarkes travels] Ellis's review of Vol. 1 appeared in *QR* for Aug., publ. after 6 Oct.

382 (c) Commission] On Scottish law courts, of which Scott had been Secretary.

382 (f) the second Volume] Vol. 2 of *Edin. Ann. Reg.* did not appear till late in 1811. An 'Advertisement', explaining the delay, is dated 27 July 1811.

383 (a) To Miss Smith] This letter cannot be correctly dated 4 Oct.: (1) Scott is replying to Sarah Smith's letter of 29 Oct. (NLS MS. 3879, ff. 243–4); (2) Scott refers to Lady Caroline Douglas's marriage as having taken place and she was married on 27 Oct. Scott is replying immediately (opening of his letter). Date, therefore, is 4 Nov.

386 (a) change of printers] See above, p. 372 and *SL* i. 415, 415 *n.*

386 (d) Appollonius] This is *Life of Apollonius of Tyana*, by Philostratus, tr. by Berwick.

386 (e) Jeffery] Jeffrey did not review it in *ER*.

386 (e) Secrets of their prison house] Shakespeare, *Hamlet*, I. 5: 'secrets of my prison-house'.

386 (f) the *Quarterly*] The review in Vol. 3, May 1810, was by Thomas Fanshaw Middleton (*Shine*, No. 95).

387 (b) 20,000 Copies] The 5th ed. of 6,000 copies brought the total to date to 20,000.

387 (b) hang my harp on the willow] *Bible*, *Psalms* 137: 2.

387 (d) the *British* Review of your work] In the *British Critic*, Vol. 35 (Jan.–June 1810), pp. 569–74.

388 (a) the elegant verses] This is the poem *To Walter Scott, Esq.*, beginning 'To thee shall Erin's lay belong,' used as a dedication to Hartstonge's *Minstrelsy of Erin*, published by John Ballantyne in 1812.

388 (e) Miss Seward . . . correspondence] See my note to *SL* ii. 273 (c).

388 *n.* 1] Delete last sentence. Scott had made no promise beyond using his 'little interest' and, although there was a hitch later (below, p. 400), the work was eventually published by Ballantyne in 1812.

389 (d) Mr. Collins] Presumably Anthony Collins. Laidlaw met at Clovenfords 'Dr Anthony, Carlisle' mistaking surname for the town (Laidlaw, *Recollections*, in *Trans. Hawick Arch. Soc.*, 1905, p. 72). Carlyon records in his *Early years and late reflections*, ii. 91, that Dr Collins (no forename) died at St Ewe, 14 Aug. 1831, formerly for many years a physician at Exeter. See also *SL* i. 207 *n.*

390 (b) I add the little collection] If this is *English minstrelsy* Scott is very late in sending it. He had already referred to it in Jan. and Mar. (above, pp. 286, 312).

391 (c) cool-headed practical farmer] Robert Laidlaw who farmed Peel next to Ashiestiel.

391 (d) Lady Hamilton] Her son, James Hamilton, who succeeded his grandfather as 2nd Marquess and later became 1st Duke, was born on 21 Jan. 1811.

391 (e) prove a little girl] Shakespeare, *Henry VIII*, V. 1: ''tis a girl,/Promises boys hereafter.'

391 *n.* 1] For pamphlets on Fiorin grass (lines 8–9) see above, p. 327.

392 (a) Edinr. Annual Register] The *History* was written by Southey. The *View of the changes proposed and adopted in the administration of justice in Scotland* (I. ii. 342–72) is almost certainly by Scott, though he here denies it.

392 (e) to write to you yesterday] That would be 14 Oct. But Scott's letter above (p. 388) is dated 11 Oct.

393 (f) the sculptor] John Bacon (1777–1859). See Partington, *Post-bag*, p. 66.

394 (c) To Lady Abercorn] This letter should be dated 1806 as the references to Dryden, the Monks of Bangor, Charlotte's transcripts and the quill pens show.

394 (e) Lord Whitworth] Lord Whitworth married in 1801 the Duchess of Dorset, widow of the 3rd Duke. Hence Scott's desire for an introduction to him. On the papers, see *SL* i. 318, 350, ii. 179.

397 (c) Crabbe] The review in *QR* for Nov. 1810 was by Sir Robert Grant. (*Shine*, No. 115.)

397 (d) my Newspaper man] For the *Courier* which was sent to Scott from London. If the same newsagents as formerly they would be Messrs Wood & Green (above, p. 48).

397 *n.* 1] The two reviews in *QR* were not of Grahame and Evans but Maturin and Evans. Grahame was reviewed by Southey but *Shine* (No. 98) gives Scott as second alternative on the strength of Grierson's note. Mrs Barbauld's work is: *The British novelists. With an essay, and biographical and critical prefaces*, 50 vols., London, 1810. Hunt's work is: *Classic tales . . . with critical essays on . . . the authors*, 5 vols., London, 1806–7.

398 (a) To Miss Clephane] To Margaret.

398 (a) appropriate mottoe] See above, p. 379.

398 (d) Northern Antiquities] *Illustrations of Northern antiquities* [ed. by Robert

Jamieson and Henry Weber] (1814). The Carslogie hand was not used for this work. Weber, however, made a drawing of it for *The Border antiquities.*

398 (d–e) my song of the Clans] It is not known if Scott had actually written such a song at this time. He may simply have been contemplating a song such as the one in *Waverley*, chap. 22. See also my note to *SL* iii. 285 (b).

398 (e) three already] (1) *War-song of Lachlan, high chief of Maclean.* See above, pp. 189–90; (2) *Coronach on Sir Lauchlan, Chief of Maclean.* See above, pp. 226 *n.*, 230; (3) *Farewell to Mackenzie, high chief of Kintail.*

398 *n.* 1] In line 3, for 'Carlogie' read 'Carslogie.' The steel hand is referred to in *The Fair Maid of Perth*, chap. 17.

399 (b) Swiss music] *Schweizerische Volkslieder mit Melodieen*, 4to Zürich, 1788. Skene bought it for himself and later presented it to Scott. No. 1 in this collection is *Schlacht den Sempach.*

399 (e) Anne Jane] Should be Anna Jane.

400 (a) your packet] John Ballantyne published Hartstonge's *Minstrelsy of Erin* in 1812.

400 (e) Ashestiel] The tack (lease) of Ashiestiel was made by Alexander Pringle and Dr Daniel Rutherford on behalf of James (later Sir James) Russell of Ashiestiel, absent in India. The original contract is in NLS (Ch. 2477).

401 (e) your kind and valued letters] Of 8 Aug. and 27 Oct. (NLS MS. 3879, ff. 156–8, 236–9).

402 (a) saith old Martin] Martin Martin, *A description of the western islands of Scotland*, etc., 2nd ed., 8vo London, 1716, p. 263. First published in 1703. St Columba is called Columbus by Martin.

402 (e) my sharers [?]] Lockhart printed 'shearers' which is obviously the correct reading. Cf. *SL* xii. 487.

402 (e) So every servant] Matthew Prior, *An epitaph*, lines 25–6.

403 (b) the poor princess] Princess Amelia, daughter of George III. She died on 2 Nov. (*Edin. Ann. Reg.* III. ii. 217–23.)

403 (d) I was delighted with the man that rememberd me] In her letter of 27 Oct. Joanna Baillie tells Scott about a neighbouring clergyman in Gloucestershire: 'He read Don Quixote a great many years ago but cannot well converse even upon this book as he has forgotten all about Sancho Panca; he has read another book not very long ago, namely the Lady of the Lake, and on that he speaks with greater freedom.' (NLS MS. 3879, f. 237b.)

403 (e) Morton] *The Knight of Snowdoun*, by Thomas Morton, was produced at Covent Garden on 5 Feb. 1811 (*White*, p. 240) and at the Theatre Royal, Edinburgh, on 18 Mar. 1811 (Dibdin, *Annals*, p. 265).

403 (e) carmining [?]] This is obviously 'careening' as Grierson notes, *SL* xii. 487.

403 (f) Mr. H. Siddons] The version of *The Lady of the Lake*, produced by Siddons on 15 Jan. 1811, was written by Edmund John Eyre. (Dibdin, *Annals*, p. 264.)

403 (f) our parish smith] John Culbertson. See *SL* iii. 154.

404 (a) "Patience cousin . . ."] Cervantes, *Don Quixote*, Pt II, chaps. 23 and 24 (Lockhart's ed., 1822, iv. 77, 86).

404 (a) N. Longman wrote me a civil letter] Thomas Norton Longman wrote on 4 Sept. 1810 (NLS MS. 3879, f. 180) that *The Lady of the Lake* was being dramatized by Morton and Reynolds and that he had told his uncle, Henry Harris (manager of Covent Garden Theatre), that Scott would read over their dramatization.

404 (b) Jeffrey] See above, p. 381, 381 *n.* and *SL* xii. 324.

404 (c) Drama on Fear] *Orra.*

404 (f) "grinning honour . . ."] Shakespeare, *I Henry IV*, V. 3.

405 (c) the Garb of old Gaul] The tune 'In the garb of old Gaul' was composed by General John Reid (1721–1807). It is in *Johnson*, Vol. 3 (1790), No. 210.

405 (f) this bald disjointed chat.] Shakespeare, *I Henry IV*, I. 3.

406 (b) Mnr Hunter] Read 'Mrs Hunter.'

406 (d) your Manuscript] Of the *Minstrelsy of Erin*.

406 *n.* 1] Delete 'probably'. See above, p. 403.

407 (d) The first things I published went to paper bandboxes.] This refers to *The chase, and William and Helen*. A sufficient quantity, however, was preserved to form a second ed., from the 1796 sheets, in 1807.

408 (a) Nichols] John Nichols. See *The lucubrations of Isaac Bickerstaff, Esq. A new ed., with notes* [by J. Nichols], 8vo London, 1786, v. 143. Nichols's note is on the *Tatler*, No. 188.

408 (b) having attempted a rape] See Scott's *Swift*, 2nd ed., i. 40 *n*. (*MPW* ii. 32 *n*.). Dean Allott wrote to Scott, 2 Feb. 1826, giving evidence which inferred Swift's guilt. The letter is in Partington, *Letter-books*, pp. 329–31. 'Rev. Mr. P—r' on p. 331 is Parker.

408 (d) The worthy and revd Mr. B—] Rev. Edward Berwick.

408 *n.* 1] See 2nd ed., 8vo London, 1792, pp. xlv–liii.

409 (d) the newspapers accompt] See above, p. 397.

410 (b) Petrarch] *Essay on the life and character of Petrarch*, by Alexander Fraser Tytler, Lord Woodhouselee. 'Lord W.', two lines below, stands for Lord Woodhouselee. It was published by John Ballantyne & Co. in 1810 and went into a second ed. Reviewed in *QR* for Sept. 1812 by Rev. John Penrose (*Shine*, No. 218).

410 (d) To Miss Smith] The Abbotsford Copy in NLS (MS. 852, f. 127ᵛ) is dated 18 Dec. although *FL* i. 196 dates it 10 Dec. The most recent letter from Sarah Smith is dated 29 Oct. (NLS MS. 3879, ff. 243–4, 247). There must be a missing letter of Dec. as Scott says here, in his reply, 'I hasten . . . to your inquiries.' In this letter Scott is giving her advice on dramatizing *The Lady of the Lake*. According to O'Donoghue's *The poets of Ireland*, a dramatized version was made by Sarah Smith and this, presumably, was the version performed at the Theatre Royal, Crow Street, Dublin. The play was published as *The Lady of the Lake; a grand dramatic romance, in three acts*, 8vo Dublin,

1811. Ellen was played by Miss Smith. See also below, p. 471 *n.* 1.

411 *n.* 1] This note is taken mainly from Dibdin, *Annals*, pp. 264–5.

412 (b) the Surrey] The Surrey Theatre version was by Thomas J. Dibdin. (*White*, p. 240.)

412 (e) "rowing you in your plaidie"] A variant of a line in *Bonny Lizie Baillie*. See my note to *SL* i. 382 (b). The line, with variations, is common in Scots songs.

413 (a) Mr. C.] Probably Charles Connor who took the part of Malcolm Graeme in the play.

413 (e) There is a balance of nearly £1000] The sum of £500 had been paid to Scott, 16 July 1809 and his receipt is dated 20 July. (MSS. in Edinburgh Univ. Lib. La III. 826/8.) See also *SL* vii. 458.

413 (f) *our* Marquis] In her reply (undated) Lady Abercorn wrote: 'I doubt not that you know by this time that Lord Abercorn is not to be the Lord Chamberlain. I should have supposed you know him well enough to give no credit to such a report.' (NLS MS. 3880, ff. 7–8.) The Earl of Dartmouth had been Lord Chamberlain since 1804. He was succeeded in 1812 by the Marquess of Hertford.

414 (d) Covent Garden] See my note to *SL* ii. 403 (e).

415 (b) Two days ago . . . two frigates] The *Pallas* and *Nymphe*, lost off Dunbar on 18 Dec. 'Two days ago' should be 'Four days ago.' For an account of the disaster see *Edin. Ann. Reg.* III. ii. 258–9.

416 (a) Milton . . . grand dungeon of fire] *Paradise lost*, Bk I, lines 61–9.

418 *n.* 1] For 'of the year' read 'for 1808.'

419 (c) a finger in every man's pie] *Ray*, p. 244.

419 *n.* 1] On mermaids on coast of Caithness, see *Scots Mag.* lxxi. 734–6, lxxiii. 910–13; *Edin. Ann. Reg. for 1809*, II. ii. 286–7; see also *Minstrelsy* (ed. Henderson), iv. 282.

420 (a) Darius] For explanation, see above, p. 219 and my note.

420 (e) Reynolds and Morton] See my note to *SL* ii. 403 (e).

422 *n.* 1] In last line, for '6 vols.' read '2 vols.'

423 (a) Edinburgh Annual Register] Scott fulfilled his promise very lamely by making a brief reference to *Influence of local attachment* in his *Of the living poets of Great Britain* in the *Edin. Ann. Reg. for 1808*, I. ii. 442–3 (publ. 1810).

423 (e) Swiss war songs] See above, p. 399 and my note and below, p. 432.

424 (b) to review it for the Quarterly] The *Illustrations of northern antiquities* was not reviewed in *QR*.

425 (a) To Robert Surtees] The letter is dated 7 Jan. in Taylor, *Memoir of Robert Surtees*, p. 112. The concluding paragraph in *SL* is not in Taylor and is taken from the Abbotsford Copies. The letter to which Scott is replying is in Taylor, op. cit., pp. 108–9.

425 (e) Weber] His work referred to here is *Metrical romances*, 3 vols., Edinburgh, 1810, not *Tales and popular romances*, 4 vols., 1812, as given in Taylor, *Memoir of Robert Surtees*, p. 108.

425 *n.* 1] Surtees's *Verses* ('And shall the minstrel harp in silence rest') was printed in the *Edin. Ann. Reg. for 1810* (1812), III. ii. lxxxviii–lxxxix.

426 (c–d) Ailred de Bello Standardi . . . Twisden] This should be Aelred, *De Bello Standardii*. See *Historiæ Anglicanæ scriptores X* [ed. by Roger Twysden], 2° Londini, 1652, Tom. 1, cols. 337–46. The illus. of the standard is in cols. 339–40.

427 (c) an unfeeling accnt.] See *SL* i. 356.

427 (c) Somers] Surtees, in his letter of 14 Dec. 1811, says he did not receive it. (Taylor, *Memoir of Robert Surtees*, p. 117.)

427 (e) your Pensioner] Sir Thomas Conyers, Bart. He was dead by this time. See my note to *SL* ii. 317 (d).

428 *n.* 1] The review of Sinclair's *Observations on the Bullion Committee* appeared in *QR* for Nov. 1810 (publ. Dec.). For author, see *Shine*, No. 129.

The article on Huskisson was Art. 10 (*Shine*, No. 124).

429 (b) Mountown thou sweet retreat] There are a few verbal slips. In line 18 for 'marke' read 'make.' The poem is in Ritson's *English anthology*, London, 1793, i. 144–5.

432 (a) Swiss battlesongs] See above, pp. 399, 423 and my note at first reference.

432 (d) D. of Argyle's marriage] Caroline Elizabeth, daughter of 4th Earl of Jersey, had married the Marquess of Anglesey. The marriage being dissolved she married the Duke of Argyll on 29 Nov. 1810.

432 *n.* 1] They were probably intended for Vol. 2, projected but never published.

433 (a) Mr. Knight's idea of a poem] In her undated letter Lady Abercorn had written: 'I enclose you a singular book. Mr Knight dared me to get it. He said if such a case had been in Ariosto's hands he would have made something very grand of it' (NLS MS. 3880, f. 8). She does not say what the book is. She does not identify 'Mr Knight' and he is unidentified by Grierson (above, p. 431 *n.* 1) but I think he is Richard Payne Knight (rather than Henry Gally Knight) as he is mentioned in a letter to Lady Abercorn (above, p. 94).

433 (b) addition to your family] James Hamilton, born 21 Jan., son and heir of Lord Hamilton, Lord Abercorn's elder son. His father predeceased the 1st Marquess and he succeeded his grandfather as 2nd Marquess and became 1st Duke.

433 (d) Lord Chief Baron & Mr. Dundas] Robert Dundas of Arniston and Robert Dundas who became 2nd Viscount Melville in May of this year.

433 (f) now fixed at allowances of £1300] See my note to *SL* ii. 355 (c–d).

434 (c) go where the D—— drives] *Heywood*, p. 135; *Ray*, p. 126; Ramsay, *Proverbs*, p. 25. Used by Shakespeare in *All's well*, I. 3. Also quoted in *SL* iii. 206, vii. 308.

434 (d) my colleague] George Home.

434 (d) £200 . . . in my favour] This was the additional grant by the Exchequer. See my note to *SL* ii. 355 (c–d).

434 (e) To Lord Dalkeith] Date is 7 Nov. 1811: (1) Scott is going to Edinburgh on Monday, i.e. 11 Nov., for opening of Courts on 12 Nov.; (2) the plan of the cottage indicates the autumn, not Jan.; (3) Dalkeith's letter of 29 Jan. cited in note 1 does not refer to this letter but to the sale of the vote for Laretburn (*SL* vii. 460).

435 (b) Vicar of Wakefield] Goldsmith, *The Vicar of Wakefield*, chap. 1: 'from the blue bed to the brown.'

435 *n.* 1] Delete this note which is not applicable.

435 *n.* 2] In line 2, for 'chief' read 'Principal.'

436 (c) Lord Chief Baron Robert Dundas] This, as it stands, is obscure. A comma should have been inserted after 'Baron.'

437 (f) Sinbads old man of the Sea] See my note to *SL* i. 369 (b).

437 (f) reversion Act] Bankes's Act of 1808 (48 Geo. III, c. 50).

438 (a) rather dwell in my necessity] Shakespeare, *Merchant of Venice*, I. 3.

438 (a) £200] See above, p. 434 and my note to p. 355 (c–d).

438 (c) a maiden aunt] Miss Jean Home. She died later in this year.

438 (e) R. Dundas] Robert Dundas who succeeded as 2nd Viscount Melville in May.

439 (b) his candidate] Alexander (afterwards Sir Alexander) Don.

441 (b) Your letter of the 10th January] Printed in *FL* i. 161–3 and in *An Anglo-Indian poet, John Leyden*, by P. Seshadri, Madras, 1912, pp. 105–9.

441 (d) a son of Mr. Pringle of Whitebank] John Alexander Pringle. See below, p. 534.

441 *n.* 2] Amend this note which contains two errors. (1) The print which Scott sent was the small line engraving by Raimbach; (2) The original was painted for Archibald Constable and was later acquired by the Duke of Buccleuch.

442 (a) Scotch terrier] Wallace. See above, p. 205.

442 (b) our woodland walks by Eskes

romantic shore] Leyden, *Scenes of infancy*, Pt II, 11th line from end: 'The wild-wood walks by Esk's romantic shore.'

442 (b) the Chinese affair] *Dissertation on the character and sounds of the Chinese language*, by J. Marshman, 4to Serampore, 1809. Leyden in his letter (*FL* i. 161) explains that this is 'only the preface of the first volume of *Confucius* in Chinese and English . . . The first volume of *Confucius* will follow in the next ship.'

442 (b) *Quarterly Review*] Leyden in his letter (*FL* i. 162) hoped that Scott would get Marshman reviewed. It was reviewed in *QR* for May 1811 by Sir George Thomas Staunton (*Shine*, No. 147).

442 (e) [Constable?]] Delete query.

442 (e) Jeshurun] *Bible, Deuteronomy* 32: 15: 'But Jeshurun waxed fat, and kicked.'

442 (f) partner's insolence] Alexander Gibson Hunter.

443 (b) 1871 *Exhibition Catalogue*] Add: pp. 155–6.

443 (c) late Act of Parliament] Bankes's Act (48 Geo. III, c. 50).

443 *n.* 1] This note, with omission of 'Dr' before 'Leyden', is copied verbatim from the 1871 Exhibition catalogue, p. 156.

446 (f) *flapper* [?]] Delete the query. Scott is quoting Swift. See my note to *SL* ii. 213 (c).

448 (d) Superannuation Act] 50 Geo. III, c. 117, passed 21 June 1810. See Index under Parliament. Acts.

448 (e–f) The judicature Act] 50 Geo. III, c. 112, passed 20 June 1810. By Sect. XVI salaries of Principal Clerks were fixed at £1,000 and by the Schedule at end of Act they were allowed £100 extra as compensation.

450 (a) Two of the enclosed] Engraving by Raimbach of Raeburn's 1808 portrait. The mezzotint to which Scott refers was by Charles Turner. See my note to *SL* ii. 441 *n.* 2.

450 (d) L. Advocate] Archibald Campbell Colquhoun. He never became a Baron of Exchequer.

451 (a) Manna in the wilderness] *Bible, Deuteronomy* 8: 16.

451 (b) Jorick] Yorick in Sterne's *A sentimental journey* (in section 'The passport. The Hotel at Paris'). Cf. Yorick in *Tristram Shandy*: 'I might say with *Sancho Pança*, that should I recover, and "Mitres thereupon be suffered to rain down from heaven as thick as hail...".' (Bk I, chap. 12.)

451 (c) Cowley] See my note to *SL* vii. 56 (c–d).

452 (f) out of the fullness of the heart] *Bible, Matthew* 12: 34: 'out of the abundance of the heart the mouth speaketh.'

452 (f) would like to have my Sheriffdom] See also *SL* i. 405, 406. Later Scott admitted that he held 'two offices not usually conjoined' (*SL* iii. 336, 345).

453 (e) Lady Hamilton & the little boy] See above, pp. 391, 433 and my note at second reference.

455 (b) Mr. Walker] James Walker of Dalry.

459 (f) the Lord President] Robert Blair who died suddenly on 20 May.

460 (b) (one being a mere novice)] David Hume. The other is James Walker of Dalry.

461 (c) "that call it folly . . ."] Scott is paraphrasing part of Home's letter of 6 Mar. (addressee not given) in which he wrote: 'It may be obstinacy or folly or weakness or what you or my friends please, but I shall never be prevailed upon to apply for a Pension while the Joint Commission subsists' (NLS MS. 19, f. 38).

461 (c) In lifes last stage] Samuel Johnson, *The vanity of human wishes*, lines 315–16.

462 (a) To Sophia] Why is this included? It is not a letter.

462 *n.* 1] Her letter quoted here is in NLS (MS. 81, f. 61). Scott read her *Cottage dialogues* (below, p. 511).

463 (b) [*O'Donoghue's Tour in Ireland*]] Add: pp. 13–14.

463 (d) Our attempt at the Lady of the Lake] The version by Edmund John Eyre, produced on 15 Jan. The

title-page stated 'now performing with undiminished applause, at the Theatre Royal, Edinburgh'. Dibdin, however, says it was played only 'about six times.'

464 (a) the Knight of Snowdoun] This version, by Thomas Morton, was produced on 18 Mar.

464 (d) Terry] played Roderick Dhu] In E. J. Eyre's version.

464 (f) Portugal] Scott had told Joanna Baillie (above, p. 404) and Lady Abercorn (above, p. 432) of his desire to go to Portugal. Either of these correspondents could have spread the report. The source for the Sheffield papers was probably Montgomery.

466 (a–b) Act 30. c. 117] For '30' read '50'. Scott is referring to the statute 50 Geo. III. c. 117. See above, p. 448.

469 (c) To Mrs. Aprice] Scott is replying to her letter of 4 Mar. which is printed in Partington, *Letter-books*, pp. 122–3.

469 *n.* 2] This note should have come at the first reference to her, above, p. 359. The quotation from Mrs Fletcher comes from her *Autobiography*, pp. 102–3.

470 (b) Mrs. W——] Mrs Waddington.

471 *n.* 1] The play as published was called *Border feuds; or, the Lady of Buccleuch*. The music was by Sir John Stevenson and the play was produced at the Theatre Royal, Crow Street, Dublin, the part of the Lady of Buccleuch being played by Miss Smith. According to O'Donoghue's *The poets of Ireland* the play was written by Sarah Smith.

472 (f) Our ancient English tragedy . . .] This is probably a parody of *Now ancient English melody*, st. [1], lines 1–4: 'Now ancient English melody / Is banished out of doors, / And nought is heard in our good day, / But Signoras and Signors.'

472 *n.* 1] Delete and substitute: *Gilmanscleuch*, by James Hogg, st. [55–8]. In his *The mountain bard*, Edinburgh, 1807, p. 46.

473 (d) flourishing like a green bay tree] See *SL* i. 23 and my note.

474 (a) Excabbar] Read 'Excalibar.'

474 (a) that all of Coleyne] *King Arthur's death*, st. [35], lines 1–2. (Percy's *Reliques*; also in Lewis, *Tales of wonder* (1801), ii. 386, printed from Percy.)

474 (d) Longman's new review] The *British Review*.

474 (d) Roscoe] William Roscoe's *Brief observations on the address to His Majesty, proposed by Earl Grey, in the House of Lords, June 13, 1810*. It was reviewed by Lord Dudley in *QR* for Feb. (publ. Mar.) 1811. (*Shine*, No. 134.)

474 (e) Barrossa] Sir Thomas Graham, afterwards Lord Lynedoch, with a combined force of British and Spanish troops, defeated the French at Barrosa in Mar. 1811.

474 (e) "Gallant Graeme"] 'Gallant' was a common epithet for the Grahames but Scott may be referring more specifically to the ballad, *The gallant Grahams* (*Minstrelsy*, ed. Henderson, ii. 227).

474 (f) King William] Scott also, in *SL* iii. 77, attributes the complaint to 'our King William,' but in *The Bride of Lammermoor*, chap. 25, he attributes it correctly to Prince William of Orange who commanded Spanish troops, in alliance with Queen Mary I of England, against France.

475 (a) while it is called today] *Bible, John* 9: 4.

475 (b) To Coimbra . . .] Robert Southey, *Queen Orraca*, st. [5], lines 1–2. In *English minstrelsy* (1810), i. 270.

475 (c) an officer of our flying artillery] William Norman Ramsay.

475 (f) as Justice Shallow says] Shakespeare, *II Henry IV*, V. 5: 'A colour, I fear, that you will die in.'

476 (b) To Charles Erskine] Date is Thursday, 11 Apr.

476 (c) Mr. Warrender] Hugh Warrender, W.S., Crown Agent.

476 (c) Agnes Murray] Agnes Baillie, whose correct name is given on the following page. She was tried at Jedburgh for theft in Oct. 1808 but released, being 'in a state of insanity.' See *Scots Mag.* Vol. 70 (Oct. 1808), p. 796.

476 *n.* 1] This work was reviewed by Southey and John Wilson Croker in

QR for May 1811 (*Shine*, No. 148). Southey in his *History of Europe* in the *Edin. Ann. Reg. for 1809*, recommended his book (II. i. 345).

476 *n.* 2] For 'Raeburn' read 'Maxpoffle.' The index figure 2 in the text should be at 'Willies', not at 'Raeburn.'

477 (a) Act respecting a Numbering] 'An Act for taking an account of the population of Great Britain, and of the increase or diminution thereof.' 51 Geo. III, c. 6, Mar. 1811.

477 (b) King David] *Bible, II Samuel* 24.

478 (b) "Silver and gold . . ."] *Bible, Acts* 3: 6.

478 (d) Chairman of the Committee] John Whitmore, Chairman of the Committee of Subscribers for Relief of the Portuguese Sufferers, to whom Scott dedicated *Don Roderick*.

479 (d) To J. B. S. Morritt] Printed out of order. Morritt's letter (NLS MS. 3880, ff. 84–6) is undated, although he has the date 12 Apr. at start of the second portion.

479 (f) my new desk] Made by Messrs Gillow. See above, pp. 343, 369.

480 (a) Captain Payne] Morritt in his letter gives no clue to his identity.

480 (e) the *Grand Secret*] Scott wrote on French tactics in *Edin. Ann. Reg.* See below, p. 503.

480 (f) "my soul and body . . ."] Shakespeare, *II Henry VI*, V. 2.

481 (a) these dwellers upon the isthmus] See *SL* xii. 322 and my note.

481 (c) Lady Hood] Morritt in his letter told Scott that Sir Samuel Hood had been appointed to the Jamaica Station and will go there in Nov. Lady Hood says she must go with him.

481 (e) verily she has her reward] *Bible, Matthew* 6: 2.

481 *n.* 1] This note belongs to note above, p. 208.

482 (a) your loss at Barosa] Morritt had described him simply as the only son of 'a very old friend of ours Mr Eyre.' He was Gervase Anthony Eyre, only son of Col. Anthony Hardolph Eyre of Grove. Had Scott been told that he was a nephew of Lady Alvanley he would probably have said more.

482 (b) "Silver and gold . . ."] *Bible, Acts* 3: 6.

482 (d) Clarkes new volumes] Edward Daniel Clarke's *Travels in various countries of Europe,* etc., Cambridge, 1810–23. Not reviewed in *QR* till Mar. 1813. Reviewed by Reginald Heber (*Shine* No. 242).

482 *n.* 1] The correct reference is: *Edin. Ann. Reg. for 1809,* Edinburgh, 1811, Pt 2, pp. 526–41. Scott was assisted by Patrick Murray of Simprim. See below, p. 503 and *SL* iii. 232.

483 (a) a few tawdry stanzas] The incident on which *The bold dragoon* was based occurred between Badajoz and Campo Mayor and is described in the *Edin. Ann. Reg. for 1811,* IV. i. 271–2. The title applies to one dragoon but the poem does not mention him and deals with the dragoons collectively. The title in Thomson's *Collection (Ruff,* No. 79), *The British Light Dragoons,* is more appropriate than the title given to it by Lockhart.

483 (f) I have it hung up by S' Fillans Spring] *The Lady of the Lake,* Canto I [opening stanza, lines 1–2] and Canto VI [conclusion].

483 *n.* 1] Lockhart, in his ed. of *The poetical works,* is wrong in associating the poem with the siege of Badajoz in Apr. 1812, and wrong in saying it was written for a Cavalry dinner. See above, p. 483 (a).

484 (e) "Chirke Castle"] Thomson had asked for a song to this Welsh tune in his letter of 15 Apr. (Hadden, *George Thomson,* p. 160.)

485 (a) Minstrelsy] Minstrelsy of Chirke Castle, the full title of the tune.

485 (e) A Colleague] John Pringle.

485 *n.* 1] In line 3, for 'Barnett' read 'Barrett.'

486 (b) Hare with many friends] *The hare and many friends* is No. 50 of John Gay's *Fables,* Part I.

487 (a) Epigrammatic Pamphlet] *A sketch of the state of Ireland, past and present,* 8vo Dublin, 1808. A new ed. was published at London by John Murray in 1822. The style is definitely epigrammatic.

487 (b) adieu to the Prince of the Brasils] *On the emigration of the Prince of Brazil to his dominions in South America* in the *Edin. Ann. Reg. for 1809* (publ. 1811), II. ii. 657–8.

487 (b) Don Roderick . . . is to make his first entree . . . in the same register] *Don Roderick* was published in book form before it appeared in the *Edin. Ann. Reg. for 1809.*

487 (d) curious task for a Scotchman] Alluding to Swift's persistent rudeness to Scotsmen.

488 (e) Braham] John Braham, the operatic singer. In his letter of 2 May (NLS MS. 3880, ff. 97–8) Clarke Whitfeld complains that he had been offered 100 guineas for the Boat Song if Braham sang it with approval in London; that Braham said he liked the song and would sing it; but that after much delay he refused, saying 'he did not like it.' He concludes: 'The caprice of favorite singers is almost past bearing.'

488 *n.* 1] For 'the Melody you told me of,' see above, p. 375.

489 (b) Carslogie reliques] See above, p. 398 and my note.

489 (d) To George Thomson] Date must be 27 Apr. Scott went to Ashiestiel on Monday, 29 Apr. (above, p. 483) and returned to Edinburgh on 13 May (below, pp. 491, 492).

489 *n.* 1] In line 8, delete 'Scott's friends are all of Torloisk.' See also my note to *SL* ii. 162 (b).

490 (a) Sketch of a little Border tale] Probably *Lord Langley* (p. 491).

490 (c) wean the child] I have found no record of a birth.

490 (c–d) under such distress of mind] Their son William had died on 28 Apr. (*Scots Mag.* lxxiii. 399.)

490 (f) "bread we shall eat or white or brown"] Matthew Prior, *Alma,* Canto III, line 587.

491 (d) To George Thomson] The date is 8 May, Wednesday being the 8th. Hadden, *George Thomson,* p. 161, wrongly says the letter is a reply to one of Thomson's of 23 May.

491 (d) Lord Langley] This may be the song which eventually became *Jock of*

Hazeldean, in st. II of which we are told that Young Frank is 'lord of Langley-dale.' Hadden, *George Thomson,* p. 161, says it probably was to be written to the tune of 'The bed in the barn.' See above, pp. 483, 484.

492 (c) I received your letter] There are no letters for 1811 in NLS.

493 (e) the 4th Stanza . . . a short note may be necessary] Scott wrote a *long* note to st. IV of the 'Introduction' to *Don Roderick.* It begins: 'This locality may startle those readers who do not recollect . . .'—James Ballantyne being one of these readers!

494 (c–d) play the *frog* in the fable] See L'Estrange, *Fables,* No. 35. *A frog and an oxe.* By Aesop.

494 (d) "patience Cousin . . ."] *Don Quixote.* See my note to *SL* ii. 404 (a).

494 *n.* 1] Cathcart's wife was Anne, daughter of John Cadell of Cockenzie.

495 (a) To Lady Abercorn] There is nothing to show why this is called an 'Extract.' The text is fuller than that of *FL* i. 217–19.

495 (c) German romance entitled Hermann of Unna] By C. B. E. Naubert. Scott refers to this novel in the Preface to his *Goetz.* See V. Stockley, *German literature as known in England, 1750–1830* (London, 1929), pp. 221, 325.

495 (d–e) She is engaged in copying the *Vision*] This transcript (16 pp., 4to) was sold by auction by Parke-Bernet, New York, Jan. 1948 for $9.

497 (e) filly & her mama] Lady Wallace and her filly.

498 (a) To John Ballantyne] A transcript of the complete letter, which is dated 6 May 1811, is now in NLS (MS. 6080).

498 *n.* 1] Delete this note which is not applicable. Scott wanted the text for his ed. of *The Castle of Otranto,* pp. xxxvii–xxxix. See also my note to *SL* i. 134 (d).

499 (d) a copy of the play] *The House of Aspen.* See above, p. 495.

499 *n.* 1] It was not the frontispiece but the title-page vignette which was drawn by Terry.

500 *n.* 1] The Mr Pringle of the letter

is Alexander Pringle of Whytbank and Yair. In last line, delete '[Edinburgh]'.

501 (c) a farm immediately east] Abbotslee.

501 (d) 3000 guineas for a new poem] *Rokeby.*

502 (a) *humana perpassi sumus*] Not traced, but Anderson (*Journal,* 25 Oct. 1827) suggests Horace, *Odes,* I. iii. 25. Also quoted below, p. 507 and in *SL* vii. 386, *Waverley,* chap. 64 and *The Monastery,* Introd. epistle.

503 (a) To Patrick Murray] Murray's letter, which Scott is answering, is not known to be extant. The NLS, however, has a photostat of Scott's letter (MS. 8494, ff. 238–9) which shows that the opening sentence relates to Adam Ferguson. Scott again wrote to Murray about Adam as is shown by Murray's reply of 7 July (NLS MS. 3880, ff. 162–3), but Scott's letter is not in *SL* and Murray's allusion to Ferguson is obscure.

503 (a–b) by near relationship] There can be little doubt that Scott is referring to the death, on 26 Apr., as the result of a hunting accident, of Murray's first cousin, Sir James Pulteney Murray, 7th Bart. of Clermont. Murray's father, 5th Lord Elibank, was the brother of Janet, Sir James's mother.

503 (c) a few separate copies for my friends] This was a small quarto with '(Author's Copy)' printed on the title-page. (*Ruff,* No. 110.)

503 (c) our tactical essay] *Cursory remarks upon the French order of battle, particularly in the campaigns of Buonaparte* in the *Edin. Ann. Reg. for 1811,* II. ii. 526–41. As Scott calls it 'our' essay, Murray presumably supplied facts and ideas, but the style shows that the essay was finally written by Scott.

503 *n.* 1] NLS MS. 3880, ff. 162–3. See also below, p. 509.

504 (a) To Archibald Park] The date is almost certainly 1816: (1) Park was not seeking a post in the Customs till 1816; (2) Scott did not become acquainted with Earl till 1816 (*SL* iv. 189); (3) from the letter it is clear that Park has been promised a post and has been given a choice but Park's name does not appear in the list of Customs officers till 1816. I cannot explain the address 'Ashestiel.'

505 (d) To Miss Clephane] To Margaret. Date must be Monday 24 June. Private copies were to be ready 'in the end of the week' and Scott was able to send one to Lord Melville on 30 June (above, p. 504).

505 n. 1] This anonymous poem, *Monody on the death of . . . Viscount Melville . . . and of . . . Robert Blair*, 4to Edinburgh, 1811, was by the Rev. Robert Buchanan. St. VIII is addressed to Scott, asking him why his Muse is silent on the death of Melville. Reviewed in *Scots Mag.* lxxiii. 452–3.

506 (a) "the lovely isle again to see"] Leyden, *The mermaid*, st. 62, line 2. For 'lovely' read 'lonely.' First printed in Scott's *Minstrelsy* (ed. Henderson), iv. 299. This quotation proves that 'lovely' so often printed by Grierson is wrong.

506 (e) To George Thomson] This letter should be dated June.

507 (a) To J. B. S. Morritt] Scott is answering Morritt's letter of 1 July, printed in Partington, *Letter-books*, pp. 19–21. Scott may absent-mindedly have copied Morritt's date. The date is probably 2 July.

507 (c) 'Tis vain to name him] Thomas Parnell, *Verses on the Peace* (1712), line 122: ' 'Tis grief to name him whom we mourn in vain.'

507 (d) humana perpessi sumus!] See above, p. 502.

507 n. 1] John Du Bisson, Surgeon-Dentist to the Prince of Wales, died at Edinburgh, 21 June 1811.

508 (a) French Ambassador] Scott probably got the anecdote from a recent letter from Lydia White. See Partington, *Letter-books*, p. 121.

508 n. 1] The Bishop's house was at Ickworth Park. See Morritt's letter in Partington, *Letter-books*, pp. 19–21.

509 (d) To Patrick Murray] Date is about 2 July. Murray acknowledged the gift on 7 July (above, p. 503 n.).

509 (f) rejoice therefore!] *Bible, II Corinthians* 7: 16.

510 (d) Miss Edgeworths Tales] Reviewed in *QR* for Aug. 1809. Several writers are suggested, priority being given to Henry John Stephen and

William Gifford. (*Shine*, No. 42.) The Irish journey is described in chap. 3 of *Ennui* (*Tales*, Vol. 1).

511 (e) To Mrs. Scott] Date must be 24 July. 'I left all our lawyers about a fortnight ago' (p. 512), i.e. 14 days after the rising of the Courts on 12 July. Wednesday was 24 July. This date corresponds with the letter to Lady Abercorn of 25 July (p. 519).

511 (f) Lady Wallace] Lady Wallace and her filly had been sent to Mertoun in May (above, p. 497). The filly must have been a gift to Mrs Scott and Scott is now taking back her mother. James Stewart is probably a groom at Mertoun. In line 2, p. 512, 'him' should be 'her.'

512 (b) Citizen Scott] William Scott of Whimpson, son of Rev. James Scott and brother of Lady Oxford.

512 (c) Charlotte & Anne] Scott surely means Sophia and Anne.

512 n. 1] Delete the last sentence which is an uncalled-for editorial comment.

514 (b) offices adjoining to the house] Cf. the views of the Marquis de Hautlieu in the 1823 introd. to *Quentin Durward*.

514 (c) Twisting of collars] See above, p. 92 and my note.

519 (b) last Sunday] 30 June. Scott's letter to Melville is printed above, pp. 504–5, but the one to Arbuthnot is not in *SL*.

519 (f) showing him my play] Scott has apparently forgotten that Kemble had considered and rejected it as far back as 1800. See *SL* i. 124 n., xii. 157 n., 170 n.

522 (a) A larger farm bounds my little patch] This was Abbotslee, owned by Mercer and tenanted by William Leithead. It was advertised in the *Edinburgh Evening Courant* of 11 July to be sold in Melrose Town Hall on 10 Aug. 1811. See below, p. 530.

522 (c) Miss Wortley] I assume that this is Miss Mary Stuart-Wortley who married in 1813 William Dundas, Lord Melville's nephew. For biographical details, see Index.

522 (e) Your letter of the 16th] In NLS (MS. 3880, ff. 188–9).

522 (f) To Mr. Mayo] Thomas Mayo. In Symington, *Some unpublished letters*, p. 16, where it is dated 2 Aug. Mayo's letter is in NLS (MS. 3880, f. 208).

523 n. 1] See also above, pp. 348–9.

524 (b) Johnsons prophecy] Samuel Johnson, *Prologue and epilogue spoken at . . . Drury-Lane*, line 46. In *Oxford Book of Eighteenth Century Verse*, p. 323, where there are notes on Hunt, a pugilist, and Mahomet, a rope-dancer.

525 (e) article by a Mocking Bird] *The inferno of Altisidora*, for which see my note to *SL* i. 412 (c).

525 n. 1] There is no need to refer to Chalmers's *Caledonia*. That Scott is referring to *Albania* is shown by his quotation, which is line 263 of that poem.

526 (d) his peasant promise] A misreading, presumably, for 'his present promise.'

526 (d) fable of the dying peasant] See L'Estrange, *Fables*, No. 108. By Aesop.

526 n. 1] In 5th line from end, for '*Altesidora*' read '*Altisidora*.' In last line, for '416' read '412.'

526 n. 2] Delete and substitute: William Howison, who published in 1817 *Fragments and fictions*, which was supposed to be translated from the French of Jean Pocucurante de Peudemots. Lockhart in *Peter's letters*, iii. 138, and Gillies in *Memoirs*, ii. 50, both say he was nicknamed Monsieur de Peudemots.

527 (c) He has beat me in the matter of the brooch] In her letter of 9 July (NLS MS. 3880, f. 176) she apologizes for not sending Edward Coxe's verses on the brooch. She enclosed them with a letter of 5 Dec. (NLS MS. 3881, ff. 122–6). The MS. has been removed and is in MS. 921, f. 28. The verses are headed 'Addressed to Miss Joanna Baillie on her shewing me a Present to her by Walter Scott of a Golden Harp.' For the brooch, see above. pp. 379, 398, 401–2, 418, and *SL* iii. 39.

527 (c) St. Columbus] i.e. St Columba. See above, pp. 362, 402 and my note at latter reference.

527 (f) tent of Peri Banou] In *The story of Prince Ahmed and the Fairy Pari Banou* in *The Arabian Nights* (Weber, *Tales of the East*, i. 449–51).

528 (c) my old friend Abou Hassan] In *The story of the sleeper awakened* in *The Arabian Nights* (Weber, *Tales of the East*, i. 316). See also my note to *SL* ii. 523 (d).

528 (d) My friend who piqued himself] See *Lockhart*, iii. 344 and *SL* v. 225 and n. Scott in his *Journal*, 25 Mar. 1829, says his friend was R. Ainslie.

530 (a) To Charles Erskine] The date, Thursday, 8 Aug. is correct and Scott is not giving himself much time as the sale was to be on 10 Aug. It is odd that he should say 'A report has reachd me', for he had been interested in Abbotslee (above, pp. 501, 522) and the sale had been advertised as early as 11 July. See my note to *SL* ii. 522 (a). Scott bid £6,000 but failed to acquire it. It was presumably bought by Nicol Milne of Faldonside as Scott bought a portion of Abbotslee from him in 1816.

530 n. 1] For '*Eclectic Review*' read '*Iris* of 1 Aug.' See *Memoirs of . . . James Montgomery*, ii. 309.

531 (a) *Life of James Montgomery*] Add reference: Vol. 2, p. 309.

531 (b) your change of state] His marriage on 5 Aug.

531 (e) "busk her & come to the braes of Yarrow"] *Braes of Yarrow*, st. [1], line 4. In *Herd*, i. 194.

532 (c) Two days ago] Four days ago, the sale being on 10 Aug. The farm was Abbotslee.

532 (f) Mr M. Montgomery] Mathew Montgomerie, a writer, died at George Street on 8 Aug.

533 (a) Fergusons clerk] Clerk of James Fergusson, W.S., who had been dilatory in winding up estate of Walter Scott, W.S. Fergusson had died on 26 May.

533 (f) Purves] James Purvis, an old school friend of Leyden at Denholm, was purser on the East India Co.'s *Castle Eden*. Leyden addressed a poem to him.

533 (f) your valued dagger] See *SL* xii. 309.

533 n. 1] I do not understand this note. Lockhart has 'revenge than generosity'

which is correct. Grierson prints 're-venge and generosity' which is wrong.

535 (c) "poor Scotland's gear"] Lady Wardlaw, *Hardyknute*, st. 34, line 2. (In Percy's *Reliques*.)

535 (c) poor and bare as Sir John Fal-staff's regiment] Shakespeare, *I Henry IV*, IV. 2.

535 (d) "it is a poor thing, but mine own"] Shakespeare, *As you like it*, V. 4.

535 (e) brighten the chain of friend-ship] This is a common expression used by the Five Nations of Canada. See Cadwallader Colden, *The history of the Five Nations of Canada*, 2nd ed., Lon-don, 1750, pp. 45, 51, 56, 101, 117 and elsewhere. Scott uses the expression in *SL* ii. 542, iii. 88, 197, 455, iv. 24, v. 279, viii. 260, xi. 156, 464, xii. 333. Scott uses the words 'brightened the chain of attachment' in *Waverley*, chap. 6, and 'the chain of friendship' in the *Journal*, 20 Feb. 1826.

535 (f) To Charles Carpenter] Printed, in part, in *Lockhart*, iii. 341–2, where the date is 5 Aug.

537 (a) obliged by law] Scott inter-preted the law differently later on. In a letter to Willie Scott of Max-poffle [1 May 1825] he wrote: 'In fact neither King nor Exchequer have any thing to do with my residence.' (NLS MS. 2890, ff. 49–50; not in *SL*.)

538 (c) "being so far into the bowels . . ."] Shakespeare, *Richard III*, V. 2.

539 (e) "A Proposal for A Hospital . . ."] *A serious and useful scheme, to make an hospital for incurables*. Dublin, 1733.

539 *n*. 1] In line 3, for 'Robert' read 'Richard.'

540 (b) grove . . . honoured by the name] There never was a grove at Abbotsford named after her.

540 (b) a letter . . . from dear Lady Hood] Of 22 July referred to below, p. 543 *n*. 1.

540 (e) As for Bandello] In Lady Stafford's letter of 14 Aug. (NLS MS. 3881, ff. 7–9) she says she is un-acquainted with *The Duchess of Amalfi* but will endeavour to consult it. This suggests that there is a missing letter from Scott to her in which he had re-ferred to the play.

541 *n*. 1] Delete from 'Bandello' to the end and substitute: *La prima (-terza) parte de le novelle del Bandello*, 3 tom., 4to Lucca, 1554; *La quarte parte*, 8vo Lione, 1573.

542 (b) *Morritt grove*] There never was a Morritt Grove at Abbotsford.

542 (c) to brighten the chain of friend-ship] See above, p. 535 and my note.

542 (c) so many good things which rot in one's gizzard] Cervantes, *Don Quixote*, Pt I, Bk III, chap. 7. (Lockhart's ed., 1822, i. 236.) Scott refers to this again in *SL* vi. 89, xi. 367, 419 and at the second and third references says wrongly that this was said in the Sierra Morena.

542 (e) mountains on their apex] See James Bruce, *Travels to discover the source of the Nile*, 2nd ed., Edinburgh, 1804, iv. 317.

542 (f) a brother of Lord Balcarras] The brothers alive at this time were Robert, Charles and John. Scott's visitor is almost certainly John.

543 (a) The Edinburgh reviewers] Francis Jeffrey in *ER* Vol. 18 (Aug. 1811), pp. 379–92.

543 (e) An application was made] By William Miller. See *SL* iii. 3.

544 *n*.] Morritt later recommended that Walter should be sent to Shrews-bury where Butler was headmaster. See Partington, *Post-bag*, p. 121.

VOLUME III

1 *n*. 1] Delete this note and see *SL* ii. 356 *n*. and vii. 445.

2 (b) the Kembles] J. P. Kemble wrote to Scott on 11 Sept. (NLS MS. 3881, ff. 54–5). Odd that Scott makes no reference here to the letter.

2 (d) about the review] Of her *Woman; or, Ida of Athens* in *QR*. See *SL* ii. 166 *n*. 2, 284, 284 *n*.

2 (d) the "wild romance"] A para-phrase of Logan, *On the death of a young lady*, st. [13], lines 3–4: 'The wild

romance of life is done; / The real history is begun.'

3 (b) Mrs. Grants work] *Essays on the superstitions of the Highlanders*, 2 vols., 8vo London, 1811.

3 (c) Miller] See *SL* ii. 543.

3 (d) Campbell] It was said that Bonaparte offered Campbell (through Miller, the bookseller) £2,000 to translate it. (M. R. Mitford to Sir William Elford, 15 Oct. 1811. *Life of M. R. Mitford*, London, 1870, i. 157.)

3 (f) Chief Baron] Robert Dundas of Arniston, Lord Chief Baron, retained his position till his death in 1819. Charles Hope of Granton was appointed Lord President on 10 Oct. 1811.

3 *n.* 1] Delete. The note has nothing whatsoever to do with the subject of Scott's letter.

4 (a) Will. Dundas] He was not appointed a Baron of Exchequer.

4 (d) The verses in the Register] *The poet released from the law*, by Rev. John Marriot [*sic*]. It was written in 1806 and published in the *Edin. Ann. Reg. for 1809*, II. ii. 652–3 (publ. 1811).

4 (f) To Mrs. Scott] The date is Friday, 6 Sept. 1811, as is proved by the words 'I am going to the Circuit next week.' The Circuit opened at Jedburgh on Monday, 16 Sept. (*Scots Mag.* Vol. 73, p. 793). Scott would go to Jedburgh on Friday, 13 Sept., to meet the Judge. The Friday of the letter, therefore, must be the previous Friday, i.e. 6 Sept.

5 *n.* 1] Delete the first sentence which is inaccurate and confused. The 'present occupant' (lines 11–12) was William Hutchinson who had been Paymaster since 19 Apr. 1799. Delete second last sentence and see *SL* vii. 511 *n.*

6 (a) To Mrs. Scott] This letter should come before the letter on p. 4 above. The letter from Scott's mother, which Scott is answering, appears to be the first intimation of Tom's paymastership and must have come before Scott wrote to Tom (above, p. 5) some time before 6 Sept. Scott's letter to Tom is not in *SL*.

7 (b) Hawthorn] Vans Hathorn, W.S.

9 (d) expects a Government] He was made Governor of Demerara.

10 (c) Stark] See below, p. 65 *n.*

10 (c) "cauk & keel"] *The gaberlunzie man*, st. [10], line 1. In Ramsay, *Teatable miscellany*; or, Burns, *Verses on the late Captain Grose's peregrinations*, st. [2], line 6.

11 (b–c) the precious box] A box of Swift's papers which Thomas Steele is going to lend to Scott. See Index under Steele.

11 (c) Lord Bathurst on 3rd Sept. 1735] His letter is in Scott's *Swift*, 2nd ed., xviii. 372, where it is dated 13 Sept.

11 *n.* 1] In line 2 from foot, for 'Clovenford' read 'Clovenfords.'

12 (a) verses from Clovenford] The poem is headed: 'Written upon the departure of the author from Ashestiel, (then) the charming residence of Walter Scott, Esq., in Ettricke Forest, Selkirkshire, September 6, 1811.' It was printed in his *Ode to desolation: with some other poems*, 8vo London, 1815.

12 (c) your poems are gone to press] *Minstrelsy of Erin*, printed by James Ballantyne and published by John Ballantyne, 1812.

13 (a) Thompson] James Thomson, the poet, born at Ednam.

13 (c) Dr. Hill] In his reply of 27 Nov. 1811 (NLS MS. 881, ff. 82–5) Hartstonge said *'our Dr. Hill'* was not *'your Dr. Hill.'* In a letter of 13 June 1814 (NLS MS. 3885, ff. 104–6) he identifies Scott's Dr Hill who remembered Scott when a boy. For Dr Edward Hill, see Index.

14 (d) Maxwell of Carriden] William Maxwell of Carriden was M.P. for Selkirk Burghs 1807–12. He was defeated in 1812 by Sir John Buchanan Riddell.

15 *n.* 1] May be a 'favourite expression' but it is used only twice in *SL*.

16 (a) To C. K. Sharpe] Sharpe's letter of 22 Oct. which Scott is answering is in *Sharpe's Letters*, i. 473–5. The verses mentioned in line 3 of Scott's letter were *Ode on the death of a military officer killed in Portugal* (ibid. i. 474 *n.*).

16 (d) as Touchstone says] Shakespeare, *As you like it*, V. 4.

16 (e) our kind Marchioness] Marchioness of Stafford.

16 (f) So runs the world away] Shakespeare, *Hamlet*, III. 2.

17 (a) I have not yet read Miss Seward's letters] True in one sense; but he had read at least letters from her to himself in MS. for Constable about 1810. See *SL* ii. 273.

17 (a) imitate the ancient romans in brevity] Shakespeare, *II Henry IV*, II. 2.

18 (a) To Mrs. Scott] Date is Saturday, 30 Nov., the day he received Tom's letter of 27 Nov. cited in *n.* 1.

18 (e) Irish song] *The return to Ulster.* See below, p. 24 and *n.*

18 *n.* 2] This is a quotation from Hadden's *George Thomson*, pp. 162–3. All except the last sentence should be in inverted commas.

19 (a) Monypenny] David Monypenny, afterwards Lord Pitmilly. He is the Solicitor-General mentioned in this letter.

19 (e) my nephew's bond] William Scott, natural son of Daniel.

19 (e) poor Peter] Patrick Erskine, surgeon in Edinburgh, had died on 21 Oct. He may have been a relative of Charles Erskine.

19 (f) Dunlop] William Dunlop, Sheriff Officer of Selkirkshire, was suspended for misconduct. The solicitors petitioned against the sentence but Scott on 13 Mar. 1811 refused the petition (*Chisholm*, p. 137). The suspension must have lasted till Scott wrote this letter in November. In second last line 'reprove' (which does not make sense) should be 'repone.'

20 (a) put a fever on my conscience] Probably a misreading for 'face'. In *SL* xi. 437 Scott uses the phrase 'putting even a face upon their conscience.'

20 (b) Commendator's house] The Commendator's House, attached to Melrose Abbey, was Erskine's home.

21 (c–d) *tota re perspecta*] The whole matter being clearly had in view. A Scots law phrase. Trayner, *Latin maxims.* Also used in *SL* xi. 150 and in *Guy Mannering*, chap. 49.

21 (e) proof-print of the late Lord Melville] I have not found this at Abbotsford.

23 (f) Lucca 1553] Read 'Lucca 1554.' See my note to *SL* ii. 541 *n.*

24 *n.* 1] The quotation from Hadden is a garbled version. And there should have been a note on *Glencoe* which, Scott says, 'I am very glad you like.' According to Hadden, Thomson, in his letter, had expressed dissatisfaction with it.

25 (e) the poem] *The minstrel.*

26 (e) To C. K. Sharpe] In reply to his letter of 26 Nov. (*Sharpe's Letters*, i. 500–4.)

26 (f) the Brazen Head] See *SL* v. 446 *n.*

26 (f) R. Allan] Read 'R. Allen.'

26 *n.* 1] Delete and substitute: *The perplex'd Prince*, 12mo London, Printed for R. Allen, n.d.

27 (c) "Fugitive Statesman"] *The fugitive statesman, in requital for the Perplex'd Prince*, 12mo London, Printed by A. Grover, 1683.

27 (d) "The Life and Heroic Action..."] Correct title is: *An historical account of the heroick life and magnanimous actions of the most illustrious Protestant Prince, James Duke of Monmouth*, etc. 12mo London, Thomas Malthus, 1683.

27 (e) provide you] Read 'provide[d] you.'

27 (e) the legend of the "Black Box"] The black box which was said to contain the marriage certificate of Charles II and Lucy Walter. See Scott's *Dryden*, ix. 253; Macaulay, *History of England*, i. 251.

27 (f) as Shakespeare's clown says] In *Titus Andronicus*, IV. 4.

28 (a) your second query] This was: 'Did you ever fall in with an older poem than that of Ramsay on Bessie Bell and Mary Gray which concludes with this stanza: "They thought to lie in Methven kirk-yard / Amang their royal kin, / But they maun lie in Stronach Haugh / To beik fornent the sin."' (*Sharpe's Letters*, i. 503–4.) In a note contributed by Sharpe in *Johnson*, new ed., 1853, iv. *203, he gives this stanza as 'another stanza of the old

song remembered in Perthshire.' 'Messen kirkyard' is substituted for 'Methven kirkyard,' but this is probably a misprint. The stanza quoted by Sharpe is the same as the one in the exhibition catalogue (see next note). Did Sharpe get the stanza from the catalogue or did he learn it from another source?

28 (c) they must have been in that for 1810] Scott's supposition is correct. They are in *Third public exhibition of paintings, &c. in Scotland . . . [Edinburgh] April 9, 1810*, 4to Edinburgh, 1810, No. 198. Scott was wrong in correcting Sharpe. In the catalogue the line is given as 'But they maun lye in Stronach Haugh.'

28 (e) As for your amicable debate] Sharpe had written: 'How I grieve that I once in your classical mansion shocked his Presbyterian spirit with praises of Lord Dundee and the other persecutors of the primitive Whigs. He thought me in a state of utter reprobation' (*Sharpe's Letters*, i. 503).

29 (a) Patagonian baby] Lady Hood was of large stature. For Sharpe's 'raillery,' see *Sharpe's Letters*, i. 502.

29 (e) seventh volume of Somers] In his reply of 14 Dec. Surtees says he has never received Vols. 4 and 6. Taylor, *Memoir of Robert Surtees*, p. 117.

29 (f) family of Ogle] For Mrs Ogle, see Index. 'Prideaux's connections' was not coined by Scott but by Lady Margaret Fordyce. See Stuart, *Letters*, i. 211, 214. Ballantyne printed *An account of the family of Ogle; and of their estates and possessions in the county of Northumberland*, the privately printed work to which Scott refers.

31 (a) Jacobite tunes] See also below, p. 257 and my note.

31 (c) To Miss Smith] She had written from Liverpool on 23 Sept. 1811 (NLS MS. 3881, ff. 69–70).

32 (a) when you were butchered there] This probably refers to 27 July 1807 when Miss Smith played Desdemona. Dibdin, *Annals*, p. 251, does not say who played Othello.

32 (a) Daniel Terry] From the way Scott writes it looks as if he had forgotten that Sarah Smith had met Terry in Liverpool (*SL* ii. 471 *n.*).

32 (c) boat-song] The music was by Sir Henry R. Bishop.

32 (e) To Henry Weber] The date, I think, is 25 May.

35 (b) To Joanna Baillie] She replied on 2 Jan. 1812. A brief extract is in Partington, *Post-bag*, pp. 78–9.

35 (f) the iron and the earthen pitchers] See L'Estrange, *Fables*, No. 229: 'Two pots.' By Avianus. Also quoted in *The Bride of Lammermoor*, chap. 1.

35 (f) Tis mirk midnight] Scott cancelled the lines, thinking they were too close to a song in Joanna Baillie's *Orra*, III. 1. See also below, pp. 59 *n.*, 61, 199.

36 (b) Osterloo] An imperial general, a character in Joanna Baillie's *The dream*.

36 (b) a petty prince of Italy] Duke of Ferrara. *Lockhart* (iii. 352 *n.*) says the story is told by Montaigne.

36 (d) the comedy and the Beacon] *The siege; a comedy* and *The beacon; a serious musical drama*.

36 (d) my purse] This red knitted purse with a silver mouthpiece supplied by Scott may be seen in the Library at Abbotsford.

38 (e) an Israelite without guile] *Bible, John* 1: 47.

38 (f) the lady] Miss Wight. See below, p. 62 and my note.

39 (b) verses of our good friend Mr. Coxe] See *SL* ii. 527 (c).

39 (e) the Bantling at Rokeby] For an account of this, see extract from Morritt's letter of 8 Dec., in which he tells of the experience of Mrs Charlton at Rokeby, in Partington, *Post-bag*, p. 76.

39 (e) My wife had once . . .] This story proves that Sophia was born at Lasswade and not in Edinburgh as Scott recorded in the family Bible. The *Scots Mag.* Vol. 61 (1799), p. 908, recorded the births of a son to Mrs Dundas of Arniston and a daughter to Mrs Walter Scott, both on 22 Oct.; but if Sophia was the second birth and after midnight the date would be 23, not 24 as is usually given. Anne was born on 2 Feb. 1803 but Mrs Dundas had no child at that time.

39 *n.* 2] For '1758–1829' read '1758–1819.'

40 (c) Bob Acres] Sheridan, *The rivals*. It was David, however, who said this about his honour. See my note to *SL* ii. 73 (e).

41 (b) yeomans service] Shakespeare, *Hamlet*, V. 2.

41 (c) my poor old nurse] Scott (*Lockhart*, i. 20 *n.*) says she died in 1810.

41 (d) Dogberry] Shakespeare, *Much ado about nothing*, IV. 2.

42 (a) To Dr. Clarke Whitfeld] In line 11 for 'any' read 'my'; in line 17 for 'guts' read 'reels'; in line 19 for 'natural' read 'national'. Dr Clarke replied on 5 Jan. 1812 (NLS MS. 3882, ff. 20–1). He says it was not himself but his daughter Marianne who had met Lord Clarendon and that the 'friend' (in last paragraph of Scott's letter) was James Broadwood, the pianoforte manufacturer, who had heard about the Edinburgh Chair of Music from Sir George Smart who had by this time left Edinburgh. (For Sir George Thomas Smart, see *DNB*.)

42 (a) musical professorship] The Reid Chair of Music founded by General John Reid. He died in 1807 but the Chair was not founded till 1839. See Sir Alexander Grant, *The story of the University of Edinburgh*, Edinburgh, 1884, i. 348–54, 382–4.

42 (d) *keeping our own fishguts . . .*] Kelly, p. 118; Ramsay, *Proverbs*, p. 41.

42 (e) Miss Clarke] Marianne, Dr Clarke's daughter.

43 (a–b) The chough & crow . . .] *Orra*, III. 1.

43 (d) To M. W. Hartstonge] This letter is out of order. It should be placed under the date of its postscript, 5 Jan. 1812.

43 *n.* 1] In line 6, for 'a form' read 'three letters and a poem by Swift.' In line 10, 'General Plunkett' should be 'Plunket, the late Attorney-General.' Plunket's wife had two brothers and Hartstonge's letter shows he is referring to the younger, William James MacCausland, who was an Attorney in Dublin. (NLS MS. 881, ff. 82–5.)

44 (a–b) a knoll to which they shall give a name] There was no plantation named after Hartstonge.

44 (b) endeavouring to trim your Laurels] *Minstrelsy of Erin*.

44 (d–e) Mr. Tickell . . . Mr. Steele] Scott's letters to these correspondents are not in *SL*. They may never have been written. See below, p. 47.

45 (a) Wilsons affidavit] For account of Wilson's alleged attack on Swift, see Scott's *Swift*, 2nd ed., xix. 258–61. The affidavit is given in a footnote, 259–60. For the text of affidavit of Richard Brennan, Swift's servant, see letter from Maxwell B. Gold in *Times Lit. Suppl.* for 17 May 1934, p. 360.

45 (c) the square Box] See above, p. 11 and my note.

46 (a) brazen utensil] Sent by Rev. Robert Douglas. For Scott's letter to Douglas, see *SL* xii. 409–10.

46 (b) Benvier] Robertson's letter of 5 Nov. (NLS MS. 3881, ff. 105–6) shows that his name was Herview. He was a French refugee studying medicine at Edinburgh and he took his M.D. in 1812.

46 (d) a Scotch lady of the name of Moray] This should be Stuart, not Moray. The Bishop married Jane Stuart, granddaughter of Francis Stuart, 7th Earl of Moray.

46 *n.* 1] See also *John Hookham Frere and his friends*, by Gabrielle Festing, London, 1899, pp. 156–8.

47 (d) To George Thomson] The date is taken from Hadden's *George Thomson*, p. 164. There is no other evidence for this date.

47 (f) To the Duke of Buccleuch] The familiar tone of this letter shows that it could never have been written to the 3rd Duke. It was written to the 4th Duke and the correct date is Tuesday, 28 Dec. 1813. The reference to 5 Jan. is to the ball at Dalkeith House on Twelfth Night, 5 Jan. 1814. See below, pp. 398, 400.

48 (b) Mrs. Siddons] I have failed to find any other reference to this snuff-box. According to the *Edinburgh Evening Courant*, 12 June 1784, she was presented with an elegant silver tea vase, inscribed 'As a mark of esteem for

superior genius and unrivalled talents
. . . 9 June 1784.'

48 (d) Boswells . . . Johnson] The dispute between Beauclerk and Johnson
was over Hackman who shot Miss
Ray. See also *Minstrelsy* (ed. Henderson), iv. 8.

48 (d) a pound of snuff at my expence]
Scott must have already confessed that
he was wrong, for Cuthill wrote on
27 Dec. 1813 (NLS MS. 3884, f. 314)
saying the Duke was pleased that he
had won the bet but that he would not
claim the pound of snuff for what was
sold in Edinburgh as snuff was *not* snuff.
Scott later evidently found out that he
was right; hence this letter.

50 (c–d) £2800] An error for £1800,
the sum (excluding £100 interest)
given below, p. 321.

51 (e) To the situation of the deceased]
When McLeay, an Extractor in Scott's
office, died in 1808 Scott could have
appointed Tom, but he appointed
William Carmichael in March. On
4 Apr. 1808 Alexander Stevenson,
Deputy Clerk, died and Scott appointed
William Pringle, an Extractor, in his
place. The extractorship, thus vacant,
was given to Tom.

53 (b) to throw stones] See *SL* ii. 60.

54 (a) which connected me with good
company] The distinction between a
'man of letters' and a 'gentleman' is
more fully elaborated in his 'Essay on
imitations of the ancient ballad' (1830)
in *Minstrelsy* (ed. Henderson), iv. 21–2.

57 (b) a Scotch phrase *as bare as the birk
tree at Yule-even*] Ramsay, *Proverbs*, p. 25.

57 (b) facturae nepotibus umbram]
See above, p. 16.

57 (c) Lewis to Swift] See Scott's
Swift, 2nd ed., xix. 309 *n.*

57 (d) a certain square box] See above,
p. 11 and my note.

58 (c) Bishop of Dromore] George
Hall. He died at Dublin, 21 Nov.
1811, a few days after he had been
consecrated Bishop of Dromore.

58 *n.* 1] Delete 'Probably his.' The
work, in spite of what Scott says, was
printed by Ballantyne.

59 (a–b) I shall certainly expect the
sum] i.e. 3,000 guineas mentioned in

footnote. But Scott had already told
Erskine on 2 June 1811 that he had
been offered this sum (*SL* ii. 501).

59 (d) Sindbads Old man of the sea]
See my note to *SL* i. 369 (b).

59 (d) Mr. Bankes late superannuation
act] See *SL* ii. 448.

59 *n.* 1] For the poem cast into the fire,
see above, pp. 35–6 and below, p. 61.

61 (c) As for my *song*] See above,
pp. 35–6 and 59 *n.*

61 (c–d) dress from your one] Read
'dross from your ore.' (Corrected in
SL xii. 488.)

62 (a) *Mar him*] Timothy Marr, who
kept a lace and pelisse warehouse at
29 Radcliff-highway, London, was
murdered on 9 Dec. 1811 along with
his wife, Celia Marr, a baby four
months old and a shop boy named
James Biggs. (*Edin. Ann. Reg. for 1811*,
IV. ii. 206–11.) Scott alludes to this
in 'Preface to third edition' of *Waverley*.

62 (c) Duchess of Buccleuch] *The
Duchess of Buccleuch* (William Beatson,
Master) arrived in London on 2 Aug.
1775. (*Public Advertiser*, 3 Aug. 1775,
p. [4], c. 1.)

62 *n.* 1] Dr Wight had, in 1775, seven
sisters and I do not know which one
was Scott's companion.

63 (d–e) To Robert Shortreed] Without
Shortreed's letter (which is not in NLS)
it is difficult to date Scott's letter. It
cannot be 1812 as Scott has just attended
the Duke's funeral and the Earl of Dalkeith could not be in London at this
time. If Dr Elliot is John Elliot of Redheugh, Scott's letter cannot be later
than 18 Jan. 1809 as Dr Elliot died
in that year. Dr Elliot left no family
and 'his grandson' should probably be
'his nephew, Robert Elliot.'

65 (a) I knew his brother] James
Oswald.

65 (b) projected rail-way] Murray
approved of it. See his reply of 27 Jan.
1812 in Partington, *Post-bag*, p. 80.

65 *n.* 1] This note should have been
given above, p. 10.

66 (c) Arroyo Molinos] For an account
of the battle see *Edin. Ann. Reg. for
1811*, IV. i. 333–5 [by Robert Southey].

Scott said he was keeping Cadogan's letter for the *Register* (below, pp. 67, 76), and some details in Southey's account suggest that he was indebted to Cadogan.

67 *n.* 1] I have not seen a copy of *Catalonia*. It was published by John Ballantyne and may have the Edinburgh imprint and not London as given in this note. The work was dedicated to Scott.

68 (d) "sadly sitting on the sea-beat shore"] John Home, *Douglas*, III. 1.

68 (d) I have sent the advertizement] In her letter of 8 Jan. 1812 (NLS MS. 3882, ff. 28–9), which Scott is here answering, Mrs Clephane says she has a farm to let and wants Scott to send the advertisement to her lawyer, James Thomson, W.S. This she had discussed when at Ashiestiel and Laidlaw had agreed to accept offers. Her last visit to Ashiestiel, so far as I know, was in Sept. 1810. The employment of Laidlaw, who might be either William Laidlaw or Robert Laidlaw of Peel, suggests that the farm was in the Borders but there is no mention anywhere in the correspondence of Mrs Clephane having a farm there. If the farm were in Mull or Fife it seems odd to select either of these Laidlaws as acceptors.

68 (e) Russian trade] A treaty of peace with Russia was signed in July 1812 and Russian ports opened to British vessels.

69 (a) lovely isle] Read 'lonely isle.'

69 (c) days of murder and street robbery] See above, pp. 61–2.

70 (b) To Joseph Train] This letter belongs to 1815 as reference to *The Lord of the Isles* shows. (Date corrected in *SL* xii. 487.)

70 (c) "therein the patient must minister to himself"] Shakespeare, *Macbeth*, V. 3.

71 (f) the Architect] William Stark.

73 (d) a *hedge* about his friends] See *SL* i. 119 *n.* and my note.

76 (a) like Dog-berry] Shakespeare, *Much ado about nothing*, IV. 2.

76 (e) Arroyo Molinos] See my note to *SL* iii. 66 (c).

77 (a) Cowper] *The task*, Bk II, *The time-piece*, line 394: 'On skulls that cannot teach, and will not learn.'

77 (b) Sir Edward Pellew's naval secretary] Edward Hawke Locker. See above, p. 67, 67 *n.* 1 and my note.

77 (c) the Gods to make poetical] Shakespeare, *As you like it*, III. 3.

77 (d) Adelantado] This may be a misreading for 'Adalantado,' a title for a Spanish governor, or Scott may be referring to the Duke del Infantado who was very pro-British.

77 (e) King William] See my note to *SL* ii. 474 (f).

78 (b) politics like misery] Shakespeare, *The tempest*, II. 2: 'Misery acquaints a man with strange bedfellows.'

79 (c–d) Walter the Devil] Not identified; but he seems to be the same Walter Scott called Walter the Devil in *SL* vi. 113 and Wat the Devil, whose raids into England are referred to in *Rob Roy*, chap. 4.

79 *n.* 1] Southey reviewed *Count Julian* in *QR*, Vol. 8, No. 15, for Sept. 1812. (*Shine*, No. 211.)

80 (b) To James Ellis] The original ALS was presented to Abbotsford in Aug. 1970. It shows trifling variations of spelling and the only misreadings are: p. 83, line 6, for 'feeling' read 'finding' and in line 7 for 'a freedom' read 'a little freedom.' Grierson's text is virtually identical with the text in *Letters between James Ellis Esq. & Walter Scott Esq.*, Newcastle-upon-Tyne, 1850, pp. 15–19. The letter, which Scott is answering, is printed, ibid., pp. 11–15.

80 *n.* 1] *Confession of John Weire, prisoner in Edinburgh, under sentence of death, July 25, 1701* is printed in *The Border antiquities*, Vol. 2 (1817), Appendix, pp. xciv–ci. It was contributed by Scott from a document supplied by James Ellis. See also *SL* iii. 245, 245 (e).

82 (b) Depend upon my correcting the passage] Scott did so by cancelling and reprinting several pages in the 5th ed., 1812.

82 (e) the curious poem] *Cheviot*, a poem in heroic couplets by R. W., printed in 1817. See *Letters between James Ellis,*

Esq. & Walter Scott, Esq., Newcastle-upon-Tyne, 1850, pp. 14–15, 26.

83 (f) your poem] *The deserted village school,* printed by James Ballantyne and published by John Ballantyne in 1813. See *Letters of Sir Walter Scott; addressed to the Rev. R. Polwhele,* etc., p. 44.

84 (a) damning of a tragedy] This was *Helga,* by Sir George Steuart Mackenzie, 7th Bart. of Coul. The prologue, written by Scott, was printed in the *Scots Mag.* Vol. 74 (Feb. 1812), pp. 134–5.

85 (a) say with Mrs. Quickly] Shakespeare, *Merry wives of Windsor,* I. 4.

85 (c) "in fancy ripe, in reason rotten"] *The nymph's reply* [ascribed to Sir Walter Raleigh] st. [4] line 4: 'In folly ripe, in reason rotten.' The 'Reply' is to *The passionate shepherd to his lover* [ascribed to Christopher Marlowe]. Both poems are in Percy's *Reliques.*

85 (e) a certain lawsuit] Mrs Bell sued her husband for £600 aliment. The case was dismissed, it being held that a wife could not sue for aliment during the voluntary separation of husband and wife. The case was decided on 22 Feb. 1812. Bell and his wife had been separated since 1806. The source from which Scott's letter is printed is unreliable. If Abbotsford is correct he must have written the letter, below p. 88, in Edinburgh before he set off for Abbotsford but by 29 Feb. he should have known the result of the Bell lawsuit.

86 (b) Mr. George Baillie] He did not, however, retire and continued M.P. till 1818. Robertson did not stand and Baillie was returned unopposed.

86 (c–d) Mr. Scott of Harden] When Hugh Scott, Younger of Harden, he had been M.P. for Berwickshire 1780–4. He did not stand in 1812.

86 (f) habits of business] This opinion does not tally with Scott's opinion given elsewhere, e.g. *SL* iv. 349–50.

87 (e) George Home] An error for George Baillie?

88 (c) throwing my money] A reminiscence of the *Bible, Ecclesiastes* 11: 1: 'Cast thy bread upon the waters; for thou shalt find it after many days.'

88 (e) your Memorabilia] i.e. local information for *Rokeby,* given by Morritt in his letter of 28 Dec. 1811 (*Lockhart,* iii. 372–81).

88 (f) brighten the chain of freindship] See *SL* ii. 535 and my note.

89 (c) Lady Aberdeens . . . Lord Hamilton] Catherine Hamilton, daughter of Lord Abercorn and wife of 4th Earl of Aberdeen. She died on 29 Feb. 1812. Her brother Lord Hamilton died 27 May 1814.

90 (a) man proposes and God disposes] Origin doubtful and usually regarded as a proverb.

90 (c) Boldero's house] Lushington, Boldero and Co., London bankers, stopped payment on 2 Jan. 1812. (*Gentleman's Mag.* lxxxii. 81–2.)

91 (a) To Duchess of Buccleuch] This letter is redated 1813 in *SL* xii. 487.

91 (c) Mr. MacDonald] James Macdonald, the Duke's gardener at Dalkeith Palace.

91 (d) like Master Justice Shallow] Shakespeare, *II Henry IV,* V. 3.

91 (f) Lady Isabella . . .] These are four children of the Duchess: Lady Isabella Mary, who married P. F. Cust in 1823; Walter Francis, who became 5th Duke in 1819; Lord John Scott, 3rd son; and Lady Margaret, afterwards Countess of Romney. Scott was godfather by proxy to last.

93 (b) beautiful verses] See *SL* ii. 425, 425 *n.* and my note.

93 *n.* 1] In line 4, 'a Norman French ballad in the British Museum' refers to Scott's translation, *On the death of Simon de Montfort, Earl of Leicester, at the Battle of Evesham, 1266,* which was included in Ritson's *A select collection of English songs,* 2nd ed., London, 1813, ii. 380–4. Scott's translation was reprinted, from this source, in *Blackwood,* Vol. 17 (Apr. 1825), pp. 484–5. For another translation done for Ritson, see *SL* i. 199. The correct title in para. 2 is: *A select collection of English songs . . . By the late Joseph Ritson . . . The second edition with additional songs and occasional notes by Thomas Park.*

94 (b) *jus quæsitum*] An acquired or vested right. A Scots law phrase. See Trayner, *Latin maxims.*

95 (a) Ellis . . . says] In a letter of 22 Feb. 1812 in *Letters between James Ellis, Esq. & Walter Scott, Esq.*, 12mo Newcastle-upon-Tyne, 1850, pp. 11–15. See above, p. 80 and my notes.

95 (f) To Mrs. Apreece] There is an extract from her letter of 1 Apr. 1812 in Partington, *Post-bag*, p. 86.

96 (e) *Hawick Arch. Soc.*] Add: *Trans.* 1921, p. 23.

98 (e) "stoop to the forward and the bold"] Edmund Waller, *Of love*, line 14. In Ellis, *Specimens of the early English poets*, London, 1801, iii. 166.

98 (e) Dryden] *Epistle dedicatory* to *The Spanish friar*. In Scott's *Dryden*, vi. 376: 'that I knew they were bad enough to please, even when I wrote them.'

99 (d) The Doctors . . . attendance] Dr Matthew Baillie, Joanna's brother.

99 n. 1] The letter of 4 Mar. which Scott is answering is printed in part in *FL* i. 245–7. Grierson's extract does not make sense. The purse was not of frosted silver. It was made of red silk. The opening piece of silver had been given to her by Scott.

100 (c) "primroses paint the gay plain"] Allan Ramsay, *The yellow-hair'd laddie*. This is the version beginning: 'In April, when primroses paint the sweet plain.' In Ramsay, *Tea-table miscellany*; also in *Herd*, i. 298, and in *Johnson*, Vol. 2 (1788), No. 122, and in many other collections.

101 (c) as Elbow says] An error for Dogberry. Shakespeare, *Much ado about nothing*, IV. 2.

101 (e) the young Cantab] I cannot identify him. Joanna Baillie, in her letter of 1 Mar. 1812 (NLS MS. 3882, ff. 99–102), merely says he is a mathematician and 'son to a great Philosopher of this country.'

101 n. 1] Her farewell address on 13 Mar. to her *Edinburgh* audience is not inconsistent with a farewell address to her *London* audience on 29 June as Grierson hints. Terry was present on the latter occasion. See his letter of 30 June to Scott in Partington, *Letterbooks*, pp. 23–5.

101 n. 2] In lines 3–4, delete 'I cannot

trace his excursion into drama.' His play was *Helga*.

102 (a) Miss Eliz. Baillie] Elizabeth Margaret Baillie, daughter of Dr Matthew Baillie and, therefore, niece of Joanna.

102 (b) Cuthullin] Cuchulain, hero of Irish mythology of 1st cent. A.D. Cuthullin is the spelling in Macpherson's *Ossian*.

102 (c) This may rival the Ministers flax] For meaning, see Joanna Baillie's letter in *FL* i. 245.

102 n. 1] For 'note 2 U to *Rokeby*' read 'note to *Rokeby*, Canto IV, st. xiv.'

103 (f) a Tale of the Civil War] *Rokeby*.

104 (a) allied to my own] See suggested amendment in *SL* xii. 488.

104 (a–b) Old Macbeth] Scott spells his name MacBeath (*SL* v. 151), but he appears as a witness in 1815 as John M'Beith (*Chisholm*, p. 202).

104 (d) O'Neal of the nine hostages] See Nial above, p. 102 and note.

104 (e) Trumpet and Church Bell] Hartstonge accepted all Scott's changes and reprinted the poem verbatim from the *Edin. Ann. Reg.* in his *Minstrelsy of Erin*, pp. 47–52.

105 (b–c) the Forest] Borris Wood in co. Carlow. (Hartstonge's letter of 27 Nov. 1811. NLS MS. 881, f. 82.)

105 (e) Mr. Gassard's Cook-Maid] Hartstonge in his letter of 28 Feb. (NLS MS. 3882, ff. 85–6) says nothing about this.

107 (a) your Volume] i.e. *Minstrelsy of Erin*.

108 (a) hardly venture to enter into a personal correspondence] Scott had already corresponded with Brydges, 5 May 1807 (*SL* xii. 388–9), but that is his only letter in *SL*. Scott did, however, write later in the year (about 25 Nov.) as is shown by a letter from Brydges to R. P. Gillies (Gillies, *Memoirs*, ii. 110).

108 (e) untaught philosopher] Robert Laidlaw, tenant in Peel. See *SL* vii. 44.

109 (b) Go . . . and do likewise] *Bible*, *Luke* 10: 37.

109 (d) *Gillies's Memoirs*] Add: ii. 77–9.

111 (d) Justice Clerk] David Boyle.

111 (d) prisoners . . . at Selkirk] There is a MS. of 132 pp. in Selkirk Public Library containing names of borrowers and titles of books borrowed by French prisoners of war, Apr. 1811–Mar. 1814.

111 (e) the Sheriffs of Roxburgh and Selkirk] Scott's fears were justified. The three troops were the Eastern and Western Troops of the Roxburgh-shire Yeomanry, and the Selkirkshire Yeomanry, totalling only 159 men. (*Trans. Hawick Arch. Soc.* 1915, pp. 36 and 50.)

111 n. 1] For 'Kinrora' read 'Kinrara.'

112 (d) late increase of Lord H.'s family] Lady Harriet Hamilton, born 12 Apr. 1812. In 1836 she married William Alexander Baillie-Hamilton, grand-nephew of 7th Earl of Hadding-ton.

112 (d) poor Lord Aberdn.] Lord Aberdeen's wife, daughter of 1st Mar-quess of Abercorn, had died on 29 Feb. 1812.

112 (e) To James Ballantyne] Grierson's dating 'May–June' is too early. The let-ter is printed in Gilbert Goudie, *David Laing*, Edinburgh, 1913, pp. 250–1, from the original which had the Mel-rose postmark. The letter, therefore, was written at Abbotsford in July after the Courts rose. Scott had received the adverse verdict of Ballantyne and Erskine by 19 July (*SL* i. 417), which would date Scott's letter mid July.

113 (a) in my way as the Gudemans mother] Ramsay, *Proverbs*, p. 76.

113 (c) celebrated question of the black and white horses] This is probably Pope's *Debate upon black and white horses* (Swift's *Works*, ed. Scott, 2nd ed., xiii. 138–42).

113 (c) Benkerschorkius and Pagen-stecherus] Dutch jurists, Cornelius van Bynkershoek and J. F. W. Pagenstecher. The latter is quoted by King James in *Nigel*, chap. 31.

113 n. 1] In line 3, for '*op. cit.*' read '*Private letter-books.*'

115 (a) Edinr. Review] Jeffrey had reviewed *Childe Harold* in Vol. 19 (Feb. 1812), pp. 466–77.

115 (d) To Miss Clephane] Margaret.

116 (f) like Vanburghs house] Scott must be referring to Swift's *Vanbrugh's house* (Scott's *Swift*, 2nd ed., xiv. 80), but there is nothing in the poem cor-responding to 'clinking of noise.'

117 (b) She sate like a pistol . . .] Christopher Anstey, *An election ball*, Letter II, lines 17–20. Quoted in *Journal*, 26 Feb. 1829. As the original has 'pillow-beer', why does Grierson substitute 'case' which does not rhyme?

117 (c) Miss Jane Anne] i.e. Miss Anna Jane.

117 (d) To the Duchess of Buccleuch] This letter is printed in part in *FL* i. 321–2 where it is misdated Mar. 1814.

117 (e) "We have not seen so much . . ."] Buckingham, *The rehearsal*, V. 1.

117 n. 1] Ditton Park was destroyed by fire on Tuesday, 28 Apr. It is stated in *N. & Q.* 8th ser. vii. 303 that 'many' letters from Scott were de-stroyed. In the Walpole Coll. in NLS there are 6 letters from Montagu to Scott, 1806–8, but the earliest letter from Scott in *SL* is for 1814.

119 (b) Mark Pringle] Mark Pringle of Clifton and Haining died on 25 Apr. 1812.

119 n. 1] The verses (NLS MS. 3882, ff. 145–8) were headed 'Introduction to Book Second September 1811' and were printed as *Fragment* in his *Childe Alarique*.

120 (a) the Vicar of Wakefield] Gold-smith, *The Vicar of Wakefield*, chap. 1: 'from the blue bed to the brown.'

120 (b) Sir Egerton Brydges . . . whose domestic calamity] His sixth son, Grey Matthew Brydges, a midshipman on H.M.S. *Malta*, died at Minorca in Feb. Brydges refers to this 'dreadful loss . . . in the Spring' in a letter to R. P. Gillies, 28 Nov. 1812. (Gillies, *Memoirs*, ii. 112.) See also my note to *SL* iii. 108 (a).

120 (f) Crabbe says somewhere, "As labour lets, we live."] *The borough*, Letter IX, line 9: ''tis labour, but we live.'

121 (a) copy of Douce's unique romance of Vergilius] *Virgilius. This boke treateth of the lyfe of Virgilius, and of his deth*, etc., 8vo London repr., 1812. This had a preface by E. V. Utterson.

121 (b) *Gillies's Memoirs*] Add: ii. 80–2.

121 (c) your . . . catalogue] Of over 15,000 vols. for sale. See Oliphant, *William Blackwood*, i. 27–30.

123 (a) To Lady Alvanley] This is obviously part of the same letter as on previous page which should not have been split into two.

123 (a) Miss Smith] Sarah Smith's first appearance this year was on 16 May. Her benefit night was Wednesday, 27 May when she recited Collins's *Ode to the passions.*

123 (f) Lord Chamberlain] 2nd Marquess of Hertford, appointed 5 Mar. 1812.

125 (a) I had your letter] Of 30 May. An extract is given in Partington, *Post-bag*, pp. 86–7.

125 (c) Canning and Wellesley] Canning was never in Perceval's administration and Wellesley was superseded as Foreign Secretary in Mar. In the new ministry (formed by Liverpool in June 1812) Canning became a member of the cabinet in 1816 and Wellesley joined it as Lord Lieutenant of Ireland in 1821 but without a cabinet seat.

126 (c) the Review] *Edinburgh Review*. See Partington, *Post-bag*, pp. 86–7 and *ER* xviii. 390 *n.*, 421 *n.*

126 (c) the Chamberlain] 2nd Marquess of Hertford.

126 *n.* 1] A fuller extract on Botany Bay etc. is in Partington, *Post-bag*, pp. 87–8. In line 8, for 'last sentence' read 'second last paragraph.'

127 (e) To Daniel Terry] Terry replied on 30 June reporting that he had delivered the letters to Heber and Joanna Baillie. See Partington, *Letter-books*, pp. 23–5. *Lockhart* (iv. 5–6, the source of Grierson's text) must have omitted the reference to Heber. Scott's letter to Heber of 11 June, which is in *SL* xii. 335–6, says: 'This will be delivered to you by Mr. Terry.'

128 (e) Marnock] This should be Marnoch.

128 *n.* 1] The tombstone is still on the right-hand side of the road leading to the stables.

129 (a) Mr. Hay] From Sharpe's letter

to Scott, 10 June 1812, we learn that Mr Hay is John Hay, afterwards Sir John Hay, 6th Bart. of Haystoun. See *Sharpe's Letters*, i. 545.

130 (b) Chronicle of the reign of James II] This was among the Auchinleck MSS. and was sent to Thomson by Sir Alexander Boswell. See Cosmo Innes, *Memoir of Thomas Thomson*, [Bannatyne Club] 1854, pp. 127–8.

130 (c) King's declaration to Parliamt.] King James V's Declaration, 6 July [1528], following the Battle of Melrose, 1526, is printed in Sir William Fraser, *The Scotts of Buccleuch*, Edinburgh, 1878, ii. 151–2. The exact words, which Scott quotes in this letter, are 'ane leadern cote and ane blak bonet on his heid.' He also quotes these words in *The Border antiquities*, Appendix II, p. xv, in *SL* iv. 468, and in *Tales of a grandfather*, chap. 26 (*MPW* xxiii. 6).

130 (e) knocked him on the head like a second Jael] *Bible, Judges* 4: 21. See also below, p. 143.

130 *n.* 1] Delete this note which copies the inaccurate entry in *ALC*. The editor's name is not given in the work. The correct title is: *A short chronicle of the reign of James the Second King of Scots.* [Ed. by Thomas Thomson.] 4to [Edinburgh, 1819.]

131 (b) *Sharpe's Letters*] Add: i. 547–9.

131 (c) To Miss C. Rutherford] The letter should be dated Thursday, 29 Oct. 1812. The General Election was held on Monday, 2 Nov. and the Thursday before that was 29 Oct. Peter apparently brought back word that she could not come to Abbotsford and Scott wrote again on 3 Nov. (below, pp. 192–3).

131 (c) Jane] Jane Russell, Scott's cousin.

131 (e) twenty other As's] Shakespeare, *Hamlet*, V. 2.

131 (f) the counseller] William Erskine.

131 *n.* 1] Delete this note, which is not now applicable.

132 (c) To Miss Clephane] Margaret.

133 (c) Fludjer] Read 'Fludyer.'

135 *n.* 1] Murray's letter is in Smiles, *John Murray*, i. 213–14.

135 *n.* 3] Add reference for D'Israeli: i. 208–10.

136 (b) for Heber and another for Thos. Park] The letter of 1 July to Heber is in *SL* xii. 336–7. The letter to Park is not in *SL*.

137 (e–f) Esurit, intactam . . .] Juvenal, *Satires*, VII. 87: 'Esurit, intactum Paridi nisi vendat Agaven.'

138 *n.* 1] Byron's letter of 6 July is in *Lockhart*, iii. 398–400.

139 (d) To C. K. Sharpe] For 'Kilpatrick' read 'Kirkpatrick'. The reference to Johnston's speech shows that this letter is later than the one below, p. 142.

140 (a) "more last words of the worthy Knight"] See below, p. 142 and *n.* 1.

140 (d–e) Jeffrey] Cf. above, p. 115.

141 (c) "Threadneedle Street has some charms"] This is a slip for Blowbladderstreet. In Foote's *Taste*, I. 1, Lady Pentweazel says: 'if . . . Blowbladderstreet has any charms.' Repeated by Puff at end of Act II. Scott quotes correctly in *SL* xi. 345.

141 (d) "its cloudy canopy"] Byron, *Childe Harold*, Canto I, st. 61, line 8.

141 (e) Ali Pacha's military court] Ali Pashaw. Byron, *Childe Harold*, Canto II, st. 72.

141 (e) Dogberry] See *SL* ii. 320.

142 (b) copy of the Chronicle] See above, pp. 129 *n.*, 130.

142 (b) declaration of the King] See above, p. 130.

143 (a) Sisera & Jael business] *Bible*, *Judges* 4: 21. See also above, p. 130.

143 (b) propensities . . . ascribed to Sappho & . . . to Madselle Hobart] See Anthony Hamilton's *Memoirs of Count Grammont*, Scott's ed., 1811, ii. 123–5.

143 (c) As to the Douglasses Chalmers has fallen into a great error] See Scott's note to chap. 37 of *The Monastery*.

143 (d) as Partridge says is a *gratis dictum*] I have failed to find this in Fielding's *Tom Jones*.

144 (f) Up in the air] Allan Ramsay, *Up in the air*, st. [1], lines 5–7. In *Teatable miscellany*. Sung by Madge Wildfire in *The Heart of Mid-Lothian*, chap. 18.

145 (c) Ohe jam satis] Horace, *Satires*, I. v. 12–13.

145 *n.* 3] Sharpe's genealogy differs from that in *Burke* under Queensberry. See also *Sharpe's Letters*, ii. 25–6.

147 *n.*] Scott and Galt met in London in Sept. 1831. There is another letter from Scott to him in *SL* x. 489.

148 *n.* 1] Galt's letter of 4 July is partly printed in Partington, *Post-bag*, pp. 90–1, where 'Greenock' is misprinted 'Newark.' The 'few stanzas in the Greenock paper' were *To Walter Scott, Esq. Author of Marmion*, printed in *Greenock Advertiser and Clyde & West Country Chronicle*, Vol. 7, Wednesday, 9 Mar. 1808. The MS. of this, showing variations from the printed version, is in the Watt Library, Greenock, having been presented in 1939 by Thomas P. Galt, grandson of John Galt.

149 (c) Roy] William Roy, a Franciscan friar, and Jerome Barlow wrote a satire in verse against Wolsey, printed in 1528. It begins: 'Rede me and bé nott wrothe / For I saye no thynge but trothe.'

150 (a) General Malcolm] See my note to *SL* xii. 334 (a).

150 *n.* 1] The queried date in line 9 is given as definitely 1816 in *SL* iv. 78 *n*.

151 (e–f) General Gowdie] Francis Goudie lived at Priorbank, Melrose. Mrs Hughes mentions him in 1824. (Hughes, *Letters*, p. 74.)

151 *n.* 1] *FL* is correct.

152 (a) officer who is at the head of the department] Charles Holland Hastings.

153 (d) To Daniel Terry] Scott is replying to Terry's letter of 7 Sept. (NLS MS. 3883, ff. 77–8) in which he lists a number of books in a bookseller's catalogue. Scott would receive Terry's letter about 10 Sept., which is probably the date of Scott's reply as he would want to waste no time if he were to secure the items chosen.

153 (e) Retford] Read 'Redford.' Redford was the tenant of Cartleyhole when Scott bought it. (See NLS MS. 1750, ff. 107–8.) There were a number of Redfords in Melrose parish but I have failed to find his Christian

name. Scott called the cottage 'Mother Redford,' no doubt punning on Mother Redcap. See *SL* iv. 335, v. 4, 63, vii. 159.

154 (a) Doctor's barn] The Rev. Robert Douglas, former owner of Abbotsford, had erected a large barn on the south side of the farm steading.

154 (a) building up the well] This well is in a field (still known as Fountain's Park) on the other side of the public road opposite Abbotsford House. Scott decorated it with stones from Melrose Abbey, but these stones are no longer there.

154 (c) John Cuthbertson] Probably Lockhart's misreading for Culbertson. The Culbertson family were blacksmiths for several generations in the Borders. See Tancred, *Rulewater*, p. 304.

155 (a) "The Dreamer"] i.e. Treatise on Dreams, mentioned on preceding page.

155 (b) a gallant son of the church] Rev. George Thomson.

155 (c) To Lady Abercorn] Her reply is printed in part in *FL* i. 258–9, where it is dated 'Sept. 1812'. The original MS. in NLS (MS. 3883, ff. 85–8) is dated 10 Sept.

155 (d) the Kembles] Kemble played in Addison's *Cato* at Theatre Royal, Edinburgh, 3 Aug. and in Shakespeare's *Coriolanus* on 5 Aug.

156 (d) Red glared the Beacon] James Hogg, *Lord Derwent*, st. [29]. In his *The mountain bard* (1807), p. 134. Also quoted in *The Antiquary* (motto to chap. 45).

157 (d) one of the young ladies] Lady Katherine Frances, 4th daughter, who died 6 June 1814.

157 (e) To James Ballantyne] Scott was at Edgerston on Friday 25 Sept. and this dates the letter.

157 (e) feelings *true*] This is in Canto I, st. II, line 12 of *Rokeby*.

159 (b) Collins] See my note to *SL* ii. 389 (d).

160 (a) To James Ballantyne] As this letter refers to Canto IV of *Rokeby*, date is about Nov.–Dec. 1812.

160 (b) We had been shooting &] This

should be '"We had been shooting &c." is a flat line.' This is line 19 of st. XXI of Canto IV of *Rokeby*.

160 (b) Sir Fretful] Sir Fretful Plagiary, a character in Sheridan's *The critic*.

160 (d) To William Laidlaw] The references to Laidlaw and planting show that 1812 is impossible. Part of the letter belongs to a letter of 21 Nov. 1818 (*SL* v. 226–7) and Carruthers has amalgamated it with a portion of another letter not known to be extant.

160 (e) George] Probably George Waynes.

162 (c) To Lady Louisa Stuart] Scott is answering her letter from Rokeby, 14 Sept. 1812. The letter begins with 52 lines of verse. The original is in NLS (MS. 3883, ff. 91–2). The complete text is in Stuart, *Gleanings*, iii. 224–7.

162 (c) I wrote to Morritt] The letter is not in *SL*.

162 (d) upon the 5th] i.e. on 5 Oct. The Head Court met on Tuesday, 6 Oct., at Jedburgh.

162 *n.* 1] Bindon in line 4 is Francis Bindon. The verses 'Mollis abuti', referred to in line 5 (Scott's *Swift*, 2nd ed., xiii. 476) were addressed to Samuel Bindon.

163 *n.* 2] See above, pp. 128–9.

164 (a) Capt. Scotts wound] Captain George Scott, R.N. (afterwards Admiral Sir George Scott), was Lady Douglas's son-in-law.

164 (a) Gothic front to a well] See my note to *SL* iii. 154 (a).

164 (b) some acres of ground] Scott did not acquire the side of Cauldshiels Loch till 1816 when he bought 90 acres from Nicol Milne.

164 (b) lake of the fisherman] *The story of the fisherman* in *The Arabian Nights* (Weber, *Tales of the East*, i. 23). Actually the description does not fit Cauldshiels Loch.

164 (e) "Have mercy mighty Duke . . ."] Shakespeare, *Henry V*, III. 2.

164 *n.* 1] Delete and refer to Index, under Abbotsford. II. Estate. (2) Separate Parts. Fountains Park.

165 (e) To James Ballantyne] Date of letter is 1 Nov., which was a Sunday.

'Tomorrow is the election' refers to the General Election on Monday, 2 Nov.

167 (a) sell all he has & bestow it on the poor] *Bible, Matthew* 19: 21; *Mark* 10: 21; *Luke* 18: 22.

168 (b–c) hewers of wood & drawers of water] *Bible, Joshua* 9: 21, 23.

169 (a) milliner] Mrs Gill. See *SL* i. 422.

169 (a) *Wednesday* [6 *October*, 1812]] Read 'Wednesday [7 October, 1812.]'

169 (b) Bold Heskets] Probably misreading for 'Robt Hesketh.'

169 (c) this accommodation] There is no mention of it in the letters. Scott probably arranged it during his recent visit to Rokeby.

170 (b) transeat quoth I cum cæteris erroribus] John Arbuthnot, *Law is a bottomless pit*, Pt 5, chap. 5. In Scott's *Swift*, 2nd ed., vi. 148.

170 (d) Burnfoot] Home of Sir John Malcolm's family in Dumfriesshire.

170 (d) Iskendiar Rustan] Persian hero in *Shahnameh* by Ferdusi, mentioned in next line.

170 (f) as Slender says] Shakespeare, *Merry wives of Windsor*, I. i.

170 *n*. 1] See Partington, *Post-bag*, pp. 93–4. Lockhart, as cited here, is merely taking his information from Morritt's letter.

172 (e) Woggarwolfs] Woggarwolfe is a character in Joanna Baillie's *Ethwald*.

172 *n*. 1] *Henriquez* was not included in the third series of *Plays on the passions*. It was first performed on 19 Mar. 1836 at Drury Lane when Vanderhoff took the part of Henriquez.

173 *n*. 1] The review was by John Wilson Croker (*Shine*, No. 196).

174 (a) a noble spring] See above, p. 154.

174 (d) Dogberry] See *SL* ii. 320.

175 (a) the lost engraving] See above, p. 161.

176 (c) "things must be as they may"] Shakespeare, *Henry V*, II. i.

177 (b) Dogberry] See *SL* ii. 320.

177 (b) Windsor forest] For Joanna Baillie's comments on the threatened disparking, see Partington, *Post-bag*, pp. 92–3.

177 *n*. 1] Delete this note which applies to the novels but not to the acknowledged poems.

178 (a) Johns Atlas] Presumably an atlas belonging to John Ballantyne.

178 (c) To James Ballantyne] Date is 20 Sept. 1812. (Only partially corrected in *SL* xii. 487.) Scott was to set out for Rokeby on Thursday, 24 Sept. The Sunday before that was 20 Sept.

179 (a) To John Ballantyne] The year is 1815. (Corrected in *SL* xii. 487.) The month is probably Oct. as indicated by the references to Sass and *Harold the Dauntless*. This letter follows a letter to John (*SL* i. 491) which, I think, should be dated 21 Oct.

179 *n*. 1] Delete this note. Scott is not referring to Bandello, but to François de Rosset, *Histoires tragiques*, as is shown by his words 'which you quote so well in your poems,' i.e. in his *Metrical legends* (1807) pp. 71–6. In 1808 Scott confessed that he had never seen a copy of Rosset (Scott's *Dryden*, vii. 9), but by 1812 he had acquired an imperfect copy referred to in this letter. This imperfect copy, 12mo Paris, 1615, was later discarded. It was offered for sale by Francis Edwards. (*N. & Q.* 10th ser. xi. 159.) Pp. 49–68 are wanting.

180 (d) "accommodate"] Shakespeare, *II Henry IV*, III. 2.

180 *n*. 1] Berguer was the author of *Stanzas, inscribed to Walter Scott, Esq.*, 4to Edinburgh, 1815, and of *Trifles in verse*, 8vo Edinburgh, 1817. Pp. 11–26 of the latter consist of *Stanzas, occasioned by a visit to Edinburgh in 1815, inscribed to Walter Scott, Esq*. There is no record of a meeting then. For suggested correction in the Latin quotation, see *SL* xii. 488.

181 (b) To George Crabbe] In the footnote it is stated that this is the third letter from Scott; but, from the contents, it is obviously the *first*. The two earlier letters, referred to, were written to Hatchard, not to Crabbe, but were shown by Hatchard to Crabbe. This is made quite clear from Crabbe's letter of 13 Oct. 1812 (*Lockhart*, iv. 29–30). There is a facsimile of Scott's letter in Symington, *Some unpublished letters,*

between p. 18 and p. 19, from which the text here can be corrected.

181 (d) Dodsley's Register] *Annual Register*, published by Dodsley.

181 *n*. 1] Crabbe's reply of 21 Dec. is in Partington, *Letter-books*, pp. 224–7.

182 (e) Abhorson's] Shakespeare, *Measure for measure*, IV. 2.

182 *n*. 1] We know that his uncle Robert bought the *Annual Register*. See *SL* i. 16.

183 (f) To James Ballantyne] There is a transcript of the rest of this letter in NLS (MS. 6080).

184 (e) a good engraver] The portrait by Bindon for Vol. 1 of Swift's *Works* was engraved by W. H. Lizars.

185 *n*. 1] This is impossible. Scott says he is 'ballasting this parcel with a poem', i.e. something bulkier than *The poacher* which was a small poem. Scott means *Don Roderick* which, as he says, was printed in the *Edin. Ann. Reg.*

186 (d) our Election] General Election on 2 Nov.

186 *n*. 1] The two quotations from Gillies's *Recollections* are from p. 143 and pp. 173–4 respectively.

187 (c) Jocky fou & Jenny *fain*] 'Jocky fou, Jenny fain' is the opening line of a song in Ramsay's *Tea-table miscellany*. Also in *Johnson*, Vol. 4 (1792), No. 381.

187 (d) the Vision] i.e. *The bridal of Triermain*, originally called *The vision of Triermain*.

188 (a) To James Ballantyne] On date, see next note.

188 (c) Fanny West] Probably Fanny Cooke, the actress, who had recently come to Edinburgh and married W. West of the Edinburgh Theatre Royal. Scott, it would seem, is asking Ballantyne to praise her in one of his dramatic criticisms. See *The Drama; or, Theatrical Pocket Mag.* Vol. 2, pp. 157–63 (with a portrait of Mrs West). The date of Scott's letter must be after 12 Nov. as the theatre opened for the winter season on that day.

190 (c) Siddons' last bowstring] The only fire in Bishop's Land about this time which I can find occurred on 14 Feb. 1813. (See *Edinburgh Evening Courant*, 15 Feb. 1813, p. 3, c. 4.) The copyist's memory (see *n*. 2 below) may have been at fault. From the wording of the letter I think Scott is not referring to an actual fire but to some spectacular representation of a fire in the Edinburgh Theatre which Scott calls 'Siddons' last bowstring,' i.e. a poor bid for popularity.

190 *n*. 2 Bishopsland] See preceding note.

191 (a) To James Ballantyne] As this letter refers to the proofs of the concluding stanzas of the poem, its date must be Jan. 1813. The second correction was made, but not the first.

191 (a) *locus penitentiae*] Opportunity for change of intention. A Scots law phrase. See Trayner, *Latin maxims*. Used in *Journal*, 1 Dec. 1825.

191 (e) what d'ye call it] John Gay, *The what d'ye call it: a tragi-comi-pastoral farce*.

191 *n*. 1] Scott's corrections refer to stanzas 32 and 34 of 1st ed. (now numbered 31 and 33) of Canto VI.

192 (c) The counseller] William Erskine.

192 (d) the Tods] Archibald Tod of Drygrange, W.S. (1758–1816), Thomas Tod, Advocate (1771–1850), and John Tod, W.S. (1773–1856), all sons of Thomas Tod of Drygrange, W.S. (1726–1800).

193 (b) To Rev. R. Polwhele] Letter may have been finished on 16 Nov. but Scott returned to Edinburgh on 11 Nov. (above, pp. 184, 192) and two days before would date the letter 13 Nov. The election of Peers was on 13 Nov. That Scott had not been in Edinburgh for 'six months' is a misstatement.

194 *n*. 1] Polwhele's anonymous work, *The deserted village school, a poem*, which John Ballantyne published in 1813.

195 (d) To Clarke Whitfeld] In *SL* xii. 487 it is correctly stated that this letter should come before the letter on p. 194; but I do not think Oct. is correct. Scott's words 'sent you some time ago' suggest a period of more than a month. The date may be Aug. or Sept.

196 (b) To C. K. Sharpe] This letter must be between Mar. and July.

Sharpe asked for Johnston's speech in a letter which is dated Mar. 1812 in *Sharpe's Letters*, i. 530. Scott sent a copy on 6 July (above, p. 142) and a better copy on 10 July (above, pp. 139–40). As Scott is in Edinburgh, the date is after 12 Mar.

196 (c) And in his hand] St. [7] of *Virtue in danger*.

197 (a–b) brightening the chain] See *SL* ii. 535 and my note.

198 (d) A starving German literatus] Rudolf Erich Raspe.

198 (f) *Familiar Letters*] i. 263–4.

199 (b–c) re-writing my robbers song] See above, p. 35.

199 *n.* 1] Delete.

201 (e) "So York shall overlook . . ."] Shakespeare, *III Henry VI*, I. 4.

203 (b) To James Ballantyne] The suggested dating is approximately correct but, as Drummond was married on 14 Apr., the marriage party seems to have been delayed a long time.

203 (d) what Moliere calls un petit pendement tres jolie] *Monsieur de Pourceaugnac*, III. 3: 'un petit pendement bien choli.' Also quoted in *Waverley*, chap. 28.

204 (b) To Duchess of Buccleuch] As Scott was not in the habit of giving a month only, this date seems to be an interpolation. Date is more likely to be Jan. 1813.

204 (e) To J. B. S. Morritt] The date of the letter is the same as the postmark, Thursday being the 10th.

205 (e) topaz seal] The seal has unfortunately been torn off the letter which is now in NLS (MS. 144, Letter 17).

206 (a) go whom the Devil drives] See *SL* ii. 434.

206 (c) Sophia . . . a letter of acknowledgment] Not sent till 5 Apr. 1813. See below, p. 248.

206 (c) "it skills not much when it is delivered"] Shakespeare, *Twelfth Night*, V. 1.

206 (d) and *n.* 1 Rush] This is a misreading for Bushe. Charles Kendal Bushe was Solicitor-General in Ireland, 1805–22.

206 (e) Terry] Dibdin (*Annals*, p. 266) says *The clandestine marriage* was to be performed on 14 Nov. with Terry as Lord Ogilby but that the performance was cancelled owing to Terry's illness. Mrs Smollett, C. K. Sharpe's aunt, gave another interpretation of Terry's 'illness.' She wrote to Sharpe in Nov.: 'By the way, Terry shou'd have play'd Ld. Ogilby on Saturday but wrote Siddons she [he?] was under the necessity of going to Bath for a few days. I am evil-minded enough to suspect poor Vining's horns will sprout afresh. His wife was *chère amie* of Mr Terry while here.' (*Sharpe's Letters*, ii. 47–8.)

207 (a) things must be as they may] Shakespeare, *Henry V*, II. 1.

207 (b) none of the quarter to] Read 'none of the quarto at'.

208 (c) new edition of the Border ballads] This is 5th ed., 1812, in which Scott cancelled pages relating to Otterburn as a result of James Ellis's letter. See my note to *SL* iii. 82 (b).

208 (c) for your second volume] i.e. of his *Rhymes of northern bards*, etc., 8vo Newcastle, 1812. This second volume was never published.

208 (d) The Mumming Dialogue] For other references, see Index under Guisers.

208 *n.* 1] Bell is acknowledging Scott's letter of 11 Dec. which is not in *SL*. Bell's letter in NLS is MS. 3883, f. 159.

210 (a) To George Crabbe] Crabbe replied to this letter on 5 Mar. (below, p. 279 *n.*). Scott's letter is probably mid or late Feb.

210 (e) action for augmentation of stipend to him and to his brethren] This was an action brought in 1810 by the ministers of Edinburgh against the Magistrates and not settled till 1814. See the *Scots Mag.* Vol. 76 (Feb. 1814), pp. 92–7.

210 *n.* 1] It is printed, almost in full, in Partington, *Letter-books*, pp. 224–7, and there is an extract in *Lockhart*, iv. 31.

211 (e) The opinions of reviewers] This is a comment on Crabbe's complaints, in his letter of 21 Dec. (Partington, *Letter-books*, pp. 225–6.)

212 (b) as Corporal Nym wisely observes] Shakespeare, *Henry V*, II. 1.

212 (c) it is a poor thing but mine own] Shakespeare, *As you like it*, V. 4.

212 (d) The Vision of Triermain] As the *Bridal of Triermain* was not published till Mar., Jeffrey must have been basing his opinion either on the extracts in the *Edin. Ann. Reg.* or on proof-sheets distributed by Ballantyne.

212 *n.* 1] In line 2, for 'in 1811' read '*for 1809* (publ. 1811).' In line 4, for 'a month after' read 'two months after'. The review in *QR* for July (publ. Aug.) was by George Ellis (*Shine*, No. 259). Lady Louisa acknowledged *Rokeby*, before she had read it, on 17 Jan. Her letter is in Stuart, *Gleanings*, iii. 229. For her letter of 22 Apr., see *FL* i. 281–3.

213 (a) To James Skene]. Date is doubtful. The copy of *Rokeby*, which was being sent to London, had to be forwarded to Southampton; yet this copy is inscribed by Skene: 'James Skene. A present from Mr. Scott, Southampton, Jan. 7, 1813.' This dating, too, is doubtful as *Rokeby* was not published till 11 Jan. If Skene regarded the date of Scott's letter as the date of the presentation, the letter should be dated 7 Jan. This presentation copy, with twelve water-colour drawings by Skene dated 1835 inserted in the volume, was sold by Sotheby's on 2 July 1962, Lot 96. Scott was at Abbotsford, 3–11 Jan. 'Edinburgh,' therefore, should be 'Abbotsford,' if the date is 7 Jan.

214 (c) *Skene's Memories*] pp. 41–2.

214 (d) To Marchioness of Stafford] This and the next have doubtful dates. After correcting the last proofs of *Rokeby* Scott went to Abbotsford (below, p. 223) on 3 Jan. The letter to Lady Stafford is dated 6 Jan. from Abbotsford (though from the contents Scott is in Edinburgh) and the letter to Lord Clarendon (p. 215) is dated 7 Jan. from Edinburgh (though from contents Scott is at Abbotsford).

215 (b) Major Weir's house] Thomas Weir, head of Edinburgh Guard (hence title of 'Major'); condemned to death as a wizard, 1670. See Scott's *Demonology*, pp. 329–33. The frontispiece to this work is an engraving of Major

Weir's house. See also John Maclaurin, Lord Dreghorn, *Arguments and decisions*, etc., 4to Edinburgh, 1774, No. 1, and *Minstrelsy* (ed. Henderson), ii. 338 and notes.

215 (c) topaz cut for a seal] See above, p. 205.

217 *n.* 1] The election was held on Friday, 13 Nov. 1812. See *Edin. Ann. Reg. for 1812*, V. ii. 186–7.

217 *n.* 2] See William Baird, *John Thomson*, 2nd ed., Edinburgh, [1907], p. 84. See also *SL* iv. 27.

218 (d) epigram on the *fracas* with Ld. Lauderdale] *Stanzas on a lady weeping*, first printed in the *Morning Chron.* 7 Mar. 1812. See Morritt's letter of Apr. 1812 (Partington, *Letter-books*, p. 183) in which he gives the lines, explaining that Princess Charlotte had wept 'when her papa scolded Lord Lauderdale.'

218 (e) in possession of a person] John Murray. See above, pp. 134–5, 139.

218 *n.* 1] Amend this note to read: Margaret Mercer Elphinstone, daughter (by his first wife Jane Mercer) of George Keith Elphinstone (fourth son of 10th Lord Elphinstone) who was created Baron Keith in 1797 and Viscount Keith in 1814.

219 (b–c) Lord Hamilton] James Hamilton, Viscount Hamilton (courtesy title), eldest son of Lord Abercorn. He predeceased his father in 1814.

219 (d) a superb spring] See my note to *SL* iii. 154 (a).

220 (c) To George Ellis] For rest of letter, see *SL* xii. 339–40.

220 (e) "indifferent hone st"] Shakespeare, *Hamlet*, III. 1.

220 (f) like the son of Lancelot Gobbo] This should be 'like the father of Launcelot Gobbo.' Shakespeare, *Merchant of Venice*, II. 2. See *SL* xii. 339 *n.* and my note to it.

222 (c) Canning] He did not return to the Cabinet till 1816.

222 (e–f) But shall we go mourn] Shakespeare, *Winter's tale*, IV. 2.

223 (a) tell it not in Gath] Bible, *II Samuel* 1: 20.

223 (b) my new old well] See my note to *SL* iii. 154 (a).

223 (f) Twelfth Night] It was performed on 2 Jan. and repeated on Jan. 5, 9, 25 and 28. Scott must have attended on 2 Jan.

224 (a) Family Legend] It was performed at Theatre Royal on Monday, 4 Jan. Scott could not attend as he was at Abbotsford. Between this and its first production in Jan. 1810 it had been produced at the Haddington Theatre on 25 Jan. 1811. There is a playbill for the latter in Edinburgh Univ. Lib.

224 (d) To J. B. S. Morritt] The date appears to be taken from *Lockhart* (iv. 51–3), where the letter is dated 'Edinburgh, 12th January 1813.'

224 (f) The book has gone off here very bobbishly] See my note to *SL* iii. 262 (d–e).

225 (c) one in Galloway] The murder of the girl took place in the Stewartry of Kirkcudbright in the autumn of 1786. The murderer, William Richardson, was discovered in the way Scott describes, was tried at Dumfries in the spring of 1787, found guilty and hanged. The story is told in *Chambers's Edinburgh Journal*, Vol. 1 (10 Mar. 1832), p. 41. Scott mentioned this story to John Morrison. See Morrison's *Random reminiscences of Sir Walter Scott* in *Tait's Mag.* Vol. 10 (Sept. 1843), p. 572.

225 (c) print of his foot] This is obviously the source for a similar incident in *Guy Mannering*, chap. 56.

225 (d) Sheriff] Sir Alexander Gordon of Culvennan, 1747–1830, was Sheriff of Kirkcudbright, 1784–1830. Scott uses the nickname again in *SL* viii. 348.

225 *n.* 1] Delete and substitute: Rape and murder of Hannah Leatham, servant to Mr Jackson of Brignal, near Greta Bridge, on 1 Jan. 1813. See *Edin. Ann. Reg.* VI, Chronicle, p. i.

227 (b) Chevy Chase] A mezzotint by Young is recorded as hanging in the Breakfast Parlour at Abbotsford about 1840 but it is no longer there. See also my note to *SL* iii. 232 *n.* 5.

227 (b) Mr. Eagle] Scott's letter of 8 Dec. 1811 to Thomas Eagles is in *SL* xii. 410–14.

227 (c) our pleasant men of Tiviotdale] The quotation is appropriate as this line comes from *Chevy-chase*, st. [14], line 1. Scott normally, as here, transfers 'pleasant' from 'Teviotdale' to 'men.' Cf. *SL* vi. 56 and *The Monastery*, Introd. Epistle. The ballad is in D'Urfey, *Wit and mirth*; Percy's *Reliques*; Herd, and elsewhere.

227 *n.* 1] The Raid of the Reidswire took place on Scottish soil more than 20 miles from Otterburn in Northumberland.

228 (b) "He rose and rax'd . . ."] This is from st. IX–X of *The Raid of the Reidswire* (*Minstrelsy*, ed. Henderson, ii. 24).

228 (e) Mr. Eagle] Thomas Eagles.

229 (e) note on Littlecote Hall] Note to *Rokeby*, Canto V, st. 27. Lord Webb Seymour's name was not given in 1st ed. It was inserted in later eds.

231 (a) Major Howard Raes brother-in-law] As in similar cases, a comma should have been inserted after 'Howard.' Scott is referring to Major Thomas Phipps Howard.

231 (c) & will now dare] For suggested amendment, see *SL* xii. 488.

231 (e) Downie] General Sir John Downie had just returned from Spain. His arrival at Portsmouth is reported in *Edinburgh Evening Courant*, 30 Nov. 1812.

232 (a) Tactique] Scott and Murray collaborated on the subject of Napoleon's tactics. See *SL* ii. 482 *n.*, 503.

232 (b) to what I wrote yesterday] Scott's letter of 24 Feb. is in *SL* iv. 34–6.

232 *n.* 1] In line 2, for 'Fergusson' read 'Ferguson.'

232 *n.* 2] There are four errors in the title; '16vo' is an impossible format; and there are three eds., not two. The first is: *The letting of humors blood in the head-vaine. With a new morissco, daunced by seven satyres, upon the bottome of Diogenes tubbe.* Imprinted at London by W. W. 1611. The second is: *The letting of humours blood in the head vaine, &c.* Edinburgh, reprinted by James Ballantyne and Co. for William Blackwood, 1814. The third consisted of the same sheets with a new title-page with the imprint: Edinburgh, reprinted by

James Ballantyne and Co. for William Laing, and William Blackwood, 1815. Scott is not given as the editor but the 'Advertisement' has, at the end: 'Abbotsford, 1st April, 1814.' Delete the quotation from Swinburne.

232 *n.* 5] The original was presented to Scott (not sold, as *DNB* says). Pichot noted it in the Dining Room in 1822 and it is recorded as being in the Breakfast Parlour about 1840. It is no longer at Abbotsford.

233 (b) To Miss Clephane] To Margaret. Her letter, written at Dumbreck's Hotel, Edinburgh, is dated 11 Mar. and describes their 'rough journey' from Mull and their disappointment at finding Scott away from Castle Street (NLS MS. 3884, f. 100).

233 (d) I have built a well] See my note to *SL* iii. 154 (a).

233 (e) like the regiment of Sir John Falstaff] Shakespeare, *1 Henry IV*, IV. 2.

235 (c) [Edinburgh, *March* 13, 1813]] Delete. The date of a letter is the date on which it is finished, i.e. 21 Mar. (p. 237). In any case, Scott was at Abbotsford on 13 Mar. (See p. 233.)

235 (f) some prejudices to be got over] See *SL* ii. 240, iii. 21.

237 (c) Scrub] A servant in Farquhar's *The beaux' stratagem*. He has a different duty for each day of the week— a coachman on Monday, ploughman on Tuesday and so on. (Act III, sc. 3.)

237 *n.* 1] The MS. of Gillies's epilogue is in NLS (MS. 1712).

238 (a) the Mysterious Mother] By Horace Walpole.

238 (a) P. . . . shewed [me] the Ms.] Scott's reply to Pinkerton when returning the MS. is in *SL* xii. 414–15.

238 (c) To the Duchess of Buccleuch] This letter also appears in *SL* ii. 281 under the wrong date, 1810.

238 *n.*] See also *SL* xii. 414 *n.*

239 (b) my little god-daughter] Lady Margaret, afterwards Countess of Romney.

239 (c) ancient and simple brooch] See above, p. 102.

239 (e) *Rokeby* was written as fast as my hand could write it] The evidence of the letters does not support this statement.

239 *n.* 2] When the Earl of Dalkeith became 4th Duke his eldest-surviving son should have become Lord Dalkeith. He is mentioned only thrice before he became 5th Duke, here as Lord Whichester and twice (*SL* iv. 317 and v. 44) as Lord Dalkeith.

240 (b) the spring] See my note to *SL* iii. 154 (a).

240 (c) gravel-pit . . . exhausted quarry] The gravel-pit, a little to the south of the house, became Joanna's Bower. I do not know anything of the exhausted quarry.

241 (b) a little novel] From Scott's description this must be John Ballantyne's *The widow's lodgings; a novel*, 2 vols., 12mo Edinburgh, 1813. Scott's verdict is nearer the truth than Lockhart's (*Lockhart*, iii. 118 *n.*).

241 (c) *Rejected Addresses*] A few days before (18 Mar.), John Ballantyne had written to Scott saying James had received an order for printing 2,000 copies of the 14th and 15th eds. There is a transcript of Ballantyne's letter in NLS (MS. 6080).

242 (a) the Prince's Librarian that his R.H. desires his library to be open to me] The Librarian, Rev. James Stanier Clarke, sent the Prince Regent's message through William Wilson, the artist. See Wilson's letter of 5 Feb. 1813 to Scott in NLS (MS. 3884, ff. 58–9).

243 (d) 25 March [1813?]] Delete the question-mark. The year is definitely 1813.

245 (d) Robin of Risingham] i.e. on 26 Sept. 1812, after Scott, Mrs Scott, Walter and Sophia had stayed overnight, Sept. 25/26 at Otterburn Castle. For a brief account of the visit see *Letters between James Ellis Esq & Walter Scott Esq*, 12mo Newcastle-upon-Tyne, 1850, p. 19.

245 (e) curious confession of the horse-stealer] John Weir. See my note to *SL* iii. 80 *n.*

245 (e) *Luck-in-a-Bag*] Thomas Armstrong. See *The Border antiquities*, Vol. 2, Appendix, p. xciv. Luck-in-a-bag and Douglas (p. 246) are both mentioned in *The Black Dwarf*, chap. 13.

247 (e) denied his faith, and made a strange exit] Patten was naturally biased. He turned King's evidence and was a witness against Hall. Hall said Patten 'swore not one true thing against me.' He did not deny his faith but testified his adherence to the only true Church of England, i.e. the non-juring church. See *A true copy of the papers delivered to the Sheriffs of London by William Paul . . . and John Hall . . . hang'd . . . at Tyburn . . . July the 13th 1716*, 4to London, 1716.

248 (b) *Rokeby*] This word, I think, is either Scott's slip or the transcriber's error for *Sadler*.

248 (c) [1813?]] Delete query. Date is definitely 1813.

248 (d) a letter of Sophia] See above, p. 206.

248 (d) childrens epistles] Shakespeare, *Twelfth Night*, V. 1.

248 n. 1] Delete '*Rokeby* was issued in December 1812, four editions . . . 1815.' *Rokeby* was issued on 11 Jan. 1813. For correct list of eds., see *Ruff*, Nos. 119–29.

249 (c) a tragedy] *The heiress of Strathearn*. See *SL* iii. 237.

249 n. 1] *Remorse* was acted in Edinburgh on Saturday, 10 Apr.

250 (a) To R. P. Gillies] According to Gillies's *Memoirs*, ii. 135–6, he lived in Heriot Row from the summer of 1813 till June 1814. The correct year seems to be 1813 but April is too early. The month is probably July, by which time Gillies was living in Heriot Row and Scott was preparing to go to Abbotsford for the summer vacation.

250 (c) 'Skill to soothe the lagging hour . . .'] William Gifford, *To the Rev. John Ireland*, st. [13], lines 5–6. In his *Baviad and Mæviad* of which Scott had 6th and 8th eds., 1800 and 1811, the lines quoted being respectively at p. 129 and p. 118. Scott printed the poem in his *English minstrelsy* (1810), ii. 126–30.

250 n. 1] In line 1, for '1743' read '1744.'

251 (b) *Gillies's Memoirs*] Add: ii. 82–3.

251 (d) yeoman's service] Shakespeare, *Hamlet*, V. 2.

251 (d) Jeffrey] *The Bridal of Triermain* was not reviewed in *ER*.

251 n. 1] Morritt's letter is printed in Partington, *Letter-books*, pp. 109–10.

252 (b) ungallantly neglecting some verses] See *SL* ii. 301–2 and 301 n.

252 (c) Sir Lucius O'Trigger] Sheridan, *The rivals*, IV. 3.

252 n. 1] In last line, for '*op. cit.*' read '*Letter-books*, p. 110.'

253 (d–e) two views . . . by Miss Arden . . . Mrs. Morritts drawing] I have not found these at Abbotsford.

253 (e) Collector of the Customs at Leith] Robert McNair.

253 n. 1] Delete this note. Miss Arden is the daughter of Lady Alvanley frequently mentioned in the correspondence.

254 (d–e) about the verses] These verses, with the title *To discretion*, were printed in the *Edin. Ann. Reg. for 1808* (publ. 1810), I. ii. xxxix–xl, with a note: 'We do not understand that his [Swift's] northern editor [Scott] was imposed on by the joke.' In her letter of 2 Apr. (NLS MS. 3884, f. 116) Lady Abercorn had written: 'I know who wrote them, tho I am not at liberty to say' and in another letter of the same month (NLS MS. 3884, f. 118) she says: 'Since I last wrote, I find you had been already informed of the Quiz on L. White.'

254 n. 1] Delete the last sentence. Both vols. were issued in May 1817 as is shown by Whitfeld's letter to Scott of 11 May 1817 (NLS MS. 3888, f. 67). Scott contributed only two poems: *The foray* in Vol. 1 and *The romance of Dunois* in Vol. 2. Clarke had taken the name of Whitfeld in 1814 but the title-page has 'John Clarke,' perhaps because the composer felt he would be better known by his old name (*Ruff*, No. 156).

255 n. 2] The correct title and place of publication are: *Poetical epistles, and specimens of translation*, 12mo London, 1813. Petrarch and Dante are not mentioned.

256 (a) Mrs. Clarke] In *Horace in London*, Ode VIII of Book II was *To Mrs. Mary Anne Clarke*.

256 (d) A volume of popular romances] *Popular romances . . . To which is prefixed an introductory dissertation by H. Weber*, 8vo Edinburgh, 1812.

257 (a) *causes célèbres* . . . The criminal records of Scotland] Cf. *The Heart of Mid-Lothian*, chap. 1: 'Oh! do but wait till I publish the *Causes Célèbres* of Caledonia.'

257 (b) collection of songs] Scott lent his collection to Hogg for his *Jacobite relics*. See also above, pp. 30–1 and below, p. 285 and *SL* iv. 190–1.

257 *n.* 1] In line 1, for '1782' read '1780.' See *N. & Q.* Vol. 195, p. 302.

258 *n.*] Delete two last lines. Fuller information is given in p. 256, *n.* 1–2.

259 (a) To Henry Brevoort] This letter is printed in *The life and letters of Washington Irving*, ed. by P. M. Irving, London, 1862–4, i. 197–8, where 'sore' is given for 'tense' (line 12 of *SL* text). The former seems to be the better reading.

259 (c) two ladies who are our guests] Mrs Clephane and Margaret were in Edinburgh in March (above, p. 233) and may have gone to Abbotsford in April.

259 *n.* 1] Washington Irving's brother is Peter. For an account of books presented by Brevoort to Scott, see *The Bibliotheck*, Vol. 4, No. 2 (1963), pp. 44–65; and for American books presented by Scott to Brevoort, see James Wynne, *Private libraries of New York*, 8vo New York, 1860, pp. 105–9.

260 (b) hermit of Prague] Shakespeare, *Twelfth Night*, IV. 2.

261 (a–b) Crabbe] Crabbe had written on 5 Mar. (below, p. 279 *n.*).

261 (c–d) Your poems] *Minstrelsy of Erin*, published by John Ballantyne in 1812.

262 (b) "heaven-directed to the poor"] Pope, *Moral essays, in four epistles to several persons*, Epistle II, line 150.

262 (c) a porter] William Begbie.

262 (d–e) about ten thousand copies] A slight exaggeration. The *Eclectic Review* for May 1813 said: 'We are desired by the publishers to state the following comparative sale of Rokeby

and the Lady of the Lake.' It is then stated that 8,000 copies of the former were sold in three months and of the latter in four months.

262 notes] The notes are reversed and one is missing. Note 2 should be note 1 with reference to 'guinea note' in line 7 of text. No. 1 should be 2 with reference to British Linen Company's Bank. Index figure at 'Gillies' in last line of text should be 3 with a note, 'See above, p. 213 *n.*'

263 (a) *confess and be hanged*] Ray, p. 116; Ramsay, *Proverbs*, p. 15.

266 (e) Terry . . . print] I have not found this engraving of Terry at Abbotsford.

266 *n.* 1] Delete 'A' before 'Charles.' He married Terry's widow.

268 (e) heaps coals of fire upon my head] *Bible, Proverbs* 25: 22; *Romans* 12: 20.

269 (a) come down to Edinr.] Harts-tonge did come to Edinburgh, for it was announced in the *Edinburgh Evening Courant*, 12 Aug. 1813, p. 3, c. 2, that he had left the London Hotel. It is odd that there is nothing in the correspondence about Scott and Hartstonge meeting or missing each other in Edinburgh.

270 (c) curious volumes] Only one is mentioned above, p. 268 *n.* It is *Histoire du règne de la Reine Anne d'Angleterre . . . Traduit . . . par M**** [i.e. M. A. Eidous]*, 8vo Amsterdam, 1765.

270 (f) To Miss Clephane] Margaret. The Clephanes had been in Edinburgh since the middle of March (above, p. 233) but there is no record of Scott's having met them unless the 'two ladies' at Abbotsford (above, p. 259) were Mrs and Margaret Clephane.

271 (a) Cossack pike] See below, p. 378.

272 *n.* 4] Delete. Information already given, p. 271 *n.* 2.

274 (a) to visit my friends the Morritts] This visit was cancelled owing to Mrs Morritt's illness. Some details of Scott's journey are in *SL* i. 431–5.

274 (c) ill-health of the wife of . . .] There is nothing in *SL* to identify this Clerk.

274 (d) Thomsons painting] See above, p. 217.

275 (c) an uncle of my neighbour . . . Scott of Gala] George Scott, afterwards Admiral Sir George Scott. See Index, under Scott. II. Gala.

275 (e) Monm[ou]lth] This should be Monreith. The Duchess of Gordon was a daughter of Sir William Maxwell of Monreith, 3rd Bart. Margaret, daughter of the 2nd Bart., married Carruthers of Dormont.

278 (c) this strange eventful history] Shakespeare, *As you like it*, II. 7.

279 (c) your three volumes] *Poems*, 7th ed., 1812; *The borough*, 5th ed., 1813; *Tales*, 1812.

279 *n.* 1] In line 2, for 'vi. 39' read 'NLS MS. 3884, ff. 90–3.' There is an extract from Crabbe's letter in Partington, *Post-bag*, pp. 96–7.

280 (c) *Virginibus puerisque*] Horace, *Odes*, III. i. 4.

280 (c) Pope] Pope wrote to James Craggs, 15 July 1715: 'I (like the *Tories*) have the Town in general, that is the Mob, on my side . . . I fear no arbitrary high-flying Proceedings from the small Court-Faction at *Button's*.' (*Mr. Pope's literary correspondence*, 3rd ed., London, 1735, i. 223–4.)

281 (b) "cairn and the scaur"] See my note to *SL* i. 224 (d).

281 (e) as Dogberry says] Shakespeare, *Much ado about nothing*, IV. 2.

282 (d–e) Brass for gold] Homer, *Iliad*, Bk VI. See *SL* vii. 197 and viii. 151 and *n.* 3.

282 (f) Paul I know & Apollos I know but who are ye?] The words 'Who then is Paul, and who is Apollos' occur in the *Bible*, *I Corinthians* 3: 5, but Scott seems to have been thinking of *Acts* 19: 15: 'Jesus I know, and Paul I know, but who are ye?'

283 (b) To Morehead] Printed in *Memorials of the life and writings of the Rev. Robert Morehead*, Edinburgh, 1875, pp. 376–7. This letter, said to be original, was offered for sale by Halliday, Cat. 225 (1938).

285 (b) my Jacobite songs] See also above, pp. 30–1, 257, and below, p. 391 and *SL* iv. 190–1. Mrs Clephane

replied on 27 June. An extract from her letter is in Partington, *Post-bag*, pp. 99–100, where Partington wrongly says that she is alluding to *Waverley*.

285 (b) So ro Morag] In Nov. 1813 Margaret translated this song and called it simply 'Translation of the Gaelic song Agus o Mhòrag.' It is printed in her *Irene, a poem . . . Miscellaneous poems*, priv. pr. 8vo London, 1833, pp. 170–1. I feel sure it formed the basis of Flora Mac-Ivor's song ('There is mist on the mountain') in *Waverley*, chap. 22.

285 (d) My Grieve] Tom Purdie. Scott calls him 'my Grieve' in *SL* v. 432.

285 *n.* 1] In line 7, delete reference to Abbotslee. He did not buy any part of Abbotslee till 1816.

287 *n.*] The undated letter (line 11) cannot belong to this period if Cadell actually wrote 'Sir Walter.' Delete the uncalled-for comments in lines 8–4 from foot.

288 (e) go South] To meet Lord and Lady Abercorn and then go on to Rokeby Park.

289 *n.* 1] The 'object' (p. 291) may not necessarily refer to land.

291 (c) Scottish Songs] *Songs: chiefly in the rural language of Scotland*, 8vo London, Printed for the author, 1813.

291 *n.* 1] Constable's name does not appear on the title-pages of *Edin. Ann. Reg.* till 1816.

291 *n.* 2] In line 7, for 'The following year appeared his *Remains*' read 'In the same year appeared Cromek's *Remains*.' In line 10, for '*dialect*' read '*language*.'

294 *n.* 1] For extracts from Morritt's letter, see *FL* i. 297–8 and Partington, *Post-bag*, pp. 100–1.

295 (a) Abbotswell] This is the spring in Fountain's Park but it is not so named on Scott's map of the estate and this is the only time I have found the name used.

296 *n.* 1.] In line 3, for 'Abbotslee in 1812' read 'Abbotsford in 1811.' In line 4, for '1816' read '1815.' In line 6, for 'Abbotslee' read 'Abbotsford.'

298 (a) To John Murray] In Smiles, *John Murray*, i. 241–2, with Murray's reply of 8 July, i. 242–3.

298 (f) The property I have purchased]
This can refer only to Cartleyhole
purchased in 1811 for £4,200.

298 n. 1] For these bills, see below,
pp. 369-70, 379-80, 385-6, 395.

299 (d) a very pretty panegyric] In
*Epistle first, from a Scotchman in London
to his friend in Scotland. Written in the
year 1799*. In *Poetical epistles and specimens of translation* [by Robert More-
head], 12mo London, 1813, pp. 7-9.
There is nothing in the poem to indicate that the Maclean mentioned is
Maclean of Torloisk. Scott must have
had private information that he was
Mrs Maclean Clephane's father.

300 (c) *parcus et infrequens deorum cultor*]
Horace, *Odes*, I. xxxiv. 1.

301 (c) about the 25th] But he did not
set out for Drumlanrig till Monday, 26
July (*SL* i. 429).

302 (c) the awful spell] Scott's description was: 'feathers, parings of nails,
hair, and such like trash, wrapt in a
lump of clay.' See Boswell's *Johnson*,
ed. Hill-Powell, v. 164 n. 1.

302 (d) the Stanhopes] Of Cannon Hall,
Yorkshire. See *SL* ii. 379, 380 and my
notes.

303 (a) to wed a wife and bring her
home] Probably a variation of *Willie's
lady*, st. 1, line 2; also used in *Guy
Mannering*, chap. 11.

303 (c) I am of opinion with Olivia]
Shakespeare, *Twelfth Night*, I. 5.

303 (d) I have your letter] Of 17 July,
of which an extract is given in Partington, *Post-bag*, p. 103. Scott's reference
to Lady Caroline Lamb is in answer to
Morritt's account of her stabbing herself out of jealousy of Byron.

303 n. 1] Delete the sentence beginning
'Scott always' and see my note to *SL* i.
302 n.

303 n. 2] Delete this note and see my
note to *SL* i. 435 n.

304 n. 3] Delete and substitute: Smollett, *Roderick Random*, chap. 18.

305 (a) Baron Smith] Sir William
Cusack Smith.

305 (a) Dr. Barratt] This is Dr John
Barrett.

306 (d-e) whether I do not well to be
angry] *Bible, Jonah* 4: 9.

309 (e) *Saturday 25 July* 1813] Saturday
was 24 July.

310 (c) To Joanna Baillie] Date should
be April instead of Summer.

311 (b) Herbert] Sir Thomas Herbert.
See his *Memoirs of the two last years of the
reign of King Charles I. To which is added,
a particular account of the funeral of the
King*, 8vo London, 1813.

311 (c) the bible] There is a good illus.
of this Bible in E. C. Rickards's *Felicia
Skene of Oxford*, London, 1902, facing
p. 8, where it is wrongly described as a
prayer-book.

311 (c) *Remember*] It has been suggested
that Charles I wished Juxon to remember his promise to urge his son,
Charles II, to forgive his enemies.
Scott had the word 'Remember' engraved on the ring which he had made
to contain Charles I's hair. See below,
p. 391, and *The Heart of Mid-Lothian*,
chap. 34.

311 (d) if he sowd the wind] *Bible,
Hosea* 8: 7.

315 (d) To Rev. R. Polwhele] Scott
had not reached Abbotsford by 12
Aug. Date may be 12 Sept. The
source from which this letter is printed
dates it 2 Aug. The only 1813 letter
from Polwhele I can find is dated 16
May (NLS MS. 3884, ff. 147-8). In
it he asks Scott to read his *Fair Isobel* but
does not mention the Reviews. This
letter would reach Scott before he set
out on his tour and Polwhele must have
written again at the end of July.

316 n. 1] The correct reference to the
Satires is II. vi. 1.

318 (c) "Fair Kitty blooming young
and gay—"] Catherine Hyde, daughter
of Earl of Clarendon and wife of 3rd
Duke of Queensberry. Though the quotation is not exact, Scott is probably
referring to Prior's *The female Phaeton*,
st. 1, line 1: 'Thus Kitty, beautiful
and young.' See also below, p. 356.

321 n. 1] Delete. Lockhart is obviously
wrong. See amended note in *SL* xii.
488.

323 (a) Lay] This is a mistake. The *Lay*
had been sold to Longman in 1805.
See *SL* i. 269, 269 n., ix. 371.

323 (c) Morritt] Mrs Morritt's illness was not the only reason. Scott had recently applied to him without getting all he wished. See above, pp. 293–4, 294 n., 300, 300 n.

323 n. 1] It was not Scott of Raeburn who wished to sell his vote, but Scott of Maxpoffle. See below, pp. 382, 383. The quotation from the Duke's letter (NLS MS. 3884, ff. 142–3) is not quite accurate.

324 (c) poet laureate] The Duke's reply of 28 Aug. is in Partington, *Letter-books*, p. 285. The Duke advised Scott not to accept.

326 (c) To be a hedge . . .] See *SL* i. 119 n. and my note.

326 n.] Amend last sentence. Scott received the letter on 31 Aug. See below, p. 334.

327 (b) your London Shylock] Shakespeare, *The Merchant of Venice*, I. 3.

327 (c) these tirrits and frights] Shakespeare, *II Henry IV*, II. 4.

333 (a) in his new vocation] As auctioneer.

333 (a) "put not your faith in princes"] *Bible, Psalms* 146: 3.

334 (e) Cross-lee toll-bar] Midway between Torsonce Inn and Galashiels on the Edinburgh–Jedburgh coaching road. Scott seems to be completing his letter at Abbotsford. ('about four miles' means 'about five or six.')

334 n. 1] Delete whole note and see first sentence at top of page.

335 (b) To Robert Southey] Lockhart's date, 4 Sept. (*Lockhart*, iv. 116) must be wrong, for this letter, sent to Keswick, had to be redirected to London in time for Southey to send a transcript of it to his wife on 5 Sept.

335 n. 1] Southey's reply (line 9) is dated 5 Nov. and is in NLS (MS. 3884, ff. 295–6).

336 (b) two offices not usually conjoined] Scott, however, had resented the suggestion made previously that he should resign his Sheriffdom while holding his Clerkship. See *SL* i. 405, 406, ii. 452–3 and cf. below, p. 345.

336 (d) like Dogberry, a fellow with

two gowns] Shakespeare, *Much ado about nothing*, IV. 2.

336 (d–e) like a cock at a gooseberry] Ray, p. 286. Also used in *Redgauntlet*, Letter 13.

337 (b) To James Ballantyne] Perhaps this letter belongs to 1812 like the preceding one.

337 (d) To Thomas Scott] Cancel. The letter, dated 29 Jan. 1811, is given in full in *SL* vii. 457–9. Error noted, *SL* vii. 393.

337 (f) Lady Maria] Lady Maria Hamilton, 4th daughter of Lord Abercorn.

338 (c) Whitehead] *A pathetic apology, for all laureats, past, present, and to come*, lines 9–14. (Chalmers, *The works of the English poets*, London, 1810, Vol. 17, p. 227.)

339 (d) "profaned by Cibber and contemn'd by Gray"] George Huddesford, *Monody on the death of Dick, an academical cat*, line 122. In his *Salmagundi*, London, 1793, p. 138, and his *Poems*, 2 vols., London, 1801, i. 137. Scott printed an extract headed *On Warton*, containing this line, in his *English minstrelsy*, Edinburgh, 1810, ii. 161.

339 (f) my answer to the Lord Chamberlain] The Marquess of Hertford, below, p. 342.

340 (a) Lady Lucia] This, I think, must be Lady Julia Gore, Lady Abercorn's youngest half-sister. She would be aged 13 at this time and in 1821 she married Robert Manners Lockwood.

340 (f) Sebastian] François Horace Sebastiani.

341 (b) "It is long time to the saddling of a foal"] Ramsay, *Proverbs*, p. 43. See also *SL* ii. 349.

341 (f) Smith & Jenyns [?]] Delete '[?]' and see my note to *SL* ii. 15 (b).

345 (c) not usually conjoined] See *SL* i. 405, 406, ii. 452–3, and above, p. 336.

347 (c) Queensberry] This is Charles Douglas, 5th Marquess, who succeeded in 1810 when the dukedom of Queensberry went to the Duke of Buccleuch. His wife was Caroline, 3rd daughter of 3rd Duke of Buccleuch, and, therefore,

sister of the Duke of Buccleuch to whom Scott is writing.

347 (e) Lord Melgund] Courtesy title. Afterwards 2nd Earl of Minto.

347 (e) Sheriff Clerk of Roxburghshire] James Potts.

348 (d) Yeomans service] Shakespeare, *Hamlet*, V. 2.

349 (b) "Ah, Freedom is a glorious thing"] John Barbour, *The Bruce*, Bk I, line 228; 'Ah! freedom is a noble thing.'

350 (a) Dr. Hill . . . Patrick] See below, p. 407 *n.* 1. Patrick is Hume, commentator on *Paradise lost*.

350 (c) To J. B. S. Morritt] Scott is answering his letter of 18 Aug. (NLS MS. 3884, ff. 230–1).

351 (f) fought the good fight] *Bible*, *I Timothy* 6: 12, or *II Timothy* 4: 7.

352 (c) To unknown correspondent] This is Edward Hull. Tom had visited him at Donaghadee in August. See *SL* vii. 401. His letter, which Scott is acknowledging, is not in Walpole Coll.

354 *n.* 1 Scott wrote to Lord Forbes] His letter is not in *SL* but Scott in a letter of 14 Sept. says he has written (*SL* vii. 468). Lord Forbes's reply is dated 28 Sept. (NLS MS. 3884, ff. 258–9). 'his father' is Tom's father. It was Lord Forbes's father who was born in 1760. Lord Forbes was born in 1785. General Hewett is Sir George Hewett, appointed Commander-in-Chief in Ireland in 1813 and created a Baronet on 6 Nov. of the same year. Sir John Hope later became 4th Earl of Hopetoun.

355 (d) the laurel] It was announced on the previous day (11 Sept.) in the *Edinburgh Evening Courant* that Scott had declined the honour. The wording of the paragraph suggests that Scott supplied the information.

356 (b) "profaned by Cibber . . ."] See my note to *SL* iii. 339 (d).

356 (c) old Q.] William Douglas, 4th Duke of Queensberry, 1724–1810.

356 (e) Priors "Kitty, blooming young and gay"] See my note to *SL* iii. 318 (c).

365 (c) "We of the right hand file"] Shakespeare, *Coriolanus*, II. 1, and in the *Journal*, 13 Dec. 1825.

366 (b) "O war to those who never tried thee sweet"] The order of the words suggests that this is a line from a poem, but I have not traced it. 'Dulce bellum inexpertis' is a proverb. In *The Antiquary*, chap. 28, Edie Ochiltree says 'war's sweet to them that never tried it.'

367 (c) Never mind these dunderheads] In his letter of 22 Sept. (NLS MS. 3884, ff. 254–5) Terry had complained of critics who accused him of imitating Kemble, King and Munden.

368 (a) flourishing like the green bay] See *SL* i. 23 and my note.

368 (d) Falconer] See below, p. 515 *n.* 1 and my note to it.

368 (d) "cow-heel, quoth Sancho"] Cervantes, *Don Quixote*, Pt II, chap. 59 (Lockhart's ed., 1822, v. 177).

368 *n.* 1] Delete last sentence. Blore contributed virtually nothing to the designing of Abbotsford.

369 (f) the first bill] i.e. of the three bills recorded above, p. 298 *n.* See p. 370 for second and third bills. Only the first was due in Oct. See also below, pp. 379–80, 385–6, 395.

372 (a) lottery ticket] See below, p. 375 and my note.

374 (f) pitcher . . . fountains . . . broken] *Bible*, *Ecclesiastes* 12: 6.

375 (e) chance of the ticket] See above, pp. 371–2. The whole ticket cost £46. 13s. 0d. The original document, dated 3 Nov. 1813 and signed by John Ballantyne and Archibald Constable, is now in NLS (MS. 6080).

376 (b) To Lady Abercorn] Scott is answering her letter of 7 Oct. (NLS MS. 3884, ff. 271–5).

376 (c) Barataria] See above, p. 155 and *n.* 2.

376 (d) Blackstone] *The lawyer's farewell to his Muse*, lines 81–2, 87–8. For sources, see my note to *SL* i. 73 (d).

376 *n.* 1] See the *Edinburgh Advertiser*, Vol. 100 (2 Nov. 1813), p. 281, for an advertisement of Ballantyne's sale beginning on 18 Nov. and continuing for the next '34 succeeding lawful days.' The sale included the libraries of 1st Duke of Queensberry and of Alexander Gibson Hunter. There is

a letter from Hunter to Constable, 25 Feb. 1812, on the sale of his books, in *N. & Q.* Vol. 191 (24 Aug. 1946), p. 78.

376 n. 2] For sources, see my note to *SL* i. 73 (d).

378 (d) Minstrel they said] Bishop Percy, *The hermit of Warkworth*, Fit the third, st. [32], lines 1–2: 'Minstrel, he said, thou play'st so sweet, / Fair entrance thou should'st win.' In Thomas Evans, *Old ballads*, new ed., 4 vols., London, 1810, iv. 283.

378 (e) one of his lances] See above p. 271.

379 (a) leave] Should be 'live.'

380 (d) Xeres sack] In addition to a salary the Poet Laureate had been entitled to a tierce of sack but by Southey's time it had been commuted for £26.

380 (f) Smollett's baggage] *Travels through France and Italy*, Letter I. There is nothing in the text corresponding to 'one small portmanteau.'

380 n. 1] Add: II. 1.

382 (b) insurance on my own life] This is not listed among the insurance policies in the *Sederunt Books* (NLS MSS. 111–14) where the following are given: taken out by Constable & Co. for £5,000, 18 Aug. 1818, with the Pelican; £5,000, 8 Dec. 1817, with Royal Exeter; £5,000, 9 Feb. 1821, with Globe; by James Ballantyne for £3,000, 5 Dec. 1821, with West of England; £2,000, 9 Jan. 1822, with Atlas; by the Trustees for £2,000, 7 Aug. 1826, with Norwich Union. See also my note to *SL* xi. 449 (f).

382 (e) Lady of the Lake] 10th ed., 1814 (*Ruff*, No. 97). With this ed. Longman took over publication; Constable's name appeared in second place; and John Ballantyne & Co. took third place instead of first.

382 (f) note . . . from Scott] i.e. Willie Scott of Maxpoffle who was trying to sell his vote. See *SL* iii. 323 n., 383.

383 (a) Wight on Elections] Alexander Wight, *An inquiry into the rise and progress of Parliament, chiefly in Scotland, and a . . . system of the law concerning the elections of the representatives from Scotland*, 4to Edinburgh, 1784.

383 (d) To J. B. S. Morritt] NLS MS. 144, f. 25.

383 n. 1] Delete the sentence beginning 'Morritt was a'. It is an uncalled-for comment.

385 (a) Lady of the Lake & Rokeby] For the former, see my note to *SL* iii. 382 (e). The latter is 5th ed. (*Ruff*, No. 126 or possibly No. 125).

385 (e) there is no living with them nor without them] A reminiscence of Addison's translation of Martial's epigram (xii. 47) in the *Spectator*, No. 68, 18 May 1711: 'There is no living with thee, nor without thee.'

386 (f) orange ribbons] In honour of the Dutch rising. See p. 388.

388 (b) opend the windows of heaven . . .] *Bible, Genesis* 8: 1–2.

388 (e) The sword . . . like that brandishd across the road of Baalaam] *Bible, Numbers* 22.

389 (b) power pomp and circumstance of war] Shakespeare, *Othello*, III. 3.

389 (d) "officious innocent sincere"] Samuel Johnson, *On the death of Robert Levett*, st. [2], line 3.

391 (a) "to mine exceeding refreshment"] Robinson Crusoe nowhere says this either in the *Adventures* or *Further adventures*. Scott makes the same mistake elsewhere in *SL* and his *Journal*.

391 (b) a friend of mine] Sir John Malcolm. See *Lockhart*, iv. 141. For Charles I's hair, see Index. The ring, with the hair, is in the octagonal showcase in the Library at Abbotsford. See also above, p. 311 and my note.

391 (d) To Miss Clephane] Margaret's letter, which Scott is answering, is in Edin. Univ. Lib. (La. III. 584, Letter 24). It is dated at the beginning 'Torloisk Novr. 9th 1813' but the 12 pages of which it consists must have been written in instalments for the PM is 18 Nov. The letter consists almost entirely of her translations in verse and prose of Gaelic songs.

391 (e) a musical French prisoner] Joubert. See following page.

392 (a) Monsr. Joubert] He was a French prisoner of war stationed at Kelso. See *Trans. Hawick Arch. Soc.* 1912, p. 28.

392 (a) Lord Compton] He had returned to England in time to speak in the House of Commons (as M.P. for Northampton) on 4 Nov. See the *Scots Mag.* Vol. 75 (Nov. 1813), p. 859.

393 (c) card from Miss Stanley] Not found. This seems to be an error for Miss Stanhope. See above, p. 302.

393 (d) cannon of Berwick are called her auld black bells] *The sege of the Castel of Edinburgh*, st. [1], line 8: 'auld blak bellis.' In *Scotish poems, of the sixteenth century* [ed. by Sir John Graham Dalyell], Edinburgh, 1801, ii. 287. The author was Robert Sempill. A facsimile of the original ed., printed by Robert Lekprevick at Edinburgh, 1573, had just been issued before Scott wrote this letter.

393 (d) battle of Glenlivet] In his note to chap. 44 of *Waverley* Scott gives the same account of the battle and Highlanders' fear of cannon.

393 (e) flung them silver] Read 'flung themselves.'

394 (a) 'fears of the brave and follies of [the] wise"] Samuel Johnson, *The vanity of human wishes*, line 316.

394 (e) Don Quixote] Cervantes, *Don Quixote*, Pt I, Bk I, chap. 1. (Lockhart's ed., 1822, i. 20.)

394 *n.* 1] Delete and see my note to *SL* i. 337 (c).

395 (c) in town in spring unless] Scott must have been contemplating going to Holland via Harwich. The Holland and London trips were to be alternatives. (Cf. below, p. 398.) Neither was fulfilled.

395 *n.* 2] Delete 'Probably.'

396 (c) To J. B. S. Morritt] NLS MS. 144, f. 26.

396 (e) walk through the highlands] In 1813. See W. M. Parker's article, *A Scott amanuensis: Henry Weber and his Highland tour* in the *Scotsman*, 20 Nov. 1937, p. 15.

396 (e) potations pottle deep] Shakespeare, *Othello*, II. 3.

396 (f) a sister I think or near relation] She was a first cousin.

396 *n.* 1] Delete the uncalled-for comment 'Lockhart treats poor Weber with his usual brutality.'

398 (a) Lord Provost] Sir John Marjoribanks of Lees, Bart. Scott received the freedom of the City on 3 Jan. 1814 at 12 Charlotte Square. The silver tankard was not ready in time for the ceremony.

398 (a–b) done the genteel thing (as Winifred Jenkins says)] I cannot find these words in Smollett's *Humphry Clinker*. Scott was probably thinking of her last letter (20 Nov.) in which she says: 'the captain has done the handsome thing by me.' Scott also uses the words 'genteel thing' in *SL* vii. 473.

398 (c) English Tankard] This silver cup was first put on display in the Drawing-Room at Abbotsford during the bicentenary celebrations, 1971, and is still on view.

398 (d) Dalkeith] There is a brief account of the Duchess of Buccleuch's fête at Dalkeith House on 5 Jan. in the *Scots Mag.* Vol. 76 (Jan. 1814), p. 73.

398 (e) like Master Silence] Shakespeare, *II Henry IV*, V. 3.

398 *n.* 1] Delete. The address was presented by the Lord Provost in London on Friday, 10 Dec. The text is given in the *Edin. Ann. Reg. for 1813*, VI. ii. cxlvi–cxlviii.

399 (b) the advantage you gave my verses] Her letter of 18 Nov. 1813 (NLS MS. 3884, ff. 286–7) tells that the verses she recited at Frogmore were those beginning 'The way was long, the wind was cold.'

399 (b) I see by to-day's Courier] The *Courier* of 3 Jan. reported a party given by the King on New Year's Day at which Sarah Smith was invited to give readings from various comedies 'with which the Royal Party appeared highly delighted.'

399 (d) Terry] See above, p. 366.

399 (f) Coleridge] *Remorse; a tragedy.* See above, p. 249.

400 (a) verses on Love] Scott printed them under the title *Fragment* in his *English minstrelsy* (1810), ii. 131–9.

401 (c) *Sharpe's Letters*] ii. 107.

401 *n.* 1] The allusion to Squire Sullen is not very appropriate. In Act IV, sc.

2 Boniface refers to one of Sullen's tankards as 'near upon as big as me.' Later (*SL* iv. 201) Scott says Justice Shallow.

402 *n.* 1] In line 10, for '*Lives of Messala Valerius, Messala Corvinus . . .*' read '*Lives of Marcus Valerius Messala Corvinus.*'

403 (a) the lives] See above, p. 402 *n.* and my note. Scott had already written to Berwick on 5 Sept. 1813 on this subject (*SL* xii. 417). Not reviewed in *QR*.

403 *n.* 1] *The toast* (i.e. *Orpheus and Eurydice*) was published in 1704, not 1730. The words 'I find' down to 'decus' should be in quotation marks. See also my note to *SL* vii. 246 *n.*

404 *n.* 1] In Swift's *Works*, ed. Scott, 2nd ed., xii. 475–6.

405 (b) To J. B. S. Morritt] NLS MS. 144, f. 27.

407 (b–c) Wood's halfpenny . . . medal . . . seal . . . Cantata] The engraving of Wood's halfpenny, inscribed 'To Walter Scott Esqr from Doctor Hill Reg. Prof. Phy. T.C.D.' is in Scott's *Swift*, 2nd ed., vi. 347; the medal and seal are on one plate (ibid., frontispiece to Vol. 2); the Cantata, with music, is engraved on two sheets (ibid., Vol. 19, between p. 261 and p. 262).

407 *n.* 2] Delete last line and see my previous note.

410 (e) squibs respecting the Bank] See *SL* ii. 323.

412 (c) White House Street] Read 'White Horse Street.'

412 *n.* 1] Add: i.e. *The bold dragoon.*

413 (b) To John Ballantyne] Cancel. It is printed from original in *SL* iv. 36–7.

414 (d) To Hay Donaldson] The date is almost certainly Sunday 13 Mar. 'Tomorrow' would be Monday 14th, and he received Mrs Tom's letter on 13th. He wrote to her on Monday, 14 Mar. (*SL* vii. 474 where he says 'I received your letter yesterday,' i.e. 13th) and had his letter franked the same day.

414 (e) I enclose a letter from Mr. Keith] It must not have been returned as it is not in the Walpole Coll.

414 *n.* 3] The Scheme is much more likely to have been connected with the estate of Walter Scott, W.S., whose trustees were Alexander Keith and the Doctor (Daniel Rutherford).

416 (a) Kean] See *SL* iv. 41 and *n.*

418 (c) To J. B. S. Morritt] This letter in *FL* i. 318–21 is dated Jan. but I think it should be dated mid Feb. Morritt's 'two last letters', giving better news of Mrs Morritt's health, are dated 22 Jan. (NLS MS. 3885, f. 20) and 8 Feb. (NLS MS. 3885, f. 71). Scott wrote again on 4 Mar. (above, p. 416) saying he had not heard about Mrs Morritt for 'some time', i.e. since 8 Feb.

419 (b) Two Russian friends of Lord Pembroke] The second wife of 11th Earl was a Russian.

419 (d) the pamphlet] Frederick Shoberl's *Narrative of the most remarkable events which occurred in and near Leipzig . . . from the 14th to the 19th October, 1813,* 8vo London. *FL* i. 319 *n.* gives the name wrongly as Shobert. Scott mentions the pamphlet in *For. Quart. Rev.* 1827 (*MPW* xviii. 299).

420 (b) Sir Jemmy] Sir James Mackintosh. He was in India, 1804–12.

420 (d) muddling work] See above, p. 275 and *n.* 1.

420 (d) Joseph Surface] In Sheridan's *School for scandal.*

420 (f) Burns] A meeting had been held at Dumfries on 13 Jan. to promote a mausoleum over his grave in that town. See *Edin. Ann. Reg. for 1814,* VII. ii. x–xi.

422 (a) coming back first] Correct reading must be 'coming back fast.'

422 (d) Mr. Alexander's . . . card] His letter is not in the Walpole Coll.

422 (e) Advocate] Scott is anticipating. David Anderson was not called to the Bar till 7 June.

423 (a) Of all funds re-funding] According to *Nigel,* chap. 24, it was a 'Scotch wag' who said this.

423 *n.* 1] Cancel the whole of this note and see my articles on *The Border antiquities* in the *Bibliotheck,* Vol. 1, No. 1 (Autumn 1956) and Vol. 3, No. 1 [1960].

424 (b) Don Roderick] 3rd ed., 1815 (*Ruff*, No. 116).

424 (c) Douglas's Banner] The original drawing of this by Henry Weber is still at Abbotsford. It was engraved for *The Border antiquities*, Vol. 2, facing p. 207. For the banner, see Sir Herbert Maxwell, *A history of the House of Douglas*, i. 112 *n.*

425 (b) Barlowe] Probably a misreading for Barbour.

426 (b) To James Scott Walker] The date must be 1816. Walker did not return from South America till 1815 and, when in Edinburgh, he wrote to Scott on 6 May 1815 as an 'entire stranger,' sending some samples of his poetry (NLS MS. 870, f. 34). Parts of Scott's letter are quoted by Walker in a letter to Scott of 3 Mar. 1828 (NLS MS. 3906, ff. 121–3) and Walker quite clearly dates Scott's letter as 1816. This letter is in Symington, *Some unpublished letters*, pp. 72–3, with a note by Mrs Scott which is not in *SL*. On Walker, see *N. & Q.* 3rd ser. x. 354, 462–3. See also my notes to *SL* viii. 191 *n.* 2 and *SL* xi. 303 *n.*

426 *n.* 1] In last line delete 'probably.' Walker, in his letter of 3 Mar. 1828 (see my previous note), says he had asked permission in 1816 to dedicate his *South American* to him. As Scott declined the dedication, Walker dedicated his work to Major William Millar.

427 (d) To R. P. Gillies] The reference to *Childe Alaric* suggests that this letter was written at Abbotsford on Tuesday, 9 Nov., the week before Scott returned to Edinburgh for the opening of the Courts.

427 (d) Irish tour] This may be *Tour through Ireland*, by Rev. James Hall, 2 vols., 1813. Hall was a Scot and had published *Travels in Scotland*, 2 vols., 1807.

428 (e) lawful rule, and right supremacy] Shakespeare, *Taming of the shrew*, V. 2.

429 (b) another person who has claims on me] Rev. Edward Berwick. See below, p. 449.

429 (c) by two Friends] Robert Jamieson and Henry Weber.

429 *n.* 1] This is an odd place to quote Robert Shortreed.

430 (e) To Miss Sophia Scott] Thursday was the 14th. As PM is 15th, Scott would arrive in Edinburgh as soon as the letter. The candles were for the illuminations in celebration of Napoleon's downfall.

433 *n.* 1] Delete. Scott did not write the articles till much later.

434 (a) like a sparrow on the House top] *Bible, Psalms* 102: 7.

434 *n.* 2] Grierson fails to correct the reference to Owen. The Owen mentioned in the correspondence is William Owen-Pughe (1759–1835).

436 (f) Owen . . . *Mabinogion*] According to *QR* xxi. 94, Owen's MS. was lost.

437 (b) Dr. Robt. Jamieson] This should be John Jamieson.

437 (c–d) One relates to . . . Robert the Bruce . . . The other relates to . . . William Wallace] John Barbour's *The Bruce; The life and acts . . . of Sir William Wallace*, by Henry the Minstrel ('Blind Harry').

437 (e) Mr. Pinkerton] *The Bruce; or, the history of Robert I . . . With notes and a glossary by John Pinkerton*, 3 vols., London, 1790.

437 (e) Dr. Jamieson . . . to give us such an edition] John Jamieson's *The Bruce and Wallace*, 2 vols., Edinburgh, 1820.

438 (c) The Register, 8 volumes] Vols. 1–4 (each in 2 vols.), 1808–11, published 1810–13.

439 (a) Berlin collection of Kindermärchen] *Kinder- und Haus-Märchen*, 8vo Berlin, 1812.

441 (a) If he writes his own history] In his farewell address to his soldiers at Fontainebleau Napoleon said: 'I will write the history of our achievements.' (*Edin. Ann. Reg. for 1814*, VII. ii. xliii.)

441 (e) chamber in the wall] *Bible, II Kings* 4: 10.

441 *n.* 1] In line 9, for 'Farmer' read 'Fairley.'

442 (a) iron sleep] Virgil, *Aeneid*, x. 745–6: 'ferreus . . . somnus.'

442 *n.* 2] For a longer extract, see Partington, *Post-bag*, pp. 104–5.

443 (a) To Matthew Weld Hartstonge] This letter begun 1 May was not completed till after 17 June and should be placed at p. 455 below. Scott had written another letter on 3 June (below, p. 448) and it should precede the two fragments finally dated 17 June.

443 (e) to record his own deeds] See my note to *SL* iii. 441 (a).

443 (f) The last of our Scottish Douglasses] James Douglas, 9th Earl of Douglas, captured by James III in 1484 and secluded in Lindores Abbey, where he died in 1488.

443 *n.* 1] *Adelaide* was published at Dublin in 1811. In line 2, for 'O'Neil' read 'O'Neill.'

444 (c) Edinburgh, 17*th June*] By the time Scott began this portion he had received Hartstonge's letter of 28 May (NLS MS. 3885, ff. 97–8) and his letter of 13 June (NLS MS. 3885, ff. 104–6). The letter, therefore, could not be finished till 20 June at the earliest.

445 (d) Dr. Hill] Scott is referring to Hartstonge's information in his letter of 13 June. See my note to *SL* iii. 13 (c).

445 (d) "little prating Boy"] Shakespeare, *Merchant of Venice*, V. 1: 'a prating boy.'

445 (f) To Miss Clephane] To Margaret. Scott is answering her letter of 8 Dec. 1813 (NLS MS. 3884, f. 300) in which she gives a list of books ordered from Miller, the Edinburgh bookseller, and tells of the gift, said to be a snuff-box, but actually a toothpick case.

446 (b) spill] Read 'spell.' See above, p. 302.

446 (d) like honest John Bunyan] *The Pilgrim's progress*, Pt I, concluding sentence.

447 (a) Captain Barclay] Robert Barclay-Allardice, the famous pedestrian, commonly known as 'Captain Barclay.'

447 (c) fears and trivets] For 'trivets' read 'tirrits.' Shakespeare, *II Henry IV*, II. 4.

447 (d) Platon] Should be Platov or Platoff.

448 (a) toothpick case] See my note to *SL* iii. 445 (f).

448 (c) my younger acquaintance] Williamina, the youngest daughter of Mrs Clephane.

448 (e) professions in Jupiter] Read 'professors in Laputa.' (Corrected in *SL* xii. 488.) *Gulliver's travels*, Pt III, chap. 5. (Scott's *Swift*, 2nd ed., xi. 235–6.)

448 (f) I have left a long letter at Abbotsford half finished] The first portion dated 1 May is printed out of order, above, p. 443, along with its completion on 17 June.

449 (b) Pitt Club] Instituted 20 May 1814. The dinner was held on 28 May. As Scott says 'yesterday', this part of the letter must have been written on 29 May and the letter concluded on 3 June.

449 (e) Border Antiquities] See my note to *SL* iii. 423 *n.*

449 (f) they have published the songs together] *Songs sung at the anniversary dinner of the Pitt Club of Scotland, May 28, 1814.* Printed by James Ballantyne. (*Ruff*, No. 136.) There were five songs, two being by Scott: *O dread was the time* and *Though right be aft put down by strength*. Ruff records copy in NLS but does not note that it is imperfect. The first song was also issued as a broadside of which there is a copy in Edinburgh University Library (not recorded in *Ruff*).

450 (b) To Robert Southey] Scott is answering Southey's letter of 27 Apr. (NLS MS. 3885, ff. 83–4) which is printed in *The life and correspondence of Robert Southey*, London, 1849–50, iv. 68–71, and of which there is an extract in Partington, *Post-bag*, pp. 104–5. See also above, p. 442 *n.* 2.

451 (c) Bottom the Weaver] Shakespeare, *Midsummer Night's dream*, I. 2.

451 (c) I think it is Strap] Smollett, *Roderick Random*, chap. 10. It was for a guinea, however, that Strap proposed to cudgel or box the highwayman.

451 (d) Palm] A bookseller in Nuremberg, shot for publishing a pamphlet

against Napoleon. See *Scots Mag.* Vol. 68 (Oct. 1806), pp. 789–90, and Scott's *Napoleon* in *MPW* xii. 158–9.

451 (d) Hoffer] Andreas Hofer, patriot leader of the Tyrolese in 1809. His rifle is at Abbotsford. It was given to Sir Humphry Davy by Hofer's lieutenant whom Davy had cured of a fever and Davy gave it to Scott.

452 (b) An intimate friend] Adam Ferguson.

452 (c–d) fought the good fight] *Bible, I Timothy* 6: 12, or *II Timothy* 4: 7.

452 (d) To M. W. Hartstonge] Date is 1812 as is shown by the contents. There are at least eight clues which point to 1812. Two clues are given in *SL* xii. 487.

452 (e) The Amphi Theatre] Scott is thanking Hartstonge for a copy of Charles Vallencey's *Account of the ancient stone amphitheatre lately discovered in Kerry*, Dublin, 1812.

453 (a) Duns] See *The Pirate*, chap. 27.

453 (e) 3d Vol. of Gulliver] *Travels into several remote nations of the world. By Capt. Lemuel Gulliver. Vol. III*, 8vo London, 1727.

453 n. 1] *Histoire des Sevarambes* was the anonymous work of Denis Vairasse, called 'd'Alais en Languedoc'; hence the form Alletz.

454 (a) Anthologia] *Anthologia Hibernica; or, monthly collections of science, belles-lettres, and history.* 4 vols., 8vo Dublin, 1793–4.

454 (b) Croker's Theatrical Poem] *Familiar epistles on the state of the Irish stage* [addressed to F. E. Jones], Dublin, 1804.

454 (c–d) Brackenridge] Hugh Henry Brackenridge (1748–1816). His letter to Scott (1 Mar.–4 May 1812) is in NLS (MS. 3882, ff. 93–6).

454 (f) flourished like green bay trees] See *SL* i. 23 and my note.

455 (b) To William Hayley] There is no 1814 letter from him in Walpole Coll. in NLS.

455 (b–c) the chain of friendship] See *SL* ii. 535 and my note.

455 (e) I have had a letter lying by me . . . from Sophia] Sophia's letter is printed in *Trans. Hawick Arch. Soc.* 1921, p. 24.

455 (e) children's epistles] Shakespeare, *Twelfth Night*, V. 1. See amended text in *SL* xii. 488.

456 (b) *Hawick Arch. Socy.*] Add: *Trans.* 1921, pp. 23–4.

456 (c) your very entertaining letter] Of 13 May, cited above, p. 447 *n.*

456 (d) a very good reply of Louis] Scott, in his *History of Europe* in *Edin. Ann. Reg. for 1814*, VII. i. 289, gives this anecdote slightly altered.

456 n. 1] Delete 'Surtees was urging him to write a poem on the '15 or the '45.' See my note to *SL* i. 341 *n.*

458 (e) earn²] Index figure should be 3. Add '3' in note.

458 (f) to be confined . . . late domestic distress] A daughter was born at Dalkeith on 13 Aug. Katherine Frances had died on 6 June.

459 (a) Political Memento] By Walter Henry Watts. See *SL* xii. 418, 418 *n.*

459 (d) I John Lyster] This is earlier than Joe Miller. It relates to Ben Jonson and Sylvester. See Byron's note to his *Don Juan*, Canto I, st. XI.

459 n. 1] See also *Edin. Ann. Reg. for 1814*, VII. i. 345–50.

460 (b) to my exceeding refreshment] See my note to *SL* iii. 391 (a).

461 (b) per aversionem] A Scots law phrase meaning a quantity of unspecified amount. See Trayner, *Latin maxims*. Used in *Nigel*, chap. 27.

461 (c) sloop belonging to the Northern Light Commissioners] The *Regent*.

461 n. 1] Scott is not referring to the number of copies sold but to the second edition which was to consist of 2,000 copies. The second edition was not ready till after 28 July (below, p. 479).

462 (c) in a hay-loft] This is the bureau in which the MS. of *Waverley* was found; i.e. in the Doctor's Barn and not in the attics of the cottage as Martin Hardy's picture depicts it.

463 n. 2] Twice in line 1, for 'Baillie' read 'Bailie.'

464 (c) "just going to sea for a trip"]
Charles Dibdin, *The lucky escape*, st. I,
line 6. A ballad in *Private theatricals*.
In his *A collection of songs*, London
[1792], ii. 129.

464 *n.* I] In lines I and 4, for 'Shiel'
read 'Sheil.' Scott had already received a copy of *Adelaide*. See above,
p. 443 and my note.

465 (e) Sheill's violent love] See above,
p. 443.

465 (e) Boswell fair] Fair at St. Boswells, Roxburghshire. Held annually
on 18 July.

466 (b) A Parody on the Lay] *The lay
of the Scottish fiddle*, by James Kirke
Paulding.

467 (d) excluded from the London
boards] Not strictly true. Joanna
Baillie's *Family legend*, produced first
at Edinburgh in 1810, was produced at
Drury Lane in 1815.

468 (c) the Excursion] There is no
letter in *SL* acknowledging this. Wordsworth wrote to R. P. Gillies, 22 Dec.
1814: 'I sent him the "Excursion" and
am rather surprised that I have had no
letter from him acknowledging the
receipt of it' (Gillies, *Memoirs*, ii. 153).

468 (d) Roderick] By Robert Southey.

468 (d–e) Up wi' the bonny blue bon-
net] See *SL* ii. 306 and my note.

470 (b) swept and garnished] *Bible,
Matthew* 12: 44; *Luke* 11: 25.

470 (d) To Miss Clephane] To Margaret.

471 (e) Saint of the Green Isle] Thomas
Moore, *A Canadian boat song*, st. [3],
lines 3–4.

473 (f) "The boat rocks . . ."] Burns,
My bonny Mary, st. [I], lines 5–8, slightly
varied. In *Johnson*, Vol. 3 (1790), No.
231.

475 (d) Elvira] Pizarro's mistress in
Sheridan's *Pizarro*. Young (mentioned
in the next paragraph) played the part
of Rollo.

476 (a) To Joseph Train] If date is
correct Scott was in Edinburgh, not
at Abbotsford.

477 (a) To J. B. S. Morritt] Date is 24
July, the day before he went to Edinburgh (below, p. 480).

477 *n.* I] Morritt's letter of 14 July
is in *Lockhart*, iv. 397–9; *FL* i. 325–7;
and Partington, *Letter-books*, pp. 111–12.
The letter of 21 July is in *Lockhart*, iv.
399 (extract) and in *FL* i. 328–9.

478 (b) We sail on the 27.] The yacht
left on the 29th.

479 (a) indifferent honest] Shakespeare, *Hamlet*, III. I.

479 (d) I shall whistle it down the wind]
Shakespeare, *Othello*, III. 3: 'I'd
whistle her off, and let her down the
wind / To prey at fortune.'

479 (f) I wish for poor auld Scotlands
sake] *Lockhart* (iv. 177) says this is from
Burns's *On my early days*. He probably
means *To the guidwife of Wauchope
House*, st. [2], line 4: 'That I, for poor
auld Scotland's sake.'

480 *n.* 2] *Cona* was written by James
Gray.

484 (a) bald disjointed] Shakespeare,
I Henry IV, I. 3.

484 (d) the thing that is not] A phrase
taken from *Gulliver's travels*. See Scott's
Swift, 2nd ed., xi. 299, 304, 305, 314,
330.

487 (c) killed by Hieland bodies]
Robert Burns, *Lines written in a wrapper,
enclosing a letter to Captain Grose*, st. [3]:
'Is he slain by Highlan' bodies? / Igo
and ago, / And eaten like a wether-
haggis? / Iran, coram, dago.'

487 (d) strong on scenery] i.e. on *The
Lord of the Isles*.

488 (c) D. and S.'s failure] Doig and
Stevenson. See below, p. 527.

489 (c) love-begotten babe] *Waverley*.

489 (d) melancholy incident at Dal-
keith] Death of the Duchess of Buccleuch.

490 (e) loss of world's gear] Burns, *The
death and dying words of poor Mailie.
The elegy*, st. [2], line 1: 'It's no the loss
o' warl's gear.'

493 *n.* I] The Duke's letter is in *Lockhart*, iv. 382–4.

495 (b) mention the subject of your
letter] McCulloch's letter is not in NLS.

496 (b) a Light Set upon a Hill]
Perhaps a garbled version of *Bible,
Matthew* 5: 14: 'Ye are the light of the

world. A city that is set on an hill cannot be hid.'

496 (f) "an iron man of iron mold"] Spenser, *The Faerie Queene*, V. I. xii, lines 2 and 6: 'An yron man ... / ... made of yron mould.'

497 (e) "poor Tom I cannot daub it further"] Shakespeare, *King Lear*, IV. I.

497 (f) another Mackenzie] Hugh Mackenzie who died at London on 27 Aug.

497 n. 1] For 'September' read 'August.'

500 (a) in a friend] Duke of Buccleuch.

501 (d) I now return the MS.] Polwhele had asked Scott to read the MS. of *Fair Isabel* in his letter of 16 May 1813 (NLS MS. 3884, ff. 147–8) and Scott had replied that he would (above, p. 315). Scott has thus kept the MS. for over a year.

501 n. 2] See *SL* iv. 117.

502 (d) To Thomas Scott] The correct date, 9 Dec. 1814, is given in *SL* vii. 406. For rest of letter, see *SL* vii. 477–8. Tom's reply is in *FL* i. 344.

503 (b) If you are not Sir John Falstaff] Shakespeare, *II Henry IV*, IV. 3.

503 (d) I beg my compliments . . .] I feel sure that this is an interpolation in *Lockhart* (iv. 402). It bears no relation to the rest of the letter and is meaningless without Tom's letter (cited by Grierson in footnote) which probably prompted Lockhart to invent the sentence. Lockhart made no comment on the sentence.

503 n. 1] Tom's reply, postmarked 15 July 1815, is in *FL* i. 344–5. The letter from Tom cited in this note is *not* a reply to Scott's letter of 8 Dec. 1814 and probably belongs to late 1815. Under Mar. 1816 in *Edin. Ann. Reg.* IX. ii. xxiii–xxiv, it is announced that Norton is publishing a History of the late war in Canada. The misdating by Grierson seems to arise by linking it with the concluding sentence of Scott's letter (for which see my previous note).

505 (c) To John Ballantyne] Cancel. Not indexed. For correct version, see *SL* i. 472–4.

506 (b) To John Ballantyne] Cancel. Not indexed.

507 (b) To John Ballantyne] Cancel. For complete letter, see *SL* i. 464–6.

507 n. 2] In last line, for 'dates' read 'debts.'

508 (c) "God bless that good friend..."] Shakespeare, *Timon of Athens*, III. 2.

511 n. 1] There is an extract from her letter in *Lockhart*, iv. 400–1. In line 1, for 'Kelly' read 'Kelty.'

512 (e) Mrs. Clephane] Read 'Miss Clephane.'

515 (a) Mrs. Smollett] This is presumably Mrs Alexander Telfer Smollett, C. K. Sharpe's aunt. See *Sharpe's Letters*, ii. 46–8.

515 (a) MS. Tragedy of Maturin's] *Bertram*.

515 n. 1] In second last line, between 'Terry' and 'Yet' insert three dots to indicate Lockhart's omission of reference to another work. The author was William Rufus Chetwood.

516 (a) Lady Raeburn] Mrs Walter Scott of Raeburn. 'Lady Raeburn' is a Scottish courtesy title.

516 n. 1] Southey (*Common-place book*, iii. 711) says he saw this copy at Ashiestiel. This is impossible.

517 (a) To Maria Edgeworth] This letter should not have been included. It must be regarded as Ballantyne's own. *Lockhart* (iv. 405–8) dates it 11 Nov.

521 (a) Sinbad's old man of the sea] See my note to *SL* i. 369 (b).

522 (d) caviare to the multitude] Shakespeare, *Hamlet*, II. 2.

522 (d) Robert Jameson] This should be John Jamieson.

523 (a) Mr. Park] George Park, tenant in Carterhaugh and later in Oakwoodmill. Lord Montagu in his reply of 11 Dec. (NLS MS. 3885, ff. 234–5) said: 'Nothing will I trust prevent my Brother's getting Carter Haugh into his own hands, indeed so far as Mr Park is concerned it is settled.'

523 (e) Mine Broder is de bestest Poet] *More lyric odes to the Royal Academicians*, Ode VII, st. [8]. In *The works of Peter Pindar* [pseud. of John Wolcot], London, 1812, i. 66. The lines are based on

the Dutchman's remark in Smollett's *Peregrine Pickle*, chap. 65.

524 (d) death of a Friend] Duchess of Buccleuch.

525 (c) Bedingfield and Pickering] See my note to *SL* iv. 15 (f).

525 *n.* 1] In line 16, Shanks should be Foster. See my note to *SL* iii. 526 *n.* 2.

526 *n.* 1] For 'Rob Roxby' read 'George Rokesby' and delete 'See Note H to *Rokeby*.' Rokesby was Clerk in the Tyne Bank, Newcastle, and, suffering from paralysis, was indigent. The title of his poem is *The lay of the Reedwater minstrel . . . By a son of Reed*, 4to Newcastle, Printed for the author, by D. Akenhead and Sons, 1809.

526 *n.* 2] Delete this note. Robin of Redesdale and Robin of Risingham are alternative names for the same person. The 'perpetrator', who destroyed the stone, was Foster (not Shanks as given above, p. 525 *n.*). On the destruction of the stone, see also *SL* iv. 271, note to *Rokeby*, Canto I, st. 20, and *Ivanhoe*, Dedicatory Epistle.

527 (d) two of £300] One to Rev. Dr Douglas for the balance of Abbotsford (3 lines above, and cf. *SL* i. 516, where the letter should probably be dated 1814); and one to Charles Erskine (cf. *SL* i. 472, 516).

529 (c) piping days of peace] Shakespeare, *Richard III*, I. 1.

529 (f) huge cave] Smoo Cave. See Scott's *Diary* in *Lockhart*, iv. 280–90, and *SL* iv. 22.

530 (b) Another cave] See Scott's *Diary* in *Lockhart*, iv. 320–1.

531 (a) the old gentleman] Thomas Coutts (1735–1822), whose daughter Frances married on 17 Sept. 1800, as his second wife, the 1st Marquess of Bute who died on 16 Nov. 1814.

531 (f) Mandeville] Scott is at fault here. There is no reference to frozen words in his *Voiage and travaile*. John Macculloch in his *Highlands and Western Isles of Scotland*, 1824, quotes same story from Mandeville. The story is a fiction of Addison and Steele, based on an imaginary manuscript of Mandeville, in the *Tatler*, No. 254, 23 Nov. 1710. Their idea was no doubt taken from Butler's *Hudibras*, Pt I, Canto I, line 148, 'Like words congeal'd in northern air,' which they quote. But these writers may have taken the idea from Rabelais, *Gargantua and Pantagruel*, Bk IV, chaps. 55–6. This theme, however, is an ancient one. See *N. & Q.* Vol. 176, pp. 154–5.

531 *n.* 1] Delete this note, which is inapplicable. Scott is referring to Thomas, not John, Coutts.

532 (d) Marmion] This is 9th ed., published in Apr. 1815.

532 (d) to refresh the machine] Lockhart three times refers to this (v. 14, 15, 21) as if Scott were referring to *Guy Mannering*. But Scott, as it will be noticed, definitely means that he is going to take exercise, not that he is going to write. Furthermore, Lockhart 'quotes' words which do not occur in the letter.

532 (f) Ferrier] Archibald Campbell Ferrier, W.S., died on 25 Dec. His father, James Ferrier, was a Principal Clerk of Session.

533 (b) Camiestone] William Riddell of Camieston.

535 (d) To Joanna Baillie] The date is about 24 Mar. 1815 as the contents show.

536 (c) Richardson . . . in summer] Mr and Mrs Richardson visited Scott in Oct. 1814 and stayed more than 'one day or two'. They were at Abbotsford, 25–8, and perhaps longer.

536 (d–e) the Hermit Fincal] *Mirglip the Persian; or, Fincal the Dervise of the Groves*. In Weber, *Tales of the East*, iii. 573.

536 (e) to dedicate a seat to you] For other references to Joanna's Bower, see Index under Abbotsford. II. Estate. (2) Separate Parts. Joanna's Bower.

536 (e) walk under their shade] Virgil, *Georgics*, II. 57–8.

536 (f) the more classical and interesting posture] Virgil, *Eclogues*, I. 1.

537 (a) her namesake in Tom Jones] Sophia Western in Fielding's *Tom Jones*, Bk IV, chap. 5.

537 (f) sale of prints] The sale of Alexander Gibson Hunter's prints began on Friday, 24 Mar. 1815. Advertised

in *Edin. Weekly Jour.* Vol. 18 (15 Mar. 1815), p. 81. See also above, p. 232.

538 (e) To George Thomson] Scott's date, 19 Dec., is correct and should not have been changed. Scott refers to the meeting of the Speculative on Saturday and this Saturday meeting was 17 Dec. at Fortune's at which Scott took the chair after Dr Baird left. (*Scots Mag.* Vol. 77 (Jan. 1815), pp. 69–71.) There

was a *second* meeting on Saturday, 24 Dec., but this is not the meeting to which Scott is referring as Grierson erroneously assumes in his footnote.

539 *n.* 2] Delete this note, which is no longer applicable.

542 (b) "*Lady of the Lake*"] Read '*Lord of the Isles.*'

VOLUME IV

2 (b–c) when I am dull there is a design] The *Tatler*, No. 38. See also *SL* vii. 284.

2 (d) To Lord Byron] The words on p. 3, 'owing to my absence from Edinburgh, where it had been lying . . . in Castle Street' correspond to 'a general jail delivery' in a letter to Polwhele, 4 Nov. 1815 (below, p. 117). The date of this letter is probably Nov. 1815.

2 *n.* 2] The only copy of *The Giaour* at Abbotsford is the first ed. The vol. of this work with Byron's inscription 'To the monarch of Parnassus' went amissing in Scott's day. It was borrowed by James Ballantyne and probably never returned.

3 *n.* 1] See *SL* i. 391 (a) and my note.

5 (c) Indian Jugglers] It was advertised in *Edinburgh Evening Courant*, 5 Jan. 1815, that the Indian Jugglers would commence their performances in Corri's Rooms on Friday, 6 Jan.

7 (b) Lawrence] Sir Thomas Lawrence painted portraits of Lord and Lady Abercorn. One, of the former, had been exhibited at the Royal Academy in 1814. See *Walpole Society*, Vol. 39, London, 1964, p. 13.

7 (c) To Daniel Terry] Date is July 15. (Corrected in *SL* vi. 262 *n.* 3 and *SL* xii. 488.)

7 *n.* 1] Delete note. Terry's only wife was Elizabeth Nasmyth whom he married on 23 June 1815. Scott's reference to her art (p. 8) alludes to her as an artist, not as an actress as Grierson supposes.

8 (d) the strange eventful history] Shakespeare, *As you like it*, II. 7.

8 *n.* 1] The correct quotation is: 'That

e'er a full-pot of good ale you can swallow, / He's here with a whoop, and gone with a holla.'

9 (e) my harp is . . . hung upon the willows] *Bible, Psalms* 137: 2.

10 (a) Your kind remembrance] Berwick wrote on 23 June and again on 21 Oct. The former would reach Scott *before* he set out on his Lighthouse tour and the latter *after* he returned. Scott's excuse, therefore, is invalid.

11 (d) Lines] Read 'Lives'; i.e. *Lives of Marcus Valerius Messala Corvinus*, etc.

12 (a) To J. B. S. Morritt] Since Scott's last letter of 14 Sept. 1814 (*SL* iii. 495–8), Morritt had written three letters: 22 Sept. (NLS MS. 3885, ff. 168–70), 21 Nov. (NLS MS. 3885, ff. 215–16) and 12 Jan. 1815 (NLS MS. 3886, ff. 20–1). This present letter of 19 Jan. is Scott's first reply to all three. Scott's answer to the first was probably written Sept.–Oct. although dated by Lockhart 11 Nov. (v. 12–13) and is printed below, pp. 18–19.

12 (c) Tom Thumb] Tom Thumb, in the nursery tale, was swallowed by a cow. See *Tom Thumb*, st. [32–8]. In Thomas Evans, *Old ballads*, new ed., 4 vols., London, 1810, iv. 6–7.

12 (f) Solve jam senescentem] Horace, *Epistles*, I. i. 8–9. 'Solve senescentem mature sanus equum, ne / Peccet ad extremum ridendus, et ilia ducat.' (Unyoke the aged horse in time, if you are wise.) Also quoted in *SL* xi. 335, 337.

13 (d) as in a glass darkly] *Bible*, I *Corinthians* 13: 12.

14 *n.* 1] For '314' read '316.'

14 *n.* 3] Delete 'surely.' Scott wrote to Morritt at Worthing (*SL* iii. 495).

15 (d) Orator Higgins] Fletcher, *Beggars' Bush*, II. 1.

15 (f) Pickering . . .] *Poetry, fugitive and original; by the late Thomas Bedingfeld, Esq. and Mr. George Pickering*, etc., 8vo Newcastle, 1815. The 'friend' who edited it was James Ellis. It has a printed dedication to Scott. I have a copy with MS. notes by Ellis.

16 (d) inaugural speech] Scott received *First annual report of the Antiquarian Society of Newcastle upon Tyne*, 4to Newcastle, 1814, but it does not contain anything called an inaugural speech.

17 *n.* 1] The Scottish History Society also issued Macfarlane's *Geographical collections relating to Scotland*, ed. by *Sir Arthur Mitchell and James T. Clark*, 3 vols., Edinburgh, 1906–8.

18 (a) the beautiful verses] Morritt's poem was included in his letter of 22 Sept. 1814 (NLS MS. 3885, ff. 168–70). It consists of four four-line stanzas beginning: 'Loves not the heart the quiet scene / Of affluent Ocean's deep repose?'

18 (f) Who boast their native filabeg] See my note to *SL* ii. 353 *n.* 1.

19 (b) I wrote you a few days since] i.e. on 19 Jan. (above, p. 12). For 'since the above scrawl' read 'since. The above scrawl.'

22 (d) Edinburgh Register] *Edin. Ann. Reg. for 1812* (publ. 1814) V. ii. 438–42.

24 (a) "these knights will hack . . ."] Shakespeare, *Merry wives of Windsor*, II. 1.

24 (a–b) "I like not such *grinning* honour . . ."] Shakespeare, *I Henry IV*, V. 3.

24 (d) burnish the chain of friendship] See *SL* ii. 535 and my note.

24 *n.* 1] In line 1, for 'Fergusson' read 'Ferguson.'

25 (a) Mr. Cadells note] Mr Alan Bell tells me that this is not in NLS and that the Constable letter-books contain nothing to explain 'Mr. Murrays business.'

27 (d) Mr. Thomson] Rev. John Thomson. He was painting a picture of Duddingston for Lord Abercorn. See *SL* iii. 217, 217 *n.*, 274.

27 (e) Bruce] Bruce's accuracy was also vindicated by Edward Daniel Clarke in his *Travels*, Pt II, Sect. II. The relevant portion of text was reprinted in the *Scots Mag.* Vol. 76 (Oct. 1814), pp. 752–5. Bruce's account of eating raw flesh was also substantiated.

28 (e) Pitt from Hoppner's fine painting] Though called an Indian ink drawing (below, p. 34 *n.*) this seems to be the sepia drawing (6·6 × 5·85 in.), signed 'W. Behnes 1815' at Abbotsford.

28 *n.* 1] For the reference to raw beef, see Bruce's *Travels to discover the source of the Nile*, 2nd ed., Edinburgh, 1804, iv. 482–5. Cf. *SL* xi. 273.

29 (a) To Mrs. Clephane] Date is probably July, just before Lord Compton's marriage to Margaret Clephane on 24 July.

29 (e) Mr. Seabright] Seebright, a character in Maria Edgeworth's *Patronage*, chap. 22.

29 (e) Horace] *Odes*, I. iii. 9–10: aes triplex / circa pectus erat.

30 (b) as Corporal Nym says] Shakespeare, *Henry V*, II. 1.

31 (a) Lord Presid.] Robert Blair.

31 (e) For many a lad I loved] Charles Morris, *The toper's apology*. Also quoted in *Chronicles of the Canongate* [1st ser. Chrystal Croftangry's introd., chap. 1] and more fully in *SL* ix. 501.

34 *n.* 1] See also above, p. 28 and my note.

35 *n.* 1] In line 6, for 'Mundy' read 'Munday.'

36 (c) To John Ballantyne] This letter has already been printed with date 26 Feb. 1814 in *SL* iii. 413–14. Either year would suit the contents, but as 26 Feb. was a Sunday in 1815 I have accepted the latter year. Cancel the letter in *SL* iii.

36 *n.* 1] William Blackwood issued the reprint in 1814. William Laing and William Blackwood issued the reprint in 1815. Both are identical in size (small quarto).

37 (d) the London journey] i.e. of John Ballantyne.

38 (a) To Lady Macleod] There is a facsimile of this letter in *Dunvegan Castle; a poem*, by H. S. Rathbone, London, 1900, between p. 22 and p. 23. It shows that the letter was addressed to 'Mrs. Macleod of Macleod,' not to 'Lady Macleod.'

38 (b–c) Strathaird] A district in S. of Skye. From the Lighthouse yacht, lying in Loch Slapin, Scott wrote on 25 Aug. to Alexander Macallister of Strathaird, apologizing for visiting a cave without permission. The letter is not in *SL* but the original is in NLS (MS. 3653, ff. 162–3).

38 (f) treatise on the second sight] Robert Kirk's *Secret commonwealth*.

39 (a) the little tartan chief] Norman Macleod, born in 1812, later 25th Chief.

40 (e) The Castle of Vincennes] For explanation of this allusion, see below, p. 71 and *n*. 1.

41 (b) To Daniel Terry] Year is 1814. (Correction in *SL* xii. 488.)

43 (b) To Miss Clephane] Margaret.

44 (c) sale of the farm] Powguild. See below, p. 62.

45 (c) early put out] Read 'easily put out.' (Correction in *SL* xii. 488.)

46 (e) Benmore or Bentalla] Benmore and Ben Talaidh, two mountains in Mull.

47 (c) the Fife farm] Powguild. See below, p. 62.

49 (c) politics] Scott must mean poetical works.

49 (f) cruel letter] Grierson suggests (*SL* xii. 488) that this should be 'civil letter.' But 'cruel' might be a more appropriate epithet for Northampton's letters than 'civil.'

50 (b) on her bended knees] Scott means 'on my bended knees.'

50 (b) *argent* comptoreal] Read '*argent* comptant.' (Correction in *SL* xii. 488.)

51 (c) your Fifeshire farm] Powguild. See below, p. 62.

52 (e) J. Whishaw] Scott met him the following month at a dinner given by the Carrs at Frognal, Hampstead (*Memoirs of Lucy Aikin*, 1864, pp. 99–100), but from this letter it seems they had already met.

54 *n*. 2] For 'Fergusson' read 'Ferguson.'

55 (b) To Mr. Wilkie] Scott could not receive a letter of 22 Apr. (see *n*. 2) till at least 25 Apr. and 'two days since' would make Scott's letter at least 27 Apr. In any case Scott's 'two days since' refers to date of receipt, not to date of letter.

57 (a) Kean's . . . ONeil] Drury Lane approached Mrs Henry Siddons in Edinburgh to play Juliet to Kean's Romeo. She declined. See Dibdin, *Annals*, p. 269.

57 (d) To John Richardson] This letter should be dated Mar. 1820. (Correction in *SL* xii. 488.)

60 (c) to love God and our Neighbour] A paraphrase of *Bible*, Mark 12: 33.

60 (d) excuse if] Read 'excuse it.'

60 (e) the humour of forty fancies] Shakespeare, *Taming of the shrew*, III. 2. It is Biondello who says this.

62 (c) Powguild] This farm in Fife has been mentioned before (above, pp. 44, 47, 51), but this is the first time its name has been given.

65 (a) corning] See suggested amendment in *SL* xii. 488.

66 (a) Laird of Logan] For fuller details of the anecdote, see *SL* vii. 137.

67 *n*. 1] There are no brilliants in the snuff-box. The date engraved on it is 23 May 1815, the date of Scott's letter to MacMahon, the Prince Regent's Private Secretary.

69 (a) Madame Simon] Probably Mme Simond, wife of Louis Simond. Lady Louisa Stuart spelt her name 'Simon.'

69 *n*. 2] To this reference add *SL* i. 465 *n*., iv. 277–8, 279–80, 294.

70 (c) Wordsworth] Scott, while in London, wrote to Wordsworth. The letter, dated only Saturday, is in Morley, *The correspondence of H. C. Robinson with the Wordsworth circle*, 1927, ii. 845. It is not in *SL*. A letter from Wordsworth to Scott, 24 May 1815, is in *Heber letters*, p. 269. Wordsworth, Heber and Scott were invited to

Sir George Beaumont's on Friday, 26 May.

70 (c) flourishing like a green bay tree] See *SL* i. 23 and my note.

71 (c) To Miss Bond] The date must be Spring 1814. Her *Letters of a village governess*, 2 vols., London, 1814, was issued about Apr. 1814 (*ER* Vol. 23, p. 251). Also John Ballantyne (p. 72) was going to London about that time. Among the subscribers were Scott and his wife, Lady Douglas and Lady Louisa Stuart. Morritt and his wife each subscribed for five copies, no doubt through Scott's good offices.

72 (e) To Mrs. Clephane] She wrote from Edinburgh on Tuesday, 18 July, that Allan Maclean would arrive at Abbotsford on Wednesday evening or Thursday morning with Oberon, a pony. (NLS MS. 3886, ff. 173–4). Scott's letter, therefore, should be dated 20 July or, possibly, 21.

72 n.] Miss Bond's work has a printed dedication to Scott.

73 (d–e) "a Giant with one idea"] Not traced in any of Coleridge's published works. Scott may have heard of his remark from Southey or Wordsworth or from some other oral source.

75 (b) highland article] Review of *Culloden papers* for *QR* of Jan. 1816.

75 (d) a young person] Probably Thomas Wilkie. See letter to him above, p. 55.

75 n. 2] *The dance of death* was published in the *Edin. Ann. Reg. for 1813*, VI [not V]. ii. cccxxxv–cccxxxix. It is dated 'Abbotsford, October 1, 1815.' It cannot, therefore, be the 'Gaudeamus poem' to which Scott refers. I think this 'Gaudeamus poem' was a projected work on the victory of the allies but that it was superseded by the *Field of Waterloo*.

77 (b) I wrote her a long letter and her father another] The former of 17 Feb. is above, pp. 29–33, and the latter of 18 Feb. is in *SL* xii. 421–4.

77 n. 3] Correct this note as follows: *Ode to desolation: with some other poems. By* Matthew Weld Hartstonge, Esq., 8vo London, Longman, 1815.

78 n. 2] Malcolm's letter has been already cited in *SL* iii. 150 n., where it is dated 23 Feb.

79 (b) two handsome cuirasses] These are in the Entrance Hall at Abbotsford. In a room not open to tourists are kept other Waterloo relics: a memorandum book, the MS. collection of French songs and a German prayer-book. The cross of the Legion of Honour was for many years in the Kelso Museum and is now in Paris.

81 (d–c) John Dacosta] Jean Baptiste de Coster. See *Paul's letters*.

85 (e) federe's] Read 'federés' [i.e. fédérés].

87 (c) third packet] Sent under Lord Castlereagh's cover. See *SL* xii. 142–3.

87 (f) the national guard . . . Ro: Miller] In *Paul's letters* (*MPW* v. 264–5) Scott wrote: 'the National Guard, who, in dress and appearance, remind me very much of the original or blue regiment of Edinburgh Volunteers.' Robert Miller, bookseller, Parliament Square, was a member. (*A view of the establishment of the Royal Edinburgh Volunteers*, Edinburgh, 1795, p. 45.)

88 (d) things must be as they may] Shakespeare, *Henry V*, II. 1.

89 (a) The soldier dwells] *Turnimspike*, st. [5], lines 3–4. In *Herd*, ii. 187.

90 (b) To Lady Alvanley] As the verses were written 'last night', the letter should be dated 13 Aug. 1815.

90 (d) Dogberry] See *SL* ii. 320.

91 (a) To James Ballantyne] Date must be August, for Scott wrote to him on 30 Aug. saying he hoped he had got the 'poem complete' (above, p. 87).

91 (a) sends abroad Don Roderk.] An ed. of *Don Roderick, The field of Waterloo and other poems* was publ. in 1815 (*Ruff*, No. 116). But *The field of Waterloo* was also published separately (*Ruff*, No. 147).

92 (c) John D'Accosta] Jean Baptiste de Coster. See above, p. 81 and my note.

94 (c) the Eastern tale] *The adventures of Aboulfouaris, surnamed the Great Voyager. First voyage.* (Weber, *Tales of the East*, ii. 474–6.)

96 (b–c) rich in corn wine and oil]

Mentioned many times in O.T. See a Bible concordance.

97 (a) To M. W. Hartstonge] From the contents the date must be Nov. 1815. Hartstonge replied to the letter on 21 Nov. (NLS MS. 3886, ff. 235–6).

97 (d) a large farm . . .] The farm is Kaeside and the great lake is Cauld-shiels Loch.

97 *n.* 1] *Review: or his memoirs of his engagement and carriage in the Irish wars.* Repr., Dublin, 1815.

98 (e) copy of] Read 'copy for.'

99 (a) Judge Osborne] In his *Swift*, 2nd ed., xix. 316, Scott refers to Judge Marshal but makes no reference to Judge Osborne.

99 (a) verses addressed to Sophia] *Address to Miss Scott on her return to Scotland*, by Ian Vich Hay, 24 June 1815, was printed in the *Monthly Mag.* Vol. 40 (1 Sept. 1815), pp. 141–2.

99 (d) Col. Stanley] Col. Thomas Stanley, M.P. for Lancashire, Mrs Morritt's brother.

100 (d) tirrets and frights] Shakespeare, *II Henry IV*, II. 4.

101 (b) an inn at Carlisle] Old Bush Inn. Hume's verses, with slight variations, were printed in John Preston Neale's *Views of the seats of noblemen*, etc., 2nd ser. Vol. 2 (1825) under the section 'Corby Castle,' where it is stated that the lines were 'communicated to Mr. Howard by Sir Walter Scott.' Scott wrote to Howard in 1806 (NLS MS. 3875, f. 148) but his letter did not concern Hume's verses. The pane of glass is now in Corby Castle. See Hughes, *Letters*, p. 82 and *n.*

101 (e) century of inventions] Perhaps a reference to the work by the 2nd Marquess of Worcester (1601–67): *A century of the names and scantlings of such inventions*, etc., popularly called 'A century of inventions.'

102 *n.* 1] Delete. See my note to *SL* iv. 75 *n.* 2.

103 (a–b) Nimrod . . . a mighty . . . hunter before the Lord] *Bible, Genesis* 10: 9.

103 *n.* 2] Delete the last sentence. Sir John Malcolm has already been mentioned a number of times.

104 (b) To Robert Shortreed] Campbell's third journey to the Borders took place between 8 and 31 Oct. 1816. (MS. in Edin. Univ. Lib.) This letter is, therefore, probably Friday, 4 Oct. 1816.

104 *n.* 1] Delete this note. Thomas o' Twizzlehope was 'Auld' Thomas in 1792 and would be dead by 1816. 'Mr. Thomas' must be Thomas Shortreed, Robert Shortreed's eldest son, almost 21 at this time and old enough to be called 'Mr. Thomas' and old enough to take down tunes.

105 (e) I sent a thing] *The dance of death.* See *SL* i. 494.

105 (e) *what thou doest do quickly*] *Bible, John* 13: 27. Scott was severely criticized in contemporary reviews for his irreverent use of Scriptural language, but he did not reform. He used this quotation in *Woodstock*, chap. 34.

105 *n.* 1] 'Mr. Hogarth' is Robert Hogarth whose daughter, Christina, Ballantyne married on 1 Feb. 1816.

106 (b) the enclosed pamphlet] *The Field of Waterloo.*

106 (c) as Tony Lumpkin says] Goldsmith, *She stoops to conquer*, Act V: 'there's not a pond or slough within five miles of the place but they can tell the taste of.'

106 (d) the "lovely isle"] For 'lovely isle' read 'lonely isle.' See my note to *SL* ii. 506 (a).

107 (e) the old housekeeper] Mrs Home, a servant of the family for seventy years. By showing visitors over the castle she realized over £30,000 and died in 1834, aged 93. (*Ann. Reg.* 1834, Chron., p. 233.)

108 (d) Who is't mount guard] John Scott in his *Journal of a tour to Waterloo* (London, 1842), p. 222, gives Scott's addition to *Bannocks of barley meal* as: 'Who is't keeps guard / At Versailles and at Marli? / Who but the lads / That eat bannocks of barley?' See also below, p. 126.

109 (e) coals of fire] *Bible, Proverbs* 25: 22; *Romans* 12: 20.

110 (b) son of Mr. Robert Shortreed] Robert, born 1801.

112 (b) Mossknow] Scott has been writing of Kaeside. The former owner,

Moss, gave his name to Moss's Stripe and Moss's Park, but there was no Mossknow. Scott is probably inventing the name for the nonce as a companion to Parnassus.

112 (d) great musical festival] First Edinburgh Musical Festival, 30 Oct.– 5 Nov. 1815. See George Farquhar Graham, *An account of the first Edinburgh musical festival*, 12mo Edinburgh, 1816.

113 (c) To Lady Louisa Stuart] Lady Louisa's letter of 29 Oct., which Scott is answering, is in *FL* i. 347–9.

114 (f) Dogberry] See *SL* ii. 320.

115 (d) an Edition of Waterloo not exceeding 3000] 3rd ed. (*Ruff*, No. 149).

115 (e) to print 6000 instead of 3000 Paul] Constable must have discussed this with Murray, for Murray in his letter to Scott of 8 Nov. wrote: 'As to the enlargement of the edition of "Paul's Letters" to 6000, I can only assure you that, in my opinion, such an impression will be sold in a fortnight.' (Smiles, *John Murray*, i. 286.)

115 (f) a few 4to. Rodericks] This proposed ed. apparently did not materialize. It is not recorded in *Ruff*.

115 n. 1] Amend. Three eds. were published in 1816.

117 (a) a grand musical festival] See above, p. 112 and my note.

117 n. 1] The book was printed at Truro and published at London. The volume contains two poems addressed to Scott (pp. 3–8, 342–50). Scott is suggested as the reviewer of the poem in *QR* for Jan. 1816 (*Shine*, No. 369).

120 (a) wild sheet of water] Cauldshiels Loch.

120 (d) "some yet untasted spring"] The nearest to this I can find is: 'A new repast, or an untasted spring.' (Addison, *Cato*, I. 4.)

121 (b) the Gods have not made her poetical] Shakespear, *As you like it*, III. 3.

121 (e) Mrs. Scott and she are . . . in Edinburgh] At the First Edinburgh Musical Festival. See above, p. 112 and my note.

121 (f) "things must be as they may"] Shakespeare, *Henry V*, II. 1.

121 (f) You cannot expect grapes from thorns] Bible, *Matthew* 7: 16.

122 (d) letter from Lady Compton] Of 7 Oct. from Castle Ashby (NLS MS. 3886, ff. 192–4).

123 (b) I am soliciting Lady Compton to help me] The music was written by Lady Compton and her sister Anna Jane Clephane. It was copied into Mrs Hope-Scott's MS. Music Book, still at Abbotsford (Vol. 2, pp. [i–ii]).

123 (c) Miss D.] Miss Dalrymple. See above, p. 29.

123 n. 1] The titles of the poems are wrongly given here. Scott's was *The lifting of the banner* and Hogg's was *To the ancient banner of the House of Buccleuch*. They were printed together under the joint title, *The Ettricke garland*. (*Ruff*, No. 150.)

124 (b) To Mrs. Clephane] As Scott is now in Edinburgh, the letter should come at p. 127, after the letter to Lady Compton. The portion beginning 'Farewell' must be a separate letter. It was written between 12 Nov. and 1 Dec. I have seen a MS. of the song (not in Scott's hand) dated 'Abbotsford 1st Dec. 1815' which shows that the version sent to Mrs Clephane was later than the one sent to Lady Compton. In the MS. stanza 3 is wanting.

125 (c) Gae warn the waters] *Jamie Telfer*, st. 25. In *Minstrelsy* (ed. Henderson), ii. 8.

125 (e) adapting musick to immortal verse] A reminiscence of Milton, *L'allegro*, line 137.

125 n. 1] See also above, p. 123 and my note.

126 (c) The two odd lines about Versailles] See above, p. 108.

126 (c) Johnstone] *Johnson*, Vol. 5 [1797], No. 475, *Bannocks o' bear-meal*.

126 (e) She twind the Bullies] John Grubb, *St George for England*, Pt II, st. [7], line 8. In D'Urfey, *Wit and mirth*, Vol. 3 (1719), p. 319.

126 (f) brick of the first head] Read 'buck of the first head.'

127 (b) "the Laird of the Cairn and

NOTES IV

the Scaur"] See my note to *SL* i. 224 (d).

127 (d) 100 acres more] Part of Abbotslee.

127 (f) Walter the first Earl] See my note to *SL* i. 330 (e).

128 (a) Douglas Banner at Carrse] See my note to *SL* iii. 424 (c). For 'Carrse' read 'Cavers.'

128 (d) To John Murray] Murray's letter of 8 Nov. is in Smiles, *John Murray*, i. 286–7.

128 (e) like Falstaff] Shakespeare, *I Henry IV*, III. 3.

129 (a) a brother in the banking line] This brother has always been identified with Alexander Park (1774–1814). He was usually described as 'Writer in Selkirk' but like many country writers he probably engaged in banking.

129 (d) Mr. Wishaws address] Scott apparently wrote to Whishaw (though the letter is not in *SL*). See Smiles, *John Murray*, i. 288.

129 (f) Waterloo presses to another edition] See below, p. 131 and my note.

129 (f) to keep the wolf from the door] *Heywood*, p. 143; *Ray*, p. 30.

131 (d) the new edition of Waterloo] 3rd ed. (*Ruff*, No. 149).

132 (e) Come weal come woe] Lines 3–4 of the chorus of *O'er the water to Charlie*. In *Johnson*, Vol. 2 (1788), No. 187.

133 (a) To Sir John Malcolm] Date is more likely to be early 1816. Malcolm's *Persia* had been Scott's winter reading, 1815–16 (below, p. 185) and Gladswood was sold to Wedderburn Webster in 1816.

133 (c) Sibbald] William Sibbald.

133 (d) *Life of Sir John Malcolm*] Add reference: ii. 94–5.

133 *n.* 2] In line 6, for '27th November' read '17 Jan. 1816'; in line 7, for 'William' read 'Mr. William'; in line 8, transfer inverted commas to 'years)' in line 9; in line 10, for 'am disposed' read 'am rather disposed.' At end of note add: 'NLS MS. 866, ff. 52–3.'

134 *n.* 1] In line 6, 1819 should be 1820.

136 *n.* 1] The Rev. William Meyrick, who had been at Manchester School along with Morritt, lost his wife, Marianne Wishaw, in Dec. 1812.

137 (c) To Mr. James Bailey] There is no letter from Bayley in the Walpole Coll. in NLS.

140 (a) A friend of mine] Robert Jamieson.

141 (c) to marry my verses to immortal notes] A reminiscence of Milton, *L'allegro*, line 137. Cf. above, p. 125.

141 *n.* 2] Delete. See above, p. 123 and my note.

142 (b) Torwoodlie Toftfield] James Pringle of Torwoodlie and James Usher of Toftfield.

142 (d–e) "other sport to bide"] Lady Wardlaw, *Hardyknute*, st. [9], line 6.

142 (e) Berwick Water] A slip or misreading for Borthwick Water.

143 (b) borrowed from Burns] Scott means his *Buy braw troggin: an excellent new song. Tune—Buy broom Besoms.* The four first lines have no corresponding lines in Burns but the remaining four lines correspond: 'Here's the Worth o' Br[oughton] / In a *needle's* e'e: / Here's a reputation, / Tint by B[almaghie].'

143 (d) The Souters of Selkirk] Scott's grammar is not always accurate, but here his singular verb 'has' means correctly that he is referring to the ballad *The Souters o' Selkirk*. See *Johnson*, Vol. 5 [1797], No. 438.

144 (b) lonely isle] See my note to *SL* ii. 506 (a).

145 (e) considerable addition] Part of Abbotslee bought from Nicol Milne. The 'little farm' is Kaeside and the 'wild lake' is Cauldshiels Loch.

145 *n.* 1] Shakespeare, *The tempest*, II. 2.

146 (b) I have more than one scull] There is one in the Entrance Hall at Abbotsford.

146 (d) Knight of Cessford] See *The lay of the last minstrel*, Canto I, st. xxx.

148 (a) Homer] Transfer index figure from date to this word.

149 (a) To John Murray] Date is Mar. or Apr. The 'sheets corrected' refer to the review of *Culloden papers*, published

in *QR* in May. *Paul's letters* was published in Feb. and other references to its success occur in letters of Apr. (*SL* i. 495, iv. 215, 225–6).

149 (d) Mr. Loftly Swift] 'Loftly' should be 'Lenthal.' His *Waterloo and other poems*, 8vo London, 1815, was reviewed along with Scott's *The Field of Waterloo* in the *Antijacobin Review*, Vol. 49 (Nov. 1815), pp. 471–9; (Dec. 1815), pp. 521–37. See also *SL* viii. 232 *n.*

149 (e) To John Murray] Date is mid Jan. 1817. Scott had sent his review of *Childe Harold*, Canto III on 10 Jan. 1817 (below, p. 363). He is still using the letters of Croker and Malcolm which he returned on 22 Jan. (below, p. 378). When he writes this letter he has received Murray's approval, which fixes the date about 16 Jan.

149 (f) reflections on Waterloo] These are at pp. 191–6 of the review in *QR* Vol. 16. Cf. *Shine*, No. 407. There is nothing in Scott's text to show how he was indebted to Croker and Malcolm. See also below, p. 378.

150 (c) the mode in which Gulliver extinguishd the conflagration] Swift, *Gulliver's travels*, Pt I, chap. 5. (Scott's *Swift*, 2nd ed. xi. 73.)

150 (e) tract upon fairies] See above, p. 38.

151 (d) letter from Lord Cranstoune] This letter, dated 1671, from William, 3rd Baron Cranstoun, is now in NLS (MS. 1560, f. 93).

151 (e) Elphinstone] *The Kingdom of Caubul*, by Hon. Mountstuart Elphinstone, which Murray had sent to Scott (Smiles, *John Murray*, i. 286).

154 (a) Kirkton] Presumably Sharpe's MS. of James Kirkton's *The secret and true history of the Church of Scotland.*

154 (d) To Rev. Mr. Polwhele] The reference (p. 155) to Lord Scott shows that this letter was written before 11 Mar. 1808. The first paragraph refers to *Marmion*, which Scott sent shortly afterwards (*SL* ii. 43). 'Messrs. Cadell and Davies' (p. 155) refers to Polwhele's order to them to supply Scott with his works (*SL* ii. 43). Date is, therefore, end of Feb. or beginning of Mar. 1808.

156 (a–b) I never did touch upon any

poetical production] See *SL* i. 398 and my note.

156 (c) To James Ballantyne] The date is about 4 Aug. See Oliphant, *William Blackwood*, i. 64–6.

157 (a) We go to Sir Giles] To the Theatre to see Sir Giles Overreach in Massinger's *A new way to pay old debts.*

157 (b) To James Ferrier] Date is probably Feb. as shown by reference to *Paul's letters.* Sunday, 11 Feb. is a possible date.

158 (b) To Duke of Buccleuch] Date is probably Thursday, 8 Feb. The letter should come before the letter to Ferrier (p. 157) as Scott says (p. 159) 'I hope to be at Abbotsford on Monday.'

159 (a) Buccleuch papers] Here and elsewhere Scott refers to five documents relating to the feuds between the Scotts and the Kers: (1) Bond of alliance, 16 Mar. 1529; printed in *Minstrelsy* 1st. ed. 1802, i. cxxvi–cxxix; not mentioned in *SL*; (2) Petition of the Kers to the Dowager Queen Mary for protection against the Scotts, 8 Dec. 1552; printed in *Border antiquities*, Appendix, pp. xxxi–xxxiii; referred to below, p. 434; (3) Contract between Scotts and Kers, 23 Mar. 1564, by which Sir Walter Ker of Cessford is required to appear in St Giles' Kirk, Edinburgh; printed in *The Border antiquities*, Appendix, pp. xviii–xxv and in Pitcairn's *Criminal trials*, iii. 390–4; referred to in this letter and below, p. 251; (4) Contract of 9 Mar. 1568 by which the parties are to meet in parish church of Melrose; printed in *The Border antiquities*, Appendix, pp. xxvi–xxx; referred to in this letter and below, p. 251; (5) Band of Association, 3 June 1589, between Scotts and Kerrs; summary by Scott printed in Pitcairn's *Criminal trials*, iii. 381–2; not mentioned in *SL*.

159 (b) the Laird of Buccleuch] Sir Walter Scott, killed in Edinburgh, 4 Oct. 1552, was predeceased by his son and heir and was succeeded by his grandson. Scott means 'slaughter of his grandfather.'

159 (c–d) General Kerr] Walter Ker of Littledean, unsuccessful claimant of Roxburghe peerage.

160 (a) the other a keen jacobite] Walter Scott, known as 'Beardie,' 2nd son of 1st Laird of Raeburn.

160 (d) oportet vivere] Horace, *Epistles*, I. x. 12.

160 (d) *Micat* inter omnes] Horace, *Odes*, I. xii. 46. Scott stole the pun from George Huddesford's *Monody on the death of Dick, an academical cat*, a poem quoted in *SL* iii. 339, 356.

160 *n.* 1] Beardie's nephew, who was killed in a duel in 1707, was Walter Scott, 3rd Laird of Raeburn. The 'late' Mark Pringle was the Mark Pringle of Clifton and Haining who died in 1812. His grandfather was Mark Pringle (3rd son of Andrew Pringle of Clifton who died in 1702) who became Pringle of Crichton and died in 1751. The place where the duel took place was called the Raeburn-Meadow-Spot.

161 (a) *The Sutor gae . . .*] Kelly, p. 338, gives this couplet as a Scottish proverb and says it is 'spoken of those whose service we suppose to be mercenary.' It also forms lines 1–2 of *The soutar and the soo* in Sharpe's *Ballad book*, [1823], p. 36.

161 (b) in one of our papers] *Edinburgh Evening Courant*, 4 Jan. 1816, p. [3].

162 (a) enthusiastic letter] Maturin's letter is dated 27 Dec. 1815 and is in Edinburgh Univ. Lib. (La. III. 584, Letter 27). It is not in *Maturin Corr.*

165 (b–c) seen through the bargain] Read 'run through the bargain.' (Correction in *SL* xii. 488.)

166 (a) "A light heart . . ."] Lines 3–4 of the chorus of a song beginning 'How pleasant a sailor's life passes.' Scott could have got the poem from a number of anthologies, e.g., *The Syren, The merry companion, The Blackbird*, or from Smollett's *Roderick Random*, chap. 5.

166 (c) John Dowie] An innkeeper in Liberton Wynd, Edinburgh. Hunter of Blackness wrote a poem called *Johnnie Dowie's ale*. There is a portrait of Dowie in the *Scots Mag.* Vol. 68, Apr. 1806, with a brief note including Hunter's poem, pp. 243–4.

166 (d) Bishop] Robert Bishop, one of Ballantyne's compositors, who transcribed Scott's MSS. He died young in 1819.

166 (f) To Charles Erskine] Date, I think, should be Thursday, 7 Nov. 1816. It is before 11 Nov., for Scott is still at Abbotsford and the purchase of Abbotslee is recorded in the *Trust Disposition* under 2 Dec. 1816.

167 *n.* 1] Although the review of *Emma* was published in the *QR* for Oct. 1815, the number did not appear till Mar. 1816. Murray's suggestion was in his letter of 25 Dec. 1815, in Smiles, *John Murray*, i. 288.

167 *n.* 2] For 'Wishaw' read 'Whishaw.'

168 (a) Wurz & Fruttel] For 'Fruttel' read 'Treuttel.' At this time the firm was called Treuttel & Wurtz.

169 (b) to suit your effort] Terry's play, *Guy Mannering; or, the gipsey's prophecy*, was first produced at Covent Garden on 12 Mar. 1816.

169 (b) Dumple it as you list] Massinger, *A new way to pay old debts*, III. 2.

169 (d) the Pitt meeting] On Saturday, 3 Feb. The 'wine tasting dinner' must refer to the Burns anniversary dinner which he attended on 25 Jan.

170 (a) apply for a song to Mrs. Baillie] Her *Gipsey glee and chorus* appears, with acknowledgement to her, in Act II, sc. 3. Scott had used this song for the motto of chap. 28 of *Guy Mannering* and this probably suggested to Terry the idea of getting the complete song for his play.

170 (c) We are mistified] Read 'We are mortified.' (Correction in *SL* xii. 488.)

170 (c) "Out you villains play out the play"] Shakespeare, *I Henry IV*, II. 4.

171 *n.* 1] No need to quote *DNB*. If Scott had said 'wife' (as this note implies), Campbell would have been guilty of bigamy! Scott means 'offence of her husband's family' and he later (below, p. 304) calls her 'Widow.'

172 (b) Why weep you . . .] In last line, for 'Fer' read 'For.'

172 (c) Allan Muidyart] More correctly, *Allan Moidart*, by Lady Compton. (Corrected to Moidart in *SL* xii. 488.)

172 (e) *better a finger off as aye wagging*] See *Kelly*, p. 56, who explains it as 'Better put an end to a troublesome business, than to be always vexed with it.' Also used in *SL* viii. 463, ix. 316, *Rob Roy*, chap. 18, *The Heart of*

Mid-Lothian, chap. 20, and *Redgauntlet*, chap. 2.

172 (e) concerning the Mermaid] See below, p. 176 and *n.* 1.

173 (a) lonely isle] See my note to *SL* ii. 506 (a).

173 (b) O'Gorman] With his letter of 17 Jan. 1816 (NLS MS. 866, ff. 52–3) Hartstonge sent a pamphlet, *Faction unmasked*, for which the publisher was prosecuted. A libel action against O'Gorman arose out of the pamphlet. Hartstonge referred to 'Mr North's celebrated speech' for the plaintiff.

173 (e) your own opinion of that Gentleman's character] Hartstonge's opinion of Monck Mason was unfavourable in his letter of 17 Jan. 1816 (NLS MS. 866, ff. 52–3).

173 (f) increasing kindness] Read 'unceasing kindness.' (Correction in *SL* xii. 488.)

174 (b) extended my wings] By the purchase of part of Abbotslee between Kaeside and Cauldshiels Loch.

174 (c) stubbing of the Oxmoor] Sterne, *Tristram Shandy*, Bk V, chap. 7.

174 (d) Lord Castlehaven's work] See above, p. 97 and *n.* and my note.

175 (c) To Miss Clephane] This letter is to Anna Jane Maclean Clephane.

175 (c) lovely isle] Read 'lonely isle.' See my note to *SL* ii. 506 (a).

176 (a) like the nobility of Laputa] Swift, *Gulliver's travels*, Pt III.

176 *n.* 1] In line 2, for 'Cousin Jane' read 'Anna Jane' (NLS MS. 866, f. 48). A MS. of *An old Factor's new garland* was copied, with the music, into Mrs Hope-Scott's MS. Music Book (Vol. 2, pp. 37–8), still at Abbotsford.

177 (c) "with dirk and pistol by his side"] *Mistress mouse*, st. [2], line 2: 'Puddy he'd a wooin' ride / Sword and pistol by his side.' Later printed by C. K. Sharpe in his *Ballad book* [1823] but Scott would know it from recitation.

178 (e) these words] Read 'these winds.' (Corrected in *SL* xii. 488.)

178 *n.* 1] Delete. Allan Maclean, called 'Allan-a-Sop' or 'Allan of the Straw,' illegitimate son of McLean of Duart.

His mother later married Maclean of Torloisk. Scott tells the story in *Tales of a grandfather*, chap. 38 (*MPW* xxiii. 299–305).

179 (a) To Clarke Whitfeld] Whitfeld's letter, which Scott is answering, is not in NLS so that I cannot say with certainty what the 'song from the French' is, but it is presumably *Romance of Dunois* which Whitfeld would see in the *Edin. Ann. Reg. for 1813*. The other poem, from *Paul's letters*, is presumably *The troubadour*. Only the former appeared in Whitfeld's *Twelve vocal pieces* (*Ruff*, No. 156). Whitfeld's first mention of this collection was in a letter of 26 Apr. 1815 (NLS MS. 3886, ff. 135–6). There must have been at least one other letter between that date and this letter of Scott's. See also below, p. 352 and my note.

180 (a) To Miss Clephane] To Anna Jane. From internal evidence the date is May.

180 (b) two political poems] But one volume, viz. *The vision of Don Roderick, The Field of Waterloo, and other poems*, 8vo Edinburgh, 1815 (*Ruff*, No. 116).

180 (c) Caduil gu la] The Gaelic tune for *Lullaby of an infant chief* which Scott had given to Terry for his dramatized version of *Guy Mannering*.

180 (d) deer-hound] Maida.

180 (f) Ballad at Carter-haugh] *The Ettricke garland*, issued privately in 1815 (*Ruff*, No. 150).

181 *n.* 2] In line 11, for 'Dugald Stuart' read 'Dugald Stewart.'

182 (f) To J. B. S. Morritt] Date is about the end of Feb. as Morritt replied on 6 Mar. His advice on a school for Walter (pp. 185–6) is given in Partington, *Post-bag*, pp. 120–1.

183 (b) corn-bill riots] There were riots in London in Mar. 1815. See *Edin. Ann. Reg. for 1815*, VIII. i. 79–84. Morritt had spoken in Parliament on the Corn Bill. See ibid., pp. 37, 81.

184 (e) best of possible worlds] Voltaire. See my note to *SL* i. 186 (a–b).

186 (b) Bullocks labours] The cabinet which served as a pedestal for Shakespeare's bust was made by George Bullock. It still serves this purpose in

the vestibule between the Entrance Hall and the Study at Abbotsford. See also below, pp. 289, 295.

187 n. 1] *Where shall the lover rest* from *Marmion* was set to music in 1810 by Barham Livius, presumably Weber's cousin.

188 (d) To Archibald Constable] Mar. should be Apr. Friday was 12 Apr. and the Circuit began on Monday, 15 Apr.

189 n. 1] In line 7, for 'Earle' read 'Earl.'

190 n. 1] This note is copied, with the error in line 2, from *Johnson*, new ed., Edinburgh, 1853, iv. 253-4. In line 2, for '170' read '179.' In last line, for 'slightly' read 'considerably.'

191 (c) "Charley fond of Popish Blessing"] John Bell, in his reply, 12 May 1816 (NLS MS. 3887, f. 57), said he had failed to find this song in the *Gentleman's Mag.* I, too, have failed to find it.

192 (c) yesterday] "three days ago", i.e. 7th (above, p. 188), unless the letter dated 7th should be 9th or a letter of the 9th is missing.

193 (a) To John Scott] If this letter is correctly dated it was written in Edinburgh though dated from Abbotsford.

195 (a) Adam . . . & the Chief Baron] William Adam of Blair-Adam and Robert Dundas of Arniston.

195 (a) Jury Clerkship] The Baronet (i.e. William Clerk) was one of three clerks to the Jury Court instituted in 1815.

195 (b) a good large farm] Kaeside. But the Fergusons had to give way to William Laidlaw.

195 (c) Soft sleeps the mist . . .] See *SL* iii. 255 and *n*. 2.

195 n. 1] The date 1800 must be wrong. Ferguson was Collector of Widows Fund to W.S. Society 1803-5 and must have been in residence. The correct date is probably 1808. In the *Army List* he is still on full pay on 10 Mar. 1817.

196 (a) There is an old man] John Moss.

196 (b) Castle Studs cottage] This must be a misreading for Castle Steads cottage. Beside Kaeside farmhouse there is a spot called Castlesteads.

196 (c) David Walker] Scott's old companion at Wooden, Kelso. He was Lt.-Col. of the 58th Foot (Rutlandshire), Adam Ferguson's regiment.

198 (a) To Alexander Macdonell] In Symington, *Some unpublished letters*, pp. 76-7, where it is dated '[19 Feb. 1816].' Symington prints a covering letter to Glengarry from J. H. Forbes which is not in *SL*.

198 (b-c) the Earldom of Rosse] If Glengarry had prosecuted the claim, he would have had a formidable rival in the Duke of York. See *The Croker papers*, ed. by L. J. Jennings, London, 1884, i. 152.

201 (d) like the dog in the child's tale] Scott would know this story from recitation. See *The wife and her bush of berries* in Robert Chambers, *Popular rhymes of Scotland*, new ed., London, 1870, pp. 57-9.

201 (e) Lipsius] This is an old story but Scott probably got it from Sterne's *Tristram Shandy*, Bk VI, chap. 2: 'But you forget the great Lipsius, quoth Yorick, who composed a work the day he was born.' See Sterne's note. Scott also refers to the story in *SL* x. 300, and *MPW* xviii. 153.

201 (e) Justice Shallow] In Shakespeare's *II Henry IV* and *Merry wives of Windsor*. But in *SL* iii. 401 he compares his tankard with that of Squire Sullen.

201 (f) the Provost] William Arbuthnot (later Sir William Arbuthnot, Bart.).

202 (c) To Joanna Baillie] The date is towards the end of Mar. Scott is replying to her letter of 17 Mar. That this is a fragment, ending on p. 206, is proved by Joanna's letter of 4 Apr. which is a reply to Scott's letter. (See next note.) The fragment, occupying pp. 206-7, belongs to another letter dated 12 Apr.

203 (e) Mrs. Baillie] Mrs Matthew Baillie. In her letter of 17 Mar. Joanna wrote: 'You would have been amused some time ago when, after talking of Lord B. my good sister-in-law, tho' she delights in poetry, began to abuse all the men of genius of the present day for selfishness, excentricity, and

affectation—yourself only excepted.' (Partington, *Post-bag*, 117–18.) On 4 Apr. Joanna replied: 'I . . . have been some what amused at your taking up so seriously the defence of the whole Brotherhood and Sisterhood of poets' (NLS MS. 3887, ff. 36–8).

204 (a) with freaks and caprioles] Cervantes, *Don Quixote*, Pt I, Bk III, chap. 11.

205 (a) play fantastic tricks before high heaven] Shakespeare, *Measure for measure*, II. 2.

205 (b) Afra's and Orinda's] Afra is Mrs Afra Behn (1640–89) and Orinda is Mrs Katherine Philips (1631–64), known as the 'Matchless Orinda.'

205 (f) as Hamlet says] Shakespeare, *Hamlet*, III. 1.

206 (c) . . . MORE forward] This is the beginning of a new letter, distinct from the fragment on pp. 202–6. See my note to *SL* iv. 202 (c).

207 (b) "The chough and crow"] *Gipsey glee and chorus* in Terry's *Guy Mannering*, II. 3. In the printed version, Terry acknowledged his indebtedness to Joanna Baillie. The song appears in her *Orra*, III. 1.

209 (a) who displayed so much patience] Referring to Margaret's accident at Melrose in 1810. See *SL* ii. 379, 380.

209 (b) furrish fit] Read 'feverish fit.' (Corrected in *SL* xii. 488.)

209 (b) mutual similies] Read 'medical similies.' (Corrected in *SL* xii. 488.)

209 (c) Henry] Henry Clephane, W.S. Scott repeats the story below, p. 245.

209 (d) the Knight of the Mantle Green] Sir Joseph Banks.

209 (d) peging oaks] Read 'pigmy oaks.' (Corrected in *SL* xii. 488.)

209 (e) the circuit] At Jedburgh, 15–17 Apr.

209 (e) to turn] For suggested amendment, see *SL* xii. 488.

210 (a) Judger] Read 'Judges.'

210 n. 1] Scott could not have access to a work published in 1839! See Sir Alexander Boswell's *Songs in the Justiciary opera*, 4to Auchinleck, 1816.

211 (a) execute them first] This is traditionally known as Jeddart Justice.

212 (a) To Robert Southey] The original MS. was presented by Carlisle Public Library to NLS in 1968. There are a number of errors in the Abbotsford Copy, the most important of which are: p. 212, line 17. For 'spared' read 'saved'; p. 213, line 3. For 'commenced' read 'encurred'; line 13 from foot. For 'principle' read 'principal'; line 4 from foot. Delete 'interest'; p. 214, line 21. For 'particular' read 'portenteous'; p. 215, line 3. For 'Think' read 'Do think.'

214 (f) a small property] Kaeside.

215 (b) 1500 of the work] *Waverley*, 6th ed. See *SL* i. 495 and my note there.

215 (c) the price of the other] *The Antiquary*. See *SL* i. 495.

215 n. 1] Delete. See my note to *SL* iv. 115 n.

216 (d) "dandle Dickie on your knee"] This is probably 'To dandle Jacky on my knee,' st. [5], line 4, of a song beginning 'When I've money I am merry' in John O'Keefe's *The Highland reel*, I. 1.

218 (c–d) from whom I had the air] See above, pp. 38, 180.

219 (c) I will settle with Campbell] As a result, the *Lullaby of an infant chief* was printed without Scott's name. But Scott had already written a prospectus for the work in which the poem was announced as 'by Walter Scott, Esq.' A copy of this printed prospectus is in NLS (MS. 677, ff. 139–40).

219 (e) To James Ellis] This letter should be dated 1818. It is a reply to Ellis's letter of 12 Apr. 1818 (NLS MS. 870, ff. 43–4), which was a reply to Scott's letter of 4 Mar. 1818 (not in *SL*).

219 n. 1] By Coleridge. Part the fifth, st. [25], lines 1–2.

220 (a) look for a needle in a Bottle of hay] *Ray*, p. 261.

220 (a) Allan] By the 'Alnwick work' Scott means *The life of James Allan*, new ed., 8vo Blyth, 1818. It was printed at Alnwick.

220 (b) "the Knave" as Davie . . .] Shakespeare, *II Henry IV*, V. 1.

220 (c) Allan's Grandfather or perhaps Great Grandfather] As James Allan's father, William, was born in 1704, Scott must be referring to his great-grandfather.

221 (d) lines on the North Tyne . . . Shepherd] Ellis, in his letter of 12 Apr. 1818 (NLS MS. 870, ff. 43–4), had quoted lines from 'Dialogue between the North and South Tyne Northumberland,' written by Rev. George Shepherd, Aug. 1817, with additions by Miss M. H. D., Oct. 1817.

221 (e) Polyolbion] By Michael Drayton.

221 (e) Reedwater Minstrel] *The lay of the Reedwater minstrel* [by Robert Rokesby], 4to Newcastle, 1809.

221 (f) Lewes] Read 'Lowes.' This was Thomas William Lowes of Ridley Hall who had died in Edinburgh on 18 Sept. 1812. See *SL* ii. 61–2, 61 *n.*

221 (f) Mr. Hedley] Rev. Anthony Hedley had stayed at Abbotsford in 1817. The redating of Scott's letter to 1818 shows that Hedley's 'admirable stories' were probably told while at Abbotsford. For an anecdote relating to the visit, see the *Gentleman's Mag.* Vol. 103, Pt 1 (Suppl. to June 1833), p. 596, and John Gibson's *Reminiscences of Sir Walter Scott* (1871), p. 12.

222 (c) To John Ballantyne] Cancel and see *SL* i. 497–8.

224 (d) Mr. Shandy's Oxmoor] Sterne, *Tristram Shandy*, Bk IV, chap. 31.

225 (d) Swifts verses on Chaucer] I cannot find these in Scott's *Swift*. But in a note supplied to Lockhart by Monck Mason and printed in *MPW* ii. 414 *n.*, Mason says: 'Mr Scott was so obliging as to transmit to me an imitation, but by no means a successful one, of the style of this early English poet. This attempt was in the handwriting of Swift. I have been so unfortunate as to have lost both the document itself and the polite letter which accompanied it.' This letter may be the one noted below, p. 305. Cf. also Scott's *Swift*, 2nd ed., xiii. 291.

225 (d) "Seven and One added to nine"] *Merlin's prophecy.* In Scott's *Swift*, 2nd ed., viii. 498–502, xiv. 97–8.

225 *n.* 1] In Scott's *Swift*, 2nd ed., xii. 297–300.

227 (a) To J. B. S. Morritt] The date is 22 Mar. which was a Friday. Scott had 'just heard' from Southey (p. 229), i.e. after 17 Mar.; and 'I go to Edinr.' (p. 230), i.e. for Register House duty from 26 Mar. till 12 Apr.

227 (b) seldom comes a better] *Ray*, p. 200.

228 (f) like the fly on St. Pauls] See the *Guardian*, No. 70, 1 June 1713, by Bishop Berkeley. Cf. Thomson's *Seasons*, *Summer*, lines 291–5.

229 (b) chamber in the wall] *Bible*, II *Kings* 4: 10.

229 (b) the great trouble you have taken] On choice of a public school for Walter. Morritt's advice is given in a letter of 6 Mar. (Partington, *Post-bag*, pp. 120–1).

229 (e) like Rodrigo in Othello] Shakespeare, *Othello*, V. 2.

229 (e) If he swear he'll certainly deceive you—] Otway, *The orphan*, II. 1.

230 (b) a large house now for sale] Gladswood (or Gledswood). See above, p. 133.

230 *n.* 1] In line 1, for 'James Wedderburn Webster' read 'Sir James Wedderburn Webster' and for 'grandson' read 'great-grandson.' See Index.

232 *n.* 1] For 'Ardwell' read 'Ardwall.'

232 *n.* 2] Scott is correct in giving number as thirteen. Delete this note. For a full discussion of Scott's brothers and sisters, see my article in the *Scotsman*, *Week-End Mag.* 26 Dec. 1970.

233 (e–f) 2nd Volume of Triermain] i.e. *Harold the Dauntless.*

233 (f) in the state of the Bear and Fiddle] i.e. in the middle—an allusion to Butler, *Hudibras*, Argument of Canto I, lines 5–6.

234 (d) my old peacock] From Mertoun, given to Anne. See *SL* iii. 264, 269.

234 *n.* 1] This note should have appeared at p. 196.

235 (c) To John Ballantyne] Date is about 15 May, for Scott sent a cheque for Moss on 16 May (below, p. 236).

236 (b) short reckoning that makes long friends] *Heywood*, p. 112; *Ray*, p. 195. See also *SL* ix. 230.

236 (d) George Moss] This should be John Moss.

237 (a) Philiphaugh business] Presumably *Barrie* v. *Heiton*. See *Chisholm*, p. 177.

237 (a) Ushers business] Scott had been negotiating with Usher of Toftfield for Dick's Cleugh which, after he acquired it, he renamed Rhymer's Glen.

237 (b) Leithheads sale] William Leithhead, tenant in Abbotslee.

238 (c) I have arranged with Campbell] See my note to *SL* iv. 219 (c).

238 (c) Howe] This should presumably be Huie who published dramatized versions of the Waverley Novels.

238 (d) Emery] Emery took the part of Dandie Dinmont.

238 *n.* 1] See below, pp. 252–4.

240 (b) My mother remembers him] She could not remember the Murray who died in 1708.

240 (d) To Thomas Scott] This and the next extract belong to one letter, printed in part in *SL* vii. 478–83.

240 *n.* 2] Delete this note.

242 (a) To Thomas Scott] See above, p. 240 (d).

244 (b) Mr. Sharpe] Richard Sharp (1759–1835).

244 (c) a sort of Oxmoor] Sterne, *Tristram Shandy*, Bk IV, chap. 31.

244 *n.* 1] Rogers's reply is in Partington, *Letter-books*, pp. 184–5, where Partington wrongly surmises that the portrait was by C. K. Sharpe. In line 7 from foot, for 'Sharp[e]' read 'Sharp.'

245 (f) your cousin Harry] Her uncle Henry Clephane, W.S. Scott had already told this to Lady Compton (above, p. 209).

245 (f) letter of a Lady Compton] This was printed in the *Scots Mag.* Vol. 59 (Feb. 1797), pp. 90–1 (where Scott may first have seen it) and printed again in *Edin. Ann. Reg. for 1813* [publ. 1815], VI. ii. lxxix–lxxx, taken from Winwood. See also below, p. 249.

246 (b) the Lady of the Cairn and the Scaur] See my note to *SL* i. 224 (d).

247 *n.* 1] Delete the last sentence and see Scott's *Journal*, 7 Sept. 1827. Mrs MacCunn was merely quoting the *Journal* without acknowledgement.

248 (e) our new Prince George of Denmark] Identified with Prince Leopold in *SL* xii. 488. He married Princess Charlotte on 2 May. As she was next in succession to the throne he would become Prince Consort like the Prince of Denmark, husband of Queen Anne. 'Prince George of Denmark' had become proverbial for a person taking a second role.

250 (d) to lay the foundation stone] On 4 June 1816. The Marquess of Lothian had been asked to perform the ceremony and it was only because he was unable to be present that Scott took his place. The hall was for Lodge St John's, Selkirk, No. 32.

250 *n.* 1] *Molly Mog* is given by Scott in his ed. of *Swift* (2nd ed. xiii. 346–8) without any indication that it is by Gay.

251 (a) a parson whom they were obliged to initiate] Rev. James Nicol, minister of Traquair. In order that he might take part in the ceremony he was admitted, before it began, an honorary member of the Lodge.

251 (a) alluded to by Burns] *Address to the Deil*, st. [14].

251 (b) Prince Ho[u]sseins tapestry] In *The Arabian Nights*. See my note to *SL* i. 229 (e).

251 (c) three very handsome transcripts] The first is the Testament of Sir Walter Scott of Branxholme and Buccleuch, dated 18 Nov. 1574, printed in *The Border antiquities*, Appendix, pp. iii–xi. The second and third are Nos. 3–4 in the list in my note to p. 159 above.

252 (c) death of poor Meadowbank now hourly expected] Allan Maconochie, Lord Meadowbank, actually died the day this letter was written.

252 (d) Lord Register Elect] Archibald Campbell Colquhoun.

252 *n.*] For correction, see *SL* v. 348 *n.*

254 (c) To Duke of Buccleuch] Date is probably 10 June: (1) Meadowbank died on 14 June and Scott could not, so late as 16 June, be ignorant of his death; (2) 'a few days since,' referring

to his previous letter of 5 June, fits 10 June better than 16 June.

254 (d) Lord Advocate . . . solicitor] Archibald Campbell Colquhoun. James Wedderburn became Solicitor-General on 20 July 1816.

255 (a) Robert Bruce] He received no promotion at this time but he became Sheriff of Argyll, 15 Aug. 1818.

256 (b) volume—which Lady C] See above, p. 247.

259 (b) the Bart.] In *SL* xii. 488 it is suggested this is Sir James Naesmyth. This, I think, is correct as the reference to Tom shows. But Scott's letter is ambiguous for this 'Bart.' cannot be the same 'Bart.' as the one five lines above. See next note.

259 *n.* 1] Delete this note. Sir William Forbes is impossible as Scott is writing to Donaldson on politics, not on finance. Sir William Scott is impossible as he was only 13 years of age. As the 'business' is political the 'Bart.' must be Sir Alexander Don, Bart., M.P. for Roxburghshire. When Sir John Scott of Ancrum died in 1812, he was followed in the baronetcy by two young sons, the elder of whom was a midshipman and was drowned in 1814. His younger brother succeeded. During their minority the house would be unoccupied by the family and it is almost certain it was rented by Sir Alexander Don, for Lady Don gave birth to a son at Ancrum House in Apr. preceding Scott's letter.

261 *n.* 1] This long note is unneccessary as Joanna Baillie's letter is printed in Partington, *Letter-books*, pp. 124–7.

262 (c) if two people ride a horse] Shakespeare, *Much ado about nothing*, III. 5.

263 (e) I'll awa to the hieland hills] *Turnimspike*, st. [12]. In *Herd*, ii. 186–8.

265 (a) Win Jenkins] See my note to *SL* i. 337 (c).

265 (c) drunken Landlord at the Arroquhar Inn] This is probably the same as 'old Macfarlane of the Arroquhar' of the *Journal*, 22 Aug. 1826.

265 (d) "How shall we pay him honours due?"] Coleridge, *Fire, famine and slaughter*, line 71: 'How shall we yield him honour due?'

265 (e) Bath friends] This visit apparently did not materialize, for Allott wrote to Scott in 1826 as an entire stranger. See Partington, *Letter-books*, pp. 329–31.

265 *n.* 1] Arrochar is in Dunbartonshire.

266 (d) all the copy for the Annual Register] i.e. for the year 1814.

266 (f) 1816 will be comparatively light work] Yet it was not published till 1820.

267 (c) least of all possible dwellings] Variation of 'best of all possible worlds' (Voltaire, *Candide*, chap. 1).

267 *n.* 1] This note is badly worded. The visitors were Miss Dumergue and Sarah Nicolson, neither of whom, so far as I know, had been in Scotland before. Jane had been in Edinburgh.

267 *n.* 2] Cambusmore was the home of John Buchanan and Ross Priory was the home of Hector Macdonald Buchanan.

268 (a) Deadmans heugh] This should be Deadwater Heugh. The name is given correctly in *SL* v. 510. The haugh derived its name from a boat disaster in 1723 when many persons perished. Two sermons were preached on the occasion by the Rev. Henry Davidson, minister of Galashiels, and were published as *Dark providences to be admired*, 8vo Edinburgh, 1763.

268 (b) visitors and guests] Scott must mean visitors and hosts.

270 (a) your nephew] Edward Stanley of Cross Hall.

270 *n.* 1] Lady Hood (widow of Sir Samuel Hood) took the name Hood Mackenzie on the death of her father Lord Seaforth.

271 (d) the Boor] See my note to *SL* iii. 526 *n.* 2.

272 (c) The circuit] At Jedburgh on 14–15 Sept.

273 *n.* 1] The author's name is Morrier.

274 (a) To James Ballantyne] The year is 1813. The contents are virtually the same as those in Scott's letter of 28 Sept. (correctly dated 1813) in *SL* i. 447–9.

274 (f) Constable *has* a plan] The

annuity plan. See Index under Finance, 1813.

275 (d) literary fund] Royal Literary Fund, founded in London in 1790.

275 *n.* 1] Delete this erroneous note. Vols. 1–5 of the *Register* came out in 2 vols. each year, 1810–14. With Vol. 6 the two annual parts were issued together, 1815 onwards. Scott's reference to 'the *two* volumes' is obscure.

277 *n.* 4] Delete. See *SL* i. 465 *n.,* iii. 509, iv. 69, 277–8, 279–80, 294.

279 (d) *Thursday*] Thursday was 24 Oct.

280 *n.* 1] Delete 'Probably.' Scott had already referred to Lyttelton as his model. See *SL* iii. 509.

281 (a) Burns's old woman] *Halloween,* st. [15], lines 7–9: 'And aye a rantin' kirn we gat, / And just on Halloween / It fell that night.'

281 (c) To Samuel Rogers] The date cannot be 1816: (1) James Russell was too young in 1816 to go to London 'on scientific and medical pursuits'; (2) Conundrum Castle did not exist in that year. The date is probably 1823, the year Russell took his M.D. and F.R.C.S.E. Rose was at Abbotsford in 1823 and must have stayed from Aug. till Oct.

281 (d–e) My tediousness] See *SL* ii. 320.

281 *n.* 1] The dishonoured bill was the result of John's absence from Edinburgh, *not* James's. See Lockhart, *The Ballantyne-humbug handled,* pp. 56–8. It is doubtful, however, if Scott is referring to this bill in this letter to Constable.

281 *n.* 3] Amend. Scott says quite clearly that the son was James, on whom the note should have been written and not on his father.

282 (b) Rusty iron coats] Burns, *Verses on Captain Grose's peregrinations,* st. [6], line 2: 'Rusty airn caps and jinglin' jackets.'

282 (c) Rare commodities for a country smith] See below, p. 343, 343 *n.* 2.

282 (c) Robinson Crusoe] See my note to *SL* iii. 391 (a).

282 (d) topple on the warders heads] Shakespeare, *Macbeth,* IV. 1.

283 (a) To Lady Abercorn] This letter cannot be dated Nov. 1816 as the opening sentence of Scott's letter of 29 Nov. (below, p. 307) shows. The correct date is *c.* 14 June 1816 as Lady Abercorn replied to it on 17 June, the day she received it (NLS MS. 3887, ff. 73–4). She says she never received the two letters Scott wrote before he went to the Continent and from Paris. Lady Abercorn's letter, which Scott is here answering, is not in NLS.

283 (f) one of the English Reviews] The *British Lady's Mag.* Vol. 1 (1 May 1815), pp. 355–8, in a review of *Guy Mannering.* The *Critical Review,* 5th ser. Vol. 4 (Dec. 1816), pp. 614–25, in a review of *Tales of my Landlord,* also referred to Forbes.

284 *n.* 1] Delete 'Evidently'.

285 (b) return by sea] Scott returned by sea in June after his first visit but he returned by land after his second visit in Sept.

285 (d) hermit of Prague] Shakespeare, *Twelfth Night,* IV. 2.

285 (e) coals of fire] *Bible, Proverbs* 25: 22; *Romans* 12: 20.

285 *n.* 1] Delete the whole sentence beginning 'After Blore had submitted.' It is a common statement, but one without foundation, that Blore designed the first part of Abbotsford. It was designed by William Atkinson.

286 (a) least of all possible houses] A variation of Voltaire's 'best of all possible worlds.' See *SL* i. 186 (a–b).

286 (c) have, like Squire Shallow, land and beeves] Shakespeare, *II Henry IV,* III. 2.

286 (d) I have a wild Ox-moor to stub] Sterne, *Tristram Shandy,* Bk V, chap. 7.

286 (e) Pereat inter haec lux] Horace, *Satires,* II. vi. 59.

287 (d) To Daniel Terry] This letter could not have been written on 12 Nov. 1816. There are details about Abbotsford which belong to a later date and Lockhart must have amalgamated the substance of several later letters.

287 (f) Hans in Kelder] For meaning see Smollett, *Peregrine Pickle,* chap. 10. Also used in Dryden's *The wild gallant,* V. 2. (Scott's *Dryden,* ii. 98.)

287 *n.* 2] Delete and substitute: *The fortunes of Devorgoil*, later called *The doom of Devorgoil*.

288 (b) I'll tickle ye off] Shakespeare, *I Henry IV*, II. 4.

288 (c) (there is a conceit!) ... (another!) ... (another!)] G. B. Johnston in *N. & Q.* Vol. 195 (25 Nov. 1950), p. 522, suggests this is taken from Ben Jonson, *Every man in his humour*, Act I.

288 *n.* 2] Delete the whole of this note, which is inaccurate. *The Battle of Bothwell Brig*, by Charles Farley (not Fairley as given in the note) was produced at Covent Garden on 22 May 1820 and had a successful run. Dibdin's version, *Old Mortality*, was produced at the Surrey Theatre, 20 June 1820. Calcraft's version, *Old Mortality*, was produced at Edinburgh on 3 May 1823.

289 (a–b) Lord Byron's vase] The silver vase, given by him to Scott in 1815, is now in the Drawing-Room at Abbotsford. Scott's letter to Moore, describing the gift, is in *Lockhart*, v. 38–43, but is omitted in *SL*. Bullock's drawing of the stand is now in the Victoria and Albert Museum. (Information from Mr Clive Wainewright of the Museum.)

289 (c) buildings to the right of it] 'right' should be 'left.'

289 (d) Mr. Blore has drawn me a very handsome elevation] There is at Abbotsford a small water-colour drawing by Blore showing the elevation from the road. It differs from the house as erected and was no doubt drawn by Blore to let Scott see how the ideas of Skene, Scott and others would look.

289 (e) a handsome boudoir ...] Most of the suggestions which follow were abandoned or modified when Atkinson became architect.

289 *n.* 1] The cast of Shakespeare's bust is now in the vestibule between the Entrance Hall and the Study. The cast was made by Bullock at Stratford in Dec. 1814. Only one complete cast was made and the mould was broken up and thrown into the Avon. See R. B. Wheler's account in the *Gentleman's Mag.* Vol. 85, Pt 1 (Jan. 1815), p. 5. The pedestal, also made by Bullock, was the gift of Morritt (above,

p. 186 and below, pp. 295–6). Lockhart is wrong in saying Bullock was a collector. He has confused him with his brother William.

290 *n.* 1] Delete lines 1–2. There was no plan for an Armoury at this time and Scott is referring to a window in the east side of the Dining-Room, a plan which was abandoned. At a later date Mrs Terry painted windows for the Armoury. In line 3, for 'Easel' read 'Easil.'

290 *n.* 2] Abbot had brought Terry's letter of 15 July 1816 (NLS MS. 3887, ff. 88–9).

292 (b) what came they forth] *Bible, Luke* 7: 24.

292 (c) thus wears the world away] A variant of Shakespeare, *Hamlet*, III. 2: 'Thus runs the world away.'

292 (d) like any mad] This is an uncommon expression but it is used in Wycherley's *The plain dealer* (1677), III. 2; in Fielding's *The Covent-Garden tragedy* (1732), II. 12, and in his *Joseph Andrews* (1742), Bk IV, chap 15. Also used below, p. 302.

293 (c) as Falstaff ... asks] Shakespeare, *I Henry IV*, II. 4.

293 *n.* 2] Lady Louisa's letter is in *FL* i. 393–5. On the word Sentimental, see below, p. 347.

294 (d) set up his rest] See *N. & Q.* 10th ser. vi. 509, vii. 53, 175. Cf. *Journal*, 13 Nov. 1826. Scott's explanation, given in a MS. note to Beaumont and Fletcher, *Women pleas'd*, V. 1, is: 'When the arquebusier or musqueteer in ancient times took his ground of battle, he set up the rest of his piece on which he leant it during the action.' (Scott's annotated copy in my Scott Coll.)

295 (d) the land of mist and snow] Coleridge, *The ancient mariner*, Pt 2, st. [12], line 4, or Pt 5, st. [25], line 2. There is a reminiscence of this quotation below, p. 343.

295 *n.* 1] Delete and see above, pp. 186, 289.

297 *n.* 1] The Latin quotation is from Juvenal, *Satires*, X. 356.

298 (c) I am due at the roup] Possibly William Leithhead's sale. See above, p. 237.

299 (a) To Joanna Baillie] Since Scott last wrote to her he had received a letter of 13 Sept. from Fontainbleu of which there is an extract in Partington, *Post-bag*, pp. 113–14.

299 (e) "to lift us to the storms"] Goldsmith, *The traveller*, line 204.

300 (b) a certain tragedy of a certain lady] Joanna Baillie. Scott is probably thinking of Rezenvelt, who is described by Freberg thus: 'He is indeed a man, within whose breast / Firm rectitude and honour hold their seat, / Though unadorned with that dignity / Which were their fittest garb. Now, on my life! / I know no truer heart than Rezenvelt.' (*De Monfort*, III. 2.) These lines describe Morritt exactly.

300 (e) melancholy and gentlemanlike] Ben Jonson, *Every man in his humour*, I. 2.

300 (e) visiting old Abbies by moonlight] An allusion to Melrose Abbey by moonlight (*The lay*, Canto II, st. I). Scott tells us on more than one occasion that he never saw the Abbey by moonlight.

300 (f) swept and garnishd mansion] *Bible, Matthew* 12: 44; *Luke* 11: 25.

302 (e) like *any mad*] See above, p. 292.

303 (d) as Uncle Toby says] Sterne, *Tristram Shandy*, Bk III, chap. 22.

303 (f) tho/ unknown] Read 'thof unknown.' See *SL* vi. 110 and my note.

304 (c) the yellow leaf] Shakespeare, *Macbeth*, V. 3.

304 (e) Widow of a Highland Chieftain] Ranald Macdonald of Keppoch.

305 (b) Monck Mason . . . Of course I answered] See my note to *SL* iv. 225 (d).

305 (d) hey ho the wind and the rain] Shakespeare, *Twelfth Night*, V. 1.

305 *n.* 1] 'Mr. North,' in line 8, had already been mentioned by Hartstonge. (See my note to *SL* iv. 173 (b).) He was John Henry North, an Irish barrister, and John Ballantyne met him during this visit to Edinburgh. (See Ballantyne's letter to Hogg, 10 Oct. 1816, in Strout, *Hogg*, p. 115.)

306 *n.* 1] Act I, sc. 1.

311 (a) Non-entry] See below, pp. 316–17.

312 (d) the Chancellor] Lord Eldon.

313 (b) *give their own fish-guts . . .*] See *SL* iii. 42.

315 (c) O fortunatam . . .] Juvenal, *Satires*, X. 122.

315 (c) Dickie Gossip] *Dicky Gossip* was the title of a popular song. In *The charms of melody*, 2° Dublin, n.d., p. 229.

315 *n.* 1] This note is not only superfluous but confusing. The couplet, which Scott quotes, is from Swift's *Duke upon duke*, st. [17], lines 1–2 (Scott's *Swift*, 2nd ed. xiii. 321) which was written as early as 1720 and, therefore, preceded both Thomson's *Sophonisba* and Fielding's *Tom Thumb*.

316 (c) Sharpe projects a publication of original letters] This work on the Queensberry correspondence was never completed. See Index, under Queensberry (*House of*).

316 *n.* 1] This part of the Duke's letter is in Partington, *Letter-books*, pp. 285–6.

316 *n.* 2] Delete this note. An editorial note in *Sharpe's Letters*, ii. 141, says Gower was referring to *Kirkton*, but Gower was referring to the work on 'original letters,' about which Scott is writing here. See below, p. 354 and my note.

317 (e) Stellas] There is a portrait of Stella at Abbotsford (canvas, oval, 30·5 × 25 in.). There is no record of its purchase.

318 (c–d) Solomon] *Bible, I Kings* 3: 16–27.

318 *n.* 1] Murray's letter is in *Lockhart*, v. 169–70, and in Smiles, *John Murray*, i. 469–70.

318 *n.* 2] The quotation is from *Lockhart*, i. 293.

319 (a) the Gypsies] This article for *QR* was not written. See below, p. 544.

320 (b) no great arithmetician] Henry Mackenzie recorded that this was said of Professor Dugald Stewart. See *The anecdotes and egotisms of Henry Mackenzie*, ed. Harold William Thompson, London, 1927, pp. 172–3. Robert

Chambers attributed this anecdote to Scott in his *Scottish jests*, Edinburgh, 1832, p. 77.

321 *n.* 1] For the Duke's letter of 19 Dec. see Partington, *Letter-books*, pp. 286-7.

324 (c) *pit* and *gallows*] Scott's interpretation is supported by Trayner (*Latin maxims*, under 'Cum fossa et furca'): 'It signified a jurisdiction over felons to punish men by hanging and women by drowning.' Scott expounded this more fully in the following year (1817) in his introd. to *The Border antiquities* (*MPW* vii. 109 *n.*). He uses the Latin phrase in *Waverley*, chap. 10, and in *Quentin Durward*, Introd. But in *Waverley*, chap. 41, Bradwardine uses the word 'pit' in sense of 'dungeon.' There are references to 'pit and gallows' in Pitcairn's *Criminal trials*, iii. 479, 491. At the latter reference a male prisoner, having died, was carried 'out of the said pitt to ane jibbet.'

324 (f) Grantongue field] This should be Green-Tongue Park. It had been part of the Toftfield land.

325 (b) Dicks Cleuch] Renamed Rhymer's Glen by Scott.

325 *n.* 1] For 'Seton Kerr' read 'Seton-Karr.'

326 (b) Genus et proavi] Ovid, *Metamorphoses*, Bk XIII, lines 140-1: Nam genus, et proavos, et quae non fecimus ipsi, / Vix ea nostra voco. (Birth, ancestry, and what we have not ourselves done, I would hardly call our own.) Bradwardine quotes this, partly in English and partly in Latin. (*Waverley*, chap. 10.)

326 (d) a fico for the phrase] Shakespeare, *Merry wives of Windsor*, I. 3.

327 (a) The "leetle poopy dog"] This may be an allusion to J. P. Kemble's pronunciation of these words; if so, Terry would understand the allusion.

327 (c) *Tanuguay du Chatel*] See my note to *SL* ii. 336 (d).

328 (b-c) digging for coal] See also below, p. 433-4 and *SL* v. 33 and my note.

329 (d) To Miss Clephane] Anna Jane.

329 *n.* 1] Another letter to Park, dated 17 Feb. 1816, is printed in the *London Weekly Rev.* Vol. 1 (8 Sept. 1827), pp. 220-1.

330 (c) Mr. William Dundas] But Scott gives the credit for the appointment to Croker, below, p. 369.

331 (d) Allan Moidart] It was printed in Campbell's *Albyn's anthology*; Croker's ed. of Boswell's *Johnson*; *Athenæum*, 1831, p. 438; *Schoolmaster*, ii. 151.

331 (e) harmony] This should be 'learning.' (Corrected in *SL* xii. 336 *n.* 1.)

331 (e-f) thriving like a green bay tree] See *SL* i. 23 and my note.

331 (f) Captain Clephane] Captain Robert Clephane, R.N.

333 (a) between Mr. Milne and me] In the negotiations for the purchase of part of Abbotslee by Scott from Nicol Milne.

333 (c) Sanderson & Paterson . . . Smiths estimate] Messrs Sanderson & Paterson, builders, Galashiels, and J. & T. Smith, builders, Darnick. Estimates were prices of materials only. There were no plans as yet and, therefore, there could be no estimate for cost of building. John Smith recorded in his diary, 23 Dec. 1816: 'Letter from Abbotsford to give in estimate for his house' and on 24 Dec.: 'Called at Abbotsford and saw Mr Scott.'

333 (f) Mr. Atkinson] This is the first reference in the correspondence to William Atkinson, the architect of the whole of Abbotsford. Blore is given in many books on architecture as the architect of the first portion of Abbotsford. This is definitely erroneous. No part of Abbotsford was designed by Blore. Though Blore is mentioned here and elsewhere, all his ideas were rejected and those of Atkinson adopted.

334 (b) three sides of an octagon] This plan was never carried out.

334 (f) old woman in a [*illegible*]] The illegible word is 'cullender.' See *SL* iii. 515.

335 *n.* 1] Delete this note and see my note to *SL* iii. 153.

336 (c) offices at Bowhill] They were designed by William Atkinson.

336 (e) Mr. Smallwood] I have not traced him. William Froome Smallwood

(1800–34) was a Gothic architect who died at Camberwell. He may have been a son of Scott's Smallwood. In index to *Lockhart* there is an entry: 'Smallwood and Smith, Messrs, Melrose.' This is an error. Smallwood was not a member of the building firm of John and Thomas Smith, Darnick.

336 (f) ice house] Later an ice-house was built as a separate building incorporating a larder.

336 (f) gate of the Parliament house ...] This was much later incorporated in the door into the garden from the terrace on the extreme left as one looks at the house from the river.

337 (a) back door . . . out of the Tolbooth] A portion of the round stair turret from the demolished Edinburgh Tolbooth was eventually made into a doorway on the river side of the kitchen court. It was demolished when Hope-Scott built his addition on the site of the court and some of the stones are still to be seen lying on the grass at the side of the road down to the stables.

337 (b) several scutcheons in the College] One was from the Hall of the University of Edinburgh. It has a quotation from Seneca with the date 1616 and was placed on the outer wall of the Library above the bow window built in 1822. It is not known what the others were.

338 (a) Jalabad Sing] As this letter is printed from an Abbotsford Copy, I cannot say what Scott actually wrote. In a letter to William Scott of Maxpoffle, 29 Jan. 1817 (not in *SL* but original in NLS MS. 2889, ff. 133–4), Scott spells the name Salabad Jung. Neither Jalabad Sing nor Salabad Jung is given as a son of Nadir Shah in L. Lockhart's *Nadir Shah*, London, 1938. In a store in the basement of Abbotsford there is a coat of chain-mail, in very dilapidated condition, which may have belonged to Jelabad Sing. The armour was presented by John Macdonald Kinneir. See my note to *SL* vi. 335 (c).

339 (a) Doctor Diet . . .] An English proverb. See *Ray*, p. 40. Scott probably got this from Swift's *Polite conversation*: 'the best doctors in the world are Doctor Diet, Doctor Quiet, and Doctor Merryman.' (Swift's *Works*, ed. Scott, 2nd ed., ix. 456.)

339 (a) York place] Mrs Terry's father, Alexander Nasmyth, lived in York Place, Edinburgh.

339 (c) "as great as the Prince of Condé"] St. [6], line 2 of the song beginning 'The Sun had loos'd his weary Team' in D'Urfey, *Wit and mirth*, 4th ed., Vol. 1 (1719), p. 322. Also in *The Syren*, 3rd ed. (1739), p. 216, and in *The vocal miscellany*, 3rd ed., London, 1738, i. 173.

339 (f) the Chapel] Nickname for the northern range of the kitchen courtyard.

339 *n.* 1] John Alexander Ballantyne was born 29 Nov.

340 (f) His wife has come over] From Canada. She was now at Dumfries (*SL* vii. 484).

341 (d) the last Earl of Bothwell] Francis Stewart or Hepburn, 5th Earl. See Scott's *Provincial antiquities*, under 'Crichton Castle' (*MPW* vii. 179–86).

341 (d) I have in my possession] 'Proceedings at law by Francis Stuart, son of Francis Earl of Bothwell, against the Earl of Buccleuch.' Scott refers to this MS. in his note to chap. 4 of *Old Mortality*.

341 *n.* 2] Why this note? It merely repeats what Scott has said.

342 (a) At Philiphaugh the fray began] This is st. 1 of *The Battle of Philiphaugh* in Scott's *Minstrelsy* (ed. Henderson), ii. 215.

343 (b) I went on a pilgrimage] Probably to Creehope (or Crichope) Linn, near Drumlanrig, which Scott had already seen when a boy (Hogg, *Life of Allan Cunningham*, p. 203). This is more likely than a pilgrimage from Bowhill to Dobson's Linn. Both places are mentioned in a note to *Old Mortality*.

343 (d) mists and snows] A reminiscence of the quotation from Coleridge above, p. 295.

343 *n.* 1] Add: lines 203–4.

344 (b) mess [?]-earth] Read 'moss-earth.' Scott refers to marle-mosses above, p. 146, and to moss earth in *Guy Mannering*, chap. 23.

345 (b) To Lady Louisa Stuart] Scott is replying to her letter of 5 Dec.

1816, cited above, p. 293 *n.* 2, and printed in *FL* i. 393–5.

345 (b) Now their fame is up] See my note to *SL* i. 380 (c). It was Dulcinea's, not Don Quixote's, fame that was to go from 'Toledo to Madrid.'

346 (b) see *very far* into the mill stone] *Ray*, p. 260; Ramsay, *Proverbs*, p. 32.

346 (c) like the memorable Cobler] *The cobler* begins: 'A cobler there was, and he liv'd in a stall, / Which serv'd him for parlour, for kitchen and hall.' In Ramsay, *Tea-table miscellany*.

346 (e) Augustus] Suetonius, *Lives of the Caesars*, Bk II, chap. 29.

347 (a) sentimental] The word occurs in 1st ed., ii. 337. Scott altered it to 'fine' (chap. 13 of one-vol. eds.).

347 (b) as Win Jenkins says] In Smollett, *Humphry Clinker*. See my note to *SL* i. 337 (c).

349 *n.* 1] Scott's spelling of Hutson is correct. Lockhart is wrong in spelling the name Hudson and also wrong in calling him a forester. Hutson was one of the Duke's gamekeepers.

352 (b) Shillinglaw] George Shillinglaw, seedsman, Redpath, near Dryburgh Abbey. His son, Joseph, was a joiner at Darnick and did much of the woodwork in the second portion of Abbotsford.

352 (c) To Clarke Whitfeld] This letter is on the same subject as that of 22 Feb. 1816 (above, p. 179) and written, with considerable delay, after he had received Whitfeld's letter of 28 Oct. 1816. Scott seems to be referring to this letter in his letter to John Ballantyne (*SL* i. 527) which can be dated 7 Jan. 1817 and, if so, the date of this letter is Monday, 6 Jan. 1817.

352 (c) a volume of four hundred & fifty pages] *Paul's letters*.

352 *n.* 1] See my note to *SL* iii. 254 *n.* 1.

353 (b) To Archibald Constable] As Scott writes to Constable, 18 Aug. 1817 (below, p. 502), about possible changes in the *Farmer's Mag.* this letter must come after that one.

354 (a) To C. K. Sharpe] The date is Saturday, 21 Dec. 1816. Scott asked what print he wanted and Sharpe replied on 24 Dec. that he wanted one

of the first Duke of Queensberry. His letter (NLS MS. 3887, ff. 165–6) was addressed to Abbotsford and has the postal date 24 Dec. 1816, but on the cover is written 7 Jan. 1817 as if, for some reason, it had not been delivered till then.

354 (b) *Macte animo*] Statius, *Thebaidos*, Bk VII, line 280.

354 *n.* 1] Scott's letter deals exclusively with Sharpe's projected work on the Queensberry letters. The note, therefore, should begin with 'Sharpe was meditating' (line 4) and lines 1–4 should be made a new note (note 2) relating to 'Russell for collation' in the second letter to Sharpe on p. 354. In lines 5–6, for 'he had written' read 'he replied.'

355 (a) bargain with Ballantyne] This is John Ballantyne. At this stage he must be taking responsibility for publishing Kirkton, but by the time it was published the management was in the hands of Longman & Co. with Ballantyne's name second in the imprint.

355 (d) To C. K. Sharpe] The reference (p. 356) to holiday suggests 30 Jan. (martyrdom of Charles I). If so, date of letter is 29 Jan. Scott appears to be answering Sharpe's letter (*Sharpe's Letters*, ii. 144) which is dated '[Feb. 1817].' But the Wednesday of Sharpe's letter may actually be Wednesday, 29 Jan.

355 (e) If they are virtuous] Shakespeare, *Twelfth Night*, II. 3.

355 *n.* 2] For 'Sir David Dalrymple, Lord Hailes's *Annals of Scotland*, 1776' read 'Sir John Dalrymple's *Memoirs of Great Britain*, 1771–88,' and for 'pp. 4' read 'pp. 5.'

356 (a) We will ordain them] *The rising in the North*, st. [32], lines 3–4. In Percy's *Reliques*.

356 (a–b) All that is done in the matter of Jedediah] i.e. Scott's own review of *Old Mortality* for *QR*. Sharpe had asked for a sight of it before it went to press. (*Sharpe's Letters*, ii. 144–5.)

356 (f) a certain friend of mine] Robert Jamieson.

359 (a) *keep moving*] See my note to *SL* vi. 297 (f).

362 (a) has many mansions] *Bible, John* 14: 2.

362 (f) I have returned the precognition] i.e. on 9 Jan.; but below, p. 369, he says 'by the Mail coach of this day,' i.e. 10 Jan.

363 (e) I have this day sent] This letter to Croker follows at p. 366. But cf. *SL* xii. 426 and see my note to *SL* xii. 364 *n*.

364 *n*.] The 'undated letter' in line 10 from foot is printed in *SL* xii. 426 where it is openly dated 10 Jan. 1817; but it is given as undated in *The Croker papers*, from which it is printed.

366 (a)] Grierson could have got the conclusion from Smiles, *John Murray*, i. 376: 'stout as a lion. Yours faithfully, Walter Scott.'

366 (b–c) Byron . . . sound politics] See Scott's review of *Childe Harold*, Canto III in *QR* Vol. 16 (Oct. 1816), especially pp. 191–4. Not reprinted by Lockhart in *MPW*.

366 (e) to get his appointment] The sentence is incomplete. Scott meant to write: 'to get an exchange for his appointment.'

369 (a) entirely to your recommendation] But Scott had given the credit to William Dundas (above, p. 330).

369 (e) Hector MacDonald] Hector Macdonald Buchanan.

369 *n*. 1] See my note to *SL* ii. 213 (c).

370 (c) Mr. Watson] James Watson, a London surgeon or apothecary. See *Edin. Ann. Reg.* IX. ii. cii. He was later tried for treason but was acquitted. (Ibid., x. ii, Appendix, 6–16.)

370 *n*. 1] The explanation of Scott's 'harsh reference' to Colquhoun is wrong. See *SL* ii. 326, 335, vii. 61. Scott's dislike was not due to Colquhoun's part in reforming the law courts in 1806–8 (during which period Scott is friendly). The dislike was a personal one for which other explanations might be suggested.

371 (b) "custom of your exercise"] See my note to *SL* ii. 252 (a).

371 (c) Long ill long well] The nearest I can find is in Ramsay, *Proverbs*, p. 10: 'Be lang sick that ye be soon hale.'

371 (f) a commission granted] In 1794.

372 *n*. 2] For 'H. Ridley' read 'James Ridley.' *The history of the merchant Abudah, or the talisman of Oromanes* is in Weber, *Tales of the East*, iii. 426. See also below, p. 487, the *Journal*, 2 Aug. 1826, and *MPW* v. 3.

373 (d) curious border law] Scott used this discovery in the introduction which he wrote this year for *The Border antiquities*. The regulations were drawn up in 1249. See *MPW* vii. 117–19.

373 *n*. 1] The Duke's letter is printed in full in Partington, *Letter-books*, pp. 308–9.

374 (e) Tom Hutson's Minstrelsy] The verses were probably those given in *SL* x. 510.

374 (e) Campbell] i.e. for Alexander Campbell's *Albyn's anthology*.

374 *n*. 1] Invernahyle is in Argyllshire.

374 *n*. 3] Delete. The note (*SL* v. 347 *n*. 2) merely refers back to the present reference.

375 (c) put the saddle on the right horse] *Kelly*, p. 281; Ramsay, *Proverbs*, p. 53.

375 (f) hang him, foul coallier] Shakespeare, *Twelfth Night*, III. 4.

376 (d) From the *kist*] Shakespeare, *Hamlet*, III. 4: 'That from a shelf the precious diadem stole.'

376 *n*. 1] Lockhart, in a letter of 4 Aug. 1821 to Hogg, gave a different version of these lines. See Mrs Garden, *Memorials of James Hogg*, p. 143.

377 (b) your Grace's appeal] In the Queensberry Case (q.v. in Index). See also *SL* v. 120 *n*.

377 (e) Bailey] He does not appear as a contributor to *QR* in Shine.

378 (b) Sir John Malcolms & Crokers letters] Which Scott had used for his review of Byron's *Childe Harold III* in *QR*. See above, p. 149.

378 (b) yeoman service] Shakespeare, *Hamlet*, V. 2.

379 (a) annuity to the boy] i.e. to William Scott, Daniel Scott's natural son.

379 (d) The Solemn League & Covenant] *The Battle of Killiecrankie*, st. [4]. In Herd, i. 102–3.

379 *n.* 1] Delete. Scott is not referring to Kirkton but only to the Killiecrankie article.

381 (b) made a most energetic attack] Dr Thomas McCrie's articles appeared in the *Edinburgh Christian Instructor*, Vol. 14 (Jan. 1817), pp. 41–73; (Feb. 1817) pp. 100–40; (Mar. 1817) pp. 170–201. Scott did, however, read them and referred to them in his review in *QR*.

381 (c) "there shall be no cakes and ale?"] Shakespeare, *Twelfth Night*, II. 3.

382 (f) But all this is nonsense again] Sterne, *Tristram Shandy*, Bk VI, chap. 5.

383 (c) in my minds eye Horatio] Shakespeare, *Hamlet*, I. 2.

383 (d) blue-bank and hinny-lees] These are names of plantations at Abbotsford. On John Morrison's plan of the estate these are: No. 55. East Blue-Bank; and No. 58. Hinny-Lees.

383 (d) yeomans service] Shakespeare, *Hamlet*, V. 2.

383 (e) But shall we go mourn] Shakespeare, *Winter's tale*, IV. 2.

383 *n.* 1] Delete 'See *Lyrical and Miscellaneous Pieces*, 1817.' There is no such work.

384 (f) boute-feu] In his ed. of Dryden's *Works* (xv. 264 *n.*) Scott says: '*Boutefeu*, a gallicism for *incendiary:* in Dryden's time it was a word of good reputation, but is now obsolete.'

385 (a) The "weary knife-grinder" and your own squib] *The Friend of Humanity and the Knife-Grinder* in *Poetry of the Anti-Jacobin*; and Morritt, *Advice to the Whigs*.

388 (b) My mother as Sancho says] See my note to *SL* ii. 299 (b).

388 (d) Kaeside] Only on condition that John Moss was willing to vacate the house. See below, pp. 392–3.

389 (a) Mariners book] Mariner's *An account of the natives of the Tonga Islands* was reviewed by William Laidlaw (almost certainly with Scott's assistance) in *Edin. Ann. Reg. for 1817* (publ. 1821), X. i. 329.

389 (e) To John Richardson] This letter should be dated 1818. The snuff-box was presented to Kemble on 28 Feb. 1818. See below, p. 390 (a).

389 *n.* 2] Delete the whole note. Murray's letter, which Scott is answering, is in Smiles, *John Murray*, ii. 7. Murray says Miss Waldie's book is 'Residence in Belgium,' i.e. *Narrative of a residence in Belgium . . . By an Englishwoman*, 8vo London, 1817. The author was Charlotte Ann Waldie who became Mrs Eaton in 1822. Cf. *SL* xii. 136 *n.* and my note.

390 (a) John Kemble] A gold snuff-box was presented to him at a dinner in Edinburgh on 28 Feb. 1818. Jeffrey made the presentation. See *Edin. Ann. Reg.* XI. ii. 191–2.

390 (b) Rundell and Bridges] Rundell, Bridge, and Rundell. See my note to *SL* i. 517 (e).

391 (e) Hey ho for the green holly] Shakespeare, *As you like it*, II. 7.

391 (f) for the address at Selkirk] i.e. on 20 Feb. Addresses were being sent to the Prince Regent on his escape from assassination and on the disturbed state of the nation. The address from Edinburgh had been drawn up on 3 Feb. See *Edin. Ann. Reg. for 1817*, X. ii. 148.

392 (b) the land above Abbotsford] For want of the necessary data it is difficult to explain this passage clearly. The thicket was at the extreme SW. corner of the estate; it was part of the original land bought in 1811; and it had been planted by Dr Douglas in 1808. At this point there were two awkward triangles, one nicked out of the Faldonside estate and one out of the Abbotsford estate. Scott seems to be saying that he will buy Nicol Milne's triangle but that he will not sell his own. If Scott had succeeded in making this adjustment (which he did not) the boundary of his estate would have been straightened out.

392 (c) his brother in law Knox] John Knox. John's brother Ebenezer, who had been a tenant in Crosslee (*Chisholm*, pp. 65, 149), was convicted in 1817 of having forged notes in his possession and was sentenced to transportation for 14 years. (*Scots Mag.* lxxix. 575–6.) Ebenezer wrote to Scott from Sydney, N.S.W., 1819–21.

392 (d) the Dickies (?)] Read 'the Duke's.'

394 (b) Tale of Plunton] See below, pp. 403–6 and my note to p. 403 (a).

394 n. 1] The MS. belonged to Alexander Stewart of Appin. The *Letters from a gentleman* was by Edmund Burt. In line 6, for '1822' read '1818.' See also *SL* v. 275 n.

394 n. 2] It is inaccurate to say that this letter marks the beginning of Scott's cramp. He had complained about it in Oct. 1815 (*SL* i. 489). See also above, p. 365.

395 (d) roar like a Bull calf] Proverb.

395 (f) The hand is the hand of Esau] *Bible, Genesis* 27: 22.

396 (b) the Clowns universal exclamation of "O Lord Sir!"] Shakespeare, *All's well that ends well*, II. 2. (Said six times.)

396 (d) guerdon is better than remuneration] Shakespeare, *Love's labour's lost*, III. 1.

397 (a) *taxing man*] As this is in italics it is probably intended as a quotation. See 'Taxing man with visage grim' in *SL* v. 448 and my note to it.

398 (f) Needpath] There is no record of stone from Neidpath being used.

398 n. 1] For 'Probably Sprouston is meant' read 'The transcriber's mistake for Sprouston.'

402 (e) "The peats and turf . . ."] *The auld man's mare's dead*. In *Johnson*, Vol. 5 [1797], No. 485, and Chambers, *Scottish songs* (1829), i. 269.

403 (a) the Archbishop's homilies] Le Sage, *Gil Blas*, Bk vii, chap. 4.

403 (a) Barons of Plenton] Train told Scott the story in a letter of 19 Dec. 1814, printed in Partington, *Post-bag*, pp. 107–9. The family name, which Scott has forgotten, was Kenmore. There is no reply to this letter in *SL*.

405 n. 2] Add: respectively in *The man of the world* and *Love à la mode*, two comedies by Macklin.

406 n. 1] Delete this note. For the occasion of the letter see *SL* vii. 484–8.

408 (b) with most admired disorder] Shakespeare, *Macbeth*, III. 4.

408 (f) a stupid Scottish diary] Rev.

John Blackadder's memoirs. See above, p. 401.

409 n. 1] i.e. of Shakespeare's *Taming of the shrew*.

412 (e) Sir Terence OFay] A character in Maria Edgeworth's *The absentee*. He does not use the words Scott attributes to him but they describe the claims he made to manage affairs. See chap. 5.

413 (a) grasshopper is still a burthen] *Bible, Ecclesiastes* 12: 5.

413 (c) man of mould] Shakespeare, *Henry V*, III. 2: 'men of mould.'

413 (d) All sorts of remedies] Le Sage, *Gil Blas*, Bk I, chap. 10.

415 (a) proposal in the Quarterly Revw] See *Tracts on saving banks* in *QR* Vol. 16 (Oct. 1816), pp. 89–116. *Shine* (No. 404) gives author as either Rev. William Sidney Walker or Rev. Robert Lundie. The latter is the more likely author. Scott is referring to pp. 113–14. It is not the *QR*, as Scott's words imply, that is advocating right of depositors in a savings bank to claim parish relief. This provision is in George Rose's Bill before Parliament and *QR* gives only qualified approval.

415 (e) Gold & silver] *Bible, Acts* 3: 6.

415 (f) damned measurements] See above, p. 396.

415 n. 1] Delete 'never accepted by any manager.' It was produced at the Caledonian Theatre, Edinburgh, in May 1830. In May 1952 it was produced at the Pitlochry Festival Theatre, when it was wrongly advertised as a world première.

416 (e) Coriolanus for the last time] Kemble played Coriolanus for the last time on 27 Mar. and his last appearance was in *Macbeth* on 29 Mar. when he spoke the farewell address written by Scott. Dibdin, *Annals*, pp. 277, 279.

417 (e) Lady Julia] Lady Julia Gore, half-sister of Lady Abercorn and afterwards Lady Julia Lockwood.

417 n.] For '*Life of Kemble*' read 'Scott's review of Boaden's *Memoirs of Kemble* in *QR*, Apr. 1826.' Grierson's quotation will be found in *MPW* xx. 198–9.

418 (c) on my red beam like one of Fingal's heroes] This is not an exact

quotation. Spirits of the dead appear in clouds and beams but nowhere in the poems on 'red beams.' The nearest approaches to this idea are in *Fingal*, Bks II and IV, *The death of Cuthullin*, and *Sulmalla of Lumon*.

418 (c) sent by Prospero] Shakespeare, *The tempest*.

418 (e) praise the bridge] *Ray*, p. 106.

419 (a) Allan of Moidart] A poem by Margaret, now Lady Compton.

419 (a) funny verses on St. Mary's well] The verses are not attached to Anna Jane's letter of 20 Jan. (NLS MS. 3888, ff. 10–11.)

419 (b) Collector's place] M. C. McCallum. He was Collector for only one year. In 1816 Dr Haliburton was Collector; McCallum in 1817; in 1818 the post was vacant; in 1819 it was held by Archibald Park. *Edinburgh Almanack for 1816 (–1819)*.

419 (c) sit at Rome and strive with the Pope] *Kelly*, p. 194; Ramsay, *Proverbs*, p. 39. See also *SL* vii. 106.

420 (d) renewed his youth like the eagles] *Bible, Psalms* 103: 5.

421 (b–c) "sit on silken seat"] Lady Wardlaw, *Hardyknute*, st. [16], line 2: 'To lean on silken seat.' (Percy's *Reliques* and Herd, i. 123.)

421 (d) Demon who wasted Sir Vista's wealth] Cf. Pope, *Moral essays, Epistle IV*, lines 15–16: 'What brought Sir Visto's ill got wealth to waste? / Some Dæmon whisper'd, "Visto! have a Taste".'

421 n. 1] The address was printed in the *Literary and Statistical Mag.* Vol. 1 (May 1817), pp. 212–13, with the parts omitted by Kemble indicated. This was not Kemble's last public appearance. See above, p. 390 (a).

422 (e) If two niches could be made] This plan was never carried out.

422 (f) beggars . . . ought not to be chusers] See *SL* ii. 225.

422 n. 1] Delete 'I think.' Mrs Scott was definitely Mrs Tom Scott. See below, p. 426.

423 (b) Doctors Quiet, Diet & Merryman] See my note to *SL* iv. 339 (a).

423 (f) To Daniel Terry] The date here is taken from *FL* i. 423. The correct date is mid May.

423 (f) iron beams] These were for the bow window in the Dining Room, the only iron beams used in the building.

424 (a) death of one of my brethren] James Walker who died on 9 May.

424 (b) on Saturday 7th May] This should be 7th June.

424 n. 1] There is nothing in the play to justify the remark that 'at the age of seventy he fancies himself an Adonis.' The reference to 'ugly twinges' comes from Act II, sc. 1, where Ogleby says: 'that's an ugly twinge.'

424 n. 2] Delete. The reading 'furnished' is correct. The windows were made in London by Bullock & Co.

425 (a) Ariostos excuse] See *Orlando furioso in English heroical verse by Sr John Harington*, 2° London, 1634, p. 421.

425 (b–c) balcony . . . of cast Iron] This plan was never carried out and Scott did not have gas lighting till 1823.

426 n. 1] The reference is to *Devorgoil*. The letter is too early for *Rob Roy*.

426 n. 3] Mrs Scott sailed on 21 Apr. See *SL* vii. 492 n.

427 (b) To James Ballantyne] *The search after happiness* appeared in *The Sale-Room* of 1 Feb. The letter, therefore, was written a day or two before that and almost certainly on Wednesday, 29 Jan., and written on the same day as the letter to Sharpe (above, p. 355) which can also be dated Wednesday, 29 Jan.

431 (c) fraud & suet] Scott calls Constable this in *Journal*, 15 Nov. 1827.

431 (d) his puritanical magazine] With Vol. 8 (1814) Blackwood took over the *Edinburgh Christian Instructor* in which McCrie had attacked *Old Mortality*.

432 (d) Browns . . . Donaldsons] William Brown and James Donaldson. The latter was proprietor of the *Edinburgh Advertiser*.

432 n. 2] In line 1, for 'Johnstone' read 'Johnston.' The date of Johnston's birth

is usually given as 1766, but it probably should be about 1771 as, in a letter to Scott, 5 Nov. 1817 (NLS MS. 3888, f. 221 b), he refers to the time when they went together to the High School.

432 *n.* 3] The purchase was concluded on 18 Apr. The agreement made by Scott, James Ballantyne and Hogarth as joint proprietors is dated 27 May and 2 June. Ballantyne was appointed editor with a salary of £200 p.a. A copy of the document, made by Hogarth in 1826, is now in NLS (MS. 6080).

433 (d) blue granite] From the quarry at Kaeside. Later Scott had to confess that it was not granite but graywacke. See below, p. 515. The freestone came from Sprouston.

433 (f) Florence] Joseph Florence, cook to successive Dukes of Buccleuch. Scott mentions him in a footnote to *Guy Mannering*, chap. 46. A portrait of him by J. Ainslie, 1817, was at Dalkeith House (A. Francis Steuart, *Pictures at Dalkeith House*, Dalkeith, 1890, p. 101). The portrait is illustrated in *Scotland's Mag.* Vol. 58 (Mar. 1962), p. 16.

433 (f) Thrift—Thrift—Horatio] Shakespeare, *Hamlet*, I. 2.

333 (f) coals] See also above, p. 328 and *SL* v. 33 and my note.

434 (a) a very curious petition] This is No. 2 in the list in my note to p. 159 above. 1553 should be 1552.

434 (c) To Adam Ferguson] Date is 24 Apr. [1818]. Scott appears to be replying to Ferguson's letter from St. Andrews, 15 Apr. 1818 (NLS MS. 866, ff. 180–1), but there is nothing in his letter about Spalding or Maxwell.

434 (c) Knight of Riddel] Sir John Buchanan Riddell, 9th Bart. of Riddell, who died the following year (1819).

434 (e) what it is that does *not* butter parsnips] i.e. words. 'Fair (or fine) words butter no parsnips.' *Ray*, p. 220. Also used in *A legend of Montrose*, chap. 3, and in the *Journal*, 15 Apr. 1826.

435 (a) "the half thereof had not been told to him"] *Bible*, *I Kings* 10:7.

435 (b) a cousin of mine] James Scott, son of his Uncle Thomas.

435 (d) Sir John] Sir John Buchanan Riddell.

435 (f) my grapery] The plan for a grapery was abandoned.

435 *n.* 1] For 'Fergusson' read 'Ferguson.'

436 (f) the square tower] This plan was abandoned. The top of the tower was finished off with a parapet copied from Melrose Abbey.

437 (f) Keans squeezes] At Theatre Royal, Edinburgh, where Edmund Kean was acting.

437 (f) an old lady] Lady Douglas. See below, pp. 450, 458.

438 (c) The little pickaninny] Scott's godson, Walter Scott Terry.

438 (d) The eldridge knight] *Sir Cauline*, Pt I, st. [32], lines 1–2. In Percy's *Reliques*.

441 (a) having Moses & the Prophets] *Bible*, *Luke* 16: 29.

441 (e) Sancho's physician] Cervantes, *Don Quixote*, Pt 2, chap. 47 (Lockhart's ed., 1822, v. 32).

441 (f) Prospero visited Caliban] Cf. above, p. 418.

442 (a) as Augustus did at Rome] Suetonius, *Lives of the Caesars*, Bk II, chap. 29.

442 (c–d) Two kind remembrances] One was Panter. The other was probably *A report of the proceedings . . . against Waller O'Grady*, etc., 8vo Dublin, 1816.

442 *n.* 1] If the Latin form of Panter had to be used it should have been in the nominative case.

443 (a) "Get thee a wife—get thee a wife"] Shakespeare, *Much ado about nothing*, V. 4.

443 (f) To Robert Southey] The address is in the handwriting of William Elliot-Lockhart, who franked the letter on 2 May. See facsimile in Symington, *Some unpublished letters*, facing p. 14. The letter was redirected to London and the PM date (7 May) may be a London one.

444 (d) William Smith] For an amusing account of Smith, see Stuart, *Letters*, ii. 183. See also *SL* xii. 488–9.

444 (e) the ancient and eternal strife of which the witch speaks in Thalaba] Southey, *Thalaba*, Bk IX: 'This the eternal, universal strife!'

444 *n.* 2] Southey applied to the Court of Chancery on 18 Mar. 1817 for an injunction to restrain Messrs Sherwood, Neely and Jones from printing and publishing *Wat Tyler*. See *Edin. Ann. Reg. for 1817*, X. ii. 64–7. The quotation is from *Lockhart*, v. 221 *n.*

448 (d) Mr. Scott of Linton] Lockhart prints Scott of Sinton, which is the correct reading. He is John Corse Scott of Sinton.

448 *n.* 1] Robert Gilmour was also the author of *Tales in verse* and *The Battle of Waterloo*. In the review of *Lothaire* in the *Augustan Rev.* Vol. 1 (May 1815), p. 28, the reviewer called it an imitation of Scott.

448 *n.* 2] These lines are given as Dr Delany's in Scott's *Swift*, 2nd ed., xiv. 167. Scott had used the same misquotation in 1806 (*MPW* xix. 159). The same idea occurs at the end of *Rob Roy*, written in 1817.

449 (c) kindest regards] Read 'kindest respects.'

450 (a) a place of public amusement] Theatre Royal, Edinburgh. See above, p. 437, and below, p. 458.

451 (c) To John Richardson] This letter is printed from *FL* i. 427–9 where Douglas dates it as given here. But Douglas's dating is not to be trusted and although 19 May in 1817 was a Monday I think the year is 1818. The letter, which deals with Aitken, must follow the letter, on the same subject, to Charles Erskine (*SL* v. 132–3) which is docketed by Erskine 1818. 'About two years ago' is inconsistent with 'this twelvemonth' (*SL* v. 132) unless we date the letter to Richardson as 1818.

452 *n.* 2] This note is copied from *FL* i. 429, but from the wording in Scott's letter it would seem that the reference to the medallion is to something else.

453 (c) res domi] 'Res angusta domi.' Juvenal, *Satires*, III. 165.

453 *n.* 1] In last line, for '*Songs*' read '*Pieces.*'

454 (e) Robt. Dundas] Robert Dundas of Beechwood.

459 (d) The creature's at his dirty work again] Pope, *Epistle to Dr Arbuthnot*, line 92.

459 *n.* 1] In lines 4–5, for 'Lady Stewart-Mackenzie' read 'Mrs Stewart-Mackenzie.'

460 (a) To Laidlaw] Date is 11 July. Scott returned to Abbotsford on 26 July and 'a fortnight' before that brings us back to 12 July. Friday of the letter, therefore, would be 11 July. On that day he had an attack of cramp (below, p. 493). The word underlined, '*Interrupted*', almost certainly refers to this attack.

460 *n.* 2] It was not till Apr. 1819 that *Blackwood* (Vol. 5, p. 105) announced that it would be delivered to subscribers 'in a few days.'

461 (a) born under a six penny planet] In the form of the proverb given here Scott has altered its meaning as given in *Ray*, p. 104, and in Ramsay, *Proverbs*, p. 27. Ramsay has: 'He that's born under a Tippenny Planet will ne'er be worth a Groat.'

461 (c–d) his bookseller turnd bankrupt] George Goldie. See *SL* xii. 447, 448 *n.*

462 (e) Dis aliter visum] Virgil, *Aeneid*, II. 428.

463 (c) Venetians before they were Christians] See *SL* ii. 56.

463 *n.* 1] For 'had just been destroyed by fire' read 'had been destroyed by fire in 1812.'

464 (c) under the shade . . . pastoral posture] Virgil, *Georgics*, II. 58; *Eclogues*, I. 1.

464 (d) Lady Montagu . . . confinement] I can find no record of a birth in 1817.

464 *n.* 1] Delete 'as well as the artist ultimately employed in arranging Scott's interior at Abbotsford.' Atkinson was the architect for the whole of Abbotsford, both exterior and interior.

466 (c) an old friend] Robert Jamieson.

468 (e) "with ane leathern coat"] See *SL* iii. 130.

468 *n.* 1] Delete this note. Scott's mother could not know a man who died in 1737. Sir Hew is Sir Hew Hamilton-Dalrymple, 3rd Bart., who succeeded in 1790 and died in 1800. The incident must have taken place before 1790 while his wife was still Mrs Dalrymple.

468 n. 2] Delete and see *SL* v. 354 n.

469 (a) To H. M. Buchanan] Date is 8th July [1820]. (Corrected in *SL* vi. 285 n.)

469 (c) Howard] George William Frederick Howard, afterwards 7th Earl of Carlisle.

470 (d) Macconochie who insinuates hopes] In the Queensberry Case (q.v. in Index). See also *SL* v. 120 n.

470 (e) Lord of Linne] *The heir of Linne.* In Percy's *Reliques.*

471 (a) Satchells] The couplet does not occur in the work cited in n. 1. By 'Satchells' Scott may mean the tenant of Satchells in 1817; if so, n. 1 should be deleted.

471 (c) To shine the bright palladium] Samuel Johnson, *The vanity of human wishes*, line 84.

471 n. 1] Also published at Hawick, 1786, at Edinburgh, 1892, and at Hawick, 1894.

471 n. 2] The excursion ended on 26 July, not 20. See below, p. 479.

472 (e) N'allez pas dans cette galere] Varied from Molière, *Les fourberies de Scapin*, II. 11: 'Que diable alloit-il faire dans cette galère?'

473 (c) jump with their humour] Shakespeare, *I Henry IV*, I. 2: 'it jumps with my humour.'

474 (d) Since the rest of our courts] Read 'Since the rise of our courts.'

474 n. 2] Wordsworth's poem refers to Neidpath, not to Drumlanrig. If Grierson had to quote verse, he should have quoted Burns's *Verses on the destruction of the woods near Drumlanrig.*

475 (b) death of a brother in office] James Walker who died on 9 May.

475 n. 1] Delete this note. The legend of Columbus was published in her *Metrical legends of exalted characters*, 1821.

476 (a–b) stuff of the conscience] Shakespeare, *Othello*, I. 2.

477 (e) poor auld Scotlands] Burns, *To the guidwife of Wauchope House*, st. [2], line 4.

477 (e–f) this disjointed chat] Shakespeare, *I Henry IV*, I. 3: 'This bald unjointed chat.'

478 (e) the Scotch military musician] Andrew Hope in *The rose, thistle, and shamrock*, the third play in *Comic dramas*, London, 1817.

478 n. 2] *Thoughts on bores* was not included in *Comic dramas.*

479 (a) this kiver] See my note to *SL* i. 337 (c).

479 (c) remit of the Chancellors] Of Lord Eldon.

479 (c) selling the Fife land] This must refer to Lady Compton's farm, Powguild.

479 n. 1] For 'A W.G. Phillips' read 'G. Phillips.' Phillips had written to Scott on 28 July 1817 (NLS MS. 3888, ff. 126–7) and secured an interview. Phillips wrote again, from Edinburgh on 25 Sept. 1817 (NLS MS. 3888, ff. 172–3), thanking Scott for his advice and adding that he was proceeding with his novel.

480 (d) his novel] *Women, or pour et contre.*

481 (d) writing for the quarterly Review] This is his review of Sheil's *The apostate*, which appeared in *QR* for Apr. 1817 (publ. Aug.). Scott had suggested that Maturin should write reviews (*SL* xii. 361–2). Maturin thanked Scott for the advice, 19 Apr. 1817 (*Maturin Corr.* p. 77).

481 (f) the two Mr. Pringles] James Pringle of Torwoodlee and Alexander Pringle of Whytbank and Yair.

482 (a) the Loch] Strictly speaking 'lochs'. There were two—Loch of the Lowes and St Mary's Loch.

482 (e) flapper] Swift. See my note to *SL* ii. 213 (c).

482 (e) Head Court] Claims by freeholders to vote at a parliamentary election had to be made to the Head Court two months before its annual meeting in October. Objections by other freeholders could be lodged.

483 (a) the grand Cause] The Queensberry Case (q.v. in Index). See also *SL* v. 120 n.

483 (a) hetacombs] Scott presumably wrote, or meant to write, 'hecatombs.'

483 n. 1] Johnston's letter, dated 30 July, is postmarked 30 Oct. (NLS MS. 3888, ff. 128–9). It looks as if Johnston had absent-mindedly copied Scott's date. It is usually stated that the door and keys were presented by the Magistrates. Johnston's letter shows that Scott bought them from Inglis, the contractor. See also *SL* v. 9.

484 (d) chamber in the wall] *Bible, II Kings* 4: 10.

484 n. 1] For 'McIvor' read 'Mac-Ivor.'

485 (c) To Francis Jeffrey] Jeffrey did not reply till 14 Oct. His reply is in *FL* i. 439-40.

485 (e) to plague poor Caliban] See above, pp. 418, 441.

486 (c) like one of Miss Edgeworth's heroines] Mrs Raffarty in *The absentee*, chap. 6.

486 (d) the minister was mobbed by his parishioners] Rev. Robert Douglas, in his account of the Parish of Galashiels in Sir John Sinclair's *The statistical account of Scotland*, Vol. 2, Edinburgh, 1792, p. 299, said it was 'here an inconsiderable river.'

486 (e) Thomson or Jo. Murray] Thomas Thomson, Deputy Clerk Register, and John Archibald Murray (later Sir John), both Whigs.

487 (d) Merchant Abudahs hag] See above, p. 372 n. 2.

487 n. 1] In line 1, 'this month,' i.e. Aug., is taken from *Sharpe's Letters*, ii. 150, but Sharpe's letter must have been written in July as Jeffrey wrote to Scott on 1 Aug. Sharpe's reply is in ibid. ii. 157-60. For 'Ballantyne...cheated... at Brussels' [by Douglas Watt] (lines 6–7), see below, p. 511 and *SL* vi. 198 n.

488 (b) D. of Monmouth] Sharpe (*Letters*, ii. 151) had told Scott that he had made copies of letters from her to the Earls of Leven and Melville. Transcripts of these copies were made by A. C. [Alexander Campbell ?] for Scott.

488 (c) He should have had my hearty vote] Swift, *On the same* [i.e. *Verses on the upright judge*], lines 3–4 (*Works*, ed. Scott, 2nd ed., xii. 391.)

488 (d) Andw. Stuart] Andrew Stuart was the author of *Genealogical history of* the Stewarts, London, 1798, against which Sir Henry Steuart wrote *The genealogy of the Stewarts refuted: in a letter to A. Stuart*, Edinburgh, 1799. In a *Supplement*, London, 1799, Andrew Stuart replied to Sir Henry.

489 (b) Queen Mary] Sharpe replied on 21 Aug.: 'Where didst thou find that odious anecdote of the "Ferry Boat of Kinclevin"? I will not believe a word of it.' (*Sharpe's Letters*, ii. 158.)

489 (d) with more noise . . . than the temple of Solomon] *Bible, I Kings* 6: 7.

490 (a) To unknown correspondent] He was William Scott, Northumberland Street, and the PM is 1820. (*SL* xii. 488.) His 'Defence of Swift' appeared in the *Edinburgh Monthly Review*, Vol. 4 (July 1820), pp. 1–37.

492 (b) Muller] Peter Erasmus Müller.

492 (d) letter from Mathurin] Of 2 Aug., printed in *Maturin Corr.* pp. 81–2.

492 n. 2] For '*The Heart of Midlothian*' read '*Rob Roy*.' (Corrected in *SL* xii. 489.)

494 (a) Monsr. de Porceaugnac's treatment] Molière, *Monsieur de Porceaugnac*, I. 11.

494 (d) Spillsbury or Godbold] Francis Spilsbury and Nathaniel Godbold, 18th-cent. writers on medicine.

496 (d) the sons of Zeruiah] *Bible, II Samuel* 3: 39.

496 (e) Lord Lindsay] Afterwards 7th Earl of Balcarres and 24th Earl of Crawford. See *SL* ii. 542.

497 (c–d) guess my meaning by my mumping] Ramsay, *Proverbs*, p. 71: 'We may ken your meaning by your mumping.'

497 (e) To Lady Byron] She sent a note on 13 Aug. See below, p. 522 n.

497 (f) like the fairy tent] Of Pari Banou. See my note to *SL* ii. 527 (f).

499 (e) harping & carping] See my note to *SL* i. 262 (b).

499 n. 3] *The Border antiquities* had been appearing in parts since 1812.

500 (b) Thistle & fleur de lis] The thistle was put on the west gable of the Dining Room block in 1817 but the fleur-de-lis was reserved for the second

portion of the house and was put on the west side in 1822. See also below, p. 538.

500 (b–c) Fountain of the Lions] *The Story of Prince Ahmed and the Fairy Pari Banou* in *The Arabian Nights* (Weber, *Tales of the East*, i. 447, 451, 452). At the present day there is no lion presiding over a well. There are, however, *two* sculptures of red stone, which look like lions, above the door from the Terrace to the Garden. See also *St Ronan's Well*, chap. 7.

502 (a) respecting the Chronicle] With Laidlaw. See above, p. 465.

502 (c) Miss Constable] Elizabeth, eldest daughter, who married Robert Cadell on 14 Oct. 1817 and died in 1818.

502 (e) letter . . . from Mathurine] Of 2 Aug. See above, p. 492 and my note and below, p. 503 *n.* Maturin did not ask for a London bill. He said he would like Constable's bill to be discounted in Edinburgh.

502 *n.* 1] For 'Scott was to write' read 'Scott had written'.

503 (d) Your poor fathers death] John Ballantyne died on 23 Aug.

503 *n.* 1] Delete 'Probably.' The tragedy Maturin was preparing was *Fredolfo*, produced in May 1819. Maturin's letter is in *Maturin Corr.*, pp. 81–2.

504 (b) To James Ballantyne] The date of the letter must be Monday, 1 Sept. and the date of visit of Hogarth and Ballantyne, Thursday, 4 Sept. Scott must have expected his letter (p. 505) to reach Ballantyne on the 4th before he set off for Abbotsford.

504 (e) let his loss be loss] He had been robbed on the Continent. See above, p. 487 *n.* and below, p. 511. See also *SL* vi. 198 *n.*

508 (a) desireable purchase] Toftfield.

508 (c) "Doubt truth to be a liar"] Shakespeare, *Hamlet*, II. 2.

509 (b) a letter from James V] Mrs Hughes says James IV. See Hughes, *Letters*, p. 79.

509 (c) *carta supellex*] This should be *curta supellex* (broken household goods).

509 (d) cedant arma togae] Cicero, *De officiis*, Bk I, sect. 22.

509 (f) Solomon's temple] *Bible, I Kings* 6:7.

509 *n.* 1] John Riddell as is shown by Grierson's own note, above, p. 488. (Correction in *SL* xii. 489.)

511 (e) his swindling losses] See above, pp. 487 *n.*, 504 and *SL* vi. 198 *n.*

512 (b) Half a loaf] *Ray*, p. 171.

512 (e) my arrondissement] Toftfield.

512 (e) Journal] *Edinburgh Weekly Journal.*

513 (a) claims on the Roxburghshire roll] See my note to *SL* iv. 482 (e).

513 (f) two letters] Scott wrote to Willie on 9 Sept. (NLS MS. 2889, ff. 141–2) explaining why he had delayed applying to the Duke, and asking for a full statement of 'your situation & views.' This letter is not in *SL*. Willie, in reply, wrote a long letter on 11 Sept. (He kept a copy which is now in NLS MS. 2889, f. 143.) This is undoubtedly one of the letters sent on to the Duke but I do not know what the second was. Scott wrote again to Willie on 3 Oct. (NLS MS. 2889 ff. 144–5; not in *SL*) saying his application to the Duke had been unsuccessful.

515 *n.* 1] Delete this note, which merely follows Lockhart's error.

515 *n.* 3] The monument which Scott saw was not the one dedicated on 30 June 1815. The first one collapsed and Scott saw the second.

516 (a) burnt the water] See below, p. 531 *n.*

516 *n.* 1] The author was W. K. Wesly, not Villiers. See *SL* viii. 469.

518 (d) author of Belshazzars vision] W. K. Wesly. See above, pp. 516–17 and *SL* viii. 469.

518 (e) Inclosed is a letter to Constable & one to Hay Donaldson] The one to Constable is on the following page. The one to Donaldson is not in *SL* but it is in the *Antiquary*, Vol. 49 (Jan. 1913).

519 (e) Stirling Heads] Copies of some of them were painted by Mrs Terry for the window in the ante-room to the Armoury.

520 (a) Mr. Pringle wrote me] His letter of 9 Sept. 1817 is in NLS (MS. 3888, ff. 150–1). Scott's reply is not known to be extant. A printed *Notice of the transactions between the publisher and editors of the Edinburgh Monthly Magazine* was sent to Scott with PM 30 Oct. 1817 (NLS MS. 3888, ff. 213–14).

520 (f) *amicus omnium bonorum*] This should be 'amicus omnium horarum,' used in the *Journal*, 23 Jan. 1826, and given in English as 'the companion of all hours' in *SL* v. 268, and as 'the friend of all hours' in *St Ronan's Well*, chap. 18.

523 *n*. 1] The quotation from Joanna Baillie's letter is repeated, with variations, in *SL* v. 27 *n*.

524 (b) Ilka man buckles his belt his ain gate] Wording varies. *Kelly*, p. 92, gives it in its English form: 'Every man wears his belt in his own fashion.' Also used in *The Heart of Mid-Lothian*, chaps. 28 and 35, and in *SL* v. 178, vii. 335.

524 *n*. 1] These are the four opening lines of her *The heathcock*, which Scott had printed in his *English minstrelsy* (1810), ii. 248–9.

525 (b) The bower] For other references, see Index under Abbotsford. II. Estate. (2) Separate Parts. Joanna's Bower.

526 (b) drawing room] This is obviously a slip, or misreading, for dining room.

526 (c) men of mould] Shakespeare, *Henry V*, III. 2.

526 (e–f) Highlanders gun] Thomas Carlyle is sometimes credited with this saying, but Scott certainly anticipated him. Even Scott was probably not the first perpetrator of the joke. See also *SL* v. 4.

527 (a) a clever mode of uniting] This plan was never carried out.

527 (e) guess my meaning by my mumping] A Scots proverb. See above, p. 497.

527 *n*. 1] Not necessarily 'Mother Redford's.' Mr Redford was the previous tenant from whom Scott took over.

528 (b) To Daniel Terry] This should not have been printed as a separate letter. See above, p. 525 *n*.

528 (b) MacDonald] Rev. Andrew Macdonald.

528 (c) "home is home"] Ramsay, *Proverbs*, p. 22.

529 (a) in treaty for a considerable addition] Toftfield.

529 (c) Shadrach Meshach & Abednego] *Bible, Daniel* 3.

530 (b) to settle with Longman] For *The Heart of Mid-Lothian*.

530 *n*. 1] Tobin's letter from 2 Adelphi Terrace, London, 21 Sept. 1817, is in NLS (MS. 3888, ff. 164–5). It is postmarked 22 Sept. twice and also 25 Sept. so that Scott would not receive it till several days after he had written to Richardson. Tobin gives details of the two bills drawn by Tom. Caesar Tobin was a Captain and James Tobin an Ensign in the Royal Manx Fencibles, presumably relatives of Richard Tobin. Emma, daughter of Patrick Tobin, married in 1813 Sir William Hillary about whom Tom had written in 1811 (*SL* vii. 461, 461 *n*.). I have not established the relationship, if any, of these Tobins. See also *SL* vii. 409 (c).

531 (b) Clemitson] Read 'Clementson.' Isaac Clementson was a Navy Agent. As the name is uncommon he may be the same man as the Clementson who visited Abbotsford on 24 Oct. 1833 and signed the Visitors' Book as 'Mr Clementson London.'

531 (e) a still further extension] Toftfield.

533 (b) They must do a little more] A parody of the nursery rhyme beginning 'There was a little man,' st. [2], lines 4–6: 'You must say a little more, / And produce a little ore, / Ere I to the church will be led, led, led.' (I. and P. Opie, *The Oxford dictionary of nursery rhymes*, repr., Oxford, Clarendon Press, 1973, p. 290.) See also *SL* ix. 494 and *Journal*, 14 Mar. and 25 Nov. 1827. Scott quotes from the same nursery rhyme in *SL* viii. 486.

533 (f) To Mrs. Scott] This letter should be dated Saturday, 18 Oct. Wilkie arrived on 14 Oct. (Cunningham's *Wilkie*, i. 480) and Scott visited St Catherine's on Thursday, 16 Oct. (*SL* i. 522, 524).

535 (a) the price] For 'price' read 'piece'. Scott refers to a picture as a 'piece' in *SL* v. 10.

538 (c) *crescent* . . . Thistle] The crescent was put on the west side of the second portion of the house in 1822. For the thistle, see above, p. 500.

538 (c–d) crop] Twice for 'crop' read 'cross.' The first one mentioned surmounts the east end of the gable in the first portion of the house. The second may be the same as the cross surmounting the gable of the staircase turret in the second portion.

538 (e) consultation over *Law*] Sharpe had asked Scott for advice and sent his letter with Ballantyne. It is in *Sharpe's Letters*, ii. 177–8, where it is wrongly dated Jan. 1818. Constable left Abbotsford on 2 Oct. Sharpe's letter, therefore, must have been written at the end of Sept.

539 (b) rod of Aaron which made the heart of the widow to sing for joy] An amalgamation of *Bible*, *Exodus* 7–8 and *Job* 29: 13.

539 (f) dainty Davie himself] Rev. David Williamson, who is said to have had seven wives though his great-granddaughter would confess to only six. (*Sharpe's Letters*, ii. 160.)

540 (a) Roman forceps] See *SL* xii. 153 and my note.

542 *n.* 1] The proprietor of Darnick Tower was John Heiton.

543 (b) fountain] The basin was originally part of the Edinburgh Mercat Cross demolished in 1756. Scott's plans for the antique masks and inscription were not carried out. The structure, now moved to the centre of the courtyard, is not connected to a water supply.

543 (e) headless lady] The figure, which Scott inserted in the niche, is not headless.

544 (a) To John Murray] Date is late Feb. or early Mar. 1817, and very probably Friday, 21 Feb. (cf. above, p. 392). The first paragraph relates to Scott's review of *Tales of my Landlord* for *QR* and this, along with Scott's going to Edinburgh 'tomorrow', helps to fix the date approximately. The second paragraph is printed in Smiles, *John Murray*, ii. 5–6, where it is wrongly dated as *after* 28 Mar. 1818. Hogg, in a letter to Murray, says he met Scott on 28 Mar. 1818 and that Scott promised to write an article on Hogg for *QR* (ibid. ii. 5).

544 *n.* 1] Delete the whole note. Date of letter could not be 1815 as the reference to *Blackwood* shows. The first paragraph of the letter clearly relates to the 'Killiecrankie' article for *QR* (see my previous note) and not to Dunlop. The article on Hogg was never published. Strout (*Hogg*, pp. 127–8) prints a letter from Hogg to Blackwood, 4 Jan. 1817, in which he refers to an anonymous article on his poetry written for *QR*. Strout has a footnote that the anonymous 'gentleman' was Scott, but gives no authority for this statement. The author was probably Hogg himself and he hoped that Blackwood would use his influence with Murray. I suspect that Blackwood declined and suggested Scott as a better channel through which to approach the *QR*. Grieve, as an intermediary, is mentioned both by Hogg and Scott in their letters.

544 *n.* 2] Scott contributed several articles on the Scottish Gipsies in Vol. 1, Apr.–Sept. 1817.

VOLUME V

1 *n.* 1] 4th ed. of former and 7th ed. of latter.

2 (d) This settles the whole affairs of Jo: B & Co] Actually the business had been dissolved on 1 Feb. 1816. (*Edinburgh Evening Courant*, 20 June 1816, p. 1, c. 2.)

3 (e) the fountain shall be out of doors] Originally it was to be inside the conservatory. But Scott had just received the basin from the Edinburgh Mercat Cross (*SL* iv. 543); hence the change of plan.

3 *n.* 1] Delete. The carved heads of Scottish kings, which had been at Stirling Castle, and hence known as 'Stirling Heads', were copied by Mrs Terry from engravings in *Lacunar*

Strevelinense, published by Blackwood in 1817. Blackwood presented a copy to Scott (*SL* iv. 519). Only four of Mrs Terry's drawings remain in the window of ante-room to the Armoury: (1) Margaret Tudor (*Lacunar*, No. VI); (2) King James V (ibid., No. I); (3) probably Jane Beaufort (ibid., No. IV); (4) probably Sir William Wallace (ibid., No. VII).

4 (c) Highlandman's gun] See *SL* iv. 526.

4 (d) "the cabin is convenient"] Ben Jonson, *Every man in his humour*, I. 4.

4 *n*. 1] Scott got the basin but not the four grotesque heads.

4 *n*. 2] Delete and see my note to *SL* iii. 153.

5 (a) To William Blackwood] Mrs Oliphant (Oliphant, *William Blackwood*, i. 148–9) prefixes this extract with a paragraph on an earlier part of the letter (not printed by her) in which Scott refers to 'the first of some articles' on Rob Roy in *Blackwood*. This first article was in the number for Oct. which Blackwood sent to Scott on 20 Oct. (Mrs Oliphant, op. cit. i. 149). Quite clearly Scott's letter cannot have been written in Oct. from the evidence given in my note to *SL* v. 6 (a). It must have been written later, after the storm over the Chaldee MS. had blown over, and Scott may have been referring to the second or third articles on Rob Roy which appeared in Nov. and Dec. Cf. also Laidlaw's letter to Blackwood (Oliphant, op. cit. i. 148) which seems to be out of order.

5 (d) Mr. Pringle] For Constable's *Edinburgh Magazine . . . A new series of the Scots Magazine*, Vol. 1 of which was coming out at this time.

5 (d) expect me to favour them] For 'favour' read 'father.'

6 (a) To William Blackwood] Scott was at Bowhill on 20 Oct. and had visitors up to 30 Oct. The letter which Laidlaw showed Scott 'this morning' is probably Blackwood's letter of 29 Oct. to Laidlaw (Oliphant, *William Blackwood*, i. 150). Date of letter is, therefore, about 30 Oct.

7 (c) To Duke of Buccleuch] Date must be about 26 Oct. as Ballantyne's grandmother died on 23 Oct.

7 (f) Mr. & Mrs. S. & Lord Lifford] Hon. and Rev. Richard Bruce Stopford and Hon. Mrs Eleanor Stopford, sister of 2nd Baron Lilford.

7 *n*. 1] For 'November' read 'October.

8 (b) an English Solicitor at Law] John Richardson.

8 (e) To the Duke of Buccleuch] Date is 12 Nov., the day Sophia, Walter and Charles went to Edinburgh. See below, pp. 9, 12.

9 (c) To Robert Johnston[e]] Delete '[e]'. The first paragraph is a reply to Johnston's letter of 30 July [PM 30 Oct.] cited in *SL* iv. 483 *n*.

9 (d) Mr. Inglis] John Inglis, Edinburgh builder, who bought the Tolbooth from Edinburgh Corporation. It was Inglis who gave the Tolbooth relics to Scott, and not the Corporation as is usually stated. Inglis would not accept money in payment and so Scott gave him a present of books.

10 (b) To Sir David Wilkie] Date cannot be 1817. Wilkie was at Abbotsford, Oct.–Nov. 1817, but Scott says 'we have not had the pleasure of seeing you here.' The year is probably 1818.

10 (b) Love me love my dog] *Ray*, p. 126; Ramsay, *Proverbs*, p. 46.

10 *n*. 1] The letter of 2 Aug. cited was from Scott, not from Wilkie.

11 (d) *Sunday Even* [8 [9] *November* 1817]] I do not understand '8[9]'. Sunday was 9 Nov.

12 (b) the cramp which visited me last week] Sophia put his attack a week later but her memory was probably at fault. See *Letters to their old governess*, pp. 43–4.

14 (b) one for M. Douce . . . and one for Madame Schubart] The letter to Douce is in *SL* xii. 430–1. The one to Madame Schubart is not in *SL*.

14 (d) To Robert Johnston[e]] Delete '[e]'. The date is Tuesday, 11 Nov. Princess Charlotte died on 6 Nov. and Scott returned to Edinburgh on Monday, 17 Nov. The only Tuesday which fits is 11 Nov.

15 *n*. 1] Delete this long note. 'Creech's Land' was a tenement near St Giles Church and the Tolbooth in the High Street. On 21 July 1817 Creech's Land

was sold for £194 and demolition began immediately. (*Scots Mag.* Vol. 79 (July 1817), p. 581.) 'Creech's lintel' has not been identified among the old stones built into the walls of Abbotsford House.

17 (b) To John Ballantyne] This, the following letter to Ballantyne and the letter to Cadell, p. 18, must all come after the letter to Erskine, p. 18. In the letter to Erskine of 28 Nov. Scott is uncertain as to the amount to be paid to Milne. In these three letters he knows the sum is £500. 28 Nov. was a Friday. The Monday, Tuesday and Wednesday of the three letters are likely to be 1, 2 and 3 Dec. respectively.

18 (a) To Robert Cadell] See previous note.

18 (e) Mr. Kerr] Andrew Seton-Karr who succeeded to Kippilaw in 1815.

20 (a) The minstrel's pipe] This, if included at all, should have been printed in Vol. 1 under 1799.

21 (f) Mrs. [. . .]] Read 'Mrs [Campbell].'

22 (a) To Duke of Buccleuch] The letter is correctly dated 1817 as is shown by the contents: (1) reference to blackcocks (above, p. 8); (2) trouble over buildings on North Bridge began in Dec. 1817. See *Edin. Ann. Reg.* X. ii., App. 180–7 and XI. ii., App. 86–93; (3) Courts rose on 20 Dec. in 1817.

22 n. 3] Delete this note, which is not now applicable.

23 (c) So runs the world away] Shakespeare, *Hamlet*, III. 2.

24 (a) Culvenan who is a near relation of my brothers wife] The relationship is explained in *SL* viii. 348 n.

24 (f) setting his knighthood . . . aside] Shakespeare, *II Henry IV*, I. 2.

25 (a) Sophia] This may be a slip for Anne who was the wit of the family.

25 (d) the Trade would give the thousand pounds] This is an early reference to *Metrical legends*, published in 1821. See *SL* iv. 475 n. 1, vi. 95, 95 n., 468.

25 n. 2] Chap. 5.

26 (b) hold the candle to you] A proverb.

26 (c) The Bacchanalian song] 'There's no drinking in the grave' is the last line of *Banish sorrow*, by George Ogle. In *The charms of melody*, 2° Dublin, n.d., p. 273.

27 (a) Dr. Johnson] See Boswell's *Johnson*, ed. Hill-Powell, v. 343 n.

27 n. 1] The quotation from Joanna Baillie's letter is a repetition, with variations, of quotation in *SL* iv. 523 n.

28 (a) "Cocks of the North so wildly shy"] Joanna Baillie, *The heathcock*, line 4.

28 n. 1] The gift was probably *La cité de Dieu, traduite en françois par Raoul de Preulles*, 2 vols. (in 1), 2° Abbeville, J. Du Pre et P. Gerard, 1486. With inscription on flyleaf: 'Charles Kirkpatrick Sharpe Esq. from his sincerely attached friend Walter Scott.' It was sold at the Gibson-Craig sale at Sotheby's, 23 Mar. 1888, Lot 245.

29 (d–e) roaring like King Corny] Maria Edgeworth, *Ormond*, chap. 5.

29 (f) Richard is himself again] Colley Cibber, *Richard III*, V. 3. The whole line is given as the motto to chap. 40 of *Ivanhoe*: 'Shadows avaunt!— Richard's himself again.'

30 (d) To Thomas Scott] In a footnote (p. 33) Grierson says: 'The passages omitted from this letter are of little interest.' But he printed the omitted passages in *SL* vii. 493–7!

30 n. 1] Delete. An illustration of Ariosto's inkstand is given in Hoole's translation of *Orlando furioso*, 5 vols., London, 1783, Vol. 1, facing p. lxxxix.

32 (e) as Sancho was] See my note to *SL* i. 304 (d–e).

32 n. 1] The stag's feet are no longer in the Armoury.

32 n. 2] Act I, sc. 1.

33 (b) Mr. Kerr retaining his right to the minerals] Andrew Seton-Karr of Kippilaw. There was an advertisement in the *Caledonian Mercury*, 30 June 1746, p. [4], c. 2, by the proprietor of Huntleywood and Toftfield for working coal which it was thought could be found on these lands. See also *SL* iv. 328, 433–4.

33 n. 1] See my note to *SL* v. 30 (d).

34 (d) Currie Lambe] Carrie Lamb, Mrs Thomas Mitchell.

36 (f) Toftfield] i.e. the new house, renamed Huntlyburn.

37 (a) To James Ballantyne] This letter cannot be 31 Dec. *Rob Roy* was reviewed in the *Scotsman*, 3 Jan. 1818. *Lockhart* (v. 267–8) dates it *c.* 21 Dec., a more likely date.

37 *n.* 1] The song appears as *Johannot's Grinder* in *The charms of melody*, Dublin, n.d., p. 269.

39 (a) To Mr. Anderson] Date is *c.* Aug. 1829 when Scott is working on the Magnum Opus. Such a letter in 1818 would have revealed his authorship.

39 (d) To William Laidlaw] I suspect that Lockhart has amalgamated two letters. The second paragraph fits his date, Jan. 1818. (See footnote here and my note to it.) But the first paragraph appears to belong to a later period. John Smith recorded in his diary, 28 Sept. 1818: 'Made a petition for widening the road thro' the village [of Darnick]. Got it signed by most of the people. Went to Abbotsford with it.' If Scott is referring to this, the first part of the letter must belong to late 1818 or early 1819.

39 *n.* 1] Delete first sentence.

40 (a) Beechland] Lockhart's error for Bauchland.

40 (d) lord of the "beast and the brute"] Perhaps a variation of Cowper's *Alexander Selkirk*, st. [1], line 4: 'lord of the fowl and the brute.'

40 (d–e) St. John's Well . . . Carline's Hole] St John's Well is in Wrights Meadows, midway between Faldonside and Huntlyburn. Carline's Hole, though marked on Scott's own plan of the estate as in the Upper Thicket at the extreme SW., is shown on the Ordnance Survey maps as being outside the estate.

40 *n.* 1] Delete the whole of this note, which does not contain a single correct statement. Bauchland was the park in the SW. corner of the estate and formed the boundary. The Bauchlin Cottages of the present day have no connection with Bauchland. They sit on the road from Abbotsford House

to Kaeside on the north side of the estate. The Bauchland mentioned in the passage quoted from the *Journal* [26 July 1827] is *not* Bauchlin Cottages but the Bauchland already described above. It is true that there are now no cottages called Abbotstown but there were in Scott's day. Adjoining Bauchland on SE. was Abbotstown Park at north end of which stood the farm steading of Abbotslee, converted in 1818 into cottages (continuous on three sides of a rectangle) and named Abbotstown by Scott. John Smith, the Darnick builder, recorded in his diary for 21 Mar. 1818: 'At Abbotslea measuring at set of old offices. Planning to make them into cottages.'

41 (a) To the Duke of Buccleuch] Cancel. This extract is part of a letter of 25 May 1818, printed below, pp. 153–8. For a note on this extract, see *SL* xii. 489.

42 (b) Kerr] Andrew Seton-Karr of Kippilaw.

43 (a) Bishop of Granadas sermon] Le Sage, *Gil Blas*, Bk vii, chap. 4.

43 *n.* 1] It was produced at Edinburgh in 1830. See my note to *SL* iv. 415 *n.*

45 (c) highland terrier] Ourisk. See *SL* x. 169.

45 (d) Chandler] His letter is not in Walpole Coll. But the Duke replied on 15 Jan.: 'I will take care of your Chamois boot hooks' (NLS MS. 866, f. 165).

46 (a) To Robert Johnston[e]] Delete '[e]'.

46 *n.* 1] Mrs John Ballantyne (*née* Jean Barclay), *c.* 1745–1818.

48 (b) *Minuit presentia famam*] Claudius Claudianus, *De bello Gildonico*, line 385.

48 (b) every crow thinks her own egg [whitest]] A variation of the proverb. *Heywood*, p. 106; *Ray*, p. 120; *Kelly*, p. 91; Ramsay, *Proverbs*, p. 17.

49 (b) Fifteen or twenty years ago] 1794, i.e. twenty-fours years ago.

50 (b–c) too much flax on my distaff] See *SL* ii. 171.

50 (c) two stories] The first is *The Heart of Mid-Lothian*. The second, on the Regalia, was never written.

51 (a) one good turn merits another]
Kelly, p. 269; Ramsay, *Proverbs*, p. 2.

51 (c) Denzill] i.e. Denzil in *Rokeby*.

52 (a) To make a can / For brandie
Nan] This is an inaccurate quotation
from a poem called *The metamorphosis,
or the Royal Honours of Scotland*.

53 *n*.] Lady Douglas died on 31 Mar.,
not in June. Scott had already written
on her death (*SL* iv. 449) in a letter
dated 11 May but which should probably be dated 11 Apr.

55 (c) like the Committee appointed]
Churchill, *The ghost*. See below, p. 60.

55 (d) tale founded upon . . . Regalia]
See my note to *SL* v. 50 (c).

56 (a) the Minister] Rev. James
Granger.

56 *n*. 2] The reference should be to
Act V, sc. 11. Grierson follows Douglas's
error in his ed. of the *Journal*, 16 Dec.
1826.

57 (e) My medical adviser] Dr Ebenezer
Clarkson of Selkirk.

57 (f) Dr. Scott's bath] Dr James
Scott of Ellem who settled at Darnlee
outside Darnick. His muriatic bath was
later recommended for the Duke of
Buccleuch.

61 (c–d) "tout genre est permis hors le
genre ennuyant"] Voltaire, *Œuvres
complètes*, 70 tom., [Kehl] 1785–9, tom.
7 (1785), p. 51: 'Tous les genres sont
bons, hors le genre ennuyeux.' Also
quoted, with variations, in 1830 Introd.
to *The Monastery*, *The Sale-Room*, No. 1
and *MPW* xviii. 323.

61 *n*. 2] Delete and substitute: Buckingham, *The rehearsal*, I. 1: 'Besides, Sir,
I have printed a hundred sheets of
paper, to insinuate the plot into the
boxes.' See Scott's *Dryden*, ii. 293 and *n*.

62 (e) leather and prunella] Pope,
Essay on man, *Epistle IV*, line 204.

63 *n*. 1] Delete and see my note to *SL*
iii. 153.

64 (a) your valuable picture] 'The
Abbotsford family' which Wilkie exhibited at the Royal Academy this year
(No. 117, as 'Walter Scott, Esq., and
two sons'). This explains why Scott is
here sending it to him. I have no
record of an engraving before 1827.

65 (e) To Messrs. Sanderson and
Paterson] The builders of the first
portion of Abbotsford, 1817–19. Scott
had written an important letter to
them on 16 Jan. It is, unfortunately,
not in *SL*, but it is printed in the *Scots
Mag.* N.S. Vol. 7 (Sept. 1927), pp. 478–9.

67 (c) Poins . . . Moor or a Bertram]
Poins in Shakespeare's *I Henry IV* and
II Henry IV; Moor in Schiller's *Die
Räuber*; and Bertram in *Rokeby*.

67 (e) To C. K. Sharpe] This belongs
to series printed under 1816 in *SL* iv.
150–4.

67 (f) hot in the mouth] Shakespeare,
Twelfth Night, II. 3.

69 (a) To William Laidlaw] The
reference to Blackwood's being sent to
Coventry (p. 70) because of the Chaldee
MS. and Blackwood's letter (p. 70 *n*.)
indicate that the date of the letter is
about Nov. 1817.

69 (b) birch-hedge] This must be a misreading for beech-hedge.

69 (c) I am glad the saws are going]
The sawmill, established by Scott at
Huntlyburn, was still functioning till
recently. It has now been demolished.

69 (e) Packwood] George Packwood,
a London cutler, whose advertisements,
mostly in verse, attracted attention.
See also *SL* vi. 239 *n*., 240 *n*.

69 *n*. 2] Andrew Mercer owned Loch-
breist (below, p. 118). Rutherford
owned Sunnyside.

70 (c) sent to Coventry] Scott also uses
this proverb in *SL* ix. 457 and in 1826
he asked Thomas Sharp for its origin
(*SL* ix. 447).

71 (d) Somewhat too much of this]
Shakespeare, *Hamlet*, III. 2: 'something
too much of this.' Cf. below, p. 352.
Correctly quoted in *SL* vii. 357.

73 (d) Sincerely] Scott probably wrote
'Seriously.' He frequently began a sentence with 'Seriously' when switching
from the gay to the grave.

73 *n*. 2] Lockhart should not be quoted.
Grieve did come to Abbotsford. See
below, p. 92.

73 *n*. 3] The thumbikins mentioned in
this letter were not presented by
Gabriel Alexander. At one time there

were three pairs at Abbotsford: (1) a facsimile of those used on Principal Carstairs (referred to in Lord Fountainhall's *Chronological notes*, footnote to pp. 101–2; and illus. in the *Scots Mag.* for Aug. 1817); (2) a pair given by Gabriel Alexander in May 1819; (3) a pair which had belonged to Douglas of Stenhouse given by Train in Dec. 1819. Only No. 3 is now at Abbotsford, in the Armoury. No. 1, to which Scott must be referring in this letter, has disappeared. No. 2 was stolen by a tourist in 1974.

74 (b) Thomson's work] See *SL* iv. 372, 372 *n*. 1.

74 (b) St. Thomas] An allusion to *Bible*, *John* 20: 24–9.

74 (d) To J. W. Croker] *Lockhart* (v. 279–82) dates it 5 Feb. Scott here refers to his letter 'of yesterday', 4 Feb. There seems to be no reason for changing it to 7 Feb.

76 (a) Ogilvie of Barra] Ogilvy of Barras.

77 (a) the poor clergyman nothing] See above, p. 56 *n*. 2.

77 (a) *the hare's foot to lick*] This seems to be a variant of 'Kiss the hare's foot,' said of a person who comes late to dinner. (*Kelly*, p. 229.) Kelly says: 'I know not the reason of the expression.' The meaning is quite clear from Scott's use of the proverb.

78 (e) Tom] Laidlaw, in a letter dated 'Sunday' [8 Feb. 1818], reports trouble between Tom Purdie and his wife Mary over the tending of the cows. Laidlaw recommends additional wages to Mary in payment for the work to be done by one of her daughters. (Edin. Univ. Lib. La. III. 584, ff. 102–3.)

78 (e–f) jump particularly well with my humour] Shakespeare, *I Henry IV*, I. 2.

78 *n*. 2] An odd place to put this note! There is no reliable evidence that Purdie had been a poacher.

79 (c) have lands and burns] For 'burns' read 'beeves.' Shakespeare, *II Henry IV*, III. 2.

79 (d) Eagle and Henderson] It was through Mrs Eagle, seedmerchant in Edinburgh, that Constable commenced

his career in Edinburgh. See *Archibald Constable*, i. 6–7.

80 (e) Land laws] Read 'Laidlaws.' (Corrected in *SL* xii. 489.)

81 (d–e) Lord Chief Commr. . . . Presidents . . . Chief Baron] William Adam of Blair-Adam, Charles Hope, Lord Granton, and Robert Dundas of Arniston.

81 *n*. 1] Delete 'Probably'.

82 (a) pomp & circumstance] Shakespeare, *Othello*, III. 3.

82 *n*. 1] This note should be transferred to the previous page as a note to 'Capt. Adam Fergusson.' The passage on p. 82 to which the note is attached refers to Scott himself, not to Ferguson. See below, p. 83.

82 *n*. 2] Scott's epilogue beginning 'A cat of yore (or else old Aesop lied)' was included in Scott's *Poetical works* (1820), x. 239–41.

84 (c) "the mother of mischief . . ."] A Scottish proverb. See my note to *SL* ii. 116 (a).

84 *n*. 1] In line 1, for 'under-clerk' read 'Deputy Clerk.'

85 *n*.] In line 3, for 'Dunnottar' read 'Edinburgh.'

87 *n*. 1] Adam did not reveal the whole truth to Lockhart. See articles by Arthur Aspinall in *Rev. of English Studies*, Vol. 22, pp. 319–22, and in *Times Lit. Supp.*, 1947, p. 556.

88 (c) when I say with Falstaff] Shakespeare, *Merry wives of Windsor*, III. 5.

88 (c) Mr. Bayes's feelings] Buckingham's *The rehearsal*.

90 (c) Gil Blas] See Le Sage, *Gil Blas*, Bk II, chaps. 3–5.

90 (d) land of mist and snow] Coleridge, *The ancient mariner*, Pt 2, st. [12], line 4, or Pt 5, st. [25], line 2.

90 (d) "long hid from those who search the main"] Collins, *Ode to liberty*, line 82: 'Mona, once hid from those who search the main.' Quoted in *Minstrelsy* (ed. Henderson), iv. 279, and used as motto to *Peveril*, chap. 11.

91 (d) Lord Binnings mad houses] Lord Binning, afterwards 9th Earl of Haddington, had, on 4 Feb.,

introduced a bill in Parliament for the establishment of lunatic asylums in Scotland.

91 (f) Galashiels old Kirk] Lindean Church.

92 n. 2] Delete. The Cameronian preacher is Walter Grieve. See above, p. 73. (Wrongly 'corrected' to George Grieve in *SL* xii. 489.)

93 (a) celebrated Border piper] John Bruce. Though he had lived in the Borders, he originally came from Skye.

93 (d) Minister of Cupar] The holder of the First Charge in 1818 was the Rev. George Campbell.

93 (e) I was at Blair Adam two days in last summer] At the first annual meeting of the Blair-Adam Club. It is odd that this is Scott's first reference to it.

93 (f) charter or grant] See *Blackwood*, Vol. 1 (Apr. 1817), p. 65, *Grant of the Land of Kyrkenes*. It is odd that Scott does not refer Lady Compton to this printed source either here or in a later letter (below, p. 245).

94 (e) bestowed . . . my tediousness] See *SL* ii. 320.

94 (e–f) to *harp and carp*] See *SL* i. 262.

95 (c) To Mr. Mathurine] The letter is not dated, but *Lockhart* (v. 300–3) has the correct date 26 Feb. 1818. A better text (from the original) is in *Maturin Corr.*, pp. 87–9, and Maturin's reply of 9 Mar. is printed, ibid., pp. 89–90.

96 (c) current] Read 'torrent.'

98 (c) To C. K. Sharpe] The date is taken from *Sharpe's Letters*, ii. 182, but Scott would not be at Abbotsford in Feb. 1818. Even if he were for a day or so he would not send Blackadder and Law but would bring them to Edinburgh. I think the date should be 1817. Scott had been reading Blackadder in Mar. of that year (*SL* iv. 401, 408) and would not delay till Feb. 1818 sending 'transcript and original.' Walker's letter is not in the Walpole Coll. in NLS so that we are deprived of this help in dating Scott's letter. Walker belonged to the Scots Greys who were stationed at Piershill Barracks till about Aug. 1818 and Sharpe's letter of Aug. 1818 (*Sharpe's Letters*, ii.

185–6) shows that he was on intimate terms with the regiment, suggesting that he had met the officers in Edinburgh during the previous winter. Walker would deliver the Swift immediately on arrival, probably in 1817. Sharpe's letter which 'in part explains' must be a letter of 1817 and not the letter cited in note 2 and printed in *Sharpe's Letters*, ii. 181–2, for in it Sharpe says the Scots Greys are 'under marching orders' which makes that letter about July 1818, before Scott left Edinburgh on the rising of the Courts (Sharpe's 'I know not when you intend leaving Edin.').

98 (d) Mr. Walker] Thomas Walker was a Cornet in 2nd Dragoons (Scots Greys), 29 June 1815. See Index. Sharpe's sister Susan married, as her second husband, 1800, William Walker of Erdington Hall, Warwick, Captain in 8th Dragoons, who was dead by 1806. If Thomas Walker was a son, he would be Sharpe's nephew; but if so it is strange that Sharpe does not mention the relationship.

98 n. 2] I do not think Scott is answering Sharpe's letter referred to here. See my note to *SL* v. 98 (c). In second last line, delete '*L.P.*'

99 (f) does not come me twanging off] Scott may be thinking of Massinger's *A new way to pay old debts*, III. 2: 'came twanging off.'

99 n. 1] Delete this note. The verses were written on the title-page of Satchells. The MS. in Lib. B. 5. 30 at Abbotsford has nothing whatsoever to do either with the verses or with Satchells.

99 n. 2] The words above, from 'HISTORY OF SCOT' down to 'March 1818', should have been put as part of this footnote and not printed in the text as if it were a part of Scott's letter.

100 (a) "God mend me"] See *SL* ii. 520.

100 (f) I wrote Mr. Atkinson yesterday] i.e. on 1 Mar. This letter is not known to be extant but it was acknowledged by Atkinson in his reply of 7 Mar. (NLS MS. 3889, ff. 17–19).

101 (b) To Archibald Constable] Maturin's letter was dated 9 Mar. (above, p. 95 n.). Scott could not receive it in time to write this letter by

Wednesday, 11 Mar. He was at Abbotsford on Wednesday, 18 Mar. and at Maxpoffle on 19 Mar. He had to pay Sanderson & Paterson on 28 Mar. (See next note.) Date of letter, therefore, is 25 Mar.

101 (b) some mason work etc to pay] To Messrs Sanderson & Paterson. A bill accepted on 29 Dec. 1817 became due on 28 Mar. 1818.

101 (f) two children of Mr. Walter Scott of Wauchope] Charles, his eldest son, and Anna both died in Dec. 1817.

103 n. 1] The prize poem was *Demosthenes, contemplating the ruins of Athens*, 8vo Dublin, 1818. In the poem Elgin is satirized (though not by name) both in the text and in a full-page woodcut.

103 n. 2] The correct title is: *The hill of caves, in two cantos. With other poems.*

104 (b) To C. G. Gordon] There is no letter from him in NLS.

105 (a) long-delayed verses] Scott's contributions to Thomson's *A select collection of original Scottish airs*, Vol. 5, London [1818], were: p. 209. *The maid of Isla*; p. 215. *The sun upon the Weirdlaw Hill*; p. 217. *Farewell to the Muse*; p. 227. *On Ettrick Forest's mountains dun.*

105 (a) smell less of apoplexy] Le Sage, *Gil Blas*, Bk VII, chap. 4.

107 (b) To Charles Erskine] Delete '[Edinburgh]' at end of letter. From contents it is clear Scott is writing from Abbotsford. The words 'I leave this place on tuesday to return in ten days' indicate that he is going to Edinburgh for Register House duty. He was in Edinburgh on Saturday, 28 Mar. (Smiles, *John Murray*, ii. 5). The Tuesday before was 24 Mar. Scott probably wrote to Erskine on Sunday, 22 Mar. He returned from Edinburgh on 10 Apr. (NLS MS. 2889, ff. 156–7.)

108 n. 1] Murray's letter of 17 Mar. is in Smiles, *John Murray*, ii. 7–8. For full title of *Whistlecraft*, see my note to *SL* v. 168 (e).

108 n. 2] In line 5, for 'May 1818' read 'Jan. 1818, publ. June.'

109 n. 2] Scott's review appeared in *QR* Vol. 18 (May 1818), pp. 423–31; not reprinted in *MPW*.

111 (a) mend his musket] Read 'mend his market.'

112 (c) To John Murray] The letter enclosed for Boswell (below, pp. 126–30) is dated 25 Apr. This letter to Murray, therefore, should be 25 Apr. or perhaps a day or two before.

112 n. 2] This passage (with some inaccuracies) is from *QR* Vol. 18, pp. 423–4. (See above, p. 109 n. 2.) The quotation from Joanna Baillie is from Act III, sc. 1.

113 (a) Walpole] See above, p. 109.

113 (c) "we do know that sweet Roman hand"] Shakespeare, *Twelfth Night*, III. 4.

114 (d) like the snakes of your eastern tyrant] Scott may be alluding to Zohak in Southey's *Thalaba*, Bk V.

116 (a) two yoke of huge oxen] Gog and Magog.

116 (b) circular saw] The sawmill established by Scott at Toftfield.

116 (b) intended rail road] Railroad from Dalkeith to St Boswells. There is a letter (not in *SL*) from Scott to Pringle, 31 Jan. 1819 in the *Border Mag.* Vol. 4 (Nov. 1899), p. 209, where some details of this railway are given. The wagons were to be drawn by horses. See also Index under Railways.

116 (b) Perditur inter haec . . .] Horace, *Satires*, II. vi. 59.

116 (d) interview with Bony] For Croker's account, see his letter to Peel, 26 Nov. 1817, in *The Croker papers*, ed. L. J. Jennings, London, 1884, i. 111. See also *MPW* xvi. 260.

117 n. 1] Bullock is called Prince of the Black Marble Islands only once (below, p. 139) and once Prince of the Black Islands (below, p. 133).

118 n. 2] Graham's letter of 29 Apr. 1817 is in NLS (MS. 866, ff. 137–8) and his letter of 6 Apr. 1818 is also in NLS (MS. 866, ff. 177–8). In the latter he says of Miss Edgeworth: 'She was so fascinated with it' but the words 'with which Miss Edgeworth is delighted', quoted by Grierson, are not in Graham's letter. In line 4, delete 'evidently.' See below, p. 146.

119 (d) I should not like my letter to be published] Graham respected Scott's

wish during the latter's lifetime. But the letter appeared as *Original communication of Sir Walter Scott relative to the Clan Graham* in the *Dublin University Mag.* Mar. 1833.

119 *n.* 1] Delete. John Guillim, *A display of heraldrie* (1610). There is no copy at Abbotsford and I am surprised Scott declined the gift. He had recently referred twice to the work in *Rob Roy*, chaps. 10 and 11.

121 (a) a Jedburgh circuit] On 21 Apr. This was the first time the new Jury Court sat at Jedburgh and there was only one case. William Reid, writer and messenger in Coldstream, sued Thomas Ormiston in Glenburnhall for assault. Reid was awarded £30 damages. (*Kelso Mail*, 23 Apr. 1818, p. [4].)

121 (b) honors of Yarrow] They would go up Yarrow to Tinnis (just short of Deuchar Tower) and cross over by the track from Yarrow Church to Kirkhope in Ettrick and pass Oakwood Tower on the way back to Selkirk.

121 (c) Sir John Riddell] Sir John Buchanan Riddell, 9th Bart. of Riddell, M.P. for Selkirk Burghs. Peebles was one of the constituent burghs.

121 (d) the tough tugger] Adam Ferguson. See *SL* iv. 434, where the letter should be dated 1818.

122 (d) Lady Anne . . . Lady Charlotte] The former was the eldest daughter of the Duke. The latter, his second daughter, became Lady Stopford.

122 (e) Mirabile dictu] Virgil, *Aeneid*, II. 174.

122 (f) Reaburn] Walter Scott, 5th Laird of Raeburn, Scott's uncle. His interests were chiefly centred in hunting.

123 (b) my highland trip] With Miss Dumergue and Miss Sarah Nicolson. See *SL* iv. 267.

125 (f) Macconochie] Maconochie was not installed as Lord Advocate till 12 Nov. 1816. He must have been early with his appointments of Advocates Depute.

128 (a) Selkirk] The Royal Company of Archers competed for the Selkirk Silver Arrow on 28 Aug. 1818. (Hay, *History of the Royal Company of Archers*, p. 113.)

128 (c) with maimed rites] Shakespeare, *Hamlet*, V. 1.

128 (d) old Logan] Hugh Logan of Logan. For fuller details of the anecdote, see *SL* vii. 137.

130 (b) quotation from D'Israeli] There is no quotation from D'Israeli in Scott's review.

130 *n.* 1] Delete 'doubtless' and 'and December'; and for '110' read '109.'

131 (a) Arnot or Maclaurin] Hugo Arnot, *Collection and abridgment of celebrated criminal trials in Scotland, from 1536 to 1784*, 4to Edinburgh, 1785. John Maclaurin (Lord Dreghorn), *Arguments and decisions in remarkable cases before the High Court of Justiciary*, 4to Edinburgh, 1774.

131 (c) the Magazine] The *Scots Magazine*. See below, p. 325.

131 *n.* 2] Charlotte Champion Willyams became later Mrs Pascoe (q.v. in Index). There are letters from her to Scott in NLS. Fifteen letters to her from Scott were presented to NLS in 1956 by Col. E. N. Willyams, her great-great-nephew.

132 (b) Mr. Erskine Major Pott] Mr Erskine may be William Erskine, Charles Erskine's younger brother, and Major Pott is probably Charles Erskine's brother-in-law George Pott of Todrig.

132 (b) half a loaf] *Ray*, p. 171.

132 (e) this twelvemonth or so] According to a letter to Richardson (*SL* iv. 451), Aitkin entered Scott's service about 1816.

133 (b) *Tuesday* 28/29 *April*] Tuesday was 28 Apr.

134 (b) "So bolt upright, / And ready to fight."] First line (all in one line) of chorus of *Pillycock* in D'Urfey, *Wit and mirth*, Vol. 4 (London, 1719), p. 311. The words 'bolt upright and ready to fight' are used in *Woodstock*, chap. 15 but not as a quotation.

134 (d) I have a brave old oaken cabinet] Scott bought through William Scott of Maxpoffle an old cabinet for which he thanked him in a letter of 11 Apr. (Not in *SL*; original in NLS MS. 2889, ff. 156–7.)

134 (e) Mrs. Murray Keith] She died on 26 Apr. Scott received the news

from Miss Mary Agnes Pringle. See below, p. 161 *n*. 2.

135 (b) "call me *horse*"] Shakespeare, *1 Henry IV*, II. 4.

135 *n*. 1] Delete. *Rob Roy Macgregor; or, auld lang syne*, by Isaac Pocock, was produced at Covent Garden, 12 Mar. 1818, and ran for 32 nights. See *White*, pp. 34–42, 243.

135 *n*. 2] Delete this note from *Lockhart* which is inaccurate. *The Heart of Mid-Lothian* came out in July, not June, and the second story was not to be *The Bride of Lammermoor* but a story based on the Scottish Regalia.

137 (e) To M. W. Hartstonge] Hartstonge replied on 20 Aug. with apologies for his long silence (NLS MS. 3889, ff. 174–5).

137 *n*. 1] This should be Hugh Scott of Harden as Hartstonge's letter of 20 Aug. shows (NLS MS. 3889, f. 174). Hartstonge had been investigating the fate of 'Poor Capt. Jock Home' (below, p. 320) for Scott of Harden.

139 (a) furniture were placing] Might not 'placing' be 'playing'?

139 (d) "airy tongues that syllable mens names"] Milton, *Comus*, line 208.

139 (d) Sadducismus triumphatus] Joseph Glanvil, *Saducismus triumphatus; or full and plain evidence respecting witches and apparitions*. (Originally published under a different title in 1666.)

140 (b) D'Israeli] There was no quotation from D'Israeli in Scott's review. See above, p. 130 and my note.

140 (c) Queens Wake] See my note to *SL* iv. 460 *n*. 2.

140 (c–d) failure of the bookseller] George Goldie.

140 *n*. 1] Delete this note. Scott is not referring to *Dramatic tales*, which had been published in 1817 by Longman, but to *The Brownie of Bodsbeck and other tales*, published this year by Blackwood and Murray.

141 (a) 2nd post bag] Read '2d post bag' (i.e. twopenny post).

141 (a) article on D'Israeli] This, if written, was not published.

142 *n*.] The funeral of Steenie is in *The Antiquary*.

143 (c) Kilvenan (?)] This is Culvennan.

143 (d) that the pancakes are naught] Shakespeare, *As you like it*, I. 2.

144 (a) the lines in dispute] See below, p. 198, 198 *n*.

145 (a) I am afraid to think] Shakespeare, *Macbeth*, II. 2.

145 *n*. 1] For 'Wilhelmina Belches' read 'Williamina Belsches' and for '*Journal*, i. 404' read 'Douglas's note to *Journal*, i. 404 *n*.'

146 *n*. 1] Delete 'in 1822 published views of places described by the author of *Waverley*' and substitute: Constable published in 1821 *Sixteen engravings from real scenes supposed to be described in the novels and tales of the Author of Waverley*. Except for the title-page vignette the engravings were all from drawings by Nasmyth. In second last line, for 'about 1821' read '1815.' See corrections in *SL* vi. 262 *n*. 3 and xii. 489.

148 (b) Glanville or Aubrey's Collection] For Glanvill, see above, p. 134, 134 *n*. 2. For Aubrey, see John Aubrey, *Miscellanies . . . 1. Day fatality. 2. Local fatality*, 2nd ed., London, 1721.

150 (d) Dundas] Robert Dundas of Beechwood.

150 (e) the little French lawyer] *The little French lawyer*, by Beaumont and Fletcher.

150, *n*. 2] For 'vol. i., p. 5' read 'vol. i, pp. 278–9.'

152 (c) Mr. Morrison] John Morrison.

152 *n*. 1] Delete and see my note to *SL* v. 140 *n*. 1.

154 (f) But mark how midst] Swift, *Duke upon duke*, st. [16], lines 1–2 (*Works*, ed. Scott, 2nd ed., xiii. 320).

154 *n*. 1] Delete and see above, p. 41 *n*. 1.

154 *n*. 2] See also above, p. 150.

155 (c) The mountain bard . . . publishd a letter] Strout (*Hogg*, p. 151) cites *Edinburgh Advertiser* of 15 and 22 May 1818. A letter, dated 13 May 1818, was printed in the *Glasgow Chronicle* and repr. in *N. & Q.* 2nd ser. Vol. 9 (12 May 1860), p. 366.

155 (d) "reproof valiant"] Shakespeare, *As you like it*, V. 4.

156 (e) His Tales] *The Brownie of Bodsbeck; and other tales,* 2 vols., Edinburgh, 1818. The dedication consists of a long poem, *To the Right Honourable Lady Anne Scott, of Buccleuch,* to which Scott refers.

157 (a) Don Quixote] Cervantes, *Don Quixote,* Pt II, chap. 67 (Lockhart's ed., 1822, v. 260).

157 (b) the invocation is somewhat musty] Shakespeare, *Hamlet,* III. 2: 'the proverb is somewhat musty.'

157 (c) the poor Queen] Charlotte, Queen of George III, died on 17 Nov. 1818.

158 (a) Regalia] The Commissioners appointed were: Duke of Gordon; Viscount Melville; Archibald Colquhoun, Lord Register; Alexander Maconochie, Lord Advocate; and David Boyle, Lord Justice Clerk. Adam Ferguson was appointed Deputy Keeper on 19 Aug. See *Edin. Ann. Reg. for 1818,* XI. ii. 227.

158 (b) To William Laidlaw] Date, Friday, 29 May, is correct, 'Saturday se'nnight' being 6 June. (See p. 159.) This arrangement was cancelled (below, p. 161).

159 (c) as Tony Lumpkin says] See my note to *SL* i. 524 (a).

161 (a) To Charles Erskine] Scott was to be at Abbotsford on Saturday, 6 June (above, pp. 158, 159) but this was cancelled owing to Dundas's journey to Bath. Scott is now writing on Sunday, 14 June, from Abbotsford, *not* from Edinburgh.

161 (b) begging him not to . . . go to law] This probably refers to a dispute over feu rights which Willie was having with Newbigging, from whom he had bought Maxpoffle. There is a letter (not in *SL*) from Scott to Willie, Oct. 1818, on this subject in NLS (MS. 2889, ff. 160–1).

161 (c) To. J. Hume, W.S.] John Home, W.S.

161 (e) To Mrs. Lindsay] Elizabeth Dick, wife of Hon. Robert Lindsay, second son of 5th Earl of Balcarres.

161 *n.* 1] Delete and substitute: William Scott of Maxpoffle.

161 *n.* 2] The letter from Mrs Lindsay

of 8 June 1818 is in NLS (MS. 3889, ff. 113–14).

162 (d–e) the bowl was broken at the cistern] *Bible, Ecclesiastes* 12:6: 'bowl be broken, or the pitcher be broken at the fountain, or the wheel broken at the cistern.'

162 *n.* 1] For '*The Highland Widow*' read '*The chronicles of the Canongate.*'

163 (d) I have both your kind letters] There are no letters from Terry in the Walpole Coll. between 15 May and 16 Sept.

163 (e) letter from Mr. Atkinson] Neither this letter nor Scott's reply is known to be extant.

164 (b) Hanover Square] George Bullock's address was 4 Tenterden Street, Hanover Square, London.

164 (c) Buggins] Read 'Bridgens.'

165 (a) "Walter ill to haud"] I have not found a Walter with this epithet, but there was a John Scott called 'Jocky ill to had' in Scott of Satchell's *True history* (Hawick 1894 ed., Post'ral, p. 61).

165 (b) To the Rev. Principal Baird] Principal Baird read an extract from this letter to the General Assembly of the Church of Scotland in 1828 and the extract was printed in the *New Scots Mag.* Vol. 2 (Sept. 1829), pp. 150–1.

167 (d) Locky] A misreading for 'Lochy,' i.e. Andrew Mercer.

167 (e) *Saturday* [Edinburgh]] Read '*Saturday* [Kaeside].'

168 (e) I hope to send Harold next week] Scott's letter enclosing his review of Byron's *Childe Harold* is not in *SL.* It is printed in *N. & Q.* Vol. 206 (Feb. 1961), p. 68. Unfortunately it is not dated.

168 (e) 2d part of the National poem] John Hookham Frere's *Prospectus and specimen of an intended national work, by William and Robert Whistlecraft . . . intended to comprise the most interesting particulars relating to King Arthur and his Round Table,* 8vo London, John Murray, 1817. As this contains the third and fourth cantos, Scott has regarded it as a '2d part.'

169 (c) To Daniel Terry] Date is probably 16 July. The Court of Session

broke up on that day and Scott was at Abbotsford on 17 July if the letter on p. 168 is correctly dated.

169 (d) reform the old MS.] *The doom of Devorgoil.*

169 n. 1] Scott is not referring to Rose's book, but to the original work by G. Casti from which Rose made his translation.

170 (d) If the gods have made you poetical] Shakespeare, *As you like it*, III. 3.

171 (f) Budgins] This is a misreading for Bridgens. Scott had already written to him on 23 July. I have a copy of his letter which is not in *SL*.

171 (f) Allans assistance] Sir William Allan.

172 (c) I have answerd your friends letter] Scott's letter to Halls is not in *SL*.

172 (c) Sir James Cockburn] Sir James Cockburn of Langton, Berwickshire. Walter Scott, W.S., was factor on the sequestrated estate. (MSS. in possession of Major P. I. C. Payne.)

172 (d) Mr. Halls] Thomas Halls. Joanna Baillie, in her letter of 6 July (NLS MS. 3889, ff. 135–6), says she is sending on Halls's letter at the request of his sister 'once a very kind neighbour of ours' without saying who he is.

172 n. 1] In last line, for 'many people' read 'few people.'

173 (d) something rotten] Shakespeare, *Hamlet*, I. 4.

174 (d) Saracens head . . . Sir Roger de Coverley] The *Spectator*, No. 122, 20 July 1711. By Addison.

174 n. 1] Scott may have got the idea from Bunyan's *Pilgrim's progress*, Pt II (chap. 8 in eds. divided into chapters) where there is a badly worded paragraph which reads: 'Polycarp, that played the man in the fire. There was he that was hung up in a basket in the sun for the wasps to eat.' The 'he' is the first in the paragraph not to be given a name and in reading quickly one is apt to associate Polycarp with the wasps.

176 n. 1] The review was not by Jeffrey but by John Wilson. See Mrs Gordon, '*Christopher North*,' i. 239–40, Smiles, *John Murray*, i. 398, 400, and Elsie Swann, *Christopher North* (1934), pp. 70–3.

177 n. 1] The lines cited do not explain Scott's "full-blown Cardinal." Wolsey uses the compound word "high-blown" and Anna Seward quoted 'With all his full-blown honours thick upon him' (*Letters*, i. 322), but I have not found 'full-blown Cardinal.'

178 (a) To John Murray] Scott, on his way back from Rokeby, was at Longtown on Saturday, 29 Aug. and probably reached Abbotsford on the same day. Murray must have visited him this week-end, for Murray wrote to him on 3 Sept. about the visit. (Smiles, *John Murray*, ii. 14–15.) Hogg was present. (Ibid. ii. 15.)

178 (c) "Kept the Castle in a gay uproar"] James Thomson, *The Castle of Indolence*, Canto I, st. 63, lines 8–9: 'kept in a gay uproar/Our madden'd castle all.'

178 (e) "ilk man buckles his belt his ain gate"] See my note to *SL* iv. 524 (b).

178 (f) Captains commission] The Commissioners for Keeping the Crown and Regalia of Scotland met on Wednesday, 19 Aug., and appointed Captain Adam Ferguson Deputy-Keeper. (*Edin. Ann. Reg for 1818*, XI. ii. 227.)

180 (b) "a gentleman of elegant inquiry"] I have not traced this quotation but exactly the same words, though not given as a quotation, are used in *St Ronan's Well*, chap. 5.

180 (c) Wednesday 30th] Transfer index figure to '1817' at head of letter.

180 n. 1] Delete and substitute: This letter, placed among 1818 letters, belongs to 1817 as is shown by letter to Mrs Tom Scott (*SL* vii. 492–3).

181 (b) To William Blackwood] The reference to Southey's *Wat Tyler* suggests that this letter may be early 1817.

181 (f) the Antiqy.] The 5th ed. of *The Antiquary* was published in 1818.

181 *n.* 1] Delete. Footnote, p. 176, is inapplicable. Reference should presumably be to p. 180, *n.* 2.

182 (e) To Sir James Stuart] Date must be 5 Oct. 1818: (1) Scott was going to Melville Castle on Wednesday, 9 Sept. (previous letter) and could not, therefore, have Lord and Lady Melville at Abbotsford on the same day; (2) Lord and Lady Melville were invited to Abbotsford on Wednesday, 7 Oct. (below, pp. 195, 201).

182 *n.* 1] In line 1, for '1817' read '1816.' Delete the second sentence. 'Stuart' was the spelling used by the family.

183 (c–d) Far from asking what] Scott may be referring to *Etchings from Scott & Byron, by Sir James Stuart, Bart.*, published at London by Colnaghi in June 1821, and dedicated to Scott.

184 (c) Captain Fergusson] Adam Ferguson was appointed Deputy Keeper of the Regalia on 19 Aug.

185 (a) These little things] Goldsmith, *The traveller*, line 42.

186 (a) To Charles Erskine] The date must be wrong. Scott is here writing from Abbotsford as the reference to Tom and the blackcock shows. But Scott was at Melville Castle on 9–11 Sept.

186 (c) To James Ballantyne] 10 Sept. cannot be correct date. Scott was at Melville Castle on that day. The reference to the 'steps at the Rhymer's Waterfall' suggests a date about May. See above, p. 151.

186 (e) *nil desperandum*] Horace, *Odes*, I. vii. 27.

188 (d) a tragedy. I would much sooner write an opera] Scott was actually writing *The doom of Devorgoil* for Terry and Terry may have been indiscreet and let the secret out. See *The doom of Devorgoil* in Index.

190 *n.* 1] Terry's letter is in NLS (MS. 3889, ff. 189–92).

191 (e) Jane] Jane Russell, eldest daughter of William Russell of Ashiestiel. She and her sisters, Anne and Eliza (mentioned p. 192), lived with Miss Rutherford. Their brother, Alexander Pringle Russell, died at Madras in Jan. 1818. The news would reach

them about this time. The death was announced in *Blackwood*, Vol. 4 (Oct. 1818), p. 117.

192 (e) there is a good time coming] Regarded as a proverb, but not in *Heywood, Ray, Kelly* or Ramsay, *Proverbs.*

193 (e) Your oak is superb—he will need] These were the roots of oak trees from Drumlanrig, out of which Bullock made the Dining Room table still on view at Abbotsford. See below, pp. 364–5. 'he will need' is a mistake for 'it will need.'

194 (c) Tanguy du Chatel] See my note to *SL* ii. 336 (d).

194 (f) Dr. Last] Scott is at fault here. Dr Last in *Dr Last in his chariot*, a farce by Bickerstaffe and Foote, uses a mixture of Latin and English words, but the words quoted by Scott were not used by him. They occur in Fielding's *The mock doctor*, where Dr Gregory says: 'as we say in Greek, distemprum bestum est curare ante habestum' (Act II, sc. 1).

195 (a) Cattle show] On 6 Nov. See below, pp. 201, 213. The oxen are Og and Bashan.

196 (a) To Daniel Terry] Date would be about 20 Sept. Scott would receive Terry's letter about 19 Sept. and write immediately so that Terry would receive the letter before he set out at the beginning of Oct.

196 (b) Mr. Harris] Terry, in his letter of 16 Sept. (NLS MS. 3889, ff. 189–92), quotes letter to him from H. Harris of Covent Garden Theatre ending Terry's contract.

196 (c) windows . . .] The windows were for the Hall and Armoury to left and right respectively of the greenhouse. The former became a door. Of other items mentioned later in this paragraph, the sideboard was designed by Atkinson and the marbles refer to fireplaces.

197 (c) painted glass] By Mrs Terry for the Armoury ante-room windows.

197 (c) Mr. Bruce] J. Bruce & Co., Wine Merchants, Leith.

198 (a) To Maria Edgeworth] The visit of Mr and Mrs Hamilton must have been on Sunday–Monday, 6–7 Sept. Scott was at Melville Castle 9–11,

NOTES

V

and, as he is writing in the same week, the date is probably 12 Sept.

199 (b) touching the hem of your garment] *Bible, Matthew* 9:20; 14:36.

199 (d) temple of Solomon] *Bible, I Kings* 6:7. Also referred to, p. 200.

202 (a) To G. H. Gordon] See my note to *SL* vi. 208 (c).

203 (a) imitate the antient Romans in brevity] Shakespeare, *II Henry IV*, II. 2: 'I will imitate the honourable Roman in brevity.'

203 (c) To Lady Compton] The Yeomanry dinner was on Saturday 24 Oct. Date of letter is Friday, 23 Oct.

203 (c) Naesmythe and his daughter Mrs. Terry] This statement should have prevented the misdating of Terry's marriage in *SL* iv. 7 *n.* and v. 146 *n.*

203 (f) To J. G. Lockhart] This letter is in reply to Lockhart's letter of 20 Oct. which is printed (with some omissions) in *FL* ii. 28–30.

204 (c) circum pectus æs triplex of Horace] *Odes*, I. iii. 9–10.

204 *n.* 1] *Hypocrisy unveiled* was written by James Grahame, Advocate. Lockhart suspected he was the author. See Mrs Oliphant, op. cit., p. 169. Note 1 on p. 212 below should have formed part of this note.

205 (d) To John Ballantyne] Date is 7 Nov. 1818.

206 *n.* 1] Delete two final sentences.

207 (a) To C. K. Sharpe] Date of letter is 1817. (Corrected in *SL* xii. 489.)

207 (a) Cur me exanimas querelis tuis?] Horace, *Odes*, II. xvii. 1. These are the opening words of *Redgauntlet*.

208 (b) the offensive article] The Chaldee MS.

208 (e–f) like the man in the tales of the Genii] *The enchanters; or, Misnar, Sultan of the East* in James Ridley's *Tales of the Genii*. (Weber, *Tales of the East*, iii. 507.)

210 (c) il a un grand talent pour le silence] Maria Edgeworth in *Ormond*, chap. 27, has: 'Ce monsieur là a un grand talent pour le silence.' Cf. another possible quotation from *Ormond*, below, p. 367.

210 (e) Forest yeomanry] The Selkirkshire Yeomanry Cavalry dined at Abbotsford on Saturday, 24 Oct.

211 (e–f) flat and unprofitable] Shakespeare, *Hamlet*, I. 2.

212 (a) an idle cousin] James Scott, son of Thomas Scott. See below, p. 221 *n.* 1.

212 (c) the pamphlet] *Hypocrisy unveiled*, by James Grahame, Advocate. See above, pp. 204, 204 *n.* The letters of Wilson and Lockhart, separately challenging the writer, and the writer's reply were issued (presumably by Grahame) as a single sheet folded (4 pp.), without title-page, as *Correspondence on the subject of Blackwood's Magazine*.

212 (d) The person to whom the public ascribed the answer] Macvey Napier. See below, p. 221.

212 (e) When first they set] Shakespeare, *Henry VIII*, V. 2.

213 (a) glass windows in their heads] See *SL* ii. 60.

213 (e) Graham] Dr Andrew Graham, physician in Dalkeith. A portrait of him was painted by J. Ainslie in 1817 (29·75 × 24·75 in.). See A. Francis Steuart, *Catalogue of pictures at Dalkeith House*, Dalkeith, 1890, p. 102.

215 (f) his lifetime] This should presumably be 'her lifetime.'

217 (d) a certain Mr. Cunninghame] George Cunninghame. He was uncle of McCulloch of Ardwall; hence his interest in him. The application was unsuccessful. Cunninghame was succeeded by George Forrester.

218 (a) Swifts rule] *Journal to Stella*, Letter 20 (*Works*, ed. Scott, 2nd ed., ii. 235).

219 (e) long litigated estate of Knowsouth] John Rutherford of Knowesouth died in 1788 but the estate lay in nonentry till 1798, when his grandson, John Rutherford, W.S., was served heir. The latter died in Apr. 1801 and again the estate lay in nonentry till his uncle, Capt. John Rutherford, was served heir in July 1815.

220 (f) a nod is as good as a wink] A common proverb, but not found in *Heywood, Ray, Kelly* or Ramsay, *Proverbs*.

Used in *The Heart of Mid-Lothian*, chap. 16 and *Nigel*, chap. 25.

221 (c) the pamphlet] *Hypocrisy unveiled*, by James Grahame, Advocate.

222 (b) the Harleian miscellany] Princess Caroline wrote in a letter to Lady Charlotte Bury: 'Lady Oxford (De Miscellany Harleyan, as all de world does call her now)' (Bury, *Diary illustrative of the times of George the Fourth*, iv. 89).

222 (c) Jeremy in Love for Love] In William Congreve's *Love for love*, I. 1, Jeremy refers to creditors but not exactly in same sense as Scott implies.

222 (d) third daughter] Ismene Magdalene, third daughter of William Glendonwyn of Parton who died 18 June 1809.

223 (a) academical institution] See *Prospectus of a new academical institution at Edinburgh* in *Blackwood*, Vol. 4 (Nov. 1818), pp. 217-20. The article is ascribed to John Wilson.

223 (e) Edinburgh Encyclopedia] *Drama* was for *Encyclopædia Britannica*.

224 (a) Suave mari magno] Lucretius, *De rerum natura*, Bk II, line 1. Quoted in *The Antiquary*, chap. 8. The whole passage means that it is pleasant, when the waves of the great sea are being tossed about by the wind, to watch from the shore another's heavy toil.

224 (b) like a mouse below a firlot] Not found as a proverb. Scott attributed the expression to a farmer. See *Guy Mannering*, chap. 2. Also used in *SL* ix. 380.

224 (c) dining & sleeping at Huntlyburn] This arrangement was cancelled. Scott arrived at Bowhill on Friday, 27 Nov. and left on Monday morning.

225 n. 1] See my note to *SL* ii. 528 (d).

226 (a) a very good article] The last article in Vol. 4, No. 20, Nov. 1818, p. 228, was *Is the Edinburgh Review a religious and patriotic work?* [By John Wilson.]

226 (d) To William Laidlaw] There is a garbled version, combined with another letter, in *SL* iii. 160-1, where it is wrongly dated 1812. This letter cannot be 1818 as Sir John Buchanan

Riddell did not die till Apr. 1819, and Riddell was not sold till 1823. I think the date should be 1821.

228 (c) Dr. Scott . . . son of . . . tenant at Singlee] Scott could not be mistaken and we must accept his statement that Dr Scott of Darnlee was the son (second) of William Scott of Singlee (recorded by K. S. M. Scott, *Scott*, p.121). K. S. M. Scott, however, has (p. 164) James Scott of Ellem, a second son of John Scott of Midgehope, W.S., where he says: 'No particulars are available of James Scott's birth, marriage or death,' showing that he never saw James Scott's tombstone in Melrose Abbey churchyard. This James Scott of p. 164 could not be James Scott of Darnlee for he could not have been born earlier than 1784, whereas Scott of Darnlee was born in 1776.

229 n. 1] Ferguson was Deputy Keeper.

230 (e) to urge any request] About his cousin, James Scott. See above, pp. 219-20, 221 n.

231 (d) "Your love and fear . . . to them"] Shakespeare, *III Henry VI*, II. 6.

242 (a) A.M. bath] Possibly mistake for N.M. bath (i.e. Nitro-Muriatic bath, p. 243).

242 (f) To Lady Compton] This letter is dated 2 Dec. But Scott says (p. 243) that he had already written to Mrs Clephane and the letter to her (below, p. 246) is dated 3 Dec.

243 (b) iron sharpeneth iron] *Bible*, *Proverbs* 27:17.

245 (d) patience cousin] See my note to *SL* ii. 404 (a).

245 n. 1] For '94' read '93.'

246 (b) Lord Compton] I have not found his sketch of Abbotsford.

247 (a) Rinaldini] *Rinaldo Rinaldini; der Räuber-Hauptmann; eine romantische Geschichte* [By Christian August Vulpius]. 6 Thle, 12mo Leipzig, 1802. An English trans. with title *Rinaldo Rinaldini, Captain of Banditti*, was published in 3 vols. at London, 1831.

247 (a) Allan of the Straw] See my note to *SL* iv. 178 n. 1.

247 (b) Clementina] This is surely a misreading for Williamina.

247 (b) lovely isle] Read 'lonely isle.' See my note to *SL* ii. 506 (a).

249 (a) her sister] Williamina, the third daughter.

249 (b) "rejoice therefore"] *Bible, II Corinthians* 7:16.

249 (d) "things must be as they may"] Shakespeare, *Henry V*, II. 1.

249 (e) To Adam Ferguson] This letter should be dated from Edinburgh, *not* Abbotsford.

251 (a) "there's honour for you Sir Walter"] Shakespeare, *I Henry IV*, V. 3.

251 (a) the Advocate . . . his Mother] Alexander Maconochie. His mother was Elizabeth, daughter of Robert Wellwood of Garvock.

252 (d) Hogg] He was at this time preparing his *Jacobite relics*.

252 (e) He thought it best] Adam Skirving, *Tranent Muir*, st. [6], lines 7–8. In *Herd*, i. 110; and in *Johnson*, Vol. 2 (1788), No. 102.

252 (f) Douglas] John Douglas of Barloch. See above, pp. 150, 154. The epithet 'grim' is an allusion to Archibald Douglas, 3rd Earl of Douglas (1328?–1400?), called 'The Grim.'

253 (c) To unknown correspondent] Almost certainly addressed to Bullock & Co. This letter should come after the one to Laidlaw on p. 254, which should be dated 11 Nov. In the letter to Laidlaw, which Scott is writing at Abbotsford, he gives Laidlaw his final instructions—sending in potatoes for the winter supply, ploughing and so on. At the same time he had begun a letter to Bullock & Co. which he dated 11 Nov. After writing the first sentence he stopped to write to Laidlaw. By the 6 Dec. he had received Laidlaw's report of 5 Dec. and thereupon completed his letter to Bullock which he dated 6 Dec. without (as in other cases) changing the date 11 Nov. at the beginning.

253 *n.* 2] Delete from 'Scott's letter' down to 'Scott's slips.' The letter could not be written to Atkinson for two reasons: (1) Scott would never have written such a letter to Atkinson; and (2) Atkinson had nothing to do with the dispatch of material from London. The word 'advises' [*sic* for 'adviser'] does not fit Atkinson who was the architect, not the 'adviser.'

254 (d) To William Laidlaw] For dating see my note above, p. 253 (c).

254 (e) Patersons] As Paterson was a mason, Scott must mean Messrs Sanderson & Paterson.

254 *n.* 1] Delete this note. The two dates are explained in my note above, p. 253 (c).

255 (f) return to India] Should be 'return from India.'

255 *n.* 1] Delete. This is a misreading for Charge Law as the reference to Stobs meadow shows. These two sections of the estate were contiguous.

256 (a) Mr. Heath] Josiah Marshall Heath who married a sister of Mrs Carpenter.

257 (d) Miss Kitty Hert Reading] For 'Hert' read 'Hort.' See Index under Packe-Reading.

257 (e) *rich* Miss Brodies] These were probably the nieces of Alexander Brodie (1733–1811), a rich iron-founder of London who established woollen mills at Innerleithen about 1786. He left the bulk of his immense fortune to his nieces and nephews. (*Gentleman's Mag.* lxxxi. 89; *Scots Mag.* lxxi. 798; Buchan, *Peeblesshire*, ii. 333, where daughter is given instead of niece.) The William Brodie of Inner-leithen who rented Ashiestiel, after Scott left it for Abbotsford, was prob-ably one of the nephews. (*Chisholm*, pp. 97, 201.)

258 (b) Capt. Florence & Lincoln] i.e. Captain Adam Ferguson, Joseph Flor-ence (the Duke's cook) and Dr Lincoln (the Duke's doctor).

258 (c) the bonds] i.e. Adam Ferguson's bonds for safe keeping of the Regalia. See pp. 251, 267.

259 (b) from Dan to Beersheba] *Bible, Judges* 20:1 and elsewhere in O.T.

260 *n.* 1] Delete this note. Scott is referring to James III. Robert Lindsay of Pitscottie says he 'delighted more in music and policies of bigging.' (*History of Scotland*, 3rd ed., Edinburgh, 1778, p. 115.) Scott also quotes this in his note to Canto IV, st. xiv of *Marmion*.

261 (d) "I like not such *grinning* honour as Sir Walter hath"] Shakespeare, *I Henry IV*, V. 3.

262 (c) To Joanna Baillie] The date is about 11 Dec. as Joanna Baillie received the letter on 14 Dec. (NLS MS. 3889, ff. 279–80.)

264 (a) The crescent at whose gleam] Only the second line is from Southey's *Madoc*, Pt II, sect. XVIII. See also *SL* vii. 121 for another version of the lines.

264 (f) like Sir Roger de Coverley's portrait] See above, p. 174 and my note.

266 (c) Who left his poor plough] Charles Dibdin, *The lucky escape*, st. I, line 10. A ballad in *Private Theatricals*. In his *A collection of songs*, London [1792], ii. 129.

266 (e) Mine Aunt] Christian Rutherford.

266 (f) Sir William Bingham] This is Scott's error for Sir George Bingham. Sir George Ridout Bingham was half-brother of Richard Bingham. Both became Generals.

267 (a) Mrs Clarke a certain revd. Dr O Mara] Mrs Clarke, when examined before the House of Commons, was asked if she had communicated Dr O'Meara's offer for a bishopric to the Duke of York and she replied that she had but that the King 'did not like the great O in his name.' See *Scots Mag.* Vol. 71 (June 1809), p. 451 and *Edin. Ann. Reg. for 1809*, II. i. 149 and cf. ibid., pp. 155, 300–1.

267 (c) I send the Bond] Adam Ferguson's bond for the safe keeping of the Regalia. See above, pp. 251, 258.

268 (b) companion of all hours] Scott gives the Latin, 'amicus omnium horarum,' elsewhere. See *SL* iv. 520 and my note.

269 (d–e) *worlds gear*] As this is in italics it is probably a quotation from Burns. See my note to *SL* iii. 490 (e).

272 (b) To James Skene] Dating in Skene's *Memories* is erratic. In 1818 Tuesday was 8 Dec. and Scott was not at Abbotsford either on 8 or 10 Dec.

273 (c) the Duchess] The Duke's mother, Elizabeth, wife of 3rd Duke.

274 (c) To Archibald Constable] The date is probably 8 Dec. This letter is now in NLS (MS. 4880, ff. 143–4) and is clearly dated 18 Dec. 1818. Constable's reply (below, p. 276 n. 1) is also in NLS (MS. 866, ff. 193–4) and is clearly dated 18 Dec. 1818. Both cannot be right and as Scott was more guilty of misdating than Constable we must accept Constable's dating and reject Scott's. Scott's reference to Abbotsford (p. 276) shows that he is writing a considerable time before Christmas and a considerable time before 18 Dec. His reference to being occupied in the country (p. 275) refers to his recent vacation at Abbotsford which ended on 12 Nov. The reference to his tour abroad (p. 275) is to the agreement with John Ballantyne and Constable for a continuation of *Paul's letters*, 7–11 Nov. (*Archibald Constable*, iii. 114–18). The Yeomanry dinner at Abbotsford (p. 276) was on 24 Nov. Such topics were comparatively fresh news on 8 Dec. but rather stale by 18 Dec.

275 (d–e) State Trials] The vol. wanted was Vol. 24, not 22, and it did not complete the set, which consisted of 32 vols.

275 n. 1] For 'Edward' read 'Edmund.' There is no need to cite Bibl. Nat. catalogue. The 5th ed. was published by Fenner.

277 (b) Black cock Cleugh] Another name for Cappercleugh.

277 n.] Water on the chest had not been entirely overlooked. Dr Scott had suspected it. See above, p. 239.

278 (d) Cogie and the King come] Concluding stanza or second chorus to *Carle, an the King come*. In *Johnson*, Vol. 3 (1790), No. 239.

279 (b) *pieds de mouche*] Scott also describes Heber's handwriting thus in *SL* vii. 339, viii. 111, and his own in *SL* vi. 510, x. 206, xi. 277. This is the only time Scott attributes the description to Ellis.

279 (c) brighten the charm of friendship] See *SL* ii. 535 and my note. The misreading 'charm' is corrected in *SL* xii. 489.

279 (d) on the *Tirtea-fuera* system]
Cervantes, *Don Quixote*, Pt 2, chap. 47
(Lockhart's ed., 1822, v. 32).

279 (d) land & beeves] Shakespeare,
II Henry IV, III. 2.

280 (b) Sir Jo: Malcolm] He returned
to India in 1817.

280 (c) Achilles's shout] Homer, *Iliad*,
Bk 18.

280 (d) To John Ballantyne] May
1818 is too late, as reference to the bond
shows. This seems to be an early
reference to 2nd ser. of *Tales of my
Landlord* and must be about Apr.
1817. See *SL* iv. 431.

280 (d) I have hungered and thirsted]
A reminiscence of the *Bible*, *Matthew*
5:6.

281 (a) To John Ballantyne] The date
is the end of May 1820. See my note to
SL v. 281 *n.* 1.

281 (c) lacked but you—as the witches
song says] Thomas Middleton, *The
witch*, III. 3.

281 (c) "steer him up and haud him
gaun"] Altered from the first line of an
old Scottish song: 'O steer her up, and
had her gawn.' In Ramsay, *Tea-table
miscellany*.

281 (d) a bird in the hand] Heywood,
p. 64.

281 (e) the Solicitor] The Solicitor-
General, James Wedderburn.

281 *n.* 1] The copy sent was of the
second ed., 1820. Inserted is a piece of
paper with an inscription to Scott by
Bowdler, 20 May 1820. On the back of
this paper Lockhart has written: 'This
book was given by Sir Walter Scott to
his daughter Sophia & it is now given to
her daughter Charlotte Lockhart on
Xmas day 1837 by her affectionate
father J. G. Lockhart.' This edition,
which Scott did not wish to add to his
Library, found its way back to Abbotsford and is now among Lockhart's
books.

286 (b) Ptarmigan sailed from Inver-
ness] See above, p. 265. Joanna reported
on 7 Jan. that they had arrived. See
extract from her letter in Partington,
Post-bag, pp. 126–8.

288 (e) To Lord Melville] This letter
is dated 14 Jan. but Scott says in his

letter to Ferguson (p. 291) that he
'will write' and dates that letter 15
Jan.

289 (b) patrimonial] Grierson has not
queried use of this word here though
he does so at *SL* viii. 153. Scott uses the
word, not in the sense of inherited
property, but with the meaning 'financial.' A writer in the *Scotsman*, 30 Mar.
1935, cited examples from Scott,
Cockburn and Jeffrey, and pointed out
that Juvenal used 'patrimonium' in the
sense of lawyers' fees.

290 (a) whom the prince has delighted
to honour] *Bible*, *Esther* 6:6, 7, 9, 11.

290 (c) whet like Hamlets ghost]
Shakespeare, *Hamlet*, III. 4.

291 (a) To Adam Fergusson] On date
see my note to *SL* v. 288 (e).

291 (b) Otium cum dignitate] Honoured
leisure. A proverbial expression based
on Cicero, *De oratore*, I. 1: 'in otio cum
dignitate.'

291 *n.* 3] No need to quote Goldsmith.
It is a Scottish proverb in *Kelly*, p. 373;
Ramsay, *Proverbs*, pp. 25, 79. It is also a
Gaelic proverb. See Donald Mac-
intosh, *Gaelic proverbs*, 1775, C. 342.

292 (c) as the learnd Partridge says]
Fielding, *Tom Jones*, Bk IX, chap. 6.

293 (a) Macculloch] James Macculloch.

293 (b) To C. K. Sharpe] The year
must be 1820 as Spence's *Anecdotes*
did not come out till Jan. 1820.

293 *n.* 1] Hislop should not be cited as
many of his so-called 'proverbs' are
merely quotations from Scott and other
writers.

293 *n.* 2] The volume lent was probably
*Life, intrigues and adventures of the
celebrated Sally Salisbury*, by C. Walker,
1723, with a MS. poem of nine verses
on her by Sharpe. It was sold at the
Gibson-Craig sale at Sotheby's, 7 July
1887, Lot 2733.

294 (f) To J. Richardson] The date is
12 Jan. 1819. In his reply of 19 Jan.
(NLS MS. 3890, ff. 10–12) Richardson
wrote 'I was very happy to receive
your letter of the 12th inst.' This letter
is cited below, p. 295, *n.* 2 as a reply to
a letter of 18 Jan., an impossibility.

294 (f) Mrs. *****] The only judge
whose surname began with a T was

Alexander Fraser Tytler, Lord Wood-houselee. Mrs Tytler was a widow at this time.

295 *n.* 2] Richardson has overestimated the amount of fees. I have a transcript of the original MS. of 'Account of Fees of Sir W. Scott's Baronetcy, May 1820.' The total comes to £259. 11*s.* 6*d.*

297 (d) Polwarth title] But Scott of Harden did not get the decision of the House of Lords till 1835.

299 (a) the poor Count] As Mrs Scott's letter is not in NLS, I do not know to what Scott is referring.

299 *n.* 2] According to Burke's *Landed gentry*, the family originally came from Sweden. In line 2, for 'Wordsworth' read 'Wadsworth.' In line 9, for '1820' read '1819.' The Abbotsford catalogue (last line) gives 1819, not 1829.

300 (b) a fair artist] The frontispiece and vignette on title-page are signed 'Maria invent.'

300 (d) some bit of a book] 'book' must be a misreading for 'box.'

301 (e) To Miss C. Rutherford] The date cannot be Feb. 1819 as the Scotts of Harden were in the South (above, p. 298). It cannot be 1820 as Eliza Russell and Chritty were both dead by that time. Sir John Buchanan Riddell died on 21 Apr. 1819 and his brother-in-law, the Earl of Romney, who was his trustee, came to Scotland to inspect the estate of Riddell. (*Hist. Berwickshire Nat. Club*, Vol. 8, p. 326.) The date of the dinner, therefore, might be during the summer session of the Courts, i.e. between mid May and mid July.

301 *n.* 1] Murray's name appears in the imprints from Aug. 1818 till Feb. 1819 inclusive. With the number for Mar. 1819 T. Cadell & W. Davies displace Murray. As *Blackwood* was published at the end of each month, the quarrel must have occurred in Mar., not Jan. as Mrs Oliphant says.

302 (d) Taymouth] Scott had stayed at Taymouth Castle about 1797. See his letter (not in *SL*) in *Rev. of Eng. Stud.* Vol. 25, p. 248.

302 *n.* 1] In first line, delete 'I presume.' In line 6, for '1819' read '1820.'

304 (d) I will follow Iagos rule] Shakespeare, *Othello*, I. 3.

305 (b) Donald Cargill] He was wound-ed but not mortally.

305 (c) *Here follows Genealogy and Claim of Arms*] This part of the letter, here omitted, is printed with the letter in Symington, *Some unpublished letters*, pp. 94–6.

305 (d) To Charles Mackay] As first performance of *Rob Roy* was on 15 Feb., date of letter is probably 16 Feb.

307 *n.* 1] The Duke's letter of 15 Feb. is in Partington, *Letter-books*, pp. 287–8.

309 (b) To unknown correspondent] This is Alexander Young and the date of the letter is 2 Mar. 1824. See *SL* viii. 138 *n.*

309 (b) your Indian book] See *SL* viii. 138 *n.*

309 *n.* 1] This note is not now applic-able. It should be noted, however, that Scott could not be answering in Mar. a letter written in India in Feb. (NLS MS. 3890, ff. 42–5). On Macdonald Kinneir's gifts, see my note to *SL* vi. 335 (c). In line 10, the reference is to Hector Macdonald Buchanan's son of the same name who died on 22 Oct. of the same year, i.e. 1819.

310 *n.*] The long paragraph on Col. Norton is a repetition of *SL* iii. 503 *n.*

310 *n.* 1] Keith died at Ravelston, not at Dunnottar. The same mistake is made in *SL* v. 85 *n.*

312 (a) Lord Errol] Scott is strangely at fault here. The 18th Earl of Errol, who had succeeded on 26 Jan. 1819, was simply asking for the position his father had held since 1805. When Sir Alexander Keith died, Errol succeeded him.

312 (e) loaves & fishes] *Bible, Matthew* 14: 17–19; *Mark* 6: 38–41, 8: 6–7; *John* 6: 9–11.

313 (c) Lord Beresford] William Carr Beresford, 1st Viscount Beresford.

313 (d) The Lord President] Charles Hope, Lord Granton.

313 (d) from his son] *Lockhart* (vi. 34) interpolates 'Captain Charles Hope, R.N.' Hope was appointed Lieut. on H.M.S. *Liffey* on 22 Feb. 1818 and

cruised in Mediterranean and off Lisbon.

316 (c) Kennedy's latin song] Herbert Kennedy's *Prælium Gillicrankianum*. In *Johnson*, Vol. 2 (1788), No. 102, p. 105.

316 (e) *non valentia agendi*] Inability to act through some legally recognized impediment. A Scots law phrase. See Trayner, *Latin maxims*.

316 *n.* 1] Hogg's fabrication was *Donald M'Gillavry*. See Edith Batho, *The Ettrick Shepherd*, pp. 38–9.

317 (b) American Sachem] See above, p. 315.

317 *n.* 1] For '*Humphrey*' read '*Humphry*.'

317 *n.* 2] Delete this note. Alexander Keith (son of Alexander Keith, 1705–92) had married in 1811 Margaret, daughter of Laurence Oliphant of Gask and died on 26 Feb. 1819. It was his nephew, son of his younger brother William, who was the Knight Marshal.

318 (f) a meeting of Burns' admirers] In Assembly Rooms, George Street, Edinburgh, on 22 Feb. 1819. See *Edin. Ann. Reg. for 1819*, XII. ii. 284.

320 (d) Harden's affair] Polwarth peerage claim.

320 (d) Poor Capt. Jock Home] Home cannot be identified from Hartstonge's letters in NLS. The only John Home I can find, who might fit, is an officer in the army (1711–38), grandson of 1st Earl of Marchmont.

321 (f) I sighd and howld] Perhaps a parody of Coleridge's *Ancient mariner*, lines 61–2 (Pt I, st. 15, lines 3–4): 'It cracked and growled and roared and howled, / Like noises in a swound.'

322 (b) Take *thou* the vanguard] *The Battle of Otterbourne*, st. 25, lines 2–4, in Scott's *Minstrelsy* (ed. Henderson), i. 291.

322 (c) like old Sir Anthony Absolute] Sheridan, *The rivals*, II. 1.

322 (c) temperament] In the MS. (NLS MS. 142, No. 6) the reading is 'temperament.' But Scott obviously meant to write 'constitution' (as he did below, pp. 325, 329) as is shown by his words 'an eye to my ribs as glorious hoops for a skeleton.' The application is physical, not mental.

322 *n.* 2] There are extracts from Lockhart's letter of 3 Apr. in Partington, *Post-bag*, pp. 129–30 and *FL* ii. 40.

323 (b–c) my nose is held to the grindstone] *Ray*, pp. 262, 380, Ramsay, *Proverbs*, p. 41.

324 (c) primrose path of poetry] Cf. 'primrose path of dalliance' in Shakespeare's *Hamlet*, I. 3.

324 (c) *intus et in cute*] Persius, *Satires*, III. 30.

324 (e) Ross] Dr Adolphus Ross.

325 (a) the Lay] There was no edition of *The Lay* between 1816 and 1821. Scott is referring to the text for *The poetical works*, 1820.

325 (b) I have written to Baillie] Scott probably is referring to Dr Clarkson's letter to Matthew Baillie (below, pp. 327, 359).

325 (d) like Sir Anthony Absolute] See my note to *SL* v. 322 (c).

326 (a) "The voice is the voice of Jacob . . ."] *Bible, Genesis* 27:22.

326 (a) a young medical friend] James Burnet Clarkson, son of Dr Ebenezer Clarkson. He stayed at Abbotsford during Scott's illness. See letter of Sophia to Miss Millar, 11 May 1819 (*Letters to their old governess*, pp. 52–3).

326 (b) betwixt the Devil & the deep sea] Ramsay, *Proverbs*, p. 13.

327 (c) Doctor Clarkson] Dr Ebenezer Clarkson of Selkirk. His son, James Burnet Clarkson, is the 'young medical friend' of p. 326. James later practised in Melrose and attended Scott.

327 *n.* 2] For 'p. 360' read 'p. 359.'

328 (d) To J. B. S. Morritt] Date is Friday, 26 Mar.

329 (d) *intus et in cute*] Persius, *Satires*, III. 30.

330 *n.* 1] Scott's letter cannot be addressed to Hickie: (1) Hickie in his letter (NLS MS. 3890, ff. 48–9) gives his address as 'Record Tower, Dublin Castle' but Scott says his correspondent has given 'no direction' (p. 331); (2) Hickie is asking for a subscription, not for an opinion. The addressee has not been ascertained.

332 (f) Rodwell & Martin] This firm was publishing Scott's *Provincial antiquities*.

333 (a) "But shall we go mourn . . ."] Shakespeare, *Winter's tale*, IV. 2.

333 (a) doff the world aside] Shakespeare, *I Henry IV*, IV. 1.

333 (b) Moriturus te salutat] Suetonius Tranquillus, [*Lives of the Caesars*], *Tiberius Claudius Drusus*, chap. 21: 'Ave imperator, morituri te salutant.'

333 (e) abstemious Miss in the Arabian tales] Amina, wife of Sidi Nonman. *The story of Sidi Nonman* in *Adventures of the Calif Haroun Alraschid* in *The Arabian Nights* (Weber, *Tales of the East*, i. 387–8).

333 n. 2] Sharpe's letter of 7 Apr. is in *Sharpe's Letters*, ii. 197–200, and in Partington, *Letter-books*, pp. 28–30.

334 (c) Fountainhall's Diary] Sharpe's proposed ed. was Robert Mylne's version. See letter from Constable to Sharpe, 26 Jan. 1819, in *Sharpe's Letters*, ii. 194–5.

335 (d) bowl in the act of breaking] *Bible, Ecclesiastes* 12: 6.

336 (b) your latest pledge of affection] Birth in Feb. of Southey's second son, Charles Cuthbert Southey.

338 (e) "The game is done . . ."] Coleridge, *The ancient mariner*, lines 197–8 [Pt 3, st. 12].

338 (f) like Sancho] Cervantes, *Don Quixote*, Pt I, Bk III, chap. 1. (Lockhart's ed., 1822, i. 149–59.)

338 n. 1] Delete.

339 n. 1] For 'Buckie' read 'Bucke.' Charles Bucke printed for private circulation in 1838 *A letter intended (one day) as a supplement to Lockhart's Life of Sir Walter Scott*. Bucke exonerates Scott but blames Lockhart for printing Scott's letter of 4 Apr. to Southey (*Lockhart*, 1st ed., iv. 240). Lockhart, however, retained the letter in the 2nd ed., 1839 (vi. 44).

339 n. 2] Except for the four first lines, this note has nothing to do with Scott's text. Incidentally, the poem which was used as a test was, according to Skene, a translation from Bürger. See Skene, *Memories*, p. 70.

340 (a) a friend, who had been lately on the Continent] David Constable. See following page.

340 (b) *experto crede*] For possible sources, see *N. & Q.* 7th ser. iii. 17.

340 (b) Bishop of Grenada's sermon] See my note to *SL* iv. 403 (a).

342 (e) Mrs. Scott] She went to Edinburgh to engage a cook and bring back Charles, who was unwell. See below, pp. 355, 364.

343 n. 2] Scott is returning the MS. of Turner's *Memoirs* which belonged to Constable. In May 1810 (*Scots Mag.* Vol. 72, pp. 364–5) Constable had announced its publication in 1 vol. 8vo with portrait. This project had been abandoned. See also *SL* xi. 269.

344 (a) To James Ballantyne] Date is Sunday, 11 Apr.

346 (d) a white poney] *Bible, Revelation* 6: 8.

346 n. 1] *Peregrine Pickle*, chap. 27.

347 n. 3] Two portions of the letter of 29 May 1816 are in *SL* iv. 240–3 from *FL* and *Lockhart*. The letter printed from the original is in *SL* vii. 478–83. In line 3 from foot, 'raisd' is 'levied' in *SL* vii. 482.

348 (c) as Tony Lumpkin says] See my note to *SL* i. 524 (a).

348 n.] The complete letter of 21 Aug. 1807 is in *SL* vii. 416–17.

349 (b–c) *age of brass*] Horace, *Odes*, I. iii. 9–10.

349 (c) has twice made a very chowder-headed person of me] The 1808 portrait for Constable (now at Bowhill) and the 1809 portrait for Scott (at Abbotsford).

350 (b) Rathillets] David Hackston of Rathillet. See *SL* iv. 341.

350 (d) Constable has offerd Allan three hundred pounds] For *Illustrations of the novels and tales of the Author of Waverley from designs by William Allan*, 4to Edinburgh, Archibald Constable and Co., 1820.

350 n. 1] This portrait of the Duke (11·5 × 9·5 in.) was at Dalkeith. See A. Francis Steuart, *Catalogue of pictures at Dalkeith House*, Dalkeith, 1890, p. 76.

351 (e) parson Abraham Adams]
Fielding, *Joseph Andrews.*

351 (e) notorious Mr. MacLagan] Rev.
Frederick Maclagan, minister of Melrose, 1768–1818, was charged with
adultery about 1785 but was acquitted
by the Presbytery.

351 (f) Let us all be unhappy together]
St. 1, line 8 of Charles Dibdin's song
beginning 'We bipeds, made up of
frail clay,' in *The Wags.* In Dibdin's *A
collection of songs,* London [1792], ii.
50.

352 (d) Somewhat too much of him]
Shakespeare, *Hamlet,* III. 2: 'something
too much of this.' Cf. above, p. 71.
Correctly quoted in *SL* vii. 357.

353 (a) the loss of two fine young men in
India] Hugh, the 5th son, who died at
Bombay, May 1818, and John, the 6th
son, who died in India, June 1818.

353 (c) "like a haulded saumon"]
For explanation, see below, p. 357.

355 (b) Death on the pale horse]
Bible, Revelation 6: 8.

356 (a) his whimsical uncle] Joseph
Hume who succeeded to Ninewells in
1786 and died unmarried, 14 Feb.
1832.

356 (b) after his wife's death] Janet
Alder had died on 23 May 1816.

356 (d) Old Kennedy] William Kennedy who was tried at Jedburgh 15
Apr. 1819 for the murder of William
Irving at Yarrowford on 23 June 1818.
He was sentenced to transportation
and when he returned to Jedburgh he
travelled the country making and selling
baskets. He was still alive about 1860.
The old feud dated back to 1772 or
1773 when a fierce battle (known as
'The battle of Hawick Brig') was
fought between the Kennedys and
Taits with Jean Gordon among the
latter. Scott here says Irvings instead of
Taits. See the *Kelso Mail,* 15 Apr. 1819,
p. 4; Simson, *History of the Gipsies,*
1865, pp. 190–2; *Trans. Hawick Arch.
Soc.,* 1916, pp. 35–6; Hughes, *Letters,*
p. 256.

356 (f) An old soldier of the Dukes]
Old soldiers, st. [1], lines 4–5: 'That we
are old Soldiers of the Queens, / And the
Queens old Soldiers.' In D'Urfey, *Wit
and mirth,* Vol. 5, London, 1719, p. 217.

356 *n.* 1] Lockhart may be right. Scott
below, p. 394, uses the word 'Commie.'

357 (c) the spectre of Death] *Bible,
Revelation* 6: 8.

360 (c) To John Forbes Mitchell]
Mitchell's letter is not in NLS.

360 (c) monument to be erected at
Edinr.] See *Festival in commemoration of
Robert Burns, and to promote a subscription
to erect a national monument to his memory
at Edinburgh, held in London, June 5, 1819,*
8vo London, 1819.

360 (d) ten guineas if I recollect] £5.
See above, p. 334.

362 (b) Bishop of Grenada's homily]
See my note to *SL* iv. 403 (a).

364 (c) Bullock . . . advertises his
museum for sale] William Bullock's
museum in Piccadilly was sold, 29
Apr.–11 June 1819.

364 *n.* 1] The scarlet paper was hung
in the Dining Room in 1819 and was
still there during the lifetime of the late
Sir Walter Maxwell-Scott. There never
has been scarlet paper in the Drawing
Room. The Chinese wallpaper was hung
when the room was built and still
remains there. The curtains in the
Drawing Room were silk but the curtains in the Library were woollen.

365 *n.* 2] Mrs Shedden's letter is in
Partington, *Letter-books,* pp. 228–30.

366 (f) To Archibald Constable] In
Archibald Constable, iii. 125–6. Thomas
Constable, in his commentary (ibid.
iii. 127), implies that the subject of
dispute was *Tales of my Landlord,* Third
ser. The dispute was over *Novels and
tales,* 12 vols., 1820 [1819].

367 (b) as the man said to the queen of
France] This is a free translation of
what Calonne said to Marie Antoinette.
As the wording varies in different
reports it becomes practically certain
that Scott is quoting from Maria
Edgeworth's *Ormond* (1817) chap. 9,
where Corny uses the words almost
exactly as Scott does. Cf. another
possible quotation from *Ormond,* above,
p. 210.

368 (b) To John Ballantyne] Note that
date is 28 Apr. 1821. The correction
is made in the footnote but not on
p. 370.

368 *n.* 1] See my note to *SL* v. 366 (f).

370 (c) Campbell of Kailzie] Robert Nutter Campbell, 1761–1845, who acquired Kailzie in Peeblesshire in 1794.

370 (d) Pringle] John Pringle of Clifton and Haining. He was elected M.P. for Selkirk Burghs in 1819.

370 *n.* 1] Delete this note, which is inapplicable, the correct date of the letter being 1821.

372 (a) To Archibald Constable] In *Archibald Constable*, iii. 126–7, but Thomas Constable does not print his father's letter to which Scott is replying. The trouble arose over the printing of *Novels and tales.* See above, p. 366 and my note.

372 *n.* 1] For 'this year' read 'on 23 Apr.'

373 (c) To James Ballantyne] *Lockhart* (vi. 68–9) says it is written on an envelope containing a chapter of *The Bride of Lammermoor.* The implication is that Scott's letter relates to that novel. I think, however, that Scott is referring to *Novels and tales* (above, pp. 366–8, 372). As Scott has pledged his word (above, p. 367) that Ballantyne could undertake the work, he is now urging Ballantyne to get on with the job.

373 (d) my trust is constant in thee] Cf. *SL* vii. 43: 'As the king said to Mac-Donnell of the Isles, "My trust is constant in thee".' There is a tradition that Robert the Bruce said this at the Battle of Bannockburn. See Scott's note to *The Lord of the Isles*, Canto VI, st. xxviii.

373 *n.* 2] In line 2, delete '(1762).'

377 (b) young Walter] The 5th Duke, who had just succeeded to the title.

377 (c) Tulloch of Ellieston] Thomas Tulloh of Ellieston. See *SL* xi. 445 *n.*

378 (b) the Queensberry question] The Queensberry Case (q.v. in Index). See also above, p. 120 *n.*

378 (f) Tulloch] Tulloh.

379 (b) Mr Short] William Short.

379 (c) To John Ballantyne] Date is Sunday 9 May: (1) letter written after 5 May; (2) Scott would be in Edinburgh on Tuesday evening, 11 May, for opening of the Courts. The letter in NLS (MS. 863, ff. 269–70) has no address or PM, having presumably been enclosed in a cover which has been lost.

380 (b) To James Ballantyne] The date is almost certainly 10 May as Scott wrote on that day about the obituary of Duke of Buccleuch to Lord Montagu (p. 381). The main part of the letter refers to the dispute with Blackwood over the 5th ed. of first ser. of *Tales of my Landlord.*

381 (a) a few pages] Put index figure 1 here so as to refer to note 1 on p. 382.

382 *n.* 1] In lines 3–4 for '*Prose Miscellanies*, vol. iv' read '*The miscellaneous prose works* (1827) iv. 339–352.'

385 (d) our club] See *SL* i. 9 *n.* 1.

385 (d) poor Reston] David Douglas, Lord Reston, who died on 23 Apr.

385 (e) James Bruce perishd yesterday] The accident occurred on Friday, 21 May. Though the letter is dated 23 May, Scott may have begun it on 22 (making 'yesterday' correct). For an account of the catastrophe, see the *Edinburgh Evening Courant*, 24 May 1819, p. [3].

385 (e) Burnet] Burnett Bruce, younger brother of James. James was a naval officer and Burnett was an Advocate. The latter had died in 1813. They were sons of Robert Bruce, Lord Kennet.

386 *n.* 1] For 'Fergusson' read 'Ferguson.'

387 (a) remain in the family] The Marquess of Lothian married, as his second wife in 1806, Harriet, daughter of 3rd Duke of Buccleuch.

387 (b) W Thompson] This is Rev. George Thomson.

387 (c) To C. K. Sharpe] Date is Monday, 24 May 1819.

388 (b) *carmina cum melius*] For '*cum*' read '*tum.*' Virgil, *Eclogues*, ix. 67. (Correction in *SL* xii. 489.)

390 (a) The Farrier's Garland] The MS. of this, in Sophia's hand, is in NLS MS. 876, f. 30.

391 (c) in complying with his wishes] To be made Knight Marischal.

391 *n.* 2] For 'Dunnottar' read 'Edinburgh'. For 'probably his son' read 'his nephew.'

392 (a) To John Ballantyne] *Tales of my Landlord* was published on 10 June. In this letter Scott has nearly finished *The Bride of Lammermoor*, but he has still to write *A legend of Montrose*. The date is more likely to be Apr. than May or June.

392 *n.* 2] After 'published' insert 'along with *A legend of Montrose.*'

394 (b) the Commie] See above, p. 356, *n.* 1, where Grierson says Lockhart was wrong in printing 'Commie.'

394 (b) D. of G.] Read 'D. of Y.' [i.e. Duke of York]. (Corrected in *SL* xii. 489.) The MS. (Edin. Univ. Lib. La III 585, ff. 19–20) has 'D. of Y.'

394 (c) Iago's rule] Shakespeare, *Othello*, I. 3.

394 *n.* 3] From the context it is clear that Lockhart dates it 13 June. (*Lockhart*, vi. 85.)

396 (a) Mr. Bullock] William Bullock. For note on Bullock's sale, see *SL* v. 364 (c).

397 (a) the grasshopper being at present a burthen] *Bible, Ecclesiastes* 12: 5.

397 (a) *H. of M.L.* has done but so so] According to *White*, p. 236, Terry's play ran for only 15 nights, whereas Dibdin's version at the Surrey ran for 170 nights.

397 (d) To Abel Moysey] Date must be wrong. Scott did not go to Abbotsford till 16 June (above).

397 *n.* 1] For '*The Legend*' read '*A legend.*'

397 *n.* 2] For '1818' read 'issued in 10 parts, 1819–26.'

397 *n.* 3] See W. M. Parker's article, "*Forman*": *a forerunner of Scott's "Nigel*" in the *Scotsman*, 16 Apr. 1938, p. 13.

399 (b) Mr. Anderson] Samuel Anderson, partner in Sir William Forbes & Co.'s bank. See Index.

400 *n.* 2] Delete this note. Scott is referring to his pamphlet, *Description of the Regalia of Scotland*, Edinburgh, printed by James Ballantyne & Co.,1819. The article which he later wrote for *Provincial antiquities* was a different work.

401 (d) To John Murray] This letter is wrongly dated. In the first sentence Scott refers to his letter to John Ballantyne (below, pp. 427–8) which was written on Sunday, 25 July. Secondly, 3 July is impossible as Walter did not leave Abbotsford till 14 July. Date is probably 3 Aug.

404 (d) To John Ballantyne] This letter belongs to Dec. as reference to *Ivanhoe* shows. (Partially corrected in *SL* xii. 489.)

404 (e) so there is a plug fitted] This must be a misreading for 'so there is a play fitted.' (Shakespeare, *A midsummer night's dream*, I. 2.)

405 (b) you and Miss W. Clephane] Scott has omitted reference to Anna Jane, who also came. See below, p. 479.

405 *n.* 1] Lockhart's date is probably correct as Scott is writing after Walter left, and Walter left on 14 July.

407 (a) To Miss Millar] Margaret Millar had asked for this testimonial at the suggestion of Mrs Tovey of Stirling, as Miss Millar later explained to Sophia Lockhart in a letter of 7 Apr. 1837. (Private collection at Abbotsford.)

408 (f) Bohemia and its seven castles] Scott may be alluding to Corporal Trim's unfinished story, 'The story of the King of Bohemia and his seven castles' in Sterne's *Tristram Shandy*, Bk VIII, chap. 19.

408 *n.* 1] In line 3 and last line of note, for 'Hochmar' read 'Stockmar.'

411 (b) Mr. Stanley] Morritt's nephew, Edward Stanley of Cross Hall, Lancashire, married on 3 Sept. 1819 Lady Mary Maitland, 2nd daughter of 8th Earl of Lauderdale.

411 (b) grasshopper is a burthen] *Bible, Ecclesiastes* 12: 5.

411 (e) "prophet's chamber"] *Bible, II Kings* 4: 10.

411 *n.*] Delete four last lines. Fuller references are in Index.

412 *n.* 1] The building of the inn was completed this year, following the opening, in 1818, of the new road down the left bank of Gala Water. (Thomas Wilson, *The Stow of Wedale*, 1924, p. 192.) Hitherto Scott had gone to Abbotsford by the right bank.

413 (d) John . . . might go up with the cornet] By the time James Ballantyne had received this letter John had sailed to London on 10 July (above, p. 403 n. 1).

414 (c) To Robert Surtees] The letter was probably written in the second half of July. When Surtees and Raine were in Edinburgh, Raine went to the Theatre and heard Miss Stephens sing *Auld Robin Gray*. (Taylor, *Memoir of Robert Surtees*, p. 157 *n*.) It was announced in the *Edinburgh Evening Courant*, Thursday, 29 July, that Miss Stephens, who had been engaged for a few nights, would make her third appearance that evening. The *Scotsman* of Saturday, 31 July reported on performances since Saturday, 24 July, including Miss Stephens's singing of *Auld Robin Gray*. The Thursday, suggested for the visit to Abbotsford, would probably be Thursday, 5 Aug.

416 (a) Scenery] *Provincial antiquities*.

417 (d) Triphooks] Triphook issued Part 2 of *Catalogue of rare books* in the following month.

418 (b) Saint Boswells fair] The Fair was normally held on 18 July, but that being a Sunday this year it was held on Monday 19, the day that Scott is writing.

418 (f) To John Ballantyne] The date is Monday, 19 July. The half bank note sent with the letter was sent on Monday (below, p. 424). The letter, however, could not be posted before 21 July as Scott enclosed letters of 21 July to Walter (p. 418) of 20 July to Maria Edgeworth (p. 420) and of 21 July to Hartstonge (p. 421).

421 (b) *dignus vindice nodus*] Horace, *Ars poetica*, 191.

422 (d) "like a tether"] Burns, *The holy fair*, st. [24], line 8.

424 (a) I wrote you on Monday] 19 July. See above, p. 418.

424 (d) To James Ballantyne] This letter is now in NLS (MS. 2526, ff. 13–14). Folio 14 consists of the statement with a note 'I have just received your letter and one from John which alters the result of the foregoing statement.' The corrections follow.

426 (b) To John Ballantyne] In NLS

(MS. 863, ff. 299–300). The date of this letter, coming between two letters of 26 July, might be presumed to be of the same date; but John was in London on that day and the letter is obviously written to John in Edinburgh. The references to July and 'you out of town' suggest June or earlier for the date.

427 (b) To John Ballantyne] In NLS (MS. 863, ff. 277–8).

428 (c) To J. G. Lockhart] Date is 26 July which was a Monday.

428 n. 3] In line 5 from foot, for 'Miller' read 'Millar.'

430 n. 1] Add: lines 69–70.

430 n. 2] For 'Blacklock, the blind minister and poet' read 'Black' and for 'Fergusson' read 'Ferguson.' On Erskine, see *SL* xii. 489.

431 (c) *dignus vindice nodus*] Horace, *Ars poetica*, 191.

431 (e) To John Ballantyne] The references to Ricardo and Constable's loss (the latter not referring to Constable's mother) do not help to date the letter. It can be dated approximately July 1818: (1) by the reference to payment to Usher on 2nd., i.e. 2nd Aug. 1818 (above, p. 131); (2) Scott went to Drumlanrig in Aug. 1818 but not in 1819; (3) John Ballantyne was at London or Brighton in Aug. 1819, but the letter (NLS MS. 863, ff. 256–7) is addressed to Edinburgh.

431 n. 1] There is nothing in *Peter's letters* to link the description of his visit to Abbotsford with his visit of 10 Apr. 1819 when Scott was unwell. His description of the house, it may be noted, is extremely inaccurate.

432 (e) to *appropinque an end*] Butler, *Hudibras*, Pt I, Canto III, line 590. Read '*appropinque*.'

432 n. 1] Delete this note, which is not applicable. Scott's reference to Constable's loss is to a financial one and, in any case, Constable's mother did not die till 17 Aug., after this letter was written.

432 n. 2] The land was bought from Nicol Milne to give to Andrew Seton-Karr of Kippilaw.

433 (b) To Walter Scott] Date cannot be

1 Aug.: (1) Scott knew that Walter had to be at Cork by 1 Aug. and would not address a letter written on that day to London; (2) He received Murray's letter 'two days since' and Murray, in his letter to Lady Shelley of 30 July, says Scott must have received his letter 'some time since.' Date must be about 25 July.

434 (c) have written to Col: Murray] See above, p. 433 *n.* 3. The portion of that note beginning (line 5) 'In his letter' belongs to this reference, not to p. 433.

440 (a) proofs of scenery] Proofs of *Provincial antiquities*. No. 2 was published this month (Aug.). No. 3 did not appear till Mar. 1820.

443 (d) A New Novel] *The Monastery*.

446 (b) a letter from Mr. Freeling] Scott's letter to Freeling and Freeling's reply are not known to be extant. On 29 Oct. 1819 Freeling sent a reply (NLS MS. 3890, ff. 202–3) to a letter from Scott (not in *SL*) saying he knew nothing about the proposed road between London and Edinburgh, which seems strange in view of what Scott says in this letter.

446 (b) Rainie] John Rennie, civil engineer.

446 (b) Reedwater survey] For a new road to speed up the mailcoaches.

447 (a) To R. W. Elliston] Printed in the *New Monthly Mag.* 1837, Pt 3 (Vol. 51, Nov.), p. 328. Elliston's letter, to which this a reply, is printed, ibid., p. 328.

448 (c) The Newspaper] *Edinburgh Weekly Journal*.

448 (d) "Taxing man with visage grim"] *The duke and the taxing-man*, st. [3], line 1: 'The taxing-man, with grim viságe.' In *Poetry of the Anti-Jacobin*, 2nd ed., London, 1800, p. 32.

450 (e) the very moral] i.e. double. *OED* gives 1757, but Smollett, *Peregrine Pickle* (1751), chap. 13, uses the word in this sense. Also used in *The Bride of Lammermoor*, chap. 16.

450 *n.*] In the Edinburgh *Directory* for 1819/20 there are two of this name, both in Fowlis Close. J. P. Pierotti is given as a teacher of music and he may also have taught Italian.

452 (b) paragraph on the poor Duke of Buccleuch] i.e. a reprint in pamphlet form of Scott's obituary in the *Edinburgh Weekly Journal*. This was done, and Scott distributed copies (*SL* v. 472, vi. 249). Scott's copy is now in NLS (Abbot. 104 (1)).

454 (c) Blackwoods copies] i.e. of 4th ed. of *Tales of my Landlord*, first ser.

459 (a) Newspaper] The *Courier*.

460 (a) Your Pay Mr.] William Deane, Paymaster of 18th Hussars.

460 *n.* 2] Scott could not have written 'Laurence fair.' Instead of putting 'Probably' in this note the word should have been corrected in the text. The fair was held annually on 12 Aug.

461 (c) "poor wounded Hussa-a-r"] A nickname for Walter which Scott took from Thomas Campbell's *The wounded hussar*.

461 (e) Fleet Street] Should be Fleet Market.

462 (c) James Biggs] His letter of 3 Aug. is in NLS (MS. 866, ff. 234–7). He is soliciting subscriptions for three great-grandchildren of the Duke of Monmouth and Lady Henrietta Maria Wentworth, Baroness of Nettlestead. Their father, John Frederick Dalziel Smyth Stuart, had been run over by a carriage and killed.

462 (d) Messrs. Dowson] Emerson Dowson and John I. Hawkins had registered a patent for improved grates and stoves in 1816. (*Edin. Ann. Reg. for 1816*, IX. ii. cxcvii.)

462 (e) His R. Highness] Prince Leopold of the Belgians.

462 (f) pruning knife] See below, p. 499.

464 (a) a settlement for the newspaper] *Edinburgh Weekly Journal*.

466 (a) To Lord Sidmouth] This letter should be dated 1821: (1) The reference to the disbanding of the 18th Hussars belongs to 1821; (2) Scott is right in saying 'pleasant occasion' for he is referring to the King's state visit to Ireland in Aug. 1821 when Lord Sidmouth was in attendance as Home Secretary; (3) This is the letter which Scott sent to Walter on 21 Aug. 1821 (*SL* vii. 5).

466 n. 1] Delete reference to Manchester massacre, which is not now applicable. In second last line, for '1821' read 'Jan. 1822.'

467 n. 1] David Walker, farmer at Timpendean, had married, 30 Nov. 1815, Mary, daughter of Robert Hogarth, Carfrae, and sister of Mrs James Ballantyne.

469 n. 1] Scott is sending to Richardson a copy of the printed version, dated 1820 but printed in 1819.

471 (e) man of mould] Shakespeare, *Henry V*, III. 2: 'men of mould.'

472 n. 1] There is no need for the first part of this long note as Lady Louisa's letter is in *FL* ii. 48–50.

475 (c) "tis my occupation to be plain"] Shakespeare, *King Lear*, II. 2.

475 n. 1] This play was first acted at Covent Garden, London, 25 Feb. 1836.

476 (c) To Mrs. Clephane] Scott met Lord Montagu at Langholm on Wednesday, 25 Aug. (above, pp. 466–7, 470–1, 472). The letter must have been written on 24 Aug.

476 (f) Lady Grace and Mrs. Douglas] Lady Grace Douglas, dowager of Cavers, and her daughter-in-law, Mrs Douglas, wife of the new laird.

477 (e) To Mrs. Scott] Date is 28 Aug. which was a Saturday.

478 n. 1] Delete the whole note. Scott wrote to William Stewart Watson on 30 Nov. 1820 concerning his petition to the Duke of York. From this evidence it is almost certain that Scott is writing to his mother about him and that the Captain mentioned (p. 477) is W. S. Watson's uncle, Captain James Watson. Scott's letter to Watson, which is not in *SL*, is in *N. & Q.* Vol. 206 (Feb. 1961), p. 69.

479 (a) her two daughters and two other girls] Anna Jane and Williamina Clephane and the Misses MacAllister. See below, p. 483.

479 (d) To James Skene] From the contents the date seems to be 29 Aug.

479 (e) Lizars] He was engraving Skene's drawing of St Mary's Aisle, Dryburgh Abbey, for the *Memorials of the Haliburtons*.

480 (a) two, with themselves, are now in the grave] Lord Scott (died, 1808), Lady Katherine Frances Scott (died, 1814), the Duke (died, 1819) and the Duchess (died, 1814).

480 (b) Macleods] Read 'Maclean Clephanes.' (Correction in *SL* xii. 489.)

480 n. 1] Delete this note, which is no longer applicable. In any case, the Macleod who was at Abbotsford in 1819 was Col. George Francis Macleod.

481 (b) Your adjutant . . . is a foreigner] Henry Duperier.

482 (f) your two colonels] The Scottish one was Hon. Henry (afterwards Sir Henry) Murray. The other was Major Hay who had held brevet rank of Lt.-Col. since 1814. Scott calls Major Hay 'Colonel' in *SL* vi. 373, 437, 443.

484 (e) the Journal] In *Blackwood*, Vol. 5 (Sept. 1819) in the article *The tent*, p. 639, there is a discussion on James Ballantyne's criticism in the *Edinburgh Weekly Journal*: 'We were both sorry to observe, that the ingenious Editor of that paper was still quite on the wrong key about the Manchester affair . . .' Reference is then made to a reply in the *Journal* from L.T. which 'has already tickled him [James Ballantyne] pretty closely.' 'L.T.' probably stands for Laurence Templeton, the pseudonym adopted at this time by Scott for *Ivanhoe*. If so, Scott is the correspondent who has 'tickled' Ballantyne. The allusion to the *Journal* was probably by Lockhart, prompted by Scott.

485 n.] In lines 6–7, for 'John Ballantyne' read 'James Ballantyne.'

486 (e) Battle of Tranent] Caused by the passing of the Militia Act. The rioting occurred on 28 Aug. 1797. See the *Scots Mag.* Vol. 59 (Sept. 1797), pp. 704–5. At the trial on 11 Oct. Scott was counsel for Neil Redpath. Ibid., p. 778.

487 (c) too old a dog] Ray, p. 184. Also used, *SL* vi. 181.

488 (f) Mr. Bell] This may be John Bell, printer, Edinburgh, who married Jean Ballantyne, perhaps a relative of James. His widow died at Edinburgh 14 Sept. 1829.

489 (d) To Robert Johnston[e]] Delete '[e]'.

490 (a) at Mr. Allans] In 1820 William

Playfair designed a house for Alexander Allan, banker, who owned the lands of Hillside on the Calton Hill, Edinburgh. (The plans are in Edinburgh Univ. Lib.) The present Hillside Crescent is named after Allan's land.

490 (b) To Mrs. Scott] Date is Monday, 27 Sept., the day Chritty left Abbotsford (below, p. 498).

491 *n.* 1] The complete text of Wordsworth's letter has since been printed in *The letters of William and Dorothy Wordsworth: the middle years* . . . ed. by Ernest de Selincourt, Oxford, 1937, Vol. 2, pp. 915–16. 'Tax' in line 13 is given as 'tap.'

494 (c) I am farming] Read 'I am forming.'

495 (a) would not march through Coventry] Shakespeare, *I Henry IV*, IV. 2.

495 (b) sour plumbs] 'Sour plums' is the motto in Galashiels Coat of Arms, in allusion to a tradition that the Scots surprised and defeated a band of Englishmen while eating the wild plums of the district in 1337.

495 *n.* 2] And why not? Plumb was an old spelling, very common in literature before Scott's day.

496 (d) Mrs. Chisholm whose brother Col. Ellis] 'Ellis' should be 'Ellice.' Helena, sister of Edward Ellice, M.P. for Coventry (*DNB*) and Charles Ellice of the 6th (Enniskilling) Dragoons, married Charles Chisholme, natural son of William Chisholme of Chisholme (near Hawick). Col. Ellice would know Walter's regiment as the 6th and 18th Dragoons were both Irish regiments.

498 (e) about the wife] She was Mary Yellowlees whom Andrew Mercer had married in the West Kirk, Edinburgh, on 18 Aug. 1816.

499 (b) untill his girl comes of age] Isabella Mercer was born in 1817. She was afterwards Mrs George Rutherford, wife of the farmer at Sunnyside.

499 (c) Cappercleuch] Cappercleugh (or Black-Cock Cleugh) was on the Toftfield ground.

500 (b) very knife I wished for] But it was not a coincidence. Scott had asked John Ballantyne in London to get a knife and Ballantyne would tell Terry. Hence the gift. See above p. 462.

500 *n.* 1] On 25 Nov. 1819 Mary Goodfellow died at Broomielees, aged 64. From an examination of Melrose Parish Registers I have been unable to establish the relationship of William and Mary.

501 (a) [Lauchie] . . . his child being a minor] See my note to *SL* v. 499 (b).

503 (a–b) Scottish scenery] i.e. *Provincial antiquities*. There were two illustrations of Dunbar Castle in it. One was by Turner. The other was by Schetky, and his original oil painting for it is still at Abbotsford.

503 (e) To George Craig] Mr William Rutherford, owner of the letter in 1933, has since presented it to Selkirk Public Library.

503 *n.* 2] For 'Sharpe' read 'Sharp.'

504 (c) Buxton letter] Of 30 Sept., cited above, p. 495 *n.*

504 (d) in Roxburghshire] i.e. precautions against disturbances.

504 (e) proposed plantation] Chiefswood. See above, p. 303.

504 (e) Elliot from Goldielands] James Elliot, the Duke of Buccleuch's factor, was well known as a draughtsman.

504 *n.* 3] Delete this note, which is inapplicable. Scott is not referring to the Peel tower of Goldielands but to the farm of that name.

506 (d–e) *warnd* the waters] i.e. to have summoned his friends. A ballad expression; e.g. *Jamie Telfer*, st. 25, line 1: 'Gar warn the water, braid and wide.'

506 (e) young Clifton] John Pringle of Clifton and Haining. The Haining is an estate on outskirts of Selkirk.

506 (e–f) march them through Coventry] Shakespeare, *I Henry IV*, IV. 2.

507 (c) Lady Anne] Eldest daughter of 4th Duke of Buccleuch. She died unmarried 13 Aug. 1844.

507 *n.* 1] Delete. There is no connection between Powheid's 'muniments' (a Malapropism) and Scott's 'monuments' for Scott meant 'monuments.' There

were no muniments in the ruins of Jedburgh Abbey.

508 (a) Erskine] William Erskine whose wife had died on 20 Sept.

510 (a–b) Deadwater Heugh] See my note to *SL* iv. 268 (a).

510 (d) I have a letter from your Uncle Tom] Scott is writing this on 14 Oct.

but according to *SL* vi. 1 he did not receive Tom's letter till 15 Oct.

511 (d) Greentongue park] See *SL* iv. 324–5.

511 *n*. 1] Henry Francis Scott, eldest son of Hugh Scott of Harden, was admitted a Fellow Commoner of St. John's Coll., Cambridge, in 1818.

VOLUME VI

1 *n*. 1] Tom could not reply on 9 Nov. to a letter written on 16 Oct. For 'replies' read 'wrote.'

2 (c) to go up about Christmas] In a letter to George Craig (original at Abbotsford; but not in *SL*) Scott wrote on 4 Dec.: 'I must set out for London on 24th.'

2 (d) 1794 and 1795] Scott usually elsewhere cites 1793 and 1794. See Index under Politics, Domestic.

3 *n*. 1] Though *Lockhart* (vi. 138–41) is given as the source here, the source must be the original letter as the omitted portions, indicated by dots, show. There are no dots in *Lockhart*. Another omitted portion, which must also be from the original, is in *SL* vii. 410.

4 (c) To James Ballantyne] This letter should be dated 4 July 1819, the day Scott wrote to Constable (*SL* v. 402). (Date is corrected in *SL* xii. 489.)

4 *n*.] Reference to Lang's *Lockhart* should be i. 225.

5 (c) ornamented edition] *Novels and tales*, 12 vols., 1820 [1819]. See *SL* v. 366–7, 372.

5 (e) John Clarke] John Clerk, afterwards Lord Eldin.

6 (a) To John Ballantyne] Alexander's daughter (p. 7) was born on 4 Dec. Date of letter, therefore, is 5 Dec., which was a Sunday.

6 (c) cannot get out I[vanho]e till the next month] i.e. Jan. and the title-page has 1820. But the novel was published in Dec.

6 (e) will make two parts of three volumes each] i.e. *The Monastery* and *The Abbot* together in 4 vols. or separately in 3 vols. each.

7 (b) a Second part of I[vanho]e] This is a mistake for *Monastery*, the second part being *The Abbot*.

7 (f) Sandy . . . a girl] Christina Hogarth Ballantyne (1819–26).

8 *n*. 1] In lines 2–3, the reference to Lang's *Lockhart* is ambiguous. For 'see note on this letter from Lang's *Lockhart*, pp. 3–4' read 'See note above, pp. 3–4.' The Christie and Wilson are Jonathan Henry Christie and William Wilson of the Scott–Christie duel.

10 (a) To J. G. Lockhart] Scott had written about Murray's letter on Monday, 8 Nov. (above, pp. 8–9). On Tuesday he sends the letter. Date is, therefore, 9 Nov.

10 (c) best of all possible worlds] Voltaire. See my note to *SL* i. 186 (a–b).

10 *n*. 2] Delete and see above, p. 8 *n*. 1.

12 (c) Chuce & Chennery] This should be Chase & Chinnery. (*N. & Q.* Vol. 199, p. 213.)

14 *n*. 2] In line 1, for 'Musclie' read 'Muselee.'

15 (b) Eldon hall] Should be 'Eildon Hall.' Also on p. 14, *n*. 2.

15 (b) The Galashiels weavers] Cf. Scott's letter to Walter, 14 Oct. 1819 (*SL* v. 509–10).

15 (c) like Wallace and Bruce across the Carron] An apocryphal story. See Scott's note to Canto III, st. VIII of *The Lord of the Isles*.

15 *n*. 1] Delete this note which is obviously erroneous. The reverse is the case. The lines in *The doom of Devorgoil*, II. 1 (1830) and the lines quoted here and in *Rob Roy*, chap. 23, are all taken from *Jockey's escape from Dundee* of which there are versions in broadsides

and in D'Urfey's *Wit and mirth*, 4th ed. (1819), v. 17–19.

16 (d) Lady Anne] Lady Anne Scott, eldest daughter of 4th Duke of Buccleuch.

17 (f) Sally] Walter's horse.

19 *n.* 1] In line 4 from foot, for 'Mackerstoun' read 'Makerston.'

20 (c) To Washington Irving] The postscript in i. 366 of the work cited has been omitted in this transcript.

20 (c) when your letter reached Abbotsford] Irving's letter from London, 3 Nov., is in *Studies in Scottish Literature*, Vol. 3, No. 2, Oct. 1965, p. 116.

21 (a–b) "and for my love I pray you wrong me not"] Shakespeare, *Merchant of Venice*, I. 3.

21 *n.* 1] Scott did not preserve the 'three numbers of . . . the Sketch Book' (line 3).

23 *n.* 1] In line 15, for 'Short [?]' read 'Street.' In last line, for 'seven' read 'nine.'

24 *n.*] Scott is not referring either to Croxall or to Wagstaffe, but to the *Guardian* (as his text shows) in which Steele took the name of Nestor Ironside. Sparkler appears in No. 43, 30 Apr. 1713, but Scott's allusion is obscure.

25 (a) John Forbes] John Hay Forbes, afterwards Lord Medwyn. At this time he was Sheriff of Perth. See *Sir Walter Scott Quarterly*, p. 196.

26 *n.* 1] The Bishop of London (line 4 from foot) is William Howley.

27 (d) like Sir Andrew Aguecheek] Shakespeare, *Twelfth Night*, III. 4.

27 (d–e) "I like not such grinning honour . . ."] Shakespeare, *I Henry IV*, V. 3.

28 (a) beggars must not be chusers] See *SL* ii. 225.

28 *n.* 2] The author of the article on Pontefract Castle was W. M. Parker.

29 (c) no fool like an old fool] *Heywood*, p. 96; *Ray*, p. 140; *Kelly*, p. 256; Ramsay, *Proverbs*, p. 49. Also used *SL* x. 300.

31 (e) cannot make bricks without straw] *Bible, Exodus* 5.

33 (b) To James Ballantyne] The reference to Lord Grenville's speech, which was on 30 Nov., shows that this letter was written after that date, say 4–5 Dec., and it should be placed at p. 47.

34 (b) Lord Grenvilles excellent speech] In House of Lords, 30 Nov. 1819, opposing Lord Lansdowne's motion for the appointment of a Committee to inquire into the state of the country. See *Edin. Ann. Reg. for 1819*, XII. i. 235–7. It was published as a pamphlet, *Substance of the speech*, etc. For a Whig analysis of the speech, see *ER* Vol. 33, Jan. 1820, pp. 187–225.

35 (d) invention of Sheepface] Sheepface was a character in *The village lawyer*, a farce popular at this time and Scott again referred to him later (*MPW* xxi. 341). It was one of the parts played by Rayner at the Haymarket Theatre, London. I have not found the author of the farce.

36 (b) I have a vast mind to dream a vision] This became the *Visionary*.

36 *n.* 1] Lines 13–14.

36 *n.* 2] There is no justification for combining two letters. In any case, Carruthers gives the two paragraphs chronologically in reverse order.

37 (c) *Chambers's Journal*] N.S. Vol. 4 (2 Aug. 1845), p. 73.

39 (b) Charles XII] This half-length oil painting (50 × 41 in.) is in bad condition and is kept in a store at Abbotsford. A MS. at Abbotsford of about 1840 (when the picture still hung in the Dining Room) states that it was 'said to be from the Queensberry Collection.' In another Abbotsford MS. dated 1932 it is stated that it is a copy of the original by Lionel, Count de Dysart, at Marchmont House, believed to have been acquired by 2nd Lord Marchmont who was a diplomatist. For John Elliot Shortreed's account of the picture, see *Chambers's Jour.* 7th ser. Vol. 15 (7 Nov. 1925), p. 774.

39 (c) like the Barber of Bagdad] *The story told by the taylor* in *Story of the little Hunchback* in *The Arabian Nights* (Weber, *Tales of the East*, i. 133).

40 (b) "brogues and brochan and a' "] James Hogg, *Donald Macdonald*, st. [1],

line 9. In his *The mountain bard* (1807), p. 179.

40 (c) his weekly paper] *Edinburgh Weekly Journal*.

41 (c) a troop of cavalry] Lord Elcho's troop. See below, pp. 57, 79, 109, 234, 235.

43 (a) To J. W. Croker] Croker wrote on 29 Nov. (above, p. 23 *n*.) that he would send the prospectus. Scott here thanks him for it and sends *Visionary*, No. 1, printed 1 Dec. Letter is about 3 Dec. 1819.

44 (a) Lady Anne] Lady Anne Scott, eldest daughter of 4th Duke of Buccleuch.

44 (c) Charles XII] See my note to *SL* vi. 39 (b).

44 *n*. 2] Irving's letter of 20 Nov. is partly printed in *FL* ii. 60–1.

45 (d) *quart d'heure* de Rabelais] See *Petit Larousse illustré* under 'Quart.' Scott refers to Rabelais in *MPW* xvi. 205.

47 (d) Capt. Huxleys promotion] As brevet Major. He was still Capt. in 70th when he went on half-pay in 1826 with brevet rank of Colonel. (*Gentleman's Mag.* Vol. 96, Pt 1, p. 558.)

48 (a) Mr. Erskines debt] See *SL* vii. 479.

49 (d) Kinloch of Kinloch] His trial came on in High Court of Justiciary on 22 Dec. Having failed to appear, he was outlawed. See *Edin. Ann. Reg. for 1819*, XII. ii. 405–6.

49 *n*. 1] The 'earlier letter,' in line 3, is of 13 Dec. 1817, partly printed in *SL* v. 30–3. But 'the last sentences, omitted by Lockhart' (and also omitted by Grierson) are in *SL* vii. 497. Delete 'Scott would seem to have met or heard of the Colonel.' Scott had received a letter from Norton in 1816 when Norton was in Edinburgh (NLS MS. 3887, f. 102).

49 *n*. 2] Helen was his cousin once removed. Her grandmother was Cecilia Kinloch who married James Smyth of Balhary, John Smyth's father.

50 (a) doomd the long isles] Thomas Campbell, *The pleasures of hope*, Pt II, line 411.

50 (b) The event of this trial] See my note to *SL* vi. 49 (d).

50 (e) To Walter Scott] This letter should come at p. 60 as the P.S. is dated 18 Dec.

51 *n*. 2] The Misses Russell did not live at Ashiestiel, the house being let after the death of Col. William Russell.

52 (c–d) Much of her moderate income was spent in charity] John Howell in his *Life of Alexander Alexander* recorded: 'In this child of misery [Alexander Alexander] I recognised an old playfellow . . . Fortunately I knew one whose heart and hand were ever open to pity, and to relieve the unfortunate, —"Hallowed for ever be her memory!" Many partook of her bounty who never knew the source from whence it flowed. The proudest boast of my life is, that I had her confidence, and the honour to be one of her almoners. The excellent person to whom I allude was Mrs. Ann Scott, mother of the justly celebrated Sir Walter Scott. To her I applied in the poor soldier's behalf. Never shall I forget the angelic look of pity, and the tear that graced her venerable face, as I related the tale of woe. I made no request, I named no sum. Her purse was put into my hand: "John," she said, "take what you think he may require." Much as I knew of her goodness, I was so overpowered my heart was too full to thank her. He was clothed, nor was I allowed to say who was the generous donor. Many other deserving individuals she relieved through me, under the same restraint.' (Edinburgh, 1830, Vol. 1, pp. ii–iii.)

53 (a) loss of his eldest son] John, lost in *Earl of Abergavenny*, 5 Feb. 1805. See *SL* i. 239.

55 (e) *Inter arma silent Musæ*] A variation of 'Silent leges inter arma,' Cicero, *Pro Milone*, 4.

56 (a) the pleasant men of Teviotdale] *Chevy Chase*, st. [14], line 1. See my note to *SL* iii. 227 (c).

56 *n*. 1] Cockburn is a partial and unreliable witness and should not be cited.

58 (e) the other appears today] The three articles of *The visionary* appeared in the *Edinburgh Weekly Journal* for

Dec. 1, 8, 15. 'today' indicates that the first portion of this letter was written on 8 Dec.

58 (e) the fate of Kotz[e]bue] August Friederich Ferdinand von Kotzebue (1761–1819), German dramatist. He was a strong reactionist; and a fanatical youth, Karl Ludwig Sand, thinking it an act of patriotism, stabbed Kotzebue to death, 23 Mar. 1819. Hence Scott's allusion to what his own fate might be.

59 (a) Kinloch] See my note to *SL* vi. 49 (d).

60 (a–b) On tuesday the Doctor] This should be 'On Wednesday.'

60 (c) this morning] She died Saturday 18 Dec.

61 (d) Gala . . . Torwoodlee] John Scott of Gala and James Pringle of Torwoodlee.

62 (e) Lord Lothian] He was an invalid at this time. See Stuart, *Letters*, i. 35.

66 (c) Morrison] John Morrison, who was surveying the Abbotsford estate at this time.

66 (c) John Usher . . . or his son] John Usher (1776–1847) formerly of Toftfield and his son James. His only other son, John, was born in 1809 and was too young to be an ensign.

66 (e) The auld captain] Adam Ferguson. He is called this in *Lockhart*, v. 390.

66 n. 1] Nicol Milne did not become an Advocate till 1827.

67 (c) Tom Jamieson . . .] He was later gamekeeper to William Scrope. See C. S. M. Lockhart, *Centenary memorial*, p. 65; Gordon Waynes who married Elspeth Young in Morebattle. His niece, Elizabeth Young, knew Scott as a girl and died at Jedburgh, 11 Apr. 1915, aged 93. See *Border Mag.* Vol. 20, p. 132; Walter Dickson had been a ploughman in Cartleyhole and several children by his wife Edgar Hislop had been born there between 1799 and 1804. (Melrose Parish Registers.)

67 n. 1] John Scott, hosier in Hawick, was known as 'John the Turk' (*Hawick Arch. Soc. Trans.* 1915, p. 24). Scott's employee may have been a relative and

Lockhart's explanation may, therefore, be wrong.

68 (b) died yesterday morning] She died on 18 Dec. This is another example of a letter written in instalments.

68 (e) old Carey] Patrick Cary (1623?–85), author of *Trivial poems and triolets*, a copy of which Scott had presented to Surtees (SL v. 503).

70 n. 1] He was M.P. for Selkirkshire, 1806–30.

72 (b) On Tuesday] Should be 'On Wednesday.'

73 n. 2] Lockhart was wrong.

74 n. 1] This note is unnecessary. The discrepancies in dates can be accounted for by the fact that Scott wrote many letters in instalments.

75 (f) Kinloch] See my note to *SL* vi. 49 (d).

77 n. 1] The date of the letter does not affect Scott's statement that his mother died on Friday [i.e. 24 Dec.], which is correct. The letter was begun on 28 Dec. for he says (p. 78) that the funeral is 'tomorrow' and we know that his mother was buried on 29 Dec. The letter may not have been completed till some days after 28 Dec.

79 (b) the Turk Darnick Tommie [?]] John Scott called 'the Turk' and probably Tom Jamieson.

79 (c) March in good order] These exact lines are not in *General Lesly's march to Longmarston Moor* (in Ramsay's *Tea-table miscellany*). Scott is evidently quoting his own song in *The Monastery*, chap. 25. The two lines correspond to st. [2], line 7 and st. [1], line 4 respectively.

80 (a) a set of my works] *Poetical works*, 12 vols., 12mo Edinburgh, 1820. (*Ruff*, No. 160.) Though dated 1820 they were available in 1819.

80 (c) Henzie [?]] Hinse, or Hinzie, Scott's cat.

81 (a) If they are] Read 'If there are.'

81 (b) To Lord Melville] On the same day Scott wrote two letters which are not in *SL*: (1) to John Scott of Gala (*Scotsman*, 23 Dec. 1907, p. 9, c. 2); (2) to Lord Lothian (*N. & Q*. Vol. 209 (Nov. 1964), pp. 413–14).

82 (f) Dr. Rutherford] Scott's uncle Dr Daniel Rutherford married Harriet Mitchelson, daughter of John Mitchelson of Middleton, Advocate, and sister of Isabella Mitchelson who married Robert Hepburn of Clerkington.

83 n. 2] Mrs Swinton was Margaret, 2nd daughter. Her husband, John Swinton (judge as Lord Swinton), died in 1799 and she died in 1812.

85 (a) I inclose a copy . . . new modelld] See above, p. 64 n.

86 (c) To Dr. Kerr] William Kerr.

87 (b) *Hawick Arch. Soc.*] *Trans.* 1921.

87 n. 1] Delete 'Probably.' Scott said they were related. See *SL* viii. 222.

89 (a) Allans rafle] See *SL* v. 349.

89 (c) Sierra Morena] See my note to *SL* ii. 542 (c).

89 (f) admirable flapper] Swift. See my note to *SL* ii. 213 (c).

90 (b) *Thursday*] Thursday was 8 Apr.

90 n. 1] Dick's letter of 23 Aug. is partly printed in *FL* ii. 53–5.

91 n.] In lines 6–7, Colonel Harris is William George Harris who succeeded as 2nd Baron Harris in 1829.

92 (d) To John Ballantyne] Cancel. The letter is printed in full in *SL* i. 528–9.

93 (f) youngest daughter] Anne Rutherford.

95 (b–c) I certainly think Longman] Longman published her *Metrical legends of exalted characters* in 1821. It consisted of *William Wallace*; *Christopher Columbus*; *Lady Griseld Baillie*; and four ballads.

95 n. 1] There is an extract from her letter of 12 Nov. in Partington, *Post-bag*, pp. 138–9. Partington's comment requires to be corrected.

96 (b) "War has broke in on the peace of auld men,"] Susanna Blamire, *The veterans*, st. [1], line 1. In R. A. Smith, *The Scotish minstrel*, Vol. 5, Edinburgh, n.d. [*c.* 1823], p. 24.

97 (a) send them under Crokers frank] See below, p. 107.

97 (d) To H. M. Buchanan] The date is about Dec. 1820. Buchanan passed

on Scott's request to Charles Clark of Cupar Angus, who passed it on to John Halkett. In NLS there is a letter from Halkett to Clark, 25 Jan. 1821, on this subject (MS. 3892, ff. 19–20). By the time Scott received it, it was too late for his ed. and he endorsed it: 'Information for Francks Northern Memoirs —came too late.' Scott edited Franck for the benefit of George Huntly Gordon. See Scott's letter of 27 Aug. 1829 to Burn, bookseller, London, in the *Athenæum*, 1832, p. 666 (not in *SL*).

97 n. 3] Scott probably sent proofs of his own edition.

99 (a) Dogberry] See *SL* ii. 320.

106 (a) Edinburgh papers] These are the *Edinburgh Evening Courant*, the *Caledonian Mercury*, the *Edinburgh Advertiser*, the *Edinburgh Correspondent*, the *Edinburgh Weekly Journal* and the *Scotsman*.

107 (a) packet for Mrs. Joanna Baillie] See above, p. 97.

107 (e) new burial ground] For a plan of this, see C. S. M. Lockhart, *Centenary memorial*, facing p. 51.

110 (b) Commodore Trunnion] Trunnion, in Smollett's *Peregrine Pickle*, uses the word 'thof' (a very common 18th-cent. word) several times but he nowhere says 'thof unknown.' The nearest source is *Roderick Random*, chap. 41, where Bowling says 'tho'f I know him not.'

110 notes] There should be three notes. Add index figures 2–3 to refer to Williams and MacCulloch respectively. When renumbered amend as follows:

1. Colonel Norton. See Index.

2. H. W. Williams, *Travels in Italy, Greece and the Ionian Islands* [1816–17], 2 vols., Edinburgh, 1820.

3. John Macculloch, *A description* [. . . as in *SL*]. This and the preceding work were published by Constable.

111 (e) disease] Read 'decease.'

112 (a–b) 12 or 13 children] She had thirteen. See my note to *SL* iv. 232 n. 2.

112 (b) actions of charity] See my note to *SL* vi. 52 (c–d).

113 (c) Walter the Devil] See my note to *SL* iii. 79.

113 (d) Cock up your bonnet] *Cock up your beaver*, lines 7–8. In *Herd*, ii. 205.

113 (f) Dr. Kerr] William Kerr, physician at Manchester. See above, p. 86.

115 (d) To Lady Louisa] After 19 Jan. Elizabeth Jane Russell (p. 117) died on 19 Jan.

115 *n.* 1] Lockhart does not definitely assign the letter to Dec. He says it is undated but evidently written when the events (death of Scott's relatives) 'were fresh and recent.' His running title 'December 1819' is misleading. (*Lockhart*, vi. 169.)

116 (a) giddy-paced time] Shakespeare, *Twelfth Night*, II. 4.

117 (b) fellow of little mark or likelihood] Shakespeare, *I Henry IV*, III. 2.

117 (d) of whom only one now survives] James (later Sir James) Russell of Ashiestiel, 1781–1859.

117 (d) three daughters] Jane Boston Russell (1778–1849), Anne Russell (1780–1849) and Elizabeth Jane Russell (1791–1819).

117 (d) was in summer so much shocked] This implies the summer of 1819. But it was in the autumn of 1818 that the news came of Alexander Pringle Russell's death. See *SL* v. 191 and my note there.

119 (c) in well-chosen charities] See my note to *SL* vi. 52 (c–d).

120 (e) Catherine] Sophia's maid. See below, pp. 387, 390.

120 (f) a double columnd Shakespeare] *The plays of Shakespeare. Printed from the text of Samuel Johnson, George Steevens, and Isaac Reed*, 2 vols., 8vo London, Printed for Hurst, Robinson, & Co., Edinburgh; By James Ballantyne & Co., Edinburgh, 1819. I do not know why Scott should call it John Ballantyne's. His name is not mentioned. Scott had suggested a Shakespeare in 1810 (*SL* i. 413) and I thought that sheets printed about that time might have been used for this ed. of 1819 but I find the watermarks (there are very few) are 1817 and 1818.

120 (f) situation to the 10th] 10th Hussars who were or had been stationed at Piershill Barracks, Edinburgh. See above, p. 41. Christie is John Christie.

121 (e) Margaret Macdonald] i.e. Margaret Macdonald Buchanan. 'Mr. Price' is Rose Lambart Price. She did not marry him. I do not know who the vinegar manufacturer is.

126 (d) Egerstane, Gala and young Whitebank] John Rutherford of Egerston, John Scott of Gala and Alexander Pringle, Younger of Whytbank. Whytbank is pronounced 'Whitebank' so that Scott here (as elsewhere) is spelling phonetically.

127 (a) their brother] Sir James Russell of Ashiestiel (1781–1859).

127 (c) To William Laidlaw] As Scott had sent £60 on 19 Jan. (above, p. 122) it is unlikely that he would be sending £50 on 25 Jan. In each case the basic sum is £50. The reference to Maida suggests that this letter is much earlier. Laidlaw would know the habits of Maida long before Jan. 1820.

128 (a) without an introduction] Scott has forgotten that he had told Dick that he was sending the volumes. See above, p. 92.

131 (b) To George Craig] The original MS. with others were presented by Mr Archibald Rutherford to Mrs Maxwell-Scott of Abbotsford, 14 Oct. 1970. In line 3, for 'subjoined draw' read 'subjoin drat' [contraction for 'draft'] The letter was written on 3 Feb. and has PM 4 Feb. The bill was accepted on 3 Aug. 1819 and became due on 3/6 Feb. 1820.

131 (c) Sanderson & Paterson] Builders, Galashiels. They built the first portion of Abbotsford, 1817–19 and this letter relates to a part payment.

131 (d) To Charles Erskine] 6 Feb. was a Sunday. Erskine's dating, therefore, is wrong. Scott went to Abbotsford on 4 Feb. and could have given Erskine the Haliburton MS. then. It also seems a long time for Scott to learn of the Selkirk incident of 31 Dec. The letter probably belongs to early Jan.

131 *n.* 1] Delete this note, which is now unnecessary.

131 *n.* 2] This note is misleading. Scott sent the original MS. to Erskine. Curle owned a copy of the printed version.

132 (a) Mrs. Rutherford . . . Samuel Russell] Catherine Russell, wife of Dr John Rutherford of Middlehall. Her brother Samuel Russell was a watchmaker in Selkirk.

132 (c) Laird of Harden's resurrection] There was apparently a rumour that Scott of Harden, who had earlier represented Berwickshire, would stand again for the new Parliament, but he declined (below, p. 137).

132 (d) To A. B.] *Alfred* has a printed dedication to 'Sir Walter Scott.' It must have come out after 1 Mar. and Scott could not be thanking the author on 5 Feb. The year must be 1821. Except for the first paragraph, this letter was printed in Allan's *Life of Scott*, p. 260. By the time this part of the *Life* had been reached Allan had taken over from William Weir. Allan gives the date correctly as 1821. How did Allan get the letter? From a friend, or was Allan the author of *Alfred*? *Alfred* has an Edinburgh imprint but there is no printer's name.

132 (f) revisal] Should not this be 're-viewal'?

133 (b) weightier matters of the law] *Bible, Matthew* 23: 23.

133 (e) Monteaths seat] Henry Monteith of Carstairs was elected M.P. for Selkirk Burghs.

136 (a) *locus delicti*] The place where the crime was committed. A Scots law phrase. See Trayner, *Latin maxims.*

136 (d) the Knight of the Mirrors] Cervantes, *Don Quixote*, Pt II, chap. 14 (Lockhart's ed., 1822, iii. 263).

138 (b) his own grandfather] Gustavus III, assassinated in 1792.

138 (e) take a fools word for it as Sancho says] Cervantes, *Don Quixote*, Pt I, Bk IV, chap. 4. (Lockhart's ed., 1822, ii. 122–3.)

139 *n.* 2] In line 2, delete 'and attended him in his last illness.'

140 (a) has gaind his lawsuit] Queensberry Case (q.v. in Index). See also *SL* v. 120 *n.*

140 (d) Merry doings in London] Cato Street conspiracy led by Arthur Thistlewood.

140 *n.* 1] For 'Act I, sc. 2' read 'Act II, sc. 1.'

142 (a) Lamb] William Lamb, seedsman in Selkirk. See Index.

142 (a) *Hawick Arch. Soc.*] *Trans.* 1921.

142 (b) To Washington Irving] The text, from which this letter is printed, is obviously incomplete and the '*Unsigned*' at the end is, therefore, without justification.

143 (c) "Your name is up . . ."] See my note to *SL* i. 380 (c).

143 (d) Dinarzades . . . Scheherezade] In the *Arabian Nights.*

144 (b) Sister Pegg] Adam Ferguson, *History of the proceedings in the case of Margaret, commonly called Peg, only lawful sister to John Bull, Esq.*, 12mo London, 1761. The work was anonymous. The allegory is based on Arbuthnot's *Law is a bottomless pit; or, the history of John Bull.* Mackenzie printed the letter, written to Dr Carlyle and dated 3 Feb. 1761, in which Hume owned (jocularly) that he wrote it, in *The life and works of John Home*, i. 155–6.

144 (e) as he glided from the stage] This is a reminiscence of Robert Morehead's line, 'Home's pale ghost slow gliding from the stage.' *Epistle first*, line 202, in *Poetical epistles*, 1813, p. 14.

145 (b) Siddons] His novels published by the Minerva Press were : *Leon* (1791), *Somerset* (1792) and *Reginald de Torby* (1803). No work called *The mysterious bridal* was published by Lane. In the previous year Scott had told the same anecdote to James Ballantyne but gave the name of the novel as *The mysterious warning.* The letter is not in *SL* but there is a transcript in NLS (MS. 6080).

145 (f) the Fair Unknown] I cannot explain this. Rose's letter is not in NLS.

146 (c) out of all cess] Shakespeare, *I Henry IV*, II. 1.

146 (e) Marchmont estate] Polwarth peerage case.

147 (d) Lord Lauderdales Boroughs] Jedburgh Burghs returned one member to Parliament. The burghs were Jedburgh, Haddington, Lauder, Dunbar and North Berwick. Dudley Long

North (1748–1829), a prominent Whig, was M.P. 1818–20.

147 (d) since the trees walkd forth to chuse a King] *Bible, Judges* 9: 8–15.

147 (e) Drummond . . . Dalrymple] Sir Hew Hamilton Dalrymple (or Sir Hew Dalrymple Hamilton) was elected. Henry Home Drummond of Blair Drummond became M.P. for Stirlingshire in 1821.

149 (c) To Archibald Constable] Tuesday was 14 Mar., but, in any case, Scott was at Abbotsford by that time. He first announced Sophia's engagement on 17 Jan. and 'a fortnight' (p. 150) after that brings us to Tuesday, 1 Feb., which is probably the date of the letter.

151 (a) "Burned bairns dread the fire"] *Heywood*, p. 94; *Ray*, p. 106; Ramsay, *Proverbs*, p. 13.

151 *n.* 1] There should be no dots between '*romantic*' and '*Translated*' and the imprint is: William Blackwood, Edinburgh, and T. Cadell, London, 1823.

151 *n.* 2] In order to make the statement correct delete 'married' in second line.

152 (a) some of the Ross-shire lairds] The tenants of Monro of Novar resisted eviction from the estate of Culrain. See *Edin. Ann. Reg. for 1820*, XIII. ii. 316–18.

153 (c) Israelites went to Philistia] A free paraphrase of *Bible, I Samuel* 13: 20.

153 (e) To Mrs. Scott] Correct date is Monday, 19 Mar. 1821. Mrs Carpenter had not arrived from India by Mar. 1820 and the references to her health relate to Mar. 1821. See, for example, below, pp. 380–1.

154 (e) Chief Baron] Sir Samuel Shepherd.

158 (f) the judge is own sister . . .] Hunt was tried by Mr Justice Bayley. *The unfortunate Miss Bailey* is a song by George Colman, the Younger, in *Love laughs at locksmiths*, Act II. Scott's allusion is obscure.

159 (b) 3 months days] 'months' should presumably be deleted.

159 (d) "They let them care that come

ahint"] 'Let them care that come behind.' Ramsay, *Proverbs*, p. 44.

159 *n.* 1] Delete the last sentence. The Miss Baillie of the song has nothing to do with Joanna Baillie. See my note to *SL* vi. 158 (f).

160 (b) Sir Francis] Sir Francis Burdett.

161 (b) To Charles Scott] Date is Wednesday, 12 Apr. 1820.

161 (c) Walter and I go to Woolwich tomorrow] According to date of letter this would be Wednesday, but Croker reported that the visit was on Thursday, 13 Apr. (*N. & Q*. Vol. 185, 11 Sept. 1943, p. 156). Scott's reference to the Admiralty Barge shows that this visit was with Croker. Scott gives the day correctly as Thursday below, p. 167.

162 (a) To Lady Abercorn] This letter is probably Thursday, 23 Mar.

163 (d) leave off sack] Shakespeare, *I Henry IV*, V. 4.

163 (e) Sir Terry O'Fay] The note is on p. 164.

163 *n.* 1] In lines 1 and 8, 'Johnstone' should be 'Johnston.'

164 *n.*] The anecdote of the knighting 'by an Irish lord-lieutenant in some convivial frolic' was current at the time and was no doubt known to Maria Edgeworth. See my note to *SL* x. 2 (d). In line 8, for 'chap. 17' read 'chap. 2.'

167 (b) Sir William Scott's son] William Scott, son of Sir William who became Lord Stowell in 1821.

167 (c–d) To Lady Abercorn] Date is 15 Apr. Scott was going to Ditton on the following day, Sunday, 16 Apr. (below, p. 174).

169 (a) Lockharts translations] His translations of Spanish ballads in *Blackwood*, subsequently published as *Ancient Spanish ballads*.

169 *n.* 2] There is no need for this note when we remember that Scott wrote letters in instalments. He wrote this one on 2 and 3 and concluded it on 4 Apr.

172 (c) To Rev. H. H. Milman] The correct date of letter is 6 Apr. 1821. Milman's *The fall of Jerusalem* was presented in Mar. 1821.

173 (c) To Hector Macdonald Buchanan] There is no letter from him in NLS that Scott might be answering and Buchanan's reply of 3 May (NLS MS. 3891, ff. 49–50) makes no reference to Stonefield's protégé. Stonefield is presumably John Campbell of Stonefield. Hector Macdonald Buchanan, a Cornet in the Madras Cavalry, was already dead. He died at Bombay on 22 Oct. 1819 but the news had not yet reached Britain.

174 (a) drawing three souls] Shakespeare, *Twelfth Night*, II. 3.

174 *n.* 1] Surely a comma was unnecessary!

174 *n.* 2] There is an extract from Buchanan's letter in Partington, *Postbag*, p. 141, which deals with the Radical disturbances.

175 (b) To John Wilson] A letter from Wilson of 17 Apr., which crossed Scott's, is in Symington, *Some unpublished letters*, pp. 88–9.

175 (c) Dugald Stuart] Professor Dugald Stewart objected to Scott's poem on Lord Melville's acquittal.

175 *n.* 1] Blair (last line) is not mentioned in *SL*. Grierson is probably referring to *Christopher North*, by Elsie Swann, Edinburgh, 1934. She was a student of Grierson's at this time, and Blair takes a prominent place in her thesis.

176 (a–b) what Tony Lumpkin calls] See my note to *SL* i. 524 (a).

176 (c) he has more wit in his anger] Ramsay, *Proverbs*, p. 59. Also used in *The Heart of Mid-Lothian*, chap. 24 and *Nigel*, chap. 23. The meaning is made clearer in the form used in *The Bride of Lammermoor*, chap. 7: 'have more reason in your wrath.'

177 (a) "on and awa' "] There can be little doubt that Scott is thinking of *O Kenmure's on and awa, Willie*. (*Johnson*, Vol. 4 (1792), No. 359.)

179 (c) no grass grow under my feet] Ramsay, *Proverbs*, p. 24: 'He'll no let Grass grow at his Heels.'

179 (e–f) To Lord Montagu] Date is Sunday, 23 Apr.

180 (a) I inclose Lady H's Po.] See below, p. 449, where Scott seems to

imply that the verses were written by Theodore Hook.

180 (a) To you Sir and your honour I bequeath her] Otway, *Venice preserved*. See *SL* ii. 334 (e).

180 (b) Lady Hume] Scott's phonetic spelling. She was Elizabeth Scott, 2nd daughter of 3rd Duke of Buccleuch and wife of 10th Earl of Home.

180 (b) Duchesses pew] Dowager Duchess of Buccleuch (the only Duchess at the time). She lived at Richmond.

181 (a) To Hay Donaldson] Date is 28 Apr. Scott arrived in Edinburgh on evening of 27 and wedding was on 29.

181 (b) these Burghs] Jedburgh Burghs. See my note to *SL* vi. 147 (d).

181 (b) too old a dog to learn new tricks] *Ray*, p. 184. Also used, *SL* v. 487.

181 (c) To Sir James Russell] This letter cannot be addressed to James Russell who did not return from India till 1825. It must be addressed to James Scott, son of Scott's uncle Thomas Scott (1731–1823) who resided at Monklaw. James Scott had a sister Anne, mentioned at the end of the letter.

181 *n.* 1] Delete this note, no longer applicable.

183 (b) "Ah me! the flower and blossom . . ."] Joanna Baillie, *The family legend*, IV. 1. Also used as motto to chap. 12 of *Kenilworth*.

184 (a) Prince Oscar] He became King of Sweden and Norway as Oscar I in 1844. His father, Charles XIV, supplanted Prince Gustavus's father. Hence Scott's remark.

186 (d) old Duke of Q.] William Douglas, 4th Duke of Queensberry (1724–1810), known as 'Old Q.'

186 (d) Mrs. Scott] Lady Scott, surely!

186 *n.* 1] Lockhart's father's first wife was Elizabeth Dinwiddie of Germiston. Delete last sentence. On the three first occasions that Scott writes the name he spells it Jermiston; thereafter (six times) he spells it Germiston. 'Jermiston' was an older spelling of the name.

187 (a) your very attentive letter] Not in NLS.

187 n. 1] For 'William Park' read 'Archibald Park.'

189 (e) James IId. . . . in his own Memoirs] *Life of James II, collected out of memoirs writ by his own hand. Published by J. S. Clarke*, 2 vols., 4to London, 1816. For a discussion of James's Memoirs, see *ER* Vol. 26 (June 1816), pp. 402–30.

189 n. 1] In 1819 Padua struck a gold medal to commemorate his discoveries. In 1821 Belzoni sent two examples to Scott, one for himself and one for the University of Edinburgh. The letter, dated 6 June 1821, accompanying the gift, is in NLS (MS. 3892, ff. 153–4). I have not found the medal at Abbotsford.

194 (a) Wight . . . two bills] James Wight from whom Scott bought Broomielees. On 29 May Scott drew on James Ballantyne to Charles Erskine's order for £360. (Scott's letter to Ballantyne of that date; not in *SL* but there is a transcript in NLS MS. 6080.) The second, for £233. 6s. 9d., was paid by Craig. (Letter to Craig, 28 Aug. 1820, the original of which is at Abbotsford but is not in *SL*.)

195 (e) a beautiful seal] This amethyst seal, engraved 'Walter Scott—Gustaf 1820', was sold at Christie's, London, 21 July 1930, for twenty-five guineas.

196 (a) land adjoining to the Burnfoot cottage] Shearingflatts, bought from John Heiton, carpenter and builder in Edinburgh. See below, p. 209.

196 (e) To James Ballantyne] From the contents this letter should be dated 18 June. This letter and the letter to John, below, p. 210, were written in Edinburgh in the morning before the family set off for Abbotsford.

196 n. 1] The first mention of Chiefswood Cottage but not of Chiefswood.

198 (c) Dogberry] See *SL* ii. 320.

198 n.] In line 16, delete 'one.' James Barclay was his cousin.

198 n. 1] i.e. *Edinburgh Weekly Journal*.

200 (b) Lady C.] Lady Conyngham, mistress of Prince Regent. See *SL* i.

327 n. 1. She was known as the Vice-Queen.

200 (c–d) Burnet . . . Nell Gwyn . . . decencies of a mistress] Scott used this passage in *Peveril*, chap. 31. The King said to the Duke of Buckingham: 'It is harder that a wench's bright eyes can make a nobleman forget the decencies due to his Sovereign's privacy.' 'May I presume to ask your Majesty what decencies are those?' said the Duke.

201 (a–b) Prince Oscar] See my note to *SL* vi. 184 (a).

201 (b) new edition of the books] *Novels and tales*, 12 vols., 1820 [1819]. See my note to *SL* vi. 252 (a).

201 n. 2] There is nothing in the play corresponding to 'solitary stupidity.'

201 n. 3] For 'youngest sister' read 'youngest half-sister.'

202 (a) Lithgow] Linlithgow.

202 (a) the Silver vase] See above, p. 180.

202 (e) Mr. Reader] William Reader. Abraham Thornton was tried and acquitted for the murder of Mary Ashford in 1817. Her brother, William Ashford, dissatisfied with the verdict, raised an action against Thornton who, in the Court of King's Bench, threw down a glove and challenged Ashford to trial by combat. See *Edin. Ann. Reg.* X. ii. App. 174. Reader was a counsel at the original trial but I have not found that he was author of any of the works on trial by combat which were subsequently published. A play called *The mysterious murder; or, what's the clock?* was based on this murder and was published at Birmingham in 1817. The suggestion that Reader was to appear as Royal Champion must have been a joke for the office was hereditary and at the Coronation Henry Dymoke, acting for his father the Rev. Henry Dymoke of Scrivelsby, appeared as the Royal Champion.

202 (e) hard case for any impugner] This follows the argument of Beau Tibbs in Goldsmith's *Citizen of the world*, Letter 104.

203 (a) a flaming letter] Not in NLS.

203 (b) Droits] I cannot explain the reference to 'draining the canal,' but

the reference to the 'Droits' relates to the recent debates in the House of Commons on the 'Droits of the Admiralty.' See *Edin. Ann. Reg.* XIII. i. 44–52.

203 (e) Mr. H. Warrender] Hugh Warrender, W.S., died on 8 June.

208 (c) To G. H. Gordon] This letter bears such a strong resemblance to the letter in *SL* v. 202 that one wonders if Lockhart has done some manipulation.

208 (f) Milligan] This is Richard Milliken, bookseller in Dublin.

209 (b) Tomorrow I go there with Mr and Mrs. John Prevôt] John Smith, in his diary, says he met Scott alone on 19 June and Scott, Lady Scott and Mr and Mrs Lockhart on 20 June. The entries in his diary for 17–21 June deal with planning and preparing estimates for the cottage. He submitted a very detailed estimate on 23 June.

209 (c) Heitons grounds] Shearingflatts, which Scott bought from John Heiton. See above, p. 196.

209 (e) Commission of Oyer and Terminer . . . a temporary court] By the Treaty of Union, 1707, the English law of treason was made law for the whole of Britain. There had been no treason trials in Scotland since 1707 (those of Watt and Downie in 1794 related to sedition) so that a special court had to be set up in Scotland in 1820. See *Edin. Ann. Reg. for 1820*, XIII. ii. 187–8.

209 n. 1] In line 3, '1796' should be '1794.'

210 (d) To John Ballantyne] See above, p. 197, n. 2.

210 (d) Doctor Baillies report] In the following month Lockhart referred to this in his *Testimonium*, st. xlviii: "Twas said, some weeks ago, that Ballantyne / Hop off in some affection iliac would, / But, thanks to Dr Baillie's skill and mine, / John's now quite well—though not so stout as Blackwood.' (*Blackwood*, Vol. 7 (July 1820), p. vii.)

211 (c) Mons. Porçeaûgnac] Molière, *Monsieur de Pourceaugnac*, I. 11. Not an exact quotation.

212 (e) to—Rutherford] Jean Rutherford, who died at Jedburgh, 2 Feb. 1824.

212 (e) one poor fellow was blown up in the Queen] See my note to *SL* i. 106 (e).

213 (d) Moffat] James Mackcoull, alias Moffat, was tried on 12 June. See *Edin. Ann. Reg. for 1820*, XIII. ii. 279–87. Scott referred to him in the 'Introductory Epistle' to *Nigel*.

216 (d) Hays or the Brawl] The hay and branle are dances. Scott uses the form 'branle' in *The Abbot*, chap. 31, and 'bransle' in *Anne of Geierstein*, chap. 31.

217 (c) To Lady Abercorn] Scott is answering her letter of 10 June (NLS MS. 867, ff. 23–6) in which she writes of the Queen and of her own intention to go abroad. The part relating to the Queen is in Partington, *Post-bag*, p. 140, and supplements the portion quoted above, p. 200 n. 1.

218 (a–b) "Long may she live to disgrace her husband"] See below, p. 237 and my note.

222 (d) parodies upon Scripture . . .] In *Hypocrisy unveiled* (1818) the anonymous author [James Grahame] wrote (p. 46 n.): 'The Leopard entertains the *Dilletanti Society* with imitations of preachers of the gospel, and *obscene parodies on the Psalms.*'

223 (f) [*circa* 19 *July* 1820]] Delete. The date is at end of letter—Wednesday, which was 19 July.

224 n. 2] Delete and see *SL* iv. 415.

225 (c) Rome of Augustus] Suetonius, *Lives of the Caesars*, Bk II, chap. 29.

225 (d) go through the night air] i.e. from the cottage to his bedroom in the 'chapel' in the kitchen courtyard.

225 (e) Sangrados] Sangrado is a character in Le Sage, *Gil Blas*. See my note to *SL* v. 90 (c).

226 (c) good accounts of Walter] A complete extract from Brisbane's letter is given above, p. 213 n. It will be seen that Scott embellishes the report.

226 n. 2] Read '*Every Man in his humour.*' (Corrected in *SL* xii. 490.)

227 (b–c) as Sancho did on the cowheel] Cervantes, *Don Quixote*, Pt II, chap. 59 (Lockhart's ed., 1822, v. 177).

227 (b–c) geese are all swans] *Ray,* p. 246; *Kelly,* p. 8; Ramsay, *Proverbs,* p. 31. Also used in *St Ronan's Well,* chap. 7.

230 (d) the harvest is small and the labourers numerous] *Bible, Matthew* 9: 37: 'The harvest truly is plenteous, but the labourers are few'; *Luke* 10: 2.

230 *n.*] In line 1, 1820 should be 1821.

231 (b) a sword into a pruning-hook] *Bible, Isaiah* 2: 4; *Micah* 4: 3.

231 (e–f) voyage of his life] Shakespeare, *Julius Caesar,* IV. 3.

234 (a) Miss Peterson] Read 'Paterson.'

234 (c) surviving sisters] Jane Boston Russell and Anne Russell.

234 (d) There is in Edinburgh a squadron] Lord Elcho's Troop. See above, p. 41(c).

234 (f) ten hussars and as many yeomen] 10th Hussars under command of Lieut. Edward Hodgson, and Kilsyth Troop of the Stirlingshire Yeomanry under command of Lieut. John James Davidson. See *Edin. Ann. Reg. for 1820,* XIII. i. 21–2. At the trial Hodgson is called Ellis Hodgson. See ibid., XIII. ii. 201. He may have been the son of Lieut. Thomas Ellis Hodgson of 4th Dragoons who went on half-pay in 1814 and his full name may have been Edward Ellis Hodgson.

235 (e) 'make my grass mow . . .'] A variation of a line in a song beginning 'Since Times are so bad, I must tell thee Sweet-Heart' in *The Syren,* 3rd ed., London, 1739, p. 193: 'To make our Corn grow, and our Apple-Trees bear.' Scott's allusion to London and a country life is paralleled in the song where Collin finds London a snare and returns to his farm.

236 *n.* 1] In line 3, Wm Scott is William Scott, Younger of Woll, who died at Quebec on 12 Jan. 1820. General Lewis Grant had been appointed Governor of the Bahama Islands on 1 Jan. 1820.

236 *n.* 2] For '*Humphrey*' read '*Humphry.*' Scott is possibly thinking of Tabitha Bramble but she nowhere in the novel refers to 'this side Jordan.' Scott was probably confusing her with Mrs Trunnion who, according to Hatchway's report, was 'palavering about

some foreign part called the New Geereusalem, and wishing herself a safe birth in the river Geordun.' (Smollett's *Peregrine Pickle,* chap. 86.)

237 (c) like Hermione and her husband] Shakespeare, *Winter's tale,* V. 3.

237 (d) Lady C] John Fitzgibbon, 1st Earl of Clare, was Lord Chancellor of Ireland, 1789–1802. In 1786 he married Anne Whaley who may be the Lady C. of this anecdote. See also above, p. 218.

238 (d) Mr. Kerrs cover] William Kerr, Secretary, General Post Office, Edinburgh. He occasionally franked letters for addressees in Scotland.

240 *n.*] For 'Lunch'em' in line 3, see below, p. 248 and *n.* 1. In line 3 from end, Lockhart was not referring to Cranstoun's song on Packwood but to his own *Testimonium* in *Blackwood,* Vol. 7 (July 1820), pp. i–viii.

241 *n.* 1] In line 3, for 'No. 37, April 1820' read 'No. 40, July 1820.'

242 (b) "Strike up our drums . . ."] Shakespeare, *II Henry IV,* IV. 2.

242 (e) "the gambol has been shown"] Thomas Parnell, *A fairy tale, in the antient English stile,* st. [17], line 3. In Lewis's *Tales of wonder* (1802), ii. 275, the poem is called *Edwin of the Green.* Also quoted in *SL* ix. 494, xi. 100 and in 1830 Introd. to *Ivanhoe.*

242 *n.* 1] Also *II Chronicles* 3: 17.

243 (a) yeoman's service] Shakespeare, *Hamlet,* V. 2.

243 (b) Galwegian Stot] J. R. McCulloch, called 'The Stot' in *Blackwood.*

244 (d) the *Review*] The historical section of the *Edin. Ann. Reg.,* first written by Southey, then by Scott and now by Lockhart.

244 *n.* 1] I do not think Scott is referring to a post for Lockhart. Scott probably means that Lockhart should get on with his novel and leave the Whigs alone.

246 (b) Milligan] Richard Milliken, bookseller in Dublin.

248 (b) the Exhibition] Annual piping competition held by the Highland Society of London at Falkirk Tryst and since 1784 at Edinburgh.

249 (d) To Lady Abercorn] Scott wrote to her on 2 Aug. (below, p. 252), which was a Wednesday, that the picture had been sent off. If the Wednesday of this letter was a week before, the date would be 26 July.

249 n. 3] Delete. See above, pp. 201, 217, 217 n.

251 (b) To James Ballantyne] Part of the omitted portion reads: 'I have sent Mr Hogarth direct the £296–14/- produce of the second bill. It has cost me about £80 to purchase Walter's second charger and put him in marching trim for Dublin.' (NLS MS. 6080.)

251 (c) Kenilworth . . . Gordon] George Huntly Gordon transcribed *Kenilworth*. There is a letter in Yale University Library from John Ballantyne, 30 Dec. 1820, to Gordon, answering his request for additional payment.

251 (e) hunt[?]] Read 'land.'

252 (a) received the books] Lady Abercorn's letter of 23 July (NLS MS. 3891, ff. 103–4) shows that the books were the first collected ed. of the Waverley Novels in 12 vols., 1820 [1819], and not the pamphlets referred to in n. 1.

252 (b) The picture] Portrait of Scott by Sir John Watson-Gordon, painted for Lady Abercorn.

252 (c) Highland terrier] Ourisk.

252 (f) Lady ——] Lady C—— of Lady Abercorn's letter (below, p. 253 n.), i.e. Lady Conyngham.

252 n. 1] Delete this note, which is not applicable.

254 (e) The drawings] Sir William Allan's *Illustrations of the novels and tales of the Author of Waverley*, published by Constable in 1820. She had referred to the drawings in her letter of 23 July.

255 (b) Francis Walker] Francis Walker Drummond.

257 n. 2] Scott misquotes. In the play Betty always takes a nap when she wants to watch 'for I watch much better so than wide awake.' (Act V, sc. 1.) Scott gives the correct version below, p. 481, and in *Journal*, 27 Feb. 1831.

260 (b) Irish author] I have gone over all Scott's Irish correspondents and cannot identify this one. He cannot be either Hartstonge or Maturin, for they are both mentioned on the same page.

260 (c) a couple of lines to Mr. Maturin] This letter is not known to be extant.

260 (f) Kippilaw] Andrew Seton-Karr of Kippilaw.

261 (f) measures than men] Goldsmith, *The good-natur'd man*, Act II: 'Measures, not men, have always been my mark.'

262 (a) £400 clears all the expenses] For the historical section of the *Edin. Ann. Reg.* See above, p. 244, 244 n. 3.

262 (b) books and K.] Read 'books for K.'

262 n. 3] The mistake about Terry's marriage was made in *SL* v. 146 n. as well as in *SL* iv. 7 n. In line 10, for '8th' read '8vo.' This 8vo ed. was published in 10 vols. in 1821. A vignette of Mortham Castle appears in Vol. 8 and a vignette of Abbotsford in Vol. 10. (*Ruff*, No. 164.) In line 3 from foot, 'Swift' should be 'Dryden.' See below, p. 265.

264 (b) Ken] Read 'Rose.' (Corrected in *SL* xii. 490.) Delete n. 1.

265 (c) yeoman's service] Shakespeare, *Hamlet*, V. 2.

265 (d) Sidney Papers] The work with this title was not published till 1825. Here Scott is referring to *Letters and memorials of state*, ed. by Arthur Collins, London, 1746.

266 (b) To James Ballantyne] Date is after 12 Nov. as reference to 'Session work' shows.

266 (b) conduct of a paper] *Edinburgh Weekly Journal*.

268 (b) Water Company] The Edinburgh Joint Stock Water Co. in which Scott held 5¾ shares. (NLS MS. 112, f. 59.)

268 (e–f) To James Ballantyne] The date September is impossible as Scott refers to 'early August' as a date in the future. The date is probably mid July after the Courts rose and when Scott was at Abbotsford. 'Lambs remittances' may be Lammas remittances, that is, his salaries as Sheriff and as Clerk.

268 *n.* 1] Read 'Pope, *Eloisa to Abelard,* line 124.'

269 (b) To Lady Compton] Her letter, to which Scott is replying, is not in NLS.

269 *n.* 1] Delete this note, which is no longer applicable.

269 *n.* 2] The reference should be to *The Psalms of David in metre according to the version approved by the Church of Scotland,* Psalm 74, st. [3], lines 5–8. In the text 'held' should be 'had.'

269 *n.* 3] Hoddam was not C. K. Sharpe's estate. It belonged to his elder brother, Major-General Matthew Sharpe.

270 (b) Mr. Grants cover] Charles Grant, afterwards Lord Glenelg, was Irish Secretary at this time.

270 *n.* 1] Maturin's letter is in *Maturin Corr.* pp. 97–8.

273 (a) we have company] Lord and Lady Compton. See above, p. 269.

275 (a) To Walter Scott] As in many other cases in *SL*, the putting of address and date at top of letter instead of at end leads to confusion. Date of letter is 18 Oct. It was begun on Friday, 13 Oct., by which time Scott had received Walter's letter of 6 Oct. and *before* Charles set off on 15 Oct. (p. 277). It was finished on 18 Oct. which gives date for the whole letter.

275 (b) hill of MacGabbett] This is a misreading for Meigallot, one of the old ways of spelling Hill of Meigle, Galashiels. Scott uses the form Meiglet in *SL* viii. 262.

275 (c) sand ditch] Read 'said ditch.'

275 (f) Sir James Soulis] Read 'Sir James Foulis.' (Corrected in *SL* xii. 490.)

276 *n.* 1] Delete and substitute: In 1754 Davidona Haliburton, daughter of Lord Provost Haliburton, married William Dallas of North Newton, younger son of Dallas of St. Martin's. She had six sons and three daughters, Henrietta, Margaret and Davidona. Margaret married Sir James Foulis, 14 June 1791, as his second wife. See James Dallas, *The history of the family of Dallas,* 1921, pp. 370–6.

276 *n.* 2] Scott is probably referring to William, Graf von Lippe-Schaumburg, who commanded British forces sent in 1761 to help Portugal against Spain. Foulis's first wife was a Spanish lady (name not given in *Burke*).

278 (a) Home] John Home, Hay Donaldson's partner.

278 (c) handsome cup] For this silver cup given by the Duke of Buccleuch to Selkirk, see *SL* iv. 150–1, 158–9, 160–1, 255.

278 (d) "malevolent in all aspects" Shakespeare, *I Henry IV*, I. 1.

278 (e) The maltman he is cunning] *The maltman*, st. [3], lines 1–4. See *SL* i. 496 and my note.

279 (a) Minister of Sanquhar] William Ranken.

279 (c–d) a cursed scrape . . .] Scott is referring to Queen Caroline.

279 (f) Diva Messalina] Valeria Messalina, daughter of Valerius Messala Barbatus, and wife of Claudius, Emperor of Rome; put to death A.D. 48.

280 (b) Privy Garden] i.e. Montagu House, the Duke of Buccleuch's London house in Privy Gardens.

280 *n.* 1] Donald Robertson, proprietor of the Black Bull Coffee-House, 1 Catherine Street.

282 (c–d) Morningside] i.e. Boroughmuir Head, Morningside, where John Ballantyne was residing in the Autumn of 1820. See *SL* v. 368 *n.* 2.

283 (e) one's own chaff] 'King's chaff is better than other men's corn.' *Kelly,* p. 226. Also used in *SL* ix. 194, in *Rob Roy*, chap. 34, and *Nigel*, chap. 3.

284 (e) Cathrail] Catrail. The accident was on Meigle Hill. See above, p. 275. The pony was Sybil Grey. 'He' and 'his' should be 'She' and 'her.'

284 *n.* 1] For 'middle of October' read '18th October'.

285 *n.* 2] Lord Morpeth succeeded as 6th Earl of Carlisle in 1825. His eldest son, referred to by Scott, was Mr Howard who became 7th Earl in 1848.

286 (d) going to the devil with a dishclout] *Kelly,* p. 264, who explains it as

'If you will be a knave, be not in a trifle, but in something of value.' Also in Ramsay, *Proverbs*, p. 51. See also below, pp. 310, 453.

286 (e) Lady Julia] Lady Abercorn's half-sister, Lady Julia Gore, afterwards wife of Robert Manners Lockwood.

286 (f) picture of two or three dogs] 'Alpine mastiffs reanimating a distressed traveller,' by Sir Edwin Landseer. The British Institution, 1820, No. 277.

287 (e) Genl. MacQuarrie] On the same day that Scott wrote this letter he also wrote to Macquarie and the letter (not in *SL*) was delivered by George Harper (p. 288). Macquarie acknowledged this letter of 28 Oct. 1820 in a letter to Scott, 24 Nov. 1821 (NLS MS. 3893, ff. 165–6). Harper's letter to Scott from Sydney, 14 Aug. 1821, is in NLS (MS. 3893, ff. 41–2).

288 (a) Harper] George Harper, a youth in Darnick who was employed as a gardener at Abbotsford for a short time. He got into trouble, was befriended by Scott, and went to New South Wales where he made good. There are a number of letters from him to Scott in NLS. He arrived in New South Wales in May 1821 and announced his arrival in a letter of 14 Aug. 1821 (NLS MS. 3893, ff. 41–2).

288 (b) To James Ballantyne] Scott reached Edinburgh on Monday, 13 Nov. (below, p. 295) and 'Monday sennight' makes the date of this letter Sunday, 5 Nov.

288 (e) To John Ballantyne] The Abbotsford Hunt was on Wednesday, 8 Nov. The date of this letter, therefore, is 8 Nov.

289 (a) John shall have the binding] This may be John Stevenson who had been a clerk with John Ballantyne & Co. and was now a bookseller and probably undertook bookbinding.

289 n. 1] Brockett visited Abbotsford on 20 Sept. 1833 and signed the Visitors' Book.

292 (d) to drill her youngster] Mrs Dennistoun had five sons and six daughters. 'Youngster' perhaps should be 'youngsters.' If Thomson is still tutoring the same family in 1822 (*SL*

vii. 54), there were six pupils. Thomson's pupil, mentioned in *SL* ix. 110, 146, cannot be of this family.

293 (d) Wheat or barley] *The story of Ali Baba and the Forty Thieves* in *The Arabian Nights*. (Weber, *Tales of the East*, i. 402.) '*sesamum*' should be '*sesame*.'

294 (e) Halidon and Prieston] Holydean and Prieston, farms in Bowden Parish, Roxburghshire, SE. of Abbotsford.

295 (a) Mr. Craig] George Craig, agent at Galashiels of the Leith Banking Co. Writing to Craig next day (15 Nov.) Scott said: 'I trust you are now quite recovered from the effects of your accident.' (Original owned by Mrs Maxwell-Scott of Abbotsford; not in *SL*.)

296 (d) Mr. Watt] The cast of Chantrey's bust of Watt is no longer at Abbotsford.

296 n. 2] There is no apparent connection between the *Songs of Scotland* and *The Mermaid of Galloway*. It was after *Sir Marmaduke Maxwell; the Mermaid of Galloway*, etc. was published in 1822 that Scott suggested that a dramatic version 'with music, scenes, &c' might be made out of *The Mermaid of Galloway* (*SL* vii. 147).

297 (f) *Push on, keep moving*] Lockhart, who prints this letter, has a footnote (*Lockhart*, vi. 279): '*Punch* has been borrowing from *Young Rapid* in the "Cure for the Heart-ache."' It is true that these words are constantly used by Young Rapid in Thomas Morton's farce, but Lockhart might just as well have said that Morton was copying Punch. But Gifford had attacked, in his *Baviad and Mæviad*, (*Baviad*, lines 135–6), catch words such as 'keep moving' used by Morton, Holcroft and Reynolds.

300 (a) Brown] Captain James Brown. See *Letter to the Lord Provost . . . on the subject of the late investigation into the Police Establishment*, 8vo Edinburgh, 1820. Brown was Superintendent of Police.

301 (d) suffer my windows to be broken] For a brief account of the illuminations for the Queen in Edinburgh and the

riots which ensued see *Edin. Ann. Reg. for 1820*, XIII. ii. 363–4.

301 *n.* 1] In last line August should be July.

302 (a) like true Scotsmen wise behind the hand] Ramsay, *Proverbs*, p. 44. See also *SL* ii. 203.

302 (c) the Dukes inquest] Ceremony of serving Walter Francis as heir to his father, which took place on 15 Jan. 1821. See below, pp. 330, 336–7.

302 (e) I cannot avoid [to] send your] Editorial amendment should be: 'I cannot avoid send[ing] your.'

302 (e) the Sutors] i.e. the townsfolk of Selkirk.

302 *n.* 1] Ritson, in a letter to Scott, 10 June 1802 (*Letters of Joseph Ritson*, London, 1833, ii. 225–6), assured him 'on the most decisive authority' that this parody was written by Capt. Philip Lloyd. Ritson was commenting on Scott's note in the *Minstrelsy*, 1st ed., ii. 187. Scott accepted Ritson's attribution and made the correction (Henderson's ed., ii. 322). It is interesting that in 1820 Scott reverts to his original attribution to Wharton.

303 (c) Monteith] Henry Monteith of Carstairs, Lord Provost of Glasgow, who had been elected M.P. for Selkirk Burghs.

304 (a) Ohe jam satis!] Horace, *Satires*, I. v. 12–13.

304 (c) *friday*] Letter should be dated 1 Dec., which was a Friday.

304 (d) To William Laidlaw] In *Chambers's Edinburgh Journal*, N.S. Vol. 4 (2 Aug. 1845), p. 73.

304 *n.* 1] Scott was elected on 27 Nov. 1820.

305 (a) To William Laidlaw] This letter must be about Feb. 1821. The park is Tinder-Coal Yards. Scott closed the transaction in his letter of 25 Feb. 1821 to Hay Donaldson (below, p. 365). Mr Dunlop is William Dunlop, brother-in-law of John Usher, formerly of Toftfield. Mr. Drummond is John Drummond who was Scott's tenant in Shearingflatts which Scott had bought from John Heiton in Nov. 1820. John Drummond was apparently

contemplating buying Tinder-Coal Yards. (Information partly from *Trust Disposition*.)

305 (b) To James Ballantyne [?]] The letter is written to William Laidlaw and 'James' is a slip for 'Willie.' The James and George, mentioned in the letter, are Willie Laidlaw's brothers. The date is Dec., probably the middle.

305 (c) Richardson's accompt] Probably Robert Richardson, Selkirk, who supplied linen, cotton and other cloths.

305 (c) I have seen Lambe's account] Read 'I have not seen Lambe's account.'

305 (f) Walter] A surprise visit of 10 days to Edinburgh. See below, pp. 313, 317.

305 (f) Laidly worm] See my note to *SL* ii. 317 (e).

306 (a) newspaper] A misreading, surely, for 'vacation.'

306 (e) hast any philosophy in thee] Shakespeare, *As you like it*, III. 2.

307 (a) And Log the second] This may be a genuine quotation of a line based on the well-known fable but I have not traced it. It appears in other forms: Dryden, *Epistles, Epistle XII*, line 48: 'For Tom the second reigns like Tom the first'; Pope, *The Dunciad*, Bk I, line 6: 'Still Dunce the second reigns like Dunce the first.'

309 (c) witt] Scott probably wrote 'wut.'

309 (c–d) Haining . . . Reaburn-meadow-spot] Walter Scott, 3rd Laird of Raeburn, was killed in a duel with Mark Pringle (later of Crichton), 3 Oct. 1707. Mark Pringle was an ancestor of 'young Haining' of Scott's letter. The field, where the duel took place, is now a housing estate within the burgh of Selkirk.

309 (d–e) Ils seront recus Biribi] The lines 'Biribi, / A la façon de barbari, / Mon ami' occur a number of times in the plays of Le Sage. See, e.g., *Le théâtre de la foire, ou l'opéra comique*, 12mo Amsterdam, 1723, i. 22, 100, 101, 127, 224, 289; ii. 13, 65, 303, 339, 417.

309 (e) Copagné [?]] Read 'Cossaqué.' (Corrected in *SL* xii. 490.) See above, p. 302.

309 *n.* 1] The whole of this note is given as an extract from Lady Louisa's letter in Partington, *Post-bag*, pp. 146–8.

310 (b) popish plot] Correct date is 1678.

310 (b–c) Net Currency] David Douglas, in his own copy of *FL* (now in my Scott Coll.), has corrected this to Bet Canning [i.e. Elizabeth Canning].

310 (c) going to the Devil with a dishclout] See above, p. 286 and my note.

310 *n.*] Spence's *Anecdotes* (line 17–18) was reviewed in *QR* Vol. 23, No. 46 (July 1820), publ. in Oct. According to Shine (No. 550) the review was by Isaac D'Israeli. Though Lady Louisa did not assist Dallaway she made contributions (anonymously) to *The letters and works of Lady Mary Wortley Montagu, ed. by her great grandson, Lord Wharncliffe*, 3 vols., London, 1837.

311 (b) "a pleasant tragedy stuffed with most pitiful mirth"] A variation of *A lamentable tragedy, mixed full of mirth conteyning the life of Cambises, King of Percia*, by Thomas Preston. Also quoted in *SL* viii. 29. Cf. *MPW* xix. 215.

311 (c) as Capt. Bobadil says] Ben Jonson, *Every man in his humour*, Act IV. Scene numbering varies in different eds.

312 (c) There is a comical meeting] On Saturday, 16 Dec. 1820. For an account of it, see *Edin. Ann. Reg. for 1820*, XIII. ii. 373–6.

313 (c) My youngest son . . .] Lady Holland wrote to her son, 26 Feb. 1821: 'He [Scott] has a stubborn boy who will not learn Latin. To induce him to that pursuit, he is to be placed in a village where Welsh alone is spoken; & Scott flatters himself he will thus be driven to the language of Cicero in preference to that of Shenkin & Cadwallader.' (*Elizabeth, Lady Holland to her son, 1821–1845*, London, 1946, p. 2.) This slightly garbled version would be got third or fourth hand through Lady Louisa.

314 (b) Mr. Parish] Woodbine Parish, Chairman of the Board of Excise, Scotland.

314 *n.* 1] For 'taxes' read 'excise.'

317 (b) at the Pantheon] See my note to *SL* vi. 312 (c).

317 (c) a loyal Address] Drawn up by Scott. See below, p. 325. Issued as a pamphlet of 16 pages, without title-page. The address, headed 'Address to the King!', occupies pp. 1–2 and the list of signatories, pp. 3–16.

317 (e) Irish giant] Patrick Cotter or O'Brien (1761?–1806).

321 (a) acceptance] Read 'accession.'

321 (d–e) Lindsay of Pittscotti] Robert Lindsay of Pitscottie's *Chronicles* had been edited by J. G. Dalyell in 1814.

323 (b) To James Skene] Date corrected to 1823 in *SL* xii. 489. The date is determined, not by reference to Sophia's baby, but to the stone screen. The date is almost certainly Sunday, 20 Apr.

323 (a) To William Laidlaw] Date is 28 Dec. (or about 28 Dec.) 1816. Cf. *SL* iv. 333.

323 *n.* 2] The screen erected at Abbotsford differed from the one described here. The heavy iron, which was undermining the foundations, was removed in 1958.

324 (a) Blore] Blore, like others at this early stage, was merely contributing ideas. Actual planning was carried out by Atkinson when he was chosen as architect for Abbotsford.

324 (d) Ils seront recus] See my note to *SL* vi. 309 (d–e).

324 (f) south-country *cub*] This is James Scott who painted a portrait of Tom Purdie. He made the copy of the 'Wedding,' referred to on p. 325. Both paintings are now in my Scott Coll.

324 *n.* 1] The date is 20 Nov. 1820. The main rioting was on Sunday, 19 Nov. which would be Mrs Clephane's occasion for appealing to Scott. There was a little rioting on the evening of Monday. See *Edin. Ann. Reg. for 1820*, XIII. ii. 363. Mrs Clephane was in Edinburgh in Nov. 1820 (above, p. 300).

325 (c) To Lord Melville] This letter continues the subject of Simpson and James Scott of Scott's letter of 1 Dec. 1820 (wrongly dated 1821 in *SL* vii. 35–6).

325 (d) My cousins matter] James Scott, son of Scott's uncle Thomas.

326 (b) Gray] i.e. Grey. Charles Grey, 2nd Earl Grey.

328 (a) To Lord Montagu] Montagu in his reply of 23 Jan. (below, p. 338 *n.*) refers to Lang and Hogg, both mentioned in this letter. Scott's letter, therefore, is of 7 Jan. 1821.

329 (b) Old Gaffer Gray] Charles Grey, 2nd Earl Grey.

330 (a–b) one of our sweet voiced Sutors] Andrew Simpson, M.D., seeking an appointment in India.

330 (d) On Monday God willing] Scott is writing on Sunday. By 'Monday' he means 'Monday week,' i.e. 15 Jan. when the Duke would be served heir.

331 *n.* 2] The mural tablet to Lord Charles Scott, 1727–49, 2nd son of 2nd Duke of Buccleuch, is on the north wall of the Cathedral cloister. The Latin inscription consists of 29 lines. There is also a small square tablet to him in the floor of the Cathedral.

332 (b) "God be with your labour!"] Scott attributes these words to Ophelia four times in the letters (here and *SL* viii. 404, ix. 509 and xi. 177) but Ophelia nowhere uses these words. In Chapman's *Eastward hoe*, III. 2, we have: 'God be at your labour' and in *Kenilworth*, chap. 24, we have: 'as the play says "God be with your labour!"'

332 *n.* 1] Wilkie's painting was 'Chelsea pensioners reading the gazette of the Battle of Waterloo', painted for the Duke of Wellington and finished in 1822. See Allan Cunningham, *Life of Sir David Wilkie*, iii. 526.

333 (c) Turner's Holm] See Index. Mentioned also in *The Black Dwarf*, chap. 9.

335 (a–b) spurring the willing horse] *Ray*, p. 205.

335 (c) John Kinnear MacDonald] John Macdonald (afterwards Sir John Macdonald Kinneir) sent armour to Scott on at least three occasions: (1) armour of Jalabad Sing at end of 1816, mentioned in *SL* iv. 338 and in a letter from Scott to Willie Scott, 29 Jan. 1817 (NLS MS. 2889, ff. 133–4; not in *SL*); (2) in 1818 (*SL* v. 309 *n.*); (3) and now in 1821.

336 (c) "no very fou but gaily yet"] *We're gayly yet*, st. [1], line 2. In *Herd*, ii. 121.

336 (c) Sir W. W. Macdougal] This is a mistake for Sir H. H. Makdougall.

336 (d) Harden & his son Gala] Grierson has forgotten to insert a comma after 'son' to 'make the meaning clear.' Scott is referring to Hugh Scott of Harden; Henry Scott, Younger of Harden; and John Scott of Gala.

337 (d) Canning] Canning, as President of the Board of Control, resigned in Jan. 1821. He returned to the Cabinet as Foreign Secretary in Sept. 1822.

338 (a) On friday I had . . .] Meeting of Pittites in Edinburgh on Friday, 12 Jan. (above, pp. 329, 336–7); meeting of jury on Monday, 15 Jan. to serve Duke of Buccleuch heir to his father (above, pp. 336, 337); meeting of Celtic Society on Friday, 19 Jan. (below, p. 343).

338 (d) Roger] George Rodger, Town Clerk of Selkirk.

338 (d) Provost of Eton] Rev. Joseph Goodall.

338 *n.* 1] Lang and Hogg are Andrew Lang and Walter Hogg.

341 (a) letter . . . which I have written] Not in *SL*.

341 *n.* 1] 'This is the first allusion' (line 1) is incorrect. Scott had referred to it on 19 Jan. (top of same page).

342 (b) our very true proverb] *Ray*, p. 9, with 'family' for 'Clan'; Ramsay, *Proverbs*, p. 38, with 'Kin' for 'Clan.'

342 (c) a bill] This became 'An act for establishing regulations respecting certain parts of the proceedings in the Court of Session,' 1 & 2 Geo. IV, c. 38, 28 May 1821. By Sect. 17–18 of this statute decrees previously signed by the Principal Clerks of Session were, after 20 June 1821, to be signed by the Extractors.

343 (b) the noble Kerne of Ireland] For explanation of this allusion, see *SL* ii. 329 *n.*

343 (c) all plaided and plumed in their tartan array] Thomas Campbell, *Lochiel's warning*, line 51.

344 (e) their eldest son Robert] Lord Melville's eldest son was Henry. Robert was the third son.

345 (b) Mr. Dundas] Robert Dundas (later in the year Sir Robert) of Beechwood.

346 n. 2] Scott is probably not referring to the inclusion or exclusion of the Queen's name in the Church of England liturgy but to the Order in Council forbidding ministers of the Church of Scotland to pray for her. Such an Order was unconstitutional and was opposed by the Scottish clergy. See *Edin. Ann. Reg. for 1821*, XIV. i. 35–9.

351 (c) a statement by Lockhart] This 'statement' was a pamphlet, without title or imprint, regarding Lockhart's connection with *Blackwood*, in reply to John Scott.

351 (c) Milligan] Richard Milliken, bookseller in Dublin.

352 n. 1] This note means that Scott set off on Monday, 12 Feb., but Scott left on Thursday, 8 Feb. and was able to see Christie in London on 12 Feb. Ballantyne's note (below, p. 355 n. 2) shows that Scott had left before 12 Feb.

354 (a) one of my brethren] Robert Dundas of Beechwood.

354 (f) *haud alienum a Scaevolae studiis*] Cicero, *Ad Atticum*, IV. xvi. 3: 'Sermo non alienus a Scaevolae studiis.' Tom Jones, like Scott, says 'alienum' and Partridge retorts: 'You should say *alienus*.' (Fielding, *Tom Jones*, Bk XII, chap. 13.) Also quoted in *The Antiquary*, chap. 39.

356 (f) Lady Anne . . .] Montagu's nieces, daughters of 4th Duke of Buccleuch: Lady Anne Elizabeth, died unmarried, 1844; Lady Isabella Mary, afterwards Lady Isabella Cust; and Lady Charlotte, afterwards Lady Charlotte Stopford.

357 (c–d) dine with old Sotheby . . .] Insert commas after Sotheby and Wellington to show that Scott will dine with Sotheby on Monday, 19 Feb.; with Wellington on Tuesday and Croker on Wednesday.

357 (d) progress through Parliament of a bill] See my note to *SL* vi. 342 (c).

358 (e) a cup made of a Buffalos horn]

This is now on display in a showcase in the Drawing Room at Abbotsford.

360 (b) "Patrick Fleming"] The first stanza is copied from st. 8 of *On the first Rebellion*: 'Mackintosh was a valiant soldier, / He carried his musket on his shoulder; / Cock your pistols, draw your rapier, / And damn you, Forster, for you are a traytor.' See *SL* i. 343. Sharpe refers to the song in a letter to Scott. See *Sharpe's Letters*, ii. 346.

361 (d) as Jack Cade says] Shakespeare, *II Henry VI*, IV. 6. It is Smith, not Cade, who says it. Scott makes the same mistake in a note to chap. 4 of *The Bride of Lammermoor*.

361 (e) Scotts surgeon] Dr T. G. Pettigrew. Scott met him in London later but did not connect him with the Scott–Christie duel. See *Journal*, 29 Apr. 1828.

363 (a–b) die like the deil at a dykeside] i.e. that he will survive. *Ray*, pp. 125, 389; Ramsay, *Proverbs*, p. 40.

364 (b) He gat them frae his daddy] *The surprise*, st. [1], line 2: 'I gat him frae my daddy.' In *Herd*, ii. 151, and in *Johnson*, Vol. 2 (1788), No. 185, under the title *I had a horse, and I had nae mair*.

364 (d) the Institution] The British Institution. The pictures to which Scott refers were: No. 12. 'The importunate author, from *Les Fâcheux* of Molière,' by Gilbert Stuart Newton, and No. 72. 'Belshazzar's Feast,' by John Martin.

365 (b) sale of a field] See letter to Laidlaw, above, p. 305, and my note to it.

366 (b) neither force nor prevent] Read 'neither foresee nor prevent' (NLS MS. 859, f. 1).

367 (b) to his father] Rev. Alexander Christie. Letter is not in *SL*.

368 (c) Nicol] This passage is obscure. I think it means that Nicol Milne planned to buy the field and, by threatening to build a house on it, force Scott to buy it from him at an enhanced rate. Cf. above, p. 365.

368 (d) Lawrence . . . Maida] There is no dog in Lawrence's portrait.

368 (e) Maida & Panick] I think this is a misreading for 'Maida & Ourisk,' the two dogs depicted in Wilkie's 'The Abbotsford family.' If so, Scott is asking for that picture to be sent to London.

368 (f) the date of this letter] See *SL* ix. 450 *n*. 2 and my note.

368 *n*. 1] Delete. Nicol is Nicol Milne of Faldonside. The field was owned by William Dunlop, who acted for himself and his son John.

369 (a) Daniel in the Lyon's den] *Bible, Daniel* 6: 7–23.

369 (a) little Ligin [?]] Probably Scott's tailor, William Goodfellow, who had been ill. See above, p. 344.

370 *n*. 1] Delete. If Stanhope became Earl of Harrington Scott would have called him Lord Petersham. The Stanhope to whom Scott is referring is Col. James Hamilton Stanhope (1788–1825).

373 (b) Major in place of Col. Hay] Philip Hay was Major of 18th Hussars at this time with Brevet rank of Lt.-Col. It was announced in *Blackwood* in Apr. 1821 that he had exchanged with Major Synge, half-pay, of 25th Dragoons.

373 (b) I inclose a letter to Mathurine] Not known to be extant.

373 (c) Ballantyne Crosslie] In 1821 George Bryden was tenant in Crosslie. His mother was Agnes Ballantyne and the Ballantyne of the text may be Bryden's cousin.

373 *n*. 1] Delete this note. The part of the letter (p. 373) beginning 'He is certainly a little mad' belongs (as Mr Alan Bell confirms) to another letter written at Abbotsford. Grierson should have suspected that Maturin, in Ireland, would not want a pony from Scotland. From the context it is quite clear that 'He is certainly a little mad' refers to Willie Scott of Maxpoffle.

374 (c) "O'Connor's Child"] This allusion to Campbell's poem has a double meaning. Mrs Christie was Irish and her maiden name was Conner and she had two uncles who changed their name to O'Connor.

376 (b) Seged Emperor of Ethiopia] Samuel Johnson, *The Rambler*, No. 205, 3 Mar. 1752.

376 (e) To Lord Compton] His son was born on 6 Mar., the day on which Scott wrote this letter.

378 (b) Home, Creevey, Lambton] Joseph Hume; Thomas Creevey; J. G. Lambton, afterwards 1st Earl of Durham.

378 (e) Richd. Maine Esq] Possibly Sir Richard Mayne who, like Christie, was soon to be a barrister of Lincoln's Inn.

380 (a) "Where shall I gae dine the day"] *The twa corbies*, st. 1, line 4. In Scott's *Minstrelsy* (ed. Henderson), ii. 417.

380 (c) of great importance] After 'importance' insert index figure 2.

380 (e) nothing.[2]] Read 'nothing[3].'

380 *n*. 1] Delete the whole sentence beginning 'Mr "Loftus" should be' and substitute: [2]'Loftus' should be 'Lofty.' See Goldsmith's *The goodnatur'd man*, Act II, where Croaker says of Lofty: 'He is a man of importance.'

380 *n*. 2] Change index figure to 3.

382 (b) Lambe] William Lamb, seedsman in Selkirk.

382 *n*. 1] Cockie Pistol was the name of a small public house in Melrose. (*Border Mag.* ix. 27.)

384 *n*. 1] The drawing of Wayland Smith's cave has not been found at Abbotsford. For another drawing see *SL* xi. 230, 258, 260 *n*. 1, 261.

384 *n*. 1] John Hughes's poem is *Pompeii, a descriptive ode*, n.p., n.d. [1820]. It is a quarto of 14 pp.

384 *n*. 2] Scott is answering Mrs Hughes's letter of 19 Feb., of which there is an extract in Partington, *Postbag*, pp. 150–1. As she replied on 15 Mar., Scott's letter must be before 12 Mar. It is almost certainly Tuesday, 6 Mar. which approximates to Mrs Hughes's dating of 7 Mar. in her *Letters*, pp. 31–2.

385 (a) the trial] For an account of the trial on 13 Apr. at the Old Bailey, see *Edin. Ann. Reg. for 1821*, XIV. ii, Appendix, pp. 60–5.

387 (b–c) a capital amulet] Described and illustrated in colour in Mrs M. M. Maxwell-Scott's *Abbotsford: the personal*

relics, London, 1893, plate 21. The stone is exhibited in the Library at Abbotsford.

387 *n.* 1] Milliken is Richard Milliken, bookseller in Dublin. His letter in NLS is MS. 3892, ff. 71–2.

390 (b) friend & companion] Villiers Surtees. See above, p. 386 and *n.*

390 (e) as you are strong be merciful] 'As you are stout be merciful' is a Scottish proverb. See *Kelly*, p. 39.

390 *n.* 1] Delete this pointless note and see above, p. 387 and my note.

391 (c) To William Laidlaw] Date is about 4 Mar. as reference to John Scott shows. It could hardly be later as Scott had to allow time for making the survey.

391 (c) Mr Smith or Mr Paterson] John Smith of Darnick who built the second portion of Abbotsford and Paterson of Sanderson & Paterson of Galashiels who built the first portion. It is not known who made the survey at this time but on 13 Dec. 1821 John Smith sent a very detailed survey to Atkinson.

391 (e) Sir Thomas] Sir Thomas Munro, Governor of Madras, 1819–27.

391 (f) one of the Shortreeds] See above, p. 330 and *n.*

391 *n.*] Scott's views on Catholic emancipation are expressed many times apart from the letter to Southey. See Index under Catholic emancipation.

392 (d) the Captains marriage] Adam Ferguson.

392 (d) the W.S.] i.e. the *Walter Scott*, a smack sailing between Leith and London.

393 (a) Allan's picture is much liked] William Allan exhibited at the Royal Academy exhibition which opened on 7 May 1821, No. 33, 'Death of Archbishop Sharp on Magus Moor, 1679.' It was highly praised in the *Lit. Gaz.*, 1821, pp. 296, 317. In Feb. 1822 it was exhibited in the shop of Peter Hill & Co., Edinburgh, and then engraved by James Stewart. See the *Scotsman*, 16 Feb. 1822, p. 56, c. 1 and *Blackwood*, Vol. 11 (Apr. 1822), p. 439.

393 (d) To Thomas Scott] This is a good example of a letter written over a long period. It was begun before 27 Feb. and finished on 5 Apr.

393 (e) his brother] His brother-in-law.

393 *n.* 2] Sidmouth is answering Scott's letter of 17 Feb. which is not in *SL*. See below, p. 397 (c).

394 (c) the world for the winning] See above, p. 151, where the words are given as a quotation.

395 (c) publickly went to Court] Lockhart was presented in Feb. See above, p. 345.

395 (e) Butterworths] Edmond Butterworth, writing master at Edinburgh High School, who taught Scott writing.

395 (e) as Jack Cade says] See my note to *SL* vi. 361 (d).

395 (f) whom the King delighteth to honour] *Bible, Esther* 6:6, 7, 9, 11.

396 (b) Lord Moira] This should be Lord Hastings. Lord Moira had been created Marquess of Hastings in 1816.

396 (b–c) men must die] Shakespeare, *As you like it*, IV. 1.

396 (e) To Lord Montagu] Date is 2 Apr.

396 (e) Seged] See my note to *SL* vi. 376 (b).

397 (c) To John Villiers] This letter was printed in *The Life and correspondence of the . . . First Viscount Sidmouth*, by the Hon George Pellew, London, 1847, iii. 480–7. The correct date is 6 Apr. 1821. After writing this letter Scott wrote on the same night, at 11 o'cl., to Lord Sidmouth, and this letter is printed ibid. iii. 345–6. Scott, while in London, had written to Sidmouth on Saturday, 17 Feb., and this letter is printed ibid. iii. 342–3.

399 (b) miss the tide of fortune . . .] A paraphrase of Shakespeare, *Julius Caesar*, IV. 3.

402 (a) irritable race] Horace, *Epistles*, II. ii. 102: 'Genus irritabile vatum.'

402 (b) Fabiscio's feast of the author] 'Fabiscio' should be 'Fabricio' and 'author' should be 'authors.' See Le Sage, *Gil Blas*, Bk VIII, chap. 9. At the conclusion of the feast with six authors, Gil Blas calls them 'a vil-

laneous set, I will henceforth keep to my clerks.' He recurs to this opinion in Bk VIII, chap. 13. This preference for clerks is quoted by Scott in *SL* viii. 26, 176, x. 312, 390, xi. 358.

403 (f) "were meant for *merit* . . ."] By Edward Young. See Johnson's *Lives of the poets* under Young.

404 (f) "all ill come running in . . ."] Thomas Middleton, *The witch*, V. 2.

405 (f) [7]] Delete and see my note to *SL* vi. 397 (c).

406 (a) To Walter] This letter should precede the one to Villiers on p. 397.

406 (c) the Duke] Duke of York, Commander-in-Chief.

406 n.] The letter to Villiers is correctly dated 6 Apr. The letter to Ferguson, dated 6 Apr., is also correct, and when he wrote it Scott apparently did not think he would be in Manchester till the 7th but he actually arrived there late on the evening of the 6th.

406 n. 1] Scott would be unlikely to send a work just beginning and finally extending to 15 vols. The work is almost certainly *Histoire critique et militaire des guerres de Frédéric*.

407 (b) To Adam Fergusson] This letter, written in London, should precede that written to Villiers, p. 397.

407 (c) Your business] Ferguson's salary as Deputy Keeper of the Regalia.

407 (c–d) Peartree] Sir William Rae.

408 (d) Better late thrive] 'Better late thrive than never do well.' Ramsay, *Proverbs*, p. 12.

408 (d) the proverb is somewhat musty] Shakespeare, *Hamlet*, III. 2.

408 n. 2] Delete 'Evidently.'

409 (a) To C. J. Dumergue] Date must be 13 Apr., the date of letter to Mrs Carpenter which accompanied it.

409 (d) funeral . . .] Funeral of Lt.-Col. Robert Swinton who had died on 6 Apr.; christening of John Hugh Lockhart; marriage of Adam Ferguson; and canvas for William Scott of Maxpoffle who was standing for Collectorship of Taxes for Roxburghshire.

409 n. 1] Jorlie, in line 2, is usually given as Joli or Jolly.

410 (a) Mungo] The suggestion that the child should be called Mungo must have been a joke. Mungo was the name of Lockhart's dog and the family used only traditional names. See below, p. 420.

410 (a) My God daughter] The Leith smack *Walter Scott*. Scott means to say 'betwixt Leith & London.'

410 (c) an old friend] Adam Ferguson.

411 (b) Jamieston] Read 'Samieston.' Delete footnote.

411 (d) Reaburn supports] This should be 'Maxpoffle represents.'

411 (e) Reaburn has] This should be 'Maxpoffle has'.

411 (e) [cousin]] Read '[uncle].'

412 (b) funeral . . . Christening . . . canvas] See above, p. 409.

412 (c) Daniel in the Lyons den] See above, p. 369.

412 (c) *intuitu matrimonii*] In the prospect of marriage. A Scots law phrase. See Trayner, *Latin maxims*. Used in *Waverley*, chap. 71.

412 n. 2] For '*Humphrey*' read '*Humphry*.' Lesmahagow was a Lieutenant, though he was sometimes addressed as Captain.

413 (b) Somerton] Read 'Samieston.' Delete footnote 2.

414 (a) Captain Lismahagow] See above, p. 412 n. 2 and my note.

414 n. 2] The letter was printed in the *Lit. Gaz.*, 8 July 1826, p. 431, from which *The Times* and *John Bull* probably copied it.

415 n. 1] Delete whole note, no part of which is applicable. The reference to Walter shows that the letter was written in Oct., when Walter was in Scotland and when he attended the Abbotsford Hunt (*SL* vii. 32). The 'congratulations to the Captain' must refer to William Lockhart's engagement, which probably occurred in Oct. as he was married in 1822.

417 n. 1] In line 22, delete 'I will not fail to write to the Lord President.' This has nothing to do with the Royal

Society of Literature. It refers to Scott's letter to the Lord President for leave of absence to attend the Coronation.

420 (a) two funerals] The first was that of Lt.-Col. Robert Swinton. I cannot find the other.

420 n. 1] The pamphlet by Bowles (line 14) is: *Two letters to . . . Lord Byron . . . in answer to his . . . letter on the Rev. W. L. Bowles's strictures on the life and writings of Pope*, 8vo London, 1821.

421 (d) Edgerstane] John Rutherford of Edgerston.

422 (a) Borthwickbrae . . . Torwoodlee . . . Chesters] William Elliot-Lockhart, James Pringle and Thomas Elliot Ogilvie.

422 (b) Harden, Gala, Sunlaws] Hugh Scott, John Scott and Robert Scott-Kerr.

422 (b) Sir Harry] Sir Henry Hay Makdougall of Makerston.

422 (e) as many carabines] Le Sage, *Gil Blas*, Bk X, chap. 3. The words 'to scare him out of his feathers' apply to Ferguson, not to Gil Blas.

424 (a) Sir George Murray] General Sir George Murray was Governor of the Royal Military College, Sandhurst, 1819–24.

424 (f) Lismahagow] See above, p. 412 n. 2 and my note.

425 n. 1] Delete 'Presumably.'

427 (b) Lockhart absent on the northern circuit] At Inverness. See above, p. 424.

427 (d) To John Ballantyne] The date seems to be correct; yet it is difficult to reconcile the contents with the letter of 28 Apr. (*SL* v. 368).

429 (d) Mr. Rutherford the Sheriff] A comma should have been inserted. The Sheriff was not Rutherford but William Oliver.

430 (a) Don & Elliot] Alexander Don and Gilbert Elliot (afterwards 2nd Earl of Minto), the Tory and Whig candidates respectively for Roxburghshire in 1812.

432 (a) the two Kings of Brentford] Buckingham, *The rehearsal*.

432 (c) handful of nuts] See L'Estrange, *Fables*, No. 375; *The dancing apes*. Scott quotes the fable from Lucian in *Guy Mannering*, chap. 38.

434 (e) Somerston] Read 'Samieston.'

437 (c) Colonel Hay] Philip Hay. He had transferred to the 25th Dragoons in Apr. (See my note to *SL* vi. 373 (b).) This may have been due to the trouble in the 18th.

438 (a) Mr. Machel] John Thomas Machell.

438 (f) Mr. O Grady] Capt. Standish O'Grady, 18th Hussars; afterwards 2nd Viscount Guillamore.

440 (b) To John Ballantyne] This letter cannot be dated 14 May. Scott would not send copy by Terry on that day when he was himself returning to Edinburgh (below, p. 444). Scott would not propose breakfasting at Kirklands *after* he had returned to Edinburgh. The proposed breakfast must be for Sunday, 6 May, and the date of this letter 4 May.

442 (a) your letter of May 6th] Unfortunately this letter, which might have explained some points raised in Scott's reply, is not in NLS.

443 (c) Lord Stewart [?]] This is probably Charles William Stewart who was created Lord Stewart in 1814 and who succeeded as 3rd Marquess of Londonderry in 1822. He had been Lt.-Col. of 18th Hussars, Walter's regiment.

443 (d) *Lion d'or*] I cannot explain the allusion. The lions in Londonderry's coat of arms were *gules*.

444 (b) a field] Tinder-Coal Yards, bought from William Dunlop. See above, pp. 305, 365, 368.

444 (e) To Hugh Scott] Francis is Francis Scott, 4th son of Hugh Scott of Harden. He was born 31 Jan. 1806 and eventually became a barrister. Scott's statement (p. 445) that he is 'twenty or so' would place this letter about 1826. It is probably Aug. 1827 and would be written before Harden and David Thomson dined with Scott on 30 Aug. (Scott's *Journal*). The dinner party was probably arranged as a result of this letter in order to discuss Francis's career. David Thomson, W.S., was Harden's lawyer.

445 (e–f) Sufficient for the day is the evil thereof] *Bible, Matthew* 6: 34.

445 (e–f) "All to make the haggis fat"] *The haggis o' Dunbar*, st. [3], line 1.

446 (b) His sister . . . The eldest] Former is Margaret, the youngest; the latter, Isabella, the eldest.

448 *n.* 1] The pamphlet is now attributed to Lockhart.

450 (f) Mrs. Crumpton] Presumably a slip or misreading for Crampton.

451 (c) a manuscript] In his ed. of Gwynne (p. vii) Scott says Graham presented it.

452 (b) Mrs. C.] Mrs Crampton (Mrs Crumpton above, p. 450).

452 (c) all plaided and plumed in their tartan array] Thomas Campbell, *Lochiel's warning*, line 51.

452 (e) Sir David] Sir David Baird.

453 (b) going to the Devil with a dish clout] See above, p. 286 and my note.

454 (b) He says] The 'He' is William Stewart Rose. See below, p. 479.

454 (b) to shoot young wild ducks in Saint Marys Loch] Rose had his wish fulfilled. He went with Lockhart to Altrive on 6 Aug. 1821 and spent three days with Hogg. (Mrs Garden, *Memorials of James Hogg*, pp. 142–3; Strout, *Life and letters of James Hogg*, p. 217.)

454 (c) *all plaided and plummed in their tartan array*] Thomas Campbell, *Lochiel's warning*, line 51.

454 (e) It goes to Aberdeen] This apparently is the steamship launched at Perth on 5 Apr. 1821, to run between Leith and the north of Scotland. See *Edin. Ann. Reg. for 1821*, XIV. ii. 103. See also my note to *SL* vi. 487 (a).

454 (f) I will send this . . . epistle to Will Rose under cover] The letter of 26 May 1821 which Scott wrote to Rose is not in *SL*, but it is mentioned in *The Times*, 6 Oct. 1928, p. 14, c. 1.

456 (a) Lord Lothian] Scott's letter to him, 15 May 1821 (not in *SL*), is in *N. & Q.* Vol. 209 (Dec. 1964), pp. 469–71, with Lothian's reply of 22 May, pp. 471–2, and Scott's letter of 25 May (not in *SL*), p. 472.

456 (b) The Maultman he is cunning] *The maltman*, st. [3], lines 1–4. See *SL* i. 496 and my note.

456 *n.* 1] John Morrison's plan of the Abbotsford estate has the names of all the fields and plantations written on it by Scott himself. This plan is now in my Scott Coll.

457 *n.* 1] Delete '*An Inquiry into the Corn Laws*, 1796.' (Correction in *DNB*.)

458 (c) To [William Sotheby]] It is almost certain that this letter was written, not to Sotheby, but to William Jerdan: (1) Sotheby was an Englishman but Scott says at the end of the letter 'all the Scots' showing he was writing to a Scot; (2) Jerdan was a Scot from Kelso, personally known to Scott, and was editor of the *Lit. Gaz.* In the *Lit. Gaz.*, 1821 (30 June), p. 414, there was a paragraph on the forthcoming performance. The success of the play in Edinburgh, it said, was due to Mackay 'who combined, as we learn from the *best authority*, the manufacturer, the magistrate, and the man of benevolence.' Jerdan is thus quoting Scott's letter and it is a safe guess that he was Scott's correspondent.

459 (b) To James Ballantyne] The suggested date is impossible. Scott was at Blair-Adam on 10 June 1821 and could not negotiate a bill at Galashiels and bring the produce on Tuesday. The date is 27 Aug. 1820. See *Reply to Mr Lockhart's pamphlet*, Appendix, p. 39, where Hogarth's bill for £600 and Constable's bills for £500 are recorded.

459 *n.* 1] Delete this note, which is no longer applicable.

460 (c) the Sheriff] William Oliver, afterwards William Oliver-Rutherford of Dinlabyre and Edgerston.

460 (e) vacant seat at the board of Commissioners] James Jackson, one of the Commissioners of Excise for Scotland, had died on 4 June.

460 (e) Miss Baillie who introduces in one of her plays a projector] Royston in *The trial; a comedy*. See especially Act V, sc. 1.

461 *n.* 1] In Ramsay, *Tea-table miscellany*; *Herd* and elsewhere. On authorship, see

Johnson, ed. William Stenhouse, Edinburgh, 1853, iv. *205–206*.

462 (d–e) *like a cow in a fremd loaning*] i.e. a cow in a strange lane. A Scottish proverb. *Kelly*, p. 223, gives an unusual form: 'like a cow in an uncouth loan.'

464 (f) Covent Garden] Should be Drury Lane.

465 *n.* 1] Delete and see my note to *SL* vi. 458 (c).

466 *n.* 2] Delete the word 'poor.'

467 (d) Her bower is bigged in gude green wood] This phraseology is common in ballads; e.g. in *Brown Adam*, st. III, line 3 is: 'And he's bigged a bour in gude green-wood' (*Minstrelsy*, ed. Henderson, iii. 201).

468 (a) Legends] Joanna Baillie's *Metrical legends*, published this year.

469 (d) Allan] See my note to *SL* vi. 393 (a).

470 (c) To James Ballantyne] Though this is printed from *The Ballantyne-humbug handled*, there are a number of misprints.

472 (a) Royal Bank] Security for Ballantyne's loan had been given by Scott and Rev. Robert Lundie. See *Reply to Mr Lockhart's pamphlet*, pp. 36–7.

476 (b) The Dicksons] Archibald Dickson of Housebyres, Sir Archibald Collingwood Dickson and Archibald Dickson of Huntlaw were freeholders in Roxburghshire at this time.

476 (c) The dial spoke not] Dryden, *The Spanish friar*, IV. 2. Also quoted in *The Bride of Lammermoor*, chap. 6.

477 (b) Where two men ride a horse] Shakespeare, *Much ado about nothing*, III. 5.

477 (d–e) Tutors of Buccleuch] The tutors (that is, guardians legally appointed) to the young Duke of Buccleuch were Lord Montagu and Hon. Charles Douglas.

479 (c) Covent Garden] Should be Drury Lane.

480 (c) To James Ballantyne] I think this letter should be dated 6 Nov. 1822: (1) Reference to '4th volume,' i.e. of *Peveril* (p. 481) shows that the date is about Nov. 1822; (2) The 'note at four

months for £500' refers to a bill due 7 Mar. 1823 (*Reply to Mr Lockhart's pamphlet*, Appendix, p. 74), i.e. drawn about 7 Nov. 1822. Wednesday was 6 Nov.

480 *n.* 1] The *Private letters of the seventeenth century* was not published in full till 1947 when it was issued by the Clarendon Press with an introd. by Douglas Grant.

481 (b) The labourer is worthy of his hire] *Bible, Luke* 10: 7.

481 *n.* 2] Delete and see above, p. 257 *n.* 2 and my note.

481 *n.* 3] For '*Novelists*' read '*Novelist's.*' The insurance for £5,000 with the Globe was taken out on 9 Feb. 1821 by Constable. The £5,000 mentioned in this letter probably refers to two policies taken out by Ballantyne—£3,000 with West of England on 5 Dec. 1821 and £2,000 with Atlas on 9 Jan. 1822. See *Sederunt Books*.

483 (b) Fabius *qui rem restituit cunctando*] A variation of the phrase used by Ennius about Fabius Maximus (died 203 B.C.).

483 (e) sluggards in the bible] *Bible, Proverbs* 6:6–10.

484 (b) Johnie MacDonald] John Macdonald Buchanan. He died in 1823.

484 (d) poor Frank Douglass's death] Francis James Douglas, second son of George Douglas of Cavers and a Lieut. in the Coldstream Guards, died on 29 May.

484 (e) Lady Grace] Lady Grace Douglas, Frank's mother.

486 (c) Bugenal] As Scott's u and a are alike, this should be Bagenal as above, p. 451.

487 (a) Steam Ship] The *City of Edinburgh* was launched on 31 Mar. 1821 and a similar vessel in April. They were over 400 tons and cost £20,000 each. See *Edin. Ann. Reg. for 1821*, XIV. ii. 103.

487 *n.* 2] Hogg's letter of 26 June is in Partington, *Letter-books*, pp. 95–7.

489 (b–c) Mellville] Lord Melville was at the Admiralty 1812–27 and 1828–30. C. B. Bathurst had become President of the Board of Control in Jan. 1821.

489 (d) Simson . . . his brother] William Simpson and his brother Andrew.

490 (e) false knight] Shakespeare, *As you like it*, I. 2.

493 (a) slane] See above, p. 486 *n.* 2.

493 (f) Aye theres the rub] Shakespeare, *Hamlet*, III. 1.

494 (a) To the editor of the Edinburgh Weekly Journal] This should not have been included in *SL*. It is an article, not a letter. See my note to *SL* i. 158 (b).

495 (e) "the cynosure of neighbouring eyes"] Milton, *L'allegro*, line 80.

497 (e) "every inch a King"] Shakespeare, *King Lear*, IV. 6.

498 (c) "noble horsemanship"] Shakespeare, *I Henry IV*, IV. 1.

501 (d–e) "not to man yourself with your kin"] Ramsay, *Proverbs*, p. 5: 'A man canna bear a' his kin on his back.' Also used in *SL* ix. 110 and *Journal*, 4 Aug. 1827.

503 *n.* 1] Add Lockhart reference: vi. 363.

503 *n.* 2] Correct title is: *Ballantyne's Novelist's Library*.

504 (a) To Lord Montagu] Date is Thursday, 23 Aug., when Col. Stanhope was at Abbotsford (*SL* vii. 4).

504 (a) Lady Isabella] Third daughter of 4th Duke of Buccleuch, afterwards Lady Isabella Cust.

504 (b) Chesters & Gala] Thomas Elliot Ogilvie of Chesters and John Scott of Gala.

504 (d) To Countess Pürgstall] This letter, though called original, is not in Scott's hand (NLS MS. 853, f. 330).

505 (b) The little volume] *Taschenbuch für die vaterländische Geschichte*, Erster Jahrgang 1820, 12mo Wien.

505 (d) The verses] The verses, wrote

Basil Hall, 'are no where to be found, and . . . appear never to have been written' (*Schloss Hainfeld*, p. 347).

505 *n.*] In last line, for 'Belches' read 'Belsches.'

507 (a) The gay and wild romance of life] Logan, *On the death of a young lady*, st. [13], lines 3–4. In *English minstrelsy*, ed. Scott (1810), i. 187.

507 (a–b) age dark and unlovely] Ossian, *Carthon; a poem*. In *The poems of Ossian . . . with notes . . . by Malcolm Laing*, 8vo Edinburgh, 1805, i. 346. Quoted in *SL* vii. 130, *MPW* xix. 338, and partially in *The Monastery*, chap. 17.

508 (a–b) like the slave in the poet's chariot] An allusion to the slave in the triumphal chariot at Rome. (Juvenal, *Satires*, X. 40–1.) See also *SL* viii. 338 and *Kenilworth*, chap. 21.

508 (c) To Maria Edgeworth] The reference to the royal visit shows that this letter was written in the second half of August and should have been printed in *SL* vii.

510 (b) *pieds de mouche*] See *SL* v. 279 and my note.

510 *n.* 3] The letter which she thinks has been lost (lines 8–9) was that of 27 Sept., which Scott did receive and which is cited in *SL* vii. 25 *n.* 2. The 'very curious letter' (line 5 from foot) must be a different one from the well-known one, dated 21 May 1823, in Partington, *Letter-books*, pp. 296–8. See *Lockhart*, vii. 227–9, and *SL* viii. 163 *n.* and my note.

511 (e) To J. G. Lockhart] Date must be 1820. Scoular's bust was included in the exhibition in Edinburgh which opened on 12 Mar. 1821. If the date were 1821 Scott would have had to wait till the exhibition had closed and *Valerius* had been published. But *Valerius* is still in proof, making the date about Autumn 1820 while Scott was still at Abbotsford.

VOLUME VII

3 (c) Mr. Kerr] William Kerr, Secretary to General Post Office.

3 (d) though Reaburn writes like a blockhead] Henry Raeburn, the por-

trait painter, who was going to Bothwell to paint a portrait of Lord Douglas. See below, pp. 9 *n.*, 10, 55.

4 (b–c) Man from the Sandwich islands]

Scott also refers to this Sandwich islander in the *Journal*, 13 May 1831.

4 (e) give a dog a bad name] *Kelly*, p. 124; Ramsay, *Proverbs*, p. 20. Also used in *Guy Mannering*, chap. 23.

5 (a–b) Lord Sidmouth . . . Lord Melville] Who were in Ireland in attendance on George IV during his state visit. The letter to Sidmouth, by being misdated, appears in *SL* v. 466.

8 (a) made a virtue of necessity] *Ray*, p. 214.

10 (c) "the metal of its pasture"] 'metal' should be 'mettle.' Shakespeare, *Henry V*, III. 1.

10 *n.* 3] The robbery took place on Monday, 24 Sept. The *Kelso Mail* of 1 Oct., reporting it, said: 'The robbery is supposed to have been committed by two or three men, who, from the manner in which they proceeded, appear to have been acquainted with the house.' It does not follow, from the omission in Chisholm's book, that there was no prosecution. Such a case would not have come before the Sheriff but would have been tried at the Circuit Court at Jedburgh.

11 (c) Barrowman] Read 'Borrowman.'

11 *n.* 1] For '1811 or 1812' read '26 Nov. 1811.'

12 (d) bricks with . . . straw] *Bible*, *Exodus* 5.

13 *n.* 1] Constable's letters of 15 Aug. and 3 Nov. are in *Archibald Constable*, iii. 149–51 and 165–6.

14 (b) Johns novels . . . Eastern Tales] *Ballantyne's Novelist's Library* and Weber's *Tales of the East*, both published by John Ballantyne.

14 *n.* 1] This long note is unnecessary as Constable's letter is printed in full in *Archibald Constable*, iii. 154–7.

15 (e) Dr. Johnson & Tom Campbell] Samuel Johnson, *The works of the English poets. With prefaces . . . by S. Johnson.* 68 vols., 8vo London, 1779–81; Thomas Campbell, *Specimens of the British poets*, 7 vols., 8vo London, 1819.

15 *n.* 1] Amend second paragraph. For 'Novelists' read 'Novelist's.' The essay on Charlotte Smith could not appear in the *Lives of the novelists* (Paris, 1825) which included only essays in *BNL*.

It was first printed in Scott's *Miscellaneous prose works* (1827), iv. 1–47.

17 (e) old oak panelling] Cedar was used for the Library.

18 (d) "I do well to be angry"] *Bible*, *Jonah* 4: 9.

20 (d) unless these abide in the ship] *Bible*, *Acts* 27: 31.

20 (d) James Gibson] James Gibson (afterwards Sir James Gibson-Craig) raised an action against subscribers to the bond of credit for support of *The Beacon*. The case came up in Court of Session, 22 Dec. 1821. (*Scots Mag.* lxxxix. 128.)

21 (b) *transeat* quoth John *cum cæteris erroribus*] Arbuthnot, *Law is a bottomless pit*, Pt 5, chap. 5 (Swift's *Works*, ed. Scott, 2nd ed., vi. 148).

21 *n.* 2] It was discontinued the following year.

22 (b) I did tell you] Shakespeare, *Henry VIII*, V. 2.

23 (a) garden in the fable] Aesop's *Fables*. See my note to *SL* ii. 526 (d).

25 *n.* 1] Scott may have got the line from Shakespeare's *II Henry IV*, V. 3.

27 (a) the other fellow] James Stuart of Dunearn.

28 (b) young gentleman] This should be 'young gentlemen'—not a particular person, but the 'youngsters' mentioned above.

28 (e) To Robert Jamieson] For explanation see below, p. 326 and cf. p. 128.

28 *n.* 1] Melville's letter of 4 Oct. must be a reply to a Scott letter not in *SL*. Scott's letter above, docketed 7 Oct., is a reply to Melville's letter of 4 Oct.

29 (d) Kinnoul Castle] An error for Dupplin Castle.

30 (c) To George Thomson] Date is probably 3 Dec. (which was a Monday) and the same as the letters to Murray (below, p. 37) and to John Richardson (below, p. 42).

30 (c) hung my harp on the willows] *Bible*, *Psalms* 137: 2.

30 (e) To Alexr. Young] The reference to the 'bustle of the concluding Session' shows that Scott is writing in July. If

the year is correct the Saturday was 7 July.

30 (e) Wallaces oak and of Queen Marys yew] See *SL* v. 123–4, viii. 362.

30 n. 1] It should be noted that the letter in Hadden, op. cit., is longer than the version given here from the original.

30 n. 2] Delete. The Robroyston chair was presented by Joseph Train in 1822. See below, p. 176. In any case, how could Scott put a chair beside the other tiny pieces of wood?

32 (c) Walter] His son. See below, p. 38.

32 n. 2] Lockhart does not give Waugh's Christian name. I have, however, a number of letters addressed to 'Robert Waugh, Melrose' from 1810 to 1830 which deal, among other matters, with the furnishing of a house in Melrose in 1810 and the shipment of rum from Jamaica. It is almost certain that Scott's 'melancholy Jaques' is this Robert Waugh. He also appears to be the brother of Dr John Waugh of Jamaica, whose daughter, Miss L. J. Waugh, married, at Melrose in 1820, Robert Henderson, Writer in Selkirk (q.v. in Index). Robert Waugh had a nephew, John Broomfield, and a niece, Mrs Mein Wight.

35 (a) To Lord Melville] Date is 1 Dec. 1820.

35 (a) Dr Simpson] Andrew Simpson, M.D.

37 (a) To John Murray] The date of this letter is Monday, 3 Dec. 1821.

37 (b) the other two letters] Presumably the letters to George Thomson (above, p. 30) and to John Richardson (below, p. 42); and, if so, these two letters should be dated 3 Dec.

37 (c) To John Murray] The original letter is dated 4 Dec.

39 (b) Labour's the price of our joys] This is from the chorus of a song beginning 'Life is chequer'd—toil and pleasure' in *The Blackbird*, new ed., Berwick, 1783, p. 30. Scott may also have got the line quoted from Smollett's *Peregrine Pickle*, chap. 2.

40 (a) if castles have not toppled] Shakespeare, *Macbeth*, IV. 1: 'Though castles topple on their warders' heads.'

41 (b) To James Ballantyne] This postscript was written before 10 Mar. but, as the letter to which it was attached is not in *SL*, I cannot date it more exactly.

42 (a) To John Richardson] The date is almost certainly Monday, 3 Dec. 1821. It is probably one of the 'Monday' letters sent through John Murray (above, p. 37) and written after Scott had heard of Joanna Baillie's success but before he could hear of her failure. See next note. *The pirate* was publ. in Dec. 1821 and this also helps to date the letter. (Date partially corrected in *SL* xii. 490.)

42 (a) Joanna's success] Her *De Monfort* was produced at Drury Lane on 27 Nov. 1821 and ran for only five nights. Joanna did not regard that as a success. See below, p. 58 n.

42 (a) as John Moodie says] Vanbrugh and Cibber, *The provoked husband*, I. 1. See my note to *SL* xi. 196 n.

42 (f) Capt Loch] Francis Erskine Loch.

43 (a) my cousin Raeburn] William Scott of Maxpoffle.

43 (a) "My trust is constant in thee"] See my note to *SL* v. 373 (d).

43 (a) getting rid of signing] See my note to *SL* vi. 342 (c).

43 (c) 3 volumes] *The pirate*.

43 n. 1] In line 6, for 'July 1825' read '8 Feb. 1825.'

44 (b) I saw him when he lost your brother] Scott had already referred to this, without mentioning names. See *SL* iii. 108–9.

46 (c) Minister of Castletown] Rev. David Scott who had died on 7 Jan.

46 (d) Lady Harriot] 6th daughter of 4th Duke of Buccleuch, afterwards Lady Harriet Moore.

49 (d–e) the horse can well enough carry the saddle] Ramsay, *Proverbs*, p. 27: 'He's a weak beast that downa bear the saddle.'

53 (d) for the armour & for Raeburn] See above, pp. 42–3.

54 (b) six pupils] See my note to *SL* vi. 292 (d).

55 (b) though he wrote an absurd letter]
This letter is referred to, above, p. 3.

55 (c) portrait of Walter] It was
exhibited at the Institution for the
Encouragement of the Fine Arts in
Scotland, 1822, No. 208, as 'Portrait of
an officer of the 18th Hussars.'

55 (e) Allans picture] See SL vi. 393 and
my note 393 (a).

55 n. 1] Scott had no brother-in-law
according to our definition of the
term. But in Scott's day 'in-law' was
used for any type of relation who was
not a blood relation. Here he is probably referring, not to one of the
McCullochs of Ardwall, but to William
Lockhart, for Allan's picture eventually
found a home at Milton-Lockhart.

56 (a) a new Clerk] Robert Hamilton.

56 (c–d) though Gideons fleece remains
dry] i.e. Lockhart's, referring back to
'shower' two lines above. Scott is not
quoting the Bible (*Judges* 6: 37–40)
where there are two miracles—in one
the fleece is wet, in the other dry. He is
quoting Cowley, *The complaint* (quoted
in *SL* ii. 451) st. 4, as he does in *The Heart
of Mid-Lothian*, chap. 1, where Hardie
says: 'We cannot complain, like Cowley, that Gideon's fleece remains dry. . .'

56 n. 1] Delete this note. Scott is not
quoting from Blackmore's *King Arthur*
but from his *A paraphrase on the Book
of Job*, 2° London, 1700, p. 100: 'He'll
raise thy Head now buried in the
Dust, / And make thee midst the Clouds
thy glitt'ring Turrets thrust.' Scott's
lines, however, approximate more
closely to the version given in Pope's
*Martinus Scriblerus . . . or, the art of sinking
in poetry*, in Swift's *Works*, ed. Scott,
2nd ed., xiii. 63: 'Thy head shall rise
though buried in the dust, / And 'midst
the stars his glittering turrets thrust.'
Scott, it seems certain, learned the lines,
not directly from Blackmore, but from
Pope when he was editing Swift.

57 n. 1] Joanna Baillie's letter of 2
Feb. is printed, with slight omissions,
in Partington, *Letter-books*, pp. 262–3.

58 n.] *De Monfort* was produced at
Drury Lane on 27 Nov. 1821 but ran for
only five nights. *Mother Bunch, or, the
Yellow Dwarf* was first produced at
Covent Garden on 26 Dec. 1821 and
had a long and successful run.

59 (c–d) Howison . . . has turnd meta-
physician] *An essay on the sentiments of
attraction, adaptation and variety*. Printed by
James Ballantyne & Co. for William
Blackwood, 1821. Howison's *Grammar
of infinite forms* was published in 1823.

59 (e) calld I think a night in Rome]
One night in Rome occupies pp. 79–104
of his *Fragments and fictions*, 12mo
Edinburgh, 1817.

61 (f) the half-bred swine] *Bible, Luke*
15:15–23. Scott's metaphor is confused.
He means that the theatre audience
(the prodigal son) would prefer the
husks of the swine rather than the
fatted calf, i.e. prefer *Mother Bunch*
rather than *De Monfort*.

62 (a) a dramatic scene] The story here
told became *Halidon Hill*, published
separately. Scott's contribution to
Joanna Baillie's volume was *MacDuff's
Cross*.

62 (a) Halidon hill (I think)] He
means Homildon Hill (1402). He gives
the correct battle below, p. 179.

63 (e) about ten years old] Margaret
Swinton died on 8 Nov. 1780 (*Scots
Mag.* xlii. 618). As Scott was only nine
when she died, this is another example
of his retentive memory.

64 n. 1] i.e. below, p. 498.

65 (c) To W. Laidlaw] The letter
should be dated a few days before 8
Feb. 1820, as on that day Scott issued a
single sheet, quarto, printed on one
side only, *To those inhabitants of the
Regality of Melrose, who offered, or proposed
to offer, their services to form a corps of
marksmen under Mr Walter Scott of
Abbotsford*.

65 (e) Capt. Elliots troop] This was the
3rd (or Hawick) Troop of the Corps of
Roxburghshire Yeomanry Cavalry. It
was raised in 1817 by Sir William
Francis Eliott, 7th Bart. of Stobs. See
Trans. Hawick Arch. Soc. 1915, p. 37.

66 (a) 1819 or 1820] This should be
1817 or 1819.

68 n. 1] Delete this inaccurate note.
The title of Wenlock's book is: *To the
most illustrious, high and mighty majesty of
Charles the II: . . . The humble declaration
of John Wenlock of Langham*, etc., sm. 4to
London, Printed by T. Childe and L.
Parry for the author . . . 1662.

69 (a) Lockharts Quixote] Scott had suggested (above, p. 16) that Constable should take it. In spite of what Scott says here, it was published by Hurst, Robinson and Constable.

69 (f)–70 one . . . with the gout and the other a novice] Sir Robert Dundas and Robert Hamilton.

71 (d) Mortham parapet] This bears no resemblance to the Tower of the Shields.

72 (b) Tower of the Shields] The plan was never carried out and the shields remain blank.

74 (a) Solomon . . . temple] *Bible*, *I Kings* 6: 7.

74 *n.* 1] There is an extract from this letter in Partington, *Post-bag*, pp. 162–3.

75 (b–c) like King Corney busied with pulling down and building up] Maria Edgeworth, *Ormond*, chaps. 4 and 9.

75 (c) "thof unknown"] See *SL* vi. 110 and my note.

75 (f) I wrote you so lately] The previous letter in *SL* (vii. 4) is dated 22 Aug. 1821. There must be several missing letters since Walter set off for Berlin.

75 (f) Mr. Rose's nephew] George Pitt Rose, nephew of William Stewart Rose and son of Sir George Rose.

77 *n.* 1] May not Walter have begun his letter on 16 Feb. and continued it later as his father often did? Additional evidence that the date cannot be 16 Feb. is provided by Walter's letter in which he says he is moving to Unter den Linden on 15 Mar. (Partington, *Letter-books*, p. 34.)

77 *n.* 2] Delete 'Presumably.'

79 (a) the sketches] The biographical introductions to *Ballantyne's Novelist's Library*.

79 *n.* 1] For 'Kitchener' read 'Kitchiner.'

80 (a) letters from abroad] This is a continuation of the unfulfilled 'New travels on the Continent' first projected in 1818. See *SL* i. 525, v. 205–6, 205 *n.*

80 *n.*] In line 5, for 'Kitchener' read 'Kitchiner.'

82 (b–c) the removal of David Hume . . .] This sentence is very confused. Scott means: 'the removal [on his appointment as Baron of Exchequer] of David Hume [and the absence] with a sharp fit of the gout on the part of Sir Robt. Dundas, have for the time thrown some fagg on me as [this means that] one brother of the Clerks table [Dundas] is absent & the other [Robert Hamilton is] a novice.'

82 *n.* 1] This long note is unnecessary as Constable's letter of 14 Feb. is printed in full in *Archibald Constable*, iii. 171–180.

83 (b) Lady Dumfries] Margaret Crauford who became the wife of 6th Earl of Dumfries in 1771 and died in 1799.

83 (c) So glides this world away] Shakespeare, *Hamlet*, III. 2.

86 *n.* 1] Delete 'Presumably.'

87 (b) To James Ballantyne] This letter must come after the letter to Hurst & Robinson of 10 Mar. (below, p. 94).

87 (d) the Manuscript] This must be *Historie and life of King James the Sext*. Malcolm Laing had brought out part of it in 1804 but he never completed the work. Thomas Thomson edited the whole work for the Bannatyne Club in 1825. Scott's letter is rather ambiguous but he seems to have got Thomson to do the editing for which Scott 'will venture on 250 copies.' The first paragraph of the next letter (p. 88) continues the story. After the Bannatyne Club was founded in 1823 it must have been decided that Thomson would edit the work for it. 52 copies were printed at the expense of the Club and 150 on different paper for general circulation. The plan of 150 copies for non-members seems to carry on Scott's original plan for 250 copies. See also *SL* i. 294.

87 *n.* 2] Scott, following Chalmers, gave his Christian name as Charles and the date of his death as 'about the year 1800'; *DNB* likewise. But the *Scots Mag.* Vol. 48 (Sept. 1786), p. 465, recorded the death at Chinsura, Bengal, of 'William Johnson, the reputed author of . . . the Adventures of a Guinea.'

88 (a) To James Ballantyne] In his letter of 23 Mar. (below, p. 103) Scott says he has finished a quarter of Vol. 3 of *Nigel*, but is retaining it till 'the beginning of the week.' In this letter

(p. 89) he is sending it. Date of letter, therefore, is about 25 Mar.

88 (b) Chrysal] For *Ballantyne's Novelist's Library*, Vol. 4.

88 (c) Brodies diary] I cannot find any quotation from Brodie in *Chronological notes*.

88 *n.* 1] Delete. Scott is referring to Thomas Thomson's *Historie* of James VI mentioned on previous page.

89 (b) Niggle] David MacRitchie suggested that Nigel should be pronounced 'Niggle' with a hard 'g'. See *N. & Q.* 8th ser. vi. 281, 514.

89 (f) For Walter Scott] Date must be Feb. as Walter had received the letter by 5 Mar. (p. 90 *n.* 1).

89 (f) Your letters came both together] The first was from Hamburg (mentioned p. 92), quoted in Partington, *Post-bag*, p. 162, and the second from Berlin, 27 Jan., of which there is an extract, ibid., pp. 162–3.

90 (b) Comptesse Nial] Countess Pauline Neale. She wrote to Scott from Abercromby Place, Edinburgh, 29 Jan. 1822 (NLS MS. 3894, ff. 31–2). In her letter she referred to the delightful day she had spent in Castle Street. If this is the dinner mentioned by Scott, this would confirm that Scott wrote the letter in Feb.

93 *n.* 1] Walter's letter of 22 Feb. is in Partington, *Letter-books*, pp. 33–5.

94 *n.* 1] Delete this note and see *SL* xii. 490.

95 *n.*] In line 3, for '*Prose Works*' read '*MPW*'.

95 *n.* 1] For '*Lives of the Novelists*' read '*MPW* iii. 401, 403.'

96 (e) To Lord Montagu] The date is 14 Mar., the day on which the letter was finished.

96 (f) "two blackies..."] *Kelly*, p. 321; Ramsay, *Proverbs*, p. 69.

96 *n.* 2] Delete this note. Scott is not asking for this work but for the *Manchester Transactions*.

97 (e) Sydney Smith ... "The Rectors horse..."] In his lectures to the Royal Institution in 1804–6 Sydney Smith dealt with the beautiful and picturesque. The lectures were first published in

1850 as *Elementary sketches of moral philosophy*, but the work does not contain the illustration Scott cites. His source must have been oral or a newspaper report.

97 *n.* 1] For 'see note 4 to that letter' read 'see above, p. 55, *n.* 2' and for 'see note 3 to same' read 'see *SL.* v. 323, 349.'

98 *n.* 1] It was edited anonymously by Thomas Thomson.

99 (b) a good gardiner] William Bogie. He is mentioned in an extract from Lord Montagu's letter of 22 Mar. in Partington, *Post-bag*, p. 165.

99 (d) Gala & capt Scott] John Scott of Gala and his uncle George Scott, afterwards Admiral Sir George Scott.

99 (f) I have got some Botany bay plants & seeds] George Harper, in a letter from Sydney, 14 Aug. 1821, wrote: 'Please accept a few Australian seeds which perhaps may be a rarity in Scotland' (NLS MS. 3893, ff. 41–2).

100 (b) The Provost] Rev. Joseph Goodall, Provost of Eton.

100 (c) Prince Potemkin] For similar stories of books to suit shelves, see the *World*, No. 15 (12 Apr. 1753) [Chalmers, *British essayists*, xxvi. 77] and R. P. Gillies, *Recollections of Sir Walter Scott*, London, 1837, p. 200.

100 (d) Henrietta Maria] Oil on canvas (31 × 19 in.); artist unknown. I think Scott bought this at John Ballantyne's sale, 19 Jan. 1820, Lot 855, when it was described as a Van Dyck. The portrait now hangs on the staircase in the Hope-Scott addition.

101 (a) Anne] Apparently the result of the Bachelors' Ball. See above, p. 94.

102 *n.* 1] The intelligent young man (lines 13–14) is G. P. R. James. The aunt is Mrs Churnside. See *Lockhart*, i. 140.

103 (a) more than one fourth of the volume] *Nigel*.

103 (b) Respecting funds] On 21 Mar. James Ballantyne had sent the statement for Apr., showing a deficit of £1,647. (*Reply to Mr Lockhart's pamphlet*, p. 84.) Here Scott is providing for that sum.

103 (e) To Archibald Constable] I think this letter should be dated 13 Mar.:

(1) Scott loses no time in answering Constable's letter of 9 Mar., which he would receive on 12 or 13 Mar.; (2) the storm to which he refers (p. 106) had abated by 20 Mar. (p. 101).

103 n. 1] Constable's letter of 9 Mar. is in *Archibald Constable*, iii. 203–6 and that of 27 Mar. ibid. iii. 214–15. Constable's book was printed in London by James Moyes, Greville Street. No other ed. was called for.

104 (e) They talk of a farmer] Swift, *Gulliver's travels*, Pt II, *A voyage to Brobdingnag*, chap. 6 (*Works*, ed. Scott, 2nd ed., xi. 174).

105 n. 1] For 'Roughhead' read 'Roughead.'

106 (b) Lieut. on the ½ pay of the 15th] He was gazetted Lieut. in Oct. 1821, by purchase from John Pennington, retired.

106 (d) sit at Rome and strive with the Pope] See *SL* iv. 419.

107 n. 1] For 'Kitchener' read 'Kitchiner.' There is an extract from Kitchiner's letter to Constable in Partington, *Post-bag*, p. 163. In *The Royal Scottish minstrelsy*, 12mo Leith, 1824, p. 229, there are additional lines to the national anthem said to be by Scott.

108 (e) a little tower] The Tower of the Shields. The arms were not carved on the shields and they remain blank.

108 (e) peerless blades Morritts] A comma should have been inserted. The peerless blade is William Erskine, not Morritt.

110 (d) who have thrown their bread] *Bible, Ecclesiastes* 11: 1.

111 (d) *in meditatione fugae*] Meditating flight. A Scots law phrase. See Trayner, *Latin maxims*. Used in *Nigel*, chap. 5, and *Redgauntlet*, chap. 20 (Narrative, chap. 7).

113 n. 1] There is no justification for saying that the letters crossed and that Lockhart's letter was mistakenly dated Friday. When Scott wrote on Thursday he did not know of Boswell's death. Lockhart received his letter on Friday and replied on same day that had he known that Scott had not heard the news he would have written 'yesterday', i.e. Thursday. Furthermore, Lockhart's reference to the 'bloody lesson' shows he is replying to Scott's letter.

116 n. 1] Byron's letter (line 1) is printed in Partington, *Letter-books*, pp. 188–90, where Partington notes the omission in previous eds. of '(or rather mine).' In line 3, for '1830' read '1898–1904.'

119 (d) as Christopher Sly has it] Shakespeare, *The taming of the shrew*, Induction.

120 (c) "large of limb and bane"] *Sir Cauline*, Pt I, st. [17], line 2; 'And large of limb and bone.' In Percy's *Reliques*.

121 (a) At whose glare the Cumbrian oft] See *SL* v. 264 and my note.

121 (b) in your ancestor's Narrative] The incident described here by Scott is in *The narrative of the Honourable John Byron . . . containing an account of the great distresses . . . on the coasts of Patagonia*, etc., 12mo London, 1788, pp. 82–3. There is no hint that the sailors thought they saw a mermaid, for the figure is described as 'that of a man swimming half out of water.'

121 (d) a beautiful little family property] Dryburgh Abbey.

122 (d) Lady Mary Wortley's remark] Scott cites her in almost the same words in *The Fair Maid of Perth*, chap. 1, and in the 1831 introd. to *Nigel*. The nearest source appears to be a letter to Wortley from her, 11 Dec. 1758, in which she says: 'I have found, wherever I have travelled, that the pleasantest spots of ground have been in the vallies which are encompassed with high mountains.' Scott's application of this idea is not very apt.

122 (e) one of my colleagues] Sir Robert Dundas of Beechwood.

123 (e) "*Scotland* is turned an *England* now"] *Turnimspike*, st. [6], line 1. In Herd, ii. 187.

124 (a) To James Ballantyne] Date is 30 Apr. Scott went to Jedburgh on that day for election of a Collector of Cess and wrote on his return. See opening and closing words of the letter.

124 (d) errors in Le Sage] i.e. in Vol. 4 of *Ballantyne's Novelist's Library*.

125 n. 2] Canning was nominated Governor-General of India in Mar. but

he resigned in Sept. before taking up office. Capt. Maclean is Allan T. Maclean. If he got promotion it was not immediately for he was still Capt. in 13th Light Dragoons in 1826.

126 (a) Chalmers] *Caledonia*, 3 vols., 1808–24, by George Chalmers.

126 (a) Riddell] John Riddell, Advocate.

126 (c) A worthy clergyman] This is Rev. Edmund Cartwright, whose letter to Scott of 23 Feb. 1822 (NLS MS. 3894, ff. 79–80) was passed on to Scott by Sir Thomas Bradford with a letter of 18 Mar. (NLS MS. 3894, ff. 110–11).

126 (e) John Maclean] His identity has not been established. See W. M. Parker, *A Jacobite refugee mystery* in *N. & Q.* Vol. 196 (28 Apr. 1951), pp. 182–4.

128 (a) the rascal] Probably Robert Jamieson. See above, p. 28.

128 (c) your gallant clansman] Capt. Allan T. Maclean of 13th Light Dragoons (above, p. 125 *n.* 2).

128 (d) Governor General] First Marquess of Hastings.

128 (e) To Lord Montagu] Date is 6 June 1822. (Corrected in *SL* xii. 490.)

128 (e) like Ophelia] Shakespeare, *Hamlet*, IV. 5.

129 (b–c) a cousin of mine] James Scott, son of Scott's uncle Thomas.

130 (a) age is dark and unlovely] Ossian. See *SL* vi. 507.

130 (c) residence near Jedburgh] Monklaw. See also below, p. 164.

131 (c) To Lord Montagu] The agreement, reported in this letter, was later called by Scott the 'Convention of Jedburgh.' See *SL* vii. 148, ix. 110.

133 (e) Torwoodlee] On proposed railway from Dalkeith to St. Boswells see my note to *SL* v. 116 (b).

134 (a) Melrose Abbey] This is the first reference to the repairs. There are apparent inconsistencies in Scott's accounts but these can be reconciled if we suppose that the work was carried out in two parts, the first being finished in Oct. 1822 and the second in 1823.

135 (a) Laird of Craig] James Gordon.

135 *n.* 4] For 'Clydesdale, Lanarkshire' read 'Dumfriesshire.'

136 (a) Tutors of Buccleuch] i.e. legal guardians of the young Duke. See *SL* vi. 477 (d–e).

136 (b) Riddle] Charles Riddell of Muselee, chamberlain to the Duke of Buccleuch.

137 (d) the fair bride] Lady Charlotte Scott, 2nd daughter of 4th Duke of Buccleuch. She married Lord Stopford on 4 July. See above, p. 133.

137 (d) Moulsey Hurst] Molesey Hurst, near Hampton Court, famous for boxing matches.

137 (e–f) a *fowl* (meaning I presume *fool*)] On 'dukes and fools' see Scott's note to *The Heart of Mid-Lothian*, chap. 18. See also *SL* v. 128 and *Journal*, 30 Nov. 1825.

138 (d) learnd Theban] Shakespeare, *King Lear*, III. 4. Cf. *The Abbot*, chap. 26.

138 (e) your Lordships trumpets] For suggested amendment, see *SL* xii. 490.

138 *n.* 1] The correct title is: *Anecdotes and history of Cranbourn Chase*. There is no evidence that Rose gave Scott this book. Lockhart was probably misled by Rose's later interest in it. See *SL* x. 68 *n.*

141 (a) my old bloodhound] Maida who died in Oct. 1824. He was a deerhound.

141 (e) his guardians] See *SL* vi. 477 (d–e).

142 (b) Early Popular poetry] Laing's *Select remains of ancient popular poetry of Scotland* came out in parts between Nov. 1821 and Dec. 1822. Robert Pitcairn assisted him.

142 *n.* 1] Delete the sentence beginning 'Laing is preparing.'

144 (b) Bishops famous Manuscript] Thomas Percy's folio MS. from which his *Reliques* was partly compiled.

144 *n.* 2] Laing did not procure *John the Reeve*. It was printed, however, in Small's ed. of Laing's *Select remains* (1885), pp. 42–79. See also Scott's *Minstrelsy* (ed. Henderson), i. 236.

145 (c) your little modest volume] Sir

Marmaduke Maxwell . . . The Mermaid of Galloway, etc., 12mo London, 1822, the preface of which is dated Mar. 1822. Later Cunningham sent *Traditional tales of the English and Scottish peasantry*, 2 vols., London, 1822, and an advance copy of *Sir Marmaduke Maxwell*, 2nd ed., 12mo London, 1822. Scott did not acknowledge them as is shown by a letter from Cunningham, 9 Sept. 1822, in Partington, *Letter-books*, pp. 231–2.

145 *n*. 1] Delete this note and substitute: Prince Adam Constantin Czartoryski, (1804–80), son of Constantin Czartoryski, younger brother of the famous Prince Adam George Czartoryski (1770–1861). See Index.

147 (c) "I'd rather be a kitten . . ."] Shakespeare, *I Henry IV*, III. 1.

147 *n*. 1] See my note to *SL* vi. 461 *n*.

148 (b) Convention of Jedburgh] Scott's humorous title for the letter above, pp. 131–2. See also *SL* ix. 110.

148 (c) Mr. Rutherford] From the context this must be John Rutherford of Mossburnford.

148 (e) on thursday last] This should be Wednesday, 24 Apr. John Smith recorded in his diary under 24 Apr.: 'Met Sir Walter and Major Riddell in Melrose.' Scott gives the correct date above, p. 141.

148 (e) one Smith] John Smith of Darnick was building the second portion of Abbotsford at this time and Scott would never refer to him as 'one Smith.' It is a misreading for Jno Smith.

151 (e) as plainly as Sancho's cow-heel] Cervantes, *Don Quixote*, Pt II, chap. 59 (Lockhart's ed., 1822, v. 177).

151 (f) Torwoodlees letter] See above, pp. 133–4.

152 (b) offerd me today a swan] But Scott had recorded this on 21 Apr. (above, p. 139).

152 (e) Mr. Milne] This relates to the proposed letting of Faldonside within a short distance of Abbotsford. See below, pp. 155–6, 155 *n*., 161, 294.

152 (e) rickyard] Read 'orchard.' (Corrected in *SL* xii. 490.)

153 (c) To James Ballantyne] The

date is about 29 May. The Saturday of the letter is 1 June. See below, pp. 181, 289. In Symington, *Some unpublished letters*, p. 119, where it is misdated May 1823.

153 *n*. 2] *Halidon Hill* was originally proposed for Joanna Baillie's collection. But by the time Scott writes this letter the plan had been abandoned and Scott is here referring to *Halidon Hill* as a separate publication. The MS. of this drama was given to Cadell.

154 (a) To James Ballantyne] The date is Jan. 1830 when Scott is preparing a new ed. of his poetical works. Ballantyne is printing *from* Joanna Baillie's *A collection of poems* which did not appear till 1823. Scott is now writing an introd. to *Macduff's Cross* which it did not have in Joanna Baillie's volume.

154 *n*. 1] Delete this note, which is not now applicable.

155 (a) To James Skene] There is another letter to him on these stones (not in *SL*) in Skene, *Memories*, pp. 95–6.

156 (a) not well certainly. If . . .] Read 'not well certainly if he can help himself. To the break . . .' (Correction in *SL* xii. 490.)

157 (c–d) a good picture] This paragraph refers to two portraits—one for Raeburn himself finished in 1823 and one for Lord Montagu left unfinished.

158 (f) burning bricks] Tens of thousands of bricks used in the building of the house and the fruit garden wall were made on the premises by Creelman of Portobello. Creelman visited Abbotsford on 29 May to see the operations. (John Smith's MS. diary.)

159 *n*. 1] Delete and see my note to *SL* iii. 153.

159 *n*. 2] See also James Dallas, *The history of the family of Dallas*, Edinburgh, 1921, pp. 375–6.

160 (c) To James Skene] Monday was 13 May in 1822.

160 (d) yeoman's service] Shakespeare, *Hamlet*, V. 2.

160 (d) delicate arches] Read 'delicate touches.' (Corrected in *SL* xii. 490.)

160 *n*. 1] Scott is more likely to have taken it from *The gaberlunzie man*, st.

[10], line 1, in Ramsay, *Tea-table miscellany.*

160 *n.* 2] In line 1, for '1837, v. 64' read 'vi. 314.'

160 *n.* 3] For explanation of Camul, see *SL* xii. 490, where Weber's *Tales* should be dated 1812.

161 (a) Milne] About lease of Faldonside. See above, pp. 152–3, 155–6, 155 *n.*, and below, p. 294.

163 (b) the old proverb] *Ray*, pp. 52, 350–1.

163 (d) a Daniel coming to Judgement] Shakespeare, *Merchant of Venice*, IV. 1.

163 (d) an honest gentleman] George Harper, whom Scott had befriended when he got into trouble.

163 (e) Colonel Rutherford] As Scott calls him 'Colonel' this must be John Rutherford of Edgerston. John Rutherford of Mossburnford was 'Major.'

163 (f)–164 scripture phrase with coals of fire] *Bible, Proverbs* 25: 22; *Romans* 12: 20.

164 (a) Monklaw] See above, p. 130.

164 *n.* 2] Delete 'Evidently.'

165 (c) Jeshurun] *Bible, Deuteronomy* 32: 15.

165 *n.* 2] For 'Maxpopple' read 'Maxpoffle.'

166 (c) Mr. Rose . . . Celts] Walter, in his letter of 22 Feb. (Partington, *Letter-books*, p. 34), had said: 'Young Rose wishes particularly to get into the Celtic Society.' He is not given as a member in the list of members of the Celtic Society published in 1825.

166 *n.* 1] George Pitt Rose was not the son of Hugh Rose of Kilravock. For the family connection see *N. & Q.*, Vol. 191, pp. 224–5.

167 (d) To Walter Scott] Letter belongs to end of May as reference to *Nigel* shows.

167 (e) Kyle] This is Thomas Kyle, Younger of Fens, who was served heir in 1811 to his mother Janet Kyle, wife of David Kyle of Fens and formerly wife of Alexander Fisher of Clackmaa. He continued to reside in Prussia and visited Abbotsford on 4 Aug. 1837 when he signed the Visitors' Book as 'Thos.

Kyle Late of Fens on his way for Konigsberg East Prussia.'

168 (b) more sinned against than sinning] Shakespeare, *King Lear*, III. 2.

168 (f) a Bath beauty] Mary Jane Palliser. See above, p. 165 *n.* 1.

168 (f) Put your hand into the creel] *Kelly*, p. 278, where it is thus explained: 'Spoken of taking a wife, where no cunning art or sense can secure a good choice, but must be taken for *better and worse.*' Also in Ramsay, *Proverbs*, p. 54.

168 *n.* 1] The company was formed at Dunbar in 1810. On 10 Apr. 1822 William Borthwick, the cashier, absconded with £21,000.

169 (d–e) Spain] For suggested amendment, see *SL* xii. 490.

170 (a) To James Ballantyne] As Scott told Sharpe on 9 Mar. that he would receive a copy of Fountainhall (above, p. 94) and since the work was reviewed in the *Edinburgh Mag.* for Apr., this letter must belong to the second half of Mar. after the Courts rose.

170 (b) Richard Surtees] Should be Robert Surtees.

170 (c) Corrected Waverley] For *Novels and tales* [Waverley–Montrose] 12 vols., 18mo Edinburgh, 1823. See also below, p. 245.

172 (b) ArchBp. of Armagh] For an account of his death, see *Edin. Ann. Reg. for 1822*, XV. ii. 241–2.

173 (d) Glengarry] Scott told this story, with an addition, to Mrs Hughes of Uffington. See Hughes, *Letters*, p. 290. See also *SL* iv. 12 (c).

173 *n.* 1] Delete this note and see Walter Scott of Satchells, *A true history*, Hawick, 1894, p. 52: 'If Heather-tops had been Meal of the best, / Then Buckcleugh-mill had gotten a noble grist.'

175 (d) "to whet your almost blunted purpose"] Shakespeare, *Hamlet*, III. 4.

175 (f) "auld craig back again"] See *Provincial antiquities* in *MPW* vii. 441.

176 (c) Sharpe . . . Fountainhall] Scott probably wanted Sharpe's support, for Sharpe in 1819 had made a contract with Constable to edit Mylne's transcript. Scott, however, made no

reference to this in the preface to his own ed. It is significant that the paper of Scott's ed. is watermarked 1819 except for one sheet dated 1817. See *Sharpe's Letters*, ii. 194, 197, 198 and *SL* v. 334, 334 *n.*

176 (d) the curious chair] This chair, made from wood from Robroyston near Kirkintilloch, the scene of Sir William Wallace's betrayal, sits in the Study at Abbotsford. It was made by John Stirling, cabinetmaker, Kirkintilloch.

178 *n.* 1] In line 1, for '27th' read '27th March' and in line 7, for '31st' read '31st May.' These two letters are in *Archibald Constable*, iii. 214-15, 218-21.

180 *n.* 2] This note seems to refer to Sophia's letter to Constable thanking him for books and written in the third person by 'Miss Scott' and dated from Castle Street, 'Thursday.' (NLS MS. 677, f. 37.) Thursday was 27 Apr., two days before her marriage. Scott would not retain this letter for over two years and he must be referring to another, quite recent, one relating to a gift of china. Sophia showed Mrs Hughes of Uffington the set of Scott's novels, extra-illustrated with engravings and 'splendidly bound,' given by Constable. See Hughes, *Letters*, p. 144.

180 *n.* 3] I do not see why this should come *after* the letter to Constable. Scott was at Abbotsford on Sunday, 2 June. The Sunday of the letter is probably 26 May, i.e. *before* he wrote to Constable. Lady Morton's letter in NLS is MS. 3895, ff. 251-2.

181 (d) *friday*] Friday was 31 May.

181 (e) To John Richardson] Date is probably 30 Apr.: (1) Circuits were held in Apr.; (2) Scott was in Edinburgh on 30 May.

182 (d) rite et legaliter peracta] Duly performed and completed. An English and Scots law phrase. Cf. 'rite et solenniter acta et peracta' in *Waverley*, chap. 50.

182 (f) It skills not much when it is delivered] Shakespeare, *Twelfth Night*, V. 1.

183 (a) pay for the armour] See above, pp. 42-3.

183 (c) To Hugh Scott] Date is 6 June 1824. The contents—Henry in

Germany, the 'doings' at Abbotsford, illness of Erskine and Scott of Gala, and the ice-house—all apply to 1824.

183 (c) Henry the German William] A comma should have been inserted after 'German' to show that it is Henry who is the German. See *SL* viii. 171.

183 (e) disqualified by promotion] The prospect of getting the Polwarth peerage. At that time the eldest son of a Scottish peer was disqualified from sitting in the House of Commons.

184 (a) Gala] For this accident to John Scott of Gala (which occurred in 1824) see *SL* viii. 230-1, 232, 240, 242-3, 252-3, 262, 338.

184 (c) eldest boy] Walter was almost eleven when this letter was written.

185 (b) Cranbourne Chase] By Rev. William Chafin. Montagu took Scott's advice and had some blank leaves bound in. On these Scott later wrote some anecdotes as promised. See *N. & Q.* 3rd ser. Vol. 11 (19 Jan. 1867), p. 63.

185 (c) which I got from good authority] From William Stewart Rose.

185 (c) [*blank in MS.*]] This is supplied in *SL* x. 68 *n.*—'woman behind a hedge.'

185 (e) Houses] Read 'Thanes.' (Correction in *SL* xii. 490, where reference is given to Shakespeare, *Macbeth*, V. 3.)

185 (e) Borthwickbrae has got what he wanted] William Elliot-Lockhart of Borthwickbrae. His third son, Walter, had been appointed to a writership in India (p. 184 *n.* 2).

185 (f) Anniversary of Waterloo] John Smith of Darnick noted in his diary (still in MS.) that he breakfasted with Scott on the 18th and later attended the Waterloo dinner at which Scott was present.

187 *n.* 3] A grassum is a sum of money paid periodically by a tenant, usually every nineteen years. See Trayner, *Latin maxims.*

191 (d) The Deil has lately danced off] An allusion to Burns's *The deil's awa' wi' the exciseman.*

192 (a) two copies of Halidon Hill] 2nd ed. The copy for Montagu, which has the Ditton bookplate, is now in my Scott Coll.

192 (c) Miss Morritts health] Morritt's niece, Catherine Morritt.

192 *n.* 1] Scott's works, containing his letter to Cadell, 14 June 1822 (not in *SL*), asking him to send them to the Clarendon Hotel, were offered for sale by William Downing, bookseller, Birmingham, in 1907. (*N. & Q.* 10th ser. ix. 19.)

193 (a) Dunkeld] Dunkeld House, a seat of the Duke of Atholl in Perthshire.

194 (c) in a ridiculous article] In *The Beacon*. See *Edin. Ann. Reg. for 1822*, XV. ii, Appendix, p. 22 *n.*

194 (c) the Queens supposed . . . visit to Scotland] Viscount Hood, Lord Chamberlain to the Queen, wrote to Brougham, 21 July 1821: 'Her Majesty has commanded me to say she intends visiting Scotland, but I have not as yet heard the time fixed.' See *Creevey*. Selected and re-ed. by John Gore. Repr., London, 1949, p. 213. The visit never took place. For a curious story of this proposed visit, told by Scott to Mrs Hughes of Uffington, see Hughes, *Letters*, p. 294.

196 *n.* 1] For 'Latham' read 'Lathom.'

197 (a) inclosed dramatic Sketch] *Halidon Hill*. This copy was offered for sale by H. G. Bohn in his catalogue, 1841, No. 21,114.

197 (d) Mrs. Baillie] *Halidon Hill* was dedicated to her.

197 (e) Sergeant Major] Sergeant Major Masi. See *Edin. Ann. Reg. for 1822*, XV. ii. 234.

197 (f) Taaffe . . . I knew him in Edinburgh] John Taaffe was in Edinburgh and was elected one of the Presidents of the Speculative Society. (*Scots Mag.* Vol. 73 (Dec. 1811), p. 955.) Scott must have met him at this time but I have no record of a meeting. He was the author of *Padilla, a tale of Palestine*, 8vo London, 1816, and of *Comment on the Divine Comedy of Dante*, 8vo London, 1822. Taaffe and Byron were friendly in Italy. Byron, in several letters to John Murray, urged Murray to publish Taaffe's commentary.

197 *n.* 1] For 'letter to Oehlenschläger, 16th January 1824' read '*SL* iii. 282 and viii. 151 and *n.* 3.'

198 (e) Cochrane hoax] This occurred in 1814. See *SL* iii. 459 and *n.* and my note.

199 (f) Cunningham] James Cunningham, W.S. (died, 1686). His work is *An essay upon the inscription of Macduff's Crosse in Fyfe*, Edinburgh, 1678; repr. 1716; and included in *Miscellanea Scotica*, 1719, and in *Scotia rediviva*, 1826.

200 *n.* 2] The quotation is from chap. 28. Similar views are expressed in chap. 10.

201 (b) the rumour . . . revives again] Unless the letter is wrongly dated, this is inconsistent with the statement that official notice had come on 24 June (above, p. 193). But the Lord Provost of Edinburgh did not receive official notice till 18 July. See my note to *SL* vii. 213 (b).

201 (d) To Rahbek] Printed in *The Sir Walter Scott Quarterly*, Vol. 1, Jan. 1928, pp. 179–80, where a footnote identifies Wallich as Nathanael Wallich, the botanist, instead of his brother Arnold, the artist.

202 (c) Œlenschlager] Two of his works formed the groundwork of an article in the *Scots Mag.* Vol. 90 (Nov. 1822), pp. 537–45. The article may be by R. P. Gillies and based on works recently given to Scott.

202 *n.* 1] Delete 'evidently his agent.' Feldborg, a Danish poet, was simply obliging Oehlenschlager by bringing his gift to Scott. Feldborg met Lockhart and Sophia in Edinburgh and he visited Abbotsford on 10 Oct. 1822. (*N. & Q.* 11th ser. vi. 147.) He was negotiating the publication of his *Denmark delineated*. (See Goudie, *David Laing*, Edinburgh, 1913, p. 241.) Feldborg was in Edinburgh again in Jan. 1824. (See *SL* viii. 154.) Scott had no personal interest in *Denmark delineated*, which was published by Baldwin, Cradock and Joy, London, and Oliver and Boyd and D. Lizars, Edinburgh, and printed by J. Brewster, Edinburgh.

203 (a) To B. R. Haydon] The correct date is 1 July [1829]. See my note to the footnote.

203 *n.*] The article in *Blackwood* (line 3) was in Vol. 9 (Apr. 1821), pp. 43–59,

Horae Danicae. No. V. *Masaniello: a tragedy.* By B. S. Ingeman.

203 *n.* 1] Delete whole note and substitute: Haydon married Mary Hymans in Oct. 1821. His eldest son, Frank Scott Haydon, was born on 12 Dec. 1822, but he was not christened till 13 July 1829. Scott's original letter has the PM 1829 and the words in fourth line of text above should read 'the honour you propose me in giving your son my name.' That Scott speaks (p. 204) of the 'little infant' is understandable as he would assume that his godson would be an infant and not, as he was now, six years old. The date, Jan. 1823, is impossible: (1) Scott was not at Blair-Adam then, but he went to Blair-Adam on 26 June 1829; (2) Sophia and others of the family went to Abbotsford (*Journal*, 1 July 1829) in 1829, but not in Jan. 1823, and in Jan. 1823 John Hugh was the only child but Scott here speaks of Sophia's 'family.' The evidence for the 1829 date will be found in letters from Frank Scott Haydon himself to the *Athenæum*, 1877 (21 July), pp. 79–80; (8 Sept.), p. 307.

204 (b) To J. W. Croker] For Abercromby's motion against Sir William Rae in the House of Commons, see *Edin. Ann. Reg. for 1822*, XV. i. 223–5. See also below, p. 209 *n.* 2.

205 (c) *vox signata*] A technical word. A Scots law phrase. (Trayner, *Latin maxims.*) Used in non-legal sense in *The Antiquary*, chap. 36.

206 (e) chamber in the wall] *Bible, II Kings* 4: 10.

207 (a) To Joanna Baillie] The date is Saturday, 15 June 1822, the first Saturday after the Blair-Adam trip.

207 (a) your godchild] *Halidon Hill*, dedicated to her.

207 (c) a subject in my head] *MacDuff's Cross.*

207 (c) "accoutred like a Thane"] Joanna Baillie, *Ethwald, Part I*, I. 4.

207 *n.* 1] Delete 'Scott is sending' down to 'p. 57' and see my note to *SL* vii. 153 *n.* 2.

208 (c) The bricks] See my note to *SL* vii. 158 (f).

209 (a) glass] Read 'gloves.' (Corrected in *SL* xii. 490.) The references to

gloves, above, p. 187 and *n.* 2, should have prevented this misreading.

209 (b) The Lord *will* come] I have failed to find this in their metrical version of the Psalms.

209 (c) *particeps fraudis*] Partner in a fraud. A Scots law phrase. See Trayner, *Latin maxims.*

209 *n.* 2] In first line, delete 'Presumably.'

210 (a) Abercromby's journey to Scotland] Abercromby set off from London to Edinburgh to challenge Menzies and Hope. The House of Commons dispatched messengers to all three, ordering their attendance in the House. The duel, therefore, never materialized. See *Edin. Ann. Reg. for 1822*, XV. i. 234 and XV. ii. 261.

210 *n.* 1] This obscure note apparently refers to Sir Alexander's threatened duel with Stair. See below, pp. 321–2.

211 (a) going to the Highlands] See above, p. 193.

211 *n.* 1] Crabbe's letter is in *FL* ii. 146 where it is dated 16 July.

213 (b) The King is coming after all] The Lord Provost of Edinburgh received official notice on 18 July that the King was coming about 10 Aug. A minutely detailed account of the visit is given in *A historical account of His Majesty's visit to Scotland* [by Robert Mudie], Edinburgh, 1822. This work enables us to date undated letters printed later in *SL* vii.

214 (a) To J. L. Adolphus] The original letter, now in Selkirk Public Library, shows several misreadings. 'Edinburgh, 31 July' should be at the end. In line 1, delete 'at this time'; in line 3, for 'promise' read 'offer'; in line 4, for 'very happy' read 'happy'; in line 6, for 'will not, I suppose' read 'I suppose will not'; in line 9, before 'Dear Sir' insert 'I am.' Adolphus postponed his visit till 1823. See *SL* viii. 72.

214 (d–e) St. Andrew's Cross] This elaborate piece of jewellery was made by Mrs Skene of Rubislaw. It is fully described in the *Scots Mag.* Vol. 90 (Oct. 1822), p. 500. A letter (not in *SL*) to Mrs Skene is in Skene, *Memories*, p. 236. See also Mudie (cited above p. 213 (b)), pp. 32–3.

214 *n.* 1] In his letter of 12 Nov. (NLS MS. 3895, ff. 222–3) he explains why he has delayed so long his answer. He had always been hoping to be able to fix a date for the visit before winter.

215 (a) my cousin, the Knight-Marshal] His second cousin, Alexander Keith of Ravelston and Dunnottar.

215 (b) To Mrs Stewart Mackenzie] Formerly Lady Hood. See Index under Mrs J. A. S. Mackenzie. The date is almost certainly 17 July. Col. Stephenson, Surveyor-General of Works, inspected Holyrood on Tuesday, 23 July. The Friday before that was 19 July, making Scott's letter of Wednesday, 17 July.

215 (d) To Lord Montagu] Date is 2 Sept. 1822. We learn from John Smith of Darnick's MS. diary that he met Scott and Lord Montagu at Melrose on 3 Sept. The word 'return', twice used in the letter, refers to their return from the Abbey.

215 (e) Mr. Riddell] Charles Riddell of Muselee. Major Riddell on next page is the same man. He was a Major in the Yeomanry.

215 *n.* 1 James Spence] Perfumer, 12 South Bridge, Edinburgh. *Edin. P.O. Direct. 1822–23.*

216 (b) To Lord Montagu] Date is Wednesday, 21 Aug., the day that Lord Montagu and Scott dined with the King at Dalkeith House. See Mudie (cited above p. 213 (b)), p. 188.

216 (e) To Lord Melville] The King visited Melville Castle on Tuesday, 27 Aug. It is clear from this letter that Melville has invited Scott to be present. (See Mudie, cited above p. 213 (b), pp. 270–1.) Date of letter, therefore, is Monday, 26 Aug.

217 (c) this gentlemans brother] Alexander, eldest son of Patrick McDougall of Dunolly (1742–1825), was a Captain in the 5th Foot and was killed at Ciudad Rodrigo, Jan. 1812.

217 *n.* 1] Delete this note. 'Mc.Dougal of Lorn' is John McDougall, Younger of Dunolly, who succeeded his father in 1825. He had been promoted Captain, R.N., in 1820 but his present petition was unsuccessful. He commanded the second division of the Celtic Society when the Regalia were

taken from the Castle to Holyrood on 12 Aug.

218 (a) To Lord Melville] Date is Wednesday, 7 Aug. The Regalia were taken from the Castle to Holyrood on Monday, 12 Aug.

218 (e) To William Laidlaw] Date is 20 Aug. The presentation at Holyrood was 'to-day,' i.e. 20 Aug. and Scott is going to Dalkeith 'To-morrow,' i.e. 21 Aug.

219 (c) Mama, Sophia, and Anne] See Mudie (cited above, p. 213 (b)), pp. 167–85.

220 (a) To C. K. Sharpe] Scott dined at Dalkeith on Wednesday, 21 Aug. and on Wednesday, 28 Aug. Scott must be referring here to the former, a small party, as he would not want to take Sharpe's drawings to the latter, a large and farewell party. See Mudie (cited above, p. 213 (b)), pp. 188 and 285. Date of letter, therefore, is Wednesday, 21 Aug.

220 (c) To J. G. Lockhart] This letter falls between the end of July when Crabbe arrived in Edinburgh and 14 Aug., the date of Erskine's death. It probably belongs to the very beginning of Aug.

220 *n.* 1] Delete this note, which is not now applicable.

223 *n.* 2] Erskine died on Wednesday, 14 Aug.

226 (c) "all plaided and plumed . . ."] Thomas Campbell, *Lochiel's warning*, line 51.

226 (e) Walter and Charles acted as his pages] See below, p. 351 *n.* 1, which should have appeared at this reference.

226 (e–f) Mama, Sophia and Anne were presented] See above, p. 219.

226 *n.* 1] Delete. Grierson has confused the two Keiths—the uncle and the nephew.

227 (a) Lord Londonderry] The news reached the King, through Sir Robert Peel, at Leith on 14 Aug. See Mudie (cited above, p. 213 (b)), p. 89.

227 *n.* 2] For 'Gray' read 'Cray.'

229 *n.* 1] Scott wrote to Knighton on 12 Sept. (MS. in Windsor Castle Lib.) and on 14 Nov. (NLS MS. 3653, ff. 178–80). The comment that 'it is

very dull and of no value' is a personal opinion and uneditorial.

231 (f) infliction on the Baronet] Illness of Sir George Rose's daughter. See above, p. 228, 228 n.

233 n. 1] Cunningham's letter is in Partington, Letter-books, pp. 231–2.

234 (b) que diable alloit-il faire dans cette galère?] See my note to SL i. 118(a).

234 n. 1] Cf. this quotation from FL with the same extract from the original MS., below, p. 307 n.

235 n. 3] The first-mentioned poem was printed as A riddle in Joanna Baillie's A collection of poems, London, 1823, p. 71, where the first line reads: "Twas in heaven pronounced and 'twas muttered in hell.' The second poem (on a pillion), also called a riddle, is printed ibid., p. 72. In the table of contents the author is given as 'F——'. Scott is right in calling it a charade. He uses the word in the same sense as it is used in Jane Austen's Emma, chap. 9.

236 (b–c) chamber in the wall] Bible, II Kings 4: 10.

237 (c) row betwixt Glengarry and the Celtic Society] See Blackwood, Vol. 12 (Sept. 1822), pp. 359–68, Glengarry versus the Celtic Society [By John Cay. See Strout, A bibliography of articles in Blackwood's Magazine, p. 100.] The article includes a letter from Mackenzie, 6 Sept., in which he describes himself as 'Lieut. H. P. 72d regt. and Capt. Inverness Militia.' The piper is John Bain Mackenzie.

237 (d) vox et praeterea [nihil]] Source unknown and regarded as a proverb. Also used in this contracted form in SL xi. 154, where the editor has not added 'nihil', and in complete form in SL xi. 223.

237 n. 2] William Mackenzie had been a Lieut. 72nd Foot since 15 Feb. 1811. On 25 July 1822 he was promoted Quarter Master in place of William Benton who had held the office since 1 Nov. 1804. Later he became Captain. Peel is apparently referring to his promotion as Quarter Master.

238 (a) colly-dogs] Cf. Old Mortality, chap. 22.

238 (d–e) Lord Kinedders family] Sir Robert Peel's letter to Scott about a pension to Lord Kinedder's family was at one time in Galashiels Museum but was dispersed with other items when the Museum was closed.

240 (f) Lord Erskine] He firmly believed he had spoken to the ghost of his mother's gardener in the High Street of Edinburgh. See Cockburn's Memorials, new ed., 1874, pp. 316–17.

241 (b) awaking of Abou Hassan] The Story of the sleeper awakened in The Arabian Nights (Weber, Tales of the East, i. 315–40).

244 (a) Henry Cranstoun] Elder brother of George Cranstoun, afterwards Lord Corehouse. He lived at The Pavilion near Abbotsford.

245 n. 2] The picture is now believed to be an 18th-cent. painting of John the Baptist. Anne's letter to Mrs Robert Surtees of 9 Aug. [1832] on the portrait is in Taylor, Memoir of Robert Surtees, pp. 183–4.

246 (b) Brantome] Brantôme says the attendants were not given access at any time. See Discours troisiesme: Marie Stuart, in his Œuvres, nouv. éd., Paris, 1787, ii. 344.

246 n.] The fairy feast and Mully of Mountown are two different poems. They were both printed, the former under the title Orpheus and Euridice, along with his Some remarks on the Tale of a tub [by Swift], and published anonymously by King at London, 1704. I do not know to what ed. Pitcairn is referring. For these two poems, see The original works of William King, 3 vols., 8vo London, 1776, i. xviii–xix, 211, iii. 203–17.

247 (d) little personal debt] See Reply to Mr Lockhart's pamphlet, p. 87, for an interpretation of these words.

248 n. 1] In lines 2–3, delete 'Three months before . . . note)' and substitute: 'On 8 July (above, p. 209 n. 2) Croker had written . . .'

248 n. 2] In her letter of 18 July.

248 n. 3] The 'three Memoirs' are those of Sterne, Goldsmith and Johnson. The fourth—Henry Mackenzie—is being written. The two remaining memoirs in Vol. 5 of Ballantyne's Novelist's Library—Walpole and Clara Reeve —had not yet been thought of, as is

shown by a letter to Ballantyne of 28 Oct. 1822 (not in *SL* but there is a transcript in NLS MS. 6080).

249 (a) Mr. Mackenzie & expect his answer] Scott wrote to Ballantyne on 4 Oct.: 'Mr Henry Mackenzie is to send the anecdotes today.' (Not in *SL* but there is a transcript in NLS MS. 6080.)

249 (b) make London his washpot] See my note to *SL* ii. 357 (e).

249 *n.*] The passage could not be quoted from Croker's ed. which did not come out till 1831. Grierson has copied Lockhart's reference in *MPW* iii. 242 *n.*

250 (a) To Lord Montagu] Exact date is 3 Oct. Montagu was at Bothwell Castle and his letter of 1 Oct. (NLS MS. 2895, ff. 115–16) was written in the evening and would be posted on 2 Oct. Scott would receive it on 3 Oct. and reply. This reply was received by Montagu on 4 Oct. (NLS MS. 3895, ff. 137–9).

253 (a) Mr. Godwin's conversation] Godwin spent a day with Scott at Abbotsford, 26 Apr. 1816. See *Archibald Constable*, ii. 74.

253 (a) his metropolitan preference] Lamb, in his letter of 29 Oct. 1822 to Scott (Partington, *Letter-books*, pp. 230–1), does not exactly deny the charge but from the wording it seems clear that Scott took his information from oral tradition. The idea is much older than Lamb. It may be found in Johnson's *London*, lines 9–10, and the same accusation as Scott makes may be found almost word for word in the *ER*, Vol. 7 (Jan. 1806), pp. 324–5, and Vol. 18 (May 1811), pp. 15–16.

253 (b) Olivier] Olivier de la Marche.

253 *n.* 2] Constable's letter of 11 July is in *Archibald Constable*, iii. 224–8.

254 (b) carvd chairs] For an account of these Borghese chairs, see *Archibald Constable*, iii. 224–5. See also *Andrea Brustolon: some additions to his oeuvre*, by Anthony Coleridge, in *Apollo*, Vol. 77 (Mar. 1963), pp. 209–12. The article contains two illustrations of one of the chairs.

254 (b) King James] See also *SL* xi. 490 *n.*, 491.

254 (c) mosaic marble] This forms the

top of a table in the Entrance Hall at Abbotsford.

255 (a) To James Ballantyne] For the omitted portion on the printing machine, see *Hist. of Berwickshire Nat. Club*, Vol. 25, pp. 124–5.

255 (e) Edinr. *1st October*] This is a slip. Scott was at Abbotsford. In any case he could not send a letter from Castle Street to Heriot Row 'per Blucher.'

257 *n.* 1] Montagu was at Bothwell Castle; hence his quick reply of 5 Oct. (NLS MS. 3895, ff. 137–9).

258 (a) a very remarkable circumstance] See above, p. 256.

258 (e) To Daniel Terry] The previous letter to Terry (above, p. 214) is dated 31 July. Lockhart, in this letter, which he dates 5 Oct., may be amalgamating, as in other cases, several letters between these two dates.

258 *n.* 1] The quotation is from her letter of 18 July. For '*Humphrey*' read '*Humphry.*'

260 (c) the *gratility*] Shakespeare, *Twelfth Night*, II. 3.

260 (c) mirror . . . mosaic slab] The narrow mirror which was put between the windows is still there. The mosaic slab was put in the Entrance Hall and a white marble table for Chantrey's bust was put in front of the mirror. This white marble table is no longer at Abbotsford.

260 (d) little oratory] The small octagonal room off the Study, now popularly called Speak-a-bit.

261 (c) The paper] The hand-painted Chinese wallpaper is still on the walls of the Drawing Room at Abbotsford. It arrived in Nov. (Scott to Willie Scott of Maxpoffle; NLS MS. 2889, ff. 217–18).

261 *n.* 2] In line 2, for 'William Scott of Raeburn' read 'William Scott of Maxpoffle'; in line 6, for '1820' read '1828.' The title of the work cited in last line is inaccurate. As it is long it should be cited simply as Rogers, *Genealogical memoirs*. Rogers's date, 1820, is a slip, for he correctly gives her age as 91.

262 *n.* 1] Delete this note, which is not only inaccurate but inconsistent with

n. 2 of p. 261 above. The date of the letter is correct. Mrs Scott lived till 1828.

263 (b) your old freind Clarke] I have been unable to identify him. At this time Isaac Blake Clarke was Lt.-Col. of the Scots Greys and J. F. S. Clarke was an Ensign in the same regiment.

264 n. 3] For 'Maxpopple' read 'Maxpoffle.'

265 (b) Mr. Nairne] John Gibson had been apprenticed to James Nairne, W.S.

265 (c) a tutor at Oxford] This is ambiguous for even by June 1824 it had not been decided whether the Duke should go to Oxford or Cambridge (SL viii. 300–2). The reference here is to a private tutor—Blakeney (SL viii. 47).

265 (f) Master Trotter] William Trotter of Ballindean had an upholsterer's business in Princes Street. He was responsible for many of the street and house decorations during the King's visit. See below, p. 301, n. 3.

266 (d) I expect Major Huxley] Tom's wife at Quebec wrote a distressing letter to Scott on 25 Aug. 1822, telling him that Major Huxley was coming to Scotland. Major Huxley posted this letter on his arrival at Deal on 7 Oct. and it is also postmarked 8, 10 and 11 Oct. Scott had presumably just received this when he wrote to Gibson. Huxley wrote to Scott from London on 9 Oct. saying he was coming to Scotland. Scott could not have yet received it. Both these letters—from Elizabeth Scott and Major Huxley—are now at Abbotsford.

267 (a) Will Rose whom I pumped] See SL x. 68 and n. 1 and my note.

267 (a–b) Survey of the Gala water rail road] From Dalkeith to St. Boswells. See Index under Railways.

267 (b) Kirk of Kirconnel] Scott has confused two churches. The one which may be vacant is Kirkconnel in the Presbytery of Penpont in NW. Dumfriesshire. The ballad of Fair Helen relates to the ancient parish of Kirkconnel in SE. Dumfriesshire. 'fair Kirconnel lee' is in Fair Helen, st. 1, line 4 (repeated). In Scott's Minstrelsy (ed. Henderson), iii. 126.

267 n. 1] For 'Anecdotes respecting' read 'Anecdotes and history of.'

267 n. 2] In Ramsay the song is called The young lass contra auld man. Also in Herd, ii. 33, and in Johnson, Vol. 2 (1788), No. 134.

268 (d) Genealogy] Memorials of the Haliburtons. Scott later sent a perfect copy. See below, p. 293.

271 n.] On sentence (lines 3–4): 'It is even doubted whether one copy be now in existence,' see SL ix. 385 n.

273 (a) To Walter] The letter being finished on 3 Nov. should have been at p. 278.

274 (d) The two Miss Erskines] There were three—Euphemia, Helen and Jane—but probably the two eldest are here meant. Their uncle is John James Erskine (q.v. in Index).

274 (d) promise of a pension] See above, p. 238 and my note.

275 (e) To David Laing] This letter is now in the Laing Coll. in Edinburgh Univ. Lib. along with the proofs of Laing's ed. of Select remains, Appendix, where the letter is reproduced, including parts omitted here.

275 (f) Comines] Mémoires, livre 4, chap. 10. (Les mémoires de P. de Commines, 8vo Paris, 1566, p. 284.)

276 (a) Pinky Cleugh . . .] References on this page and on the following page are to the second fytt of Tomas off Erseldoune, in Laing's Select remains.

276 (b) "Fresells free [?]"] Read 'Ffresells free.'

279 (a) The brasses for the shelves] For Scott's plan for movable shelves, see SL v. 65–6. See also below, p. 300.

279 (b) entrance-gallery] Atkinson called the Entrance Hall the 'Gallery.' Used also below, p. 334, but the name did not survive.

279 (e) superb elbow-chairs] See above, p. 254 and my note.

279 (e) in [a] carved box] Delete '[a]'. The article makes nonsense. Scott means a mirror with a frame of carved boxwood like the chairs of carved boxwood.

279 n. 1] In Scott's account with Cockburn, wine merchant, there is

a charge, under 8 Oct. 1822, for 'carriage of wood from Dunfermline, £1–5–0.' See Alan Bell, *Scott and his wine-merchant* in *Blackwood* for Aug. 1971, p. 171.

280 (b) tapestry-screen] This may be the screen shown in the illustration of the Dining Room in Napier's *Homes and haunts*, p. 167. It is no longer at Abbotsford.

280 (c) shall have another made for atlasses] This is the cabinet made by Joseph Shillinglaw, the Darnick joiner. It sits in the centre of the Library. The showcase on the top is modern.

280 n. 1] The cast of Bruce's skull sits on the mantelpiece in the Entrance Hall.

281 (a) Mrs. Terry's painting] Her painting 'Abbotsford, the seat of Sir Walter Scott' was exhibited earlier this year as No. 21 in the 4th annual exhibition of the Institution for the Encouragement of the Fine Arts in Scotland at Edinburgh. See the *Scotsman*, 20 Apr. 1822, p. 126. The painting is in the private part of Abbotsford.

281 (e) smell of the apoplexy] Le Sage, *Gil Blas*, Bk VII, chap. 4.

281 n. 2] For 'in November 1822' read 'on 7 Nov. 1822.'

284 (a) Delices de la France] *Deliciae Galliae, sive itinerarium per universam Galliam* [By Gaspar Ens], 12mo Coloniae, 1609.

284 (c) no time to look out for mottoes] This was for the title-page of *Peveril*. The motto chosen was from the *Tatler*, No. 38: 'It is to be noted, that when any part of this paper appears dull, there is a design in it.' This was quoted in the *Spectator*, No. 338. Both essays were by Steele.

286 (c) Gwynnass] A misreading for Gwennap. Scott could not have written 'Gwynnass' as he gives the name as Gwynnap in *Peveril*, chap. 32.

286 (e) To W.S. Rose] Scott first mentions the Scots Greys in a letter of 7 Oct. (above, p. 263). This letter, therefore, was written between 7 Oct. and 12 Nov.

286 n. 3] Rose's translation of F. Berni's version of Boiardo's *Orlando innamorato*, published in 1823.

287 (e) very clever ballad] This is Robert Surtees's *The rector's warning*. It was printed in Taylor, *Memoir of Robert Surtees*, pp. 251–2. Scott printed 40 copies, probably in 1828, for the Bannatyne Club but the sheets were not issued to members till 1848, when David Laing added them to *Captain Ward and the Rainbow* to form *Two Bannatyne garlands from Abbotsford*. See also *SL* vii. 314 and x. 407.

287 n. 4] For 'MacDougal of Makerstoun' read 'Makdougall of Makerston.'

288 (a) a small legacy] £2,000 from John Ballantyne, which Scott never received.

288 n. 1] Delete this note and see my note to *SL* vii. 56 (c).

288 n. 2] There is no doubt about the date. The letter should have appeared at p. 250.

289 (a) Tomorrow I go to Abbotsford.] Because of a hitch in his building. See above, p. 153.

289 n. 2] On the contrary, I think these two letters belong to the end of 1822. The first is about Sept. or Oct. when Ballantyne is at Scremerston. The second (p. 291) is probably Oct. as Ballantyne had returned to Edinburgh by 1 Nov. (Letter from Scott to Ballantyne in Edinburgh, 1 Nov. 1822, not in *SL* but in *Reply to Mr Lockhart's pamphlet*, Appendix, pp. 52–3.)

292 (d) George] Probably George Waynes.

292 (f) To David Laing] Though the dedication to Scott in his *Select remains* is dated 6 Nov. 1822, the volume was not completed till Dec. and Laing sent the last part to Abbotsford on 31 Dec. Scott would receive it on Wednesday, 1 Jan. 1823, which might be the Wednesday of Scott's letter. But if Scott actualy wrote from Castle Street the date would be 15 Jan., the first Wednesday in 1823 on which Scott was in Edinburgh.

293 (a) imperfect copy] This is probably the copy which Scott gave to Sir James Stuart on 27 July 1824, now in my Scott Coll.

293 (c) To David Laing] Date is 15 Feb. The Bannatyne Club met on 27 Feb., i.e. in 'the week after next'. The

reference to the 'Bannatynians' shows that the date could not be Jan., as by 2 Feb. the name had not yet been chosen (below, p. 324).

293 (e) To James Skene] Skene's dating of letters can never be trusted. As Scott's letter to Croker is dated 5 Jan. his letter to Skene is probably Sunday, 5 Jan. likewise.

293 *n.* 1] For '*Early*' read '*ancient*' and for 'in the course of the year 1822' read 'during 1821 and 1822.'

294 (a) "nipped foot and clipped foot"] This is the first line of a rhyme which occurs in the prose nursery story of *Rashiecoat* (the Scottish version of *Cinderella*), which Scott would know from recitation. The story is told in Robert Chambers, *Popular rhymes of Scotland*, new ed., London, 1870, pp. 66–70. King James in *Nigel*, chap. 9, refers to 'the "nippit foot and clippit foot" of the bride in the fairy tale.'

294 (a) foot's space. . . .] Read 'foot's space bestowed on exterior decoration.' (Correction in *SL* xii. 490.)

294 (a) with neighbour Milne] About renting Faldonside House.

295 *n.* 1] Scott probably had known Nagle when he was in command of the Leith Station, a command he held till Sept. 1810.

296 (c–d) "Patience cousin & shufle the cards"] Cervantes, *Don Quixote*. See my note to *SL* ii. 404 (a).

296 (f) hasty transcript] Of *MacDuff's Cross* for Joanna Baillie's volume.

297 (a) Thus said the old man] This is a variation of *Sair fail'd hinny* in John Bell's ed. of *Rhymes of Northern bards*, 8vo Newcastle upon Tyne, 1812, pp. 257–8. Also quoted in *Journal*, 13 Aug. 1826. A version is given as a nursery rhyme in J. O. Halliwell-Phillipps, *The nursery rhymes of England* [Percy Soc.], London, 1842, p. 140.

297 (f) tell it not in Gath] *Bible, II Samuel* 1:20.

298 (b) our Member] If Scott was referring to Roxburghshire, the member was Sir Alexander Don.

298 (d) To Daniel Terry] Date cannot be 9 Jan. Below (p. 304), Scott refers to a letter from London written on 8 Jan. He could not receive it before Saturday, 11 Jan., and as he says he will be in Edinburgh on 14 Jan. the date of this letter is probably Sunday, 12 Jan.

299 (b) Peter's garret] The stables, down in the haugh.

299 *n.* 1] The 'Roslin drops' used in the Library ceiling were casts in Roman cement from Roslyn Chapel.

300 (a) brass notches] On movable shelves, see above, p. 279 (a), and my note.

300 (b) the Roslin drop] It was put in the bow window of the Library. The ceiling of the Oratory had to be lowered to allow for the spiral stair from the Study gallery to Scott's dressing-room.

301 (b) The silk damask] In spite of what Scott says here, the curtains were made in London by Messrs Potts & Collinson. Lockhart wrongly follows Scott. (*Lockhart*, vii. 217.)

301 (d) The chairs] Here, as elsewhere, Lockhart seems to have amalgamated letters to Terry. On 3 Feb. 1823 Terry wrote about solid ebony chairs (Partington, *Post-bag*, p. 176) and on 8 Mar. he announced that they had been dispatched (NLS MS. 3896, ff. 79–82, cited in Partington, op. cit., pp. 176–7). In a letter, which Lockhart dates 10 Nov. 1822, Scott refers to 'one or two pair of the ebony chairs you mention' (above, p. 280) and here in this letter, which Lockhart dates 9 Jan. 1823, Scott says 'The chairs will be most welcome' but there is no mention of chairs in the letter of 14 Feb. (below, p. 329) which falls between Terry's two letters of 3 Feb. and 8 Mar. cited above. The two armchairs and three of the others (with cane bottoms and scarlet cushions) are still in the Drawing Room at Abbotsford.

301 (d–e) O Lord, sir!] Shakespeare, *All's well that ends well*, II. 2.

302 (a) anchovies] This seems to be a variant of the story of the duel fought over the assertion that anchovies (confused with capers) grew on trees. See Charles Marsh, *The clubs of London*, London, 1828, i. 99–107. Scott told Mrs Hughes a different version of this anecdote. See Hughes, *Letters*, p. 164.

302 (a) "Miratur novas frondes . . ."]
Virgil, *Georgics*, II. 82.

302 (b) My new gardener] William
Bogie.

303 *n.* 1] In line 4, for 'Gourlay' read
'Gourley.'

303 *n.* 2] The large painting of Fast
Castle (30 × 41·5 in.) is in very bad
condition and is now stored in the
basement.

304 (d) Dogberry] See *SL* ii. 320.

304 (e) Beddoes] An error for Beckford.
*Popular tales of the Germans. Tr. by
William Beckford from the German* [of
J. K. A. Musäus]. 2 vols. 8vo London,
1791. Scott also gives Beddoes as the
translator in *Foreign Quart. Rev.* 1827
(*MPW* xviii. 287).

305 (a) Beit Weber] Scott means Veit
Weber, the pseudonym of Georg
Philipp Ludwig Leonhard Wächter.

305 (b) Sintram and his Comrades] La
Motte Fouqué's *Sintram and his com-
panions*, 8vo London, 1820.

305 (d) Lady Anne] Lockhart (*Lockhart*,
v. 390 *n.*) says Anne's nickname, 'Lady
Anne,' dates from childhood, but this
is the earliest use in *SL*. It was used in
letters to Scott from Edward Everett,
23 Nov. 1818 (NLS MS. 3889, ff. 254–5)
and 28 Mar. 1820 (NLS MS. 3891,
f. 41).

305 *n.* 1] Delete and substitute: See *SL*
ii. 290 (e).

306 *n.* 3] Morritt's letter of 8 Jan. is in
NLS (MS. 3896, ff. 5–6).

307 *n.*] The interview with Brougham
(lines 7–8) has already been quoted
above, p. 234, *n.* 1, from *FL*, though
the present quotation is from the
Walpole Coll.

308 (c) needs must go when the Devil
. . . drives] An English and Scottish
proverb with a pun on printers' devils.
See *SL* ii. 434.

309 (a) Gas . . . bells] A plant to make
gas from oil was installed in the summer
of 1823. The plant has all been dismantled and only two retorts remain.
The bells still function perfectly.

309 (a) in Laputa] The Grand Academy
of Lagado, described in Swift's *Gulliver's*
travels, Part III, chaps. 5–6. (Scott's
Swift, 2nd ed., xi. 225–46.)

309 (b) like that of the Diable Boiteux]
Le Sage, *The devil upon two sticks*, chap. 3.
'We embraced,—and from that time
became mortal foes.'

310 *n.* 1] In line 5, for '1824' read
'1823.' In line 6 from foot, the correct
title and reference are: *Autobiography
and other memorials of Mrs Gilbert,
(formerly Ann Taylor)* . . . *Ed. by Josiah
Gilbert*, 2 vols., London, 1874, Vol. 1,
p. 233. The letter, here quoted from,
was written to Josiah Conder, probably
in 1810 when Conder presented to
Scott a copy of *The associate minstrels*,
by himself and Ann and Jane Taylor.

311 *n.* 1] If Scott had read Taylor's
book more carefully before he wrote he
would have omitted this long account
of Prince Paddock, for Taylor, in his
notes (pp. 237–8), refers to it and
quotes the same four lines as Scott does
from Leyden's ed. of *The complaynt of
Scotland* (1801), Introd. p. 234. The
lines had also been quoted by Sir
Francis Palgrave in an article in *QR* Vol.
21 (Jan. 1819), p. 99. Scott would
know the story from recitation as well
as from Leyden. There are variants.
See Robert Chambers, *Popular rhymes of
Scotland*, new ed., London, 1870, pp.
103–5. The couplet, with variations, is
quoted in the *Journal*, 2 Aug. 1827.
Delete sentence in this note (which is
confusing) from 'The tale' down to
'Roxburgh.'

312 (d) Waste not, Want not] Scott had
these words carved in large letters over
the fireplace in his kitchen at Abbotsford.

313 (e) Do you remember the story]
This story was told of Lord Panmure
(q.v. in Index). See John Kay, *Kay's
Edinburgh portraits*, London, 1885, ii. 263.

312 *n.* 1] These two authors are mentioned in Taylor's Preface, pp. ix–x.

314 (a) the penitence . . .] *The rector's
warning.* See my note to *SL* vii. 287 (e).

314 *n.* 2] For 'Sharpe' read 'Sharp.'

315 *n.* 1] Pitcairn's father was a writer
in Edinburgh but not a W.S.

315 *n.* 2] In line 1, for 'collegerunt'
read 'colligerunt.' The number of
copies for Nos. 5, 9, 18 are not given.

For the others the number varies from 10 to 30. The work cited at the end of the note should be *Notices relative to the Bannatyne Club*. It was edited anonymously by Maidment in 1836. In *N. & Q.*, 3rd ser. Vol. 10 (17 Nov. 1866), p. 387, Maidment said 'not above eight copies were thrown off for private distribution.'

315 *n.* 3] Amend the opening sentence. The Club had been mentioned in 1822. See above, p. 268. Also add that the MS. minutes of the Club, 1823–61, were deposited in the NLS by the Society of Antiquaries of Scotland (NLS MSS. 2046–8).

316 (d) Mr Homes death] William Montagu Douglas Home, 2nd son of the 10th Earl of Home, died at Madras on 22 July 1822. The news had just reached Britain.

316 (d) Duchess] Widow of 3rd Duke of Buccleuch.

317 (a) poor Scotts death] Lord Scott, eldest son of 4th Duke of Buccleuch, died in 1808.

317 (c) Major Huxley of the 71] Major of the 70th.

317 (d) A gentleman whom I do not know] Major William Claud Campbell. He claimed the Crawford peerage as descendant of Lady Mary Lindsay Campbell, sister of John, 17th Earl of Crawford. His claim was unsuccessful.

317 (e–f) a needle in a bottle of hay] *Ray*, p. 261.

317 *n.* 2] Chap. 41. See also *SL* ii. 23, xii. 353 *n.* 2.

318 *n.* 1] Though *Lays of the Lindsays* was suppressed, *Auld Robin Gray* was issued alone by the Bannatyne Club in 1825. See also *SL* viii. 37–44.

319 (b) It's hame & it's hame] The Gaelic air is in R. A. Smith, *The Scotish minstrel*, Vol. 1, pp. 18–19.

319 (d) English Minstrelsy] No part of *Auld Robin Gray* was printed in this.

320 (d) about 1801] If Doctor Mac-Knight is Rev. James Macknight the incident must have been earlier as he died in 1800.

320 *n.* 3] Scott is referring to sisters, who are not recorded by K. S. M. Scott at the reference cited.

321 (f) Don] For an account of Sir Alexander Don's trip to Paris, see Partington, *Post-bag*, pp. 171–2. See also above, p. 210, 210 *n.*

321 *n.* 2] For '1812' read '1814–26.'

322 (b) To Archibald Constable] Date is probably Thursday, 30 Jan. Scott says 'I have also suggested to Mr. Cadell' and this suggestion was made in a letter of 29 Jan. (below, p. 323).

322 *n.* 2] Constable's letter of 22 Jan. is in *Archibald Constable*, iii. 248–9.

323 *n.* 1] Delete this note, which is not applicable. Scott is referring to A. O. Exquemelin's *Bucaniers of America*, 4to London, 1684.

323 *n.* 2] Delete and substitute: See above, p. 284.

325 (c) Second Person] Read 'Sacred Person.'

325 (d) I had a great regard for his father] William Anderson, Writer in Advocates' Close. See *SL* i. 43, 43 *n.*

326 (c) securities] Read 'searches.' (Correction in *SL* xii. 490.)

326 (e) till it brings on cruel suffering] This was the effect of calomel. See *SL* viii. 323.

327 (a) C. G.] i.e. Christ God, alias of William Anderson. See above, p. 325 *n.* 2.

327 *n.* 1] No comma is required.

329 (e) To D. Terry] From the contents the date is probably Jan. Cf. my note above, p. 301 (d).

329 (f) Don Diego Snapshorto] In Colley Cibber's *Love makes a man; or, the fop's fortune*, Act I, Don Lewis says: 'Tho' I can speak no Greek, I love and honour the sound of it.' Several times in the play Clodio, his nephew, calls Don Lewis 'Testy' and in Act V he calls him Don Cholerick Snapshorto de Testy. Diego is Scott's error. Cibber's play is based on Beaumont and Fletcher's *The elder brother* in which, Act II, sc. 1, Miramont says 'Though I can speak no Greek, I love the sound on't.'

331 *n.* 2] Fox Maule became 2nd Baron Panmure in 1852 and 11th Earl of Dalhousie in 1860. In *Ann. Reg.* 1825, Chron. p. 77, the sum allowed by his father is given as £100.

332 (d) to Simpson the success of his brother] William Simpson and his brother Andrew. The latter had been appointed Assistant Surgeon in Bengal in 1821.

333 (a) cousin of his a gauger] Andrew Vair. See above, p. 191.

333 (b) an utterly radical paper in Kelso] *The Border Courier* which was short-lived.

333 (d) Campbell] See above, pp. 317–18.

334 (b–c) Timeo Danaos] Virgil, *Aeneid*, II. 49.

335 (c) I buckle my belt my ain gate] See my note to *SL* iv. 524 (b).

336 (d) Lochend] Scott was prevented from purchasing this farm by the death of Andrew Mercer who left only a young girl, Isabella (the 'little maiden' of the next sentence). See *SL* v. 501.

337 (b) Mr. Milne's sketch] This is the sketch for the Gas House made by James Milne who installed the oil gas lighting at Abbotsford. There is a rough sketch in NLS MS. 1750, f. 366.

337 n. 2] An ambiguous note. The Messrs Smith were building Abbotsford at this time.

339 n. 1] The 'pieds des mouche' is Ellis's description, not Scott's. See *SL* v. 279 and my note.

340 (b) "why Come ye not to Skotland"] Probably a parody of John Skelton's *Why come ye not to court?* which Scott had used about this time as the motto to chap. 45 of *Peveril*.

342 (a) like that of Banquo] Shakespeare, *Macbeth*, III. 4.

343 (a) the draught of the deed] Relating to Mrs Carpenter and Charles Carpenter's bequest to the Abbotsford children.

343 (d) knight dub'd] See previous page.

343 (d) Banquo] See my note to *SL* vii. 342 (a).

343 (e) except 1794] Hogg's story *Storms* (*Winter evening tales*, 1820) relates to this snowstorm of 1794.

344 (b) To James Ballantyne] As the 'drinkables' are mentioned only in a postscript, this letter should probably come after the letter on p. 345. Its date is probably early Mar.

344 n. 1] A facsimile of the 1572 ed., ed. by William Beattie, was issued by the National Library of Scotland in 1966 for members of the Edinburgh Bibliographical Society.

344 n. 2] For 'June' read 'May.'

345 (c) To James Ballantyne] On 14 Feb. Ballantyne had ordered, from Cockburn, claret to the value of £65. 14s. od., as a present to Scott. (Alan Bell, *Scott and his wine-merchant* in *Blackwood* for Aug. 1971, p. 173.) As Scott is writing in Edinburgh and refers to the wine being sent to Abbotsford in a 'fortnight or three weeks' (i.e. when the Courts rose), the letter was probably written in the second half of Feb.

346 (d) To D. Terry] It is impossible to date this letter accurately but the suggested date March is impossible. Gas was not installed till Sept. The workmen left on 12 Sept., leaving one mechanic to fix burners and globes. In a letter to Maria Edgeworth of 22 Sept. Scott said the installation was working (*SL* viii. 90) and in a letter to Walter of 23 Oct. (*SL* viii. 107–8) Scott describes the gas in terms similar to those in this letter to Terry. The words 'about twice a-week the gas is made' suggest that Scott was writing a considerable time after 12 Sept., probably at the same time that he wrote to Walter, i.e. 23 Oct.

346 n. 4] Delete this note, which is a worthless and a ludicrously inaccurate description of Abbotsford.

348 (b) young MacDonald Buchanan] John, son of Hector Macdonald Buchanan. He died at Gibraltar on 11 May.

348 n. 1] Delete and substitute: William Orman, young Walter's batman, had been in the 18th Hussars, served in the Peninsula and was discharged after being wounded at Waterloo. Later he was batman to Walter, but the dates are not known. It is not known who got him a post as a guard nor when, but Orman was never at Abbotsford in Sir Walter's lifetime. After Scott's death the second Sir Walter installed him at Abbotsford as caretaker (unpaid) and he remained

for about 20 years, making annually about £400 in tips.

351 n. 1] This is an odd place for this note. It should have been given above, p. 226.

352 (b) To Henry Wells] This letter and the letter of 28 Feb. from the boys are printed in *The Antiquary*, Vol. 49, Jan. 1913.

352 n. 1] Wells's letter in NLS is MS. 935, No. 96A.

353 (a) To Archibald Constable] The original was missing in 1873. See *Archibald Constable*, iii. 252.

353 n. 1] The two statements of Lockhart and Thomas Constable are not inconsistent. In line 5, for '442–43' read '443.'

355 (a) To Archibald Constable] The date is probably Wednesday, 12 Mar., the day the Courts rose. 16 Mar. was a Sunday.

355 (a) Lady Howards book] See below, p. 390 n.

355 (c) to bestow the tediousness] See *SL* ii. 320.

355 (c–d) Miss Edgar] Scott apparently wrote to her, for Constable in his letter of 25 Mar. said: 'I forwarded the letter to Miss Edgar.' *Archibald Constable*, iii. 254.

355 n. 2] Constable in his letter of 25 Mar. wrote: 'A complete set of honest John Nichols' literary anecdotes shall be sent to you.' *Archibald Constable*, iii. 255. This work is not at Abbotsford.

355 n. 3] *Tranquillity* was first published in 1810. *Chinzica; or, the battle of the bridge*, by Henry Stobert, was published at London in 1822. Stobert was the pseudonym of Stuart Maxwell who issued a 2nd ed. under his own name and with the title changed to *The battle of the bridge*, published at Edinburgh by Archibald Constable and printed by James Ballantyne, in 1823. The *ALC* has failed to note that Stobert and Maxwell are one and the same man. There is a brief obituary of Maxwell in *Edin. Ann. Reg. for 1824*, XVII. iii. 453. See also below, p. 360 and my note.

357 (e) Some thing too much of this] Shakespeare, *Hamlet*, III. 2. Scott quotes phrase as 'Somewhat too much' in *SL* v. 71, 352.

359 n. 1] For other eds., see my note to *SL* iv. 471 n. 1.

359 n. 2] Constable's letter of 31 Mar. is in *Archibald Constable*, iii. 258–62.

360 (d) Only one letter] From Helen Lawson, Mrs Thomas Goldie.

360 n. 1] Delete this note and see my note to *SL* vii. 355 n. 3. See also *Archibald Constable*, iii. 255.

360 n. 2] The novel was published in May 1823.

360 n. 3] Helen Walker was the daughter of a day-labourer at Cluden. Crockett (*Scott originals*, 3rd ed., p. 233) points out Scott's error.

361 (b) Your Scheme] Sent to Scott on 25 Mar. See *Reply to Mr Lockhart's pamphlet*, Appendix, p. 40.

361 (b) I trust *Durward* will be out this month] This is impossible as Scott is writing on 28 Mar. and has reached only a third of Vol. 3 (p. 362). He must mean 'next month.'

362 (c) Calloghan] George Callaghan, Paymaster of 15th Hussars.

362 (e) who owe us I think a harvests day] A proverb, but not found in the usual sources. Also used in *Old Mortality*, chap. 33, and *Rob Roy*, chap. 23.

364 n. 1] Constable's letter of 31 Mar. is in *Archibald Constable*, iii. 258–62.

365 (a) To James Skene] In this extract the very important reference to the stone screen at Abbotsford is omitted. For complete letter, see Skene's *Memories*, pp. 104–5.

365 (c) Dr. Hamilton] James Hamilton, Professor of Midwifery, Edinburgh University, 1800–39.

367 n. 1] Scott's letter creates a problem which cannot be easily solved. Laing's volume was not completed till Jan. 1825. I should date the letter 1825 were it not for the references to the Circuit (p. 368) and to the Bannatyne Club (p. 369), which both apply to 1823. Scott's 'little volume' must refer to a collection of some of the tracts which were separately printed at different times, as the varying types of paper show. The tracts were reprinted

directly from the originals and the suggestion that Scott had received 'the manuscript volume' is, therefore, untenable. The three tracts, to which Scott refers, come late in the volume as completed, but Laing probably rearranged the collection when he had printed all he wanted to print. In line 1, for '*Scottish*' read '*Scotish*.' In line 6, for 'Pill' read 'Pil.' It does not follow from Laing's note that he had adopted Scott's suggestion. Laing would know Drury's book independent of Scott. Drury's *Pleasant and surprising adventures*, etc. had been published at London in 1743. A new ed. was published at Edinburgh in 1808. In a note to *Tales of a grandfather*, 2nd ser. iii. 277, Scott casts doubts on the genuineness of Drury's work. 'A work with the same title' suggests that it might be different, but the *Pil for porkeaters* is the same poem as that printed by Laing.

368 *n.*] After 'pp. 102–5' at end of note, add: 'and his *Historical mysteries*, London, 1904, pp. 193–213.'

368 *n.* 2] Scott is not referring to this printed ed., but to the MS.

369 (b) cast a leglen girth] Ramsay, *Proverbs*, p. 56.

370 (a) I hear from Mrs. Baillie] In her letter of 2 Apr. 1823 (NLS MS. 3896, ff. 104–5).

371 *n.* 1] Maria Edgeworth's letter of 10 Apr. is partly printed in *FL* ii. 169–70.

372 (a) To James Skene] Date is 1822: (1) The Circuit was 2–5 Apr. in 1823 but 20 Apr. in 1822; (2) the letter of 21 Apr. 1822 (above, p. 139) is a continuation of this letter; (3) reference to Skene's renting a house relates to 1822; the 'election for our collector' relates to 1822. (Date corrected in *SL* xii. 490.)

373 (d) the young Oxonian] John Hughes, their only son.

373 (d) "bearded like the pard"] Shakespeare, *As you like it*, II. 7.

374 (a) To [unknown correspondent]] I think the date should be 1824. James Ballantyne paid a subscription for £5. 5s. 0d. on 3 Mar. 1824. (Lockhart, *The Ballantyne-humbug handled*, p. 88.)

376 (a) in for a penny] 'in for a penny, in for a pound.' (*Ray*.) Used also in *SL* viii. 347.

376 (a) the proverb is something musty] Shakespeare, *Hamlet*, III. 2.

376 (d) Come with a whoop] Nursery rhyme beginning 'Boys and girls come out to play,' lines 5–6. (I. and P. Opie, *The Oxford dictionary of nursery rhymes*, repr. Oxford, Clarendon Press, 1973, p. 99.)

376 *n.* 1] Delete. Lauchie stands for Andrew Mercer. He had died in 1819 but the name was apparently still used for the bog.

379 (c) the Cooper of Stobo] Scott means the Cooper of Fogo. See Robert Chambers, *Popular rhymes of Scotland*, new ed., London, 1870, p. 211.

379 (e) as Tony Lumpkin says] See my note to *SL* i. 524 (a).

380 (c) Westminster Hall] Westminster Abbey.

380 (d) To James Ballantyne] In spite of *n.* 1 on p. 381, it is clear that this and the following letter on p. 381 are quite separate. The second relates to the finale of *Quentin Durward* which was finished at the end of Apr. The first letter cannot refer to that novel, as Vol. 1 was finished by 25 Mar. (above, p. 354). Secondly, the reference to Constable does not fit Apr. 1823 when Scott's relations with him had been friendly. I think 'Vol. I' refers to *St Ronan's Well* and the reference to Constable as the 'late correspondence' referred to by Constable in his letter to Cadell of 9 Sept. 1823 (*SL* viii. 85 *n.*). If 'Vol. I' (*SL* viii. 11) refers to *St Ronan's Well*, Scott must have set it aside all summer and resumed it about Sept.

381 (a) picture of poor John] Probably the posthumous half-length portrait (7·5 × 6·15 in.) by Sir William Allan. Reproduced in *The Ballantyne Press and its founders*, Edinburgh, 1909, frontispiece, where it is wrongly described as a portrait of James Ballantyne. It hangs in the ante-room to the Armoury at Abbotsford and is wrongly described in the inventories as a full-length.

381 (b) To James Skene] Letter should be dated 1819. (Correction in *SL* xi. 485 *n.* 2, and xii. 490.) The dirty

Burgh contest is Selkirk Burghs following on the death of Sir John Buchanan Riddell on 21 Apr. 1819; and reference to Rae is to his probable appointment as Lord Advocate which actually took place on 24 June 1819. There is a facsimile of this letter in Skene's *Memories* which shows some trifling variations.

381 (c) Turner's palm is as itchy] A. J. Finberg in his *The life of J. M. W. Turner, R.A.*, 2nd ed., Oxford, 1961, p. 257, quotes this letter with disapproval. But see *Turner and his works . . . By John Burnet . . . The memoir by Peter Cunningham*, London, 1852, pp. 33–4.

381 *n.* 1] Delete this note, which is no longer applicable.

383 *n.* 2] The letter was first printed in Allan's *Life of Sir Walter Scott* (1834), pp. 444–5.

384 (a) "by the lug and the haun" as Mr. James Hogg says] The word 'haun' should be 'horn.' (*The Brownie of Bodsbeck*, chap. 17.) The phrase 'by the lug and the horn' is also used, without reference to Hogg, in *Old Mortality*, chap. 7 and *The Fair Maid of Perth*, chap. 19.

385 (b) Good Master Lieutenant] Nicholas Rowe, *Lady Jane Gray*, V. 1.

386 (b) humana perpessi sumus] See *SL* ii. 502.

386 (e) "Each one fast asleep in bed"] This approximates to the variant reading 'All our household are at rest, / Each one sleeping in his bed' which became 'All our household are at rest, / The hall as silent as the cell.' (*Christabel*, lines 116–17.) See *The complete poetical works of Samuel Taylor Coleridge*, ed. by E. H. Coleridge, i. 219–20.

386 *n.* 1] Caroline Eliza Mackenzie died at Brahan Castle on 24 Apr.

387 (b) "Mon âne parle, et même il parle bien"] Scott at this time was writing the first vol. of *St Ronan's Well* and in chap. 7 he quotes these words.

388 *n.* 1] The 'very interesting young friend' is Catherine Morritt (Morritt's niece) whose illness is referred to above, p. 376. Anne Morritt could not have been called 'young.'

390 *n.* 1] The part of this note relating

to Lady Suffolk should have appeared above, p. 355. Delete the sentence beginning 'Scott reviewed the work.' He reviewed it in *QR* for Jan. 1824 (*Shine*, No. 718).

391 *n.* 1] There is a long extract from her letter in Partington, *Post-bag*, pp. 179–81.

395 *n.* 1 (b) When the eldest child, Jessie, was born is not on record . . .] The birth is recorded in the *Scots Mag.* Vol. 62 (Dec. 1800), p. 848. She was born at Edinburgh on 16 Dec. 1800. The birth of Eliza is recorded in the *Scots Mag.* Vol. 66 (Jan. 1804), p. 78: 'At Midfield near Edinburgh, Mrs Thomas Scott, a daughter.' Midfield was the Duke of Abercorn's farm.

396 (a) apparently] Delete. Walter Scott, W.S., wrote on 12 Nov. 1789 that he was busy settling affairs on death of 8th Earl of Abercorn. (MS. in possession of Major P. I. C. Payne.)

397 *n.* 2] On Riddell and Gillon, see my note to *SL* vii. 455 (a).

398 (a) June 1808] June is too early. The date has been taken from *SL* ii. 74, but that letter dated 20 June should be Oct. See my note to *SL* ii. 74 (f).

399 (c) Ferguson] Read 'Fergusson.'

399 *n.* 1] Delete reference to *SL* ii. 345 (where the extract is now cancelled) and see *SL* vii. 435, 439.

399 *n.* 2] Tom must have written earlier to Scott about the Demerara appointment since Scott is able to reply about it on 1 Nov. See below, p. 451. Colonel Ross is Andrew Ross.

401 (a) an introduction to Daniel Terry] *SL* iii. 297.

401 (d) Walter replied] *SL* vii. 465–6.

404 (c) *Rokeby* was composed in the same year] It was finished in 1812.

405 (e–f) in April Mrs. Tom] She sailed on 28 Mar. (*SL* iii. 429 *n.*)

407 (a–b) Assaragoa] An article in *Queen's Quart.* xxxvii. 337 gives the name as Assarapa.

409 (c) in favour of a Dr. Tobin] The bill was in favour of Torrance and McLeod (NLS MS. 3888, f. 164). See also *SL* iv. 530 *n.* 1.

418 (d) Hull] Thomas Hull. Drury Lane should be Covent Garden.

419 (a) Duke of Athole . . . Mr. John Hay] John Hay became 5th Bart. of Haystoun in 1810. His wife's sister, Marjory, married in 1794 the 4th Duke of Atholl.

419 (c) Ilay] Sir Ilay Campbell, Lord Succoth.

419 (c) as Falstaff] Shakespeare, *II Henry IV*, IV. 3.

419 (c) Archd. Campbell] Archibald Campbell (afterwards Sir Archibald Campbell, 2nd Bart. of Succoth) succeeded Lord Dunsinnan as Lord of Session, 8 Apr. 1809.

419 (e) Mr. Scott] William Scott, Tom's banker at Ayr.

420 (e) Archie Campbell] See my note to *SL* vii. 419 (c).

421 (a) Bannister] In a letter of 1 Jan. 1809 to Henry Bunbury, Bannister wrote: 'I have given up all thoughts of the Edinburgh theatre.' See Dibdin, *Annals*, p. 258.

421 (b) to Albany] 1 Albany Street, Edinburgh, Tom's house.

421 (d) Carrie Lamb] Mother of Daniel's illegitimate son William. She became Mrs Mitchell.

422 (e) fight with wild beasts at Ephesus] *Bible, I Corinthians* 15: 32.

422 (e) my worthy Senior] George Home.

422 (f) Frere] It was not till 8 Oct. that John Hookham Frere was appointed Envoy-Extraordinary and Minister-Plenipotentiary to Ferdinand VII of Spain. *Edin. Ann. Reg. for 1808*, I. ii. 250.

424 (e) loss of a faithful servant] See *SL* ii. 141.

425 (a) Mr. Sibbald] I think this is William Sibbald of Gladswood, merchant in Leith, who would be in a position to report on ships coming into Leith.

425 (f) Lewis's tales . . .] See *SL* ii. 136.

434 (b) To Thomas Scott] The correct date of this letter is 1812. Janet Rutherford died on 19 Dec. 1812. (*Scots Mag.* Vol. 75 (Feb. 1813), p. 158.)

435 *n.* 1] Delete and see preceding note

438 (a) annuity of £130] 50 Geo. III, c. 112. Tom is listed in the final Schedule to the Act which was not passed till 20 June.

439 (d) James Gibson] Afterwards Sir James Gibson-Craig, 1st Bart. of Riccarton. Like Lauderdale he was a Whig.

439 (d) Lord Lauderdale] On 21 May the House of Lords, on the motion of Lord Lauderdale, ordered that the date of Tom's commission in the Manx Fencibles and the periods of his absence from the corps should be laid before the House. (*House of Lords Journal*, xlvii. 681; *Scots Mag.* lxxii. 457.)

439 *n.* 2] There is nothing in the extract in *SL* ii. 345–6 which is not in this letter. The extract should be cancelled.

441 (e) potiphar's wife] *Bible, Genesis* 39.

442 (e) The proper study of Mankind is MAN] Pope, *Essay on man, Epistle II*, line 2. Scott was probably thinking of Boswell: 'I mentioned a scheme which I had of making a tour to the Isle of Man, and giving a full account of it: and that Mr. Burke had playfully suggested as a motto "The proper study of mankind is MAN".' (Boswell, *Life of Johnson*, chap. 30.)

443 (a) The Bill] 50 Geo. III, c. 112.

443 (b) the Chancellor] Lord Eldon.

444 (c) To Thomas Scott] Scott is answering Tom's letter of 17 Aug. 1810 (NLS MS. 3879, ff. 163–4) in which he refers to Scott's last letter from Buchanan House (not in *SL*); to the *Lady of the Lake* which he has read; to the Fiery Cross 'still in use' in the Isle of Man; to his projected history of the island to be in the form of letters addressed to Scott ('your Letters from Man,' p. 444); to the newspaper project and other matters. Scott made no use of Tom's information on the Fiery Cross in a new ed. of *The Lady of the Lake*.

444 (e) 14000] The four first eds. amounted to this number.

445 (a) Addison] Addison's *Account of the greatest English poets* was addressed to Henry Sacheverell, not to William.

447 *n.* 1] Erik Pontopiddan. The author's name should not have been given here in the Latin genitive form.

451 (c) The edition now gone to press] The 6th ed. of 3,000 which made the total 23,000.

454 (d) Charlotte] Tom's daughter, Elizabeth Charlotte, afterwards Mrs Peat.

454 (d) Walter] The 'I suppose' indicates that this is Scott's nephew.

455 (a) Gillon . . Riddells] Partners in firm of Riddell and Gillon, W.S., 37 George Square, Edinburgh. At this time there were William Riddell of Camieston and his son Thomas.

455 (e) article] See my note to *SL* xi. 302 (b).

455 (f) Mr. Johnstone] James Johnson's *A view of the jurisprudence of the Isle of Man* was published at Edinburgh in 1811.

455 (f) Laird of Logan] For fuller details, see above, p. 137.

457 (a) Sacheverel] William Sacheverell's *An account of the Isle of Man*.

457 (d) William Scott] Tom's banker at Ayr.

458 (a–b) Our case in Exchequer is to be pleaded to-morrow] By Scott's dating of his letter this would be 30 Jan. But no business was conducted on that day, which was the anniversary of Charles I's martyrdom. Scott probably was writing on 28 Jan. and finished his letter on 29 Jan.

458 (d–e) sending coals to NewCastle] *Ray,* p. 235.

458 (e) a balance of £900] See *SL* ii. 413 and my note.

459 (a)] The index figure in second line should be at 'it' in the first line.

459 (a) "Bread we shall eat or white or brown"] Matthew Prior, *Alma,* Canto III, line 587.

459 *n.* 1] In last line, for 'took' read 'may have taken.'

460 (b) Laret Burn] Lord Dalkeith's letter of 29 Jan. 1811 (cited *SL* ii. 435 *n.*) refers to this and not to Scott's letter printed in *SL* ii. 434–5.

460 (c) Fergusson] James Fergusson, W.S.

460 *n.* 1] Thomas Waugh of Laretburn died 8 Aug. 1820. (*Blackwood* vii. 706.)

461 (c) Being in love & in debt] Alexander Brome, *The mad lover,* lines 1–2. Quoted in *Waverley,* chap. 55.

461 (c) Mrs Edwards . . . Mrs. Johnstone] Tom Scott was apprentice to George Johnston, W.S. (1762–1801). He was unmarried, but Mrs Johnston may have been a sister-in-law. A Barbara Johnston married in 1770 William Edwards and she may have been the 'mad daughter.'

461 *n.* 2] Denby Park should be Danbury Place.

462 (a) roup-roll of her mothers things] Mrs Mary Johnston died at Antigua Street, Edinburgh, 17 Sept. 1802. (*Scots Mag.* lxiv. 860.) Her effects were sold in Nov. by 'Thomas Scott, W.S. head of Brodie's close, Lawnmarket.'

462 (e) do suit the time] Shakespeare, *Taming of the shrew,* IV. 3.

462 (f) your mad friend] The Mrs Edwards of previous page.

463 (d) 1652] 1651.

467 (d) your mother sister & brother] Mrs David McCulloch, dowager of Ardwall, Agnes McCulloch and presumably Alexander McCulloch. I think the brother is Alexander because James M. McCulloch in a letter to Scott of 14 Dec. 1813 (NLS MS. 3884, ff. 308–9) makes it clear that he had not met Scott this summer. Scott must have had tea at the McCullochs's house in Dumfries as James says in the letter cited that Scott had never visited Ardwall.

468 (c) Lord Forbes] George John Hastings, Viscount Forbes (courtesy title), eldest son of 6th Earl of Granard. He predeceased his father.

468 (d) my mother who is now on a visit at this place] She had left by 21 Sept. as Hector Macdonald Buchanan wrote to Scott on 22 Sept.: 'I met your excellent mother yesterday who informed me that she had been to see you at Abbotsford' (NLS MS. 3884, f. 256).

469 (d) Mr. David Scott] Tom Scott's banker at Ayr is usually given as

William Scott. But there was also a David Scott, banker at Ayr, at this time, presumably a relative and member of the same banking firm.

470 (c) a fouth of auld . . .] Burns, *Verses on Captain Grose's peregrinations*, st. [6].

470 (e) Counsellor Travers] Mrs Travers was a sister of Hartstonge's cousin, Mrs Matthew Weld. Information in Hartstonge's letter of 5 Oct. 1813 to Scott (NLS MS. 3884, ff. 265–70).

471 (d–e) I had a letter from Mr. Macculloch some weeks since] A few days later Scott received from James M. McCulloch a letter dated 14 Dec. 1813 (NLS MS. 3884, ff. 308–9) on this subject, but from the contents it is clear that this is his first communication since 24 Aug. The McCulloch mentioned here must, therefore, be another brother, probably Robert in London, but there is no letter from him at this time in NLS.

473 (c) The Magistrates have asked me] Scott should not have written 'have asked', for the Address had been presented to the Regent on 10 Dec. 1813. See my note to *SL* iii. 398 *n*. 1.

473 (d) as Winifred Jenkins says] See my note to *SL* iii. 398 (a–b).

475 (f) a Bank bill] Cf. *SL* iii. 415.

477 *n*. 1] See also below, pp. 477–8.

478 (b) To Thomas Scott] An extract is given in *SL* iv. 240–2.

478 (e) Albany] 1 Albany Street, Tom's Edinburgh house.

482 (d) the Whirligig of time] Shakespeare, *Twelfth Night*, V. i.

486 (a) 71st Regimt.] Should be 70th.

486 (f) I have directed Mr. Donaldson] In a letter of 14 Mar. 1817, in *SL* iv. 406–7.

487 (e) medicine for mine aching bones] Shakespeare, *Troilus and Cressida*, V. 11.

492 (c) Like the fox which lost its tail] See L'Estrange, *Fables*, No. 101. *A fox that lost his tail*. By Aesop. Also quoted in *Redgauntlet*, Narrative, chap. 22.

493 (e) To Thomas Scott] A different extract is given in *SL* v. 30–3.

497 (c) obliged . . . as . . . Duchess to Sancho] Should be 'Duchess to Teresa Panza.' See my note to *SL* i. 304 (d–e).

497 (d) Sergeant Kite] See *SL* v. 32 and *n*. 2.

497 (e) Willie Scott of Sunderland hall] William Scott, Younger of Woll. He was related to the family of Sunderland Hall and a Scott of Woll eventually succeeded to Sunderland Hall, but I do not know why Scott should so designate him at this time.

501 (d) Mr Patterson] Brother-in-law of George Hogarth, whose sister Jane (1792–1823) married John Patterson, 16 Sept. 1819.

501 (e) the circuit] Scott was at the Circuit, Jedburgh, 3–5 Apr.

504 (d) petition of his widow] This petition, dated 17 Feb. 1824, and addressed to the Secretary at War, is printed in *N. & Q.* 11th ser. Vol. 12 (4 Sept. 1915), p. 174.

506 (d) the Corporal] Walter, Scott's nephew.

506 (e) fancy ball] Bachelor's Ball in Assembly Rooms, George Street, Edinburgh, on Thursday 4 Mar. Scott, Lady Scott and Anne attended. See the *Scotsman*, Vol. 8 (6 Mar. 1824), p. 151, c. 2; and *Letters to their old governess*, p. 92.

507 (a) I shall write to Mr. MacCulloch] His letter of same date is in *SL* viii. 274–6.

511 (b–c) Lady S. and Anne] The attributes should be reversed. The 'Beatrice spirit' applies to Anne and the 'sincerity' to Lady Scott.

VOLUME VIII

1 (b) To Lord Montagu] The first paragraph of this letter must have been written about 24 Apr., by which time Scott had heard of Lady Courtown's death on 21 Apr., but before the news of the birth of Lady Stopford's child on 24 Apr. could reach him. If 16 May is the correct date, the letter must have been written in instalments.

2 (a) the Provost of Eaton] Rev. Joseph Goodall.

2 (b) Sheriff] James Allan Maconochie.

5 *n.* 1] The index figure should be at line 3 above. For 'Jane Nicolson' read 'Sarah Nicolson.'

10 (b) Ordnance maps] Although Scott repeated his request (below, pp. 94, 203, 343) he apparently received no more.

10 (c) King of Frances escape in French] *Relation d'un voyage à Bruxelles et à Coblentz (1791) par Louis XVIII*, 8vo Londres, 1823.

10 *n.* 1] Only the first-mentioned work is on p. 144. The second is on p. 112. Though *Edwin and Anna* is described as a Northumbrian tale, part of the story takes place in Roxburghshire. Kelso, Jedburgh and real persons such as Pringle of Clifton come into the tale.

11 (e) To Maria Edgeworth] The date is 4 June.

11 *n.* 3] This note is unnecessary as the dates can be fixed from the evidence of other letters in *SL*.

12 (a) Mr. and Mrs. Stuart] Probably Professor and Mrs Dugald Stewart who were old friends of Maria Edgeworth.

12 (c) To Lord Montagu] Scott was at Abbotsford on Monday, 2 June and this is probably correct date of the letter. He has taken it to Edinburgh for posting; hence the late PM.

12 *n.* 1] See chaps. 4 and 9.

15 (d) To Maria Edgeworth] For Edgeworth family letters describing her visit to Scott, see *Maria Edgeworth and Sir Walter Scott: unpublished letters, 1823*, by R. F. Butler, in *Rev. of English Stud.* N.S. Vol. 9 (Feb. 1958), pp. 23–40.

15 (f) kingdom of *Fife*] To the Blair-Adam Club.

15 *n.* 2] Delete this note, not now necessary.

16 (d) calling it] Read 'calling at'.

16 *n.* 1] See *SL* xii. 490.

18 (e) *escalier derobé*] It is significant (from the date of this letter and the date of *Quentin Durward*) that Scott refers to this type of stair in the 1823 introd. to the novel. The plan was never carried out.

18 (f) a new cargo of them, Lord knows from whence] This cargo undoubtedly consisted of heads and horns sent by Thomas Pringle. See *SL* x. 120 and my note.

19 *n.* 2] In line 5, for '*Scotish*' read '*Scottish.*'

21 (a–b) Harrowgate] On 20 June 1823 James Ballantyne drew £100 from the business for this trip to Harrogate. (Lockhart, *The Ballantyne-humbug handled*, p. 88.)

23 (b) chamber in the wall] *Bible, II Kings* 4: 10.

23 *n.* 1] Chambers gives the story as told by C. K. Sharpe's Nurse Jenny.

24 (f) a fourth son] John Macdonald Buchanan who died at Gibraltar on 11 May.

25 (a) one left out of five] James Graham Macdonald Buchanan who died in 1828.

25 (b) Sir Frederick Adams staff] Adam was not appointed Lord High Commissioner to the Ionian Islands till 5 Mar. 1824.

25 (c) The good lady] The only letter of 1823 before June from Morritt in NLS is dated 8 Jan. The reference to the 'good lady' must be in a missing letter.

25 (e) Simon Pure] A Quaker in Mrs Centlivre's *A bold stroke for a wife*.

26 (a) I have like Gil Blas] See my note to *SL* vi. 402 (b).

26 (c) *rara avis*] Horace, *Satires*, II. ii. 26; or rather, possibly, Juvenal, *Satires*, vi. 164, as latter is quoted in *The Antiquary*, chap. 8.

27 (d) To Richard Surtees] Surtees was in Edinburgh on 23 June (Taylor, *Memoir of Robert Surtees*, p. 175). Fridays in June were 6, 13, 20, 27. On 6th Scott was engaged with the Edgeworths; on 13th he was at Blair-Adam; 27th is ruled out as the invitation to dinner for Wednesday or Thursday would be for 2 or 3 July but Lady Scott was at Abbotsford on these days. Only Friday which fits is 20 June.

27 (d) Restituta] *Restituta; or, titles, extracts, and characters of old books in English literature revived*, by Sir Egerton Brydges, 4 vols., London, 1814–16.

29 (a) To James Ballantyne] The date must be late May or early June. Vol. I was in good progress by 24 May (above, p. 11) and Scott would have reached p. 66 before July.

29 (a) scrip and scrippage] Shakespeare, *As you like it*, III. 2.

29 (b) "a humour to be cruel"] William Congreve, *The way of the world*, I. 9.

29 (b) a pitiful tragedy, filled with the most lamentable mirth] See *SL* vi. 311.

29 (d) To C. K. Sharpe] In *Sharpe's Letters*, ii. 258. Scott wrote again on the following day, ibid. ii. 261. This latter letter is not in *SL*.

30 (a) Bishop Abercromby] 'Bishop' is a mistake. The King's limner before Raeburn was Rev. Thomas Sinclair Abercromby of Glassaugh who died at Rome on 9 Apr. 1823.

30 (a) the General] Sharpe's brother Matthew.

30 (b) "O rare guerdon . . ."] Shakespeare, *Love's labour's lost*, III. 1.

30 n. 1] Haydon's letter of 1 July is in Partington, *Letter-books*, pp. 165–8. The text does not agree with the text of this note. Haydon's reply of 12 July is given ibid., pp. 168–70.

34 (d) To unknown correspondent] The addressee is William Chisholm and date is 1828. Chisholme had written on 7 July 1828 (NLS MS. 3907, ff. 11–12) but Scott could hardly receive his letter by 9 July. Scott's letter should probably have a later date. See Scott's letter of 14 July 1828 (*SL* x. 467), in which he refers to the purchase of Terry's share of the Adelphi by Matthews, to Terry's bad handwriting and to Drury Lane. For other references to Chisholme, see *SL* x. 415, 501 n., 507.

37 n. 1] Her letter of the 8th is in Partington, *Letter-books*, pp. 201–5, and other letters from her on same subject follow, pp. 205–12.

38 (c) the late Countess] Elizabeth, wife of 6th Earl of Balcarres and 23rd Earl of Crawford. From 1780 till 1808 she was Lady Balcarres and from 1808 till 1816 Lady Crawford. She died 10 Aug. 1816.

38 (c) the lady dowager] Anne, wife of 5th Earl of Balcarres.

38 (e) "Eh! quo' the tod . . ."] There is a MS. of this song in NLS (MS. 2890, f. 221) endorsed 'Sir Walter Scott,' but not in Scott's hand. It was printed in R. A. Smith's *The Scotish minstrel*, Vol. 6 [1824], p. 94, with omission of fifth stanza. See also *The Oxford dictionary of nursery rhymes*, ed. by I. and P. Opie, repr. Oxford, The Clarendon Press, 1973, pp. 173–5.

38 n. 1] Anne is the Dowager.

38 n. 3] The note in the 1880 ed. of the *Ballad book* is merely quoting Scott.

39 (e) profitless and profane art of ballad-making] See my note to *SL* i. 274 (d).

40 (b) within these few weeks] Actually more than six months before. See *SL* vii. 318.

41 (d–e) "poor Scotland's gear"] Lady Wardlaw, *Hardyknute* st. 34, line 2. In Ramsay, *Tea-table miscellany*.

43 (a–b) Dogberry's generosity] See *SL* ii. 320.

43 (c) Solomon . . . silence] *Bible*, I *Kings* 6: 7.

43 n.] In line 5, Dearsay is Dairsie, near Cupar.

44 (b) our cake is like to be dough] Shakespeare, *Taming of the shrew*, I. 1 and V. 1.

44 n.] Lady Hardwicke (line 11) was Lady Anne Barnard's younger sister.

45 n. 1] Delete 'Probably.' See also below, p. 61.

46 n. 1] The letter was written in instalments between 9 and 17 July.

49 (e) sparrow like] *Bible*, *Psalms* 102: 7.

50 (b) shells for the excellent Provost] For Rev. Joseph Goodall, Provost of Eton.

50 (b) if *Law* had but given *both* the shells] For the fable of the oyster found by two travellers and the decision of the arbiter, see L'Estrange, *Fables*, p. 382. Not one of Aesop's fables.

50 n. 1] Scott's letter which 'came too late' is the one mentioned on p. 30 above. Peel's letter of 15 July is in Partington, *Letter-books*, p. 247.

51 (c) coals of fire on my head] *Bible, Proverbs* 25: 22; *Romans* 12: 20.

52 (d) honest men and bonny lasses] Burns, *Tam o' Shanter*, line 16.

53 (a) Fanshaws pieces] Two poems, both entitled *A riddle*. See *SL* vii. 235 and *n*. 3.

54 (a) tell it not in Epping forest . . .] A parody of 'Tell it not in Gath, publish it not in the streets of Askelon'. *Bible, II Samuel* 1: 20.

54 (a–b) Howison] See my notes to *SL* vii. 59.

55 *n*. 2] Maria Edgeworth's letter of 24 July is in Partington, *Letter-books*, pp. 263–5.

56 (d) "half proud half sad half angry and half pleased"] Joanna Baillie, *Address to a steam-vessel*, last line: 'Half sad, half proud, half angry, and half pleased.' (Joanna Baillie, *A collection of poems*, London, 1823, p. 264.)

57 (a) Prince Hosseins tapestry] In *Arabian Nights*. See my note to *SL* i. 229 (e).

57 (e) the Doctor] Matthew Baillie, Joanna's brother. He died on 23 Sept. of this year.

57 (f) Mrs Baillie] Sophia Denman who had married Matthew Baillie.

58 (a) bachellors bluff] A partial quotation. See my note to *SL* ix. 438 (c).

58 (d) Mr. Bell] William Bell, W.S. See above, p. 9 *n*.

59 *n*. 1] Delete 'Evidently.' For 'did not come out in book form till 1825' read 'was coming out in parts and completed in 1825.'

59 *n*. 2] There is a longer extract in Partington, *Post-bag*, pp. 179–81.

60 (b) Lion in the Spectator] The *Spectator*, No. 5, 6 Mar. 1711; No. 13, 15 Mar. 1711 [By Joseph Addison.] Nicolini (whose real name was Nicola Grimaldi) fought a sham lion in Francesco Mancini's opera, *Idaspe fedele*, performed in London in 1711. See Grove's *Dict. of music* under Mancini and Nicolini.

60 (c) lion . . . Knight of the woeful countenance] Cervantes, *Don Quixote*, Pt II, chap. 17. (Lockhart's ed., 1822,

iv. 1–13.) On the translation 'countenance,' see my note to *SL* ii. 368 *n*. 1.

61 (a) To C. K. Sharpe] Date is probably 28 July. In 1823 27 July was a Sunday and carpenters would not be working on that day. The letter was probably begun on Saturday and finished on Monday. Sharpe's letter which Scott is answering and which is undated (but can be dated 25 July) is in *Sharpe's Letters*, ii. 262–3.

61 (a) acceptable present] Sharpe's *A ballad book*.

61 (a) But transeat quoth John] See my note to *SL* iii. 170 (b).

61 (b) your plan of Frendraught] Scott is replying to Sharpe's letter dated 'Friday' (which can be dated 25 July 1823) in which he outlined a plan for a small volume on the Frendraught ballads. (*Sharpe's Letters*, ii. 262.) Scott had a MS., *Satyr against Frendraught* (above, p. 45, 45 *n*.). Sharpe had another MS. beginning 'The eighteenth of October.' This version was printed for the first time by James Maidment in his *A North countrie garland*, Edinburgh, 1824, pp. 4–9, from a copy supplied by 'an intelligent individual' resident in Aberdeen. The person so described was Peter Buchan. Motherwell printed a version in his *Minstrelsy*, Glasgow, 1827, pp. 167–72, with an introd. largely supplied by Sharpe, who had given up his own plan for a small volume. Finlay, in his *Scottish historical and romantic ballads*, Edinburgh, 1808, Vol. 1, pp. xx–xxi, had confessed that he had been unable to recover the ballad but quoted Scott about the keys being thrown into the well, to which Scott refers in this letter to Sharpe. Apparently the first mention of the keys in print is in Maidment's version and it is significant that the lines 'The keys were casten in the deep draw well, / Ye cannot win away' are an interpolation making a 6-line stanza, whereas all the others are in the normal 4-line stanza. A modern ballad on the same subject called *Frennet Hall* was printed by Herd, Ritson, James Johnson and Finlay and it has been attributed to Henry Mackenzie, the 'Man of Feeling.' Sharpe's reply to this letter is dated 'Thursday' [i.e. 31 July]. It is in *Sharpe's Letters*, ii. 271–3.

61 (c) an old Lady's complete set of ballads] Sharpe kept this MS. It passed to Rev. W. K. R. Bedford, who gave it to Alexander Allardyce (*Sharpe's Letters*, ii. 264 *n.*). It is now in the Hornell Coll., Broughton House, Kirkcudbright (*Studies in Scottish Lit.* iv. 5).

62 (b) your kind dedication] Sharpe's *A ballad book* was dedicated to Scott.

62 (c) "Now a' is done that man can do . . ."] *It was a' for our rightfu' king*, st. [2], lines 1–2. In *Johnson*, Vol. 5 [1797], No. 497, where it is given as anonymous. It is in Burns's *Works*, as *The farewell*.

62 (d) put in her thumb] *Little Jack Horner*, lines 4–5. (*The Oxford dictionary of nursery rhymes*, ed. by I. and P. Opie, repr. Oxford, Clarendon Press, 1973, p. 234.)

64 (b) To Lord Montagu] Date is 16 Aug. 1823. Scott expects the Buccleuchs 'tomorrow', i.e. 17 Aug., and writing to Walter on 16 Aug. he expects the Buccleuch family 'tomorrow' (below, p. 74).

64 (c) With a heigh ho] Shakespeare, *Twelfth Night*, V. 1.

64 (c) King Jemmy] King James VI's letter of 6 Dec. 1600 to the Laird of Dundas is printed in the *Scots Mag.* Vol. 69 (Jan. 1807), p. 16, and elsewhere.

64 (f) To W. S. Rose] The date is 1824.

65 (d) "And if we could but get it dressed . . ."] Scott is parodying st. [6], lines 5–8, of *Scornfu' Nansy*: 'And if I can but get it drawn, / Which will be right uneasy, / I shall lay baith my lugs in pawn, / That he shall get a heezy.' In Ramsay, *Tea-table miscellany*; Herd, ii. 80; *Johnson*, Vol. 1 (1787), No. 50; Ritson, *Scotish songs* (1794), i. 183. In line 3, Scott probably wrote 'lugs' not 'legs.'

65 *n.* 2] As the correct date of the letter is 1824, Scott might just as well have been alluding to Hogg's *The three perils of man* (1822).

66 (a) To C. K. Sharpe] The correct date is 1824. Walter was at Sandhurst on 1 Aug. 1823 and it was in Aug. 1824 that he arrived after sketching in Kent. See below, p. 342. This letter is in *Sharpe's Letters*, ii. 267–8, where it is misdated 1823. Scott is answering Sharpe's undated letter [31 July 1824],

ibid. ii. 266–7, which is also misdated 1823. In this letter Sharpe explains discrepancy between the subject of the drawing and *Auld Robin Gray*. A reproduction of this frontispiece is given as No. XI in *Etchings by C. K. Sharpe*, 4to Edinburgh, 1869, with text explaining it at p. 144.

66 (c) McBane] Sharpe replied in an undated letter [20 Aug. 1824] thanking him for permission 'to copy the portrait'. (*Sharpe's Letters*, ii. 269, where it is misdated 1823; for correct date see *SL* viii. 372 *n.*)

67 (a) fighting gear] *Pibroch of Donuil Dhu*, st. [3], lines 3–4; 'fighting gear, / Broadswords and targes.' One of the very few instances where Scott quotes himself.

67 (b) Prince Hassan's tapestry] In *Arabian Nights*. See my note to *SL* i. 229 (e).

67 (b) Be here with a hoop] Varied from Buckingham, *The rehearsal*, V. 1. See also *SL* iv. 8.

67 (d) To Samuel Warren] Printed in Warren's *Miscellanies*, 2 vols., Edinburgh, 1855, i. xi; in the *Scotsman*, 2 July 1896, p. 7, c. 4; and in *The Times*, 3 Aug. 1928, p. 17, c. 4, from the original.

70 (c) The Knight of Gattonside] Sir Adam Ferguson.

70 *n.* 1] Constable's letter of 8 Aug. is in *Archibald Constable*, iii. 274–5; of 17 Aug., ibid. 276; and letter from A. Constable & Co. ibid. 277–9.

71 (c) Napiers proof] Scott's article *Romance* which was published in the *Encyclopædia Britannica* in Apr. 1824.

72 (a) To John Adolphus] This is indexed (*SL* xii. 493) as a different man from John Leycester Adolphus; but they are the same. The letter was printed in *Recollections of . . . John Adolphus . . . by . . . Emily Henderson*, London, 1871, p. 135, where it is wrongly dated 1822.

72 (b) Here shall you see] Shakespeare, *As you like it*, II. 5.

75 (a) poor Colonel Stanhope] 'Poor' because his wife had died on 14 Jan.

76 *n.* 1] Constable's letter of 20 Aug. and his letter of 22 Aug. are in *Archibald Constable*, iii. 280, 283–4.

79 *n*.] Delete last sentence and see next note.

80 (c) To James Ballantyne] This letter belongs to early Apr. 1823: (1) 'On the 15 I lett my grass parkes.' This was on 15 Apr. (*SL* vii. 363, 364); (2) reference to getting Walter on full pay follows on similar references in letters of 28–29 Mar. to Ballantyne (*SL* vii. 361, 362).

82 (d) a good farm] Broomielees.

82 (e) Six large grass parkes] See *SL* vii. 363, 364.

85 *n*. 1] The author of the first work was not Skinner but Joseph Moyle Sherer. The error on p. 255 of *ALC* is corrected on p. 446 of the index.

85 *n*. 3] Constable was wrong. Scott's letter was written on Friday, 29 Aug. On that day he witnessed the Royal Company of Archers shooting for the Silver Arrow at Selkirk. (*Edinburgh Observer*, 1 Sept. 1823, p. 3, c. 2.)

86 (e) To C. K. Sharpe] The correct date is 1824: (1) Scott did not begin putting his books into the Library till after May 1824; (2) the visit to Drumlanrig was in 1824, not 1823; (3) this letter follows the letter of 29 Aug. 1824 in *SL* xii. 453–4.

87 (a) Bell] John Bell of Newcastle from whom Scott had received a number of volumes of ballads already bound. Scott wants his style of binding followed.

87 *n*. 1] This letter from Sharpe, dated 'Friday', was written not in 1823 but on 20 Aug. 1824. See *SL* viii. 372 *n*.

88 *n*. 1] In line 2, for 'Stewart' read 'Steuart.'

89 (a) best of possible world[s]] Voltaire See my note to *SL* i. 186 (a–b).

90 (c) Miss Sophia's beautiful Irish air] In Mrs Hope-Scott's MS. Music Book at Abbotsford this song is included with the music. It has no title but begins: 'I will tye my petticoat of red' and each stanza ends: 'Shoul shoul shoulagaroo.' The wording differs considerably from the verses quoted in the letter. One line quoted in *SL* x. 320, xi. 296 and 'Introductory' section to *The Fair Maid of Perth*, is probably a variant of a line in this song.

91 *n*. 2] See also *Trans. Hawick Arch. Soc.*, 1915, pp. 39–40.

92 (c) To James Ballantyne] This letter, I think, should be dated 1824. Scott's references to Constable's visit fits 21 Sept. 1824 (below, p. 371) and to insanity fits 'the unhappy affair' of 20 Sept. 1824 (below, p. 405). Tuesday was 23 Sept. in 1823, but Scott's dating is notoriously inaccurate.

92 (d) Waterloo Humbug tavern[?]] Delete the query. Scott held four shares in the Waterloo Tavern and Hotel, Edinburgh. (*Trust Disposition*; NLS MS. 112, f. 59.) Shares were £25 each when the company was formed in 1818. (*Scots Mag.* Vol. 81 (Mar. 1818), p. 284.)

92 (e–f) jouk & let the *jaw* go bye] *Kelly*, p. 189.

92 *n*. 2] Delete this note, which can have no bearing on the subject of Scott's letter. Scott would not be unduly upset about Constable's foot trouble but he would be over his insanity.

94 (c) acquaint] After this word insert 'me.'

95 (d) To Archibald Constable] The letter, I think, belongs to the end of Aug.: (1) the weather was bad in Aug.; (2) Constable sent 26 tracts on witchcraft on 20 Aug. (*Archibald Constable*, iii. 280). In the first sentence 'Witchcraft book' should, perhaps, be 'Witchcraft books.'

95 (d) as the wren said] *Kelly*, p. 13.

95 *n*. 1] The author tells us that he was the son of Robert Cramond, merchant, who was born in Edinburgh, 8 Apr. 1703; that his grandfather lived at Roslin Castle and had one daughter who married Dr Boswell, brother of Lord Auchinleck.

96 (b) To James Ballantyne] The date must be Sunday, 1 June: (1) 'look towards July' indicates that the letter was written in June; (2) Ballantyne went to Harrogate in middle of June; (3) only Sunday in June that Scott was at Abbotsford was 1 June. The date is given as 'end of June' in *SL* xii. 490, but this is too late.

96 *n*. 1] Delete this note, which is not relevant to date of Scott's letter. Scott does not mean that the Spanish war is over. He is referring to the 'humbug' in identical terms used in his letter of 25 June (above, p. 26).

97 (c) To David Laing] This and the following letter are printed in the right order and are presumably close to each other in time. The first, like the second, would be written from Castle Street. Scott was at Abbotsford in Oct. and, in any case, Laing's preface is dated 23 Oct. and time for printing and binding must be allowed for. Dates probably belong to the summer and before the Courts rose in July.

101 (b) when your Lordship receives your own commission] Lord Montagu became Lord Lieutenant of Selkirkshire in succession to Lord Napier who had died on 1 Aug.

101 (c) "on the outer walls"] This seems to be an amalgamation of two passages in Shakespeare: *I Henry VI*, I. 6: 'Advance our waving colours on the walls' and *Macbeth*, V. 5: 'Hang out our banners on the outward walls.'

103 (f) the Prussian lecturer] Gregor von Feinaigle, who gave lectures on mnemonics at the Royal Institution in 1811 and also in Edinburgh. (See Byron's *Don Juan*, note to Canto I, st. xi.) Scott may have read the review of his book, published London, 1812, in *QR* for Mar. 1813 (ix. 125–39).

105 (a) Stoddarts engraving] Charles Alfred Stothard's drawings of the tapestry were made, 1816–18, for the Society of Antiquaries of London. Engravings of them were issued, in 1821–3, as Plates 1–17 in Vol. 6 of the Society's *Vetusta monumenta*.

106 (d) the horse] Saint George. See Index under Horses.

106 (f) Colonel Stanhope poor fellow] 'Poor' because his wife had died on 14 Jan.

107 *n.* 1] Delete this note. Lord Barnard (courtesy title) was the eldest son of 1st Duke of Cleveland and became 2nd Duke in 1842.

108 (d) the horse] Saint George. See Index under Horses.

108 (e) To Walter] Unless Scott has forgotten the date of Walter's birth, this letter should be dated '[Abbotsford, 28 Oct. 1823]'.

108 *n.* 1] Scott should have written 'Argand lamps' which required cleaning. Argand burners were installed in 1823 and required no cleaning.

109 (a) princesse's or duchesses anxiety] I cannot explain this as Walter's letter is not in NLS.

109 (f) A verie parfite gentil knight] Chaucer, *Prologue to the Canterbury tales*, line 72.

110 *n.* 3] Amend two first sentences. Scott is referring to Sir Samuel Meyrick's *Critical inquiry into ancient armour*, which, though dated 1824, was published in 1823 in time for the *Lit. Gaz.* to review it in Oct. Furthermore, Scott refers to the work as 'Ancient Armour' below, p. 113.

111 (a) *pieds de mouche*] See *SL* v. 279 and my note.

111 (c) Mr. Baldock] See Geoffrey de Bellaigue, *Edward Holmes Baldock* in the *Connoisseur*, Vol. 189 (Aug. 1975), pp. 290–9 and Vol. 190 (Sept. 1975), pp. 18–25.

111 (d) Bower] All the grates were got from Dowson in London. Bower is a possible misreading for Dowson. See my note to *SL* v. 462 (d).

112 *n.* 2] The clouds are white on a blue sky.

113 (a) blazonry . . . eighteen in number] There are altogether thirty-six shields. On 'eighteen in number' see *MPW* vii. 49–50.

113 (b) what Robinson Crusoe calls the rainy season] Aug.–Oct. See Defoe's *Robinson Crusoe* [Everyman's Lib.], pp. 73, 77, 78, 83, 112, 134, 142, 167, 267.

114 (a–b) begging to be placed at my wits end] This is the correct reading of the MS. (NLS MS. 997, f. 69). Scott must mean 'induced me, being at my wits end, not later than yesterday to write him a long letter begging him to get Charles placed.'

115 (b) Commission] Commission on the Forms of Process, and Courses of Appeals in Scotland. The report was fully analysed in the *Edin. Ann. Reg. for 1824*, XVII. ii. 28–43.

115 (b) wax old as our garments] *Bible, Psalms* 102: 26; *Isaiah* 50: 9, 51: 6; *Hebrews* 1: 11.

121 *n.* 1] For 'vol. ii. p. 163' read 'vol. ii. cols. 1631–4.' This note does not explain Scott's words 'Caraboo reached

me safe.' Scott is referring to Maria Edgeworth's gift of *Narrative of the singular imposition practised on the benevolence of a lady by Mary Willcocks, alias Baker, alias Caraboo, Princess of Javasu*, 8vo London, 1817. Pp. 64–5 contain *Young Caraboo!—a parody* [from *Young Lochinvar* in *Marmion*] repr. from the *Bristol Mirror*.

122 (a) wild Macras] See my note to *SL* ii. 355 (f).

122 (c) Dr. King] Dr John King who married Emmeline Edgeworth, Maria's sister, in 1802. Emmeline died in 1817.

122 *n*. 1] Delete reference to Macraes.

123 (b) To James Ballantyne] As Scott has only 'two or three pages more' to write of *St Ronan's Well* and as the novel came out at the end of Dec. (reviewed in both *Lit. Chron.* and *Lit. Gaz.* on 27 Dec.), the letter probably belongs to Dec.

123 *n*. 1] Lockhart is correct. Delete, therefore, the sentence beginning 'It may have appeared.'

124 (b) your horse] Saint George. See Index under Horses.

124 (b) Principal of Brazn. Nose] Dr Ashhurst Turner Gilbert.

124 (f) Dukes levee] Duke of York.

126 (a) her two daughters] Anne and Eliza.

127 (a) Compliments to the Lady . . .] The Lady is Lady Ferguson; the Major is Col. James Ferguson; and the nuns are Bell, Mary and Margaret Ferguson.

127 (d) *Sed fugit interea fugit irrevocabile tempus*] Virgil, *Georgics*, III. 284.

128 *n*. 2] See *The Oxford dictionary of nursery rhymes*, ed. by I. and P. Opie, repr., Oxford, Clarendon Press, 1973, pp. 336–7.

129 (b) Mackenzie] Roderick Mackenzie, W.S., Secretary of the Edinburgh Oil Gas Company.

129 (b) Oil Gas Compy.] For a useful note on this company, see Anderson's ed. of Scott's *Journal* (Oxford, 1972), p. 716.

129 *n*. 1] Delete this note and see my note to *SL* vii. 56 *n*. 1.

130 (a) "no very fou but gaily yet"] *We're gayly yet*, st. [1], line 2. In *Herd*, ii. 121.

130 (f) Robert] Robert McCulloch of Kirkclaugh, son of David McCulloch of Ardwall.

131 (c) Horace] *Odes*, III. vi. 46–8. Partially quoted in *Nigel*, chap. 32.

134 (d) *circa* 19 *or* 20] Delete '*circa* 19 *or*.' Saturday was 20 Dec.

135 *n*. 1] Hook's letter of 17 Dec. is in *FL* ii. 182 *n*.

135 *n*. 2] The words 'a small spill of cash' do not occur in *Roderick Random*.

136 (d) To James Ballantyne] Another letter to Ballantyne (not in *SL*) is printed in the *Scotsman*, 28 Feb. 1930, p. 11, c. 4. It does not explain the trouble and Scott merely excuses Purdie after saying 'Tom Purdie *alias* Piper got off for the fright. To be sure, he had been abominably provoking.' 'Piper' may be a misreading for 'Pipes' and Tom Purdie may have been indulging in some practical joke like Tom Pipes in Smollett's *Peregrine Pickle*.

136 *n*. 1] There is an oil portrait of Russell on wood ($11 \cdot 5 \times 9$ in.) by Sir William Allan at Abbotsford.

137 (a) To Thomas Thomson] Scott summoned Patrick Fraser Tytler to a meeting of the committee on Friday, 28 May 1824 'at five o'clock for business: ½ past five for a haggis.' (Burgon, *A memoir of P. F. Tytler*, London, 1859, p. 163 *n*.) The only date which fits this letter to Thomson is Tuesday, 25 May 1824,

138 *n*. 1] In lines 4–5, for 'Sir John Maxwell of Broomhill' read 'John Maxwell, Esq. of Broomholm.'

139 (b) Mr. Meason] Gilbert Laing Meason.

141 (a) the two miniatures] See above, pp. 119, 122.

141 *n*. 1] Scott had met Captain Parry in London in Feb. 1821. See John S. Harford, *Recollections of William Wilberforce*, London, 1864, p. 111.

142 (a) your friend] Capt. Francis Beaufort.

142 (a) when two men ride a horse] Shakespeare, *Much ado about nothing*, III. 5.

143 (d) two uncommon fine girls] Anne and Eliza Scott.

143 (e) a puppy . . . for your medical friend] This is presumably Cribb, which Scott gave soon afterwards to Constable. See below, pp. 232, 233, 235.

144 n. 1] For 'Galashans' see *SL* ix. 446, 446 n., and my note.

145 n. 1] See Harold William Thompson, *A Scottish Man of Feeling*, London, 1931, p. 398. Thompson apparently did not know that Mackenzie had sent a MS. of *Nonnie Doo* to Scott.

146 (d) as Miss Jenkins says] See my note to *SL* i. 337 (c).

147 (c) earthen pots] These were made by William Creelman of Portobello. He is described as 'of Coats and Portobello.' His wife died 31 Jan. 1819; his son James became an Advocate 9 Mar. 1819; and his portrait by Graham-Gilbert was exhibited at the Scottish Academy, Edinburgh, in 1827.

147 n. 1] In line 5 delete 'Evidently.' Montgomery had asked for a poem. See below, p. 177.

148 n. 1] Lockhart should not be cited. He gives the impression, wrongly, that there was an ed. called the 'Variorum Classics.' What Constable presented was a miscellaneous collection of various editions, mainly published abroad but with one published at Glasgow. The dates range from 1613 to 1813. Montfaucon's work is *L'antiquité expliquée*, 10 tom. (in 15), Paris, 1719–24.

149 n. 1) At end of note delete reference and substitute: *MPW* xxi. 77–151.

150 (e) I have written to Sir Henry] The letter is not in *SL*.

151 n. 3] Delete last sentence and substitute: See also *SL* iii. 282 and vii. 197.

152 (a) Jo] See *Marmion*, Introd. to Canto VI, line 7, and Scott's note.

153 n. 1] Delete. Scott's meaning is quite clear. See my note to *SL* v. 289 (b).

154 n. 1] In last line for 'agent' read 'friend.' See my note to *SL* vii. 202 n. 1.

155 n. 2] Tobin is Sir John Tobin, a Liverpool merchant, not an architect as Scott says. The article before 'James

Milne' should be deleted. He was well known and installed the gas plant at Abbotsford.

156 n. 1] Constable's letter of 16 Jan. is in *Archibald Constable*, iii. 292–3. Scott's reference to the box of MSS. shows that the letter is after 16 Jan., but I do not think it is a reply to Constable's letter which gave a very gloomy report of his health. The word 'rejoiced' would have been inappropriate.

157 (a) To Miss Clephane] To Anna Jane.

158 (b) Some heritable security] She lent some of this money to William Scott of Maxpoffle, for on 4 Apr. 1824 Scott wrote to Willie: 'Miss Clephane would add to her loan . . . about £150 if it be wanted' (NLS MS. 2890, f. 23; not in *SL*).

158 (d) l'embarras des richesses] The title of a play by D'Allainval.

158 (d) a full sorrow] A Scottish proverb. 'Of all sorrows a full sorrow is the best.' (*Kelly*, p. 271.)

159 (e) "A thing to dream of . . ."] Coleridge, *Christabel*, Pt I, line 253: 'a sight to dream of, not to tell.'

160 (a–b) the song in the Beggar's Opera] Gay, *The beggar's opera*, I. 1.

160 (b) "Did you never hear of Captain Parry? . . ."] This and similar squibs seem to have been common in 1824. I have not traced this one but I have found another: 'Captain Parry! Captain Parry / Welcome from the Polar Sea: / Now, I hope, thou'st come to marry / Miss Brown—if she'll marry thee.'

160 (c) this bald unprofitable chat] A combination of Shakespeare, *I Henry IV*, I. 3: 'this bald unjointed chat' and III. 1: 'this unprofitable chat.'

160 (c–d) O for an hour of Dundee] Scott in his *Minstrelsy* (ed. Henderson), ii. 288 tells us that 'an ancient gentleman' told him the story of the Highland Chieftain who in despair at Mar's inactivity exclaimed 'O for one hour of Dundee!' The 'ancient gentleman' was probably John Ramsay of Ochtertyre who recorded the anecdote in his MSS. which were later published as *Scotland and Scotsmen*, ed. Alexander Allardyce (Edinburgh, 1888). See Vol.

ii, p. 49 n. Wordsworth in his *In the Pass of Killicranky* (1803), line 11, wrote: 'Oh, for a single hour of that Dundee.' He may have heard the anecdote from Scott.

161 (e) Mr Handleys] The Handley of this letter should be Hankey.

161 n. 1] Scott at this time had two portraits of Claverhouse—a small one (4·25 × 3·75 in.) and a large one (29·5 × 24·5 in.). The former is now in the ante-room to the Armoury and the latter in the Library at Abbotsford.

163 (b) "Yet not so ill . . ."] Shakespeare, *Richard III*, IV. 4: 'Nor none so bad but well may be reported.'

163 (b) On Saturday, 31st January] According to *Blackwood*, xv. 248, 250, the daughter was born on 24 Jan. and died on 27 Jan. According to Scott's date she died on 2 Feb., the day before he is writing, leaving an interval of only a day for his reference to Sophia's recovery. Scott's dating, therefore, is wrong.

163 (d–e) Anent the matter of the correspondence] See above, p. 142 n.

163 (e) I acknowledge like Sancho] Cervantes, *Don Quixote*, Pt 2, chap. 43 (Lockhart's ed., 1822, iv. 281). Don Quixote's niece also uses the proverb (Pt 1, Bk I, chap. 7; Lockhart's ed., 1822, i. 75). Scott's allusion is not very apt.

163 n. 1] The American friend is Mrs Mary Griffiths. As almost the whole of her letter is printed in Partington, *Letter-books*, pp. 296–8, it was unnecessary to print it in this note. The portion dealing with the chicken pie, which is omitted by Partington, would have been sufficient. In a letter of 9 Apr. 1824 to Mrs Rachel Lazarus, Maria quoted (in at least one passage, inaccurately) from this Scott letter of 3 Feb. See *Mod. Lang. Rev.* Vol. 23 (July 1928), pp. 296–8.

165 (b) *rugged* and *tough*] A partial quotation. See my note to *SL* ix. 438 (c).

168 (b) James Ballantyne's blarney] His theatrical criticisms in the *Edinburgh Weekly Journal*.

168 n. 1] Delete reference to *Redgauntlet*. Scott is referring only to *Tales of the Crusaders*, which consisted of two tales in two vols. each.

170 (f) *quaestio voluntatis*] Quality of intention. A Scots law phrase. See Trayner, *Latin maxims*.

171 (c) Walter . . . went back] He left Edinburgh on Saturday, 31 Jan. *N. & Q.* Vol. 206, p. 72.

172 n. 1] Jean Rutherford, Mrs Thomas Scott, died at Jedburgh, 2 Feb. 1824.

173 (b) Governor Elphinstone] Hon. Mountstuart Elphinstone was at this time Governor of Bombay.

173 n. 1] According to Croker (*The Croker papers*, i. 123), George IV kept indoors at Brighton, not because of gout or any other bodily ailment, but because he was afraid of coming into contact with Mrs Fitzherbert.

174 (b) Ossian] I have failed to find this saying in any of the poems of Ossian.

175 (b) Till she be fat as a Noraway seal] *Bannocks of barley-meal*, st. [5], lines 7–8. Attributed to John Campbell, 2nd Duke of Argyll. In *Herd*, ii. 131, and in *Johnson*, Vol. 6 (1803), No. 560. Title is sometimes given as *Argyle is my name* or *My name is Argyle*.

175 (b) the custom of her exercise] See my note to *SL* ii. 252 (a).

175 n. 1] Add: lines 137–8.

176 (a–b) reduced like Gil Blas much to the company of my brethren Clerks] See my note to *SL* vi. 402 (b).

176 n. 1] I have not found this drawing at Abbotsford. It may have been kept in Castle Street and sold in 1826.

177 (e) manner of constructing chimneys] See above, p. 147.

177 n. 1] There is a longer extract from Joanna Baillie's letter in Partington, *Post-bag*, pp. 192–3.

178 (d) Japan Blacking] Alexander Kemp, 'Poet Laureate of Warren's Blacking,' had written to Scott on 10 June 1823. See Partington, *Post-bag*, pp. 181–2.

179 (a) Mrs Hemans tragedy] See above, p. 174.

179 (c) one of my colleagues] Robert Hamilton. See below, p. 185.

180 (a) To Sir Adam Fergusson] Sir Frederick Adam was appointed on 5 Mar. Scott hoped to return to Abbotsford, on rising of the Courts, on Wednesday, i.e. 10 Mar. (Actually he went on Thursday. See below, p. 213.) Date of letter is about 10 Mar.

181 (a) white side-table] This is no longer at Abbotsford but its position is still marked on the wall.

182 (e) Duke of Queensberry] William Douglas, 1st Duke, who died in 1695.

185 n. 1] Wm. Wood (in 4th last line) should be Alexander Wood, one of the Directors.

186 n. 2] *Walladmor* was written by Willibald Alexis (pseud. of Georg Wilhelm Heinrich Häring). De Quincey's analysis appeared in the *London Mag.* Vol. 10 (Oct. 1824), pp. 353–82.

187 (c) The course of true love] Shakespeare, *Midsummer Night's dream*, I. 1.

187 (d) petticoat of red] i.e. *Shoulagaroo*. See above, p. 90.

188 (b) what Slender would call] Shakespeare, *Merry wives of Windsor*, I. 1.

189 (c) Paul Jones] See *Lockhart*, i. 189–90.

190 (c) a cousin of hers] Ginger. See above, p. 183 and below, p. 195.

190 n. 1] This quotation is taken from *The Scott Exhibition, MDCCCLXXI. Catalogue*, etc., 4to Edinburgh, 1872, p. 149.

191 (a) To John Walker] This letter is to John Allen Walker. See his letter of 14 Mar. 1823 in NLS (MS. 3896, ff. 87–8).

191 (d–e) specimens . . . of a new literary attempt] I have no record of any book written by John Allen Walker but I have found a poem by him in the *Lit. Gaz.* 1821 (8 Dec.), pp. 780–1.

191 n. 1] Scott's name is in the list of subscribers to this work, but it is extremely unlikely that Scott did not receive till 1824 a work published in 1817. I do not know what the 'elegant work' is.

191 n. 2] I had thought that 'Mr. James' might be James Scott Walker with whom Scott had corresponded in 1815 and 1816 and who was the author of *The South American, a metrical tale*, published at Edinburgh in 1815. But Walker in his letter of 14 Mar. (NLS MS. 3896, ff. 87–8) writes of 'the late Mr. James's poetical remains,' showing that he is not James Scott Walker who lived till 1850. James seems to be a surname and I do not know who he is.

192 (a) To Miss Clephane] To Anna Jane.

193 (d) Jack Thurtle] It is certain that he never was an officer in the Marines. I cannot find any other person of that name an officer between 1818 and 1821.

194 (f) bachelor uncle] Robert Scott of Rosebank.

195 (c) Fancy Ball] See my note to *SL* vii. 506 (e).

196 (a) bearded like the pard] Shakespeare. *As you like it*, II. 7.

196 (b) cadgers] *Kelly*, p. 77; Ramsay, *Proverbs*, p. 14; *Ray*, p. 364. Also used in *SL* x. 84 and *Rob Roy*, chap. 26.

196 n. 1] This note could have been compressed, for most of it is given in *FL* ii. 189–90.

197 n.] There is no promise of engravings (line 8 from foot) in any letter in *SL*. She had received the 12 vols. of the novels with engravings (*SL* vi. 201, 252, 252 (a)).

199 (a) conceal the real author] William Greenfield.

199 (a–b) German novel] *Walladmor*, by Willibald Alexis, pseud. of Georg Wilhelm Heinrich Häring.

202 (d) To James Ballantyne] The date is about the end of Apr. Ballantyne went to London in the middle of Mar. (p. 213) and he is now back (p. 202). Scott has money to pay at Whitsunday (p. 203), i.e. 15 May.

203 (c) your whirligig lamp] This was invented by a Dutch chemist, P. J. Kipp. It continued to sit on the mantelpiece in Scott's Study till 1972, when it was removed to the Dutch cabinet after a tourist had stolen the glass stopper.

203 (d) young Constables printing offices] Scott must be referring to Willison, the printer, Constable's father-in-law. Willison's business was taken over by Constable's son Thomas in

1833 but in 1824 he was only twelve and could be no more than an apprentice.

204 (a–b) ride when they put their boots on] Scott uses this proverb in a letter to Ellis (*SL* xii. 190) and in *Old Mortality*, chap. 36. I have not found it in this exact form, but Ramsay, *Proverbs*, p. 23, has: 'He does na ay ride when he saddles his Horse.'

205 (c) your cousin] Miss Hooke.

208 (c) George Home] He was appointed Keeper of the Register of Tailzies, 1 Mar. 1785. (*Scots Mag.* xlvii. 156.)

208 (c) as Jacob did] *Bible, Genesis* 29: 20.

208 *n.* 1] Ferrier did not resign the Keepership of the Record of Entails till 1827. See *SL* x. 291.

210 *n.*] On Walter's marriage, see also *SL* iv. 24. In line 6, for 'Vol. VII, p. 262 note' read 'Vol. V, p. 262 note.'

210 *n.* 1] There are two versions in *Herd* (ii. 104–5 and ii. 223), the second corresponding with the version in *Johnson*, (Vol. 5 [1797], No. 440), but with considerable differences. See Chambers, *Scottish songs* (1829), ii. 378–9 and comments on Chambers in *Johnson*, new ed., Edinburgh, 1853, iv. *449. The verses in this note are from *Johnson*, but quoted inaccurately.

212 (c) The arms which you have kindly procured to be cut for me] It is not known if this idea originated with Constable or with Scott. Scott had sent his coat of arms to Constable (above, pp. 95–6) and Constable, therefore, may have had the metal stamp cut on his own initiative.

212 *n.* 1] For the ballad, see Ramsay, *Tea-table miscellany*, or Thomas Evans, *Old ballads*, new ed., London, 1810, iv. 320–3.

213 (d) one fine mirror over the chimney-piece; a smaller one] The one above the mantelpiece was removed when Raeburn's portrait of Scott was hung there. The smaller one between the two windows is still there.

214 (b) At Baldock . . .] Scott means that just as he is whipping Terry he wants Terry to whip Messrs E. & H. Baldock, merchants in London, who were supplying Scott with furnishings for Abbotsford. 'My mother whips me' is from *Don Quixote*. See my note to *SL* ii. 299 (b).

214 (f) attaching] A word very uncommon in Scott's writings but very frequently used by Jane Austen.

215 (b) Wilson's business] Trouble over the election of John Wilson (Christopher North) to Chair of Philosophy at Edinburgh University.

216 (a) *Blackwood's Magazine*] No articles by Williams are recorded in Alan Lang Strout's *A bibliography of articles in Blackwood's Magazine, 1817–1825*.

216 *n.* 2] Delete 'Presumably.' Scott's words 'your Treasury matter' refer to Richard Mackenzie's appointment as Treasurer of the W.S. Society, an appointment he held till 1828 when he became joint Deputy Keeper of the Signet in succession to Colin Mackenzie who had been Deputy Keeper since 1820. Richard Mackenzie, W.S., was son of John Mackenzie of Dolphinton, Advocate.

218 (f) the Marplot of neat devices] Marplot is a character in Mrs Centlivre's *The busy body*. The words 'neat devices' do not occur in the play but they describe his character well enough.

219 *n.* 2] For 'Hulton' read 'Hutton.'

220 (c) Mauldon] Henry Malden.

220 (c) Wilsons class] An allusion to the Whig opposition to John Wilson's appointment as Professor of Philosophy at Edinburgh University in 1820. See Index under Wilson (John).

220 (e) Skene and . . . Dundas] The letter to Skene is given above, p. 214, but the letter to Dundas is not in *SL*.

220 *n.* 2] The couplet consists of lines 215–16.

221 (c) Mr. Mauldon] Henry Malden.

222 (a) Dr. Kerr] William Kerr died at Northampton, 3 Sept. 1824, aged 87.

224 (e) red nurse & the brown doctor] The pony is called 'black Doctor' above, p. 177.

225 (e) To Thomas Shortreed] A fuller version of this letter is in the *Scots Mag.* N.S. Vol. 5 (Feb. 1890), p. 170.

226 (a) coat of the Olivers] For the Courtyard side of the cornice round the Entrance Hall.

226 n. 1] In line 4, for '1819' read '1824.'

227 (b) Aytoun spoke fairly about] See amendment in *SL* xii. 490. Is correct reading 'Aytoun spoke fairly out about'?

227 (c) Ridley] James Ridley. A copy of his testimonial, formerly at Abbotsford, is now in NLS. (Abbot. 105 (34)).

228 (a) Lord Robert Seymour] Third son (1748–1831) of 1st Marquess of Hertford; his daughter Elizabeth by his first wife married as her second husband (1817) Major Herbert Evans of Highmead, Co. Carnarvon.

230 (a) Sir Robert] Sir Robert Dundas of Beechwood, a Principal Clerk of Session.

231 (b) your family connection with Gala] John Scott of Gala's uncle, Sir George Scott, second son of John, 5th Laird, married Hon. Caroline Lucy Douglas, daughter of 1st Lord Douglas by his second wife, Lady Frances Scott, sister of 3rd Duke of Buccleuch.

231 (e) Lord what will all the people say] See *SL* vii. 335.

232 (d) a terrier dog] Cribb. See pp. 233, 235 and cf. p. 143.

232 n. 1] In line 2, 'Loftly' should be 'Lenthal.' In line 5 'my late Father' is Theophilus Swift. This note is inappropriate here. If it had to be included, it should have appeared in *SL* iv. 149.

234 (c) *Vixerunt fortes ante*] Horace, *Odes*, IV. ix. 25–6: 'vixere fortes ante Agamemnona / multi.'

234 (c) Edgerstane] John Rutherford of Edgerston.

234 n.] Constable's letter of 16 Apr. is in *Archibald Constable*, iii. 295–7. 'Moores Baffled' (line 8) is: *The Moors baffled . . . With an abbreviate of the genealogy of the family of Rutherfurd*, 4to Edinburgh, 1738.

236 (a) To James Ballantyne] Date cannot be end of Mar. as Ballantyne was in London then. Scott says he is going to Abbotsford 'on Saturday se'nnight' and he told Willie Scott of

Maxpoffle that he was going on Saturday 14 Feb. (NLS MS. 2890, f. 15; not in *SL*). This would date the letter about 7 Feb., which would correspond with the reference to Richardson. See next note.

236 (b) Richardson's volumes] Richardson's novels occupied Vols. 6–8 of *Ballantyne's Novelist's Library*. Scott's memoir is dated 1 Jan. 1824 and the vols. were advertised in the *Lit. Gaz.* on 7 Feb.

237 (a) the young tourist] Their son, John Hughes.

237 (b) a week at the very least] Dr and Mrs Hughes visited Abbotsford, 3–6 May and later visited Scott in Edinburgh. See Hughes, *Letters*, p. 59.

237 (c) To James Skene] The meeting of the Academy directors was on Friday, 2 Apr., the 'to-morrow' of Scott's letter, confirming that the date of Scott's letter is 1 Apr.

238 (a) see as far into the mill-stone] Ramsay, *Proverbs*, p. 32.

240 (f) "their exceeding refreshment"] See my note to *SL* iii. 391 (a).

241 (b–c) red hot coals . . . on my head] A variation of *Bible, Proverbs* 25: 22; *Romans* 12: 20.

242 n.] Lady Margaret (line 4) is the 5th daughter of 4th Duke of Buccleuch. She married 3rd Earl of Romney in 1832. On her name see *SL* ii. 522.

243 (b) Petersham] Douglas House, once owned by Kitty, Duchess of Queensberry (q.v.). The Duke left it to Lady Jane Scott, who left it to her niece, Lady Douglas (q.v.), who gave it to Lady Scott, wife of Admiral Sir George Scott (q.v.). (Stuart, *Letters*, i. 19–20.)

244 (a) his nieces protracted illness] Catherine Morritt.

244 (b) two tales one of which] Both tales dealt with the Crusades. It looks as if at this stage Scott had in mind a different subject for the second.

245 (e) Lord Castlereagh] For Anne Scott's opinion of him, see her letter of 10 Mar. to Miss Millar in *Letters to their old governess*, p. 92.

246 (b) half god-daughter] 'Half

because Scott had been only proxy godfather to Lady Margaret.

247 (b) my *kiver*] See my note to *SL* i. 337 (c).

247 *n.* 1] Why cite Dr Johnson who gives no authority for his statement? Reference should be to Dryden's 'Epistle dedicatory' to his *The Spanish friar*. (Scott's *Dryden*, vi. 377.)

247 *n.* 2] See my note to *SL* i. 524 (a).

248 (d) Waterloo bridge] At 2 Nov. 1820, £100 shares gave no dividend and the current price per share was £5. 5s. 0d. See *Edin. Ann. Reg. for 1820*, XIII. ii. 437.

248 *n.* 1] Substitute: Henrietta Howard (*née* Hobart) Countess of Suffolk, afterwards Mrs Berkeley, who continued, after her second marriage, to be known as Countess of Suffolk.

249 (d) Capt. Dolittle] Lockhart's brother William perhaps, but not necessarily.

250 *n.* 1] Scott is right and Lockhart is wrong.

251 (b) *laissez faire a Don Antoine*] For this French and Italian proverb, see Scott's *Dryden*, vi. 97 and his *Swift*, 2nd ed., ii. 314. Also used in *SL* x. 493, and in *Waverley*, chap. 27, and alluded to, below, p. 335. Cf. *N. & Q.* 3rd ser. ix. 322, 400, x. 17–18.

251 (c) Riddell] See also below, p. 281.

251 (c) Battier] William Battier of the 18th Hussars, having been transferred to the 10th, was sent to Coventry by his brother officers. He eventually challenged his Colonel, Lord Londonderry, and they met at Battersea Bridge, London, on 6 May 1824. See *Edin. Ann. Reg. for 1824*, XVII. iii. 172–6, 183–4, 190–1.

251 (d) "catch no fish"] Beaumont and Fletcher, *Monsieur Thomas*, I. 3: 'no swearing; / He'll catch no fish'; *Ray*, p. 207: 'If you swear you'll catch no fish.'

251 (e) a bit and a buffet] Ramsay, *Proverbs*, p. 59: 'Take the bit and the buffet wi' it.' Also used in *Woodstock*, chap. 20.

252 (c) Captain & Mrs. Scott] Captain George Scott (afterwards Admiral Sir

George Scott), uncle of John Scott of Gala, and his wife, Hon. Caroline Lucy Douglas, daughter of 1st Lord Douglas.

253 (c–d) Royal Academicians] The dinner was held on 3 May 1815.

253 *n.* 1] This Duke was Charles Howard, 11th Duke, who died seven months after the Royal Academy incident.

254 *n.* 1] See *MPW* xx. 195–7.

255 (b) "Sir John Graeme of the West countrie"] *Bonny Barbara Allan*, st. [1], lines 3–4: 'That Sir John Graeme in the west country / Fell in love with Barbara Allan.' In Ramsay, *Tea-table miscellany*.

257 (c) "poor creature small beer"] Shakespeare, *II Henry IV*, II. 2. See also above, p. 252 *n.*

257 (c) Lady Isabella] Daughter of 4th Duke of Buccleuch. She married in 1823 Hon. Peregrine Francis Cust.

257 (e) Lady Margaret] Daughter of 4th Duke of Buccleuch, afterwards Countess of Romney.

257 *n.* 3] Delete this note. The latest date for Bruce in Scott's service is Nov. 1821. He became Pipe Major in the 72nd Foot and there is no evidence that he ever returned to Abbotsford as a servant.

258 (b) Suffolk papers] See *SL* vii. 390, 390 *n.* and my note.

259 (a) Cotton] George Cotton.

260 (c) chain of friendship] See *SL* ii. 535 and my note.

262 *n.* 1] Rink Hill is on Fairnilee estate as stated correctly above, p. 240 *n.*

266 *n.*] I have a letter from the Earl of Aberdeen, 6 Feb. 1827, to Lady Abercorn, which shows that the Abercorn claim to the dukedom of Châtellerault was being discussed at that time.

267 (d) Dogberry] See *SL* ii. 320.

267 (e) will be borrower] Shakespeare, *Macbeth*, III. 1.

269 (d) you had a wish to be introduced to her] But Scott says later (*SL* ix. 9) that Walter and Jane had met two years since, i.e. in 1823.

270 (a) a small post] Keeper of the Record of Entails. See above, p. 208.

270 (b) loaves & fishes] See *SL* v. 312 and my note.

271 (b) what arms Huxley bears] For north doorway. See next note.

271 (d) on some of the old oak pannelling] The coats of arms of 'Kith, Kin, and Ally' were painted on the wall plaster round the north doorway at the Study end of the Entrance Hall.

272 *n.* 1] Delete 'Evidently.' See below, p. 327.

273 (c) the mirrors] See my note to *SL* viii. 213 (d).

274 (a) To William Blackwood] Date is 6 May 1824. Dr and Mrs Hughes left Abbotsford that day, a Thursday, to go to Edinburgh and Scott would write this letter of introduction just before they set off.

274 (c) To James Ballantyne] Date is 10 May. Scott will be in Edinburgh on evening of 11th for opening of the Courts on the 12th.

274 *n.* 2] Add reference: Act III, sc. 2.

276 (e) To Miss Clephane] To Anna Jane.

279 (a) his decent funeral] Campbell was buried in Canongate churchyard. See Anderson, *Silences*, pp. 548–50.

280 (c) late opening in Selkirkshire . . .] In 1823 Lord Montagu had succeeded Lord Napier as Lord Lieutenant of Selkirkshire. The Duke of Buccleuch became Lord Lieutenant of Midlothian, 5 Mar. 1828.

281 (c) £13000] £15,000 according to p. 251 above.

282 (b) Sir Frederick] Sir Frederick Adam, son of the Chief Commissioner of the previous line. His 'establishment' refers to the Ionian Islands.

283 (b) Battier] See my note to *SL* viii. 251 (c).

283 (c) Ludlow [?]] Read 'Lad Lane.'

283 *n.* 2] In line 3, for '1823' read '1824.'

285 (a) the Chief Baron] Sir Samuel Shepherd.

285 (d) I trust it will have your approbation] Which suggests that the marriage of Jane Jobson and Walter was a foregone conclusion.

287 (a) birds of the air] *Bible, Ecclesiastes* 10: 20.

287 (d) subsequent Saturday] Actually a fortnight later. Scott went to Tyningham on Saturday, 29 May, and to Blair-Adam on Saturday, 12 June.

288 (b–c) popular with another R.H.] Because the Duke of Cumberland could not spare a captain from the 15th (below, p. 432).

288 *n.* 1] Delete 'Presumably.'

289 (c) A thing to dream of] Coleridge, *Christabel*, Pt I, line 253: 'A sight to dream of.'

289 *n.* 1] Delete this note and see *SL* iv. 346 and my note.

290 *n.* 1] Maturin's letter is in *Maturin Corr.*, p. 102.

291 *n.* 1] For Lord Castlereagh (line 10), see *Don Juan*, Canto I, Dedication, st. xi–xv.

292 (f) And roar Stop, Stop them] Soame Jenyns, *The American coachman*, st. [6], lines 3–4. (Chalmers, *The works of the English poets*, London, 1810, Vol. 17, p. 619.)

300 *n.* 1] There is an extract from Montagu's letter in Partington, *Post-bag*, p. 196. In line 8 delete '[?]'. The name Short is correct. Thomas Short was Tutor and his brother William was private tutor to the Duke of Buccleuch.

302 (d) Captain Dewar] David Dewar of Gilston. I do not know why Scott calls him Captain. He became a Colonel in 1812 and a Major-General in 1814.

303 (c) Joe Hume . . . the *tottle*] In *Laudes Robinsonianae* (*Blackwood*, Vol. 17 (May 1825), p. 621) occur the lines: 'Two more of claret, just to cool my throttle: / Though Hume impute this consummation rare / To his harangues on figures and sums tottle.'

306 *n.*] There are two extracts from her letter of 10 June (line 3) in Partington, *Post-bag*, pp. 197–8.

307 *n.* 6] The verses are not attached to Mrs Hughes's letter of 10 June (NLS MS. 3898, ff. 202–5). They may be *Verses on a report of the Duke of Q——'s*

death, by Sir Alexander Boswell of Auchinleck. Each stanza ends with 'The Star of Piccadilly.' (*The poetical works of Sir Alexander Boswell*, Glasgow, 1871, pp. 224–6.)

308 (c) Higgins-Neuch] Should be Higgins-Neuck.

309 (a–b) Mrs. Paterson who experienced your bounty] Scott's letter, in third person (not in *SL*), passing on the gift of £5 from Mrs Hughes, was sold on behalf of the Edinburgh Sir Walter Scott Club at Abbotsford, 30 May 1975. Mrs Paterson was a widow with six children. See Hughes, *Letters*, p. 81.

309 (c) as your friend Mungo says] Bickerstaffe, *The padlock*, I. 3.

309 n. 1] Mrs Paterson in her letter of 22 May 1824 (NLS MS. 3898, ff. 184–5) does not say who Hay is, but I suppose he is David Hay, the Edinburgh house decorator who was carrying out the interior decoration of Abbotsford at this time.

309 n. 3] For second sentence read: 'In 1801 he was created Earl of Craven and Viscount Uffington.'

310 (d–e) Robinson] There are no works by Defoe in *Ballantyne's Novelist's Library*.

310 (f) on Thursday or Friday] But Scott was already engaged, with Charles and Lockhart, to dine at Polton on Friday (above, p. 298).

311 (a) Mr Paterson] John Patterson, iron founder, Edinburgh, and brother-in-law of George Hogarth, erected the iron screen at Abbotsford. His bill for £355 2s. 1d. is entered under 18 Dec. 1824. (*Reply to Mr Lockhart's pamphlet*, Appendix, p. 78.) See also Skene's *Memories*, p. 105. In line 5, delete the query.

313 (a) let every herring] Ray, p. 154; *Kelly*, p. 240. Also used in *Rob Roy*, chap. 26. Ramsay, *Proverbs*, p. 44, gives it as: 'Let ilka sheep hing by its ain shank.'

313 n. 1] The Duke's letter (line 8) is in Partington, *Letter-books*, pp. 328–9.

318 (a) Captains commission] Walter was not gazetted Captain till 25 June 1825. See *SL* ix. 145 n. 2.

318 (d) To David Laing] The date,

I think, is 5 June 1826 for the following reasons: (1) 'Weighty matters' would apply to the financial crash of 1825/6 but not to July 1824; (2) Scott is sending the List as he cannot attend the meeting. The first election of members since Nov. 1823 took place on 30 Jan. 1826, followed by elections on 5 June and 10 July and the date of the letter must be one of these days; (3) Thomson called about the Club on 5 June (*Journal*) probably to discuss the ed. of Melville. There is no record in the *Journal* of Scott's having attended the Club on any of these days.

319 (a) famous Bulls head] 'The chancellor presented a bull's head before the Earl of Douglas, which was a sign and token of condemnation to the death.' Robert Lindsay of Pitscottie, *The history of Scotland*, etc., 3rd ed., 8vo Edinburgh, 1778, p. 28. This was the 6th Earl of Douglas, murdered on 24 Nov. 1440.

319 (c) Richardson's metaphor] See above, p. 307.

319 n. 1] Southey's letter is printed in full in Partington, *Letter-books*, pp. 80–2.

320 (a) Lay of the Laureate] Published London, 1816.

323 (b) cure almost as bad as the disease] This was the effect of calomel. See *SL* vii. 326. For the proverb, see *Kelly*, p. 336, and Ramsay, *Proverbs*, p. 60.

323 (f) Humbie] Sharpe's extracts from the Humbie Kirk Session Book, 1647–76, are in NLS (MS. 2510, ff. 66, 99).

324 (a) a joug] The jougs are still on the gate at Abbotsford but there is no motto.

325 (c) Lady in Goldsmith's Essays] *Essays* (1765), No. VI. *Adventures of a strolling player*, in *Miscellaneous works*, 4 vols., London, 1801, iv. 355.

325 (e) Caleb Williams] The prefaces to Vol. 10 are dated 1 Sept. 1824, but those of Vol. 9 (containing Cumberland's *Henry* but not Godwin's *Caleb Williams*) are dated Dec. 1824. Vol. 9 must have been delayed through the legal question of *Caleb Williams*.

326 (b) a monument for Mr. Watt] See *Edin. Ann. Reg. for 1824*, XVII. iii. 202–3, and the *Scotsman*, Vol. 8 (10 July 1824), p. 527, c. 1.

327 (b) To Mrs. J. G. Lockhart] The date is 12 July. Scott visited Sophia on Saturday (i.e. 10 July) and went to Abbotsford 'next day.' The letter to Peel of 12 July (p. 328) is dated from Abbotsford.

328 (d) To Sir Robert Peel] Peel did not reply till 6 Dec. See below, p. 454 *n.* 1.

328 *n.* 1] Scott did not sit to Lawrence for a portrait for Peel. Peel, however, secured a bust by Chantrey, now in the Scottish National Portrait Gallery.

329 (e) a share of my tediousness] See *SL* ii. 320.

330 *n.* 1] This note should be at *SL* x. 214 *n.* 2.

332 (b) Dr Meik . . . Bengal] Bengal is correct. I have the original copies kept by Patrick Meik of his letters sent to his brother Dr James Meik, Bengal, 1812–19.

332 *n.* 1] Meik is the spelling used by the family. In third line from foot, the dates '1795–1800' can be narrowed. Haliburton was home by 1797. See *SL* i. 83.

335 (c) Don Antoine] For explanation, see my note to *SL* viii. 251 (b).

336 (d) Kirkintilloch Rail road] In the *Trust Disposition* (NLS MS. 112, f. 59) it is recorded that Scott held shares in the Monkland and Kirkintilloch Railway. The number is not given. This railway was authorized by Act of Parliament (5 Geo. IV, c. 49) and was opened in Oct. 1826. (C. F. D. Marshall, *A history of British railways down to the year 1830*, London, Oxford Univ. Press, 1938, p. 126.)

336 *n.* 2] Haldane married in 1822, as his second wife, Margaret Rutherford, daughter of Scott's uncle Daniel Rutherford.

337 (a) To Lady Abercorn] Date should be 2 Aug.

337 *n.* 1] In second last line 'Ldy. C——' is the Marchioness Conyngham.

338 (a–b) two of my best friends] John Scott of Gala and Charles Erskine of Shielfield.

338 (c) slave in the triumphal chariot] See my note to *SL* vi. 508 (a–b).

338 *n.* 1] Phillips's letter (line 4) is in Partington, *Letter-books*, pp. 192–3.

339 (d) the book you inquire about] In her letter cited above, p. 337 *n.* The book is *Tales of the Crusaders*, not published till June 1825. This seems to be an admission of authorship inconsistent with his strong denial above, pp. 198–9.

340 (a) a review of the yeomanry] Review at Floors Castle on Monday, 2 Aug., of the Roxburgh Yeomanry Light Dragoons who were inspected by Major Stisted.

340 *n.* 2] Wilkie was not given a public dinner as he implied in his letter to his sister. He was merely a guest, along with Landseer, at the Third Anniversary Dinner of the Scottish Artists on Friday, 10 Sept. See the *Lit. Gaz.* 1824, p. 619.

341 (a) Lady Isabella] Lady Isabella Cust. She gave birth to a daughter on 1 July.

341 (e) Glasgow] During the troubles in 1819. See Index under Glasgow.

342 (a) my own great chamber] Shakespeare, *Merry wives of Windsor*, I. 1. This was Scott's dining-room. His study (as we now know it) was not finished till 1825 and his first study was probably being dismantled while Scott was writing this letter.

342 (b) bestow his tediousness] See *SL* ii. 320.

342 (d) bearded like a pard] Shakespeare, *As you like it*, II. 7.

343 (a) Ordnance maps] See my note to *SL* viii. 10 (b).

343 *n.* 2] Another replica was owned by John Forster and is now in the Victoria and Albert Museum. It is illustrated in *The Scott Exhibition, MDCCCLXXI. Catalogue*, etc., Edinburgh 1872, facing p. 94.

344 (a) To Owen Rees] This letter relates to Scott's entry in 5th ed. of *Debrett's baronetage*, 1824. Longman was one of the publishers.

344 (e) half yearly payment] If Scott got the Keepership of Register of

Entails, worth £200 p.a., he was going to pay it all to Mrs Scott (above, p. 270). Ferrier, however, continued to be Keeper till 1827. It looks as if Scott, having raised Mrs Scott's hopes, did not want to disappoint her, and was going to pay the £200 out of his own pocket.

346 n.] The last line is an allusion to the ballad *O Kenmure's on and awa', Willie.*

347 (b–c) Walter Scott Leith Smack or the no less nobly nominated stage] For references to the Leith smack, see Index under *Walter Scott*. The *Sir Walter Scott* was a mail-coach which ran between Edinburgh and Carlisle.

347 (d) In for a penny] See *SL* vii. 376.

347 n. 1] Scott may not be referring to any particular member of the family but merely to 'Messrs Gow's Band,' as it was called.

348 n. 2] In line 1 of continuation of note on p. 349, '1735–?' should be '1735–1815.' His father may have been a partner in Coutts & Co., but the reference here should be to his brother Edward, who was a partner 1796–1868.

349 (a) Baird] William Baird, Edinburgh plasterer, who made the Roman cement mouldings for the Library ceiling and Entrance Hall.

352 (d) Mirzas bridge] The *Spectator*, No. 159, 1 Sept. 1711. By Addison.

353 (c–d) a bed miss . . .] 'A led miss and a led doctor' is suggested as correct reading in *SL* xii. 490.

353 (e) Italian Lamp] It still hangs from the Roslin drop in the Library alcove.

355 (a) the tent of the fairy Perizade] Scott means Pari Banou. See my note to *SL* ii. 527 (f).

355 (d) Joanna's exclamation] Joanna Baillie, *Rayner; a tragedy*, III. 2: 'Poor pent up wretch! thy soul roves far from home.' Scott used the words (though not as a quotation) 'your thoughts stray far from home' in *The Abbot*, chap. 31.

355 (f) "sear & yellow leaf"] Shakespeare, *Macbeth*, V. 3.

356 (b) Miss Ferriar] I do not know why Basil Hall is inquiring about Susan Ferrier. His letter is not in NLS.

356 (c) Sir James Colquhoun] Sir James Colquhoun of Luss (1741–1805) was a Principal Clerk of Session, 1779–1805, but I cannot find that he published anything.

357 (a) Uncle Adams & Aunt Betties] Uncle Adam and Aunt Betty are two characters in Susan Ferrier's *The inheritance*.

357 (c) Lady Spensers curiosity] Spenser should be Spencer.

358 (c) Kirkhill] Should be Birkhill.

359 (b) *thof* less known] This is intended as a variation of 'thof unknown,' but see *SL* vi. 110 and my note.

359 n. 1] The four lines of verse come from *Captain Ward and the Rainbow* which was printed as the first of *Two Bannatyne garlands from Abbotsford*, and issued to members of the Bannatyne Club in 1848. Scott had written an introductory notice dated 17 Sept. 1831. In this notice Scott says the ballad was well known to him as a boy but it had not been, so far as he knew, included in any collection. There were, however, chapbooks containing it and Lady Compton may have learned the song from one of these or from Scott's recitation.

360 (a) To Lord Montagu] The Duke dined on Tuesday 28 Sept. at Abbotsford and stayed overnight. This letter, therefore, was written during the preceding week.

360 (c) mourning ring] In the showcase in the Library at Abbotsford.

361 (b) to publish any of my letters] See below, pp. 393, 400–1, 400 n.

361 (e) Sermons] Polwhele's *Sermons*, 2 vols., 8vo London, 1813.

362 (c) Wallaces oak—Sir John the Graemes yew tree] These quaichs are in the octagonal showcase in the Library at Abbotsford.

363 (a) To Alexander Peterkin] *DNB* erroneously says Peterkin was a W.S. and a friend of Scott.

363 (a) look over the enclosed] *The Scots compendium; or, pocket peerage of*

Scotland, 2 vols., 12mo Edinburgh, 1826. Peterkin added the material which Scott points out as having been omitted, but he misread Scott's handwriting. In Vol. 1, p. 72, he prints 'Kinkerry' for 'Glenkerry.'

363 (c) Merks of Melrose] Read 'Monks of Melrose.' For 'gathering wood' read 'gathering word.'

363 *n.* 1] See also *SL* ix. 7.

364 (c) Inscription on a tombstone] This wording varies slightly from the lettering on the tombstone. The inscription occupies 13 lines, not 4. This medieval poem is common. For one version from MS. Harl. No. 913, see Thomas Wright and J.O. Halliwell-Phillipps, *Reliquiæ antiquæ*, ii. 217. See also *N. & Q.* 5th ser. xii. 439, 11th ser. i. 48, 116, 156.

365 (b) Canning] Scott had written to Canning on the previous day (10 Sept.) and again on 13 Sept. Neither letter is in *SL* but Canning acknowledged both in a letter to Scott from Dublin, 17 Sept. with PS 18 Sept. (Private collection at Abbotsford.)

365 (b) young Buccleuch] The visit took place 28/29 Sept. See below, p. 378.

366 *n.* 2] Mrs Hughes had written on 15 June 1824, sending drawings of Mosely Hall and Boscobel. I have not found the drawings of Abbotsford, Mosely Hall and White Ladies.

367 (a) yeomans service] Shakespeare, *Hamlet*, V. 2.

367 (a–b) ballad about the *Stuons*] In a letter from Abbotsford, 12 Sept. 1824, C. R. Leslie wrote: 'Now that I am on the subject of songs, I must give you the fragments of a Gloucestershire ditty Sir Walter repeated the other day.' He then quotes five lines. (*Autobiographical recollections*, ii. 152.)

367 (b) D'Urfeys collection] Scott is at fault here. The song, *My dog and I*, is not in D'Urfey. He probably saw it in a Newcastle broadside. Two stanzas are sung by Oliver Proudfute in *The Fair Maid of Perth*, chap. 16.

367 *n.* 1] The drawing of Donnington Castle has not been found at Abbotsford.

368 *n.* 1] The Pallas is still in the Armoury at Abbotsford.

370 (a) Elegy on the first Earl of Roxburghe] This was printed in *The Bannatyne miscellany*, issued in 1827.

370 *n.* 1] It is stated in *Biog. Univ.*, tom. 28 (1821), p. 105, that Jean Meerman left his father's library, augmented by himself, to The Hague, 'pour être rendue publique.' For a brief account of the sale in 1824, see *Edin. Ann. Reg.* XVII. iii. 313, or *Lit. Gaz.* 1824, p. 495 (same report). The sale lasted a month and ended on 3 July.

370 *n.* 2] Constable's letter of 7 Sept. is in *Archibald Constable*, iii. 297–9. The relics from Peru cannot be identified at Abbotsford.

371 (b) *Saturday*] Saturday was 18 Sept.

371 (c–d) Miss White] I do not know who Miss White was. Lydia White was a friend of Constable but she was too ill in 1824 to travel and if Scott's visitor had been Lydia he would have said so.

371 (e) To Archibald Constable] The date is 26 Sept., the day Ballantyne left Abbotsford.

371 *n.* 2] This is probably the copy bought by Constable at the Roxburghe sale in 1812 (Lot 7849) for £1. 11s. 6d. Scott is here referring to a loan and the reference to *ALC.* is misleading. Scott did not acquire a copy till 1829. See *SL* xi. 265.

372 *n.* 1] Sharpe's letter of 24 Sept. is in Partington, *Letter-books*, pp. 310–11, and his letter of 20 Aug. ibid., pp. 309–10. Scott's letter to Henderson of 24 Aug. is mentioned in his letter to Sharpe, 29 Aug. (*SL* xii. 453).

373 (a) an old gamekeeper] The oil portrait on panel (10 × 7 in.) of Tom Purdie by C. R. Leslie is in the anteroom to the Armoury at Abbotsford.

373 (a) like Theseus himself] Virgil, *Aeneid*, VI. 617–18: 'Sedet aeternumque sedebit / infelix Theseus.'

373 (b) condiddling] A word attributed to Hunter. See *SL* vii. 81 (e).

373 (b) Fraser's] John Fraser, picture framer, North Gray's Close.

373 (c) Mrs Duguid] A character in Susan Ferrier's *The inheritance*. Everybody imposes on her kindness, sending her on messages and so on.

373 (d) Miss C.] Miss M. G. S. Crumpe. See Index.

376 (b) par[a]lell betwixt the Great Rebellion and the French Revolution] Scott developed this theme in his preface to *Memoirs of the Marchioness de la Rochejaquelein*, Edinburgh, 1827, pp. 13–16.

378 (a–b) like the ties which kept down Gulliver] Swift, *Gulliver's travels*, Part I, chap. 1. (Scott's *Swift*, 2nd ed., xi. 26.)

379 (c) Carpenter] Charles Carpenter. Carpenter was family name of Lord Tyrconnel.

379 n. 1] This letter can be dated without Leslie's evidence.

380 (c) the Wynnes] Charles Watkin Williams-Wynn became President of the Board of Control in Feb. 1822.

380 n. 1] Patrick and Peter are both correct, being synonymous in Scotland.

381 (a) Tom] Eldest son of Robert Shortreed. He died in 1826.

381 (b) *Oswyne middle . . . Hexgate Pathhead*] This is fully discussed by W. M. Parker in his article *A disputed locality: Oswyne Middle and Hexpethgatehead* in *Trans. Hawick Arch. Soc.* 1949, pp. 36–9.

381 n.] In line 1, 'Abbotsford' is a mistake. They breakfasted at Ashiestiel in 1807. See *SL* i. 381–2.

382 (c) To Maria Edgeworth] Date is end of Sept. Sophia is stout and healthy but by 6 Oct. she has been dangerously ill for 'near a week' (below, p. 390). He describes his deafness in the same way he does to Walter on 28 Sept. (above, p. 379). Maria has time to reply by 11 Oct.

382 (c–d) As the Gods have not made me philosophical] A combination of Shakespeare, *As you like it*, III. 2: 'Hast any philosophy in thee, shepherd?' and III. 3: 'I would the gods had made thee poetical.'

382 n. 1] Delete this note, which has no bearing on the subject of Scott's letter.

383 n. 1] Maria Edgeworth's letter is in Partington, *Letter-books*, pp. 265–7.

384 n. 1] Maria Edgeworth has misunderstood Scott's letter. She refers to the humour of the Lowlanders in the Waverley Novels, but Scott was referring only to the lack of humour in the Highlanders—the Gaels akin to the Irish.

386 (b) frontispiece drawn by Mr. Kirkpatricke Sharpe] See my note to *SL* viii. 66 (a).

387 (a) To Bernard Barton] Correct date is 1830. It is the only letter from Scott to Barton in *SL*, but Barton wrote seven letters to him in 1830 (originals in NLS). Barton had written about historical MSS. in possession of a friend. These MSS. relating to Scottish history (lines 12–13 in *n*. 1) belonged to W. S. Fitch of Ipswich, as Barton tells Scott in his letter of 27 Apr. 1830 (NLS MS. 3913, ff. 69–70) and subsequent letters. Barton gives a detailed account of the MSS. For Fitch, see Index.

389 (a) Broster] John Broster, his father, has already appeared in 1809 as a bookseller (*SL* ii. 146, 157, 158). His son John, also a bookseller, here appears as a curer of stammering. There is an article on him in *Blackwood*, Vol. 17 (Jan. 1825), pp. 46–7, and a poem on him, ibid. Vol. 18 (Dec. 1825), pp. 730–1, and an article by W. M. Parker in the Edinburgh *Evening Dispatch*, 5 Jan. 1943, p. 4.

389 (b) Lady Morton] Susan, wife of 16th Earl.

389 (c) A Major Stisted . . . who was inspecting our yeomanry] At Floors Castle on 2 Aug. See my note to *SL* viii. 340 (a).

389 n. 1] Stisted made a drawing of Scott reading in the Armoury at Abbotsford. This was later lithographed and published.

390 (a) Falkland] An oval miniature in gold and green enamel rim and gold and green enamel back (2 × 1·5 in.) with drop pearl, in a red leather case. This is at Abbotsford in an apartment not open to tourists.

391 (c) John Bull and Louis Baboon] John Arbuthnot, *Law is a bottomless pit; or, the history of John Bull*. In Swift's *Works*, ed. Scott, 2nd ed., vi. 1. Louis Baboon is Louis XIV of France.

391 n. 2] The poem was also printed by Hughes in his *Lays of past days*,

London, 1850, p. 173. For a drawing on the same subject, see below, p. 439.

392 (c) Maida] See *SL* x. 155 and my note.

392 *n*. 1] The drawings of Leyden and Scott by Berens have not been found at Abbotsford.

393 *n*. 2] Scott's contribution to *The Literary Souvenir* was *Epilogue. Written for a tragedy, entitled 'Mary Stuart,' and intended to have been spoken by Mrs. H. Siddons.* See below, pp. 407, 407 *n*., 409.

395 *n*. 2] Her letter is in Partington, *Letter-books*, pp. 265-7.

397 *n*. 1] Scott is not referring to the Scottish Forbes (in any case he was 18th Lord) but to the Irish Lord Forbes (courtesy title), eldest son of 6th Earl of Granard, who predeceased his father in 1836. The bronze inkstand (line 17) is still at Abbotsford.

398 (b) Mrs O'Rafferty] Scott must mean Mrs Raffarty in Maria Edgeworth's *The absentee*. See *SL* iv. 486 (c).

399 (c) inkstand dish of Petrarch] See above, p. 397 *n*.

400 *n*. 1] This letter of 10 Oct. is not the first on the subject. See above, pp. 361, 393.

401 (e) Leslie's picture] Ticknor would not allow his copy to be engraved, but a replica made for Constable was engraved many times.

402 *n*. 1] In line 1, delete 'evidently the' and in line 4, for 'It is probably she who' read 'She.'

403 *n*.] It should be noted that Lady Foulis is wrong in saying Capt. Robert Scott 'Purchas'd their Burying Place, that his Remains might mingle with Theirs.' Lord Buchan conceded the right to the Scotts to be buried in the Abbey but sold no part of it, and Capt. Scott was buried, not in the Abbey, but at Kelso. In line 7 from end, for *Sir William Wallis* read *Sir William Foulis*.

404 (b) the Conference] See above, p. 385 and *n*. 3.

404 (c) as Ophelia says] See my note to *SL* vi. 332 (b).

404 (d) Mr Curl] James Curle, Charles Erskine's partner.

404 *n*. 2] If the reader does not have access to a copy of the *Miscellany* itself, he will find a list of contents in Gilbert Goudie, *David Laing*, Edinburgh, 1913, pp. 161-2.

406 (a) a damnd song] There are three songs in *The betrothed* (Chaps. 19, 20, 31) to any one of which Scott may be referring.

406 *n*. 1] '25th next Saturday' (p. 405) also applies to Sept.

406 *n*. 2] In first line, delete 'evidently.'

407 (b) most potent grave & reverend Secretary] Shakespeare, *Othello*, I. 3: 'Most potent, grave, and reverend signiors.'

407 *n*. 2] The MS. of the *Epilogue* (line 8) in Edin. Univ. Lib. is in the Laing Coll. (La. IV. 1. 17*). On the *Literary Souvenir*, see my note to *SL* viii. 393 *n*. 2. Constable's letter of 5 Nov. (line 11) is in *Archibald Constable*, iii. 300-1.

408 *n*.] The Epilogue (line 1) was not included in *The poetical works*, 10 vols., Edinburgh, 1825 (*Ruff*, 180). (See my note to p. 393 *n*. 2 above and beginning of the note on p. 407.) In lines 9-10, 'Johnsons Willow' is the tree planted by Samuel Johnson in the garden of his stepdaughter, Lucy Porter, at Lichfield. The piece of wood has not been found at Abbotsford. John Daniel (line 11) is *A narrative of the life and astonishing adventures of John Daniel*, 12mo London, 1751. John Bowdler (line 14) should be William Bowdler. His work is *The Devil's cloven-foot*, 12mo Bristol, 1723.

408 *n*. 1] Lady Anne Barnard's letter of 27 Aug. (line 13) is printed in Partington, *Letter-books*, pp. 191-2.

409 (a) He says very truly] As Scott has not yet seen Medwin's book he may have got his information from the *Lit. Gaz.*, 1824 (16 Oct.), pp. 657-60, where (at p. 659) this passage on Lewis and *The Fire King* is quoted.

409 (d) To Walter] The date should be 26 Oct. The hunt was on 25 Oct. and Scott refers to it as 'Yesterday.'

410 (c) Mr Rosss] Dr Adolphus M. Ross.

411 (c) To Charles] This, like the preceding letter to Walter, should be dated 26 Oct.

412 n. 1] Lockhart is wrong in saying that Maida's effigy was by the gate and that it has stood there 'a year or more.' The effigy was, and is, beside the porch and the figure was put in position on 13 Feb 1824. (John Smith's MS. diary.) The inscription was cut on the pedestal, 21–3 Oct.

413 n.] There was no need to cite the *Poetical works* when Scott's verses are given below, pp. 418–20. The dog which Glengarry is presenting is Nimrod.

416 (a) Aarons serpent] *Bible, Exodus* 7: 12.

417 (d) To the editor of the Morning Post] This should not have been included in *SL*. It is an article, not a letter. See my note to *SL* i. 158 (b).

418 (a–b) Dr Johnson . . . "ignorance— pure ignorance"] Boswell, *Life of Johnson*, chap. 8, under year 1755.

418 (c) The inscription cannot now be altered] Because it had already been carved. See my note to p. 412 above.

418 (d) *Pugna est de paupere regno*] Statius, *Thebaidos*, Bk I, line 151.

418 n. 1] Scott returned to Edinburgh on 15 Nov. The 'to-morrow' of Scott's letter (p. 420) shows that it was written on Sunday, 14 Nov. The coursing match mentioned (p. 421) was the Abbotsford Hunt on 25 Oct., *not* the match at Bowhill.

419 (e) *stet pro ratione voluntas*] Juvenal, *Satires*, VI. 222: 'Sit pro ratione voluntas.'

420 n. 3] Delete and see above, pp. 368 and n., 388 n., 392.

421 (a) "the Stuons"] *George Ridler's oven* (q.v. in Index under Ballads and Songs).

421 n. 3] In line 4, the Athenaeum is the London club founded by J. W. Croker. See Brightfield, *John Wilson Croker*, pp. 156–61. Brightfield states (p. 157) that Scott was present at the inaugural meeting on 16 Feb. 1824. Scott was not in London on that date but he was elected a member. 'Bensons Journal' in line 5 from foot, is *Narrative of Lord Byron's voyage to Corsica and Sardinia . . . 1821*, published in 1824 and said to be written by 'Captain Benson, R.N.' There was no captain of that name at this time and the *Lit. Gaz.* 1824 (6 Nov.), pp. 707–9, in a review, treated the book as a hoax. If it was, it is a strange coincidence that another work on Corsica came out in 1825 by Robert Benson of Lincoln's Inn.

422 (e) The night has come upon him] *Bible, John* 9: 4.

423 n. 1] See also *SL* xi. 205, 267, xii. 4.

423 n. 2] Delete the two sentences from 'We have wrote' down to 'enclosed.' They have nothing to do with the subject of Scott's letter. I have transferred this portion of the Smiths' letter to p. 468 below.

425 (a) Miss Bacon] I have failed to identify her, but there was a Miss Bacon, a well-known toast, at this time. *A Jewish epigram. By an amorous Israelite, on seeing the beautiful Miss Bacon* appeared in a newspaper. See *The Spirit of the Public Journals for 1824*, p. 237.

425 (c) Brydone at Crosslee] George Bryden.

427 (b) Alnaschars chest or Hosseins tapestry] Alnaschar (q.v. in Index) seems to be a mistake. For Hussein's tapestry, see my note to *SL* i. 229 (e).

428 (c) Young Hay] Adam Hay, afterwards Sir Adam Hay, 7th Bart. of Haystoun, 3rd son of Sir John Hay, 5th Bart.

429 (a) Peebles the Returning Burgh] At this time, when burghs were grouped together to return one member, each burgh acted as Returning Burgh in rotation.

429 (a) much between the cup and the lip] *Ray*, p. 121; *Kelly*, p. 254; Ramsay, *Proverbs*, p. 47.

430 (a) Alnwick] This trip was cancelled. See below, p. 448.

430 (a) weightier matters of the Law] *Bible, Matthew* 23: 23.

430 (b) To Mr. Dobie] Date is 20 Nov. 1813. Scott is answering Dobie's letter of 1 Nov. 1813 (NLS MS. 3884, ff. 280–1).

430 (c) Johnstone's History] Robert Johnston, *Historia rerum Britannicarum*, 1655.

431 n. 1] Delete this note. There is no need to cite Murray on the meaning.

Scott had already given it in the *Minstrelsy*, 2nd ed., 1806, i. 218, in his introd. to *Lord Maxwell's goodnight*. (It is not in 1st ed.) It is very odd that Scott should say in this letter 'I have heard or read somewhere' when the definition is in one of his own works!

432 (b) Justice Shallows plan] Marriage of Walter and Jane Jobson.

432 *n.* 1] She died on 20 Nov.

435 (e) transeat cum ceteris erroribus] See my note to *SL* iii. 170 (b).

437 (e) "to ears polite"] Pope, *Moral essays, in four epistles to several persons*, Epistle IV, line 149: 'Who never mentions Hell to ears polite.'

437 *n.*] Delete. The pamphlet Scott wanted was *The dreadful voice of fire, begun at Edinburgh, the 3d of February, 1700*, 2° Edinburgh, 1700 (Abbotsford Lib. A. 5. 29/33).

438 (b) James Hall] Ann Fraser Tytler wrote in her diary, 24 Nov. 1824: 'Basil Hall told us, that while they were rushing to and fro in the midst of the flames, his brother James was quietly seated taking sketches of the ruins; and that eight drawings done on the spot were to be published to day, for the benefit of the sufferers.' John W. Burgon, *The portrait of a Christian gentleman*, London, 1859, p. 170.

439 (c) The Lay of the one horse shay . . . in poetry and in painting] Scott is referring to the poem (above, p. 391) and to the drawing which is still at Abbotsford.

439 (e) By torch and trumpet fast array'd] Thomas Campbell, *Hohenlinden*, st. [3], line 1.

441 (e) a good appointment in India] See *SL* vi. 109, 123, 123 *n.*

442 (b) inter silvas academi] Horace, *Epistles*, II. ii. 45.

442 *n.* 1] The persons mentioned in Charles's letter are Edward Cardwell; John Thomas Hope, who won the Newdigate Prize for his *The arch of Titus* in 1824; and Patrick Boyle. For biographical details see these names in Index.

443 (d) Ferguson] Adam Ferguson, *The history of the progress and the termination*

of the Roman Republic, 3 vols., 4to London, 1783.

446 (b) Corke] The 15th Hussars, who had been at Hampton Court Barracks since May 1822, left for Ireland in July of this year.

448 (b) Alnwick] For the proposed visit, see above, p. 430.

448 (c) So what's impossible] George Colman the Younger, *The maid of the moor*, st. [19], lines 3-4. See *SL* vi. 300 *n.* 2.

451 (a) H.R.H.] Duke of York, Commander-in-Chief.

455 (e) your lonely isle] A quotation from Leyden. See *SL* ii. 506 (a).

455 *n.* 1] Lawrence never painted a portrait of Scott for Peel.

456 *n.* 1] Coldingham is inland, *not* on the coast.

459 *n.* 1] In line 4, for '(1825–26)' read '1826 [1819–26].' See also my note to *SL* vii. 303 *n.* 2.

460 *n.* 1] Bertolini is Joseph Philip Bartolini who married Miss Johnston of Lathrisk on 30 Apr. 1821. See *Edin. Ann. Reg. for 1821*, XIV. ii. 345.

461 (c) a killing frost] Shakespeare, *King Henry VIII*, III. 2. See *SL* i. 35.

461 (d) With all the ills . . .] Charles Cotton, *Invitation to Izaac Walton*, st. 3.

462 (c) only son] Probably a misreading for 'older son.' See *n.* 3 below.

462 *n.* 1] Delete. Scott is not referring to the Hall family but only to James Hall. The meaning becomes clear if the words 'with all the activity of all the families' are put in parentheses. The 'activity' is explained in Ann Fraser Tytler's diary quoted above, p. 438 (b).

463 (a) riding on the rigging of the Kirk] *Kelly*, p. 37.

463 (c) "Better a finger off as aye wagging"] See *SL* iv. 172 (e).

463 (e) Governess dead] Miss Martyn.

463 *n.* 1] This weapon, called a hunting-knife, is in the Armoury at Abbotsford (No. 62).

464 (c) To David Laing] The date, I think, is 8 Nov. This letter and the letter

to James Ballantyne (below, pp. 467–8)
seem to have been written on the same
day: (1) both dated from Abbotsford
on a Monday; (2) both refer to *Auld
Robin Gray*; (3) Gordon carries the letter
to Ballantyne. In the letter to Laing 'by
this same opportunity' points to Gordon
as messenger; (4) in both Scott writes of
coming 'to town'. The Courts resumed
on 12 Nov. The Monday on the week
before that is 8 Nov. Except for reference
to *Auld Robin Gray*, this letter relates to
Laing's *Early metrical tales*.

464 (d) the etching] See my note to *SL*
viii. 66 (a).

464 n. 2] Anne dates her letter 'Wednesday, 23rd November.' But Wednesday was 24 Nov.

464 n. 3] Delete this note, which is not
now applicable.

465 (a) Sir Eger] *The history of Sir
Eger, Sir Grahame, and Sir Gray-Steel.* The
earliest printed text found was that of
[Aberdeen] 1711.

465 (a) To James Ballantyne] Captain
Basil Hall's evidence (cited in *n.* 2) does
suggest 1824 for the date; but the insurance for £3,000 would fit Dec. 1821
and the weather in Dec. 1821 was very
bad all over Britain.

465 (d) 1806 . . . floods] See *SL* i. 314–
15, 316. There were also floods in 1807.
See *SL* i. 377, 393, ii. 87.

465 (e) To James Ballantyne] This
letter seems to be related to the second
letter on p. 466, which should be dated
20 Dec. 1827. The 'four leaves' of the
first letter seem to be the same as the
'missing sheets' of the latter. Scott had
discovered that he had sent the sheets
to London instead of to Ballantyne
(*Journal*, 29 Nov. 1827). Date of letter,
therefore, would be about 29 Nov. 1827.

466 (f) To James Ballantyne] Date is
20 Dec. 1827: (1) the missing sheets were
sent to London by mistake (*Journal*,
29 Nov. 1827); (2) the Bannatyne Club
met on 19 Dec. 1827; (3) the Roxburghe Tract relates to 1827.

467 (a) a Roxburghe Tract] *Proceedings
in a court martial held upon John, Master of
Sinclair*, ed. by Scott for the Roxburghe
Club.

467 (a) fled from me like Quicksilver]
Shakespeare, *II Henry IV*, II. 4.

467 (b) To James Ballantyne] The
words 'before you went away' probably
refer to Ballantyne's trip to London in
Mar. (cf. above, pp. 202 *n.*, 213) and
the reference to the *Encyclopaedia* may
be linked with a Spring letter (above,
p. 203). Hamilton, who had had gout,
was recovered by 18 Feb. (above, p.
185). Date of letter, therefore, is probably late Feb. or early Mar.

467 (e) To James Ballantyne] Date is
8 Nov.: (1) Monday was 8th; (2) Scott
will be in town 'next week,' i.e. for
opening of the Courts; (3) Memoir of
Bage is dated Dec.; (4) Bill for £500 at
3 months brings us to 8 Feb. and Scott
asks Curle to take up bill on 4 Feb.
(below, p. 510). Cf. dating with that of
letter to Laing, above, p. 464.

468 (b) three small parks] In the *Trust
Disposition*, 1826, it is recorded that
parts of the lands of Darnick had been
sold to Scott by 'James Smith Ronaldson, Writer in Dunfermline with consent of his Mother and Spouse.' His
mother was a sister of Thomas, John
and James Smith of Darnick. The sale
was recorded on 11 and 13 Dec. 1824.
On 8 Nov. 1824 Messrs John & Thomas
Smith wrote to Scott: 'We have wrote
to our Brother James as desired by Mr
Laidlaw to cause Mr Ronaldson convey the whole purchase to you, & you
can convey our Brothers part in the
way it will answer best. The Missive
from our Brother to you is enclosed.'
I have transferred the preceding quotation to here from p. 423 *n.* 2 above.

468 n. 1] For '*Lives of the Novelists* (1825)'
read '*Ballantyne's Novelist's Library*, Vol.
9.'

470 (c) perils here by flood & fire] See
above, p. 465, 465 *n.* 2.

470 n. 1] The uncle of Charles Marjoribanks was Edward Marjoribanks, partner in Coutts & Co. See above, p. 348,
n. 2 and my note.

472 (b) To Sir Adam Ferguson] For
previous appearance of this letter in
print, see *SL* xi. 42 *n.*

473 (d) You have the rent-roll of Ab-
botsford] *Abbotsford valuation at Walter's
marriage, 1825* was contributed by 'C.
Inverness' [i.e. Robert Carruthers, In-
verness] to *N. & Q.*, 5th ser. Vol. 1
(24 Jan. 1874), p. 65. Rents of the different parts of the estate are given in

detail and the total is £1,428. 14s. 0d. (not £1,680 as Scott gives in this letter).

478 (f) To Lord Melville] This letter should be dated 1822 as the reference to Walter's being at sea in tempestuous weather shows. Cf. *SL* vii. 74.

480 (d) Beggars . . . must not be chusers] See *SL* ii. 225.

480 n. 2] At this time the holder of the title was Archibald Douglas, 1st Baron (1748–1827).

481 (a) Walter] Walter's journey to Berlin.

481 (c–d) To C. K. Sharpe] Date is between 23 and 29 Jan., 'four or five days' after Lady Alvanley's death on 17 Jan. and week before Walter's marriage, 3 Feb. Date, therefore, is probably 23 Jan.

481 (d) Lady Alvanley's funeral] The note on p. 482 should have been here.

481 (e) dedication] Sharpe, in an undated letter [c. Jan. 1825], had asked to be allowed to dedicate to Scott an enlarged ed. of his *Ballad book*. (*Sharpe's Letters*, ii. 325.) Sharpe's letter was a reply to one from Scott, not in *SL* but in *Sharpe's Letters*, ii. 324.) Sharpe's project was abandoned but Laing brought out an enlarged ed. in 1880, using the material collected by Sharpe.

481 (f) *res angusta*] Juvenal, *Satires*, III. 165: 'Res angusta domi.'

482 (a) "Oh, if it were a dirty thing . . ."] This is one of the variants of an old song. See, e.g., st. [4], lines 1–4 of *The fryer and the nun* in D'Urfey, *Wit and mirth*, 4th ed., iv. 177. See also *Nigel*, 'Introductory epistle,' and Chambers, *Scottish songs*, Edinburgh, 1829, i. xxxviii.

482 (b) the poor wounded Hussar] Walter, alluding to Campbell's *The wounded hussar*.

484 (b) Bell] Mrs Isabel Ormiston, servant at Abbotsford. See *Journal*, 2 Apr. 1828.

485 (c) railroad] Dalkeith to St. Boswells. See Index under Railways.

485 (c) Mr Bruce] Thomas Bruce of Langlee.

485 (f) Her own estate] But Lochore was not sold till 1867. See above, p. 238 n. 2.

485 n. 1] The name is almost certainly Winnos or Waynes.

486 (a) Will the flame . . .] Nursery rhyme beginning 'There was a little man, / And he wooed a little maid,' st. [4], lines 4–6. (I. and P. Opie, *The Oxford dictionary of nursery rhymes*, Repr. Oxford, Clarendon Press, 1973, p. 290.)

487 (a) £50,000 and possibilities] Shakespeare, *Merry wives of Windsor*, I. i. That Scott is quoting Shakespeare is shown by his references to the play, above, p. 212 and below, pp. 490, 500.

487 (b–c) My bonnie Jeanie Jobson] Parody of st. [3] of *Bonny Lizie Baillie*. See my note to *SL* i. 382 (b).

487 (c) The good lady in Shandwick place] Mrs Jobson lived at 6 Shandwick Place, Edinburgh.

487 n. 1] Delete this note. The 'She' is Lizie Baillie's mother who lived at Castlecary in Stirlingshire, as referred to in the song *Bonny Lizie Baillie* which Scott has just been parodying.

488 n. 1] Knighton's reply on behalf of the King is printed ibid., p. 181.

490 (a) "is good gifts"] Shakespeare, *Merry wives of Windsor*, I. i.

490 (d) *thought on*] For a fuller quotation, which gives a different explanation, see *SL* ix. 9.

491 (a) good Mr. Lieutenant] Nicholas Rowe, *Lady Jane Gray*, V. i.

491 n. 1] Delete and see my note to *SL* i. 382 (b).

492 (e) companionship of the Bath] Scott surely means 'commandership', which would have entitled Walter to be called 'Sir.'

493 n. 1] Almost certainly Sir John Watson Gordon.

494 (c) With a crutch in the hand] Margaret Maclean Clephane, afterwards Marchioness of Northampton, *Translation of the Gaelic song Ge fada mo choiseachd*, st. [3], line 2. In her *Irene . . . Miscellaneous poems*. Priv. pr. London, 1833, p. 172.

494 (e) the Wolf of Badenoch.] Alexander Stewart, Earl of Buchan, 4th son of King Robert II.

495 (b) the dragon of Wantley] See *The dragon of Wantley* in Percy's *Reliques*.

495 (e) A worthy clergyman] Rev. David Dickson.

495 (e) Brabantio] In Shakespeare's *Othello.*

497 (a) Your reasons for being anonymous] See above, p. 395.

497 (c) My bonny little Jeanie] Parody of st. [3] and [6] of *Bonny Lizie Baillie.* See my note to *SL* i. 382 (b).

497 n. 1] Butler is Rev. Richard Butler who married Harriet Edgeworth. Lockhart knew him at Balliol. See *FL* ii. 320.

498 (d) Mount & go] Burns, *The captain's lady,* st. [1]. In *Johnson,* Vol. 3 (1790), No. 233. Scott has substituted 'soldiers' for 'captain's'.

499 (d) "profane and unprofitable art of poem making"] See my note to *SL* i. 274 (d).

500 (b) *good gifts*] Shakespeare, *Merry wives of Windsor,* I. 1.

500 (e) Bridge of Mirza] See my note to *SL* viii. 352 (d).

501 (d) the Xth regiment] The 10th Hussars had been stationed at Piershill, Edinburgh, in 1819 (*SL* vi. 41, 53). Battier (q.v.) had been a Cornet in it. The 10th had made themselves notorious and skits in prose and verse appeared in the newspapers. For some of these, see *The spirit of the public journals for . . . M.DCCC. XXIV,* London, 1825, pp. 149–52, 357.

501 (e) an honest divine] Rev. David Dickson.

502 (c) Mount & go] See my note to *SL* viii. 498 (d).

502 n. 1] This extract is given in Partington, *Post-bag,* p. 204.

503 n. 1] The details about the railroad are of great interest and should have been printed.

503 n. 2] Erskine died at Melrose, *not* Jedburgh.

504 (a) Sheriff Substitute] William Laidlaw applied for post which Scott refused. Scott's letter of 28 Jan. is not in *SL* but it is printed in *N. & Q.,* Vol. 206 (Mar. 1961), p. 92.

504 (d) Poor Maxpopple] See next note.

506 (b) I shall not hesitate to give Maxpopple the office] Scott had written to him on 30 Jan. Scott's letter is not in *SL* but Willie Scott's answer of 31 Jan. acknowledging Scott's letter 'of yesterday' is in NLS (MS. 2890, f. 43). Scott's commissions are in NLS (Ch. 1460–1).

506 (e) Spence] I think this is David Spence, who was a writer in Melrose at this time.

508 (c) "put money in my pouch"] Shakespeare, *Othello,* I. 3.

509 (b–c) To Miss Erskine] Charles Erskine's sister, Christine (1773–1860).

510 (e) to take up my bill to Usher] This is the one at three months which is now due to be discounted (*SL* viii. 468). Scott is here getting Curle to discount it for him.

511 (e) Saturday 12] 12 Mar., when the Courts rose, was a Saturday in 1825.

VOLUME IX

1 (d) Shandwick Street] Should be Shandwick Place.

2 (b) The Gods have not made Jane poetical] Shakespeare, *As you like it,* III. 3.

2 (c) Britomarte or Bradamante] Britomart in Spenser's *Faerie Queene* and Bradamante in Boiardo's *Orlando innamorato* and Ariosto's *Orlando furioso.*

2 (e) at Edgeworthstown about the 20] i.e. 20 Mar.

5 (c) Incumbite remis] Virgil, *Aeneid,* X. 294. Also quoted below, p. 259, and in *SL* x. 155 and in the *Journal,* 11 June 1826; and as 'incumbite fortiter remis' in *SL* x. 441 and as 'incumbite remis fortiter' in *Nigel,* chap. 9.

7 (b) I wont give a hundred guineas] Montagu had referred to this sum in his letter of 11 Feb. (Partington, *Letter-books,* p. 38). A letter from her, to Edward Ellice, M.P., demanding £200 for exclusion of his name, is printed in

the *Ann. Reg.* 1825, Chron., pp. 27–8. She signs herself 'Harriette Rochfort, late Wilson.'

7 (c) a sister Lady Berwick] Harriette Wilson was a daughter of John James Dubouchet, a London shopkeeper. Her sister Sophia married 2nd Baron Berwick.

7 (d) the peerage man] Alexander Peterkin. See *SL* viii. 363.

8 (a–b) Ancient Scottish poetry] 'last year' goes with 'told,' not with 'published.'

9 (b) "tender & true"] Sir Richard Holland, *The Buke of the Howlat*, Pt II, st. VII, line 13. In John Pinkerton, *Scotish poems*, 1792, iii. 146; ed. by David Laing for Bannatyne Club, 1823.

9 (d) The lad forgot but the lass thought on] St. [2], line 3 of the song beginning 'There gaed a fair maiden out to walk.' In *Herd*, ii. 226, where the song is given the title *Up in the morning early*.

10 *n.* 1] Lady Louisa's letter is in Partington, *Letter-books*, pp. 270–1, which makes this note superfluous.

11 (a) Auto da Fe held by the relentless curate and Barber] Cervantes, *Don Quixote*, Pt I, Bk i, chap. 6 (Lockhart's ed., 1822, i. 60–71).

12 (a) value in being tall or a value in being short] Cf. *The Antiquary*, chap. 3: 'some because they were tall, some because they were short.' It is odd that Scott should repeat this error, for although tall copies may have an enhanced value, short copies never have.

12 (f) But Dib. like Tam o' Shanter] Burns, *Tam o' Shanter*, line 163.

12 (f) The *Lincoln nosegay*] This statement is confusing. What Scott means is that the old books listed in *The Lincoln nosegay* were sold for £1,800. The footnote is also confusing. A copy of the pamphlet from Beckford's collection was sold in 1823 for £1. 16*s.* 0*d.* See *Edin. Ann. Reg. for 1823*, XVI. iii. 398. Why the two dates, [1808?] and 1811?

14 (a) His Majesty's gracious and condescending message] See my note to *SL* viii. 488 *n.*

14 *n.* 1] Capt. James McAlpine of 15th Hussars. In line 2, delete 'one'. He appears often in the correspondence.

For other references to purchase of a troop, see Index.

16 (a) *fire* . . . and a *puppit show*] See below, pp. 19, 116 and 19, 95–7 respectively.

16 (f) The bird is flown] Scott's quotations are sometimes inappropriate. This is one of them. Also used wrongly below, p. 498.

17 (a) Mammon of unrighteousness] *Bible, Luke* 16: 9.

18 (d) Shandwick Street] This should be Shandwick Place.

19 (b–c) Italian puppets] Performances by the 'Théâtre du Petit Lazari de Paris de Messrs. Maffey' in the Waterloo Hotel, Regent Bridge, were advertised in the *Edinburgh Evening Courant* for Feb. to Apr. The puppets were two feet high. See *Parties and pleasures; the diaries of Helen Graham, 1823–1826*, ed. by James Irvine, [Edinburgh] 1957, p. 127, for a reference to this show and Jeffrey's comment on it. See also above, p. 16 and below, pp. 95–7.

20 (b) The picture is finished] The copy of Raeburn's portrait of Scott painted in 1823. See *SL* viii. 493.

20 *n.* 1] Except for the date of the commission this note is unnecessary. Scott has already told us that he appointed Maxpoffle. See *SL* viii. 506. The commissions are in NLS (Ch. 1460–1).

21 (a) letter of mine dated about three weeks since] This letter of 23 Jan. 1825 (not in *SL*) was not received by Morritt till 21 Apr. as announced in Morritt's letter of that date (NLS MS. 3900, f. 196).

21 *n.* 1] Miss Foote, the actress, had been the mistress of Col. Berkeley. She then became engaged to Hayne and sued him for breach of promise. Hence the significance of Morritt's grouping all three together.

21 *n.* 2] Pt I, Bk IV, chaps. 6–8 (Lockhart's ed., 1822, ii. 138–201).

22 (c) My bonny Lizie Baillie] St. [3] of *Bonny Lizie Baillie*. See my note to *SL* i. 382 (b).

22 (d) good ladys pastor] Rev. David Dickson.

22 (f) Patagonian] Walter, like his father, was over six feet in height.

23 (e) Lady Beresford] She was already dead when Scott is writing. She died near Southampton on 27 Feb. See *Edin. Ann. Reg. for 1825*, XVIII. iii. 326.

24 (a) the Great Lords manuscripts] Duke of Wellington's. See *SL* viii. 452, 452 *n*.

25 (a) I forget if you saw him] Charles did see Col. Stanhope and Lady Frederica Stanhope at Abbotsford in Aug. 1821. See *SL* vi. 504 and vii. 6.

25 (a) his last wife] Read 'his late wife.' She died in 1823.

25 (b) at Pennycuik] Presumably Penicuik House, seat of the Clerks.

26 (c) "right hand file"] See *SL* iii. 365 and my note.

27 (b) Scherazade] Scheherazade in *The Arabian Nights*.

27 *n*.] Delete from 'Evidently' (line 4) to end of note. Walter was Walter Cuming of Guiyock. See *Rob Roy*, chap. 30 and Scott's note, where the proverb quoted below, p. 28, is given.

28 (a) at Cambridge] St. John's College. Cf. *SL* viii. 300 *n*.

30 (*d*) MacDonald, and the two knights] Major-General John Macdonald, Deputy Adjutant-General; Sir Herbert Taylor, Military Secretary; and Sir Henry Torrens, Adjutant-General.

36 (d) from Dan to Beersheba] *Bible*, *Judges* 20: 1. For other references, see a concordance.

37 (a) Mr Sym of Blair] David Syme of Cartmore and Blair. See also below, p. 143 *n*. and my note.

37 *n*. 1] Betson is the old spelling but he is given as Thomas Beatson in the *Edinburgh Almanack*.

39 (b) a mans fortune depends on a wifes pleasure] *Ray*, pp. 58, 360.

39 (e) Mrs Baillie] Mrs Isaac Bayley, a daughter of Principal Baird.

40 (f) bestow his tediousness] See *SL* ii. 320.

41 (e) MacBeths *Amen*] Shakespeare, *Macbeth*, II. 2.

41 (f) intended rail-road] From Kelso to link up with Dalkeith–St. Boswell's railway (q.v. in Index). Subscriptions were opened at a meeting at Melrose,

3 Jan. 1825 and at a meeting in Edinburgh, 14 Jan. 1825, Scott was appointed one of the Committee of Management. See *Edinburgh Evening Courant*, 24 Jan. 1825, p. [1], c. 4.

42 (a) Harden the two Torwoodlees and the engineer] Hugh Scott of Harden, afterwards 6th Baron Polwarth; James Pringle of Torwoodlee (died 1840); James Pringle, Younger of Torwoodlee (1783–1859); and James Jardine, engineer.

42 (a) Maisie] Corrected to 'heaven' in *SL* xii. 490.

42 (d) Prince Hoseins tapestry] In *Arabian Nights*. See my note to *SL* i. 229 (e).

42 (f) the little pond] This is Abbotsmoss on the way to Cauldshiels Loch. When Morrison surveyed the estate it did not have a name. Abbotsmoss appears on Ordnance Survey maps.

42 *n*. 1] In D'Urfey, *Wit and mirth*, Vol. 3 (1719), p. 229, there is a song beginning 'Fairest Jenny! thou mun love me.' St. [2], line 1 is: 'For aw Fife and Lands about it.' There are different versions in *Johnson*, Vol. 2 (1788), No. 120; and in R. A. Smith, *The Scotish minstrel*, Vol. 1, p. 97.

43 *n*. 1] Scott is referring to the 7th Earl. Lord Linton did not become 8th Earl till 1827.

44 (e) your literary undertaking] Her book on travellers. See *SL* viii. 395, 497.

44 (f) Mrs. Fox Lane] This should be Mrs. Fox. Sophia Edgeworth had married Capt. Barry Fox. There was a family of Fox Lane in Yorkshire and Scott seems to have confused the names. He also calls her Mrs Fox Lane, below, p. 176, and in *SL* x. 212, xi. 123, 368.

44 *n*. 2] In last line, for '1803' read '1737.'

45 (b) a pony] Marion. See also below, p. 431 and *SL* x. 184, 214.

45 (b) "up to the fair board-head"] *Dick o' the Cow*, st. 18, line 1: 'up to the fair ha' board.' In *Minstrelsy* (ed. Henderson), ii. 79.

45 (d) the sapient Monarch] James VI of Scotland and I of England.

47 (a) at your new institution] The

School of Military Engineering at Old Brompton, Chatham.

49 (c) An unlucky foot-boy] See also below, pp. 58 *n.*, 60, 62.

49 *n.* 1] Delete this note, which is not applicable.

51 (c) dedication] To *The Eve of All-Hallows; or, Adelaide of Tyrconnel; a romance*, 3 vols., 12mo, 1825.

55 (c) mechanist in Rasselas] Samuel Johnson, *Rasselas*, chap. 6.

56 (e) "The thing may to-morrow . . ."] Matthew Prior, *Down-Hall*, st. 8, lines 3–4: 'The matter next week shall be all in your power; / But the money, gadzooks! must be paid in an hour.'

58 (b) To Henry Mackenzie] This letter was printed by its owner, Harold William Thompson, in his ed. of Henry Mackenzie's *Anecdotes*, London, 1927, pp. xxix–xxx, with a number of misreadings.

58 (d) Old Bervie] 'Bervie' is a misreading of 'Birrel.' Scott is quoting *The diary of Robert Birrel* in *Fragments of Scotish history* [ed. by Sir John Graham Dalyell], 4to Edinburgh, 1798. Under 10 July 1598 Birrel records: 'Ane man, sume callit him a juglar, playit sic sowple tricks upone ane tow, qlk wes festinit betwix the tope of St Geills kirk steiple and ane stair beneathe the crosse, callit Josias close heid, the lyk wes nevir sene in yis countrie, as he raid doune the tow and playit sa maney pavies on it.'

59 (a) five or six articles] By this time Scott had contributed about 20 articles.

59 (a–b) Donald Gunn] Scott tells the story in a note to *The Lady of the Lake*, Canto V, st. XI, where he calls him John Gunn. Mackenzie (*Anecdotes*, p. 225) thought the anecdote related to Rob Roy.

59 (b) "impeticosed the gratility"] Shakespeare, *Twelfth Night*, II. 3.

59 (c) Genl Melville] General Robert Melville. See *SL* i. 113 *n.* 1.

59 *n.* 1] Scott's account is accurate. The six who died in Anchor Close were Anne I, Robert I, John I, Robert II, Jean and Walter I. The six who grew up were Robert III, John II, Sir Walter (Walter II), Anne II, Thomas and

Daniel. The last of the children to die in infancy was not Walter I but Barbara, who died in College Wynd. For references to Barbara and Anchor Close, see Grierson's *Sir Walter Scott, Bart.* (1938), p. 8 *n.* A tablet was erected in Anchor Close about 1950. Scott, in the passage quoted, was wrong in saying his birthplace was pulled down to make way for the northern front of the new College. The new building did not extend so far as the head of College Wynd. The statement has led to the erroneous assertion, so often repeated, that Scott was born in the Latin classroom.

61 (a) Cedant arma togae] See *SL* iv. 509.

61 (c) Oh but I'm weary with wandering] *The Duke of Gordon has three daughters*, st. [15]. Incomplete version in *Johnson*, Vol. 5 [1797], No. 419 and complete in Ritson, *Scotish songs*, London, 1794, ii. 169–75.

61 (c) Mrs Scott (of Hardens) friend] Mrs Newenham of Coolmore. See below, p. 80.

62 (a) explosion] In Colin Mackenzie's house, 12 Shandwick Place. Mrs Jobson lived at No. 6. See above, pp. 49, 58 *n.*, 60.

62 *n.* 2] Thackwell had been Lt.-Col. of the 15th since 1820.

64 (b) There is life . . . in a *mussell*] *Kelly*, p. 309.

64 *n.* 1] The PM is indistinct and might be Apr. 16. This would make date of Scott's letter 15 Apr.

65 (d) pignon sur la vie] For 'vie' read 'rue'; i.e. to have a house of one's own.

65 (f) went . . . to Dalkeith] Scott also wrote to Lord Dalkeith. See *SL* xii. 392–4.

68 (a) out in 1715] Either a misreading or Scott's mistake for 1745.

69 *n.* 1] This Mrs Macleod, from the context, cannot be a Macleod of Macleod. I have not been able to identify her.

71 (d) The mill, mill O] *The mill, mill—O*, st. [4], lines 5–8. In Ramsay, *Tea-table miscellany.*

73 (f) L'homme qui cherche] See below, p. 84 and my note.

74 *n.* 2] It is inaccurate to say that Lockhart 'has proposed to take.' Lockhart, in his letter dated 'Edinburgh, Saturday,' was asking Scott's advice. On dating of Lockhart's letter, see my note to p. 64, *n.* 1 above.

75 (d) So wise and young] Shakespeare, *Richard III*, III. 1.

76 (d) Forrest] 'Mr George Forrest, gunmaker of Jedburgh, has made an ingenious improvement on the percussion lock, by which the sportsman may supply himself with priming for 80 discharges of a double-barrelled gun.' *Edinburgh Lit. Gaz.*, 15 Feb. 1823, p. 31.

77 *n.* 1] Maria Edgeworth's letter of 8 Apr. (line 2) is in Partington, *Letter-books*, pp. 267–70. *Letters from the Irish Highlands* (line 15) has been attributed to a Mrs Wood and to Mrs Henry Wood. Maria Edgeworth definitely attributes it to Henry Blake of Renvyle and his wife. See *Life and letters of Maria Edgeworth*, ed. by A. J. C. Hare, London, 1894, ii. 239.

78 (b) Arms should give way to the Gown] Cedant arma togae. See *SL* iv. 509.

78 *n.* 1] There was also Mrs McAlpine. See above, p. 48.

78 *n.* 2] Delete and see my note to *SL* ix. 84 (c–d).

79 (d) That if one should] Shakespeare, *Midsummer night's dream*, V. 1.

81 (c) To Mrs. Scott] Although this letter has the PM 21 Apr., it must, like other letters, have been written in instalments. The reference (p. 82) to his illness 'yesterday' relates to the incident before 16 Apr. (above, p. 74).

83 (a) Richard is himself again] Colley Cibber, *Richard III*, V. 3. See my note to *SL* v. 29 (f).

83 (f) the duets] With Mrs Studd. See above, p. 78.

84 (b) cartouche-box] See above, pp. 73, 78 and below, p. 88.

84 (c–d) *Trois princes de Sarendip . . . L'homme qui cherche*] *Voyages . . . des trois Princes de Sarendip*. Originally published in Italian by Christoforo Armeno. There is a French trans. in Gronier, *Voyages imaginaires*, tom. 25, Amster-

dam, 1788, pp. 223–480. I cannot find the story of *L'homme qui cherche* in this work.

85 (d) marchings and countermarchings] Foote, *The Mayor of Garratt*, I. 1. See also *SL* viii. 333, ix. 114, x. 1, 84, xi. 317.

86 (a) L'homme qui cherche] See my note to *SL* ix. 78 (c–d).

86 (e) The Breast pin] See above, pp. 16, 58.

86 (f) Nicol is again talking] i.e. Nicol Milne is again talking of selling Faldonside.

87 (d) Ettrick foot to the Carraweel] The River Ettrick enters Tweed 3 miles south of Abbotsford. Carry Weil (so spelled on 25 in. to 1 mile Ordnance Survey) to Ettrick foot was a much longer stretch than Scott would have got by the purchase of Faldonside.

88 (a) his keeper] Mrs Stisted, his wife. See *SL* viii. 389 *n.*

88 (a) Cartouche box] See above, pp. 73, 78, 84.

89 (e) have written to Edinburgh] This letter may not have been written on that day, i.e. 27 Apr. See below, pp. 97–8, and my note, for reference to letter of 29 Apr.

90 *n.* 1] State lotteries became illegal in 1826. See *The last of the lotteries*, in *The Spirit of the Public Journals, 1825*, pp. 51–2: 'No more shall we compose the sentence, terse, / Or hymn Tom Bish in floods of numerous verse.'

90 *n.* 3] Amend this note. Scott's negotiations were not a resumption of his bargaining in 1819. He had been negotiating in 1824 and earlier in 1825. See above, pp. 15 and 86–7.

91 (a) M[r] Anderson] This may be John Anderson of Gladswood.

92 (d) that cub of Sir Adams] The only stepson mentioned in the correspondence is John Lyon who was about 21 at this time and too old to be excluded from the family dinner. I cannot explain the reference.

92 (e) breastpin] See above, pp. 16, 58, 86.

93 (a) For the thing may tomorrow] See my note to *SL* ix. 56 (e).

93 (b) Walter has completed his purchase] A hitch occurred and Walter was not gazetted Captain till 25 June.

93 *n.* 1] The £1,500 was made up of £500 sent on 27 Apr., £500 sent on 29 Apr., £150 from his current salary and £350 lent by Constable and to be repaid to him on 2 May. See also my note to *SL* ix. 151 (c).

94 (c) the Buttery spirit] See Thomas Heywood, *Hierarchie of the blessed angells*, London, 1635, p. 577. The relevant passage is quoted in the *Minstrelsy* (ed. Henderson), ii. 406-7.

94 *n.* 1] *The fairy legends* was published in 3 vols., 1825-8. For 'in his notes to the 1830 edition of the Waverley novels' read 'in his note to chap. 28 of *Rob Roy.*'

95 (a-b) "pulld the old woman out our hearts" as Addison expresses it] The *Spectator*, No. 12, 14 Mar. 1711. [By Joseph Addison.] Addison is actually translating Persius, *Satires*, v. 92.

95 (d) [puppet show at Selkirk]] This is the same as the one mentioned above, p. 19, as is shown by Scott's note to the Magnum Opus ed. of *The Monastery*, chap. 3. Scott told the story to Moore. See Moore's Diary under 29 Oct. 1825. (*Memoirs . . . of Thomas Moore*, ed. Lord John Russell, iv. 331.)

95 (e) Ebenezer Beattie] Scott fined Beattie for trespassing on the Duke of Buccleuch's grounds in 1820. See *Chisholm*, p. 216.

95 *n.* 1] For 'p. 341' read 'p. 352.'

95 *n.* 2] No need to cite *N.E.D.* and Hogg. See Scott's *Demonology and witchcraft*, p. 339.

96 (f) unwashd artificers] Shakespeare, *King John*, IV. 2.

97 (e)-98 sent it into M[r.] James Ballantyne] This letter of 29 Apr. is not in *SL* but there is a transcript of it in NLS (MS. 6080).

98 (b) Wednesday 5th] Should be Wednesday 4th.

98 *n.* 1] In line 2, 'Colonel T——' is Colonel Thackwell.

99 (a) the Major] Major Lane.

99 (c) To [Gabriele Rossetti?]] Scott had not subscribed for Dante by 12

Oct. 1825 (below, p. 246). This letter, therefore, is more likely to be end of 1825 or beginning of 1826.

100 *n.* 1] Motherwell's letter of 28 Apr. 1825 is printed in the *Scots Mag.* N.S. Vol. 24, Nov. 1935.

103 *n.* 1] For one bit of omitted gossip, see below, p. 123.

105 (d) Saturday 1st. May] Saturday was 30 Apr.

105 (e) good "Mistress Lieutenant"] Nicholas Rowe, *Lady Jane Grey*, V. 1: 'good master lieutenant.' Touchwood in *St Ronan's Well*, chap. 30, says: 'So, good morning to you, good master lieutenant.' See also below, pp. 121, 124.

106 *n.* 1] The volume contains (pp. 39-53) *Ode to the Great Unknown.*

108 (a) Pasley] See below, p. 241 *n.*

108 *n.* 1] Delete this note, which is inapplicable.

109 *n.* 2] The date of the letter is the date of postscript, i.e. 10 May, the day he set off for Edinburgh.

110 (d-e) Convention at Jedburgh] See *SL* vii. 131-2, 148, and my note at latter reference.

110 (e) old proverb warning one "against manning himself with his kin"] See *SL* vi. 501 and my note.

110 (e) He has got a residence] The Shaws, Selkirk, which Erskine had used when in Selkirk on official duty. Two letters (not in *SL*) on this subject are in NLS: an undated one, but which from internal evidence is 1 May 1825 (MS. 2890, ff. 49-50) and one dated 15 June 1825 (MS. 2890, ff. 51-2).

112 (b) a brother officer & his wife] The McAlpines. See above, p. 106 *n.*

112 (e) I have orderd the gun] From George Forrest. See above, p. 76 and below, p. 228.

114 (c-d) marchings & countermarchings] Foote, *The Mayor of Garratt*, I. 1. See also *SL* viii. 333, ix. 85, x. 1, 84, xi. 317.

115 (b-c) a present of the fine bust] It was not, however, sent to Abbotsford till 1828.

115 (d) An empty house . . .] Ramsay, *Proverbs*, p. 11: 'Better a toom house than an ill tenant.'

115 *n.* 2] There is an extract from Jane's letter in Partington, *Post-bag*, pp. 205–6.

116 (c) Saul the son of Kish] *Bible, I Samuel* 9: 3.

118 (a) Catholic Emancipation Bill] The bill which was passed in the House of Commons by 248 to 227 was lost in the Lords by 130 to 178. But Parliament was not dissolved till 1826.

118 (f) Waterloo Bridge] See my note to *SL* viii. 248 (d).

119 (d) Allanbank] Sir James Stuart, 7th Bart., sold it in 1828 to Samuel Swinton (1773–1839), nephew of John Swinton of Swinton (Lord Swinton).

119 *n.* 2] This *is* Lockhart's brother William, as the reference to Riddell shows.

121 (a) And so good morrow] Nicholas Rowe, *Lady Jane Grey*, V. 1: 'And so good morrow t'ye, good master lieutenant.' On 10 Feb. 1825 'Gentleman Cadet W. Scott' was given temporary rank of 2nd Lieut. during the time he was to be under Col. Pasley's instructions in sapping and mining. See *Blackwood*, xvii. 758. See also above, p. 105, and below, p. 124.

121 (b) To John Hughes] This is an extract also printed in Hughes, *Letters*, pp. 5–6.

121 (d) I beg to offer my respects to Mrs. Hughes] i.e. young Mrs Hughes, John's wife.

121 (e) Hotspur conducts himself towards Glendower] Shakespeare, *I Henry IV*, III. 1.

121 (e) I must remind Mrs. Hughes of this] He did. See below, p. 164.

121 *n.* 1] Delete and substitute: The 1st Earl Powis had two daughters. The elder, Henrietta, married Sir Watkin Williams Wynn, 5th Bart. The younger, Charlotte, married 3rd Duke of Northumberland. Hence Wynn and the Duke were brothers-in-law. See also below, p. 164 and *n.* 3.

123 (b) the Doctors musical studies] This must be a misreading for 'your Daughter's musical studies.' In the same sentence Scott writes of 'her proficiency.'

123 (c) balm in Gilead] *Bible, Jeremiah* 8: 22.

123 (e) But the only person (lady) whom I know to be at Cheltenham] This must be one of the bits of gossip omitted in the letter to McCulloch. See above, p. 103 *n.*

124 (d) "Good master lieutenant"] See also above, pp. 105, 121.

125 (b) sabre of the redoubted Sultaun] Tipu, Sultan of Mysore. See above, pp. 103, 104 *n.*

125 (c) three Vols of your Legend] *The Eve of All-Hallows*. See above, p. 51 and below, p. 140 *n.*

125 (e) Respecting your dedication] Scott has forgotten that Hartstonge did ask permission and was given a qualified consent. See above, p. 51.

125 *n.* 2] Delete the references. They apply to a different person.

126 (a) Irish road book] William Wilson's *The post chaise companion*, 3rd ed., Dublin, 1803.

128 (d) extravagant flights a Dalilah] 'Epistle dedicatory' to *The Spanish friar*. (Scott's *Dryden*, vi. 377.)

130 *n.* 2] Delete this note. Scott's use of the word 'late' shows that he is referring to James Ferguson of Pitfour who died in 1820. He was an Advocate. There was no need to quote Pitfour who was merely quoting a Scottish proverb.

131 (e) Mousie thou art no thy lane] *Lines to a mouse*, st. [7], line 1.

132 (d) Dr. Gibson] Though the MS. (NLS MS. 140, No. 122) has 'Dr. Gibson' quite clearly, I am sure he meant to write Dr Dickson.

132 *n.* 1] Dundas (second last line) is John Hamilton Dundas. See below pp. 136, 145, 177.

133 (a) "to my exceeding refreshment"] See my note to *SL* iii. 391 (a).

133 (e) Bachelor Bluff] This is a partial quotation. See my note to *SL* ix. 438 (c).

134 (d) "fishd up pale faced honour..."] Shakespeare, *I Henry IV*, I. 3: 'And pluck up drowned honour by the locks.'

135 (d) homebred youths] Shakespeare, *Two gentlemen of Verona*, I. 1: 'Home-keeping youth have ever homely wits.'

136 (d) fishing a lady] Miss Bergan.

136 (e) "pluckd up drownd honour"]
See above, p. 134 (d).

136 (e) Suum cuique] Cicero, *De officiis*,
Bk I, sect. 5: 'tribuendoque suum
cuique.'

137 (d) lonely isle] See my note to *SL*
ii. 506 (a).

137 *n.* 1] In line 2, for 'Scandreth' read
'Scandrett.' In line 3, for 'Davies' read
'Davis.'

139 (d) Ipsis Hybernis Hybernior] The
words 'Ipsis Hibernis Hiberniores'
occur at the beginning of an Irish
statute. See *MPW* ii. 56 *n.*, xx. 39.

140 *n.* 1] The PM dates must be those of
Edinburgh, otherwise Scott could not
have replied to the letters on 16 June.
In line 6, 'what a production' refers to
Hartstonge's *The Eve of All-Hallows*.
See above, pp. 51 (c), 125.

143 *n.* 1] John Syme of Cartmore, W.S.,
died in 1821. 'Mr. Syme', therefore,
must be David Syme, Professor James
Syme's brother.

145 (b) Elliots Light Horse] 'Elliots'
should be 'Eliotts.' When Lovel would
not confess that he was a bad horseman
Oldbuck says: 'No; all you young
fellows think that you would be equal
to calling yourselves tailors at once.'
See *The Antiquary*, chap. 16. Eliott's
Light Horse were not at Minden. See
N. & Q. 8th ser. v. 413–14, 478.

146 (d) Will Honeycombes pursuit of
wealthy widows] See the *Spectator*, No.
311, 26 Feb. 1712 (by Addison) and
No. 359, 22 Apr. 1712 (by Eustace
Budgell).

147 (b) paradise of Tweedside] Gattonside House.

147 (e) son of Mr. Campbell] Rev.
Archibald Blair Campbell. He had
been licensed by the Presbytery of
Jedburgh on 8 June but his first charge
was that of colleague and successor at
Port Patrick, 1828.

148 (b) a non repugnantia] An absence
of opposition. A Scots law phrase.
(Trayner, *Latin maxims*.)

151 (c) To James Ballantyne] Probably
of same date as letter to Gibson, below,
p. 159, i.e. 1 July. The words 'my sons
Commission now gazetted' [on 25 June]
show that the letter was not written till

1 July, by which time Scott knew of the
promotion (below, p. 160); 'lying here
at my return' must mean that he is
writing on Friday, 1 July, from Edinburgh and wants the money to be at
Castle Street when he returns from
Abbotsford; 'breakfast tomorrow' must
refer to Saturday, 2 July, the day he is
to set out for Abbotsford; and the
Friday, on which Ballantyne is to dine,
must be 8 July.

152 (a) pay my law agent] See below,
p. 159.

154 (c–d) *things must be as they may*]
Shakespeare, *Henry V*, II. 1.

154 (d) One generation] *Bible, Ecclesiastes* 1: 4: 'One generation passeth
away, and another generation cometh.'

155 (f) Wilderness of Monkeys] Shakespeare, *The Merchant of Venice*, III. 1.

158 (a) "in the mind's eye Horatio"]
Shakespeare, *Hamlet*, I. 2.

158 (f) Waterloo Bridge] See my note
to *SL* viii. 248 (d).

159 (e) the horse is quite able to carry
the saddle] See *SL* vii. 49 (d–e).

159 *n.* 2] Greenhill was a temporary
address in 1827. Richardson eventually
settled at Kirklands, Roxburghshire,
about 1830.

162 (b) Captain Do Littles] William,
Lockhart's brother.

162 (e) to return on friday night] i.e.
8 July, but later he says he will be
returning on Wednesday, 6 July (below,
pp. 165, 171).

163 (b) *l'embaras des richesses*] Title of
a play by D'Allainval.

163 (d) Mr. Bowdler's note book]
Father of Henrietta Maria Bowdler
who gave the notes to Mrs Hughes. See
Partington, *Post-bag*, p. 209.

163 (d) Sunderland] See Scott's *Dryden*,
viii. 365, ix. 255.

163 (e) Annals] This should be
'Memoirs.' The 'Annals' was written
by Sir David Dalrymple.

163 *n.* 2] Some of these extracts are in
Partington, *Post-bag*, pp. 209–12.

164 (c) Hotspur & Glendower] Shakespeare, *I Henry IV*, III. 1. Cf. above,
p. 121.

164 *n.* 3] See also my note to *SL* ix. 121 *n.*

165 (d) with no hand that is idle] Swift, *The grand question debated*, lines 107–8 (*Works*, ed. Scott, 2nd ed., xv. 175): 'Because he has never a hand that is idle / For the right holds the sword, and the left holds the bridle.'

166 (b) between cup and lip] *Ray*, p. 121; *Kelly*, p. 254; Ramsay, *Proverbs*, p. 47.

166 *n.* 1] Miss Nangle (line 7 from foot) is Anne Nangle. See Index.

167 (b) *spirit of Colonelcy*] Colonel Tidcomb. See *Considerations upon two Bills* in Swift's *Works*, ed. Scott, 2nd ed., viii. 320.

168 (d) Sancho's dish of cow heels] Cervantes, *Don Quixote*, Pt II, chap. 59 (Lockhart's ed., 1822, v. 177).

169 (d) *Time* and *I* . . . saith Don Diego] See *SL* iii. 91 and *n.*

169 (e) Leader Haugh and Yarrow] A reminiscence of Nicol Burne's *Leader Haugh and Yarrow*.

170 (a) "and for my love . . ."] Shakespeare, *The Merchant of Venice*, I. 3.

170 (d) Dogberry] See *SL* ii. 320.

170 (e) the golden sceptre] *Bible, Esther* 4: 11, 5: 2, 8: 4.

171 (a) a sort of enigma] The parcel contained *Tales of the Crusaders* and the enigma is the reference in the introduction to the Author of Waverley's intention to write a life of Napoleon.

171 (c) A brother officer] Capt. McAlpine. See above, p. 106 *n.*

173 (d) Monsr. Jourdain] A character in Molière's *Le bourgeois gentilhomme*, whose desire is to pass as a perfect gentleman.

174 (b) like *Wisdom*, uplift his voice in the streets of Dublin] *Bible, Proverbs* 1: 20: 'Wisdom crieth without; she uttereth her voice in the streets.'

175 (c) Janes answer] See above, p. 160 *n.*

176 (a) Mrs. Fox Lane] See my note to *SL* ix. 44 (f).

177 (a) saved the poor woman] Miss Bergan. See above, pp. 132 *n.*, 134, 136, 155.

177 (d) alacrity at sinking] Shakespeare, *Merry wives of Windsor*, III. 5.

178 (e) the Gods have not made him poetical] Shakespeare, *As you like it*, iii. 3.

179 (a) praise the bridge] *Ray*, p. 106.

179 (c) For if I should *as Lion*] Shakespeare, *Midsummer night's dream*, V. 1.

179 (d) Bishop of Granada's appoplexy] See my note to *SL* iv. 403 (a).

180 (a) Win Jenkins] See my note to *SL* i. 337 (c).

180 (c) To Robert Chambers] 'going to the country' suggests that he wrote the letter in Edinburgh on 2 July but did not post it till 8 July, after his return.

181 (d) a daughter who has been very ill] Eliza.

183 (b) a bill of mine for £500] This sum was paid to Terry on 2 Sept. (*Reply to Mr Lockhart's pamphlet*, Appendix, p. 82.)

183 (e) neither satire nor panegyric] Swift, in his *History of the four last years of the Queen*, wrote: 'Neither shall I mingle panegyric or satire with a history intended to inform posterity.' (*Works*, ed. Scott, 2nd ed., v. 19.)

183 *n.* 2] Constable's letter of 30 Aug. is in *Archibald Constable*, iii. 323–5.

184 *n.* 1] James Skene reports this story of the challenge, saying that Scott told him it was made by 'my cousin, Mr C—— of A——'. Skene's *Memories*, pp. 53–4.

187 (f) *draw kindly*] Sheridan, *The rivals*, I. 1.

188 (a) a brother officer] Capt. McAlpine. See above, p. 106 *n.*

188 (d) Nebuchadnezars fiery furnace] *Bible, Daniel* 3.

189 (c) Lord Lieutenant] Marquess Wellesley, appointed 1821.

189 (d) "time enough to go to bed . . ."] Shakespeare, *I Henry IV*, II. 1.

190 *n.* 1] Jane's maid is Rebecca. Petitoe should be Petito.

191 (c) Courage friend . . .] Matthew Prior, *The thief and the cordelier*, st. 8, lines 3–4.

191 (c) *thof* unknown] See *SL* vi. 110 and my note.

192 (a) Cockburn] Messrs. R. & J. Cockburn, wine merchants, Leith, to whom Scott owed £354. 11s. 8d. in the *Trust Disposition*. This present sum of £425. 12s. 5d. is entered under 2 Aug. 1825 in *Reply to Mr Lockhart's pamphlet*, Appendix, p. 82.

193 (a) Brickworks . . . without straw] *Bible, Exodus* 5.

193 (d) Seven Churches] At Glendalough.

193 (f) *Monseigneur vient*] Swift, *A preface to the Bishop of Sarum's introduction* (*Works*, ed. Scott, 2nd ed., iv. 147). Swift connects this story with Boufflers and Earl of Portland, but Scott, in his article on Gourgaud in *Blackwood*, Vol. 4 (Nov. 1818), p. 220, relates it of Villars and Marlborough or Prince Eugene.

194 (a) The Surgeon Genl] Sir Philip Crampton.

194 (c) "Kings chaff being better than other folks corn"] See *SL* vi. 283.

194 *n.* 2] An extract from Cox's letter of 25 July is given in Partington, *Post-bag*, p. 213. The two letters to Cox cited by O'Donoghue are not in *SL*.

195 *n.* 1] Morritt's letter is dated 25 July (NLS MS. 3901, ff. 21–2).

196 (f) as King Lears fool says] Shakespear, *King Lear*, III. 4.

197 (a) King Malachie & the collar of gold] King of Ireland, 10th cent., who took a collar of gold from a Danish champion whom he overcame. See Moore's *Let Erin remember the days of old*, st. [1], lines 3–4: 'When Malachi wore the collar of gold, / Which he won from her proud invader.'

198 (c) To Thomas Moore] The original letter, which is in the Davis Coll., Van Pelt Library, New York, is dated 3 Aug. See John Clubbe, *After Missologni* in the *Library Chron.* xxxix. 1, note 7.

198 (d) worth the coil that has been made about me] Shakespeare, *King John*, II. 1.

199 (b) land of mist and snow] Coleridge, *The ancient mariner*, Pt 2, st. [12], line 4, or Pt 5, st. [25], line 2.

201 (f) and shame us all] Cf above, p. 196.

203 *n.* 1] There was an Irish poet of same name (1820–90) whose original name was Nolan. See O'Donoghue, *The poets of Ireland*, p. 132.

212 *n.* 1] Delete 'Probably.'

213 (a) Missie Flora] A comma should have been inserted between the names to show that Scott is referring to Margaret (called 'Missie') and Flora.

214 (a) as Falstaff did] Shakespeare, *I Henry IV*, IV. 2.

215 (a) a bowl be broken] *Bible, Ecclesiastes* 12: 6.

215 (a) the Holyrood picture] See *SL* viii. 340, 340 *n.* 2.

215 (b) the parting, I think, of the King and Louis xviii] Bird left unfinished his 'The embarkation of Louis XVIII for France.'

217 *n.* 1] Delete this note. Scott is referring to John Morritt and to his marriage which took place about Oct.

220 (d) picture . . . of James VI] An unframed portrait of James VI on panel (27·5 × 21 in.) from Abbotsford was sold by auction at Dowell's, Edinburgh, 29 Oct. 1938, Lot 70.

222 (d) There is a haunted house] Whaley House. See below, p. 228.

223 (c) De Foe to be found in the Novelist] This is an error. Defoe was not included in *Ballantyne's Novelist's Library*.

223 (f) the inclosed] The signed receipts for Scott's salaries.

224 (a) Ye ken that Maggie winna sleep] Burns. See my note to *SL* i. 529 (b).

224 (c) Charlotte Smiths . . . with Defoe] Both essays were included in Vol. 4 of *Miscellaneous prose works* (1827).

226 (c) Bardolphs security] Shakespeare, *II Henry IV*, I. 2.

227 (d) To Walter] Date must be before 28 Sept. as Scott knew by that time that Walter had been appointed A.D.C. See above, p. 226.

228 (a) stone lion of the Whalleys] Whaley House, in St Stephen's Green, was the town house of the Whaleys of

Whaley Abbey, co. Wicklow. I have not traced the story to which Scott refers above, p. 222.

228 (e) Mrs. M'A.] Mrs McAlpine, wife of Capt. McAlpine, who shared 10 St Stephen's Green with the Scotts.

229 (f) young Rose] George Pitt Rose, Lieut. in 15th Hussars; eldest son of Sir George Henry Rose.

230 (b) To William Stewart Watson] Date is 1823: (1) the miniatures were painted in 1823; (2) the painted glass windows in Entrance Hall were made in 1823.

230 (e) the Glass-painter] William Henry Brown, whose account for the stained glass windows is dated 28 Jan. 1824.

230 n. 1] In line 2, for '1825' read '1823.'

231 (d) To James Ballantyne] The references to *Woodstock* and the £600 show that this letter comes after the one on p. 277, which should be dated 30 Oct. Earliest date is Tuesday, 1 Nov., but may be later.

232 n. 2] Constable's letter of 11 Oct. (printed in *Archibald Constable*, iii. 329–31) is not a reply to Scott's letter of 9 Oct. The contents and dating show that it is in no way connected with Scott's letter.

233 (a) Blue postesses] 'Blue Post' was a popular name for taverns. The coachman in Foote's *The commissary*, I. 1, uses the form 'beastesses' for 'beasts.' Similarly Scott's 'postesses' would be the plural for 'posts.'

233 (c) "carry her through the dub and the lairie"] *The drucken wife o' Gallowa*, st. [2], line 3. In *Herd*, ii. 38, and in *Johnson*, Vol. 2 (1788), No. 191, with the title *Hooly and fairly*.

233 n. 2] Most of this note is superfluous and the reference to John Waldie of Hendersyde is omitted.

234 (c) the Russells] Anne and Jane Boston. The third sister, Elizabeth Jane, died in 1819.

235 (b) Mrs. Pringle] Mrs Alexander Pringle of Whytbank and Yair. The Russells had been staying at Yair. See Anne Scott's letter in *Letters to their governess*, p. 111.

237 (c) "burning marle"] Milton, *Paradise lost*, Bk I, line 296.

238 (e) her [sic] progress] I can see no reason for 'sic.'

240 (c) "those vast inland seas"] Spenser, *The Faerie Queene*, Bk II, Canto VI, st. 10, line 1: 'In this wide inland sea.'

240 (e) "And merry folks were we"] Perhaps a parody of 'And merry men are we' in Allan Cunningham's *A wet sheet and a flowing sea*, st. [2], line 8.

241 n. 1] He visited Abbotsford, 26 Oct. 1838, and signed the Visitors' Book.

243 (d) The story of the Flowers of the Forest] See my note to *SL* i. 121 (e–f).

243 n. 1] The 'collection printed in Edinburgh' (line 5) is: Herd, *Ancient and modern Scottish songs* (1776). *Flodden-Field* is in Vol. 1, pp. 45–9.

244 (c) seven Lairds becoming ruined] About 1760. See *Letters and memoir of . . . Mrs. Alison Rutherford or Cockburn*, Edinburgh, 1900, pp. 113–19. See also *SL* i. 333. Mrs Cockburn was Scott's mother's aunt.

244 (f) the saddle put on the right horse] *Kelly*, p. 281; Ramsay, *Proverbs*, p. 53.

246 (a) Dante] *La divina commedia. Con commento analitico di Gab. Rossetti*. Tom. 1–2. London, 1826–7.

246 (a) Baron Moncrieff Stuart] David Stewart Moncrieff, of Moredun, Baron of Exchequer, 1781.

246 (b) Calantha] Lady Caroline Lamb. Calantha is a character in her novel *Glenarvon*, of which she is largely the prototype; hence she came to be called Calantha.

246 (b) The Chew lad] Benjamin D'Israeli, who was a Jew. Scott was probably quoting Peter Pindar's *The Jewess and her son*, in which the young Jew is called the 'Chew lad.'

246 (c) the Chevaliers cover] Sir George Rose.

246 (c) Glengarrys helmet] See above, p. 243 n. 1.

246 (d) To Captain Basil Hall] There is a facsimile of part of this letter in *A week at Waterloo* (cited below p. 247

n. 2), facing p. 34, from which the text can be corrected.

246 *n.* 1] Delete '[end of April].'

247 *n.* 1 Capt. Maitland's . . . narrative] A letter dated 20 Oct. 1817 from Captain Maitland on Napoleon on the *Bellerophon* was printed in the *Edin. Ann. Reg. for 1816* (publ. 1820), IX. ii. ccccciv–cccccv. See also *Journal,* 11 Mar. 1826.

247 *n.* 2] The narrative was published as *A week at Waterloo in 1815. Lady de Lancey's narrative . . . Ed. by Major B.R. Ward,* 8vo London, 1906.

253 (b) bind your brows] Shakespeare, *II Henry IV,* I. 1.

253 (e) Lord Gifford] Who had been at Abbotsford (above, pp. 233–4).

257 (b) *beaux yeux de sa cassette*] See below, p. 413.

257 (c) your Colonels lady] Mrs Thackwell.

258 (a) in his new Capacity] As A.D.C. to the Lord Lieutenant.

258 *n.* 1] Delete this note. The Blakes referred to in *SL* ix. 77 *n.* are different people.

259 (a) *Incumbite remis*] See my note to *SL* ix. 5 (c).

259 *n.* 1] This is the franking date, the month and day of which had to be written in words.

259 *n.* 2] Delete this note. Scott is *not* quoting from his own poem. It is a common Gaelic phrase long in use.

265 (f) Dogberries & Verges] Dogberry and Verges in Shakespeare's *Much ado about nothing.*

267 (a) Muc[k]ross] Scott wrote Mucruss (his o and u being alike) and this is the contemporary spelling and should have been left unamended. Maria Edgeworth spelt the name 'Mucruss Abbey' in *Ennui,* chap. 10.

269 (b) To William Straiton] This letter is addressed to young Straiton, son of Will Straiton who died in Mar. 1826. He was still an employee in Feb. 1826 (below, p. 405). The date, therefore, cannot be 1825; and it cannot be 1826 as Scott was in France in Oct. of that year. It may be 1827.

269 *n.* 1] Delete this note, which is not applicable. Scott's letter is addressed to *young* Straiton.

270 (f) Brompton] i.e. School of Military Engineering at Old Brompton, Chatham.

273 (e) gallant efforts in favour of Marie Antoinette] See *SL* ii. 207 *n.*

273 *n.* 1] There is an extract in Partington, *Post-bag,* pp. 214–15.

274 (c) To Walter] This letter has been written in instalments. Moore (p. 275) left on 2 Nov.

276 (a) as you are strong be merciful] See *Kelly,* p. 39.

276 (f) I am at this moment in Paris] See below, p. 316.

277 (b) The Gunpowder plot] *The fifth of November,* line 1 of chorus. In Hogg, *Jacobite relics* (1819) p. 363. 'The Gunpowder Plot / Will never be forgot / While Edinburgh Castle stands upon a rock' was a rhyme which Scott would know from recitation. See Robert Chambers, *Popular rhymes of Scotland,* new ed., London, 1870, p. 154.

277 (c) To James Ballantyne] Moore was at Abbotsford 29 Oct.–2 Nov. The Sunday of this letter, therefore, is 30 Oct.

278 (b) Things must be as they may] Shakespeare, *Henry V,* II. 1.

279 (b) like a cow in a *fremd loaning*] See *SL* vi. 462 (d–e).

280 (a) To [unknown correspondent]] Joseph Jamieson Archibald. See *SL* xi. 486 *n.* 2 and xii. 490.

280 (b) winnock bunker] A cupboard in a window seat. Scott may have felt it appropriate to use this term as its only use by Burns is in his *Tam o' Shanter,* line 119.

280 (d) targing[?]] Delete query. 'Targing the bairns' is Scots for 'keeping the children in order.'

280 (e–f) Virgilium vidi tantum] *Ovid, Tristia,* IV. x. 51.

280 *n.* 1] Archibald's letter to Scott (in NLS) does not say he is sending the watch. Probably only the box was sent. In that case Scott's words 'containing the watch' must mean 'which had contained the watch.'

281 (c–d) dear little Anne] Scott means Eliza.

282 (b) the Lungs of London] A saying usually attributed to William Windham. Windham, however, in the House of Commons, said on 30 June 1808: 'It was a saying of Lord Chatham, that the parks were the lungs of London.' See *Cobbett's Parliamentary history*, Vol. 11, c. 1124.

283 (e) Brewster is at Gattonside] i.e. at Allerly.

285 (c) I have every reason to believe that he has kept his word with me] Yet, writing to Lockhart on the same day, Scott says 'I really do not know how much or how little you have been concerned in Blackwood' (below, p. 289).

285 (f) proscription] A misreading for 'prescription,' a legal term meaning that Lockhart, after this lapse of time, could not be charged with the offence.

289 (c–d) concernd in Blackwood] Cf. above, p. 285.

290 (c) play the old man and his ass] See L'Estrange, *Fables*, No. 358: *An old man and an ass*. By Poggius.

290 (e) a reed shaken with the wind] *Bible, Matthew* 11: 7.

290 (e–f) Ever Gramercy stampd paper] i.e. that the contract had been signed by Murray. See below, p. 335.

291 (a) *vestigia nulla retrorsum*] A saying ('There is no stepping backwards') based on Horace, *Epistles*, I. i. 74–5. Also used in *MPW* viii. 32.

293 (a) Dickson & Co/] Dixon & Co., Bankers, London. Title of firm varies.

293 *n*.] The evidence of the student is worthless and should not be cited.

294 (f) Wilsons & Williams] John Wilson's candidature for Philosophy Chair at Edinburgh University and John Williams's candidature for rectorship of Edinburgh Academy.

295 (b) revd. Laurence and his fair lady] Lockhart's brother had married on 16 Sept. Louisa Blair.

295 (f) like Tristram Shandys bull] Sterne, *Tristram Shandy*, Bk ix, chap. 33.

299 (c) *rectus in curia*] A legal phrase; i.e. that no charge had been made

against him. See also *SL* x. 205, 370, 469, *Waverley*, chap. 6, *Guy Mannering*, chap. 52 and *Woodstock*, chap. 5.

301 *n*. 2] This note does not refer to '25 January' of the text. The note should read 'See *Journal*, 22 Nov. 1825, where Scott refers to *Woodstock*'s being out on 25 Jan.' The note here should be transferred to the end of the letter on p. 302.

305 (d) government claims] War Office claims against Tom for Irish funds.

306 *n*. 3] The correct spelling is probably Lethem. In the Edinburgh Marriage Register, 1751–1800, there are thirteen entries for Lethem but none for Lathem.

308 (a) to meet a few family friends] This gathering did not take place. Sophia dined alone with Scott on Friday, 1 Dec. (*Journal*).

308 *n*. 1] Scott wrote in his 1830 introd. to *The Monastery*: 'Captain Clutterbuck . . . has no real prototype in the village of Melrose or neighbourhood.' The *Kelso Mail* of 21 Nov. 1836 recorded the death at Melrose of Capt. Walter Tait, R.N., 'said to be the original of Capt. Clutterbuck.'

309 (c) to Heber and yourself] Letter to Southey is above, p. 297, but the letter to Heber is not in *SL*.

313 (c–d) Hector . . . Sir Robert] Hector Macdonald Buchanan and Sir Robert Dundas.

315 (e) the Colonels Lady] Mrs Thackwell.

315 *n*. 3] No need to italicize 'Patrick.' Patrick and Peter were synonymous in Scotland.

316 (a) He and I went to the play] On 12 Nov. See Moore's *Memoirs*, v. 13–15.

316 (d) "better a finger off than aye wagging"] See *SL* iv. 172 (e).

316 (e) that I had gone to . . . Paris] See above, p. 276.

317 (a) Prince Housseins tapestry] In *Arabian Nights*. See my note to *SL* i. 229 (e).

317 (b) "My dear it hails . . ."] St. [2], line 3 of *Hunting song* in Henry Fielding's *Don Quixote in England*, II. 5: 'My Dear, it rains, and hails, and snows.'

318 *n.* 1] Scott is right and Walter is wrong. The name is Tuke.

319 (b–c) Ellis] Charles Rose Ellis, created Baron Seaford in 1826.

319 (d) as Corporal Nym says] Shakespeare, *Henry V*, II. 1.

319 (d) retu[r]nd from Melville Castle] Where he had dined on Monday, 28 Nov. (*Journal*).

320 (f) right reckoning and short reckoning make long friends] See *SL* iv. 236.

320 (f) A writer to the Signet] Hugh James Rollo.

321 (a) an old proverb] 'He that is born to be hang'd, shall never be drown'd.' *Ray*, p. 104; *Kelly*, p. 158; Ramsay, *Proverbs*, p. 27.

321 (b) More last words of Mr. Baxter] Addison, in the *Spectator*, No. 445, says 'last words' and 'more last words' related to Richard Baxter; but Brewer, in *Dictionary of phrase and fable*, says they related to Mrs Baxter.

321 (c) the Surgeon General] Philip (later Sir Philip) Crampton.

321 (e) This morning . . .] This and the two following paragraphs were written on 5 Dec.

321 (f) "What argufies snivelling . . ."] Charles Dibdin, *Poor Jack*, st. [3], line 3: 'What argufies sniv'ling and piping your eye.' This is a ballad in *Whim of the moment*. In his *A collection of songs*, 3rd ed., London, n.d. [1792?], i. 154.

321 *n.* 1] Delete this note. *The Comet*, to which Scott is referring, was lost off Greenock on 21 Oct. of this year.

322 *n.* 1] Also dated 23 Nov. in Hughes, *Letters*, pp. 204–7.

323 (a) soliciting a situation] Sheriffship of Sutherland (q.v. in Index).

324 (c) mettle of the pasture] Shakespeare, *Henry V*, III. 1.

325 (b) like a cow in a *fremit loaning*] See *SL* vi. 462 (d–e).

325 (c) lonely dowie and wae] *Flodden-Field*, st. [18], line 2. In *Herd*, i. 48; Jane Elliot, *The Flowers of the Forest*, st. 11, line 2: 'lonely, and dowie, and wae.' In *Minstrelsy* (ed. Henderson), iii. 404.

325 *n.* 2] See also above, p. 322 *n.*

328 (a) To J. G. Lockhart] Cancel here. It is printed from the original under its correct date, 8 Dec. 1827, in *SL* x. 328.

329 (c) Prince Hossein's tapestry] In *Arabian Nights*. See my note to *SL* i. 229 (e).

329 (c) *thof unknown*] See *SL* vi. 110 and my note.

329 (c) "just to drive the cold winter away"] St. [2], line 2, of song beginning 'Come, come, my Hearts of Gold' in *The vocal miscellany*, 3rd ed., London, 1738, Vol. 1, p. 163.

330 (e) dowie lonely and wae] See above, p. 325, where the quotation is more correctly given.

330 (e) Brunton] Brunton, one of Scott's employees, was a Selkirk man. See below, p. 405.

331 *n.* 3] In *St Ronan's Well*, chap. 28, Scott also attributes the proverb wrongly to Swift. It is in *Ray*.

332 (d–e) like MacBeth] Shakespeare, *Macbeth*, II. 2.

333 (a) letter from Lady Stafford] See *Journal*, 13 Dec. 1825. There is an extract from her letter, dated 8 Dec., in Partington, *Post-bag*, pp. 214–15.

333 (e) After all the Hogg . . .] This obscure sentence may mean that the Lockharts, on their way to London, gave Hogg's nephew Robert a 'lift' as far as Selkirk.

335 (b) like Mahomets coffin—or like the ass] The moral of the coffin and the ass between two bundles of hay is discussed in the *Spectator*, No. 191 (9 Oct. 1711). Scott was probably thinking of this passage.

335 (f) stamped paper] See above, p. 290 and my note.

336 (c) *ride on its rigging*] See my note to *SL* viii. 463 (a).

336 (d) King John . . . King William] i.e. Lockhart and William Gifford. But King John succeeded King John (i.e. Coleridge).

337 (a) Your nephew] Scott is here referring to the recent marriage of John Morritt.

338 (b) "put money in my purse"] Shakespeare, *Othello*, I. 3.

338 (c) You gave me one last year]
At the time of Walter's marriage. See
SL viii. 473 (d).

339 (c) To Archibald Constable] Date
is taken from the *Journal*.

341 (c) but old men . . . will be talking]
Shakespeare, *Much ado about nothing*,
III. 5.

341 (e) But grievings a folly] Charles
Dibdin, *The sailor's confession*. A ballad
in *Private theatricals*. In his *A collection
of songs*, London [1792], ii. 162. The
burden of each stanza is: 'But grieving's
a folly / Come let us be jolly / If we've
troubles at sea boys, we've pleasures
ashore.'

343 (a) food of horses] Samuel Johnson's
definition of oats in his *Dictionary*. See
also *SL* xi. 152.

343 *n.* 1] Alexander Gordon.

344 (a) To Allan Cunningham] Date
is 14 Dec. (The transcriber for the
Abbotsford Copies probably misread
the '1' as a '2', these two figures often
being very much alike.) On 14 Dec.
Scott, in a letter to Lockhart (above,
p. 334), said: 'I inclose a note to Allan
Cunninghame.' The words 'Sophia
leaves us' can mean 'Sophia has left
us' as well as 'Sophia will leave us.'
Amend *n.* 1 at foot of page.

344 (d) like a cow in a strange loaning]
See *SL* vi. 462 (d–e).

344 (f) Wordsworths bust] It sits in
the Entrance Hall at Abbotsford.

346 (c) treating with Nicol Milne] For
Faldonside.

346 (d) Lady Vice Regent] Marchioness
Wellesley.

346 *n.* 1] In line 6, for 'Sagahun' read
'Sahagun.'

347 (b) as if a dagger] See *Journal*, 26
and 27 Dec.

347 (c) Clarkson] Dr James Clarkson
from Melrose. See below, p. 366.

347 (f) I have sent a song to Jane]
Bonnie Dundee. See *Journal*, 22 Dec.

348 (d) freedom from Corke] Scott in
his *Journal* twice notes receipt—29 Dec.
1825 and 5 Jan. 1826. The former may
relate only to the intimation of the gift.
See below, p. 365, 365 *n.* 3.

348 (d) button my coat *behind*] Dougal
Graham, *The comical sayings of Paddy
from Cork, with his coat buttoned behind*
[in prose]. 'Paddy from Cork, with his
Coat buttoned Behind' was used as
a pseudonym in *Blackwood*, Vol. 11
(Mar. 1822), p. 344.

349 *n.* 1 John Clarkson] This should be
James Burnet Clarkson.

350 (a) Mr Shaw] John Shaw, surgeon.

350 (a) Dalrymples history] Sir John
Dalrymple's *Memoirs*. See below, p. 355.

350 (b) Whare gat ye . . .] *Jockey's
escape from Dundee* in D'Urfey, *Wit and
mirth*, Vol. 5 (1719), pp. 17–19. A rewritten version by Burns, with these
opening lines, appeared in *Johnson*,
Vol. 1 (1787), No. 99, under the title
Bonie Dundee. The lines in D'Urfey are:
'Where gott'st thou the *Haver-mill
bonack*? / Blind Booby can'st thou not
see' and in Johnson: 'O whar did ye
get that hauver-meal bannock? / O
silly blind body, O dinna ye see.'

351 (a) To James Ballantyne] Date
is taken from the *Journal*.

351 *n.* 2] The letter cited is NLS MS.
868, f. 236. Miss Wemyss was persistent. She wrote again in Mar. 1826
(NLS MS. 3903, ff. 250–1) revealing
(although she had said she had 'no
relatives to whom she can appeal') that
she lived with her brother and sister-in-
law. She wrote again on 15 Dec. 1828
(NLS MS. 3907, ff. 283–4).

352 (e) I send you a few sentences]
According to the *Journal*, 29 Dec.,
Scott sent four pages.

353 (b) It is well away if it bide]
A Scottish proverb. See *Kelly*, p. 164,
who gives it as 'He's well away, if he
bides' and explains it as 'Spoken when
we are glad to be quit of an ill man's
company.'

354 (a) To Mrs. Scott of Harden] The
date of this letter is 5 Jan. 1826 as
entry for that day in the *Journal* shows.
The letter is a reply to Mrs Scott's
apology for not coming to Abbotsford.

354 (d) To Mrs Scott of Lochore] Date
is about 6 Jan. 1826, the day the letter
was completed.

354 (f) receive good . . .] *Bible, Job*
2: 10.

355 *n.* 2] Scott is not quoting from *Herd* but from *Jockey's escape from Dundee* in D'Urfey, *Wit and mirth*, Vol. 5, London, 1719, p. 18. The lines quoted are not the beginning but are lines 1–2 of st. 2: 'For I have neither robbed nor stole, / Nor have I done any injury.' See also above, p. 350 and my note.

356 (a) The other] This version with title *Bonny Dundee* is in *Herd*, 3rd ed. (1791), ii. 91–2, and with title *Bonie Dundee* in *Johnson*, Vol. 1 (1787), No. 99.

358 (c) John Thomson] Bookseller and bookbinder in Edinburgh.

360 (a) Mr Dunlop] George Dunlop, W.S., agent for Mr Farie from whom Scott borrowed £10,000 on Abbotsford.

360 (c) The rental] See *SL* viii. 473 (d).

362 (f) Dunlop and Hogarth] Payment of fees to them for negotiating bond on Abbotsford. See above, pp. 359–60, and my note. George Hogarth, W.S., acted as Scott's agent.

363 (b) To James Ballantyne] Scott had already written two letters on 5 Jan. and would be unlikely to write a third. From reference to snow and his walk, date is probably 7 Jan. See *Journal* under that date.

363 (e) smack of the Apoplexy] Le Sage, *Gil Blas*, Bk vii, chap. 4.

364 (a) Mr Dunlop] See above, pp. 359–60, 362.

364 (e) To Major Walter Scott] The date is correct but the letter could not be addressed as given here. Walter was not a Major till 1828 and was not stationed at Chichester till 1829.

366 *n.* 1] Delete 'See Vol. VII, Appendix, p. 405.'

368 (b) Fergusson] Robert Ferguson, M.D., Sir Adam Ferguson's cousin, once removed.

370 (a) if my right hand should lose its cunning] *Bible*, *Psalms* 137: 5.

371 (b) £600 for the Lay] Scott sold the copyright in Nov. 1805 to Longman for £500. See *SL* i. 269 and *n*.

372 (b) as Lieut Hatchway says] Smollett, *Peregrine Pickle*, chap. 2.

372 (b) offer I had of a loan for £30,000] Laidlaw recorded: 'I heard today that the Duke of Somerset and another English nobleman have written to Sir Walter, offering him £30,000 each, which he has firmly refused.' (Robert Carruthers, *Abbotsford notanda* in Robert Chambers, *Life of Sir Walter Scott*, Edinburgh, 1871, pp. 169–70.)

373 (a) Tyne heart Tyne all] Ramsay, *Proverbs*, p. 68: 'Tine Heart and a's gane.'

375 *n.* 2] For 'peculiarly' read 'particularly.' (Correction in *SL* xii. 491.)

378 (b) the Miss Smiths] This should be 'the Messrs Smith,' i.e. John & Thomas Smith, builders, Darnick. Scott thought that the house had been fully paid for (above, p. 346). In the *Trust Disposition* (NLS MS. 112) Scott was listed as owing £900 to the Smiths. See also below, pp. 506–7.

378 (e) vanity, if not vexation of spirit] *Bible*, *Ecclesiastes* 1: 14: 'all is vanity and vexation of spirit.'

379 *n.* 1] A long extract from Walter's letter is given in Partington, *Post-bag*, pp. 219–20. It is there dated 15 Jan.

380 (d–e) like mice under a firlot] See *SL* v. 224 and my note.

380 *n.* 1] Constable took Cadell's advice, for he set off the same day, i.e. 13 Jan. See above, p. 371 *n*.

381 (e) loss of world's gear] Burns. See my note to *SL* iii. 490 (e).

383 (c) as Bobadil says] Ben Jonson, *Every man in his humour*, I. 4. But Bobadil actually says 'a cleanly and quiet privacy.'

384 (e) bread I shall eat or white or brown] Matthew Prior, *Alma*, Canto III, line 587: 'Bread we shall eat, or white or brown.'

385 (e) "And still I'll wellcome . . ."] Thomas Parnell, *The hermit*, line 213: 'And still he welcomes, but with less of cost.' In *Poems on several occasions*, 12mo Glasgow, 1752, p. 185. Also in Lewis, *Tales of wonder* (1801), ii. 272.

385 *n.* 1] This corrects error in *SL* vii. 270 *n.* 2.

388 *n.* 1] '*Ten Plays*' is the cataloguer's description of the contents of a made-up vol. and should not have been given in italics. In any case, Scott asks for 'the 3d Vol', i.e. Vol. 3 of the 4-vol. ed. on

p. 218 of *ALC*. Scott is wrong in saying the plays are on the left of Shakespeare's bust. They are on the right.

388 *n*. 3] In line 6, for 'second Baron Broughton' read 'first Baron Broughton.'

390 *n*. 1] Delete this note. Scott is quoting *Bible, Psalms* 20: 7. (See *SL* xii. 491.) Scott also writes 'This it is to put trust in chariots and horses!' in his review of Pepys in *QR* (*MPW* xx. 127) which he had just completed (above, p. 367).

392 (a) The first work] *Woodstock*.

393 (d) to Maria Edgeworth] This letter should have appeared in *SL* x, under 2 May, the date it was finished.

394 (b) "*things must be as they may*"] Shakespeare, *Henry V*, II. 1.

394 (b) things past cure should be past care] A proverb, but not traced in the usual sources. Shakespeare has: 'Past cure is still past care' (*Love's labour's lost*, V. 2). *Ray*, p. 121, has: 'that cannot be cured, must be endured' and Ramsay, *Proverbs*, p. 72, has the Scottish equivalent.

395 (d) The political letters] The Malachi Malagrowther letters on the currency which appeared in the *Edinburgh Weekly Journal* for 22 Feb., 1 and 8 Mar. 1826.

396 (a) the subscription] Rev. John Jephson's *Sermons*, ed. by the Bishop of Raphoe, was issued later in the year by C. & J. Rivington, London.

397 (e) Don Whiskerandos and the lady Tilburina] Two characters in Sheridan's *The critic*.

398 *n*. 1] In the *Trust Disposition* (NLS MS. 112) the sum given is £331. 17*s*. 9*d*.

400 *n*.] The sentence (lines 12–14) relating to the Macdonalds and Price can be related to the rumour in 1820 that Margaret Macdonald Buchanan was going to marry Mr Price (*SL* vi. 121).

400 *n*. 1] Walter's letter is in Partington, *Letter-books*, pp. 353–4.

402 *n*. 1] The 'book there noted' refers to Douglas's note in the *Journal*; viz. *The cause of truth defended*, 8vo Hull and London, 1827. Only the *Statement*,

cited here, is given in Anderson's ed. of the *Journal*, p. 74, *n*. 1.

403 (a) To James Ballantyne] The date is 3rd Feb. Under that date in the *Journal* Scott writes of the bird and potato bogle. The 3rd was a Friday.

403 (c) To James Ballantyne] The date is 26 Jan. as is shown by the reference to Shakespeare in the letter and in the *Journal* under that date.

404 (a) your objection] i.e. to *Woodstock*.

409 (d) "things must be as they may"] Shakespeare, *Henry V*, II. 1.

409 *n*. 2] See also my note to *SL* ix. 385 (e).

410 *n*. 2] See also the extract from Morritt's letter in Partington, *Post-bag*, pp. 221–2.

412 (a) Murrays paper] The *Representative*.

412 (b) the puppet show in Tom Jones] Henry Fielding, *Tom Jones*, Bk 12, chap. 5.

413 (a) One lady] Miss Macdonald Buchanan. See *Journal*, 5 Feb.

413 (b) Willie Clerke] His sister Elizabeth had died on 17 Jan.

413 *n*. 2] Sophia's letter is in Partington, *Letter-books*, pp. 354–6.

414 (c) *Things must be as they may*] Shakespeare, *Henry V*, II. 1.

414 (e) poor Walters money] Money for Scott's nephew. Sophia wrote on 1 Feb.: 'Little Walter bids me say he will sail about the 20th of this month, and that his equipment including passage will require as near as he can judge 220 £.' (Partington, *Letter-books*, p. 355.)

415 (b) Miss Russells] Jane and Anne Russell of Ashiestiel, the two surviving sisters at this time.

415 (c) Yesterday was the Cavalry ball] On 2 Feb. See Anne's letter above, p. 400 *n*. This shows that the letter has been written in instalments.

416 (c) *Iago's* words] Shakespeare, *Othello*, V. 2: 'I bleed, sir; but not kill'd.'

417 (c–d) What is written on our foreheads] Muslims believe that the

decreed events of every man's life are impressed in divine characters on his forehead but invisible to mortal eyes.

421 *n*. 1] Lady Louisa's letter of 11 Mar. is in Stuart, *Selections*, pp. 220–2.

423 (f) To Miss Clephane] To Anna Jane.

424 (c) what is sauce for the Goose] Ray, p. 148.

424 (c) the proverb is somewhat musty] Shakespeare, *Hamlet*, III. 2.

424 (f) loss of warlds gear] Burns. See my note to *SL* iii. 490 (e).

425 (d) like a tether] Burns. See *SL* v. 422 and cf. *SL* viii. 410, xi. 101.

427 (c) female burning in India] See *Journal*, 1 Dec. 1825.

431 (a) pony] Marion. See above, p. 45, and *SL* x. 184, 214.

431 (b) beggars . . . must not be chusers] See *SL* ii. 225.

431 (e) the Blakes] Mr and Mrs Anthony Blake.

431 (f) *Open Sesamum*] See my note to *SL* vi. 293 (d).

432 (a) Mr Franck] Probably Franks, who became Sir Thomas Harte Franks. See Index and also below, p. 451 and *Journal*, 10 Mar. 1826 and Anderson's note.

434 (a) a couple of pamphlets] Scott must mean 'two copies of a pamphlet.' Only the first Malachi letter had appeared by this time.

434 (c) his Sir Williams as . . . Abraham Newlands] Abraham Newland was Chief Cashier of the Bank of England. Sir William may, therefore, be Sir William Forbes. But Sir William may stand for Sir William Wallace as a symbol of Scottish rights.

434 (d) Tristrem Shandys bull] Sterne, *Tristram Shandy*, Bk ix, chap. 33.

435 (b) Aut Erasmus] Scott said the same thing in his *Journal*, 23 Feb.

435 (d) the Club] The Albyn.

436 (b) the Calton hill] i.e. the new gaol built on Calton Hill, Edinburgh.

437 (a) fortune of Mr Carpenter] Barber, one of Mrs Carpenter's trus-

tees, was a partner of a banking firm that went bankrupt at this time. See below, p. 452.

437 (a–b) *Sunday Eveng* 25 *feby.*] Sunday was 26 Feb.

438 (a) To C.K. Sharpe] Tuesday was 14 Mar., which is date of the letter. Delete note 2.

438 (c) Bachelor Bluff] St. [10], lines 5–6 of a song beginning 'The lark was up, and the morning grey,' in *The vocal magazine*, London, 1781, p. 348, where it is called *The camp-medley*. Another version of the song with the title *The soldier's medley* appears in Charles Wilson's *St. Cecilia*, Edinburgh, 1779, p. 22. The version followed by Scott is that of *The vocal magazine*.

438 *n*. 1] Delete and see *Journal*, 14 Feb. 1826: 'Promised Sharpe the set of Piranesi's views by Clérisseau in the dining parlour. They belonged to my uncle, so I do not like to sell them.'

439 (a) To James Ballantyne] Scott, above, p. 429, said Constable's meeting would be held three weeks on Monday, i.e. 6 Mar. Date of this letter, therefore, is 6 Mar. See also *Journal*, 8 Mar. At the meeting Alexander Cowan was appointed Constable's trustee.

439 (a) dumple the thing] Massinger, *A new way to pay old debts*, III. 2.

439 (c) To James Ballantyne] Cancel and see *SL* x. 22–3.

439 (d) My lot is not to die to-day] See my note to *SL* x. 23 (a).

441 (b) viis et modis] By ways and means. A Scots law phrase. (Trayner, *Latin maxims*.)

441 (f) Abercromby & Abercromby] There were two Advocates of this name, but Scott mentions only one in his *Journal*, 7 Feb. The repetition is probably a mistake.

442 (b) A Barons gown] As Baron of the Court of Exchequer.

442 (c) But who can help it Dick] Sir John Suckling, *A ballad upon a wedding*, st. [17], line 6. In Ritson, *Ancient songs*, London, 1790 [1792], p. 227.

442 (c) I cannot see the country ruind] The letter from this point is much the

same as Scott's entry in his *Journal* for 3 Mar.

443 *n*. 1] Scott uses the words 'moneyers and great oneyers' in the *Journal*, 13 Dec. 1825.

444 (a) A man's a man for a' that] Burns, *Is there, for honest poverty*, st. [2], line 4.

444 (f) To Thomas Sharp] Scott was in Edinburgh on 7 Mar. He may have given Abbotsford as his address knowing that he would soon be there.

446 *n*. 1] Versions of *Galatians* are given in *Scottish Notes and Queries*, Vol. 2, (Mar. 1889), pp. 145–7, (Apr. 1889), pp. 163–5, (May 1889), pp. 177–9.

447 (d) Scottish Chronicle] See *SL* i. 294, vii. 87, x. 220 and my notes to *SL* i. 294 (d) and vii. 87 (d). The copy presented by Scott to S. Villiers Surtees was offered for sale by Halliday of Leicester in 1938 (Catalogue 225).

448 (c) West Indian affair] Lockhart had written four articles on 'The West Indian controversy' in *Blackwood*, Vols. 14–16, Oct. 1823–Dec. 1824. The 'West India Body of London' wrote to Scott in 1824, offering payment to Lockhart for these. (See Partington, *Post-bag*, p. 200.) Lockhart wrote an article on slavery in the West Indies in his first number of the *QR* in 1826, perhaps as a result of Ellis's offer.

449 (a) like the stag in the fable] See L'Estrange, *Fables*, No. 43. *A stag drinking*. By Aesop.

450 (b) Cissy] Cecilia Street, Anne's maid. See *Lockhart*, x. 4. At Abbotsford there is a letter from her to Mrs M. M. Maxwell-Scott from 9 Walworth Street, Westbourne Terrace, London, 18 June 1873.

450 (c) "the cabbin is convenient"] Ben Jonson, *Every man in his humour*, I. 4.

450 *n*. 1] As 1826 was not a leap year, '29th February' is probably a slip for '1st March.'

450 *n*. 2] This note is wrong. 'Date' for 'address' was often used by Scott and other writers of the period. Lockhart used it in *Peter's letters*, Letter I, and Matthew Prior and Horace Walpole had used it. See Index under Date.

451 (b) invited M[r] Franck to break-

[f]ast] On 10 Mar. See *Journal* under that date. See also my note to *SL* ix. 432 (a).

451 *n*. 1] 'twenty-eight years' should be 'twenty-four years,' and the house had been numbered 39 for only 15 years.

453 (a) portrait by Raeburn] See my note to *SL* xi. 463 (a).

456 (a) the Cabinet] See below, p. 463.

456 (a) I am sorry poor No 39 has stuck in the market] See my note to *SL* x. 54 (a).

457 (c) Once about twenty years ago] In 1806, when his support of Lord Melville cost him the friendship of Lady Roslyn, Dugald Stewart and others.

457 (d) sent to Coventry] See also above, p. 447 and *SL* v. 70.

463 (f) the cabinet] See above, p. 456, and *Journal*, 10 Mar.

465 (d–e) All ill comes from the North] The nearest proverbs I can find are 'Cold weather and knaves come out of the North' (*Ray*, p. 19) and 'Three great evils come out of the North, a cold wind, a cunning knave, and a shrinking cloth' (*Ray*, p. 341, from Fuller's *Worthies*).

467 (b) "poor Margaret was a prophetess"] Shakespeare, *King Richard III*, I. 3 and V. 1. Scott was probably thinking of Sister Peg, Adam Ferguson's allegory in his *History of . . . Margaret commonly called Peg*. (See *SL* vi. 144.) See also John Arbuthnot's *Law is a bottomless pit*, in Scott's *Swift*, 2nd ed., vi. 61 et seq.

467 (f) after the manner of Seged] Samuel Johnson, *The Rambler*, No. 205, 3 Mar. 1752.

468 (a) Lady Scott and Anne] But they did not go to Abbotsford till Wednesday, 22 Mar. See below, p. 476 and *Journal*, 23 Mar.

469 (d) hanged for *incivisme*] A French word very much in Scott's mind at this time when he was writing of the French Revolution at the beginning of his *Napoleon*.

473 (a) "sharp encounter of their wits"] Shakespeare, *Richard III*, I. 2: 'keen encounter of our wits.'

473 (f) "No man bears sorrow better"]
Shakespeare, *Julius Caesar*, IV. 3.

474 (c) saved it to cool my porridge]
Ray, p. 231; *Kelly*, p. 229; Ramsay,
Proverbs, p. 42. See also *Old Mortality*,
chap. 36 and *The Heart of Mid-Lothian*,
chap. 25.

475 (d) No man bears sorrow better]
Shakespeare, *Julius Caesar*, IV. 3.

475 *n.* 1] This extract is given in
Partington, *Post-bag*, p. 222.

476 (a) lye failing Robinson] Scott must
mean 'lye, failing Robinson, between
Longman & Coy & Murray.'

476 (b) Lady Scott] She arrived at
Abbotsford on Wednesday, 22 Mar.
(*Journal*). This dates Scott's letter of
Monday.

476 (b) To Sir William Rae] Cancel this
letter and see *SL* xi. 307.

477 *n.* 1] In line 2, for 'MS. 56' read
'MS. 143, f. 56.' The final document
(5 sheets of parchment, 22 × 28·5 in.),
dated 6 Apr. 1833, is now in my Scott
Coll. It gives a detailed history of the
money which had been lying in
Chancery and which is now, with
interest, being paid to the Scott family.

478 (a) Her only children] There were
three—two boys and a girl.

478 (a–b) Charlotte M. Carpenter]
Scott has reversed the forenames. She
was Margaret Charlotte Carpenter.

478 (b) M. Carpenter died four or five
years since] Charles Carpenter died
4 June 1818, i.e. almost eight years
since.

478 (d) That the man should have some
salvage] Stallard, elsewhere wrongly
given as Sparling.

478 (f) Stirling title] See also *Sharpe's
Letters*, ii. 381.

479 (b) Mr Humphreys] Scott's
argument is unsound as Humphreys
could not show 'a title which is ex facie
unexceptionable.' The family of Humphreys had long been resident in
America and the claimant, calling
himself William Alexander, came to
this country in 1757 and was served
heir to the 5th and last Earl of Stirling
who had died in 1739. On 2 May 1760
he presented a petition to the King

but on 10 Mar. 1762 the Committee of
Privileges of the House of Lords
ordered him to discontinue using the
title till his claim could be proved,
which he was unable to do. See
William Robertson, *Proceedings relating
to the peerage of Scotland*, Edinburgh,
1790, pp. 286, 289, 296, 299, 306. The
Alexander, about whom Scott is
writing, must have been his son. He
was tried for forgery in 1839.

480 (c) Robert Riddell] A slip for John
Riddell.

480 (d) one of their generals] William
Alexander (1726–83).

481 (a) To J. G. Lockhart] This letter
must be wrongly dated: (1) if date
were 22 Mar., the 'return of Mama . . .
yesterday' (p. 481) would be on 21 Mar.
but the *Journal* gives 22 Mar.; (2) all
Woodstock is finished (p. 482), but it was
not finished till 26 Mar. (*Journal* and
see below, pp. 286, 292.)

481 (e) person who possesses this secret]
J. Stallard.

484 (a) To John Gibson] In the original
there is a postscript to the part dated
24 Mar.: 'I find Lady Scott has left
another picture of a Scotch merry
making without a frame a copy from
De Witt that I wish to preserve on
account of the dress &c.' (Transcript
made by Gibson in NLS MS. 6080.) On
this picture, see my note to *SL* vi. 324
(f).

485 (c) on one of Glanville's narrations
a story of a David Hunter] Joseph
Glanvill, *Saducismus triumphatus*, 3rd ed.,
London, 1700, Second Part, pp. 161–2.

485 *n.* 1] There is an extract from
Croker's letter in Partington, *Post-bag*,
p. 224.

486 (c) Dutch lieutenant in Glanville]
Joseph Glanvill, *Saducismus triumphatus*,
3rd ed., London, 1700, Second Part,
pp. 130–1.

487 (f) cancell necessary in Wood-
stock] Ballantyne apparently ignored
this. In the copies I have examined
'pest' is retained.

489 (a) *moderamen inculpatæ tutelæ*]
A Scots law phrase. For meaning, see
Trayner, *Latin maxims*.

489 (a) *transeat cum cæteris erroribus*] See
my note to *SL* iii. 170 (b).

489 (b) To James Ballantyne] The postscript refers to the sale of *Woodstock*. The date of the postscript is 28 Mar. and the letter should have come at p. 493.

490 (d) To J. G. Lockhart] Abercrombie's report and Croker's letter are recorded in the *Journal* under 19 Mar. and this letter may have been begun about that date. In a letter to Ballantyne of 27 Mar. (above, p. 489) Scott gives a better account of Lady Scott, and he might have added to this letter to Lockhart this better news if the letter is correctly dated 27 Mar.

491 (f) Chancellor of Excheqr.] Frederick John Robinson.

492 (a) Voila beaucoup de bruit] This anecdote is told of General Montecuccoli (1609–80).

493 (a) To James Ballantyne] The words 'send you the receipts omitted' make the dating of letter doubtful, for Scott had recorded in his *Journal* under 27 Mar. that he had lodged his salary with Craig.

493 (b) A pox on both your houses] Shakespeare, *Romeo and Juliet*, III. 1.

494 (a) "the Gambol has been shewn"] By Thomas Parnell. See my note to *SL* vi. 242 (e).

494 (d) to speak bold words] Shakespeare, *Henry V*, III. 6: ' 'a uttered as prave 'ords at the pridge.'

494 (e) do a little more] See *SL* iv. 533.

496 (b) Campbell toasted Bonaparte] At a literary dinner in 1806 he gave the toast 'here is to Bonaparte; he has just shot a bookseller!' The bookseller was Palm who had been shot by Napoleon's orders. See Curwen, *History of booksellers*, p. 171. See also below, p. 508.

496 (c) And who can help it Dick] See above, p. 442.

497 n. 1] The 'good *Lady* Waldie . . .' is an interpolation in Scott's letter of 8 June 1831. See *SL* xii. 20 n. 2.

498 (a) To James Ballantyne] Date is 5 Apr.: (1) Scott recorded in his *Journal* on Wednesday, 29 Mar. that Gibson was going to London and he was there before and up to 11 Apr. negotiating the sale of *Woodstock*; (2)

'your family distress' refers to illness of Alexander Ballantyne's daughter, Christina Hogarth, who died on 10 Apr. See below, p. 507 n. The only Wednesday which fits is 5 Apr.

498 (f) The bird is flown] Shakespeare, *Cymbeline*, IV. 2. Scott had used same quotation, above, p. 16. See my note there.

500 (c) point devise the gentleman] Not Shakespeare, although he uses the phrase 'point-de-vice.' See also *OED*.

501 (a) *wind them* a *pirn*] Used in *The Antiquary*, chap. 39; *Rob Roy*, chap. 23; *The Bride of Lammermoor*, chap. 5, where Scott explains: 'proverbial for preparing a troublesome business for some person'; and *The Fair Maid of Perth*, chap. 25.

501 (b) But this is all nonsense again] Sterne, *Tristram Shandy*, Bk VI, chap. 5.

501 (d) For many a lad I loved] Charles Morris, *The toper's apology*. See *SL* iv. 31.

503 (e) *a ganging foot is aye getting*] *Kelly*, p. 11; Ramsay, *Proverbs*, p. 3. Also used in *Waverley*, chap. 41.

504 (b) To Colin Mackenzie] The date is the date of the postscript (p. 506), i.e. 14 Apr. See *Journal* under that date.

504 n. 2] The Yorkshire bookseller is Robinson of Hurst and Robinson.

505 n. 1] The word is Ferrier. James Ferrier, Principal Clerk of Session, was able to retire on 22 June. There had been trouble with Government over his pension. See above, pp. 65, 148, 149, 150, 314, 460, 465, 469.

506 (b) Sir Robert] Sir Robert Dundas of Beechwood.

506 (e) To Messrs. J. and T. Smith] The builders of the second portion of Abbotsford. According to the minutes of Scott's trustees, Scott was a debtor for £900 to the Smiths—a relatively small sum considering what they had already received.

507 (f) yesterday] Yesterday, by the date of the letter, would be 13 Apr. but Scott in his *Journal* says he heard the news on 12 Apr.

508 (c) To John Gibson] The correct date is 4 Apr. Scott is replying to

Gibson's letter of 3 Apr. (*Journal*). The letter which Scott wrote in reply to Gibson's letter of 12 Apr. (in footnote) is dated 15 Apr. It is in the Gibson transcripts (NLS MS. 6080) but not in his *Reminiscences* or in *SL*.

508 (c) Campbell] The bookseller was Palm. See my note to *SL* ix. 496 (b).

509 (a) To Crofton Croker] Scott is replying to a letter of 8 Apr., an extract from which is in Partington, *Post-bag*, p. 224.

509 (b) "Fair Kitty, blooming, young, and gay"] See my note to *SL* iii. 318 (c).

509 (c) God be with your labour, as Ophelia says] See my note to *SL* vi. 332 (b).

509 (e) Cranbourne Chase] See Index under Chafin (William).

509 n. 1] Lockhart's undated letter is in NLS (MS. 3903, ff. 233–5).

510 (c) Yours in trust] This must be a misreading for 'Yours in haste.'

VOLUME X

1 (b) marchings and countermarchings] Foote, *The Mayor of Garratt*, I. 1. See also *SL* viii. 333, ix. 85, 114, x. 84, xi. 317.

2 (d) I am getting as fat as a Norway seal] See my note to *SL* viii. 175 (b).

2 (d) Cuffe] Charles Marsh in his *The clubs of London*, London, 1828, i. 114–24, tells an amusing story of how the Duke of Rutland, when Lord Lieutenant of Ireland, knighted a Dublin innkeeper during a drunken frolic. The innkeeper, 'Sir Darby Monaghan', had to be induced, the next day, to give up his knighthood by a bribe of £250 per annum. 'Lady' Monaghan decided for the cash instead of the knighthood. This story is almost the same as Scott's except that Scott has substituted the name Cuffe for Monaghan. The story was probably circulated in different forms. See also *SL* vi. 164 n.

3 n. 1] For 'Elliot, Bart.' read 'Eliott, 7th Bart.' For '1791' read '1793.'

4 (b) To Charles Scott] Dated from the *Journal*, 18 Apr.: 'Must write to Charles seriously on the choice of his profession, and will do it now.'

10 (a) one of the Shortreeds] Robert, son of Robert Shortreed, Sheriff-Substitute.

11 (a) To James Ballantyne] The date is almost certainly 6 Apr.: (1) Scott is answering Ballantyne's letters of 3 and 5 Apr. and he would not delay till 22 Apr. to do so; (2) Scott's reference to Sophia and the baby—John Hugh and not Walter as the footnote implies—corresponds exactly to the entry in the

Journal for 6 Apr.; (3) the reference (p. 13) to Ballantyne's 'five hours' is a reply to his letter of 28 Mar. (*SL* ix. 493 n.).

11 n. 1] With redating of the letter the quotations from Lockhart's letters do not now apply. In any case, Scott's reference to young Walter in his *Journal* of 22 Apr. follows a letter from Lockhart of 19 Apr., as Anderson shows in his ed. of the *Journal*, p. 134, n. 3; and Scott could not reply on 22 Apr. to a letter from Lockhart written on 21 Apr.

12 (b) continued edition of the novels] *Tales and romances*, 1827: 8vo 7 vols.; 12mo 9 vols.; 18mo 7 vols.

13 (c) your five hours] See *SL* ix. 493 n. 1.

15 (e) answer . . . in Blackwoods] *The letters of E. B. Waverley, Esq. to M. Malagrowther, Esq.* in *Blackwood*, Vol. 19 (May 1826), pp. 596–607. The writer was David Robinson.

16 (c) Robinsons finessed too much] Hurst and Robinson over purchase of *Woodstock*.

16 (e) small editions] See my note to *SL* x. 12 (b).

17 (d–c) Longman & Co] But Archibald Constable & Co. appear first on title-page.

17 (e) in the copy sent] i.e. of *The life of Napoleon*.

19 (c) Henry Scott] As parliamentary candidate for Roxburghshire in succession to Sir Alexander Don.

21 n. 3] For 'a Mr. Hay' substitute

'Robert W. Hay, Under Secretary, Colonial Office.'

22 (f) To James Ballantyne] Already printed in *SL* IX. 439–40. The earlier should be cancelled.

22 (f) your still more wellcome accompt of the reception of Woodstock] See *Journal*, 29 Apr.

23 (a) My lot is not to die to-day] 'My date is not to die this Day.' *The whole prophecies of Scotland, England, France*, etc. Edinburgh, 1615. Cited in *Minstrelsy* (ed. Henderson), iv. 107.

23 (c) a review for Lockhart] Boaden's *Kemble* and Kelly's *Reminiscences* for *QR*.

23 (c–d) peering on in cases] This had already been printed (*SL* ix. 440) as 'peering in [to] cases.' Neither reading is satisfactory.

23 (f) your cousin is come down] She arrived on 4 May. (*Journal*.)

24 (e) A volume of sermons] See my note to *SL* ix. 396 (a).

24 *n*. 2] For 'John Aitken' read 'James Aitken.'

25 (e–f) I hope she [Mrs Jobson] will have no more alarms] See *SL* ix. 318.

26 (b) He has two or three very dingy looking Misses] I do not have a record of his family but the eldest, Anne Kline, married at Berne, 28 Oct. 1847, Francesco Moratti, Advocate at Florence (*Edinburgh Evening Courant*, 25 Nov. 1847, p. 2, c. 5) and another daughter wrote to *N. & Q.*, 3rd ser. Vol. 2 (15 Nov. 1862), p. 397.

26 (c) Jedburgh] This is a slip for Gattonside.

27 (f) dramatic article] Boaden's *Kemble* and Kelly's *Reminiscences* for *QR*.

27 *n*. 1] Reference to Lockhart is i. 22.

28 (a) that of the porch] i.e. the Stoic philosophy of Zeno.

29 (c) Sparling] It was later found that his name was Stallard.

29 (d) The fund consists . . .] The sum mentioned is correct but the rest of the statement is contrary to facts. George Morgan lent Wyrriott Owen £1,200 on a mortgage on his estates in 1778 (not 1787). It was agreed that when Owen repaid the money, Morgan was to

purchase government securities or an annuity for Madame Charpentier. Before this was done Wyrriott Owen died, disputes arose among the Owen family and, pending a settlement, the money was lodged in Chancery. Why Wyrriott Owen should create a 'fictitious loan' to provide an annuity for Madame Charpentier remains a mystery.

29 (e) Weber] Weber died on 5 June, i.e. just over three weeks after Scott wrote about him.

29 *n*. 2] For '*Cranbourne*' read '*Cranbourn*.'

29 *n*. 3 this whole affair] Grierson was too optimistic. By the time he wrote the *Life* he had discovered very little about the Chancery 'affair.'

30 (a) Nice Valour] Act III, sc. 1.

30 (e) advice of Messrs. Longman] Scott had asked Gibson to get Longman & Co.'s advice on the size of the edition of *Napoleon*. (*Sederunt Books*, 25 May 1826; NLS MS. 112.)

30 *n*. 1] In line 2, delete 'Evidently.'

31 (a) your freindly accomodation] The loan for equipping Walter, Scott's nephew.

31 (a) Terrys matter] See *Journal*, 13 May.

31 (b) the Glass House Co/] Edinburgh and Leith Glass Company. Scott held 50 shares. (*Trust Disposition*; NLS MS. 112, f. 59.)

32 (a) twenty six years] Should be 'twenty eight years.'

32 (b) a pipe for Fortunes finger] Shakespeare, *Hamlet*, III. 2.

33 (b) *the cabbin is convenient*] Ben Jonson, *Every man in his humour*, I. 4.

33 (d) absent[minded]] No need to expand, for 'absent' was the normal word for 'absent-mindedness' in Scott's day.

36 (a) *Duram Amice* . . .] See below, p. 477 and *n*.

38 (b–c) the Keirnans] James Kiernan of South Lambeth was Charles F. Dumergue's executor. Elizabeth Kiernan was also a beneficiary under Dumergue's will. The Kiernans were early friends of the Boultons of Soho.

38 (b–c) Smiths] This is the only reference I have found to this family, but it shows that Lady Scott had kept up some sort of connection with them. John Smith, Director of the East India Co., had sponsored Charles Carpenter when he went to India. There was a Smith, Rector of Fairford and Lord Downshire was also Viscount Fairford. John Smith (1784–1812), son of John Smith, writer in Kirkcudbright, died in Charles Carpenter's house in Salem on 18 Nov. 1812. Scott sent parcels to Charles Carpenter through Smith and Jenyns. I have not yet established the relationship, if any, of these different Smiths.

39 (a) the little dog] Ourisk. See below, p. 45.

39 (c) Chancel of Dryburgh Abbey] Or rather, the north transept.

40 (e) Stevenson] In John Gibson's transcripts (NLS MS. 6080) he has scored out 'Stevenson' and substituted 'Shannon.'

41 (a) on another occasion] The funeral of Lady Alvanley. See C. S. M. Lockhart, *Centenary memorial*, p. 78.

41 (b) Mrs. Tytler . . .] Biographical details of persons in this list will be found under their names in the Index.

42 (d) *Munus inane*] 'Empty, or unavailing funeral rites.' Scott might have added, as Waverley did when citing these words from Virgil (*Aeneid*, VI. 885–6): 'Yet why not class these acts of remembrance with other honours, with which affection, in all sects, pursues the memory of the dead?' (*Waverley*, chap. 69.)

44 (a) Eliphaz and Bildad] Two of Job's comforters. *Bible*, *Job* 2: 11 et seq.

47 (a) Miss Russells] Jane and Anne Russell of Ashiestiel.

47 (a) Walter left us last Wednesday] Should be 'last Thursday.'

47 (d) I have sent the proofs] Of the article on Kemble and Kelly for *QR*.

47 (e) Chambers . . . dramatic print] These are in *MPW* xx. 197 and 202 respectively. The Christian name of Chambers was not added and the dramatic print was not more fully explained.

49 (c) To R. P. Gillies] Date may be Thursday, 6 July. See *Journal* under that date.

51 (d) Dean of faculty] George Cranstoun, later in the year Lord Corehouse.

52 (d) we must not hollo . . .] In Denham's *Dictionary of quotations*, but without source. Not found in *Heywood*, *Ray*, *Kelly* or *Ramsay*, *Proverbs*. Also used below, pp. 58, 105 and in *SL* xi. 204, 207.

52 (e) help to make the haggis fat] *The haggis o' Dunbar*, st. [3], line 1: 'For to mak this Haggis fat.' In Sharpe, *Ballad book* [1823], p. 70.

54 (a) retain old 39] Up to this date the Trustees had failed to sell or let the house. It was to be put up again on 28 June and the Trustees were still prepared to let it. *Sederunt Books*, 25 May, 1826. (NLS MS. 112.)

55 (c) Letter from . . . Dr Lockhart] This is not in NLS and Scott, in his *Journal*, makes no reference to Mrs Dalziel.

55 (d) there was also probably a Housekeeper] The Duke of Hamilton, as Hereditary Keeper of Holyroodhouse, had a housekeeper. The office was held for over thirty years by Mrs Hannah Policy, who died there on 13 Apr. 1814 and who plays a part in the Introductory chapter to *The Fair Maid of Perth*.

55 n. 1] Lady Louisa's letter is in Stuart, *Selections*, pp. 227–30.

56 n. 1] On 25 May the Trustees authorized Cadell to publish three different eds. of *Tales and romances*, each of 1,500 copies. On 1 June Cadell offered £1,500, but the Trustees decided to consult Longman and Murray before accepting. (See *Sederunt Books*.) On 12 July the Trustees intimated that they had decided to print the editions themselves and Cadell recorded: 'On every view of the matter much pleased at not getting these books.' (NLS MS. 6080.)

57 n. 1] In line 7, 'the youth's recovery' refers to Capt. William Forbes, eldest son of Sir William Forbes, 7th Bart. of Pitsligo. He died unmarried in 1826.

58 (a) we must not hallo] See above, p. 52.

58 (d) Hay, smith at Glasgow] This should be Hay Smith, agent for a branch of the Bank of Scotland at Haddington. Alex. Fraser was appointed his successor in 1801, and his house (a large mansion) was sold by public roup in Edinburgh in June 1802.

58 *n.* 2] Delete this note, which alters Scott's meaning.

59 (a) the fellow who wanted a third share] At this time called Sparling but later his name was found to be Stallard. Handley appears to have treated Stallard unfairly and Charles, Scott's son, afterwards thought so.

59 (a) with a flea in his ear] *Heywood*, p. 61; *Ray*, p. 245. Also used in *Rob Roy*, chap. 23.

59 (c) I wrote to her yesterday] i.e. 12 June, but his letter to Sophia, above, p. 53, is dated 10 June.

63 (a) the Skenes] Probably 31 May. See *Journal* under 1 June.

63 (e) Mr Bailley] Isaac Bayley.

63 *n.* 1] See also *Ray*, p. 367; *Kelly*, p. 104; Ramsay, *Proverbs*, p. 19; and *Rob Roy*, chap. 34.

63 *n.* 2] Scott is not referring to the mansion but to the inn where Scott's carriage met the coach before it turned off the Gala road to go to Clovenfords.

64 (b–c) "Maladies of not marking"] Shakespeare, *II Henry IV*, I. 2.

64 *n.* 3] The line is a parody of 'Annie's gentle cares afford,' st. 2, line 2, of George Cranstoun's *Parody* of William Erskine's *Song*. (*The Court of Session garland*, Edinburgh, 1871, p. 118.) See also my note, *SL* xii. 157 (e).

65 *n.* 1] For 'This apparently referred' read 'This refers'.

65 *n.* 2] There is no record of this picture at Abbotsford.

67 (a) Dr Shaw] See my note to *SL* ix. 350 (a).

67 (c) young Davidoff] In a letter to Denis Davydov, 17 Apr. 1826, Scott said his young friend had been unwell during the Spring. (The letter is not in *SL*; original is in State Lenin Library.)

67 (d) Prince Hosseins tapestry] *Arabian Nights*. See my note to *SL* i. 229 (e).

67 *n.* 1] The first meeting was in 1817 and Scott did not attend the Club in 1831.

68 (c) O'Connors Child] An allusion to Campbell's poem of that name.

68 *n.* 1] Lockhart's letter of 17 June is in NLS (MS. 3903, ff. 19–23). He enclosed a letter from Rose of 17 May (MS. 3902, ff. 259–60) and an additional note by Rose (MS. 3902, ff. 266–7). The information supplied by Rose is a repetition of that supplied in his undated letter of 1822 in Partington, *Post-bag*, pp. 172–3. It is the 1822 letter which supplies the blank in *SL* vii. 185, not (obviously) this letter of 1826 as Grierson implies.

68 *n.* 3] See *Journal*, 25 June, 10 July and 12 Nov. 1826.

70 (a) unmusical voice] Cf. Lockhart's *Peter's letters*, ii. 81.

70 (b) Lady Waristoun] *A memorial of the conversion of Jean Livingston, Lady Waristoun, with an account of her carriage at her execution, July 1600*, 4to Edinburgh, 1827. This was edited by C. K. Sharpe and printed privately from a MS. in the handwriting of Robert Wodrow. The author is unknown.

70 (b–c) Boswell] For 'Boswell' read 'Birrel.' The actual murderer was Robert Weir, arrested three years later. Robert Birrel in his diary under 16 June 1603 recorded that Weir was 'broken on ane cart wheel wt ane coulter of ane pleuche in the hand of the hangman.' See Birrel's *Diarey* in *Fragments of Scotish history* [ed. by Sir John Graham Dalyell], 4to Edinburgh, 1798. Dugald Dalgetty refers to torture by 'breaking your limbs on the roue or wheel, with the coulter of a plough.' (*A legend of Montrose*, chap. 13.)

70 (d) I send you a curious manuscript] C. K. Sharpe edited *A pairt of the life of Lady Margaret Cuninghame*, 4to Edinburgh, Printed by James Ballantyne and Co., 1827. Scott's MS. is now in NLS (MS. 906).

70 (e) To James Ballantyne] Alexander Cowan was appointed Constable's trustee on 6 Mar. (*SL* ix. 439 (a).) This letter, therefore, is 6 Mar.

72 (b) *Conversations of the Canongate*] Chrystal Croftangry, in chap. 7, speaks of 'our conversations of the

Canongate,' but Scott wisely substituted 'Chronicles' in his title.

72 (b) trippily off the tongue] Shakespeare, *Hamlet*, III. 2: 'trippingly on the tongue.'

72 (d) To James Ballantyne] There is a letter to Ballantyne in *SL* xii. 456–7 which is dated (correctly I think) 8 July. As this date fits both letters, one must assume that this one was written in the morning before he had seen Terry and the one in *SL* xii. after he had seen him and invited him to dinner on Sunday.

72 (f) Geruselemme] Delete the query. This is Tasso's *Gerusalemme liberata* which Scott quoted in a footnote to *Napoleon* (*MPW* x. 252 n. 2). See *SL* xii. 456.

73 (c) I did impeticos the gratility] Shakespeare, *Twelfth Night*, II. 3.

73 (c) Chester Mysteries] Scott means Coventry mysteries by Thomas Sharp. See *SL* ix. 445 n.

73 n. 1] Delete.

75 (e) To John Gibson] The reference to Lord Newton shows that the date cannot be 1826. The correct date is 10 July 1827.

76 (a) Lord Newton] Alexander Irving, who became Lord Newton on 14 Dec. 1826, was acting as arbiter in disputes between trustees of James Ballantyne & Co. and trustees of Constable & Co.

77 (c) the political task] See *Journal*, 26 July.

77 (d) Then there are two books . . .] *Napoleon* and *Chronicles of the Canongate*; reviews of Kemble and Kelly for *QR* and of Galt's *Omen* for *Blackwood*.

77 (d) do something which as Falstaff says] Shakespeare, *II Henry IV*, V. 3.

78 (b) foreign office] This should be Colonial Office.

78 n. 1] This is the first mention of trouble caused by Messrs Abud & Sons.

78 n. 2] Alexander Irving was not Lord Newton at this time.

80 (c) Lady Anna Maria] Lady Anna Maria Elliot, eldest daughter of 1st Earl of Minto. She married Lt.-General Donkin in 1832.

82 (c) To C. K. Sharpe] This letter

cannot be a reply to Sharpe's letter in which he announced the death of James Kirkpatrick (*Sharpe's Letters*, ii. 369), for in it he sends his best respects to Lady Scott, showing that the letter was written a considerable time before May 1826. The reference in Scott's letter to Drumlanrig suggests that the date is 1824.

82 n. 1] Delete this note, which cannot be applicable.

83 (d) "Sufficient for the day is the *nonsense* thereof"] *Bible, Matthew* 6: 34: 'Sufficient unto the day is the evil thereof.'

84 (b) Major Sturgeon] Foote, *The Mayor of Garratt*, I. 1. See also *SL* viii. 333, ix. 85, 114, x. 1, xi. 317.

84 (f) carriers you know must talk of pack-saddle] See *SL* viii. 196.

84 (f) Cruet—Catch-up—Sauce] The name chosen was Cruet, but he died. See below, p. 148.

85 (b) Nuns at Kilkenny . . . in strict retreat] See above, pp. 2, 58. See also *Journal*, 9 Feb. and 1 Nov. 1826.

85 (b) The clamour much of boys and dogs] 'The clamour much, of men, and boys, and dogs.' Thomson, *The seasons*, *Summer*, line 377. Scott uses exactly same words in *Rob Roy*, chap. 5 and varies them in his *Journal*, 15 Mar. 1826, as 'tumult great of men and dogs.'

85 (b) Tilburina] Sheridan's *The critic*, III. 1. It is Puff, however, not Tilburina, who says to the confidant 'keep your madness in the background, if you please.'

85 (f) such a *howlering and a powlering*] Cf. *Waverley*, chap. 60: 'they hae been houlering and poulerying.'

86 n. 1] Scott probably means Denon. See above, p. 72 and note.

87 (c) a number of sums paid by me] Two of these, viz. Bell, Ironmonger, and [Stevenson], Bookbinder, were paid on 12 July. See *Journal* under that date.

89 (c) "a paradise on Yarrow"] *Mary Scot*, st. [3], line 8. In Ramsay, *Tea-table miscellany*, and *Johnson*, Vol. 1 (1787), No. 73.

89 (d) To Lady Abercorn] A letter should be placed under the date it is

finished, i.e. at p. 110 below. The words 'on a visit here' (p. 91) refer to his visit to Melville Castle, 25/26 Sept., and the letter should be dated 'Melville Castle, 26 Sept. 1826.'

90 *n.* 1] Delete. There is no evidence that Scott was thinking of *Macbeth*.

91 (e) a visit here to Lord & Lady Melville] On 25 Sept. See *Journal*.

92 (a–b) Scottish colleges] Scott heard of this on 17 Sept. See *Journal*.

92 (b) awkward tinkers] See *SL* i. 243 (c).

93 (c) calling spirits from the vast[y] deep] Shakespeare, *I Henry IV*, III. 1.

94 (b) To John Gibson] The date 1826 is impossible as Irving did not become Lord Newton till 14 Dec. 1826. The correct date is 1827.

94 *n.* 1] Delete 'doubtless.' Gibson, who knew all the facts, wrote on his transcript: 'A. Constable & Co's Cr'ors.' (NLS MS. 6080).

95 (b) To Lady Louisa Stuart] As Scott is answering her letter from Chiswick of 4 Sept., he could not write till 7 Sept. at the earliest.

95 (b) spout] Read 'sport.' (Corrected in *SL* xii. 491.)

95 *n.* 2] Lady Louisa's letter is in Stuart, *Selections*, pp. 233–7 and Partington, *Letter-books*, pp. 271–3.

97 (a) as Tony Lumpkin says] See my note to *SL* i. 524 (a).

97 (a) Clarissa . . . Lovelace] Characters in Richardson's *Clarissa Harlowe*.

98 (a) transcript of Galatian] Now in NLS. See *SL* ix. 446*n.*

99 *n.* 2] Derrick's work should be: *The image of Irelande . . . anno 1578*, 4to London, 1581.

100 (a) grand uncle] The birth of John Morritt's only child, Isabel Elizabeth, who married in 1846 7th Viscount Barrington.

100 (a) Mr. & Mrs. Impey] They were at Abbotsford, 6–8 Sept. (*Journal*.)

100 (d) Abney] See *SL* v. 178.

102 (e) valeat quantum valere potest] For as much as it is worth. A Scots law phrase. (Trayner, *Latin maxims*.) Also

used in *SL* x. 227, 437, xi. 281, 425, xii. 453, *The Heart of Mid-Lothian*, chap. 23, and *Nigel*, Introd. epistle.

102 (f) Friar Bacons Head] i.e. Time is—time was. See *SL* v. 446*n.*

103 *n.* 1] Sir John's letter of 11 Sept. is in Partington, *Letter-books*, pp. 130–1. Just over a year later the Duchess married Lt.-Col. Walter Frederick O'Reilly.

104 (f) put their name on the title page] Constable's name does, however, appear on the title-page of *Woodstock*.

105 (f) we must not hollow] See above, p. 52.

106 (a) foreign office] This should be Colonial Office.

106 (e) I am a witness upon a trial] See above, p. 84.

106 (e) Melville Castle] 25/26 Sept. See *Journal*.

108 (a) wilder flights of fancy] Scott is probably referring to Dryden. See *SL* viii. 247 *n.* 1 and my note.

109 (d) the foul fa the gear . . .] For 'oh' read 'o't.' *Kelly*, p. 296, gives this as a proverb. The wording varies in different versions of the song, *The blathrie o't*. See *Herd*, ii. 19–20; *Johnson*, Vol. 1 (1787), No. 33.

110 (d) I would prefer the Author of Waverley] The suggestion was adopted.

110 (e) Southeys history] *History of the Peninsular War*. See above, p. 105.

110 (f) I saw the Duke yesterday] See *Journal*, 4 Oct. Scott probably means 'where he ought to have been inspecting.' But the Duke was too young and was unqualified, in any case, for the duty. The review was on Rink Haugh at Fairnielee. See *Trans. Hawick Arch. Soc.*, 1915, p. 51. The Duke was present.

111 *n.* 1] Reference to Shylock is II. 5. Reference to Budge is II. 2.

113 (b) the former] Scott means the latter.

113 (e) foreign office] This should be Colonial Office.

114 (a) I have a work in great progress] *Chronicles of the Canongate*. Scott originally thought of publishing it for his sole profit under terms of the Trust

(see above, p. 86). He later scrupled about this; hence the arrangement that he should retain only £500.

114 *n*. 1] Gibson's letter of 9 Oct. is printed in Partington, *Letter-books*, pp. 359–60.

115 (c) a good comfortable house] 3 Walker Street.

116 (a) the gentlemen] John Gibson, on his own transcript now in NLS (MS. 6080), has written: 'This last paragraph referred to Abud and Hichens of London two Creditors who it was apprehended would use personal diligence and Sir W. was advised not to leave home till an arrangement was made.'

116 (e) Mr Robert Dundas] Third son of 2nd Viscount Melville and afterwards 4th Viscount. On his illness see above, pp. 91–2.

116 (f) Mr Hay of the Foreign Office.] Scott means 'of the Colonial Office.'

117 (d) To Robert Cadell] Scott wrote to John Gibson and on the same subject of number of copies. The letter is not in *SL* but there is a transcript of it in NLS (MS. 6080).

118 (b) *Jemmy jemmy linkumfeedleness*] 'Jemmy linkum feedle' is line 2 of a song beginning 'A Clerk I was in London gay' in George Colman the Younger's *Inkle and Yarico*. Scott also uses the phrase in sense of fine writing in the *Journal*, 6 Sept. 1826, but the reference is not obvious.

118 (d) three preliminary prefaces to the British drama] *The modern British drama*, 5 vols. la. 8vo London, William Miller, 1811. Scott's anonymous *Remarks on English tragedy*, *Remarks on English comedy* and *Remarks on English opera and farce* appeared in Vols. 1, 3 and 5 respectively.

119 (b) Aicheson] Spelt Acheson in *Journal*, 25 Oct. 1826. As Scott's spelling is erratic, I have indexed this under the usual spelling Aitchison.

120 (a) To Thomas Pringle] Pringle called on Scott on Monday, 23 Oct. when Scott was out. (*Journal*.) If Scott wrote the following day, 24 Oct. is correct.

120 (a) The curiosities . . . from the Cape] These were sent in 1823. (See *SL* viii. 18–19 and my note.) The heads of South African animals hang on the walls of the Entrance Hall at Abbotsford. These were identified for me by Dr Pringle, great-grand-nephew of Thomas Pringle, the donor.

120 (a) old [new] Gothick entrance hall] The amendment is uncalled-for. As Scott always said he detested modern Gothic it seems obvious that when he wrote 'old' he meant 'old'.

120 (d) an Attaché to some foreign mission] See *Journal*, 21 Oct. 1826.

120 *n*. 1] Delete 'Doubtless.'

121 (f) Lockhart and Sophia] But they did not go to Oxford. See *Journal*, 20 Nov.

122 (a) To Sir Thomas Lawrence] This letter cannot belong to 1826. I think the date should be Mar. 1820 or, possibly, Mar. 1821.

123 (a) Mr Carey] See David Kaser, *Messrs. Carey & Lea of Philadelphia*, Philadelphia, 1957, for an account of Scott's works published by them.

123 (d) a distinguishd American author] Washington Irving.

125 *n*. 1] See *Journal*, 15 Sept. 1826.

126 (a) Monday] i.e. 13 Nov., but Scott records in his *Journal* that they dined on Sunday, 12 Nov.

127 (e) To James Elwes] For 'Elwes' read 'Elmes'.

128 (f) Lockhart Sophia] But they did not go. See *Journal*, 20 Nov.

129 (c) To Mrs. Scott] Scott says (p. 130) that he is to see the Duke of York 'today.' No record of meeting in *Journal* under 14 Nov., but he met the Duke on 17 Nov. Date of letter is probably 17 Nov.

129 (d) Proctor] Who wanted admission to Drawing Institution, Edinburgh. See below, p. 155.

129 (d) offer] Read 'effort.'

130 (a) Lawrence] His portrait, as completed, was an indoor study.

131 (e) A battle [said Wellington] . . . is "very like a ball."] See *The Croker papers*, ed. L. J. Jennings, i. 352.

132 (a) I am in possession of his skull]
The skull is not at Abbotsford and it
seems to me to be impossible that
Scott could ever have possessed it.

132 *n.* 3] Scott had used same quotation
in the same connection in the *Journal*,
1 Nov.

132 *n.* 4] Moore's reply is in Partington, *Letter-books*, pp. 234-5.

133 (d) Lawrence] Scott's last sitting
to him was on Saturday, 18 Nov.
(*Journal*.)

134 (a) The cabbin is convenient]
Ben Jonson, *Every man in his humour*, I. 4.

134 (f) Captain Baillie] William
Alexander Baillie-Hamilton, 3rd son
of Archdeacon Charles Baillie-Hamilton.

137 (e) folly of Maxpopple] See
Journal, 9 Dec. 1826. Maxpoffle's
eldest son was appointed to the *Acorn*
and was drowned when the ship was
lost in 1828. See below, pp. 471, 473,
477.

139 (c) discha[r]ge his valour as
Sancho did his penance] Cervantes,
Don Quixote, Pt II, chaps. 71-2 (Lock-
hart's ed., 1822, v. 296, 307).

140 (c) Commander in Chief] Duke
of York.

141 (a) No new attachment . . .] Logan,
On the death of a young lady, st. [9], lines
1-2.

141 *n.* 3] Lockhart's letter of 18 Dec.
could not have reached Scott by 20
Dec., and it does not mention John
Home. Scott must be answering an
earlier letter.

142 (a) John Home] Review of Mackenzie's *Works of John Home* for *QR*
June 1827.

142 (a) The faculty election] See above,
p. 139, 139 *n.* 1.

142 (e) raise a corps of light infantry]
Scott's godsons at this time were:
Spencer Scott Compton, Walter Scott
Dumergue, Walter Scott Hughes,
Walter Scott Seton-Karr and Walter
Scott Terry.

142 *n.* 1] For '*Cranbourne*' read '*Cranbourn*.'

144 (f) Prince Hosiens tapestry] In

Arabian Nights. See my note to *SL* i.
229 (e).

145 (c–d) last week] This should be
'last month.'

145 *n.* 1] Delete this note. He is William
Alexander Baillie-Hamilton. See my
note to *SL* x. 134 (f). (Gerard was too
young to be a Captain in 1826.)

146 (e) Lady Charlotte] Lady Charlotte Home, 3rd daughter of 9th Earl
of Home, who had married the Ven.
Charles Baillie-Hamilton in 1797.

147 (d) To Maria Edgeworth] This
seems to be the 'half letter' which Scott
sent on 15 May 1827. (See below,
p. 212.) It should, therefore, have been
dated 15 May and have been printed
below, p. 210.

147 (e) Huxley of the 71st] Should be
Huxley of the 70th.

148 (d) dogs of other days] A common
expression in Macpherson's *Ossian*.

149] A letter to Archibald Constable,
5 Jan. 1827 (*Archibald Constable*, iii.
434–5), should have been included
here; with references to relative letters,
ibid. iii. 432–4, and Constable's reply
to Scott's letter of 5 Jan., ibid. iii.
435–6.

149 (d) to write to Mr Canning] He
did so on 16 Jan. but the letter is not
extant. See below, p. 163, *n.* 3.

149 *n.* 2] Sophia's letter is in Partington,
Letter-books, pp. 147–8.

150 (b) the Skenes] James Skene and
his wife. See *Journal*, 5 Jan. 1827.

150 (c) Win Jenkins] Smollett, *Humphry
Clinker*. See *SL* vii. 258 and my note.

151 (d) secretary of our Ambassador]
Lord Grenville was Ambassador at
Paris. His Secretary was H. C. J.
Hamilton.

151 *n.* 1] Although it is stated here that
Scott left Walker Street on 30 June,
a letter of 7 July with this address is
printed below, p. 248. Actually Scott
finally left Walker Street on 11 July
(*Journal*).

152 (d) the mettle of their pasture]
Shakespeare, *Henry V*, III. 1.

154 (a) seams will slit and elbows will
out] Foote, *The Maid of Bath*, I. 1:

'Stitches tear, and elbows will out.'
Also quoted in *SL* xi. 24 and *Journal*,
30 Nov. 1825 and Oct. 1831.

154 *n.* 2] The title of Burns's poem is
usually given as *Lines on meeting with
Lord Daer*.

155 (b) Sir Colquhoun Grant] It was,
however, Sir Colquhoun Grant who was
appointed Colonel in succession to the
Duke of Cumberland.

155 (b) *Incumbite remis*] See my note to
SL ix. 5 (c).

155 (c) the Academy] The Drawing
Institution, founded 1 Dec. 1824.
'Academy' had originally been suggested for its title. Scott held two shares
and was a Director.

155 (d–e) beautiful study by Landseer]
'A scene at Abbotsford,' by Sir Edwin
Landseer, was exhibited at the British
Institution, 1827, No. 313, and at the
Royal Institution, Edinburgh, 1828,
No. 30. There is an engraving, by West-
wood, of this painting in *The Keepsake
for 1829* and in *Heath's gallery of British
engravings*, Vol. 2 (1836).

155 (e) Lady Charlotte] Lady Charlotte Stopford, sister of the Duke of
Buccleuch. She died the following year.

156 (d) your new situation] The Duke
had recently succeeded the Duke of
York as Commander-in-Chief.

156 *n.* 1] Scott's letter to Ballantyne is
in *Archibald Constable*, iii. 437. It was
sent by Ballantyne to Constable with
a covering letter dated 2 Feb. (ibid. iii.
436–7). Scott's letter, therefore, cannot
be later than 2 Feb. Constable's letter
of 20 (24?) Jan., is printed ibid. iii. 435-
6.

158 (b) cadet of artillery] This is a slip.
Scott, later in the letter and in the
Journal, shows that he was referring to
the Corps of Royal Engineers, not to the
Royal Artillery.

158 *n.* 1] This was James Henry Skene,
born in 1812.

159 (d) Oil Gas] Scott was later, along
with James Gibson Craig, chosen to go
to London. See *Journal*, 16 Nov. 1827.
While the Oil-Gas Company was
promoting this new bill in Parliament
there appeared in Edinburgh an
anonymous pamphlet [by Daniel Ellis]
entitled *Considerations relative to nuisance
in coal-gas works*, 1828, in which
references are made to Scott at pp.
34–7.

159 *n.* 2] Simpson, it should be noted,
took a special interest in gas lighting
and in 1819 he registered a patent for
conveying gas to the burners. To the
works listed here add *Letters to Sir
Walter Scott . . . on . . . the visit . . . of
. . . George IV*, Edinburgh, 1822. It
should also be noted that Scott did not
consult Simpson on *Waverley* as this
footnote implies.

160 (a) Only yesterday] According to
the *Journal*, the dinner party was on
12 Feb. This letter would be written in
instalments. Sir Adam's brother is Col.
James Ferguson.

160 (b) Justice Clerk] David Boyle.

160 (c) John Murray] John Archibald
Murray, afterwards Sir John and
a judge as Lord Murray.

161 (b) your family disaster] The death
of Sharpe's sister, Susan, who had
married, as her third husband, S. F. S.
Perkins of Orton Hall and Sutton
Coldfield; not James Kirkpatrick as
given in the footnote.

161 (c–d) patience cousin & shufle the
cards] Cervantes, *Don Quixote*. See my
note to *SL* ii. 404 (a).

161 (e) shot my fools bolt] *Ray*, pp. 140,
356; *Kelly*, p. 303; Ramsay, *Proverbs*,
p. 2. Also used below, p. 454.

161 (e) Sir W. Arbuthnot] Scott prob-
ably thinks he may be elected Lord
Provost for the third time, but Walter
Brown was elected.

161 *n.* 1] Delete. James Kirkpatrick
died on 20 July 1825. The note in
Sharpe's Letters, ii. 387 is wrong.

161 *n.* 2] On returning the book
Sharpe expressed the hope that Scott
would edit a new ed. and offered
a frontispiece (*Sharpe's Letters*, ii. 388–
9, 391–2). The original drawing is at
Abbotsford (not on view to tourists). It
is reproduced in *Etchings by C. K.
Sharpe*, 4to Edinburgh, 1869, p. 145
and plate 15. See also *SL* xi. 1 (b) and
my note.

162 (c) as well as we *dow*] See *SL* x.
491 *n.* and my note.

163 (a) if I do not mar the choice tale

in telling it] Shakespeare, *King Lear*, I. 4: 'mar a curious tale in telling it.'

166 (a–b) To the Editor of the Edinburgh Weekly Journal] This should not have been included in *SL*. It is an article, not a letter. See my note to *SL* i. 158 (b).

166 (b) I am no orator] Shakespeare, *Julius Caesar*, III. 2.

167 (b) as Poins's] Shakespeare, *I Henry IV*, I. 2.

167 n. 1] Balmanno went to U.S.A. A lock of Scott's hair presented to him by J. B. S. Morritt is now at Abbotsford. Although *The Bijou* has 1828 on the title-page, it was published in Oct. 1827.

168 (a) Beau Tibbs] Goldsmith, *The citizen of the world*, Letter 54.

168 n. 1] *The friend of humanity, and the knife grinder*, st. [6], line 1. Quoted on title-page of *Nigel* and in *MPW* iv. 352. In Francis Douce's copy of the *Poetry of the Anti-Jacobin*, presented to him by one of the contributors, with a key to authors, this parody is attributed to George Ellis. See *N. & Q*. Vol. 12 (3 Nov. 1855), pp. 343–4.

169 (a) Sophia Charlotte] Should be Charlotte Sophia.

171 (a) Sheets of Leyden] *Memoir of John Leyden* for *Miscellaneous prose works* (1827), Vol. 4.

171 (c) the Secretary of State] George Canning. See above, pp. 163–6 and notes.

171 (e) snowd up here] A snow-storm began all over Scotland on 3 Mar., said to be the worst since Feb. 1799. See *Ann. Reg.* 1827, Chron., pp. 47–50.

171 n. 2] The date is correct. *Cramond Brig* was advertised for 6 Mar. *Edinburgh Evening Courant*, 5th Mar.

172 (a) the habit of my exercise] See my note to *SL* ii. 252 (a).

172 (b) I would put a few lines together] He did so in Introd. to the *Chronicles of the Canongate*.

172 n. 2] Lady Louisa's letter of 1 Mar. is in Stuart, *Selections*, pp. 237–40. There is also an extract in Partington, *Post-bag*, pp. 238–9.

173 (b) mask . . . as thin as my aunt Dinah's] Sterne, *Tristram Shandy*, Bk VIII, chap. 3.

173 (e) Jack Meggots monkey which died [?]] Delete query. Hoadly, *The suspicious husband*, I. 3.

173 n. 1] Delete, being no longer applicable.

174 (d) Two gentlemen of Cambridge] Henry Parr Hamilton and John Philips Higman, Fellows of Trinity Coll., Cambridge. Scott is passing on the information he had just received in a letter from George A. Browne of 1 Mar. (Partington, *Letter-books*, p. 116, where it is wrongly dated 1829.) Browne had written to Scott in 1820.

174 (f) say some few things about the Confession] See above, p. 172 and my note.

175 (a) Morritt] See above, p. 173 n.

177 (a) Robin & Bobbin were *two* big bellied men] 'Robin and Bobbin, two great belley'd men, / They ate more victuals than threescore men.' See I. and P. Opie, *The Oxford dictionary of nursery rhymes*, Clarendon Press, 1973, p. 373. See also *The Antiquary*, chap. 16.

177 (b) doth appropinque an end] Butler, *Hudibras*, Pt I, Canto III, line 590.

177 (c) Tickell [?]] It is explained in *SL* xii. 491 that this is Tickletoby's mare in *Tristram Shandy*, Bk III, chap. 36.

178 (b) if a great man . . .] Scott attributes this saying to Swift. See below, p. 196.

179 (b) Cadwallader] A character in Foote's *The Author*. But it was Mrs Cadwallader who was 'the worst teller of a story' (Act II, sc. 1).

180 (a) a key to some of the gardens] See below, p. 216.

183 (c) The quarrel is a pretty quarrel] Sheridan, *The rivals*, IV. 3.

183 (c) We daily are jogging] Quoted very inaccurately from 'Song' in George Farquhar's *The stage-coach*, Act II. Scott refers to this play in chap. 1 of *The Heart of Mid-Lothian* and quotes part of the song as motto to Croftangry's introduction, chap. 3, in *Chronicles of the Canongate*.

183 *n.* 1] St. [2], lines 3–4 of the ballad also called *Edwin and Angelina*.

184 (b) undertaking] *Foreign Quarterly Review*.

184 (d) The Lamb] John Hugh Lockhart's pet lamb at Chiefswood. See also below, p. 214.

184 (e) which of my bad parts] Shakespeare, *Much ado about nothing*, V. 2.

185 (c) Follow this Lord . . .] Shakespeare, *Hamlet*, II. 2.

185 *n.* 1] See also below, p. 208, 208 *n.* 1 and my note.

186 *n.* 1] In 1820 he married Miss Young of Harburn. While Shortt was helping Scott with his *Napoleon*, Shortt's father-in-law (Alexander Young) was helping Scott with his financial affairs. The family connection explains a lot.

187 (d) Dryburgh] Given as a mistake for Drygrange in *SL* xii. 491. Scott's mistake is obvious and Curle's footnote was unnecessary.

187 *n.* 1] There are earlier sources. See *Kelly*, p. 12. Scott's text is an exact quotation from Beaumont and Fletcher, *The Knight of the Burning Pestle* (1613), Act I.

188 (b) the mighty huntsman before the Lord] *Bible*, Genesis 10: 9.

188 (b) Tom Tack he comd . . .] Charles Dibdin, *Tom Tack's ghost*, st. [3], line 1.

188 (d) So go thou and do likewise] *Bible*, Luke 10: 37: 'Go, and do likewise.'

189 (d) Dryburgh] Drygrange. See above, p. 187.

189 (e) My grass parks were set] Scott usually says 'let', but 'set' is also correct, though unusual, and he uses the latter again in *SL* xi. 238. The rents went to the Trustees.

190 (b) Sir Herbert Taylor is still in statu quo] He had been Military Secretary at the Horse Guards to the Duke of York since 1820. The Duke died in Jan. 1827 and Taylor continued in the office under the new Commander-in-Chief, the Duke of Wellington.

190 (d–e) London] This should be Dublin.

191 (a) Tom Tack] See my note to *SL* x. 188 (b).

192 (c) the Solicitor] John Hope.

192 (c) Hey day Hey day] The first line may be Scott's own exclamation. The second line is virtually the same as a line in Dryden's *The Duke of Guise*, III. 1: 'I know not what to say, nor what to think.'

192 (d) bursting in ignorance] Shakespeare, *Hamlet*, I. 4: 'burst in ignorance.' Also used in footnote to *Woodstock*, chap. 28.

193 (b) Will Wimble] The *Spectator*, No. 108.

193 (c) Congreve sort of direction] An allusion to Sir William Congreve's rockets which Scott had seen in 1820 (*SL* vi. 161, 167).

193 *n.* 1] He may be Edward Burrard, Capt. of 1st Regt of Foot Guards (Grenadier Guards).

194 (c) I have known many great men] See reference to Swift, below, p. 196.

194 (d) a spell of money] This should be 'a spill of money.'

194 (e) The Chancellor] Lord Eldon.

194 (e) "I cannot chuse but cry . . ."] Scott may be thinking of Pillage (impersonated by Col. Fainwell), Periwinkle's steward, who says 'my tears will flow when I think of my master.' (Mrs Centlivre, *A bold stroke for a wife*, IV. 3.)

196 (a) Canning] It is strange that Scott should write in such terms of Canning after the reconciliation. See above, pp. 192, 192 *n.*, 194.

196 (b) For Dean Swift . . . says] Swift expresses this sentiment, though not exactly in these words, in letters of 1731 and 1733. See Swift's *Works*, ed. Scott, 2nd ed., xvii. 391, 393–4, 430, xviii. 66. See also above, pp. 178, 194.

196 (d) the hunting thing] The review of Chafin's *Cranbourn Chase*. It was never written.

196 (e) Lansdowne] Lansdowne was in the Cabinet without office, May–July, and became Home Secretary in July, but Lauderdale was not appointed a Minister.

196 (f) The Advocate] Sir William Rae who disapproved of the Malachi letters.

197 (a) like the Lilliputian poet. In amaze—Lost I gaze] Though attributed here to Swift, the quotation is from Pope's *To Quinbus Flestrin*, lines 1–2. The poem was included in Scott's *Swift*, 2nd ed., xiii. 365.

197 (d) how will the Mighty be fallen] *Bible, II Samuel* 1: 19, 25, 27.

197 *n*. 1] In *Works* (1795), i. 121.

197 *n*. 2] The papers were received from Bernadotte, i.e. Charles XIV of Sweden. For Scott's correspondence with Blomfield and an analysis of the papers, see N. E. Enkvist, *Sir Walter Scott, Lord Bloomfield, and Bernadotte*, in *Studia Neophilologica*, Vol. 32 (1960), pp. 18–29.

198 (d) To James Ballantyne] This letter is earlier than 28 Apr., for on 28 Apr. Scott says in his *Journal*: 'I cannot get an answer from J. Ballantyne' and on 2 May (below, p. 199) he asks for the *third* time.

198 *n*. 4] Substitute *n*. 1 from p. 209 below.

199 (b) Border Antiquities . . . Culloden papers] Neither was included in *Misc. prose works* (1827). The *Eyrbiggia-Saga* was used for 'Buckram & binding.'

201 (c) To J. G. Lockhart] The letter which Scott is answering is in Partington, *Letter-books*, pp. 151–3.

201 *n*. 4] For '*Cranbourne*' read '*Cranbourn.*'

203 *n*. 1] Reference should be to II Samuel 3: 39.

205 (b) Rectus in Curia] See *SL* ix. 299.

206 (c) Hogg] Robert Hogg. See Index.

206 (e) I return the Sheets] Proofs of his article on John Home for *QR*. See Lockhart's letter of 6 May in Partington, *Letter-books*, p. 151.

206 (e) *pieds de mouche*] See *SL* v. 279 and my note.

207 (f) Forest article] The review (never finished) of Chafin's *Cranbourn chase*. 'Gillies' and 'Forest article' here correspond to 'Gillies' and 'hunting matter' below, p. 210.

207 *n*. 1] Delete. 'Fall back, fall edge'

is a proverb used elsewhere in the *Journal*, in the novels and in *SL* ix. 442. *Ray*, p. 243.

208 *n*. 1] I have an original letter from Scott to Hogg, 8 Feb. 1827, on this subject. This letter (which is not in *SL*) is printed with the omission of the first sentence in Mrs Garden's *Memorials of James Hogg*, pp. 223–4, where it is misdated 3 Feb.

209 (e) as Harry Wynde fought] See *Tales of a grandfather*, chap. 17 (*MPW* xxii. 244–6). He is the Henry Smith or Hal of the Wynd in *The Fair Maid of Perth*. See Scott's note to chap. 18 of the novel.

210 (a) your hunting matter] Review of Chafin's *Cranbourn Chase*. It was never written.

210 (d) like a flapper] Swift. See my note to *SL* ii. 213 (c).

210 (d–e) Davidow . . . Colyer] Sir David Brewster met them at Edgeworthstown and mentions them in a letter from that place written on 17 July 1827. See Gordon, *Home life of Sir David Brewster*, 3rd ed., p. 76. After their return to Russia, Colyer visited Maria Edgeworth in London in 1830. See *Maria Edgeworth: letters from England, 1813–1844*, ed. by Christina Colvin, Oxford, 1971, pp. 450–1.

211 (a) like the old Frenchman] In a letter of 11 Nov. 1824 W. S. Rose had written to Scott: 'I remember an old Anglicised Frenchman who, having been cured of a tapeworm, used to observe sometimes "that he began to miss his worm".' See Partington, *Postbag*, p. 202, and *Journal*, 5 Mar. 1827.

211 (d) hiding in a napkin her fine talent] A combination of *Bible, Matthew* 25: 25 and *Luke* 19: 20.

212 (c) the enclosed half letter] Printed above, pp. 147–8. It should have been printed here along with the letter of 15 May.

212 (f) "Poor Wounded Hussar"] Walter, so nicknamed by Scott after Campbell's *The wounded hussar*.

212 (f) the Squire] See above, p. 60 *n*.

214 (a) The sheep] John Hugh Lockhart's pet lamb at Chiefswood. See above, p. 184.

214 (c) John Dicksons son] David Dickson of Hartree, Lockhart's first cousin. For relationship see Index under Dickson (David) and Dickson (John).

219 (c) The rogues fly from me like quicksilver] Shakespeare, *II Henry IV*, II. 4.

219 (e) Irish Historians] Charles O'Conor's *Rerum Hibernicarum scriptores veteres.* See above, p. 144, 144 *n.*

220 (c) Sir George Rose] He acquired the library of the last Lord Marchmont. See *SL* xi. 492 *n.*

220 (d) of which a copy] Read 'of which [if] a copy.'

220 *n.* 2] *The historie and life of King James the Sext,* etc. See also my notes to *SL* i. 294 (d) and *SL* vii. 87 (d).

221 (e) a prophets chamber] A 'chamber in the wall.' *Bible, II Kings* 4: 10.

225 (b) To Mrs. Scott] The contents show that 1827 is impossible. The correct date is 1829. On Col. Thackwell, and the colonelcy, see *SL* xi. 179, 207.

227 (a) valeat quod valere potest] 'quod' should be 'quantum.' See above, p. 102.

228 (b) the Saxons] For explanation see *Journal,* 1 June.

230 *n.* 2] Her letter of 16 July is in Clara Burdett Patterson's *Angela Burdett-Coutts,* London, 1953, pp. 23–4. The beautiful silver-gilt inkstand is still at Abbotsford.

231 (a) alternated] Suggested reading in *SL* xii. 491 is 'attended.'

231 (b–c) a work] *Life of Napoleon.*

232 (b) *Bathurst*] There is a long extract from his letter of 2 July in Partington, *Post-bag,* pp. 236–7.

232 (d) To John Swinton] At this time he had no territorial designation, having sold Broadmeadows in 1825. In 1850 he became John Campbell Swinton of Kimmerghame.

233 (b) I will write Sir James] He did. See below, p. 246.

235 (b) Jane and she] Scott means Jane and Jessie [Mrs Huxley].

237 (c) the stout old Lord Mayor] Sir William Walworth, Lord Mayor of London in 1381, knighted for killing Wat Tyler.

237 *n.* 1] This note does not explain points raised by Scott. For the full text of Lady Louisa's letter, see Stuart, *Selections,* pp. 243–8, or Partington, *Letter-books,* pp. 274–6. In reference to Emperor Francis, Scott in 2nd ed. (i. 294) changed 'son' to 'brother.' But Scott was originally right and Lady Louisa wrong and in *MPW* viii. 273 the relationship was omitted. On Gordon, Scott made no alteration in the 2nd ed. but Lockhart in *MPW* viii. 307 *n.* 2 added a note that he was informed that the person concerned was Sheffield, not Gordon.

239 (e–f) lands and beeves] Shakespeare, *II Henry IV,* III. 2.

240 (b) A plague of both your houses] Shakespeare, *Romeo and Juliet,* III. 1.

240 (c) will do fast enough of itself] Shakespeare, *Merry wives of Windsor,* IV. 1.

240 (c) like Win Jenkins] In Smollett's *Humphry Clinker.* See my note to *SL* i. 337 (c).

240 *n.* 1] In line 2, 'F. A.' should be 'F. W.'

241 (c) Now Age has clawed me] Shakespeare, *Hamlet,* V. 1.

243 (b) Trinculo's solution] Shakespeare, *The Tempest,* II. 2. Said by Stephano, not by Trinculo.

245 (c) the Witch corner] Case O in alcove with the bow window.

245 *n.* 2] The address has the error '19 Hussars' for '15 Hussars.'

246 (a) Miss Wells] Walter had called her 'odious.' See above, p. 234 *n.*

246 (f) I answerd Swinton] See above, p. 232.

247 *n.* 1] For Stuart's inquiry about *Matthew Wald,* see above, p. 233.

248 (a) Lady Foulis] This was Mrs Munro. Scott uses the old Scottish custom of calling the wife of a laird by his territorial title prefixed by the courtesy 'Lady.'

248 *n.* 1] In line 6, for '141' read '145.' (Reference is p. 145 in 1st ed. and p. 141 in 2nd ed.) In lines 6–7, for

'Katherine Munro, Lady Fowlis, by birth Katherine Ross of Balnagowan' read 'Mrs Munro of Foulis (*née* Katherine Ross of Balnagowan)'.

249 *n.* 1] In line 25, 'one for Scott' should be 'two for Scott.' The two medals are still at Abbotsford. Similar extracts from the Carlyle letters are in Partington, *Post-bag*, p. 252.

252 *n.* 1] Delete and substitute: The name of Goetz's castle in *Goetz von Berlichingen* by Goethe.

254 (b) a step of fence [?]] Without seeing the MS. I cannot guess what these words are. But Scott is referring to recording of Kirkness in Record of Tailzies. See below, p. 282 and my note.

254 (b) Your miniature] This has not been found at Abbotsford.

255 (e) For Robert Cadell] This letter must be wrongly dated. It probably should be 17 July: (1) Scott first records the emus in his *Journal* for 17 July; (2) on same day he would write to Cadell (this letter); (3) Cadell replied on 18 July (*SL* x. 255 *n.* 2); (4) Scott answered Cadell's letter on 19 July (*SL* x. 258–9, where it is wrongly dated 17 July).

255 (e) Mr Harper] See my note to *SL* vi. 288 (a).

258 (b) wise fellow enough, go to] An amalgamation of two phrases—'I am a wise fellow' and 'a rich fellow enough, go to' in Shakespeare's *Much ado about nothing*, IV. 2.

258 (c) dumple as you like] Massinger, *A new way to pay old debts*, III. 2.

258 (c) Si populus vult decipi] 'Populus vult decipi; decipiatur' has been attributed to Cardinal Carafa, Legate of Paul IV. See Benham's *Book of quotations*, p. 639.

258 (c) the proverb is somewhat musty] Shakespeare, *Hamlet*, III. 2.

258 (e) To Robert Cadell] The date should be 19 July. See my note to *SL* x. 255 (e).

259 (d) To Joanna Baillie] This letter should have been dated 22 July. See *Journal* under that date.

260 (b) Via the curtain that shadowed Borgia!] Chapman, *Eastward hoe*, II. 2.

Used also in *Nigel*, chap. 17, and *Woodstock*, chap. 28, and parodied in *The Monastery*, chap. 37.

260 (c–d) Miss Douglas] Harriet Douglas. See my note to *SL* xi. 124 *n.* 2.

261 (a) the spur which the clear spirit] Milton, *Lycidas*, line 70. See also *SL* i. 165, 165 *n.*

261 (b) Elihu] *Bible, Job* 32: 18–20.

261 (c) I have forgot my misdemeanours about Allan Ramsay] Scott is reported to have said at the Theatrical Fund dinner, 23 Feb.: 'His own pastoral was not fit for the stage, but it has its own admirers . . . and it is not without merits of a very peculiar kind.' *An account of the first Edinburgh Theatrical Fund dinner*, Edinburgh, 1827, p. 21.

261 (e) Mr. Carr] It is odd that Scott makes no reference to his having dined with the Carrs at Frognal, Hampstead, on 9 May 1815. For an interesting account of the dinner, see Lucy Aikin's *Memoirs*, London, 1864, pp. 99–100.

262 (a) my Great Grandmother] Christian Shaw of Bargarran who married Rev. John Rutherford, minister of Yarrow. The Christian Shaw who was accused of witchcraft was presumably a niece of Scott's great-grandmother. See Robert Chambers, *Domestic annals*, iii. 167–74. There is a MS. on her alleged witchcraft in NLS (MS. 3278, f. 27).

263 (d) It is not lost that a friend gets] Ramsay, *Proverbs*, p. 40: 'It is not tint that a friend gets.'

264 (f) covenanters Croft] Haughhead, which Scott wanted Richardson to buy. See above, pp. 109, 110.

265 (a) "in command"] Walter Scott of Satchell's *A true history* [*Watts Bellanden*], line 8.

265 (b–c) To John Gibson] Missing portions of this letter are in John Gibson's transcripts (NLS MS. 6080). One relates to the emus and another to a meeting with Lady Compton in Edinburgh. The latter is important.

265 (c) letter of the 24th] Transfer note on p. 266 to this page.

266 (b) To John Gibson] The date of this letter is 27 Oct. Before it was mutilated the ending ran: 'But Mr

More and you will judge about this. I only rejoice I have open sea before me and we will see what we can do. I am dear Sir your obliged & faithful Walter Scott Abbotsford 27 Oct.' (John Gibson's transcript in NLS MS. 6080.)

266 *n.* 1] Transfer this note to the previous page to which it rightly belongs.

267 (c) I inclose a note to Mr Dickson] This is printed below, pp. 297-8.

267 (d) I am always vexd] See below, pp. 289, 298. These three references to Dickson show that the date 26 July could not be right.

267 (f) Mr Marr] This should be Mr More.

268 (d) Dr. Shaw] See my note to *SL* ix. 350 (a).

273 (c) Allan] Sir William Allan drew illustrations for the frontispiece and title-page vignette of Vol. 1. Scott is presumably referring to the former: 'Hugh Littlejohn at his grandfather's gate.'

273 (f) set a stout heart to a stay brae] See *Kelly*, p. 287.

274 (a) loss of worlds gear] Burns. See my note to *SL* iii. 490 (e).

274 (a) *sursum corda*] 'Lift up your hearts.' The opening words of the priest when celebrating mass. Also quoted in the *Journal*, 14 Feb. 1826.

274 (a) Walter & Jane] But they did not come. Walter came alone to Edinburgh on 12 Nov. See *Journal*, 12 Nov.

274 (c) the memorable barn] 'The Doctor's barn', part of the original farm steading of Abbotsford, in which Scott found the MS. of *Waverley* (above, p. 273 *n.* 2). The barn was destroyed by Hope-Scott.

275 (c) Mr Dickinson] For Dickinson's plan, see *Journal*, 5 Sept. 1827.

275 (d) My friend] The context would point to Gibson, but Scott is referring to Cowan. See above, p. 272.

275 (d) Allan the Upholsterer] There were two of this name: Francis Allan, 9 Hanover Street, and John Allan, 54 George Street. Scott is probably referring to the former as it is known that he dealt with that firm.

275 *n.* 1] I think Scott has mixed up two plays. Premium in Sheridan's *The school for scandal*, could not be called a hard man; but in Foote's *The minor*, II. 1, in a similar scene involving money-lenders, the actual words 'a hard man' are applied to Statute.

276 (a) Monteath] Robert Monteath, King's Forester, wrote two letters to Scott this year (NLS MS. 3905, ff. 113, 245).

278 (a) To the editor of the Edinburgh Weekly Journal] This should not have been included in *SL*. It is an article, not a letter. See my note to *SL* i. 158 (b).

282 (c) Mr Clephanes indirect offer] This is Andrew Clephane as is shown by the letter from Lady Compton, 18 Sept. 1827 (NLS MS. 3905, ff. 28-9). The offer had been made through her mother's cousin, Richard Lundin. Scott refers to the recording of the Kirkness entail in his letter to John Gibson, 26 July 1827, where he wrongly gives Clephane as Henry instead of Andrew. This portion of the letter is omitted in the version in *SL* x. 265-6, but it is in the Gibson transcript in NLS (MS. 6080).

283 *n.* 1] The index figure for this note should be at 'with' in line 8 of this page.

284 (a) Prince Houssein's tapestry] In *Arabian Nights*. See my note to *SL* i. 229 (e).

284 (b) my little Godson] Walter Scott Hughes, son of Mrs Hughes's son John.

285 *n.* 2] Though dated 1828 it was not issued till 1829. A photolithoprinted ed. was published by S. R. Publishers Ltd. in 1969.

286 (a) fancies [?]] Read 'frisks.' See p. 287.

286 (b) Warkworth] On 8 Oct. the Duchess of Northumberland presented to Scott a copy of her *Castles of Alnwick, & Warkworth, &c. From sketches by C. F. Duchess of Northumberland. 1823*, privately printed at London, *1824*. Hence Scott's desire to visit Warkworth.

287 (d) to Lord Ravensworth] At Ravensworth Castle, south of Gateshead, co. Durham.

287 n. 1] See also *SL* i. 496 and my note.

288 (a) hobbleshew] See below, p. 309 n.

288 (b) the Duke] Wellington, now Commander-in-Chief.

288 (d–e) Little Walter] The first is Walter Scott Lockhart; the second is Walter, Tom's son, who has gone to India.

288 (e) Sir Adam] Scott breakfasted with him at Huntlyburn the following day. See *Journal*, 10 Oct.

289 (b) Sir Herbert] Sir Herbert Taylor.

289 (d) He has promised . . . a visit] The Duke of Wellington never visited Scotland.

290 (e) unknown correspondent of Lincluden] Unfortunately the Duchess in her letter (NLS MS. 3905, f. 267) does not say who this correspondent is.

291 (c) Patersons Lodgings] In *Edinburgh Post Office Directory*, 1827–8, there are four: Mrs Paterson, 131 Princes Street; Mrs Ann Paterson, 4 Charles Street; Mrs Paterson, 18 Lothian Street; and Mrs William Paterson, 31 Cumberland Street. Scott is probably referring to the first.

291 (f) Ld. Register] William Dundas, Lord Clerk Register.

292 (a) Register of Sasines] This is apparently a slip for Register of Entails.

292 n.] Delete sentence beginning 'See letter to Mackenzie.' The reference should be to *SL* viii. 208–9, 208 n., 270, 344 (e).

294 (b) Chronicles] Second series of *Chronicles of the Canongate*.

294 (c) Mrs Dorset or Miss Hutton] To whom copies of *Misc. prose works* were to be sent. See above, p. 272.

294 (e) To the Rev. J. M. Turner] Scott records in his *Journal* that he wrote on 28 Oct., showing, as elsewhere, a discrepancy in dating.

296 n. 1] The reference should be to *SL* ii. 266–9.

298 (c) having shown some ill humour] See above, pp. 267, 289.

298 (e) To J. G. Lockhart] If entries in the *Journal* are correct, this letter should be dated 31 Oct. Scott says (p. 300) 'Sir Adam goes . . . today to Bowhill and tomorrow departs for Dumfries.' In the *Journal* these two facts are recorded respectively under 31 Oct. and 1 Nov.

298 (e) did impeticos the gratility] Shakespeare, *Twelfth Night*, II. 3.

299 (a) the *pendant*] *Essay on landscape gardening* published in *QR* for Mar. 1828.

299 (d) The old prelate] William Van Mildert, Bishop of Durham, 1826–36.

300 (b) No fool like an old fool] See *SL* vi. 29.

300 (d) Lipsius] See my note to *SL* iv. 201 (e).

300 (d) the book upon Homer] Lockhart in his letter of 25 Oct. (NLS MS. 3904, ff. 90–1) does not say what book this is.

301 (a) To James Ballantyne] This letter probably refers to *Tales of a grandfather*, 1st ser., for at Vol. 2, p. 234, occurs account of Battle of Flodden. But there is no footnote.

301 (c) To John Gibson] This letter, before it was mutilated, had the date 31 Nov. 1827 [*sic for* 31 Oct.]. Gibson called at Abbotsford on 31 Oct. with news of Abud (see *Journal*) and Scott, on further reflection, must have written this letter at Bowhill. The portion cut off was the conventional ending and signature, and 'Abbotsford 31 November 1827.' (John Gibson transcript in NLS MS. 6080.)

306 (a) To J. G. Lockhart] By the dates in the *Journal* Scott must have written this letter on the morning of 12 Nov. '*Monday night*' (p. 308) refers to the same day.

307 n. 1] Lady Shelley's letter is in Partington, *Letter-books*, pp. 276–8.

309 n. 1] This note should have been at p. 288 where the word is first used.

312 (c–d) these chosen . . . on the principle of Gil Blas] See my note to *SL* vi. 402 (b).

314 (d) these copyrights] Exact details of the copyrights owned by Constable and the dates when acquired are given in 'Assignation by Alexander Cowan, Esq. to the Trustees and Mr Cadell of

the various copyrights of the Waverley Novels & Scott's poetry purchased by them jointly in December 1827.' This document is dated 25 Apr. 1831 and was recorded in the Books of Council and Session, 2 May. (*Sederunt Books*; NLS MS. 113, ff. 217–24.)

315 (c) Suspension] Scott's Bill of Suspension in Court of Session to stay proceedings of Abud & Sons. See *Journal*, 12 Nov.

315 (d) luxuriant as Mr Puff says] Sheridan, *The critic*, II. 1: 'I know I am luxuriant.'

315 (d) to Mackenzies to dinner] No mention of this in the *Journal*. The 'Mackenzies' must mean family of Henry Mackenzie, for Scott says in his entry for 20 Nov. that he had called on Colin Mackenzie who was ill.

316 (d–e) house of Mourning as in the House of Feasting] *Bible, Ecclesiastes* 7: 2.

317 (c) Solomon in all his glory] *Bible, Matthew* 6: 29 and *Luke* 12: 27.

317 n. 1] Delete this note. The article which Scott is sending to Lockhart is 'On planting waste lands' for *QR* of Oct. 1827. The second part on Steuart —'On ornamental and landscape gardening'—appeared in *QR* for Mar. 1828. Scott, in this letter, is not referring to Steuart's *Planter's guide*, which did not come out till the following year, but to his 1824 report to the Highland Society (*SL* viii. 138–40, 148–50, 149 n.) to which he refers in the *Journal*, 31 Aug. By the time the article was printed it was possible to put the 1828 work at the head as if it were one of the works being reviewed.

318 (b) God bless the good Earl of Shrewsbury] Lines 3–4 of the burthen of a song beginning 'In Lancashire where I was born' in *The Syren*, 3rd ed., London, 1739, p. 322.

319 n. 1] Delete this note and see above, p. 318 n. 1.

320 (c) Pacolet] Probably an allusion to Pacolet who acted as Norna's messenger in *The Pirate*.

320 (d) To things that were long enough ago] See *SL* viii. 90 and my note.

320 n. 2] In line 7, for 'Miss Stuart' read 'Miss Belsches.' Williamina was never Miss Stuart. Two letters from Scott to Lady Jane Stuart, 26 July and 25 Aug. 1829, are in St. Andrews Univ. Lib. They are not in *SL*.

323 n. 1] Reference to Pope should be to *Moral essays, Epistle II*, lines 17–20.

323 n. 2] Croker was editing *The Christmas box*. When it came out at the end of 1827 it contained *Bonnets of Bonnie Dundee*. Did Scott change his mind and give this to him?

324 n. 1] For 'Viscount Dudley' read 'Earl Dudley.' When Scott wrote this letter the 4th Viscount had become 1st Earl.

325 (c) To John Gibson] This letter, written in the morning of 4 Dec., was read to the Trustees on the same day and was transcribed in their Minutes. (NLS MS. 112.)

325 (c) Mr Bells opinion] The 'Case for the Trustees' submitted to George Joseph Bell and his 'Opinion', dated 4 Dec. 1827, are both transcribed in the Minutes of the Trustees for 4 Dec. At the meeting the Trustees agreed to rank Scott's personal debts on an equality with company debts. (NLS MS. 112.)

325 n. 2] In last line, for 'July' read 'January.'

326 (c) 5 Shandwick Place] Should be 6.

326 (c) To Alexander Young] One cannot help associating this letter with *The surgeon's daughter*.

326 n. 1] In line 5, 'their uncle' is John James Erskine, brother of Lord Kinedder.

327 (c) Miss Helen Erskine] She dined with Scott on 19 Nov. (*Journal*) and may have discussed the Indian trip then.

328 (b) To J. G. Lockhart] Already printed under wrong date in *SL* ix. 328.

328 (b) Molieres life] Scott's article appeared in *The Foreign Quarterly Review*, Vol. 2, Feb. 1828 (*MPW* xvii. 137–215).

328 (c) grin and howl] Read 'girn and howl.'

328 *n.* 2] *Janus; or, the Edinburgh Literary Almanack*, [Edinburgh] 1826, pp. 58–97.

329 (a) To C. K. Sharpe] From the contents the year must be 1828. The letter is not in *Sharpe's Letters* but his reply is printed, ibid. ii. 403–5, where it is wrongly dated 1827. Scott required the information for the Magnum Opus ed. of *The Bride of Lammermoor* which he returned to Cadell on 28 Dec. 1828 (*SL* xi. 80).

329 *n.* 1] For '1827' read '1828.'

330 *n.* 2] Richard Dalton, of Andover, Hants, married Jane Wilkinson, sister of Margaret who married John Hughes, son of Mrs Hughes of Uffington. He is probably the 'Mr. Dalton of Bury St. Edmunds.' The lock of hair and Dalton's letter are still at Abbotsford.

331 (f) You will recognize Johnie] The frontispiece to Vol. 1 of first ser. of *Tales of a grandfather* was: 'Hugh Littlejohn at his grandfather's gate,' drawn by William Allan and engraved by J. Horsburgh.

332 (b) Mrs. Hemans— "Twas a trumpet's lofty sound"] This is *The captive knight*, a ballad by Mrs Hemans. It was published, with music by her sister, by Willis & Co. and was dedicated to Scott. There were at least 33 editions.

332 (c) "Roland the brave"] Thomas Campbell, *The brave Roland*. See also below, p. 499.

332 (c) "immortal verse"] Milton, *L'allegro*, line 137.

332 (c) Mrs. Arkwright] Mrs Arkwright was the wife of Robert Arkwright, grandson (not son) of Sir Richard Arkwright.

333 (e–f) Well betides] 'He that well bides well betides' is a Scottish proverb. See *Kelly*, p. 138.

333 *n.* 1] Many of Miss Browne's settings were published by I. Willis & Co.

334 (a) my Mother whips me] Cervantes, *Don Quixote*. See my note to *SL* iv. 388 (b).

334 (c) Duchess of Buckingham] See above, p. 283 and below, pp. 418, 447.

334 (d) Charles is . . . studying history & public law] Privately. His name does not appear as a student at the University classes.

334 (e) To John Gibson] The beginning of this letter refers to the loan by Gibson for equipment for Walter, Scott's nephew. Gibson was reluctant to accept repayment, holding that all money should go into the Trustees' funds.

335 (b) John Thomson] There is no creditor of the name of John Thomson in the *Sederunt Books* (NLS MS. 112) but John Stevenson is listed as a creditor for £110. 13*s.* 2*d.*, which is virtually the same as Scott's '£112, or thereabouts.' Scott had already paid this month £70 to John Stevenson (*Journal*, 6 Dec. 1827) and on 11 Mar. 1828 he paid £11, being 'Ballance of old accot John Stevenson' (*Journal*, 11 Mar. 1828). He paid Stevenson £96 in Sept. 1829 (*SL* xi. 249).

335 (c) Preux] This must be a misreading for 'Presd.'

338 (a) the righ[t]-hand file] Shakespeare, *Coriolanus*, II. 1.

338 (c) Vicar of Wakefields ejaculation] Probably a reference to chap. 19 of Goldsmith's *The Vicar of Wakefield*.

338 (c–d) The Rising in the North Countrie] Scott invents this name from an old ballad. See Index under Ballads. See also below, p. 393.

339 (e) Good luck for the field today] The sale of copyrights.

341 (e) his brothers may tire of his demands] By an agreement of 28 Feb. 1827 Cadell's brother, Hew Francis Cadell, and his brother-in-law George W. Mylne, became owners of Cadell & Co. Robert Cadell was merely the manager with as alary of £400 per annum. The co-partnery was dissolved on 28 Aug. 1829, when Robert Cadell became sole owner of the firm. (NLS MS. 6080.) Scott makes it clearer here than he does anywhere else in *SL* that Cadell had no money and that he was acting only on behalf of his relatives.

344 (d) As Mrs Quickly says] Shakespeare, *Merry wives of Windsor*, I. 4: 'indeed, la; but I'll ne'er put my finger in the fire, and need not.'

346 (e) To Mrs. Hughes] The date should be 21 Dec. Scott writes of going

to Arniston (p. 348) and this visit was on 22 Dec. (*Journal*), and in a letter to Lockhart of 21 Dec. (above, p. 344) he says: 'I inclose a few lines to good Mrs Hughes.'

347 (a) Taffy was a Welshman] The first line and first half of second line come from a nursery rhyme. The remainder is a parody of 'Convey, the wise it call' (Shakespeare, *Merry wives of Windsor*, I. 3).

347 (b) "Old Harden's Crest"] For fuller quotation, see *SL* iv. 529.

349 (a) I have written to the Duke of Wellington] Not in *SL*, but the Duke, in his letter of 29 Dec., refers to it (below, p. 353 *n*.).

349 (a) old Sir Davie] Sir David Baird.

349 (b) the Fergusson family] In the *Trust Disposition* Isabella, Mary and Margaret Ferguson were creditors for £4,200.

349 *n*. 1] For 'Colonel John Ferguson' read 'Colonel James Ferguson.'

350 (c) Edinburgh] This should be Abbotsford. The date is correct for Scott was at Jane's Wood on Christmas day (*Journal*).

350 (d) To G. H. Gordon] This letter, though dated 27 Dec. 1827, should not have been separated from the 'enclosed' (line 4) which is dated 2 Jan. 1828 and given separately on p. 352. The two portions should have been printed together under 2 Jan. 1828.

351 (d) my English guests] Mrs George Ellis and her nephew and niece, Col. and Mrs Charles Ellis. See *Journal*, 25 Dec.

352 *n*. 1] A fuller extract from Gordon's letter is in Partington, *Post-bag*, pp. 249–50. Delete last line.

354 (b) Mrs. George Ellis with her Nephew] The wife of her nephew was also there. See my note to *SL* x. 351 (d).

355 (a) that damnd kilted fellow] In the engraved frontispiece Douglas (a Lowlander) is shown wearing a High-land dress.

355 (f) Napoleon] Scott misunderstood Cadell. See *Journal*, 11 Jan.

356 (a) like a thief in the night] Bible, *I Thessalonians* 5: 2; and *II Peter* 3: 10.

356 (d) Saint Ronans Well] This refers to the collected ed., *Tales and romances*, in three formats, 7 vols., 8vo, 9 vols., 12mo and 7 vols., 18mo, containing the novels from *St Ronan's Well* to *Woodstock*, published in 1827. See *Journal*, 8 and 11 Jan. 1828.

356 (d) Tuesday at five o'clock] i.e. a week later, 15 Jan. See *Journal* under that date.

357 (a) summer & winter this proposal] There is a Scottish proverb, 'I am not obliged to summer and winter it' (i.e. both tell and retell a story) in *Kelly*, p. 219, and Ramsay, *Proverbs*, p. 34. But here Scott means 'ponder over it' and he uses the phrase with the same meaning in *The Antiquary*, chap. 44.

357 *n*. 1] This is the form in *Nigel* and in *Kelly*, p. 252, where he explains it as meaning 'Make your best of it.' Kelly says it does not correspond to the English proverb, 'Make a hog or dog of it,' which means 'bring it either to one use or another.' Grierson's explanation does not apply to Scott's form 'Kirk *and* Mill' but to another, and more usual form, 'Kirk *or* a Mill.' The Gaelic form is 'Make a kiln and a mill of it.' See Donald Mackintosh, *Gaelic proverbs*, D. 27.

358 (c) The young laird] William Forbes Mackenzie, Colin's eldest son.

360 (d) leave a stormy land] Thomas Campbell, *Lord Ullin's daughter*, st. [10], lines 1–2.

360 (e) The saddle would then be laid on the right horse] A Scottish proverb. See *Kelly*, p. 281; Ramsay, *Proverbs* p. 53.

361 (c) the late additional family misfortune] The death of 1st Baron Douglas on 26 Dec. following on death of the Dowager Duchess of Buccleuch on 21 Nov.

361 (d) Eckford] The outgoing minister was George Gray. His successor was Joseph Yair. Scott is wrong about the patronage. The Crown was patron.

361 (e) my poor protege] Rev. George Thomson.

362 (b) Bannatyne Club] The Duke of Buccleuch had been elected on 31 Jan. 1827 but the Duke of Hamilton was not elected till 9 Feb. 1828.

363 (b) Thomas Thomson] He was appointed a Principal Clerk in Feb. 1828 in succession to Colin Mackenzie.

364 (e) To James Ballantyne] From contents this should be dated 21 Jan. See *Journal* under that date.

364 (f) get on with him] 'him' must be a misreading for 'them.'

364 (f) Jamie Balfour] See my note to *SL* ii. 240 (a).

367 (d) T'is a rich smoke as Bobadil says] Although Bobadil in Jonson's *Every man in his humour* (III. 2) praises tobacco, he does not use the words 'a rich smoke.' For 'T'is' read ''Tis.'

367 (e) think of you when I take Tobacco] 'Think of this and take Tobacco' is the refrain of the song beginning 'Tobacco is but an Indian weed.' In D'Urfey, *Wit and mirth*, Vol. 3 (1719), p. 292. The words vary in different collections.

370 (e) rectus in curia] See *SL* ix. 299.

370 (e) blindness of those who will not see] *Heywood*, p. 154; Ramsay, *Proverbs*, p. 64.

370 n. 1] Crito is said to be Charles Knight. See Oliphant, *William Blackwood*, i. 221.

371 (c) To Miss Wagner] This letter was printed in the *Nineteenth Century*, Vol. 37 (Feb. 1895), pp. 271-2. Another letter, 3 Mar. 1828, which is not in *SL*, is printed ibid., p. 273.

372 (f) The wild romance of life was done] Logan, *On the death of a young lady*, st. [13], lines 3-4.

373 (a) Fifteen years] Actually thirteen and a half years.

373 (c) To J. G. Lockhart] Though dated 5 Feb., Scott says in his *Journal* under 4 Feb. that he wrote to Lockhart on that day.

373 (c) Horace Smith . . . seeing him once at Breakfast] Barron Field and Horace Smith breakfasted with Scott on 8 July 1827. (*New Monthly Mag.* Vol. 82 (Feb. 1848), pp. 250-7.) Not recorded in the *Journal*.

374 (e) Athenœum] See above, p. 370 *n.*

376 (a) letter from Sophia] Must be 'for Sophia.'

376 n. 1] Her letter is in Stuart, *Selections*, pp. 253-6.

376 notes 2-3] These, taken together, show that the critic was Cadell, although Ballantyne had to take the blame.

378 (f) february] Scott means Mar.

380 n. 2] See also *Journal*, 7 Feb. 1828. Cooper's water colour, 'The death of Keeldar,' is recorded as being in the Breakfast Parlour at Abbotsford in 1840. It has since disappeared.

381 (d) Nell Squeal] Scott had just bought the portrait of Nell Gwyn. See *Journal*, 8 Feb. The portrait is in a private room at Abbotsford.

381 (f) Tannachy Tullock] I have not traced this anecdote but in 1795 there was an Alexander Tulloch of Tannachie. 'Tullock' should be 'Tulloch.'

383 (b) as Puss wears whiskers] A dig at Walter's mustachios.

383 (c) Dukes levee] Wellington, appointed Commander-in-Chief in Jan. 1827, soon resigned but was reappointed, Aug. 1827-Jan. 1828.

385 (e) like Jeremy] William Congreve, *Love for love*, II. 1.

387 (c) go forth] Corrected to go 'north' in *SL* xii. 491.

388 (b) all Dickie instead of Robbie] Scott may simply mean that Gillies will be 'Dicky' Gillies (i.e. of unsound mind); or he may be alluding to Dicky Pearce, the Earl of Suffolk's fool. (See Scott's *Swift*, 2nd ed., xv. 212.) Gillies's forenames were Robert Pearse.

389 (b) Glengarrys fate] When travelling on the *Stirling Castle* from Inverness to Glasgow the vessel went aground at Corran near Fort William and he was killed when he leaped from the stranded ship, 14 Jan. 1828.

389 (d) expect me about the 20th] But Scott did not set off till 3 Apr. See *Journal*, 3 Apr.

389 (d) Knighton] For rumour of his disgrace, see above, pp. 310, 310 *n.*, 318.

390 (b) like Gil Blas] The allusion is to 'brother Commissaires,' not to 'place of eating.' See my note to *SL* vi. 402 (b).

390 (e) Wu[r]z] Read 'Wu[rt]z'.

390 (f) journey to London] See my note to *SL* x. 389 (d).

391 (c) Dignus dignis es] See *SL* xii. 491.

391 *n.* 1] Freeling was created a baronet on 18 Feb. Hence Scott was able to congratulate him in a letter of 27 Feb.

393 (a) Rising in the North Countrye] See above, p. 338 and my note.

393 (c) I have a house o' my ain] Scott must be thinking of 'I hae a wife o' my ain.'

393 (d) Millar of Dalswinton] See below, p. 401 *n.*

394 (a) Cooper's beautiful sketch] See my note to *SL* x. 380 *n.* 2.

395 (a) Callaghan] George Callaghan, Paymaster of 15th Hussars.

395 *n.* 1] It is suggested (correctly) in *SL* xii. 491 that the Black cat is an actual cat (and not Miss Wells), mentioned above, p. 383 and *n.*

396 (c) Laing whose acuteness] The quality of 'acuteness' is applied to him also in *SL* xii. 24, in *The Antiquary*, chap. 11, and in the 'Advertisement' to *The Pirate*.

401 *n.* 2] In line 4, for '*Post*' read '*Chronicle*'. (Correction in *SL* xii. 491.)

403 (b–c) faint heart] *Ray*, p. 134; *Kelly*, p. 139; Ramsay, *Proverbs*, p. 18; *Guy Mannering*, chap. 52.

403 *n.* 2] Cadell's letter is in Partington, *Letter-books*, pp. 361–2.

404 (c) uses of adversity] Shakespeare, *As you like it*, II. 1.

405 (c) particular case in all others] Alter punctuation to read 'particular case. In all others I avoid.' (Correction in *SL* xii. 491.)

407 (e) Diccon the Reaver] See my note to *SL* vii. 287 (e).

407 *n.* 3] There is an interesting letter from Scott to Willie Scott of Maxpoffle, 13 Nov. 1827, on this road through Darnick (NLS MS. 2890, ff. 66–7). It is not in *SL*.

410 (d) his grandfather] Alexander Nasmyth.

413 (e) To Robert Peel] Date is probably Fiday, 18 Apr. as Scott had an interview with Peel on 20 Apr. (*Journal*.)

413 *n.* 1] The election was for Collectorship of Cess for Roxburghshire. See *Journal* for 15 and 25 Apr. 1828 and Anderson's notes. The candidates were Samuel Oliver and Gilbert Eliott.

414 *n.* 1] Letter of 17 May. See *Journal*, 18 May.

415 (a) Miss N.] Miss Jane Nicolson, whose evidence was wanted for Chancery money.

416 *n.* 1] Scott wrote to Cooper on 9 May. The letter, which is not in *SL*, is in *The correspondence of J. F. Cooper*, New York, 1932, i. 143.

417 (c) Seged of Ethiopia] Samuel Johnson, *The Rambler*, No. 205, 3 Mar. 1752.

418 (b) what I can do for Allan Cunningham] To get cadetships for his sons.

418 (c) dogs for the Duchess] Duchess of Buckingham. See above, pp. 283, 334 and below, p. 447.

418 (e) I met Sir William Knighton to day] On 8 May according to the *Journal*. This would date the letter 8 May. Note Scott's ending 'your most obedient Servant.'

419 (c) Waverley] The passage to which Scott took exception is on pp. 151–2 of the *Library manual*.

419 (e) To Robert Cadell] Date is taken from the *Journal*.

420 (a) my contribution] *Proceedings in the court-martial held upon John, Master of Sinclair*. See above, p. 285 and *n.* 2 and my note.

420 (b) a high person] Sir William Knighton. About the dedication of the Magnum Opus to the King. See *Journal*, 11 May.

420 (c) Hamptonian frolic] Dining with Walter at his quarters in Hampton Court. See *Journal*, 25 May 1828. Wordsworth, Tom Moore and Rogers were of the party but Miss Rogers is not mentioned.

420 (d) like the Derby Dillie] *The loves of the triangles*, Canto I, lines 178–9 [by Frere or Canning] in *The Anti-Jacobin*: 'So down thy hill, romantic Ashbourn glides / The Derby dilly, carrying *three* INSIDES.' The couplet was

used for the motto of chap. 1 of *The Heart of Mid-Lothian.*

422 (b) the American] J. Fenimore Cooper.

422 (c–d) Mr Temple . . . Mr Temple] Scott's wording is ambiguous. The first 'Mr Temple' is the Major of the 15th Hussars who became Sir Grenville Temple. The second 'Mr Temple' is his younger brother John who was proposing marriage. For biographical details see Index.

423 (d) grass grow under my feet] See *SL* vi. 179.

426 (b) To C. K. Sharpe] The date is about 25 May 1829. Scott in a letter to Cadell, 8 Mar. 1829, in *SL* xi. 147, said he would send the epitaph at Dunnottar from Abbotsford. He failed to find it and on his return to Edinburgh wrote this letter about 25 May 1829. It is in *Sharpe's Letters*, ii. 398, where it is wrongly dated 'Nov. 1827.' The letter was delivered by a servant who brought back a letter from Sharpe, which is in ibid. ii. 399, and must be of same date. Scott replied in a letter dated 26 May (ibid. ii. 399, but not in *SL*).

426 (c) "Gie a thing . . ."] See J. O. Halliwell-Phillipps, *The nursery rhymes of England* [Percy Soc.], London, 1842, p. 84. Also used as a proverb. See *Ray*, p. 146; *Kelly*, p. 120; Ramsay, *Proverbs*, p. 21.

426 (d) "Cloud of Witnesses"] *Cloud of witnesses . . . last speeches and testimonies of those who have suffered for the truth in Scotland since the year 1680*, Edinburgh, 1810.

426 (f) Lords & dukes] *Gentle river, gentle river*, st. [3], lines 1 and 4. In Percy's *Reliques*.

427 (e) *post tantum temporis*] After so long a time. A Scots law phrase. See Trayner, *Latin maxims.*

430 *n.* 2] Delete 'probably.'

431 *n.* 1] Delete this note. The correct reading of the text is 'If Peele will bind his brows.' Scott is quoting Shakespeare's *II Henry IV*, I. 1: 'Now bind my brows with iron.' The same quotation, with the same meaning, is used in *SL* ix. 253.

431 *n.* 2] Miss Shelley was Fanny who became the Hon. Mrs George Edgcumbe. See *The diary of Frances, Lady Shelley*, London, 1912–13, ii. 314–15.

433 *n.* 2] There are extracts from Hobhouse's letters of 20 June and 14 July in Partington, *Post-bag*, pp. 253–4.

434 (a) Cupar in Angus] i.e. Coupar Angus in Perthshire.

434 *n.* 1] The complete text of Peel's reply is in Partington, *Letter-books*, pp. 42–4.

436 (b) the death of John Charpentier] Recent research among records in France has failed to find the date of his death.

437 (b) valeat quantum] See above, p. 102.

439 (a) Hosack] Not mentioned in the *Journal*. See Index.

441 (a) Incumbite fortiter remis] See my note to *SL* ix. 5 (c).

441 (d) my last from Sussex place] This letter is not in *SL*.

441 (f)–442 (a) Anne is sitting for her picture] This portrait hangs in the Dining Room at Abbotsford.

443 (d) Friend Williams falls . . .] A parody of Swift's *Epigram* (Scott's *Swift*, 2nd ed., xii. 455): 'Friend Rundle fell, with grievous bump, / Upon his reverential rump.' Swift's lines are themselves a parody of a couplet common in Jacobite songs.

444 (b) *Graia ex urbe*] Perhaps 'Graia . . . ab urbe,' Virgil, *Aeneid*, VI. 97. Also used below, p. 454. For longer quotation, see *SL* ii. 235.

447 (b–c) His account of Boscobel] *The Boscobel tracts*, ed. by John Hughes, Edinburgh, 1830.

447 (d) My two dogs] For Duchess of Buckingham. See above, pp. 283, 334, 418.

448 (a) two appointments] For his sons, Joseph Davy and Alexander.

448 (b) caught two trouts] Scott had already used the simile in his *Journal*, 23 May 1828.

448 (d) potent grave & reverend Seignors] Shakespeare, *Othello*, I. 3.

450 (c) *ower the water*] Over Firth of Forth for meeting of the Blair-Adam Club. Probably an allusion to the Jacobite song, *Over the water to Charlie*.

451 (a) cast of Shakespeares tomb and bust] The alcove in which the bust sat was not a cast of Shakespeare's tomb. For the bust, see *SL* iv. 289, 295–6.

451 (b) Mr Loch] John Loch. See *Journal*, 23 May 1828. His brother is presumably William Loch of the Bengal Civil Service.

451 (c) Prince Houssains tapestry] In *Arabian Nights*. See my note to *SL* i. 229 (e).

451 (e) To J. H. Markland] Date cannot be 29 June as Scott was at Blair-Adam on that day. Date is probably 27 June, which would correspond to 'two days ago' (p. 452) and entry in *Journal* for 25 June.

452 (c) Our new Rector] Rev. Thomas Sheepshanks. See above, pp. 443, 445 and below, p. 459.

454 (c) *Graia ex urbe*] See my note to *SL* x. 444 (b).

454 (d–e) *I shoot . . . a fool's bolt*] See above, p. 161.

457 (a) Foushie] Fushiebridge, Midlothian, on the Edinburgh to Galashiels road, where there was an inn.

463 (b) in Grahames hand] John Graham Gilbert, artist. Scott may be referring to one of several portraits called 'Portrait of a Gentleman' exhibited at the Institution for the Encouragement of the Fine Arts or at the Scottish Academy this year.

466 (a) To J. G. Lockhart] Begun at Edinburgh 9 and finished at Abbotsford 14 July. 'I wrote myself blind and sick last night' (p. 466) refers to his letter of 8 July (above, p. 458).

466 n. 1] The portion relating to Mary Queen of Scots is from a letter of 4 Aug. 1828 (below, pp. 483–4). The portion relating to Lockhart's *Burns* is not in *SL*.

467 (e) "I pass like night . . ."] Coleridge, *The ancient mariner*, line 586.

468 (a) desperate Duel] About three weeks after this letter was written Mrs Hughes of Uffington visited Abbotsford and Scott gave her an account of the duel. See Hughes, *Letters*, pp. 294–5.

468 (c) I got a letter from Mr. Markland] Which he answered on 14 July (above, p. 464).

468 (f) a mournful tour] See below, p. 471.

469 (b) Although I wrote today] The letter, though dated 15 July, must have been begun on 14 July (i.e. on same day as letter above, p. 466).

469 (e–f) rectus in curia] See *SL* ix. 299.

471 (a) Nelsons life] Southey had written a life in 1822 and he wrote another for *The Family Library* in 1831.

471 (c) the landscape book] See above, p. 321.

471 (d) Hector MacDonald] James Graham Macdonald Buchanan, fifth and last surviving son of Hector Macdonald Buchanan, went to Malta early in 1827 in search of health. Scott gave him a letter of introduction to Frere, dated 27 Jan. 1827. This letter, which is not in *SL*, is printed in full in Gabrielle Festing, *John Hookham Frere*, London, 1899, pp. 344–5.

471 n. 2] See above, pp. 137–8 and my note. Delete reference to Keith S. M. Scott, which gives no additional information.

472 (a) Brougham] The cheap publications of the Society for the Diffusion of Useful knowledge, promoted by Henry Brougham. See above. p. 470 n.

473 (d) "clawd me in his clutch"] Shakespeare, *Hamlet*, V. 1.

473 (f) in the language of the learned Partridge] Fielding, *Tom Jones*, Bk 15, chap. 12 and Bk 18, chap. 5. The Latin is from Horace, *Odes*, IV. i. 3.

475 (d) my Godson] Spencer Scott Compton, Lady Northampton's third son.

477 (e) Bembridge] Should be Bainbridge.

477 (f) sloop of Yen [?]] Read 'sloop of ten.'

477 (f) My poor aunt] Mrs Walter Scott of Raeburn died at Lessudden House on 20 Oct. of this year.

478 (e) his poem] *The death of Keeldar*.

478 *n.* 1] *Ray*, p. 301.

478 *n.* 3] Cooper's drawing of Davie Mailsetter was used for the title-page vignette of Vol. 5 of the Magnum Opus and the drawing of Bothwell and Burley was used as frontispiece for Vol. 10.

480 (a) half a loaf] *Ray*, p. 171.

481 (b) Hadji] J. J. Morier's *Hajji Baba* which Scott reviewed in *QR* for Jan. 1829 (*MPW* xviii. 354).

481 (d) Bob Hamilton] But he did not die till 1831.

482 (d) preacher whom he termd an Unco' Calf] *The calf. To the Rev. Mr James Steven*, st. [1], line 4.

483 (d) their pound of flesh] Shakespeare, *The Merchant of Venice*, I. 3, III. 3, IV. 1.

484 (b) as Hotspur says] Shakespeare, *I Henry IV*, II. 3.

485 (d) Le Sages Atlas] *Historical atlas*, by Lesage [i.e. by marquis de Las Cases.]

485 (f) £5000 a fair price] For Bridgeheugh which Richardson was trying to buy. He was unsuccessful. It was sold to Charles Balfour Scott of Woll. See *SL* xi. 58 *n*.

486 *n.* 1] This note has no direct bearing on Scott's letter, as Cochrane's letter of 19 Sept. 1829 was written long after *Anne of Geierstein* had been published. Cadell was probably ordering Voght from Treuttel and Wurtz; hence Scott's hope that Cochrane 'will smoke nothing.' In line 2, 'Kipp' is a misreading for 'Kopp.' (*Ueber die Verfassung der heimlichen Gerichte in Westphalen von Karl Philipp Kopp*, 8vo Göttingen, 1794.)

487 (b–c) William Scott] Daniel's son. See below, p. 489.

487 *n.* 1] In line 1, 'donor' should, presumably, be 'owner.'

488 *n.* 2] Delete. Scott meant father-in-law. At this time the expression 'in law' was used for any family connection which was not a blood one.

489 (b) Think of him when I take tobacco] See above, p. 367 and my note.

490 (b) To C. K. Sharpe] In *Sharpe's Letters*, ii. 424, where it is dated '23 Aug. [1828]'. The letter should be dated 23 Aug. 1827. See *Journal* under that date.

490 *n.* 1 Judge Kent] This is presumably James Kent (1763–1847).

491 (b) Come hither come hither . . .] Shakespeare, *As you like it*, II. 5.

491 *n.* 1] In line 2, for '*1829*' read '*1819*.' The words 'do as we dow' may have been a favourite phrase but Scott refers to his mother only once, i.e. at the reference cited (*SL* xi. 434). He uses it in *SL* x. 162, xi. 105, and in *The Black Dwarf*, chap. 9, and *Rob Roy*, chap. 28. The nearest proverb I can find is in Ramsay, *Proverbs*, p. 28: 'He that canna do as he wou'd maun do as he may.'

492 (c) Morritts niece Catherine] Lady Louisa Stuart, who was likely to be better informed than Scott, says it was Anne. See Stuart, *Letters*, ii. 110.

492 *n.* 1] There is an extract from this letter in Partington, *Post-bag*, pp. 256–7.

492 *n.* 4] Delete last sentence, which is inaccurate in facts and misinterprets Scott's words: (1) Melville at this time *was* at the Board of Control (Jan.–Sept. 1828); (2) Scott, therefore, is glad, for the sake of Scottish patronage, that Melville does not go to the 'old ship,' i.e. the Admiralty; (3) Melville was First Lord of the Admiralty 1812–27.

493 (a) Laissez faire a Don Antoine] See my note to *SL* viii. 251 (b).

493 (e) the business with Longman] Longman had purchased the large stock of poetical works from Hurst & Robinson. To avoid trouble over the proposed new ed. Cadell offered to purchase the stock. For continuation of the negotiations, see *SL* xi. 2 *n.* 1, 3, 197, 202, 209.

494 (a) The little book . . . with Leibnitz] See above, p. 484.

494 (a) I begin this very day] There are no entries in the *Journal* for this period from which we can check if Scott actually began *Anne of Geierstein* on 1 Sept. His letter of 15 Sept. (below, p. 501) suggests that he had not begun it by that date.

494 (a) The last of the Tales] *Tales of a grandfather*, 2nd ser.

494 (b) Montrose . . . Dundee . . . Fletcher] These appear as frontispieces to 2nd ser. Vols. 1–3 respectively.

494 (d) Allan Ramsay] In his preface to *The ever green* he acknowledged that most of the poems were taken from the Bannatyne MS.

494 (d) Hailes Sibbald] *Ancient Scottish poems, published from the MS of George Bannatyne, 1568*. [Ed. by Lord Hailes.] 8vo Edinburgh, 1770; James Sibbald, *Chronicle of Scottish poetry*, 4 vols., 8vo Edinburgh, 1802.

494 (e) Depy Register and . . . John Murray] Thomas Thomson and John (afterwards Sir John) Archibald Murray.

497 (a) idea of the planting] This was the work, proposed but never carried out, on planting, with a memoir of Evelyn, for Murray's *Family Library*. See above, pp. 321, 470 n., 471.

498 n. 1] There is an extract from Walter's letter of 2 Aug. in Partington, *Post-bag*, pp. 254–5.

499 (c) Roland the Brave] Thomas Campbell, *The brave Roland*. See also above, p. 332.

499 (f) your visit] Of Dr and Mrs Hughes and their son John, 25 July–5 Aug.

499 n. 2] Presumably the copy of *La jolie fille de Perth* which Cadell had given him (above, p. 485).

500 (a) Jog on, jog on] Shakespeare, *Winter's tale*, IV. 2. See also Ritson, *Ancient songs*, London, 1790 [1792], p. 186.

500 n. 2] For 'Waltham le Willows' read 'Walsham-le-Willows.' Delete 'Miss Wilkinson was possibly another of the Hughes' friends at Bury St. Edmunds.' Dorothea's sister Margaret married John Hughes, Mrs Hughes's son.

501 (c) soon in Switzerland] i.e. working on *Anne of Geierstein*. Cf. above, p. 494 and my note.

502 (d) draughts . . . Marshall] Scott's salaries.

502 (e) I have sent him the verses] *The death of Keeldar*. Sent through Thomas Hood (below, p. 504).

503 (a) the Pavilion] Vignette on title-page of Vol. 3 of *Tales of a grandfather, Second series*.

503 (e) Bridge of Mirza] See the *Spectator*, No. 159, 1 Sept. 1711. By Addison.

504 (a) Laidlaw at Wheathope] Laidlaw's wife was Janet Ballantyne, daughter of Thomas Ballantyne of Holylee, Peebles-shire. Her brother, James Ballantyne, tenanted Whitehope in Yarrow.

504 (b) To Abraham Cooper] This letter cannot be dated 2 Sept. In a letter of 21 Sept. to Cadell he says he has sent the verses 'some days since' and 'incloses a letter to him' (above, p. 502). The 'inclosed letter' must be this one which, therefore, should be dated 21 Sept.

504 (c) sett-to between Glossin & Dirk Hatteraick] This was used for title-page vignette of Vol. 2 of *Guy Mannering* (Magnum Opus, Vol. 4).

505 (a) Your brother] William Lockhart. He called his place Milton-Lockhart.

505 (b) the only certificate in my power] Copy of his marriage certificate, necessary for establishing claim to the Charpentier money in Chancery. See above, p. 436.

507 (e) the Lochs] St Mary's Loch and Loch of the Lowes, separated by a peninsula.

507 (e) Hope Johnstone] Admiral Sir William Johnstone-Hope, M.P. for Dumfriesshire.

507 (f) a Saint Kevan affair] A reference to his experience in Ireland. See Index under Glendalough.

507 (f) to Adams to our dinner] At Tinwald House.

508 (c) Deil would dance off] An allusion to Burns's *The deil's awa' wi' the exciseman*.

509 (a) the Couple of Cantire] Walter and Jane.

509 n. 2] Delete and substitute: Cospatrick Alexander Home, who became 11th Earl of Home in 1841. At this time he had the courtesy title Lord Dunglass. He was first cousin of the 5th Duke of Buccleuch.

510 (b) like Friday] Defoe, *Robinson Crusoe*. Everyman Lib., p. 174.

510 (c) The Moor cock swore . . .] This is apparently the verse which Tom Hutson supplied. See *SL* iv. 374-5. There is an old Scottish proverb: 'The muirhen has sworn by her tough skin, / She sal never eat of the carle's win.' (See Robert Chambers, *Popular rhymes of Scotland*, new ed., London, 1870, p. 196.)

511 (b) Arnot & Maitland] Hugo Arnot, *The history of Edinburgh*, 4to Edinburgh, 1779; William Maitland, *The history of Edinburgh*, 2° Edinburgh, 1753.

511 (c–d) Andw. Gemmells] See Hughes, *Letters*, p. 80, for Scott's account of him.

511 *n.* 1] The clock is in the Entrance Hall.

512 *n.* 1] *Kelly*, p. 37; Mackintosh *Gaelic proverbs*, N. 38.

VOLUME XI

1 (b) To C. K. Sharpe] This letter of 5 Oct. [1828], which is in *Sharpe's Letters*, ii. 417–18, is preceded there by a letter from Scott to Sharpe, 6 Aug. [1828] (not in *SL*) on, inter alia, a portrait of Argyll. The year is confirmed by Scott's references in the letter of 6 Aug. to Morritt's visit and to the 'wild Irish girl.' (For latter, see below, p. 479.) For the epithet 'gley'd' see *Whurry Whigs awa*, st. [7], line 4, in Hogg's *Jacobite relics*, ii. 65. For the 'South Sea,' see *Sharpe's Letters*, ii. 392.

1 *n.* 2] Delete this note. Scott was wrong in attributing the words to Win Jenkins. The words 'prudish natalibus' were used by Termagant in Murphy's *The upholsterer*, II. 2.

2 *n.* 1] Gibson's letter of 13 Jan. 1830 (second last line) should not be cited. Lord Newton had made the decision on 23 Oct. 1829 and it was reported to the Trustees on 29 Dec. (*Sederunt Books*.)

3 (b) Glass Company] See my note to *SL* x. 31 (b).

3 (e) the Arbiter] Alexander Irving, Lord Newton.

3 (f) Manuscripts] The arbiter, Lord Newton, did not give a decision till 1831. See *Journal*, 10 Apr. 1831. The MSS. were sold on 19 Aug. 1831.

5 (e) "as big as all dis cheese"] By Peter Pindar. See my note to *SL* iii. 523 (e) where the whole stanza is quoted.

6 (a) I am afraid . . .] Shakespeare, *Macbeth*, II. 2.

7 (b) Lord Melville's removal] Melville, who had been President of the Board of Control from Jan. till Sept. 1828, returned in the latter month to his old post as First Lord of the Admiralty which he had held from 1812 till 1827.

7 *n.* 1] For 'first Earl of Ellenborough' read 'second Baron Ellenborough, created Earl in 1844.'

8 (c) Haji] Scott's review of J. J. Morier's *Hajji Baba* for *QR* of Jan. 1829.

8 (d) Mr Cowper] James Fenimore Cooper.

8 (e) Mr Slades affidavit] This was unnecessary. Scott could have got Slade's certificate of 18 Dec. 1789 in which he certified that John David and Charles Carpenter were one and the same person and son of Jean François and Margaret Charlotte Charpentier. (India Office Library. Records. Written Petitions, Vol. 2 (1786–9), No. 15, item 2. Information from the late Mrs E. A. Dexter.)

8 (f) Francis Jean Charpentier] This should be Jean François Charpentier.

9 (b) The horse will carry this saddle] See *SL* vii. 49 (d–e).

9 (c) Murrays plan] *The Family Library*.

9 (e) the blood of Douglas will protect itself] John Home, *Douglas*, IV. 1.

9 (e) like the Barber of Bagdad] See my note to *SL* vi. 39 (c).

10 (b) Quantum mutatus . . .] 'Quantum mutatus' from Virgil, *Aeneid*, II.

274; and 'Singula . . .' from Horace, *Epistles*, II. ii. 55.

11 (a) your new poem] *The magic bridle*, which appeared in Cunningham's *The Anniversary . . . for MDCCCXXIX* (publ. Oct. 1828), pp. 136–56.

11 (f) Harry Wynd] See my note to *SL* x. 209 (e).

12 (b) Preliminary dedication] In the second ser. of *Tales of a grandfather* the dedication is dated 'Abbotsford, 15th October 1828.' This has probably given the date for this letter, the 15th being a Wednesday.

12 (d) the Bedesmen] See below, p. 75 and my note.

12 n. 2] In the Advertisement to *The Antiquary* Scott also confessed that he had lost his reference. He was probably thinking of Burns's letter to John Murdoch, 15 Jan. 1783. (*Letters of Robert Burns*, as cited by Grierson, i. 13–14.)

13 (a) William Scott has drawn on me] See *SL* x. 488 n. 1.

13 (d) The Clock] Presented to Scott by Cadell. See *SL* x. 510–11, 511 n. 1 and my note.

13 n. 1] In line 8, delete 'probably.' Nasmyth, Mrs Terry's father, lived at 47 York Place.

14 n. 1] Scott met Wrangham (line 7) in London on 22 May 1828 (*Journal*) and Wrangham visited Scott in Sept. 1829 (below, p. 241).

14 n. 3] Said to be by William Hamilton of Gilbertfield.

17 n. 1] 'Basely murdered' was a common expression in plays and occurs, e.g., in Franklin's *Matilda*, V. 1.

18 (d) Kuzzilbash] Published anonymously, 3 vols., London, 1828.

19 (d) the ballads] By Peter Buchan.

19 n. 2] Delete.

19 n. 3] Mrs Walter Scott of Raeburn. She died on 20 Oct. Scott's letter of 22 Oct. to her son, William Scott of Maxpoffle, with the MS. of an obituary notice of her for the *Kelso Mail*, is in NLS MS. 2890, f. 76, but is not in *SL*.

20 (a) Hector . . . Forbes] Hector

Macdonald Buchanan died on 14 Sept. and Sir William Forbes died on 24 Oct.

20 (a) Poor Rose] For meaning of 'poor' see below, p. 22 n. 2. Rose lived till 1843. Scott was at Brighton 20–2 May 1828 and met Rose then. See *Journal*.

22 n. 2] The 'Italian & her crew' probably refer to Marcella Condulmer whom Rose married. She had a son described as 'Count Zorgi of Brighton.' Rose in his will dated Brighton 27 May 1841 left everything to her. See *N. & Q.* 9th ser. vii. 68–9, 155. For Dr Yates, see Anderson's ed. of the *Journal*.

23 (d) the little parlour] This was Scott's first study at Abbotsford. When the present study was finished in 1825 the former one became a breakfast parlour; later it was a gun room and is now a dining-room.

24 (a) seams will slit] See my note to *SL* x. 154 (a).

24 n. 3] Lockhart's letter of 3 Nov. is in Partington, *Letter-books*, pp. 155–6.

25 (b) vir gravis pietate et meritis] This seems to be a paraphrase of Virgil's *Aeneid*, i. 151–2. In *MPW* xix. 164, Scott gives the form: 'vir pietate ac meritis gravis.'

26 (a) Derwentwater greyhound] Robert Southey.

28 (e) "After life's fitful fever . . ."] Shakespeare, *Macbeth*, III. 2.

29 (f) my faith is constant] Variant of 'My trust is constant in thee.' See my note to *SL* v. 373 (d).

29 n. 1] See Scott's *Swift*, 2nd ed., xiv. 359 and *n.*, and xix. 186. 'Whiston' should be 'Woolston,' a mistake due more likely to Lockhart or his transcriber than to Scott.

31 n. 2] The whole contents of the letter, apart from the letter to Aberdeen, establishes that the year is 1828.

33 (f) Mr Kidds picture] William Kidd's frontispiece to Vol. 7 of Magnum Opus. Scott's suggestion has been followed, for the engraving shows Rob Roy in breeches and leggings.

34 (c) To J. G. Lockhart] As Lockhart's letter of 3 Nov. (Partington, *Letter-books*, pp. 155–6) could not reach Scott before 6 or 7 Nov., this letter must be some days after 5 Nov.

34 (d) £100 . . . for the two articles]
Lockhart in his letter of 3 Nov. said the
£100 was for the review of Davy's
Salmonia.

35 n. 1] For the reference in the first line,
note that the letter in SL x. 490 should
be dated 23 Aug. 1827.

36 (e–f) starts the game] Heywood, p. 13;
Ramsay, Proverbs, p. 6; Ray, p. 185.

36 n. 2] Kelly, p. 62; Ramsay, Proverbs,
p. 43. Also used in A legend of Montrose,
chap. 2, and Journal, 6 Jan. 1828.

38 (e) like Ossians my dogs] This is not
an exact quotation. There are references
in Ossian's poems to dogs 'howling' but
not in 'empty halls.'

39 (a) the amount is a trifle] They sold
for one penny each. See On planting
waste lands in MPW xxi. 49.

40 (d) business in Mr Handleys hands]
Charpentier money lying in Chancery.

40 n. 1] There is a long extract from
Macfarlane's letter of 15 Nov. in
Partington, Post-bag, pp. 262–3. In this
letter he refers to one from Scott of
13 Nov. which is not in SL.

43 n. 1] There is an extract from Lockhart's letter of 16 Nov. in Partington,
Post-bag, pp. 257–8.

44 (b) Mr Slades evidence] See above,
p. 8 and my note.

44 (d) I mentiond to Sophia] This
muddled sentence should read: 'I mentioned to Sophia that Mrs Hughes
thought.'

45 n. 2] Lockhart's letter is in Partington, Letter-books, pp. 156–8. On Lockhart and Lytton, see also Lang's
Lockhart, ii. 37.

46 n. 1] There was no point in printing
this inaccurate 'Transcriber's Note.'
See SL x. 285 and n. 2 and my note.

46 n. 2] Delete 'the Hon.' or amend to
'Right Hon.' Grenville was elected on
28 Jan. 1829.

46 n. 3] There was no work issued in
1827–8 called Three Books of Scotish
Pasquils. Three vols. were issued separately as A book of Scotish pasquils, 1827;
A second book . . . 1828; A third book . . .
1828. They were ed. anonymously by
James Maidment. A new ed. was published in 1868 under the title A book of

Scottish pasquils, 1568–1715. Maidment
also printed in A third book, pp. 75–7,
Upon the long wished for and tymely death
of the Right Honble the Lady Stair, with a
reference to The Bride of Lammermoor.

47 (a–b) mirabile dictu] Virgil, Aeneid,
II. 174.

47 (b) road from Northumberland
through Roxburghshire] The rival
plans for bringing the London mail to
Scotland, either by Jedburgh or by
Wooler, had long been debated and a
number of pamphlets had been published. Scott had two of these and they
are now in NLS. (Abbot. 103 (21–2).)

47 n. 2] In Percy's Reliques.

48 (a) unprofitable chat] Shakespeare,
I Henry IV, III. 1.

50 (b) at the age of 28] Walter had just
passed his 27th birthday.

50 (d) one of the best of our London
painters] Mrs Margaret Carpenter. See
below, p. 67.

54 (b) pyne doublet] Baron de Fahnenberg (see below, p. 343) had seen this
letter in Antiq. Soc. of Perth Trans. and
wrote to Scott on the word 'pyne' in
a letter of 30 Mar. 1830 (NLS MS.
3912, ff. 280–1).

55 (c) Tom Purdie has a son] Charles
Purdie.

55 (d) Cowper] James Fenimore
Cooper.

55 (e) Mr. Slades examination] See
above, p. 8 and my note.

55 n. 1] Lockhart's letter is in Partington, Letter-books, pp. 156–8. The
deceased gazette-writer was Stephen
Rolleston. His successor was William
Gregson.

56 n. 1] In lines 3–4, 'one C. Yorke' is
Field Marshal Sir Charles Yorke. The
letter from Yorke to Sotheby is in NLS
(MS. 3907, f. 198).

57 (c–d) Gazzette keeper] Rolleston. See
my note to p. 55 above.

57 (f) finishing the publication] Proceedings in the court-martial held upon John,
Master of Sinclair. See SL x. 285 and
n. 2 and my note.

58 (a) perfervidum ingenium Scoto-
rum] See SL i. 19, and my note.

58 (d) "the bonny bit land and some planting on it"] 'A bonny piece land and planting on't.' Line 2 of a song beginning 'I have a green purse, and a wee pickle gowd.' In Ramsay's *Tea-table miscellany* and *Herd*, ii. 94.

59 (f) Tom] Thomas Campbell, the poet. He was a lifelong friend of Richardson.

60 (c) Lord Spencer . . . Thomas Grenville] They were both elected on 28 Jan. 1829.

60 (d) Now our name is up] See my note to *SL* i. 380 (c).

60 (e) Maxwell of Kir[k]connell] This MS. was presented in Oct. by John Menzies of Pitfoddells, Maxwell's nephew. See *SL* xii. 459 *n.* Scott did not carry out his intention. The MS. was edited for the Maitland Club in 1841.

61 (d) like Dogberry] Shakespeare, *Much ado about nothing*, IV. 2.

62 (d) an Angel walking upon the earth] In his introd. to *The Duke of Guise* (Scott's *Dryden*, vii. 9) Scott says: 'In the character of Marmoutiere, there seems to be an allusion to the duchess of Buccleuch.' In Act I, sc. 3, the Duke says of her: 'She dazzles, walks mere angel upon earth.' Scott probably had this in mind when he describes the late Duchess as 'an Angel walking upon the earth.'

63 (b) Captain Scott] Here and in the following paragraph Captain Scott should be Captain Cust.

63 *n.* 2] Delete this note, which is not applicable.

64 (d) Lord Hadington] As Lord Binning he had been elected on 31 Jan. 1827 and had succeeded as 9th Earl on 17 Mar. 1828.

65 (f) high-gravel blindness] Shakespeare, *The merchant of Venice,*II. 2.

66 (b–c) cut your coat according to your cloath] *Heywood*, p. 33; *Ray*, p. 115; Ramsay, *Proverbs*, p. 15.

67 (a) Mrs Carpenter] Mrs Margaret Carpenter. Her portrait of John Hugh Lockhart is still at Abbotsford in an apartment not open to tourists.

69 (c) my lampoon] See above, p. 46 and *n.* 3.

69 (d) never like to be reprinted] But *A book of Scottish pasquils* was reprinted in 1868. See above, p. 46, *n.* 3.

70 (a) Causes Celebres] *Criminal trials,* ed. by Robert Pitcairn.

70 (b) Murder of the Schaws] *Proceedings in the court-martial held upon John, Master of Sinclair.* See *SL* x. 285 and *n.* 2 and my note.

73 (f) your advice and Chantrey's] See Lockhart's letter to Scott of 28 Nov. in Partington, *Letter-books*, p. 157.

74 (a) Sancho sent acorns to the Duchess] Sancho should be Teresa Panza. See my notes to *SL* i. 304 (d–e) and *SL* vii. 497 (c).

75 (e) Account of the Blue gowns] This information was sent to Scott by Alexander Macdonald in a letter of 27 Nov. 1828 (NLS MS. 3907, ff. 237–8). Scott included it in the 'Advertisement' to *The Antiquary* with acknowledgement to Macdonald.

75 *n.* 1] John Landseer's letter is in Partington, *Letter-books*, pp. 248–9.

76 (c) old Quarter Masters] Scott himself—recalling the old days of the R.E.V.L.D.

76 (f) the House to which he is now Clerk] See my note to *SL* x. 341 (e).

78 (c) the letterpress independent of the expensive embellishments] Cadell had his own way and issued only an illustrated ed. and he also issued the plates separately. Cf. also below, p. 80.

78 (e) Stewart of Allanbank] Scott does not exaggerate Stuart's skill in depicting cavalry in action but he fails to realize that Stuart's style of indicating action by light touches could not be transferred to paper by the hard medium of steel engraving.

79 (d) yeoman's service] Shakespeare, *Hamlet*, V. 2.

80 (b–c) prints & cuts selling separately] See above, p. 78 and my note.

80 *n.* 1] The correction was not for p. 124, but for pp. 121, 122, 123 and 125.

84 (b) To C. K. Sharpe] Date is middle of Dec. 1828: (1) reference to lost spectacles (above, p. 65) and (2) reference to Burke and Hare.

84 (b) Mysterious Macfarlane horror]
Sharpe already knew the story of the
murder of Capt. Cayley in 1716 by
Mrs McFarlane. See *The letters of Sir
Walter Scott and Charles Kirkpatrick Sharpe
to Robert Chambers*, [Edinburgh] 1904,
pp. 24–6.

84 *n.* 2] The complete text of Nicolas's
letter of 10 Oct. 1828 is printed in
E. S. P. Haynes, *Life, law & letters*,
London, 1936, pp. 273–4. Scott's letter
of 1 Jan. was acknowledged in Nicolas's
letter of 28 Feb., the complete text of
which is given ibid., pp. 274–7. Scott
replied on 23 May (letter not in *SL*) and
Nicolas answered on 16 June, his letter
being ibid., pp. 278–83.

85 (b) printed for the Roxburghe Club]
*Proceedings in the court-martial held upon
John, Master of Sinclair*. See *SL* x. 285
and *n.* 2 and my note.

85 (c) To the Bishop of Llandaff]
Correct date is 1830. Scott is answering
the Bishop's letter of 9 Dec. 1829. See
below, p. 260 *n.* 3.

86 (b) *sapere est principium et fons*] Horace,
Ars poetica, line 309.

86 (d) Non sum qualis] Fielding, *Tom
Jones*, Bk 15, chap. 12 and Bk 18, chap.
5. The Latin is from Horace, *Odes*, IV.
i. 3.

86 *n.* 1] Delete this note. It is a purely
personal opinion not likely to be accepted by Scott scholars.

87 (a–b) Don Quixote's phrase] Scott
may be alluding to Pt I, Bk IV, chap.
16 and Pt II, chap. 29. (Lockhart's ed.,
1822, iii. 21, iv. 146.)

87 (f) Silver Cup] No longer at Abbots-
ford, having been sold by the late Sir
Walter Maxwell-Scott at Dowell's,
Edinburgh, 8 Mar. 1946, Lot 385. The
cup is inscribed: This cup / is most
gratefully presented / by W. Marshall /
The Proprietor of / The Gem / to Sir
Walter Scott Bart. / for his liberal con-
tribution / of a poem / The death of
Keeldar.

88 (a) Mr Cowper] Abraham Cooper,
R.A.

88 (c) Bones] This must be a misreading
for Brain. Brain printed the plate which
was drawn by Cooper and engraved by
Warren.

89 (d) Leech] Francis Edward Leech.

89 *n.* 3] *Satires*, X. 22.

91 (a–b) He is besides a cousin] Only
in the Scottish sense. Jean Campbell
(wife of Thomas Haliburton and mother
of Barbara Haliburton who married
Robert Scott of Sandyknowe) had a
half-brother John Coutts who married
Jean, daughter of Sir John Stuart of
Allanbank.

91 (b) his youngest brother] Archibald
Inglis Lockhart.

92 (c) chain bridge betwixt Melrose and
Gattonside] Still in use. Scott was asked
to lay the foundation stone but declined.
It is sometimes stated that he was present at the opening ceremony on 26 Oct.
1826 but this is an error as he was on
his way to France on that date.

93 (e) Daft Jamie] James Wilson.

94 (d) Dalkeith & Bowhill] Scott's last
recorded visit to Dalkeith was in 1822
(*SL* vii. 219, 220, 233) except once in
1824 when it was deserted (*SL* viii. 246);
but he had been at Bowhill as recently
as Oct. 1827 (*SL* x. 300).

95 (a) But whats impossible] See *SL* vi.
300 *n.* 2. Also quoted *SL* viii. 448.

95 (b) Lady Annes artist] I cannot find
from the Duke's letters who the artist
was.

95 (c) Graham] John Graham-Gilbert,
R.S.A. His address at this time was
14 George Street.

95 (d) Lockhart's murder] See *The
Bride of Lammermoor*, chap. 4, and Scott's
note to the passage.

96 (c) Francis Walker Drummond] Son
of James Walker, two lines above. See
Index under Drummond (*Sir* Francis
Walker).

97 (c) delighted to honour] *Bible, Esther*
6: 6, 7, 9, 11.

100 (a) "the gambol has been shown"]
By Thomas Parnell. See my note to *SL*
vi. 242 (e).

100 (d) Kemble threatened to play Fal-
staff] See *MPW* xx. 195–8.

100 *n.* 1] The reference should be to
Duan second, st. [14], lines 5–6.

101 (b) like a tether] Burns. See *SL* v.
422 and cf. viii. 410, ix. 425.

101 *n.* 1] There are several small plaster models of the statue. One is at Abbotsford.

103 (e) those sages who discover mens characters by their hand of writing] On the previous day (22 Jan. 1829) Scott had noted in his *Journal*: 'They say that the character is indicated by the hand writing.' The *Athenæum*, 1829 (15 Apr.), p. 225, commented on Scott's handwriting and the *Edin. Lit. Jour.* of 23 May published an article on this subject with a sample of Scott's handwriting and a comment on it. See also below, p. 123. Scott had already referred to this subject in Chrystal Croftangry's introd. to *Chronicles of the Canongate*, chap. 2.

103 *n.* 1] This note is ambiguous. Wicketshaw and Milton-Lockhart are given as two estates in Burke's *Landed gentry*, 1879. William was 'of Milton-Lockhart' and his brother Lawrence 'of Wicketshaw' until the latter united the estates when he succeeded William.

104 (c) Sir William Knighton's sketch] The small portrait begun at Abbotsford in Nov. 1824 and finished in 1829 for Sir William Knighton. See Partington, *Letter-books*, p. 250.

105 (c) age claws us in his clutch] Shakespeare, *Hamlet*, V. 1.

105 (c–d) old wives' proverb, "we must just e'en do as we dow"] See *SL* x. 491 *n.* 1 and my note.

107 (f) the She-hare] Mrs William Hare.

107 *n.* 2] The work is: *Pompeii, illustrated with picturesque views, engraved by W. B. Cooke, from the original drawings of Lieut.-Col. Cockburn*, 2 vols. 2° London, 1827. The work contains 'Pompeii, a descriptive ode,' by John Hughes, of which Scott makes no mention.

109 (c) grow old as a garment] *Bible, Psalms* 102: 26.

112 (c) "The man to thieves . . ."] John Walcot, *Bozzy and Piozzi*, lines 111–12. (*The works of Peter Pindar*, new ed., London, 1812, i. 344.) Scott improves the second line by substituting 'half a year' for 'a whole year.'

112 (d) Johnson's "Tour in the Hebrides"] Scott means *A journey to the Western Islands*.

114 *n.* 1] There is no need to cite Croker. The quotation in the note comes from Boswell's *Journal of a tour to the Hebrides*, under 6 Nov.

115 (a) Adam Smith] Whatever the subject of the dispute was, it was not over Smith's *Letter . . . to William Strachan*, which is dated 9 Nov. 1776. Johnson and Smith met in 1773 and Hume did not die till 1776.

116 (c) "If Pot says so, Pot lies!"] Scott seems to be the only authority for this anecdote and he is quoted in Boswell's *Johnson*, ed. Hill-Powell, iv. 5 *n.* 1, and in the index to that work Pot is not identified.

117 *n.* 2] Delete and substitute: Sir James Boswell, 2nd Bart. (1806–57). He was of age in 1829.

119 *n.* 2] See also *SL* xii. 2 and note.

120 (b) your brothers commission Archibald Inglis Lockhart.

120 *n.* 1] There is an extract from Lockhart's letter in Partington, *Post-bag*, pp. 268–9. I can find no record of an ed. by Andrew Lang (lines 6–7). The papers were ed., in part, by J. H. Glover in 1847 and the complete collection was calendared by the Royal Manuscripts Commission, 1902–16. See introd. to Vol. 1 of latter publication for an account of the commissions appointed to examine the MSS.

121 (d) Sir Joshua . . . Earl of Rothes] See below, pp. 134, 136, 136 *n.*

122 (b) Hobbema] From the description this is Hobbema's 'The avenue, Middelharnis.' In his *Journal*, 2 Feb., Scott wrote: 'A Hobbema much admired is I think as tame a piece of work as I ever saw.' It may have been a copy. The original is now in the National Gallery, London.

123 (b) handwriting] See above, p. 103 and my note.

124 *n.* 2] There is no entry in the *Journal* for this visit. Harriet Douglas married in 1833 Henry Nicholas Cruger and she stipulated that he should change his name to Douglas. They visited Abbotsford on 17 Feb. 1839 and signed the Visitors' Book as 'Henry D. Cruger' and 'Harriet Douglas Cruger.' She dined with Scott in Edinburgh 1 and 2 July 1828 (*Journal*) and visited

Abbotsford in Sept. 1828 (Angus
Davidson, *Miss Douglas of New York*,
London, 1952, p. 120).

126 (c) *Cantabit vacuus*] Juvenal, *Satires*,
X. 22.

127 (b) meat, clothes, fire] Scott is re-
peating what he had put into the mouth
of Maggie Mucklebackit in *The Antiquary*, chap. 11.

129 (d) like the divers in the old Ballad]
Earl Richard, st. XVII, lines 1–2: 'They
douked in at ae weil-heid, / And out aye
at the other.' In *Minstrelsy* (ed. Henderson), iii. 236.

129 (d) "things must be as they may"]
Shakespeare, *Henry V*, II. 1.

130 (e) piping times of peace] Shakespeare, *Richard III*, I. 1.

131 (b) supd full with horrors] Shakespeare, *Macbeth*, V. 5.

132 (a) an occasional answer] 'answer'
should be 'article.'

133 (c) Joseph the miller] So called in
the accounts of the Burke and Hare
murders; not known if Joseph is a surname or forename.

133 (d–e) Burke should have acted]
'should have' is written twice instead of
once. The sentence should have been:
'Burke, acted upon as he seems always
to have been by ardent spirits and involved in a constant succession of
murther, should have.'

134 (a) Sir Joshua] His portrait of the
Earl of Rothes is still at Leslie House.
The one for sale was bought, not by
Balfour, but by the Earl of Haddington.
See below, p. 136, 136 n. 2 and my
note.

134 (a) a print for a copy] Presumably
Scott meant to write 'a print from a
copy.'

134 (b) unsuspected as Caesars wife]
Suetonius Tranquillus, *Lives of the
Caesars*, Bk I, sect. 74.

134 (f) flapper] Swift. See my note to
SL ii. 213 (c).

136 n. 2] The portrait is still at Tyning-
hame.

138 (c) Newark castle] 'Newark Castle,
on the Yarrow' was No. 153 in the 1829
exhibition of the Institution for the
Encouragement of the Fine Arts in
Scotland.

138 n. 1] The couplet comes from Scott
of Satchell's *A true history*, Hawick, 1894,
p. 51. It is in the section called *Wats
Bellanden*.

139 (b) from their cradle . . .] *Songs of
the Edinburgh Troop* [By P. F. Tytler and
J. G. Lockhart], Edinburgh, 1825, pp.
15–16.

139 (c) Good with the sword . . .] *The
fray of Suport*, st. 5, line 3: 'Gude wi' a
bow, and better wi' a speir.' Scott's
Minstrelsy (ed. Henderson), ii. 163.

139 (d) Dogberry] See *SL* ii. 320.

139 (e) Eglington] See *The trial of
Mungo Campbell . . . for the murder of
Alexander, Earl of Eglintoun*, London,
1770. For Dr Johnson on this murder,
see Boswell's *Johnson*, ed. Hill-Powell,
iii. 188–9.

140 (a) Southeys great mortar] See
above, pp. 24 n., 25, 34.

140 (d) Peterborough] The *Edin. Lit.
Jour.* for 7 Mar. 1829, p. 240, announced
the forthcoming life of Peterborough by
Scott for Murray's *Family Library*.

141 (b) My trust is constant in thee] See
my note to *SL* v. 373 (d).

142 (e) I can remember the mob of
Edinburgh] On 2 Feb. 1779. See the
Scots Mag. Vol. 41 (Feb. 1779), pp.
107–8.

143 (d) reckon our chickens] *Ray*, p.
117.

145 (a) t'*ould woman*] This was how
William Hare, in his evidence, referred
to Margery Campbell, the elderly
woman who had been murdered. See
*Trial of William Burke and Helen
McDougal*, etc., 8vo Edinburgh, 1829,
p. 88.

146 (b) Wilkie] Wilkie had offered his
portrait of Scott for the Magnum Opus.
See Partington, *Letter-books*, p. 250. Instead of being included in the Magnum
it was issued in Vol. XI of the *Poetical
Works*, 1830 (*Ruff*, Nos. 165 and 166).
This was probably Cadell's compromise
because the portrait could not be removed from the Magnum which was
issued bound in cloth and required a
frontispiece to each vol., whereas the
Poetical works was issued in boards and

the portrait (if the owner did not like it) could be removed before the volume was bound.

147 (e) an Epitaph] See *SL* x. 426.

147 n. 2] For letters of Peel and Wellington on this subject, Sept. 1822, see *FL* ii. 155 n.

149 (b) Sir Henry Inglis] This should be Sir Robert Inglis. He defeated Peel at Oxford on the Catholic question in 1829.

149 (c) adhered to a very large body ... who petition for the bill] Scott signed the petition which was presented by Sir James Mackintosh. See Mackintosh's *Memoirs*, ii. 437–8. Signed also by Chambers (above, p. 144).

149 (d) facetious Peter] Patrick Robertson.

150 (b–c) tota re perspecta] The whole matter being clearly had in view. A Scots law phrase. Trayner, *Latin maxims*. Used also in *SL* iii. 21 and *Guy Mannering*, chap. 49.

150 n. 1] Delete this note. Scott is quoting a political phrase from Livy: *pedibus ire in sententiam*, i.e. to go over to another's opinion.

151 (a) rumours about the Duke of Cumberland] See *Creevy*; selected and re-ed. by John Gore, London, 1948, pp. 307–8.

151 (a) Siellis] Joseph Seillis.

152 (f) taxes etc to pay] A list of taxes in 1826 is given in the *Sederunt Books*. They amounted to about £140.

153 (d) Secretary of the Office] Augustus Godby.

153 (e) brought no *Carlisle* news] Sir William Scott was M.P. for Carlisle, 1829–30.

154 (b–c) vox et præterea] See *SL* vii. 237.

154 (d)–155 "ape and monkey climes"] Pope, *The Dunciad*, Bk I, line 233.

155 (d) Dundas . . . Dempster] Robert Dundas of Arniston and George Dempster of Skibo.

156 (a) leather and prunella] Pope, *Essay on man*. Epistle *IV*, line 204: 'The rest is all but leather or prunella.

156 (e) to burnish the chain of freindship] See *SL* ii. 535 and my note.

157 (a) Old Scott had a brother named Scott of Bavelaw] I cannot identify these persons from the genealogies in K. S. M. Scott's *Scott*.

157 (b) the son of this brother] Francis Scott (1802–66) son of Lt.-Col. William Scott (1763–1808). The father may not have made a fortune but he was successful in his profession. Neither of these two men was ever 'of Bavelaw,' the estate having been sold by William's father in 1774. In Scott's day it was owned by Johnston of Lathrisk.

157 (f) His only connection] This confused sentence should probably read: 'His only connection with me is through the son of Stewart of Invernahyle, a gallant old veteran, for whose memory ...'

158 (c) giving alms like Gil Blas] Le Sage, *Gil Blas*, Bk I, chap. 2.

159 (b) *pedibus ire in sententiam*] See above, p. 150 and my note.

160 (a) Lady Louisas grand nephew] Charles Stuart of Hoburne, grandson of 3rd Earl of Bute.

161 (a) translation from Martial] Archibald Campbell Swinton, *Translations and imitations of epigrams of Martial. A prize exercise in the Humanity Class of the University of Edinburgh, 1829*, 8vo [Edinburgh, 1829].

161 n. 1] For 'father of the owner' read 'son of John Swinton.'

162 n. 4] Delete this note. The reference to Clerk's MS does not apply. The poem, which Scott is quoting, is *Ode, imitated from the Gododin*, by Edward Williams. It was first printed in the *Gentleman's Mag.* Vol. 59, pt 2 (Nov. 1789), pp. 1035–6. Scott is quoting from memory and there are a number of errors apart from his changing 'Madoc' to 'Arthur' [i.e. the Duke of Wellington]. The lines were also quoted in the *Minstrelsy* (ed. Henderson, i. 56 n.), where Scott wrongly gives Jones as the author, and as motto to chap. 2 of *The betrothed*.

163 (a) King Arthurs horn] i.e. Wellington's.

163 (b) conclusion of the article] Review of Ritson's *Annals of the Caledonians* for *QR* July 1829.

163 (c) "I am glad" as Mrs. Quickly says] Shakespeare, *Merry wives of Windsor*, I. 4.

163 n. 1] For 'Letter LV' read 'Letter LIV.'

164 (a) As to poor Terry] It is odd that Scott makes no reference, either in his letters or *Journal*, to the birth about this time of Frederick George Terry, Terry's second son, who died at Melbourne, 29 June 1858, aged 29. (*Ann. Reg.* 1858, Chron. p. 413.)

164 (a–b) descriptive of the trumpery here] *Reliquiae Trottcosienses*, which was not published in Scott's lifetime. See my note to *SL* xi. 292 *n.* 3.

164 (b) your collection] John Murray's *The Family Library*.

164 (b) Skene] This project goes back as far as 1816. See *SL* iv. 163–5.

164 (d) "the battle's fought and won"] Probably Shakespeare, *Macbeth*, I. 1: 'When the battle's lost and won.'

164 (d) I send Skenes journal . . . by this post] Which he did. See *SL* xii. 463.

166 (a) a Captain in the Company's service] This is probably John Hamilton Dempster, Captain of the *Rose*, 1791–2, and of the *Earl Talbot*, 1799–1800. (Charles Hardy, *A register of ships . . . of the . . . East India Company*.) As Dempster was dead by 1811, he may have been lost when the *Earl Talbot* was wrecked in Oct. 1800.

166 (b) like a poisoned rat, as the old Dean says] 'die . . . like a poisoned rat in a hole.' Swift to Lord Bolingbroke, Dublin, 21 Mar. 1729. (*Works*, ed. Scott, 2nd ed., xvii. 249.)

166 (c–d) "Woe worth thee, is there no help in thee?"] See below, p. 438 and *n.* 1.

166 n. 1] According to Burke's *Landed gentry*, Joanna Dundas married George Dempster, son of Harriet Dempster of Skibo and William Soper who assumed the name of Dempster. 'son' in line 5 should, I think, be 'grandson.'

167(a) But grievings a folly] Charles Dibdin. See my note to *SL* ix. 341 (e).

167 (c) letter for Crieff] This letter (which is not in *SL*) was sold at Sotheby's 4 June 1946. Lieut. James McComish, R.N., had written from Crieff on 23

Mar. 1829 offering Scott a snuff-box made from the 'kind gallows' of Crieff (NLS MS. 3908, ff. 149–50). Partington (*Post-bag*, p. 367) gives the name wrongly as McCormish.

167 (c) To Robert Cadell] The date should be Sunday, 12 Apr. On same day he began the letter to Ballantyne, mentioned here, and finished it on 13 Apr. See *Journal* under 13 Apr.

170 n. 3] The title of Burns's poem is *Lines spoken extempore on being appointed to the Excise*.

171 (a) Two Misses Carrs] Isabella, afterwards Lady Eardley, and probably her sister Frances.

171 (c) res angusta] Juvenal, *Satires*, III. 165: 'Res angusta domi.'

171 (d) think of that Mr Brook] Shakespeare, *Merry wives of Windsor*, III. 5.

173 (a) To Rev. R. Polwhele] Scott is answering Polwhele's letter of 7 Feb. 1829 (NLS MS. 3908, ff. 61–2) in which he asks Scott for help in obtaining a cadetship in East India Co.'s Service for his son. He asks if Scott received a copy of his 'Recollections' which he had instructed Nichols to send. There is no mention of Whitaker. By 'Recollections' Polwhele must mean *Traditions and recollections*, 2 vols., 8vo London, 1826.

174 (c) *like the boul of a pint stoup*] Ramsay, *Proverbs*, p. 14. Also used in *Guy Mannering*, chap. 45.

174 n. 2] Delete 'Possibly.' He is Arthur Morton Carr.

174 n. 3] Delete. Captain Percy was the Hon. William Henry Percy (1788–1855), sixth son of 2nd Baron Lovaine and 1st Earl of Beverley who was second son of 1st Duke of Northumberland. He was a Commissioner of Excise; hence Scott's reference to him here.

176(b) To Robert Cadell] This letter is correctly dated as references to *Anne of Geierstein* and Ritson show. Bowring's visit must have been cancelled as he did not visit Scott till 23 Apr. 1830. See below, pp. 339, 340 and Bowring's *Autobiographical recollections*.

176 (e) Ritsons Chronicles] *Annals of the Caledonians, Picts and Scots*, Edinburgh, 1828. Reviewed by Scott in *QR* July 1829.

177 (c) God be with your labour] See my note to *SL* vi. 332 (b).

178 (b) Handley] Thomas Handley, the lawyer, who was looking after the Charpentier money in Chancery.

178 (b) without flapping] An allusion to Swift's *Gulliver's travels*. See my note to *SL* ii. 213 (c).

179 (a) Missie Moff] A misreading of 'Missie thof unknown.' 'Thof unknown' was a favourite expression of Scott's taken from Smollett and other 18th-cent. writers.

187 (c) bricks without straw] *Bible*, *Exodus* 5.

193 *n*. 2] Stewart visited Abbotsford, 3–5 May 1827. See *Journal*.

194 (c) he that looks to a gown of gold . . .] I have not found this proverb. It is also used in *SL* xii. 453, *The Monastery*, chap. 17 and *Redgauntlet*, Letter II.

195 (a) Alnaschar] *Story of the little hunchback:* [10] *The story of the barber's fifth brother* in *The Arabian Nights* (*Tales of the East*, ed. Weber, i. 144–7).

195 (a–b) reckon our chickens] *Ray*, p. 117. See above, p. 143.

195 (c) To Walter] The date is the date of the postscript, i.e. 3 June. See *Journal* under 3 June for the girls' visit to Hopetoun House.

195 (d) praise the bridge which carries us over] A proverb. See *SL* ix. 179.

196 (a) talk . . . to . . . Milne] i.e. resume negotiations for purchase of Faldonside.

196 *n*. 3] Delete the erroneous statement 'Moody or Moodie was an Abbotsford labourer' and see next note. Douglas's footnote to *Journal*, 9 Oct. 1826, has hitherto been accepted without questioning.

197 (a) as John Moody says] Vanbrugh and Cibber, *The provoked husband*, I. 1: 'he canno' hawld it—no, he canno' hawld it.' See Anderson's ed. of the *Journal*, p. xii, where Douglas's error that Moody was an Abbotsford servant is followed.

197 (c) in Longmans hands] This continues the negotiations with Longman & Co. over the poetical works. (See *SL*

x. 493–4, xi. 2 *n*. 3.) On 4 June Longman offered copyrights and stock for £8,000. Trustees offered £6,000 and a compromise at £7,000 was reached on 1 July. (*Sederunt Books.*) See also below, pp. 202, 209.

197 *n*. 2] Murray's letter of 8 Oct. is in Smiles, *John Murray*, ii. 275 and in *Archibald Constable*, iii. 122–3.

199 (e) Bruce's speech to David I.] Robert de Bruce, Earl of Carrick (1078?–1141). See Aelred, *De bello Standardii*, in Roger Twysden's ed. of *Historiæ Anglicanæ scriptores X*, 2° London, 1652, Tom. 1, cols. 343–4.

200 *n*. 1] Derrick's work should be: *The image of Irelande . . . anno 1578*, 4to London, 1581.

201 *n*. 2] Capt. James Watson was a cousin, once removed, of Scott's mother.

202 (c) Messrs Longman's demand] See above, p. 197 and my note.

204 (b) we must not hollo] See *SL* x. 52.

204 (c–d) It is weel away if it bide] A Scottish proverb. See my note to *SL* ix. 353 (b).

205 (d) a picture of the author] Murray already had a portrait painted by Thomas Phillips, R.A., in 1818.

205 (e) Sedet æternumque sedebit] Virgil, *Aeneid*, vi. 617–18.

205 (e) Slender shook Sackerson] Shakespeare, *Merry wives of Windsor*, I. 1.

206 (e) Alnaschar] See my note to *SL* xi. 195 (a).

206 *n*. 1] The play was *St Ronan's Well*. Dibdin does not mention it, and his date, 10 June, is apparently wrong. Scott gives 11 June in his *Journal* and in *SL* xi. 206, 208.

206 *n*. 2] Shakespeare, *II Henry IV*, II. 2: 'doth the old boar feed in the old frank?'

206 *n*. 3] By a strange coincidence Maria Edgeworth in *The absentee*, chap. 6, likewise 'misquotes': 'And panting James toiled after her in vain.'

207 (d) We must not hollow] See *SL* x. 52.

207 *n*. 1] A few months later Scott refers to Thomson Callender (*SL* xii.

470). In 1810 he had printed a poem by Thompson Callendar in *English minstrelsy*, i. 219. These two Callenders may be the same and there may be some link with Scott's phrase.

208 (f) James] James Ballantyne's complaints about his share of printing. See above, p. 192 *n*.

208 *n*. 1] Delete this note. Brush is Captain Le Brush, or Brush, in *The Register Office*, by Joseph Reed. The quotation is from Act II, sc. 1.

209 (b) Longmans stock] See above, p. 197 and my note.

209 (f) *Sic suscribitur*] This should be *Sic subscribitur*. The words occur in Vol. 1, p. cxxvi of *Rob Roy* in the Magnum Opus ed.

210 (a) poetical carreer] Scott means 'poetical career, and before the Minstrelsy.'

211 (a) keeping my niece] Anne was with Scott from 21 June 1828 till 1 July 1829. See *Journal* under these two dates.

211 (c) vile war office accompts] Trouble with War Office over Tom's accounts when in Ireland.

212 *n*. 2] This note belongs to p. 213.

214 (a) next Monday] The wedding took place on Thursday, 16 July.

216 (a) sparrowlike & companionless] *Bible, Psalms* 102: 7. See also *SL* iii. 434, viii. 49.

216 (b) To James Ballantyne] Date of this letter is 1827: (1) 'the *Childer*' refers to *Tales of a grandfather*, 1827; (2) the lines from *Don Juan* are for Vol. 4, pp. 397–8 of *The miscellaneous prose works*, 1827.

216 (c) Dumple it as you list] Massinger, *A new way to pay old debts*, III. 2.

217 (b) Highland Dictionary] John Macleod, *Dictionarium Scoto-Celticum*, 2 vols., Edinburgh, 1828.

217 (b) the etchings] Skene's *A series of sketches of the existing localities alluded to in the Waverley Novels*, Edinburgh, 1829. Although the title-page is dated 1829, the work came out in 21 parts between 1829 and 1831. Vol. 2, which has never been published, is in my Scott Coll.

217 (d) Scottish piece of artillery] A brass gun taken at the fortress of Bhurt-

pore in 1828 and presented by the Governor-General and Council of India to Capt. L. Carmichael of the 59th Regt. It has an inscription: 'Jacobus Monteith me fecit, Edinburgh, anno Dom. 1642.' It was presented on 14 Dec. 1829 to the Society of Antiquaries of Scotland by Capt. Carmichael. It is at present on display in the National Museum of Antiquities, Edinburgh.

218 (b) official letter of Lord Aberdeen] About the Stewart Papers.

219 *n*. 1] The Bishop means that Scott gave Colvin Smith a sitting for his portrait. Though Colvin Smith made about 20 replicas from the master copy, Scott, for some of these, actually gave a sitting. This copy was presented in 1854 to the University of Oxford by Rev. J. Treherne.

220 *n*. 2] The Duke's letter is in Partington, *Letter-books*, p. 289. It is said that the Duchess of Baden wanted the Duke to marry one of her daughters. See *Elizabeth Holland to her son, 1821–1845*, London, 1946, p. 102.

223 (c–d) *vox et præterea nihil*] See *SL* vii. 237.

225 (e) third son of Sir Walter Scott of Harden] Sir Walter Scott should be Sir William Scott.

228 (d) Sotheby] Two days before this, Lady Louisa Stuart had written to a friend: 'Only imagine that the House of Sotheby, after visiting Rokeby, are all gone in a body to fall on Walter Scott—poor man!' (Stuart, *Letters*, ii. 161.)

230 (a) drawing of Wayland Smith's dwelling] Mrs Hughes noted that this or a similar drawing had been presented in 1821 (*SL* vi. 384 *n*.). Scott sent it to Cadell (below, p. 258), but neither this nor any other of John Hughes's drawings were used for the Magnum.

230 (b) a Lambourne executed] See below, pp. 273–4.

230 (b–c) Sir Henry Lee's picture . . . copied] It was not used for the Magnum.

231 (b) the pride / Men put in cattle] Crabbe, *The borough*, Letter XIII, lines 211–12: 'pride / Men have in cattle.'

232 *n*. 1] In line 3, delete 'Scott's'. Scott was not the editor of *The Border*

antiquities. In line 3, for '1814' read '1814–17 [1812–17].'

232 *n.* 2] Sir James Foulis visited Abbotsford on 6 Sept. 1833 and signed the Visitors' Book as 'Sir James Foulis of Colinton.' See his biog. in Index.

232 *n.* 3] It was also issued by the Maitland Club.

233 (a) Manuscript Satir[e] on Stair] See above, p. 46 and *n.* 3 and p. 69.

233 (b) To James Ballantyne] In heading add: [or rather, Robert Cadell]

234 (a) painful business] The illness of Richardson's daughter, Christian. She died in Oct.

234 *n.* 1] Delete 'Presumably.'

235 (d) Miss Baillies volume] Joanna Baillie's *A collection of poems, chiefly manuscript* (1823) from which Scott's contribution, *Macduff's Cross*, is to be reprinted in *The poetical works.*

238 (a) about a mile off] About 1830 Richardson built the present mansion (designed by Blore) within a stone's throw of the village. In 1829 there was only a farmhouse and it may have been, as Scott says, 'about a mile off.'

238 (b) to set grass parks] On use of 'set' as synonym for 'let,' see *SL* x. 189.

238 (e–f) Brown of Rawflatt] This is David Brown, but he was not born till 1800 and Admiral Elliot died in 1808. Scott must mean 'David Brown, whose father long managed the property.' David probably carried on the management for Miss Carnegie after his father's death in 1822.

238 (f) Admiral Elliot & Miss Carnegie] Admiral John Elliot (died in 1808) was 4th son of Sir Gilbert Elliot, 2nd Bart. of Minto. His niece, Agnes Murray Elliot, married Sir David Carnegie, 4th Bart., who had unmarried sisters and unmarried daughters. The 'Miss Carnegie' of the text was probably a grandniece. Admiral Elliot lived at Monteviot, near Kirklands, and it was at Monteviot that his sister, Jane Elliot, author of *The Flowers of the Forest*, died in 1805.

239 (b) about the poems] *MacDuff's Cross, The doom of Devorgoil* and *Auchindrane* were included in Vol. 11 (*Ruff*, No. 165). The essay on the Highlands was not included.

240 (b) push on and keep moving] See my note to *SL* vi. 297 (f).

240 (d) a young man . . . Mr. MacDonald] The young man is John Buchanan, a clerk in the Register House. MacDonald is Alexander Macdonald, clerk to Thomas Thomson in the Register House. As Scott's letter to him is not known to be extant, we can only assume that it related to Macdonald's letter of 11 Aug. (NLS MS. 3910, ff. 23–4) in which he had sent to Scott a specimen of the Journal of the Duke of Cumberland's Army, Oct. 1745–Apr. 1746. Scott at this time was writing the 3rd ser. of *Tales of a grandfather.*

241 (c) brother of the order of Bannie] Archdeacon Wrangham was elected to the Bannatyne Club on 28 Jan. 1829.

241 (d) To Robert Cadell] This letter should be dated 1829.

242 (f) court Martial] At Ipswich. See *SL* xii. 466 *n.*

243 (b) Inglefield] Should be Englefield.

245 (a) Shortreed] He was Sheriff Substitute of Roxburghshire.

245 (b) sold his hen in a rainy day] A Scottish proverb. See *SL* v. 291, 291 *n.* and my note.

245 *n.* 1] In line 2, for 'Shortreede' read 'Shortreed.'

245 *n.* 3] In line 4, 'bound up with' should be 'published with.'

248 (a) your present afflictions] Illness of Richardson's daughter, Christian. She died on 29 Oct. See below, p. 261 *n.*

248 (c) Hesperides] See my note to *SL* i. 227 (d).

248 *n.* 1] Reference should be to *The Psalms of David in metre according to the version approved by the Church of Scotland*, Psalm 81, st. [4], lines 7–8.

250 (b) Lord Newton] On 19 and 23 Oct. 1829 he decided that the copyrights of *The Pirate, Nigel, Peveril, Quentin Durward* and *Miscellaneous prose works* belonged to Archibald Constable & Co.

251 (e–f) his young Lady] Lady Charlotte Thynne who had married the Duke of Buccleuch on 13 Aug.

252 (c) Tom Thumb] *Tom Thumb*, by Henry Fielding.

252 *n.* 1] *The Keepsake for MDCCCXXX* was published in 1829.

253 (b) Miss Kemble] Frances Anne Kemble (Fanny Kemble), eldest daughter of Charles Kemble.

253 (d) To John Murray] In Smiles, *John Murray*, ii. 276–7, where the ending is: 'I beg my kind compliments to Mrs. Murray and the young ladies, and am, yours truly, Walter Scott.'

254 (b) permission of a person] The King. See below, p. 255 *n.* 2.

254 (d) close of the late melancholy scene] Death of Lady Isabella Cust. See above, p. 250 and *n.*

255 *n.* 1] Boswell, chap. 34 (under 1777). Scott used the same quotation in his *Journal*, 29 Dec. 1825, and the words 'dogged, peevish, and snappish' (without quotation marks) in *Redgauntlet*, Narrative, chap. 2.

257 (a) should not move further in the submission] Lord Newton's decisions of 19 and 23 Oct. See my note to *SL* xi. 250 (b). It was reported to the Trustees on 29 Dec. that Scott acquiesced in the decisions.

257 *n.* 1] See *SL* viii. 251 and my note.

258 (c) drawing of Wayland Smiths stone] By John Hughes. See my note to *SL* xi. 230 (a).

259 (b) riding on the whirlwind] Addison, *The campaign*, line 292: 'Rides in the whirlwind, and directs the storm.' The line also occurs in Pope's *Dunciad*, Bk III, line 264. Also quoted in *MPW* v. 30 and there is a reminiscence of the line in *The Heart of Mid-Lothian*, chap. 35.

260 (c) Skene] In Vol. 2 (unpublished and in my possession) of Skene's *Existing localities* there is a pencil drawing of Wayland Smith's cave but he makes no reference to Hughes's drawing.

260 *n.* 1] The quaich is in the showcase in the bow window of the Library at Abbotsford. For the sketch of Wayland Smith's Cave, see above, pp. 230, 258 and below, p. 273. See also *SL* vi. 384 *n.* 1.

260 *n.* 3] The Bishop is Edward Copleston, Bishop of Llandaff. Scott's reply to

his letter of 9 Dec. is printed above, pp. 85–7, where it is dated 1 Jan. 1829 instead of 1 Jan. 1830.

261 (c) sitting at the receipt of custom] *Bible*, Matthew 9: 9; Mark 2: 14; Luke 5: 27.

264 (d)–265 I saw that distinguished poet only on[c]e] Scott saw him twice—in Sibbald's bookshop and at Sciennes Hill House.

265 *n.* 1] Delete 'Probably.'

266 *n.* 2] The Edin. Univ. Lib. copy is a copy of the original in NLS (MS. 874, ff. 469–70).

267 (a) two of the letters] These two letters (actually three, as the first included a second) were printed in the Magnum Opus, Vol. 7, Appendix II, pp. cxxi–cxxvii. The third [fourth], received from Peel, was printed in Vol. 8, pp. 381–3.

267 (c) Sedet eternumque sedebit] Virgil, *Aeneid*, VI. 617.

268 (a) Edinr review] Scott may be referring to the review of *Ivanhoe* in *ER* Vol. 33 (Jan. 1820), pp. 1–54, in which there is a preliminary review of *Tales of my Landlord*, 3rd ser. The passage on Dugald Dalgetty (p. 5) was cited by Scott in his introd. to *A legend of Montrose* in the Magnum Opus ed., Vol. 15, pp. xviii–xix. If, however, Scott is referring to the review of *Old Mortality* in *ER*, date of letter should be about Mar. 1829.

268 (c) To Robert Cadell] The £200 was to be ready for Walter in early Nov. (*SL* xii. 467), presumably for travelling expenses, as '£50 in Scotch notes' of this letter suggests. Scott is in Edinburgh, i.e. after 12 Nov. Walter came to Edinburgh and he and Scott went to Abbotsford, where Scott found a letter from Mrs Hughes dated 18 Nov. (above, p. 260), i.e. about 21 Nov. Date of letter is probably Thursday 13 Nov., which would give time for Walter to receive the money before setting out.

268 *n.* 1] Delete and substitute: Richard Bannatyne's *Journal*, Edinburgh, 1806. The passages, which Scott wanted transcribed, were for *Ivanhoe* (Magnum Opus ed., Vol. 16, pp. 330–5).

269 *n.* 1] Delete. Scott is not returning the Bannatyne volume. He is returning

the original MS. which had belonged to Constable. See my note to *SL* v. 343 *n.* 2.

269 *n.* 2] Delete 'See *A.L.C.*, p. 328,' which applies to the periodical, not to the memoir. It is clear from Nichols's letter (NLS MS. 3911, ff. 85–6) that he was sending a separate pamphlet, which Scott did not preserve.

270 (c) unless my right hand] *Bible, Psalms* 137: 5.

270 (e) the Invisible] Sir William Knighton.

270 *n.* 2] Delete this note. The vols. sent by Murray are not in *ALC*.

271 (a) while the wind blows] *The miller's wedding*, lines 2–3 of chorus. In *The vocal magazine*, London, 1781, p. 330.

271 (a) the song is somewhat musty] Shakespeare, *Hamlet*, III. 2: 'The proverb is something musty.'

271 (b) spoiling the Egyptians] *Bible, Exodus* 3: 22: 'spoil the Egyptians'; 12: 36: 'And they spoiled the Egyptians.'

271 (c) Mad Tom] Shakespeare, *King Lear*, IV. 1.

272 (c) Your Christmas Gift] A quaich. See above, p. 260.

272 *n.* 1] Delete 'Evidently.'

272 *n.* 5] 'State' must be a misreading for 'Stale,' i.e. strong ale in contrast with mild ale. Scott could not have written 'State', which does not make sense. Reference in D'Urfey is p. 201.

273 (b) Housseins' tapestry] In *Arabian Nights*. See my note to *SL* i. 229 (e).

273 (d) Abyssinian fashion] i.e. eating raw flesh. See my note to *SL* iv. 28 *n.* 1.

273 (e) yeoman's service] Shakespeare, *Hamlet*, V. 2.

274 (d) the Bishops tale] Edward Copleston, Bishop of Llandaff. See above, pp. 85, 260 and *n.*

276 (a–b) alterations . . . in the Court of Session] Scottish Judicature Act (1 William IV, c. 69). See Anderson's ed. of *Journal*, p. 592, *n.* 2.

276 (b) potent grave and reverend Seigniors] Shakespeare, *Othello*, I. 3.

276 *n.* 1] Amend this note. Shepherd did not retire till Feb. 1830.

277 (b) pieds des mouches] See *SL* v. 279 and my note.

277 (d) silver punch ladles] Eight toddy ladles from Abbotsford, with crest and motto, were sold at Dowell's, Edinburgh, 8 Mar. 1946, Lot 404. Presumably Cadell's gift.

278 (b) wolf from the door] *Heywood*, p. 143; *Ray*, p. 30.

278 *n.* 1] In line 1, for '171–2' read '71–2.' In line 7, 'Mrs. Bond replies' applies to her letter of same day, i.e. 16 Dec.

279 (b) To James Ballantyne] This letter should be dated 25 Jan. 1826. The references to *The doom of Devorgoil*, to Erskine's high opinion of it, to Constable (still alive), and to discussion with Ballantyne on the play, all correspond to the entries in the *Journal* for 25 and 26 Jan. 1826. See also Skene, *Memories*, pp. 141–3.

280 (c) Gilchrist & Gifford] Pamphlets by Octavius Gilchrist and Gifford's ed. of Ben Jonson (9 vols., London, 1816). For Scott's criticism of Gifford, see *MPW* vii. 373–82.

280 *n.* 1] Laing had just recently discovered Sibbald's transcript in the Advocates' Lib. and he read a paper on it to the Soc. of Antiquaries on 9 Jan. 1832. This is the paper printed in *Archæologica Scotica*, Vol. 4, Pt 2.

281 (a) *valeat quantum*] See *SL* x. 102.

281 (a–b) beggars must not . . . be chusers] See *SL* ii. 225.

282 *n.* 1] To these references add 'Vol. X, p. 98.'

283 (d) p. 220 Vol. 28] Neither page nor volume corresponds to the interleaved copy of the novels. The passage in the *Provincial antiquities*, i. 37–9, was copied verbatim as part of Scott's note to *The Abbot*, chap. 14 (Magnum Opus ed., xx. 207–9).

284 (c) Tout vient . . .] 'Tout vient à point à qui sait attendre' is given as a proverb in Wood, *Dictionary of quotations*.

284 *n.* 1] See my note to p. 283 (d) above.

287 (d) Melvilles diary] See *The diary of Mr James Melvill, 1556–1601* [Bannatyne Club 34; ed. by G. R. Kinloch], Edinburgh, 1829, pp. 174–6.

290 (c) The picture of the Duke] This must be No. 4 in Kenneth Garlick's *A catalogue of . . . Sir Thomas Lawrence* [Walpole Soc. Vol. 39], 4to London, 1964, p. 194. In his left hand the Duke holds a telescope, but in his right hand he holds his hat, not his watch as Scott says.

290 (e) a picture of the Pope] Pope Pius VII, painted at Rome in 1819. At Windsor Castle. See Garlick (cited in preceding note), p. 162.

291 (d) the Banquet at Milnwood . . . sketch of Old Mortality] Engraved for frontispiece of Vol. 9 and title-page vignette of Vol. 10 of Magnum Opus respectively.

291 (e) Et cantare pares . . .] Virgil, *Eclogues*, VII. 5.

292 (b) A thing to dream of] *Christabel*, Pt I, line 253: 'A sight to dream of, not to tell!' Scott substitutes 'thing' for 'sight' also in *SL* viii. 159, 289.

292 (e) Bothwells combat] Engraved by Charles Rolls for frontispiece to Vol. 10 of Magnum Opus.

292 n. 2] Delete 'See also Vol. X, p. 457, note', which does not apply. For other references, see Index under Ballads and Songs. *The death of Parcy Reed.*

292 n. 3] Delete 'Doubtless.' Most of it was published by Mrs M. M. Maxwell-Scott in *Harper's Monthly Mag.*, European ed. Vol. 17, American ed. Vol. 78 (Apr. 1889), pp. 778–88, and in the *Nineteenth Century*, Vol. 58 (Oct. 1905), pp. 621–33. Scott must have contemplated a much larger work, for Cadell estimated on 15 Sept. 1830 the cost of printing either 2,500 or 5,000 copies of the work in 2 vols. (NLS MS. 6080.)

293 (e) My mother was benevolent] See my note to *SL* vi. 52 (c–d).

293 n. 2] McMillan's letter (NLS MS. 3912, ff. 129–30) does not give the forename of William Borthwick's brother.

296 (c) whole Inventory] Scott printed extracts from it, with acknowledgement to Hamper, in a note to chap. 32 of *Kenilworth.*

296 (d) the tree must lie where it fell] *Bible, Ecclesiastes* 11: 3: 'where the tree falleth, there it shall be.'

296 (e) "Of the things that are long enough ago"] See *SL* viii. 90 and my note.

298 (a) dismiss any of us clerks] Under a bill pending in Parliament. See above, p. 276 (a–b) and my note.

299 (c) Mr Curls situation] James Curle, writer in Melrose, had been appointed manager of the Abbotsford estate by Scott's Trustees and he continued to act as such during Scott's lifetime. See Minutes of 27 Aug. 1832 in *Sederunt Books.*

299 (d) James] Willie Laidlaw's younger brother.

299 n. 1] Only in Douglas's ed.

300 (c) my own important name] This is the reading in the *Leisure Hour*, 1871 (5 Aug.), p. 490, where the letter is also printed. Obviously Scott wrote, or meant to write, 'unimportant.'

300 n. 1] Scott wrote to Mrs Scott Moncrieff on 17 Dec. 1830, saying he had received Dr Young's papers in Sept. and that publication was out of the question. This letter (which is wrongly dated 1829) is in the *Leisure Hour*, 1871 (5 Aug.), p. 490. It is not in *SL.*

301 (a) Stock Bridge] Stockbridge is now a district in north Edinburgh.

301 (c) the curious letter] This is probably the item sold at Sotheby's, June 1965.

302 (b) in article of Demonology] This is the correct reading (NLS MS. 859, f. 121). Scott means 'on the subject of' but his use of 'article' in this sense is unusual with him, and it was by this time obsolete. It is also used in *SL* vii. 455.

302 (d) the Advocate and his blasted bill] See above, p. 276 (a–b).

303 n. 1] In line 8, delete 'a certain'. In line 9, for 'Burkett' read 'Birkett.' In line 2 from foot, delete 'Perhaps.' I have compared the handwriting and signatures of the letters of 6 May 1815 (NLS MS. 870, f. 34) and 28 Feb. 1830 (NLS MS. 3912, ff. 189–90). They are identical.

304 (c) College Album] *The College album for MDCCCXXX. A selection of original pieces. Ed. by students in the University of Glasgow*, 12mo Glasgow, 1830.

With printed dedication to Scott, whose name appears in list of subscribers for two copies.

304 *n.* 2] In line 1, delete 'Sir.'

305 (a) Essay on Popular poetry part 2d.] i.e. 'Essay on imitations of the ancient ballad,' which was printed in 5th ed. of the *Minstrelsy*, 1830 (*Ruff*, No. 19). The text of *William and Helen* was not included in the Appendix to the 'Essay.'

305 (f) if the bill passes] The bill was not passed till after Scott's death. It was 'An Act to amend the laws relating to dramatic literary property,' 3 & 4 Wm. IV, c. 15, passed 10 June 1833.

305 *n.* 1] This note refers to 'those on the lay Marmion etc.', not to 'Essay on Popular poetry part 2d.' Move index figure above to 'etc.'

306 (d) My mother says Sancho] Cervantes, *Don Quixote*. See my note to *SL* ii. 299 (b).

306 *n.* 1] There is an extract on this subject from Cadell's letter of 17 Mar. in Partington, *Post-bag*, p. 287.

308 *n.* 1] Delete the reference to Burns, which is superfluous.

310 (a) Scottish Bill] See my note to *SL* xi. 276 (a–b).

311 (a) Theatrical bits] Read 'Theatrical bill.' See above, p. 305 and my note.

311 (d) the Byzantine books] For *Count Robert of Paris*.

312 (e) laws either of Medes or Persians] *Bible, Esther* 1: 19; *Daniel* 6: 8.

313 (b) Murray] John Murray who published the *Demonology*. It was never included in any collected ed.

313 *n.* 1] It is just as likely that Scott did mean Nectanabus, a necromancer in early literature. See Weber's *Metrical romances* (1810), iii. 291. This is probably the Shetland pony sent to Scott via John Gibson in 1827. See Scott's letter to Gibson, 20 Aug. [1827] in Gibson transcripts in NLS (MS. 6080). It is not in *SL*.

314 (d) Walter used to be a gallant] 'ten or twelve years ago' must be wrong. Helen Graham in her diary for Jan. 1824 reports Lady Scott as saying of Miss Crumpe and Walter: 'And den she

go for do dake my son Walter away from me, and I have got no good of him since he came. If she sees him in de street she say, "Come indo dis shop with me: I vant someding here." And take him by de arm and make him go vid her.' (*Parties and pleasures: the diaries of Helen Graham, 1823–1826, ed. by James Irvine*, [Edinburgh] 1957, p. 38.)

314 *n.* 3] Campbell's letter of 30 May is printed, with a few words omitted in each, in William Beattie, *Life and letters of Thomas Campbell*, London, 1849, iii. 66–7, and in Partington, *Letter-books*, p. 104. In line 1, for 'M.G.I. Crumpe' read 'M.G.S. Crumpe'.

315 *n.* 1] Win Jenkins's letter of 4 Oct.

316 (b) Lady Louisa] Lady Louisa Stuart.

317 (c) marchings & counter marchings] Foote, *The Mayor of Garratt*, I. 1. See also *SL* viii. 333, ix. 85, 114, x. 1, 84.

317 (e) Dr Abernethy] This should be Dr Abercrombie.

319 (d) I might have rhymed] Shakespeare, *Hamlet*, III. 2: 'You might have rhymed.' It is Horatio who says this. Scott should have written 'I might have rhymed like Hamlet.'

319 (e) To Charles] This, as the first of the 'family packet', should have been printed above, at p. 312.

321 (a) great disappointment] The cancelled visit to London.

323 *n.* 1] Constable and Co., Waterloo Place, Edinburgh.

324 (d) Minstrelsy] No new ballads were added.

328 (a) To Robert Cadell] Cadell's letter which Scott is answering is of the same date, i.e. 12 Apr., and is in NLS (MS. 3913, ff. 23–6). Ballantyne's letter (NLS MS. 3913, ff. 21–2) is also of 12 Apr., but as Scott does not mention it in this letter he must not have received it till 13 Apr.

329 (c) Advocates bill] See above, p. 276 (a–b).

329 (f) Help is a good dog] Variation of proverb 'Brag is a good dog but Holdfast is better.'

330 (c) Mr Dickinson] See my note to *SL* x. 275 (c).

330 (d) The London people] Charles Tilt. Tilt wrote at least three letters: (1) one perhaps in 1829, which Scott answered though letter is not in *SL*; (2) one about Mar. 1830, mentioned in this letter, which Scott did not answer; (3) one on 14 Apr. 1830 (cited *SL* xii. 471 *n.*), which Scott answered in May 1830 (printed in *SL* xii. 471). The only Tilt letter in Walpole Coll. is the third.

330 (f) your scratchings] *A series of sketches of the existing localities.*

330 *n.* 1] The *Landscape illustrations* was completed in 2 4to vols. in Dec. 1831 with the date 1832 on the title-pages. It came out serially in 20 parts between Apr. 1830 and Dec. 1831. I have the copy which was presented by the editor to James Skene.

331 (a) John Logan] Should be Robert Logan.

331 (d) the Strange family] As there are no entries for Apr. 1830 in the *Journal* it is difficult to say who are meant by the Strange family. Scott dined later in Edinburgh with Mr and Mrs James Strange and Skene (*Journal*, 30 June, 3 July). Sir Thomas and Lady Strange met Scott in Edinburgh on 6 July and were invited to Abbotsford, but the visit was cancelled. (Letter from Sir Thomas's daughter, 11 Dec. 1899, at Abbotsford.) In the showcase in the Library at Abbotsford are exhibited a green blotting case and another case said to have belonged to Napoleon. A small piece of blotting paper and a small piece of sealing wax inside them were found in Napoleon's cabin on the *Bellerophon*, but the green velvet cases were made by Lady Strange.

332 (a) to make the surrender] i.e. resign his Clerkship in Court of Session.

332 (b) the dramas] They formed Vol. 11 of the *Poetical works*. By 'the whole 12' Scott must mean 'the whole 11.' This ed. was dedicated to the Duke of Buccleuch.

332 (d) Advocates Bill] See above, p. 276 (a–b).

332 (e) MacBeth . . . who can have no successor] Shakespeare, *Macbeth*, IV. 1.

333 (d) I may have written a private letter] At least 37 letters in *SL* were written in Court.

335 *n.* 1] See *SL* iv. 12 and my note.

337 (a) whom the King has delighted to honour] *Bible, Esther* 6: 6, 7, 9, 11.

337 (d) inflicting my tediousness] See *SL* ii. 320.

337 (d) *Solve equum senescentem*] See *SL* iv. 12 and my note.

338 (a) To William Laidlaw] Scott had written to Laidlaw from Bowhill (letter not in *SL*) and Laidlaw replied, giving an account of Hogg's troubles. Laidlaw's letter is quoted in Carruthers, *Abbotsford notanda*, pp. 176–7. Scott is here continuing that correspondence.

338 (b) Mr Lacy] Apparently a misreading for Lang.

338 (d) Col. Fegusson] There are no entries in the *Journal* for this period. It seems that James Ferguson is talking of renting Kaeside.

339 (b) James's affair] Ballantyne's dispute with Cadell over printing of the Magnum.

340 (a–b) Mr Shaw] James Shaw.

340 (c) Dr. Bowring] See *Autobiographical recollections of Sir John Bowring*, London, 1877, pp. 9–10, 347–50.

342 (b) Turnimspike] This is not given as Graham's in any collection I have consulted. Stenhouse, in his notes to *Johnson* (1853 ed., iv. 22), says it is anonymous.

342 (b) six small volumes] See *The Bibliotheck*, Vol. 3, No. 6 (1962), pp. 202–18.

343 (c) One for a Baron Fahrenburgh] This letter, which is not in *SL*, is printed in the *Lit. Gaz.* 1832 (9 June), p. 361. The Baron de Fahnenberg (the correct spelling) had written from Carlsruhe on 30 Mar. 1830 (NLS MS. 3912, ff. 280–1) referring to the meaning of 'pyne' (cf. above, p. 54) and thanking Scott for his kindness to his son-in-law, Baron de Lotzbeck, and his wife when they visited Abbotsford (not recorded in the *Journal*).

343 (c) Madrid envoy] Henry Unwin Addington. See above, p. 281, 281 *n.* 2. There is a letter from him, 1830, to Scott in NLS (MS. 3913, f. 37).

344 (a) a letter to Lord Dalhousie] This letter of 26 Apr. 1830 was printed

in the *Scotsman*, 26 Jan. 1959, from the original deposited in the Register House, Edinburgh, on permanent loan from the Earl of Dalhousie. It is not in *SL*.

344 *n.* In line 4, the letter from Sir James Shaw is a transcript by McDiarmid (NLS MS. 3913, ff. 59–60). In line 11, for 'Sir John' read 'Sir James.' In line 17, Dalhousie's letter is in NLS (MS. 3914, ff. 177–9).

345 (c) Advocates Bill] See above, p. 276 (a–b).

345 (e–f) like Blow bladder street in the farce] Foote, *Taste*, I. 1. See also *SL* iii. 141.

346 *n.* 1] Lockhart's letter is in Partington, *Letter-books*, pp. 159–60.

346 *n.* 2] As elsewhere, Scott has written in instalments.

347 (a) of your going into parliament] There had been earlier references to this (*SL* ix. 253, 253 *n.*, 256), but the only reference I have found to his actually standing is in a letter from Anne to Miss Millar, 3 May 1831: 'Lockhart is standing for some Borough or other, but we have not heard if he has gained his election.' (*Letters to their old governess*, p. 134.)

347 (c) the last act . . . jurys] 'An Act to regulate the qualification and the manner of enrolling jurors in Scotland,' 6 Geo. IV, c. 22, passed 20 May 1825.

347 *n.* 3] Kenneth Mackenzie married in 1817 Isabella Roy, and, having no issue, left his estate to his brother-in-law, Robert Roy, W.S., who lost it to Kenneth's younger brother Thomas after long litigation. See Alexander Mackenzie, *History of the Clan Mackenzie*, Inverness, 1879, p. 284.

349 (b–c) Sir Toby] Shakespeare, *Twelfth Night*, II. 3.

350 (b) the cave] The Great Peak Cavern at Castleton, Derbyshire. (The Devil's Cavern of *Peveril of the Peak*, chap. 1.)

351 (a) "stupid bits"] This should probably be 'stupit bits,' the form he uses elsewhere.

351 *n.* 1] See also my note to *SL* x. 332 (c).

352 (c) as my epistles are not gospels] Shakespeare, *Twelfth Night*, V. 1.

352 (d) To Alexr. Young] This letter is in Skene's *Memories*, pp. 171–4, from a letter in Skene's collection. It must be a copy and Cresson's name is suppressed. The letter is wrongly given as addressed to Sir Alexander Young of Harburn, Bart.

352 (d) Mr Cresson] Elliott Cresson visited Abbotsford on 1 Apr. 1833. (MS. Visitors' Book at Abbotsford.)

357 (a) foxes judgement of the grapes] See L'Estrange, *Fables*, No. 129: *A fox and grapes*. By Aesop.

357 (f) John Gilpin] Cowper, *John Gilpin*, st. 58, lines 3–4.

358 (b) The drowsy Bench the babbling hall] Sir William Blackstone, *The lawyer's farewell to his Muse*. For sources, see my note to *SL* i. 73 (d).

358 (d) as Gil Blas preferrd his commis] See my note to *SL* vi. 402 (b).

358 (d) in dubio] A Scots law phrase. See Trayner, *Latin maxims*.

359 (a) *a rich fellow enough* go to] Shakespeare, *Much ado about nothing*, IV. 2. Scott is alluding to Lockhart's income as given above, p. 346, *n.* 1.

359 (b) To Anna Jane Clephane] Scott knew from Gibson's letter of 24 Apr. (*n.* 2 below) that Lady Northampton was dead. Lady Northampton died at Rome on 2 Apr. and Anna Jane would write as soon as she got the news. (News of it at the end of May would not have been a shock.) The letter should be dated about the end of Apr.

359 *n.* 2] Richard Lundin of Auchtermairnie was Mrs Maclean Clephane's first cousin. Lady Northampton, therefore, was his cousin once removed.

362 (b) Skene] In Skene's *Sketches* there is no indication that he was indebted to Walter for a sketch.

362 (e) To Mrs. Hughes] This letter belongs to 1829, as references to *Kenilworth* and the death of Terry show. The letter was begun on 30 June ('They leave Edinr. tomorrow,' which was 1 July—*Journal*) and completed on 1 July.

363 *n.* 1] Delete this note, which is not now applicable.

364 n. 2] Delete 'Probably.' Scott had already referred to Ainslie as 'a medallist'. See *Journal*, 3 Mar. 1828.

365 (a) Emperor Seg[e]d] Samuel Johnson, *The Rambler*, No. 205, 3 Mar. 1752.

365 (b) In the morning up I looks] *A song in the opera call'd The Kingdom of the birds*, st. 8. In D'Urfey, *Wit and mirth*, Vol. 2, London, 1719, p. 216.

365 n. 2] The epithet 'Ciceronian' is not explained by Sophia's letter. Scott had called him 'Ciceronian John' as early as 1828. See *SL* x. 376. See also below, p. 388.

366 (e) like the sick fox] Scott is probably thinking of Gay's *Fables*, No. 29, 'The fox at the point of death.'

367 (a) Walter *ill to hauld*] According to Scott's MS. pedigree of the Scotts of Sinton (printed in Sir William Fraser, *The Scotts of Buccleuch*, Edinburgh, 1878, i. 563), it was William Scott of Huntly who was called 'Willy Ill to Had.' According to Scott of Satchells, *A true history*, Hawick, 1894, *Post'ral*, p. 61, it was John Scott who was called 'Jocky ill to had.'

367 (b–c) as the old horse said to the broken cart] *Kelly*, p. 54, gives this proverb as: 'A careless parting, between the old mare and the broken carr.' Also used in *Rob Roy*, chap. 27.

367 (e) Sierra Morena] See my note to *SL* ii. 542 (c).

368 (b) Mrs Fox Lane] See my note to *SL* ix. 44 (f).

368 (e) Sir Toby's experiment] Shakespeare, *Twelfth Night*, II. 3.

370 n. 3] Scott's correspondent was only son of John Christian by his first wife. On his second marriage his father took the surname of Curwen. John Christian's half-brother was, therefore, Henry Curwen. Burke, *Landed gentry*, gives the estate as Ewanrigg.

371 (a) "beggard and outraged"] Wordsworth, *Sonnet. Composed at ⸻ [Neidpath] Castle* (1803), line 8.

371 n. 1 The Blair-Adam Club had their last expedition] It was Scott's last expedition, but not the Club's.

372 (c–d) we are all Johnstones and Jardines] See Scott's note to chap. 26 of *Guy Mannering*.

375 (d) I will now soon send you the work] The page proofs which Scott sent to Pitcairn are now in my Scott Coll.

375 n. 2] There was no advocate in 1792 of the name of Pest or Peat. In Anstey's *The new Bath guide*, Letter VI, there is a reference to a 'worthy old Counsellor Pest.' If Robert MacIntosh had acquired, in allusion to Anstey's character, the nickname of 'worthy old Counsellor Pest,' then Scott and his father would be referring to the same man.

378 (d) us high school boys] This incident proves that Scott was in Luke Fraser's second class in Apr. 1779.

378 n. 1] There is a song, *The Highlandmen's bloody encounter at Leith, April 20, 1779*, in a chapbook. The mutiny is referred to as 'that woful day beside Leith Pier' in Introd. to *The two drovers*.

381 (c–d) a Chief Clanronald] Scott had been involved in his proposed 'preposterous marriage with Mrs. Hall' in 1809. Scott's letter on this subject to Charles Bagot, 20 Mar. 1809, is not in *SL* but is printed in *George Canning and his friends . . .*, ed. by Captain Josceline Bagot, London, 1909, i. 294–5.

382 (a) screwed my courage to the sticking place] Shakespeare, *Macbeth*, I. 7.

382 (f) Poor dear Jane] There is no record of Scott's having seen Jane since Jan. 1827.

383 (a) singula praedantur] Horace, *Epistles*, II. ii. 55.

383 (d) Langton] Longtown.

384 (a) the tract] *Historical notices of Edward and William Christian: two characters in Peveril of the Peak*, 8vo London, 1823.

384 (c) Mr Wilkes] For a discussion on his identity by George H. Bushnell, see the *Scots Mag.* N.S. Vol. 45 (Sept. 1946), pp. 469–75.

385 (e) flapping the ears] Swift. See my note to *SL* ii. 213 (c).

386 (c) So transeat . . .] See my note to *SL* iii. 170 (b).

386 (d) prophets chamber] *Bible*, *II Kings* 4: 10.

386 n. 2] The phrase dates from a much earlier period.

387 (d) Well who cares a jot . . .] Bickerstaffe, *Love in a village*, I. 3.

388 (a) To J. G. Lockhart] Date is Nov., as is shown by the references to Charles. Charles had been at Abbotsford in the autumn before going to Naples. On 11 Nov. Scott asked Cadell to send Charles £50 (below, p. 415).

388 (d) Johnie . . . Ciceronian] See *SL* x. 376 and above, p. 365.

388 (e) Mr Scott] Probably James Scott.

388 (f) "the deils awa wi' the Exciseman"] The poem of that title by Burns.

388 (f) Mo[r]gans letter] From Francis Morgan, 51 Bedford Square, London (NLS MS. 3919, ff. 295–6).

390 (f) while the play is good] Ramsay, *Proverbs*, p. 21.

391 (a) Tales] *Tales of a grandfather*, 4th ser. (France).

391 (c) To Robert Southey] Most of this letter was printed in the *Edinburgh Sir Walter Scott Club, 20th annual report* (1913), pp. 31–2, where there are minor differences from the Abbotsford copy. The letter is there dated 'September 22 [1830].' A note points out that the anecdote had appeared in *Trans. of the Royal Soc. of Edinburgh*, 1815, vii. 495, and later in *Memoir of . . . James Currie, ed. by his son, W. W. Currie*, London, 1831, ii. 248.

391 *n.* 2] Delete first sentence. The Robison at the reference given (*SL* vii. 330 *n.*) is the son.

393 (c) like the old Giant pope] Bunyan's *Pilgrim's progress*.

393 *n.* 1] Alexander Hislop, *The book of Scottish anecdote*, 7th ed., Glasgow, 1888, p. 481, gives an anecdote of James VI at Falkland in which he uses this phrase. Hislop's authority is 'Charles Mackie' but I have not traced that source. *Kelly*, p. 233, gives it as a proverb meaning 'Omne simile est dissimile.' In Ramsay, *Proverbs*, p. 45. Scott had used this quotation in his review of Ritson's *Annals of the Caledonians* in *QR* for July 1829 (*MPW* xx. 346).

396 *n.* 1] Delete this note. Maggy Fendy was the nickname of Margaret Scott, daughter of Walter Scott of Harden ('Auld Wat'). She married Gilbert Eliott of Stobs ('Gibbie wi' the gowden garters').

397 (d) To James Skene] This letter should be dated 1829.

398 (b) Cadell should have enlarged the impression] Of Skene's *Sketches of the existing localities*, the title-page of which is wrongly dated 1829. The work came out in 21 parts, 1829–31, and Parts 1–7 were issued in 1829.

400 (a) old Age is clawing me] Shakespeare, *Hamlet*, V. 1.

400 (d) Dougal] Name of Walter's pony when he was a boy. See *SL* xii. 124.

400 *n.* 1] Lady Louisa Stuart's letter is in Stuart, *Selections*, pp. 259–62.

401 (a) deny with Lady Teazle the butler and the coach-horse] Sheridan, *The school for scandal*, II. 1.

401 (b) must eat a peck of dirt] Probably 'Every man must eat a peck of ashes before he dies' (*Ray*, p. 95).

402 (e) as Sir Hugh Evans says] Scott was perhaps thinking of *Merry wives of Windsor*, IV. 1: 'He is a good sprag memory.' Scott uses the word 'sprag' in *SL* xii. 333.

404 (f) Boscobel] *The Boscobel tracts, relating to the escape of Charles II. after the Battle of Worcester*. Ed. by John Hughes, 8vo Edinburgh, 1830.

405 (e) Mrs. Rickets story] The ghost story by Mrs Ricketts (sister of 1st Viscount St. Vincent and wife of William Henry Ricketts of Longwood, Hants) is fully told in *Diaries of a lady of quality* [Frances Williams Wynn] *ed. by A. Hayward*, 2nd ed., London, 1864, pp. 213–22.

405 *n.* 1] Mrs Hughes's letter of 15 Nov. is in Partington, *Letter-books*, pp. 339–44.

407 (a) Tales] *Tales of a grandfather*, 4th ser. (France).

407 (a) the excellent Bishop] Edward Copleston, Bishop of Llandaff.

407 (f) reverent Seigniors] Shakespeare, *Othello*, I. 3: 'reverend signiors.'

408 (e) minstrels epistles] Shakespeare, *Twelfth Night*, V. 1.

409 (d) letter from Sir John Malcolm] This letter is not in NLS. It is presumably the letter dated 15 May quoted in John William Kaye's *The life and correspondence of Major-General Sir John*

Malcolm, 8vo London, 1856, ii. 543. The portion quoted contains no reference to Walter Scott.

409 (d) unpronounceable Indian name] Mahābaleshwar, a Bombay hill station south of Poona.

409 *n*. 1] Delete. See above, p. 393 *n*. 2.

410 (a–b) roa[s]t potatoes at a volcanoe] See *SL* i. 187.

411 (a) Lady Charlotte] Lady Charlotte Hope, daughter of 2nd Earl of Hopetoun, whom Lord President Hope had married in 1793.

411 (b–c) old rat] As the context is the same, though differently worded, Scott is probably quoting Swift. See above, p. 166.

412 (e) turnpike act] A Committee of the Turnpike Road Trustees for Selkirkshire, with Scott as convener, was appointed on 7 Oct.

413 *n*. 2] The proverb is in Ramsay, *Proverbs*, p. 61. Also used in *Rob Roy*, chaps. 14 and 26.

414 (d) the ponies] Presumably Nectanabus and Marion. For these ponies, see Index under Horses. For the former see also above, p. 313 and my note.

415 (a) whipping to death] Shakespeare, *Measure for measure*, V. 1.

415 *n*. 3] Kinnear died on 20 Oct. It was later stated that 'after a long investigation before a coroner's jury, it was ascertained that his death was occasioned by the rupture of a blood-vessel in the stomach.' (*Ann. Reg.* 1830, Chron., p. 276.)

416 (c) Squire absolute] Probably an allusion to Absolute in Sheridan's *The rivals*.

417 (a) I am prickd on in mine intent] Shakespeare, *Macbeth*, I. 7.

417 (e) like [the] statue of don Juan] See Harvey's *Oxford companion to English literature*, under Don Juan. The statue is referred to, under Molière's title, *Festin de pierre*, in chap. 5 of *Rob Roy*.

418 (a) your wellcome Gratulor] Adam's letter of 21 Nov. (NLS MS. 3915, ff. 90–1).

419 (c) the symposions which I used to attend] The Blair-Adam Club.

419 (c) as Sancho says] See my note to *SL* ii. 542 (c).

419 (d) desipere in loco] Horace, *Odes*, IV. xii. 28.

420 (a) old Waterloo] Duke of Wellington.

420 (b) If by your art . . .] Shakespeare, *The tempest*, I. 2.

420 (d) robert and his sister] Robert and Barbara.

423 (a) My dogs as Ossian says] See my note to *SL* xi. 38 (e).

423 (d) publishd by Government] Read 'purchased by Government.'

424 (e) Job himself and his three freinds] *Bible*, *Job* 32.

425 (d) valeat quantum] See *SL* x. 102.

426 (e) mettled Jock Ha'] *Archie of Ca'field*, st. 5, lines 1–2. In *Minstrelsy* (ed. Henderson), ii. 149.

427 (b) two originals] Nimrod and Bran.

427 *n*. 1] Delete. See my note to *SL* iii. 526 *n*. 1.

428 (a) Mr. Dean—one word from you] Swift, *Imitation of part of the sixth satire of the second book of Horace*, line 82 (*Works*, ed. Scott, 2nd ed., xii. 324).

428 (a) open Sesamum] See my note to *SL* vi. 293 (d).

428 (b) Hill of Christie] Skene was apparently unable to help, for Scott, in his ed. of the *Trial*, p. xii, said it was a 'local name, which is probably known in the country, though the Editor has been unable to discover it.'

428 *n*. 1] Scott was assisted in this work by John Buchanan and Alexander Macdonald (for whom see above, p. 240 and my note). On 6 Dec. 1830 Macdonald wrote to Scott: 'I have read these sheets of my namesake's [i.e. Alexander Bane Macdonald] trial with the record along with Mr Buchanan and shall be glad to attend any suggestions & corrections of yours when they are returned.' (NLS MS. 3915, ff. 138–9.) Delete from 'The first part' (in line 5) to the end of the note. Scott declined to approach Sir Edward Paget but sent to Skene a letter for Macdonell. This letter from Scott, dated 24 Oct., is

not in *SL* but is in Skene, *Memories*, pp. 177–8. Skene comments (p. 178) that the letter to Macdonell had the desired effect, but Scott did not know this when he wrote the letter docketed 6 Dec. Both Skene and Grierson are ambiguous.

428 *n.* 3] Thomas Thomson. He did not become President of the Bannatyne Club till after Scott's death and this note, therefore, is inaccurate.

429 (a) Mr. Murray] James Murray, who succeeded to Philiphaugh on his brother's death in 1830.

429 *n.* 1] Delete this note. The Murray referred to at Vol. IV, p. 240 is a different man.

430 (e) Lady Mornington] For 'Mornington' read 'Mordington.' Mary Dillon married in 1704 4th Lord Mordington. He repudiated the marriage and went through a form of marriage with Catherine Launder in 1715. He died in May and she died in June 1741. The lady who kept the gambling house was his first wife. See *GEC* ix. 206–7; *Journals of the House of Lords*, xxvi. 492; William Robertson, *Proceedings relating to the peerage of Scotland*, 4to Edinburgh, 1790, p. 246. The entry in Douglas's *Scots peerage*, ed. Paul, is inaccurate.

430 *n.* 1] The ballad is *Johny Faa, or the Gipsie laddie*. It is true that Allan Ramsay's version does not mention Lady Cassilis, but in *Johnson*, Vol. 2 (1788), No. 181, the last line is 'The earl of Cassilis' lady.' Stenhouse in his notes to *Johnson* (new ed., 1853, iv. 175) gives the traditional story, according to which John Faw or Faa was not a gipsy but a member of 'a very respectable family' near Dunbar. See also *N. & Q.* Vol. 185, p. 377, Vol. 186, pp. 74, 117, 164.

431 *n.* 1] Cadell's letter of 6 Dec. is in Partington, *Letter-books*, pp. 365–6.

432 *n.* 1] Le Sage, *Gil Blas*, Bk VII, chap. 4.

433 (b) Bobadil] Ben Jonson, *Every man in his humour*, IV.

433 (e) Othello] Shakespeare, *Othello*, II. 3. But it is Cassio who complains that his reputation is lost.

433 *n.* 2] I do not think Scott himself knew what he meant. He was very fond

of Addison's *Cato* and the line in Act IV, 'Cæsar asham'd! Has he not seen Pharsalia!' may have occurred to him and was used, as in other cases, without considering whether the quotation was apt or not.

434 (c) we must *do* as we *dow*] See *SL* x. 491 *n.* 1 and my note.

434 (e) Man but a rush . . .] Shakespeare, *Othello*, V. 2.

435 (a) Baron de Housais] Baron D'Haussez described this visit to Abbotsford in his *La Grand-Bretagne en mil huit cent trente-trois*, Bruxelles, 1833, ii. 109–21 and in the English translation, *Great Britain in 1833*, London, 1833, ii. 153–66. See *Lockhart*, ix. 369, x. 14.

435 (c) put the saddle on the right horse] *Kelly*, p. 281; Ramsay, *Proverbs*, p. 53.

436 (b) Mrs Youngs morning visit] On 15 Feb. 1830. See above, p. 297 *n.*

436 (c) to use Hare's lingo the *Shot*] 'Shot' was the slang word used by Burke and Hare for the body they were going to sell to the anatomists. See *Trial of William Burke and Helen McDougal*, etc., 8vo Edinburgh, 1829, pp. 88–9.

436 (d) had a friend with me] In his *Journal*, 20 Dec. 1830, Scott says 'Lord' and omits the name.

437 (b) putting even a face upon their conscience] See *N. & Q.* 10th ser. vii. 288. See also *SL* iii. 20 and my note.

438 *n.* 1] The Master of Ruthven said to Henderson: 'Is there no help in thee?'. I have not found in the accounts of the Gowrie Conspiracy the exact words as Scott gives them. See also above, p. 166.

438 *n.* 2] Cadell's letter of 15 Dec. is in Partington, *Letter-books*, pp. 367–9.

439 (a) Baron D'Aussay] Baron d'Haussez. See above, p. 435.

439 *n.* 2] *Lockhart* (x. 17 *n.*) gives the correct spelling 'Roland.' The farce is by Thomas Morton.

440 (c) I hope we shall see Richard himself again] Colley Cibber, *Richard III*, V. 3: 'Richard's himself again.' See my note to *SL* v. 29 (f).

440 *n.* 3] This note omits the subject of Scott's letter. Forbes had conveyed the

resolution of the creditors at a meeting of 17 Dec. 'That Sir Walter Scott be requested to accept of his furniture, plate, linens, paintings, library and curiosities of every description' (NLS MS. 113).

442 (f) A very kind friend] William Adam of Blair-Adam. See *Journal* 20 Dec. 1830.

443 (e) all who run may read] Cowper, *Tirocinium*, line 80, which is a variation of *Bible, Habakkuk* 2: 2: 'He may run that readeth it.'

443 *n.* 2] This note means that Hunt became a blacking manufacturer after 1833. But Scott, in this letter of 1830, calls him 'shoeblack Hunt.'

444 (a) the new fishing act] 'An Act for the more effectual preservation and increase of the breed of salmon and for better regulating the fisheries in the river Tweed.' (11 Geo. IV & 1 Will. IV, Local & Personal, c. 54, 29 May 1830.)

444 (e) I have often wished to go to work on the Duke of Guise] Scott had already written on him in the *Foreign Quart. Rev.* vol. 4. See above, p. 132 and *n.* 3.

445 (a) The Miss Tullos] Jane and Margaret Tulloh. Scott is mentioned in letters from Naples to their aunt Helen Leslie by Jane (5 Jan. 1832) and Margaret (15 May 1832). Private information from owner of the letters, J. G. Burnett, Esq., of Powis Gate, Aberdeen (1954).

445 (e) shadow of the Evening] Biblical phraseology but not a quotation.

446 (c) Mr Marshall] James Marshall, Collector of Fees, Register House, who had paid Scott's salary as Principal Clerk and who will now pay his pension.

447 (a) a general trust] Scott's will is printed in the *Edinburgh Weekly Jour.* Vol. 35 (12 Dec. 1832), p. 396, c. 4.

449 (b) all habit of my exercize] See my note to *SL* ii. 252 (a).

449 (f) £20000 secured on my life] According to list of policies in the *Sederunt Books*, £22,000 would be due. See my note to *SL* iii. 382 (b).

451 (b) filling up] Read 'fitting up.'

452 (d) The Second series] The projected, but not published, 5th ser. (France) of *Tales of a grandfather*.

452 (e) Your *views*] Cadell, till the end of his life, kept a volume which he called 'Views.' In it he entered all his projects—cost of printing, number of copies and other details—not always fulfilled. (NLS MS. 6080.)

452 *n.* 1] It would seem from the *Journal*, 24 Dec., that he wrote to Walter on that day.

453 (c) To James Marnie] There is a facsimile of this letter in the *Arbroath Guide*, 24 Sept. 1932, p. 3. It shows that 'bearing the date' (p. 453, line 1) should be 'having the date' and that the letter should end 'Your obliged humble servant.'

453 (d) Jamieson . . . rhyming couplet] The references to Dr John Jamieson and to the couplet both refer to Scott's note in his *History of Scotland*, cited in the footnote below.

453 *n.* 1] The money, however, was not paid till 1833. See my note to *SL* ix. 477 *n.* 1.

453 *n.* 2] There is a short extract from Marnie's letter in Partington, *Post-bag*, pp. 299–300.

455 (e) an Orlando should blow the horn] i.e. anyone like Orlando who would awaken the sleeping knights. See Appendix No. 1 to the General Preface to *Waverley*.

456 (a) Johnstone of Alva] Alva is in Clackmannanshire. But Johnstone also owned Hangingshaw, which made him a freeholder of Selkirkshire.

456 *n.* 2] Walter's letter is in Partington, *Letter-books*, pp. 374–5.

458 (b) £20000] See above, p. 449 and my note.

458 (e) as Sir Anthony Absolute says] Sheridan, *The rivals*, II. 1.

459 (a) Black fishers] Prosecuted under the new Act. See above, p. 444 and my note.

459 (f) Italy] This ed. of *Italy: a poem*, published in 1830, had illustrations by J. M. W. Turner and T. Stothard. Scott did not retain the copy sent to him.

461 (a) Tilburina] Sheridan, *The critic*, III. 1.

461 (b) Sharpe] Richard Sharp.

462 (e) the custom of the exercise] See my note to *SL* ii. 252 (a).

463 (a) to have it . . . copied] Skene had a copy (71·5 × 58 in.) made by Sir John Watson-Gordon, presumably in 1831, as the bill for the frame, made by Chalmers & Son, Carvers and Gilders, 45 Princes Street, Edinburgh, is dated 16 June 1831. (Original bill in possession of Major P. I. C. Payne.) This copy was sold at Dowell's, Edinburgh, 30 June 1961, Lot 201 A, and is now in my Scott Coll.

463 (b) to have the copy] Scott surely means the original.

463 *n.* 1] G. P. R. James's father, Dr Pinkston James, married at Edinburgh, 26 Dec. 1791, Jean Churnside, whose sister was at Morton's school with Scott. See *Lockhart*, i. 139–41.

464 (b) Sir John . . . Alexr. Pringle] Sir John Hay, 6th Bart. of Haystoun, was not elected till 21 Jan. 1833. Alexander Pringle of Whytbank was elected the following day, i.e. 17 Jan. 1831.

464 (c) brighten the chain of friendship] See *SL* ii. 535 and my note.

465 (c) an Edinburgh paper] *Edinburgh Weekly Journal*, ed. by James Ballantyne.

465 *n.* 1] The letter of 12 Mar. 1830 is in Partington, *Post-bag*, p. 286. The work to which Lady Charlotte referred was published in 1833 as *The three great sanctuaries of Tuscany, Valombrosa, Camaldoli, Laverna: a poem.*

466 (b) To Anne Scott] Scott wrote to her again on 8 Feb., announcing his return to Abbotsford on 9 Feb. The letter (which is not in *SL*) is at Abbotsford.

467 *n.* 2] There is a brief extract from Cadell's letter of 13 Feb. in Partington, *Post-bag*, pp. 302–3. The work in line 3 from foot is *The memoirs of Sir James Melvil of Halhill . . . Published from the original manuscript by George Scott, Gent. The third edition corrected.* 8vo London, Printed for D. Wilson, MDCCLII.

468 (c) To Monsieur Le Chevalier] Scott could not reply on 17 Feb. to a letter from France dated 14 Feb. The date is probably much later.

468 *n.* 1] This note should have been incorporated with note 1 on p. 466.

469 (c) eat well drink well] See above, p. 439 and *n.* 2 and my note. See also below, pp. 480, 482.

470 (b) jucunda oblivia vitæ] Horace, *Satires*, II. vi. 62.

472 (b) what Wordsworth calls] *Michael*, line 189.

472 *n.* 1] In addition to the two letters cited she also wrote in Mar. after meeting Scott (NLS MS. 3917, ff. 174–5) and in May 1831 (NLS MS. 3918, ff. 81–2).

473 *n.* 1] Delete 'Surely.' Scott had already referred to the work cited here. See above, p. 390.

474 (a) 22nd February?] As Scott says in his *Journal* that Anne is returning on Tuesday, the query is unnecessary.

474 (a) Anne returned] She had been in Edinburgh since 14 Feb. to get medical advice on her sore throat. See *Journal*, 14 Feb.

474 (c) about April] The visit, fixed for 17 Apr., was cancelled owing to Scott's illness. See her *Recollections* in *Temple Bar*, Vol. 40 (Feb. 1874), p. 333. She visited Abbotsford on 12 May. See *Journal*.

475 (a) Sandie Ballantynes affair] See *Journal*, 19 Feb.

475 (a) merry wives of Windsor] Act II, sc. 2.

475 (e) When Miss Ferrier comes forth] i.e. her *Destiny*, dedicated to Scott and published by Cadell.

475 *notes*] Read '1' and '2' respectively.

475 *n.* 3[2]] Scott could not use material in 1825 from a book published in 1830. As in other notes for the Magnum Opus, Scott cited works which illustrate points in his novels but which were not available when writing the novels or not thought of at the time. The 'cancel' (line 6) was not made. 'Baker' appears in all eds.

476 (a) the new novel of Miss Crumpe] Miss Crumpe had not written a new novel and was, therefore, not seeking

a publisher and she was indignant that Scott had spoken to Cadell. Scott's letters to her are not known to be extant but of four letters from her, Jan.–Feb. 1831, three are in NLS: 13, 21, 28 Feb. (MS. 3916, ff. 149, 186, 226). These letters show that she and Scott were at cross-purposes. All she had wanted was a favourable critique from Scott on her novels which she would get inserted in a leading periodical or the daily papers. It gave her 'much pain' that he had forgotten his 'old acquaintance' and had addressed her as 'Madam.'

476 *n.* 1] Godwin's letter of 17 Feb. is in *William Godwin: his friends and contemporaries*, by C. Kegan Paul, ii. 310–12, and in Partington, *Letter-books*, pp. 237–9.

477 (f) As the sapient Nestor Partridge says] Fielding, *Tom Jones*, Bk 15, chap. 12 and Bk 18, chap. 5. The Latin is from Horace, *Odes*, IV. i. 3.

478 *n.* 2] Among the subscribers in Ottley's book are Scott and Mrs Thomas Scott, Canterbury.

479 (a) The times are out of joint] Shakespeare, *Hamlet*, I. 5.

479 (b) Sir Anthony Absolute] Sheridan, *The rivals*, II. 1.

479 *n.*] The Irish girl could not be Lady Lucy Whitmore who was aged 34 in 1826 and had been married since 1810. She was Anna M. Ottley, Ottley's sister, as Scott says. She became Mrs Arbuthnott in 1835. Anna Ottley's visit to Chiefswood and Abbotsford in 1828 is confirmed by Mrs Hughes of Uffington. (See Hughes, *Letters*, p. 300.) In line 9, for 'marriage to her mother's sister' read 'marriage to the daughter of her mother's sister.' For relationships, see Index under Whitmore. Lady Lucy's letter of 29 July 1829 (which she clearly dates 1826) is in NLS (MS. 3903, ff. 78–80). Scott's reply to Lady Lucy's letter, dated Abbotsford, 3 Aug. [1829] is in the Osborn Coll. in Yale Univ. Lib. The letter is not in *SL*.

480 (a) Upon the grun] *Willie was a wanton wag* [by William Hamilton], st. [2], lines 7–8.

480 (a) the giant Pope] See above, p. 393.

480 (b) eat well drink well & sleep well] See above, pp. 439, 439 *n.* 2, 469 and below, p. 482.

480 (c) Ardwall your [cousin?]] Ardwall was her brother.

481 (d) To Sir Francis Freeling] This letter should be dated 5 Mar. [5 Apr. 1831]. On the same day that Scott wrote this letter, i.e. 5 Apr., he wrote to Sir Samuel Shepherd (*SL* xii. 5–6). As Shepherd acknowledged the gift on 16 Apr., Scott's letter to him must have been correctly dated 5 Apr.

482 (d) My habit of exercize] See my note to *SL* ii. 252 (a).

482 (e) eat well—drink well—& sleep well] See above, pp. 439, 439 *n.* 2, 469, 480.

482 *n.* 1] There are extracts from Lockhart's letters of 28 Feb. and 5 Mar. in Partington, *Post-bag*, pp. 301, 301–2.

483 (c) Habbies how[e]] In his own plan of the estate Scott calls this Halbert's Hawe.

484 (c) Celticke harmonies] *Celtic melodies.* See Anderson's ed. of the *Journal*, p. 633, *n.* 1.

484 *n.* 1] Chambers's letter of 1 Mar. is in Partington, *Letter-books*, pp. 240–1.

486 *n.* 2] Scott's letter of the 6th (line 8) is dated 8 Nov. in *SL* ix. 280.

486 *n.* 3] The omitted portion may also be found in *Scottish Notes & Queries*, 2nd ser. Vol. 6, p. 25. It contains the interesting statement: 'I am tied by a strict regimen to diet and hours, and, like the poor madman in Bedlam, most of my food tastes like oatmeal porridge.' See also *SL* xii. 3 and Scott's note to *The Pirate*, chap. 33, 'Character of Norma,' and *Demonology and witchcraft*, 2nd ed., pp. 16–17.

487 *n.* 1] Scott had already replied to the letter of 28 Feb. See above, p. 482 and *n.* 1.

488 (a) waiters on Providence] A name given to a class of politicians in Cromwell's time. See *MPW* viii. 139.

488 (a) Henry Scott] Eldest son of Hugh Scott of Harden. He became 7th Baron Polwarth in 1841.

488 (a–b) Abraham to fire his pistol] Rather an inapt simile from the *Bible*, Genesis 22: 9–12.

488 (b–e) Sanday Pringle . . .] Alexander Pringle of Whytbank; William Elliot-Lockhart of Borthwickbrae, M.P. for Selkirkshire, 1806–30; James (not John) Johnstone of Alva. 'Old Harden' is Hugh Scott, afterwards 6th Baron Polwarth. Torwoodlee is James Pringle.

488 n. 1] *The Wyf of Awchtirmwchty*, lines 69–70, in Laing's *Select remains*, Edinburgh, 1822 (unpaginated): 'Albeit na butter he cowld gett, / Zit he was cūmerit wt the kyrne.' The wording differs slightly in *Herd*, ii. 128.

489 (b) as I now think probable] Scott must mean 'as I now think improbable.'

489 (d) debate . . . between Balaam & his monture] *Bible, Numbers* 22: 28–30.

490 (a) To David Laing] This letter should be dated 27 Mar.

491 (a) my picture] It hangs above the fireplace in the Armoury at Abbotsford. The date is on the picture but the legend is on the frame and may be much later.

491 (c) The Markise] The Marquess of Stafford. See below, p. 495.

491 (d) Dunc[a]n lauder] 'lauder' should be 'Laider.' See *A new Scott*

letter, by H. W. Häusermann in *Review of English Studies*, Vol. 25 (July 1949), pp. 248–9. Häusermann prints an undated letter from Scott to an unnamed correspondent on the subject of this poem, but was unable to date it except vaguely 1826–7. It can be placed between Feb. and July 1827, as Scott refers to Lord Glenorchy as a member of the Bannatyne Club and he was not elected till 31 Jan. 1827. The letter is probably addressed to David Laing. In 1827 Scott addressed him as 'My dear Sir' (*SL* x. 153).

492 (c) an honest name] *Bible, Ecclesiastes* 7: 1: 'A good name is better than precious ointment.'

492 n. 1] In lines 2–3, 'young Harden' is Henry Scott, afterwards 7th Baron Polwarth. Rose sold the Marchmont library to him and to John Richardson. See Anderson's ed. of the *Journal*, p. 619, n. 1.

493 (d) The success of Mr Rogers] This refers to his *Italy*. See above, p. 459.

494 (a) the Devil catches the hindmost] A proverb. 'Every man for himself and devil take the hindmost.'

494 (a) *Carpe diem*] Horace, *Odes*, I. xi. 8.

VOLUME XII

2 (b) Tis no[t] in mortals . . .] Addison, *Cato*, I. 1.

2 n. 3] If Scott, in his letter, means by 'Young's imitation . . . is not on my shelves' that the copy lent has not been returned, it must have been returned later.

3 (a) MacNicols remarks I have received safe] But it is no longer at Abbotsford.

3 (b) the state of the poor madman] Scott gives a fuller account in a note to chap. 33 of *The Pirate*. He heard the story from a friend. It will be noted that this letter is dated 1 Apr. 1831 and his preface to the novel is dated 1 May 1831. See also my note to *SL* xi. 486 n. 3.

4 (c) *climb* like Spencer's champions] Spenser used the verb *clombe* as Scott did in *Rob Roy*, chap. 27. See *The Faerie Queene*, III. iii. 61. 6; III. iv. 61. 6; IV. v. 46. 1.

4 (d) "Sedet æternumque . . ."] Virgil, *Aeneid*, VI. 617–18.

5 (c) I send you a law case] *The trial of Duncan Terig*. For this gift to Shepherd, see also *SL* xi. 481.

6 (d) Mr Gregorson of Ardtornish has vindicated] See Scott's letters to him in *SL* xi. 288–9, 301–2, where the subject of this letter is also discussed.

7 n. 2] Delete.

8 (c) To J. G. Lockhart] Scott has taken several days to write this letter. Part was written on 11 Apr. ('Here is John Smith come').

10 (a) two new bridges] One was over Ettrick Water at Lindean and the other over the Tweed just before its junction with Ettrick. Scott laid the foundation stone of the latter. The foundation stone of Ettrick bridge was laid by Charles Balfour Scott of Woll. The two

ceremonies took place on 11 Apr. The bridges were built by John & Thomas Smith of Darnick at a cost of £2,650. In 1975 the public road was diverted from both bridges. Ettrick bridge has been retained to give access to Sunderland Hall. Tweed bridge is closed but it has been decided (1975) to preserve it. Scott's orientation, when writing of Abbotsford, is always wrong. 'From the south side of the river to the north' should be 'from the east side to the west side.'

10 (b) Only think of this Master B[r]ooke] Shakespeare, *Merry wives of Windsor*, III. 5.

10 n. 1] Before 'Abbotsford' insert 'the second portion of'. The first portion was built by Sanderson and Paterson of Galashiels.

11 n. 2] Delete this note, which is irrelevant.

13 (d) Northam] This is either a slip or a misreading for Mortham.

14 (c) whilst it is called today] A reminiscence of *Bible, John* 9: 4.

14 (d) Lord Hopeton's inscription] See W. M. Parker's article, *A note on the Hopetoun Monument* in *Book of the Old Edinburgh Club*, Vol. 22, Edinburgh, 1938, pp. 28–37. It contains a facsimile of Scott's MS. draft for the inscription.

14 n. 1] The complete texts of Ballantyne's letters of 23 and 28 Apr. are in Partington, *Letter-books*, p. 370.

15 (c) when you come here] Susan Ferrier in her *Recollections* does not give the exact date. Scott mentions her visit only once, viz. in his *Journal*, 17 May.

15 (c–d) flattering dream] Shakespeare, *The taming of the shrew*. See *SL* xi. 474 n.

16 (b) by William Scott] Taylor was not to blame. A number of copies had 'William Scott' on the title-page. In Baker's *Biog. dram.*, new ed. (1812), ii. 267, *Goetz* is given as translated by 'William Scot', although it is given correctly in the entry for Walter Scott, in I. ii. 637. From Scott's remark (p. 17) it looks as if he was unaware of the printer's error.

16 (d) "My name's Tom Jenkins . . ."] Sheridan, *The critic*, III. 1.

17 n. 2] For 'Henry' read 'George.'

18 (c) *the* Key of the castle] It is engraved (2 plates) in Adam's *Blair-Adam Estate* (1834). There are two keys at Abbotsford and others elsewhere. There is no satisfactory evidence that any of them are genuine.

18 (d) an unco devel[ling]] The third word should not have been expanded as Scott is quoting Burns accurately.

19 n. 2] John Anstruther Thomson was Adam's son-in-law—which is more to the point.

22 n.] In second last line, delete 'Probably.'

23 (c) Prince Ho[u]sse[i]ns tapestry] In *Arabian Nights*. See my note to *SL* i. 229 (e).

24 (c) Laing, acute enough] He is called 'the acute Orcadian' on Ossian in *The Antiquary*, chap. 11 and 'acute' in the 1821 'Advertisement' to *The Pirate*. The quality of 'acuteness' is also applied to him in *SL* x. 396.

28 (e) pick a back like father Anchises] Virgil, *Aeneid*, II. 707 et seq.

28 (f)–29 impeticosd the gratilities] Shakespeare, *Twelfth Night*, II. 3.

30 (c) Richard's himself again] Colley Cibber, *Richard III*, V. 3. See my note to *SL* v. 29 (f).

32 (b) accurate [?]] Delete query. It is clear from the MS. that Scott has written 'accurate,' a word he often uses in the novels in the sense of 'careful.'

32 n. 2] For 'On 25th August' read 'On 30 Jan. 1826' and for 'Maitland Club' read 'Bannatyne Club.' In lines 4 and 5, for 'published' read 'issued.'

34 n. 2] Three stanzas from the 'old ballad' are quoted by Allan Cunningham in his *Traditional tales* (1822), ii. 1.

35 (a) I was a good writer] Read 'I was [never] a good writer.'

35 (c) to write some thing in . . . album] '*Tis well the gifted eye which saw*, dated 'Abbotsford 22 September 1831.' Printed in *A selection from the works of Sir Walter Scott, Bart.*, ed. by M. Collins, London, 1866, pp. 255–6.

35 n. 1] *Fleurs* was written by Nathaniel John Hollingsworth.

38 (d) Graham[s] Island] James D. Forbes wrote to Lady Brewster, 8 Jan. 1832: 'Sir W. writes that he means to make a poem on Graham's Island, to the tune of "Molly, put the kettle on!".' Mrs Gordon, *The home life of Sir David Brewster*, p. 153.

38 (f) the Club] Instituted 3 Jan. 1820 and consisted of members of the Royal Society of Edinburgh, chosen by ballot. There were originally 40 members and the Secretary was James Skene.

38 n. 2] The account sent by Scott was separate from the letter to Skene, so that 'the full description' is not in *Lockhart* as this note says. The *Athenæum*, 31 Dec. 1831, p. 851, reported that it had been 'read to a large audience of the learned.'

39 (c) the Pantaloons of the Don] Shakespeare, *As you like it*, II. 7.

42 (c) Lady Teazle] Sheridan, *The school for scandal*, II. 1.

43 (d) a choice Manuscript of Old English romances left here by Richard] David Laing contributed a valuable note on this 15th-cent. MS., dated Jan. 1841, to *Reliquiæ antiquæ*, ed. by Thomas Wright and James Orchard Halliwell [afterwards Halliwell-Phillipps], 8vo London, 1843, ii. 58–70. Scott must be referring to Richard Cœur de Lion, but the date of the MS. makes this reference impossible.

43 (d) I have got a lad can copy them] Sticchini.

44 (b) tarrying at Jericho] *Bible, II Samuel* 10: 5; also *I Chronicles* 19: 5.

45 (e) as Parson Adams says] This is a misquotation. Adams says: 'he preferred the pedestrian even to the vehicular expedition.' Fielding, *Joseph Andrews*, Bk III, chap. 12.

46 (b) "'Twas meant for merit . . ."] See *SL* vi. 403.

47 (a) a young Neapolitan priest] Sticchini. See above, p. 43.

51 (c) To Charlotte Carpenter] Date must be about 1 Oct. as the letter was written 'a few days' before a letter of about 6 Oct. (*SL* i. 70).

51 n.] The letters were discovered by Paul P. Stevens, Honorary Librarian of Abbotsford.

53 (b) translating little tales from the German] These are probably the tales and romances to which he refers in 1808 (*SL* ii. 43).

61 n. 1] John was at home in 1794. See *SL* i. 35.

62 (d) The Capt.] Robert Scott of Rosebank.

62 (e) Friends at a distance . . . agree best] Ramsay, *Proverbs*, p. 20: 'Friends gree best sindry.'

63 (b) "health on your Cheek . . ."] Samuel Rogers, *To *** on the death of her sister*, st. [4], line 6. In Scott's *English minstrelsy* (1810), ii. 239.

65 (a) two . . . half sisters of my Mother] Janet Rutherford (1753–1812) and Christian Rutherford (1759–1819).

65 (c) Claud Russell] In spite of what Scott says here, there is an interesting letter at Abbotsford from Russell, 4 Apr. 1833, to Robert Cadell in which he says that at Gilsland he had rallied Scott about Miss Carpenter 'when he was at pains to persuade me he thought more of another young lady, a very pretty girl, to whom he one day on returning from his ride presented a bunch of heath gathered on the Roman Wall in that neighbourhood accompanied by a copy of verses.' *Lockhart* (i. 365) gives a slightly garbled version of this letter. Cf. *SL* i. 80.

66 n. 1] For 'Sandyknowe' read 'Rosebank.'

67 (d) two other Brothers] Thomas and Daniel.

68 (a) Egyptian plague of *Froggs*] *Bible, Exodus* 8: 1–14; *Psalms* 78: 45, 105: 30.

73 n. 1] Delete this note. The Rev. Simon Haliburton of Ashkirk had no son named Simon. His son John was a Captain in E.I.C.S. but he died in India and cannot be the Haliburton who befriended Carpenter. Scott must mean David (not Simon) Haliburton of Muirhouselaw. See *SL* i. 83 and viii. 332 *n*.

78 n.] See *SL* i. 382 (b).

83 (d) a license must be taken out] Scott was at Carlisle on Saturday, 23 Dec., and took the necessary oaths for obtaining the licence. I have copies of the petition and the licence.

86 (c) Bridge of Boats] Kelso Bridge was destroyed by a flood on 26 Oct. 1797.

94 (b) To Mrs. Scott] Scott left Edinburgh on Sunday, 15 Mar. (*SL* i. 359, 360). He would arrive in London on the morning of Thursday, 19 Mar., which will give the date of this letter.

94 *n*. 1] Delete last line. Miller secured the lodgings, but Scott did not live with him in Albemarle Street but at 5 Bury Street, as given at end of Scott's letter.

95 (a) The Clerks &c all go] John Clerk (afterwards Lord Eldin), Solicitor-General and his younger brother, William Clerk, Advocate-Depute, both appointed in 1806.

95 (a) So the Law of Scotland will remain] Scott was wrong. Lord Grenville's bill to alter the Court of Session was dropped with the fall of the Government, but the bill was re-introduced by Lord Eldon in the new Government.

95 (b) W. Clerk has lost his Sheriffdom] Clerk was not a Sheriff and, in any case, could not be dismissed from such an office with a change of Ministry. Scott is referring to his chance of succeeding Edmonstone in Bute. See *SL* i. 339.

95 (b) poor Rae] William (afterwards Sir William) Rae had voted on the opposite side from Scott on the Bill in the Faculty, but he became Sheriff of Edinburgh in 1809.

97 (e) Lord Melville . . .] The Ministry was not formed exactly as Scott here outlines. Robert Dundas became President of the Board of Control and Perceval Chancellor of the Exchequer. But Canning became Foreign Secretary and Lord Mulgrave went to the Admiralty. Wellesley did not come into office till Dec. 1809 when he became Foreign Secretary.

99 (e) George Robinson] He never became a Principal Clerk of Session.

99 *n*. 1] In line 3, for 'Guildford' read 'Guilford.'

100 *n*. 1] Brooke is Lord Brooke (courtesy title) who succeeded his father as Earl of Warwick in 1816. Lady Sutton is the wife of Sir Thomas Manners Sutton, Baron of Exchequer in 1805. She became Lady Manners when

her husband was raised to the peerage in 1807.

101 (b) without dissolving the parliament] Parliament, however, was dissolved on 27 Apr.

101 (c–d) Colin Mackenzie has left London] He probably, however, did not return to Scotland as his wife gave birth to a son at Exeter on 18 Apr. (*Scots Mag.* lxix. 397.)

101 *n*. 2] Delete 'Probably.' See below, p. 106. Delete last sentence and substitute: William Clerk had been appointed an Advocate Depute in 1806 but lost the post in Mar. 1807 with the change of Ministry.

102 (a) Ballantyne]. This is John. See below, p. 106.

104 (c) Parliamt. must be dissolved] Dissolved 27 Apr.

105 *n*. 1] Mansfield cannot be the Capt. Mansfield of *SL* xi. 378, as he was killed in 1779. Sir James Mansfield is too old. He may be his grandson, William Rose Mansfield who became Baron Sandhurst. The Rose in his name suggests a connection with William Stewart Rose. At this time there was a James Mansfield who was a Capt. in the Mid-Lothian Cavalry along with Scott in 1807, and in 1809 Mary, daughter of James Mansfield of Midmar, married William, Colin Mackenzie's younger brother.

105 *n*. 2] Delete sentence beginning 'At this period.' Armadale at this period was both a judge of the Court of Session (1797) and of the Court of Justiciary (1799).

106 *n*. 1] Charles Grey, 2nd Earl Grey, 1764–1845. Before his father's death, 14 Nov. 1807, he bore the courtesy title of Lord Howick.

107 (b) Madras Bankruptcy] Bankruptcy of Messrs Chase & Chinnery. See *SL* vi. 12.

108 (b) Robt. Dundas, the Chief Baron] This badly punctuated sentence probably means Robert Dundas (afterwards Lord Melville) and Robert Dundas, Chief Baron.

108 (c) Lord Sidmouth] He was out of office till Apr. 1812.

109 (e) Miss W.] Jean Wedderburn-Colvile who married, in 1807, 5th

Earl of Selkirk. Her mother was Isabelle Colvile, wife of James Wedderburn-Colvile of Ochiltree.

112 (b) Sir V. Gibbs] He was Attorney-General.

112 (d) make her enemies her footstool] *Bible, Psalms* 110: 1, *Matthew* 22: 44, *Mark* 12: 36, *Luke* 20: 43, *Hebrews* 1: 13.

112 *n*. 1] Lockhart did not include the verses in the *Poetical works* of 1833–4. They were printed in *Lockhart*, ii. 323–6, and later included in Scott's poetical works.

113 (a) the whirligig of Time] Shakespeare, *Twelfth Night*, V. 1.

113 (b) "Lords & Dukes & noble Princes"] *Gentle river, gentle river*, st. [3], line 1. In Percy's *Reliques*.

113 *n*. 1] Lady Rosslyn's letter is in *FL* i. 47–8. Douglas notes that Scott's letter to her has not been preserved. Samuel Rogers recorded: ' "If Scott," said she, "instead of writing to me on the subject, had *only* paid me a visit, I must have forgiven him." ' (*Recollections of the table-talk of Samuel Rogers* (1856), p. 254.)

114 (c) Young Robinson] This is probably William Rose Robinson who had become an Advocate in 1804. His father was George Robinson of Clermiston and as Scott met the father in London in 1807 his son was probably with him.

115 (b–c) old black gentleman] Scott's dog Camp.

115 (c–d) Peter] Peter Mathieson, Scott's coachman.

117 *n*.] Delete 'It is the "Fairport" of *The Antiquary*.'

118 (d) "Boaties rows"] *The boatie rows*. In *Johnson*, Vol. 5 [1797], Nos. 425–7. Repr. from this source in Jamieson, *Popular ballads* (1806), ii. 352–4. Burns said it was written by a Mr Ewen of Aberdeen.

119 (b) Mrs. Baron Clerk] Jane Duff, sister of Sheriff Adam Duff and wife of James Clerk, afterwards Clerk-Rattray, Baron of Exchequer.

119 *n*. 3] See also the *Scots Mag.* Vol. 75 (Apr. 1813), pp. 313–14.

121 (b) "How little do the landsmen know?"] *A naval song*, st. [1], line 1. In *The vocal magazine*, London, 1781, p. 33.

121 (d) Logie of Buchan] An allusion to the song sung by Sophia. *Logie o' Buchan* is in *Johnson*, Vol. 4 (1792), No. 358.

124 (b) tell Walter Dougals relations] Here Scott is comparing Shetland ponies with Walter's pony Dougal. For another reference to Dougal, see *SL* xi. 400.

127 (c) Miss Russells] As Scott sends his compliments to them in succeeding letters (below, pp. 129, 131, 132, 133), it would seem that Jane, Anne and Eliza Russell (of Ashiestiel), or at least two of them, were keeping Charlotte company while Scott was on the tour.

128 *n*. 2] Miss Macleod of the text is Anne Eliza, the only unmarried sister in 1814.

129 (a) Rorie More] Rorie Mhor's drinking horn is illustrated in Oliver Hill's *Scottish castles*, 1953, p. 241.

130 *n*. 1] For 'one of the Miss Clephanes' read 'Margaret Clephane, afterwards Marchioness of Northampton.'

131 (d) Mr Craig] George Craig, agent at Galashiels for the Leith Bank.

131 *n*. 1] For '*The Pirate*' read '*The Lord of the Isles*.'

132 (d) James] James (afterwards Sir James) Russell of Ashiestiel had decided not to come home from India on leave —a visit which would have entailed a 'second parting' on his return.

135 (a) "My native Land Goodnight"] Byron, *Childe Harold*, Canto I, st. 13, lines 17 and 89. Used as motto to *Old Mortality*, chap. 36, *The Heart of Mid-Lothian*, chap. 28 and *Peveril*, chap. 8.

136 (b) Grahames bombardment] In Feb. 1814 by Sir Thomas Graham, created Baron Lynedoch later in the year.

136 *n*.] *Belgium and Waterloo* should be *Narrative of a residence in Belgium*. The author was Charlotte Ann Waldie, afterwards Mrs Eaton, not her sister Jane. She could not be called 'Scott's friend' for Scott told Murray that he was not acquainted with her (*SL* iv. 389).

138 *n.*] Da Costa (line 1) is Jean Baptiste de Coster.

139 *n.* 1] In line 7 from foot, Quiverain should be Quiévrain and in line 4 from foot, St. Maxence should be Ste. Maxence or more fully Pont-Sainte-Maxence.

148 (b–c) Mrs. Nickie Miss D.] Miss Sarah Nicolson and Miss Sophia Dumergue.

153 (a) To Mrs. Scott] It is odd that in a letter with PM 11 Nov. Scott should be telling his wife of the purchase of Kaeside when he has already, since 2 Nov., told three other correspondents (*SL* iv. 111–12, 116, 119–20). Incidentally, this letter should not have been included in the series 'Letters to his wife from Belgium and France.'

153 (a) M[r] Wilson . . . M[r] Wilkie] Perhaps William Wilson, the artist from London who had been sketching in Scotland this year (NLS MS. 3886, ff. 178–9), and Thomas Wilkie, surgeon, from Innerleithen. Wilkie could not be David Wilkie who was in London at this time (Cunningham, *Sir David Wilkie*, i. 440).

153 (c) a pair of tongs] See Washington Irving, *Abbotsford*, London, 1835, pp. 93–4. See also *SL* iv. 540.

157 (d) Lord Kinnaird] Scott could not know at this time that Lord Kinnaird's wife would inherit the manor, messuages, lands and hereditaments of Wyrriott Owen, whose name was to be so closely linked with Lady Scott's mother, Élie Marguerite Charpentier, in the Chancery Case.

157 (e) peerless Blade] William Erskine. He wrote a song containing the line 'Come, view the vale, my peerless maid.' George Cranstoun parodied the poem and this line became 'Come, view the meal, my peerless blade.' See *Court of Session garland* (1871), pp. 117–18.

158 (a) golden . . . sceptre] *Bible, Esther* 4: 11, 5: 2, 8: 4.

158 (b) Miss Nicolson] She was still in Edinburgh on 26 May as a letter of that date from Charlotte to Lord Downshire shows. (MS. in St. Andrews Univ. Lib.)

159 (c) the Man whom the King delighteth to honor] *Bible, Esther* 6: 6, 7, 9, 11.

160 (d) Ellis's publication] *Specimens of the early English poets.*

161 (c–d) Freston treated the Library of . . . Don Quixote] Cervantes, *Don Quixote*, Pt I, Bk I, chaps. 6–7 (Lockhart's ed., 1822, i. 60–71, 73–4).

163 *n.* 1] Scott cannot, in 1800, be referring to Jamieson's *Popular ballads*, which was not printed till 1806. He must be referring to a copy of *Lord Kenneth and Fair Ellinour* which, along with *Donul and Evir*, Jamieson privately printed in Aug. 1799 for distribution to friends. See his *Popular ballads*, i. 193. These two ballads were by Jamieson himself.

165 (a) "prisoner ta'en"] These words, exactly in this form, occur in *Jock o' the Side*, st. 1, line 4, in the *Minstrelsy* (ed. Henderson), ii. 99; but, as Scott is referring to Carlisle, not to Newcastle, he is probably quoting 'Prisoners tane' from Scott of Satchell's *A true history*, Hawick, 1894, *Watts Bellanden*, p. 28.

165 *n.* 3] See also *SL* i. 391, ii. 20, iv. 3.

166 *n.* 1] This is the title-page of Vol. 2. Way and Ellis are not mentioned on the title-page of Vol. 1.

167 (a) To Thomas Percy] For the complete letter, including the lists of ballads, see *N. & Q.* Vol. 165 (4 Nov. 1933), pp. 308–9 (mentioned below, p. 170 *n.* 1). It is unfortunate that the lists were excluded in *SL* as they are important in showing what ballads Scott had in Oct. 1800.

167 *n.* 1] The 'inclosed paper' (lines 17–19) was printed by David Laing in his *Early metrical tales*, Edinburgh, 1826, pp. xvi–xviii.

168 (a–b) volume of Metrical romances] The Auchinleck MS. A list of the 44 items, with descriptions, is given in Scott's *Sir Tristrem*, pp. cvii–cxxvii.

169 (c) Branksome] Note that Scott as early as 1800 spells Branxholm in this way, the spelling he used in the *Lay* as being 'more proper for poetry'; but perhaps only another example of Scott's bad spelling.

171 *n.* 1] See also *Journal of a tour in the Highlands and Western Islands of Scotland in 1800*. By John Leyden. Ed. by James Sinton. 8vo Edinburgh, 1903.

172 (d) as little Moshes says] Scott is apparently alluding to Moses in Sheridan's *The school for scandal*, III. i.

173 (c) "puing the birks on the braes of Yarrow"] *The Braes of Yarrow*, st. [2], line 4. In Ramsay, *Tea-table miscellany*.

174 (d) Mr. Ellis' plan] His *Specimens of early English metrical romances*, published in 1805.

175 (a) respecting the Souters of Selkirk] In his introd. to *The Souters of Selkirk* in the *Minstrelsy* (1st ed., i. 236–7; ed. Henderson, iii. 387–9) Scott quoted Ritson and replied to him. On reading this, Ritson wrote to Scott, 10 Apr. 1802: 'I lament, indeed, that I should have ever expressed myself in such intemperate language upon the subject of your favorite *Souters of Selkirk*, etc.' (*The letters of Joseph Ritson*, London, 1833, ii. 218.)

177 (c) trifles which I gave Lewis] For Matthew Gregory Lewis's *Tales of wonder* (1801).

180 (b) The name of Arthur] This is a curious statement. Scott knew that Arthur was connected with Edinburgh, the Eildon Hills and elsewhere in Scotland.

180 (b–c) tomb of Queen Genever] See Note XXI to Scott's ed. of Richard Franck's *Northern memoirs*, Edinburgh, 1821, p. 369.

180 (d–e) A very odd Monument . . . I will endeavour to get you a faithful sketch] This monument is described in Scott's *Essay on Border antiquities* (*MPW* vii. 14). There is a sketch in Pennant's *Tour in Scotland*, etc., London, 1790, iii. facing p. 167.

181 (a) the poetical History] *Specimens of the early English poets*.

182 (b) like the hart for water brooks] *Bible*, *Psalms* 42: 1.

182 (c) as iron sharpeneth iron] *Bible*, *Proverbs* 27: 17.

186 n. 2] The *Ode* first appeared in the *Microcosm*, a school magazine founded by Frere and Canning when at Eton. In line 2, for '*Poetry*' read '*Poets*.'

187 (c) to the Moon] Ellis retained the poem but added a note: 'The editor has to apologize to the authoress of the two following beautiful little poems,

Miss Scott, of Ancram, for having printed them without her permission.' (3rd ed., iii. 349 n.) Ellis presumably added the note in the 2nd ed., but I have not seen a copy.

188 (a) a singular faery Ballad] *The young Tamlane* in *Minstrelsy* (ed. Henderson), ii. 300–407.

189 n. 2] In line 2, for 'xxxvi–ix' read 'xxxvi–vii.' It should be noted that Ellis in his *Specimens of early English romances* (1805), i. 125 n., said he was convinced that Tanner and Warton were wrong in attributing the romance to Davie. Richard Price in his ed. of Warton (4 vols., London, 1824), ii. 53 n., says: 'In attributing this romance to Davie, Warton has followed the authority of Tanner . . . We are indebted to Mr. Ellis for detecting . . . this misappropriation.'

190 (a) he does not always ride when he puts on his boots] See *SL* viii. 204 and my note.

192 (a) Sir Eger] For references to this romance, see Index under *History of Sir Eger*.

192 (c) Burlesque elegy] David Laing, in his preface to *Early metrical tales*, also refers to this ed. of 1686 and he may have done so on Scott's authority but I cannot find it.

194 (a–b) Roswal & Lilian . . . the Duke of Roxburgh] The Duke of Roxburghe's copy, 12mo Edinburgh, 1663, was Lot 3233 at his sale and was bought by Constable for £9. 9s. 0d.

194 (c) To George Ellis] Should not this letter be dated '24 October [September] 1801'? See *SL* i. 117 n. 2.

194 n. 1] Ellis, op. cit., paraphrases Scott's letter on its popularity in Scotland. The Roxburghe copy (above, p. 194 (a–b)) was acquired by the Advocates' Library. David Laing reprinted it in 1822 and included it in his *Early metrical tales*, 1826.

195 (f) Turpin's history] Archbishop Turpin of Rheims (died about 800). It is now held that the *De vita et gestis Caroli Magni* has been erroneously attributed to him.

196 (e) the Lady of your choice] Ellis's marriage seems to have caused surprise

and unfavourable comments, but there is no hint of this in Scott's lengthy correspondence. See Gabrielle Festing, *John Hookham Frere*, London, 1899, pp. 84, 152.

197 (b) great grandfather] Walter Scott ('Beardie').

198 (c) our Ms] Auchinleck MS.

199 (a) our Scotish proverb] *Kelly*, p. 110.

200 (d) the Elephants] See *SL* i. 113 *n.* 1.

204 (d) Sunnyhill] i.e. Sunninghill Park, Ellis's home in Berkshire.

204 (e) coals of fire] *Bible, Proverbs* 25: 22; *Romans* 12: 20.

204 (f) on your late union] See above, p. 196 and my note.

208 *n.* 2] See also above, p. 180.

208 *n.* 3] Delete 'probably.' Scott mentions in the *Minstrelsy* (ed. Henderson, i. 163) that Ritson sent him extracts from Nash's *Have with you to Saffren-Walden*.

209 *n.* 3] For 'Arbuthnot' read 'Arbuthnott.'

210 (b) Leyden to resume his transcript] Of *Arthur and Merlin* in the Auchinleck MS.

210 (d) Academical Institution] Under Sir James Mackintosh. See *SL* i. 116, 124.

213 *n.* 1] Prof. Kenneth Jackson identifies Cattraeth with Catterick in Yorkshire. (*The Gododdin*, Edinburgh, 1969.)

214 *n.* 1] Scott is here referring to the farm called 'The Rink', not to Rink Hill.

215 *n.* 2] In lines 4–5, for 'See a later letter to an unknown correspondent' read 'See an earlier letter to John Clerk.'

216 *n.* 2] In line 3, delete 'as Scott calls it.' 'Sir Gy' is the form used in the Auchinleck MS.

217 (a) my brother] Tom. See below, p. 220.

217 (e) Sheriff of the "Cairn & the Scaur"] See my note to *SL* i. 224 (d).

217 (f) "Maitland with his auld berd graie"] This is Scott's amended line

from Douglas, *Palice of Honour.* See *Minstrelsy* (ed. Henderson), i. 236–8.

217 *n.* 1] On *Auld Maitland*, see my *Bibl.* Nos. 2205–6, 2209–11, 2214–19.

219 (b–c) *a copie of ye litel wee mon*] *The wee wee man* is printed in *Herd*, i. 95–6, and in *Johnson*, Vol. 4 (1792), No. 370.

219 *n.* 2] Lockhart prints more than a few sentences. See *Lockhart*, ii. 100–1, where two long passages are given in reverse order with a portion from Scott's letter of 10 May.

220 (b) per varios casus] Virgil, *Aeneid*, I. 204.

220 (d) *Mister* Ritson] Scott is poking fun at Ritson's habit of prefixing 'Mister' to names in his published works.

220 (e) " a whisker first, & then a claw"] Thomas Gray, *Ode on the death of a favourite cat*, st. [4], line 2.

220 (e) Ballantyne . . . is throwing off one of his publications] *Select Scotish poems.* Ballantyne printed only 24 pp. before the work was stopped. It consisted of *Susan* [i.e. *The pystyl of Swete Susan*] by Huchown of the Awle Ryale, and *Peblis to the play*, by King James I [st. 1–16 and part of 17 only]. David Laing printed *Swete Susan* in his *Select remains* (1822). In his preface he said it was printed 'about the year 1803' [1802, as Scott's letter shows] and that only a few copies survived of the two sheets printed.

220 (f) remark addressd by Festus] *Bible, Acts* 26: 24.

222 (a) Bowmaker] Bowmaker is an alternative name for Walter Bower, the continuator of Fordun.

224 (a) Thompson] Thomas Thomson.

225 *n.* 2] David Laing in a note to *Sir Eger* in his *Early metrical tales* gives evidence proving conclusively that it was printed at Aberdeen by James Nicol.

226 (b) At a sale of paintings the other day] Large collections of paintings and prints were sold by auction by William Bruce & Sons, 37 North Bridge Street, Edinburgh, 17–18, 25 Nov. 1802. (The *Edinburgh Advertiser*, Vol. 78, pp. 312, 331.)

227 n. 2] In line 3, for 'reported' read 'reputed.'

228 (a) the Pistle of the Swete Susanne] See my note to *SL* xii. 220 (e).

228 (d) the little Ms] *Cadzow Castle.* See above, p. 224.

229 (a) To George Ellis] The date is after 14 Dec., for Scott is replying to Ellis's letter of 11 Dec. (*SL* i. 185 *n.*). The date is probably 22 Dec., the same as his letter to Owen in which he mentioned Leyden's imminent departure (*SL* i. 168).

229 (c–d) the promised legendary tale] *Cadzow Castle.* See above, pp. 224, 228.

229 (d) as Sancho's wife did] See my note to *SL* i. 304 (d–e).

230 n. 3] Delete the first sentence, which is a misinterpretation of Scott's text.

231 (a) help your elephants] An allusion to General Melville. See *SL* i. 113, 113 *n.* 1.

231 (d) the little pamphlet] I cannot trace this.

231 (e) love surpassing the love of women] *Bible, II Samuel* 1: 26.

231 *n.* 1 Robert William Spencer] Read 'William Robert Spencer.'

232 (d) Hindostan] The East Indiaman which Leyden missed sailing in and which was wrecked, with the loss of many lives, on 11 Jan. 1803. (Charles Hardy, *A register of ships*, 1811, p. 223; Reith, *John Leyden*, pp. 186–7.) Leyden sailed on the *Hugh Inglis* on 12 Apr.

232 (d–e) a cousin German] Walter Scott, fourth son of Walter Scott of Raeburn.

233 (c) better acquainted with other parts of Scotland] Scott is having a dig at his Highland tour. See above, p. 171 and *n.*

233 (d) Hebers return] From France. See *Heber letters*, pp. 137–40.

234 (b–c) Gervase of Tilbury . . . Fordun] Scott had confessed he did not have the reference to Gervase (above, p. 227). He probably had now got it from Leyden's introd. to *The complaynt of Scotland* (1801), p. 237. The work is *Scriptores rerum Brunsvicensium illustrationi*

inservientes, antiqui omnes et religionis reformatione priores . . . cura God. Guil. Leibnitii, 3 tom., 2° Hanoverae, 1707–11. The passage from Fordun was from W. Goodall's ed. of the *Scotichronicon*, Edinburgh, 1759, ii. 9. Ellis utilized Scott's notes from Gervase and Fordun in his *Specimens of early English romances* (1805), ii. 176–9, and Weber quoted the whole of Ellis's text in his *Metrical romances* (1810), iii. 350–2.

234 *notes* 1–2] Delete both notes, which cite the wrong editions, and see my previous note.

235 (a) Drummelziar] See above, p. 213 *n.*

235 (f) the veteran Admiral] Sir Peter Parker, father of Mrs George Ellis.

237 (a) Mr. Ellis] Charles Rose Ellis, created Baron Seaford in 1826. On 21 Jan. 1803 he had lost his wife, Elizabeth Catherine Caroline Hervey, only daughter of Lord Hervey, eldest son of the 4th Earl of Bristol.

237 n. 2] This note should have been given as a note to the next letter to Heber, i.e. at p. 238.

238 (d) pomp and circumstance] Shakespeare, *Othello*, III. 3.

239 (a) like putting a candle below a bushel] *Bible, Matthew* 5: 15.

240 (a) "in Yorkshire near fair Rotheram"] See *SL* i. 204 (b–c).

241 (e) To George Ellis] On dating of this letter see my note to *SL* i. 204 (d).

242 n. 2] Curle, in giving this information, has failed to note that Henderson has corrected John Somerville to William de Somerville (*Minstrelsy*, ed. Henderson, iii. 297 *n.*).

243 (e) the Doctor] Henry Addington later Lord Sidmouth.

246 (b) woods which cannot be seen for the trees] *Heywood*, p. 107; *Ray*, p. 278; Ramsay, *Proverbs*, p. 76.

246j (d) artful woman] Carrie Lamb, afterwards Mrs Thomas Mitchell. Scott later spoke kindly of her.

247 (c) "fortune my foe"] This is the beginning of an old ballad which narrates all the misfortunes which fall on mankind through the caprice of Fortune. Quoted in Beaumont and

Fletcher, *The custom of the country*, I. 1 and *The Knight of the Burning Pestle*, Act. V. In the latter the Merchant says: 'Well, Sir, I'll sing,/ Fortune my foe,' which approximates to Scott's text. Also quoted in *Nigel*, chap. 16.

249 (c) not to write till] Alluding to belief that a ghost will not speak till spoken to.

250 n. 1] For 'p. 222, note' read 'pp. 215, note and 222, note.'

250 n. 2] There is no evidence that Ellis at this time knew that Daniel was Scott's brother. See my note to *SL* i. 138 n. 1, and cf. Scott's letter of 4 May, above, p. 247 and p. 247 n., where Ellis calls Daniel 'your friend' (*not* 'your brother').

250 n. 3] For 'reply of 20th May' read 'letter of 20th May.' Ellis could not reply on 20 May to a letter written on 27 May.

251 (a) "Seven wise Masters"] No. 19 of Auchinleck MS. It was analysed in the *Scots Mag.* Vol. 64 (Jan. 1802), pp. 43–6, possibly by John Leyden. A promised continuation did not appear. Weber printed the complete poem from the Auchinleck MS. under the title *The proces of the seuyn sages* in his *Metrical romances* (1810), Vol. 3.

251 (b) I have a proper person in my eye] This might be either Weber (*SL* i. 227) or Nelson (*SL* i. 229).

251 (b) young Leyden] Robert, John's brother.

251 (b) *in petitorio*] Petitioning. A Scots law phrase. (Trayner, *Latin maxims*.)

251 *n.*] Although Ellis, here and below, p. 259 *n.*, doubts Scott's identification of Bamborough (line 4 from foot), he nevertheless adopted Scott's views in his *Specimens of early English romances* (1805), i. 123.

252 (c–d) three black crows] Smollett, *Peregrine Pickle*, chap. 83.

253 (e) The omission of the Scottish Statutes . . . was very negligent] Nevertheless Scott made no change in his text of the 2nd ed. (1806).

253 n. 1] An ed. which could not be used by Scott should not be cited. Scott used *Historiæ Anglicanæ scriptores X* [ed. Roger Twysden], 2° Londini, 1652, Tom. 2, col. 2591.

255 n. 1] The title of the poem, from which Scott quotes, is given by Laing as *The awntyrs off Arthure at the Terne Wathelyn*, in his *Select remains* (1822).

256 (a) a piece of the true cross] This should be an image of the Virgin. See Rev. Thomas Wilson, *The Stow of Wedale*, Aberdeen, 1924, p. 91 and notes.

257 n. 1] The reference should be to the standard ed., Hawick, 1894, p. 35.

258 (d) little villa] Rosebank, Kelso.

259 (a) the good old Admiral] Sir Peter Parker, father of Mrs George Ellis.

259 n. 1] On Castel Orgueilleux (line 5) see my note to *SL* xii. 251 *n.*

260 (a) as Burns says] *The Brigs of Ayr*, line 160.

261 (b) as Gil Blas says] Le Sage, *Gil Blas*, Bk VII, chap. 4.

261 n. 1] Jessie Stewart (Miss Stewart, line 10 from foot) was the daughter of John Stewart, merchant in the Water of Leith, who died in 1796 (*Commissariat records of Edinburgh, Register of testaments*, Pt III, p. 262, Scottish Record Soc.) and Janet Cattanach, who died at the Water of Leith, 1 Dec. 1823. (*Blackwood*, xv. 131.) Mrs Stewart, after her husband's death, was described as 'Grocer, Water of Leith' in Edinburgh Post Office directories. Scott's quotation from Buckingham supports the identification, the reference to 'selleth ale' and 'Town walls' (Water of Leith being a village in the western outskirts of Edinburgh at that time) being appropriate. Percy is right in calling her Jessy and Scott is equally right in calling her Adeline for the latter name was her pseudonym when she contributed poems to the *Scots Mag.* Henry Boyd in his *Woodman's tale*, London, 1805, pp. 235–8, included a poem *On reading some manuscript poems written by Miss Stewart, a young lady in Edinburgh, communicated by Robert Anderson, Esq.* Jessie Stewart was a friend of James Hogg. See Strout, *The life and letters of James Hogg*, Lubbock, Texas, 1946, pp. 48–52.

263 (b) Laird of the Cairn & the Scaur] See my note to *SL* i. 224 (d).

263 (d) a very good amanuensis]

Henry Weber. See my note above, p. 251 (b).

264 (e) Critical Review] The review of *Sir Tristrem* in the *Critical Review*, 3rd ser. Vol. 3, Sept. 1804, pp. 45–52, was by William Taylor of Norwich.

264 *n.*1] For 'must mean' read 'means.'

266 (d) To George Ellis] Lockhart had dated a portion 30 Dec. 1804 (*SL* i. 231), although he had dated the letter as 4 Jan. 1805 on the MS. We are told (p. 268 *n.*): 'It depends a little on whether Scott is setting out from Edinburgh or from Mertoun.' But Scott clearly indicates in the earlier extract (*SL* i. 231–2) that he is setting out from Edinburgh 'for our farm' and had sent forward minced pies (which he would not do on 4 Jan.). Furthermore he refers to Heber spending his Christmas in the country (*SL* xii. 267). The date, therefore, is about 20 Dec. 1804.

269 *n.* 2] 20th Nov. (line 1) is given as 24th Nov. below, p. 283.

273 (c) Hamlets apology] Shakespeare, *Hamlet*, V. 2.

273 (e) Clerk Ellis] Scott's details are wrong. Late in 1316 the Earl of Arundel marched against Sir James Douglas at Lintalee, where Sir Thomas de Richmond (*not* Earl of Richmond) was slain. See Maxwell, *House of Douglas*, i. 48–9.

273 (e) with mirth and princely cheer] *The boy and the mantle*, st. [2], line 2. In Percy's *Reliques*.

273 *n.* 1] Scott is not referring either to the estate or mansion of Lintalee but to the locality of that name in the 14th cent.

274 (c) Like as the hart] *The Psalms of David in metre . . . approved by the Church of Scotland*, Psalm 42, st. [1], lines 1–2.

274 (e) Mrs. Gilpin] Cowper, *John Gilpin*, st. [4].

275 (d) Ritsons publication] *Ancient Engleish metrical romanceës*, 3 vols., 8vo London, 1802. Scott reviewed it in *ER*. See below, p. 281.

275 (d) Libius Desconius] Printed in Ritson's *Ancient Engleish metrical romanceës*, London, 1802, ii. 1–90, as *Lybeaus Disconus*, with notes, iii. 253–64.

277 (b) Count of Artois] See my note to *SL* i. 259 (d).

277 *n.* 1] Greenough could not be one of the bachelors, for at this time he was travelling in the Highlands with Skene (*SL* i. 255). In any case, Carlyon's letter refers to 1804.

277 *n.* 2] Reference should be to Part I, Bk III, chap. 4.

277 *n.* 3] This note is obscure. Does it mean that the letter in *SL* i. 258–9, dated 'about 5th September' belongs to this letter of 17 Oct.?

278 (b) "Adam, Adam . . ."] See my note to *SL* i. 264 (a).

278 (b) Hey (Hay)] In the *Miscellany of the Abbotsford Club*, Vol. 1, p. 60, the name is given as Hieg, Hague or Hyheg (different forms of Haig).

278 (b–c) the vision[s] of one Tundale] Delete '[s]'. Scott is referring to *Tundalus Hibernicus libellus de raptu animae Tundali et eiusdem visione*, etc., printed in 15th cent. See the *Miscellany of the Abbotsford Club*, Vol. 1, p. 60.

278 (c) "stans puer ad mensam"] *Stans puer ad mensam* is the title of a Latin poem, translated (probably by Lydgate) and printed by Caxton. It was one of Captain Cox's books. See *Captain Cox, his ballads and books*, re-ed. by by F. J. Furnivall [Ballad Soc.], London, 1871, pp. xcix–c.

279 (a) Edinr. Review being discontinued] Scott is replying to Ellis's report in a letter of 28 Aug. (cited *SL* i. 251 *n.*). This rumour persisted and it was attributed to Brougham. See letters between Alexander Murray and Constable in *Archibald Constable*, i. 249, 250–1.

280 (b) "cœlum non animum"] See my note to *SL* i. 266 (d).

280 (b) the proverb is somewhat musty] Shakespeare, *Hamlet*, III. 2.

281 (a) the Romances] Scott reviewed Ellis's *Specimens of early English metrical romances* and Ritson's *Metrical romanceës* in *ER* Vol. 7 (Jan. 1806), pp. 387–413. (*MPW* xvii. 16–54.)

281 (b) Macphersons valuable book] David Macpherson's *Annals of commerce* was reviewed in *ER* Vol. 8, July 1806, by Ellis. Ellis also reviewed his *History*

of *European commerce with India* in *QR* Vol. 8, Sept. 1812 (*Shine*, No. 213).

281 (c) in case of dissolution] Parliament was not dissolved till 24 Oct. 1807.

282 (b) Places lonely now] Wordsworth, *Musings near Aquapendente*, lines 50–2, written in 1837. As Wordsworth incorporated verses written much earlier, these lines may have been recited to Scott in or before 1806. Lines 56–84 are on Scott, prompted, no doubt, by his allusion to the 'Border Bards.'

282 *n.* 1] In line 2, for 'The' read 'A.' The essay was printed as *A sense of honour, a prize essay, recited in the Theatre, Oxford, June 26, 1805.* It has no place, date or printer's name.

283 (e) never rains but it pours] Ramsay, *Proverbs*, p. 37.

283 (e) Cavers-Douglas] George Douglas of Cavers.

283 (f) Sweet Little Cherub] Charles Dibdin, *Poor Jack*, st. [2], lines 11–12: 'There's a sweet little cherub that sits up aloft, / To keep watch for the life of poor Jack.' This is a ballad in *Whim of the moment*. In his *A collection of songs*, 3rd ed., London, n.d. [1792?], i. 154. The first line had been quoted by Leyden in his letter of 24 Oct. 1805 to James Ballantyne. (See *MPW* iv. 179.) *Lockhart* (v. 346) refers to this song.

284 *n.* 1] Leyden's letter is printed in full in *Heber letters*, pp. 202–8.

285 (c) Sir John Trott[er]s servant] A curious editorial amendment. Scott is quoting from Garrick's *Bon ton*, II. 1, where Davy says to Sir John Trotley: 'give me more wages, less work, and the key of the ale cellar.' Also quoted in *SL* iii. 380.

285 (c) an idle report] Scott has been censured for his 'Tally-ho to the Fox.' It may have a much more innocent meaning if linked with this 'idle report.'

285 (e) inclosd squibs] *Health to Lord Melville* and *The lawyer and the Arch-bishop of Canterbury.*

287 (a) have fancy fun and fire] Burns, *Elegy on Captain Matthew Henderson: The epitaph*, st. [7], lines 1–2: 'If thou hast wit, and fun, and fire, / And ne'er guid wine did fear, man.'

288 (a) Moorhall] In the ballad *The dragon of Wantley.*

288 (e) yeomans service] Shakespeare, *Hamlet*, V. 2.

289 (a) "The Whip and Key"] See above, p. 282 *n.* 1.

292 (d) a German Sir Tristrem] In the 3rd ed. of *Sir Tristrem* (1811), pp. 249–62, Scott printed *Account of the German romances on the story of Sir Tristrem*, by Henry Weber.

293 (b) Myller] Peter Erasmus Müller.

293 *n.* 1] Amend last sentence to read: '. . . by Richard Price in his ed. of Warton's *History of English poetry*, 8vo London, 1824, i. 181–98.' *ALC* wrongly gives the editor as William Price.

296 (d) Caxton] At least one perfect copy of Caxton's edition is extant.

296 *n.* 1] In line 2, for 'Millar' read 'Miller.'

297 (b) unwashd hands as Falstaff says] Shakespeare, *I Henry IV*, III. 3.

298 (b) as the deaf Adder] Bible, *Psalms* 58: 4–5.

298 *n.* 2] In line 1, for 'p. 101' read 'p. 401.'

300 (d) Eleu loro] Fitz-Eustace's (not Constance's) song in *Marmion*, Canto III, st. x–xi. See also Index under Music.

301 (d) To Richard Heber] Year confirmed by Scott's letter of same day to Francis Douce, below, p. 391.

301 (d) Ritsons failure] *Ancient Engleish metrical romanceës* (1802).

302 *n.* 1] See *SL* ii. 92 and my note.

303 (c) Charles Ellis] Charles Rose Ellis, who became Baron Seaford in 1826.

304 *n.* 1] From the letter to Miller of 30 Oct. 1808 (*SL* ii. 113) it would seem that Scott had abandoned the project by that time. In 1811 John Ballantyne published a small ed. of *The seasons*, for which Scott probably wrote the brief memoir.

308 (a–b) Copenhagen question] Scott was right. The *ER* for Jan. 1809 (Vol. 13, pp. 488–99) reviewed *An examination of the causes which led to the late expedition*

against Copenhagen, by an Observer, London, 1808.

308 (c) The Cid] Southey's ed. of *The chronicle of the Cid*, reviewed by Scott in *QR* Vol. 1, No. 1. (*MPW* xviii. 44–73.)

308 (c) Currans speeches] See note to *SL* ii. 136.

308 (c) McNeil] Scott, 30 Dec. 1808, asked C. K. Sharpe for a review. See *SL* ii. 142.

308 (e) Douglas] William Douglas, Younger of Orchardton. There is no article in *QR* by him recorded in *Shine*.

308 (f) a gentleman recently arrived from India] James Purvis, purser on Indiaman *Castle Eden*, which arrived in England on 18 Aug. 1808.

309 (a) A book on the Indo-Chinese tribes] *On the languages and literature of the Indo-Chinese nations.*

309 (d) To George Ellis] Date must be 19 Dec. See my note to *SL* ii. 137 (d).

310 (c–d) The Books went to a most atrocious price] George Paton's sale. See Scott's letter to Miller of 9 Mar. (*SL* ii. 178). The books were sold by Ross. See *Archibald Constable*, i. 21 *n.*

310 (e) Thompson] Thomas Thomson.

310 *n.* 3] Correct title is: *Europe: lines on the present war.*

311 (b) "spent in my service dying at my feet"] Dryden, *Don Sebastian*, III. 3. Scott used this quotation as his motto to chap. 38 of *Woodstock*, the chapter in which Sir Henry Lee dies at the feet of Charles II.

311 *n.* 2] Delete this note, which contains no useful information. The lines on the back of Scott's letter should have been printed. The text is printed in Mrs Florence MacCunn's *Sir Walter Scott's friends*, p. 73.

312 (b) the damnd armistice] Between Napoleon and Emperor of Austria, 12 July 1809. See *Edin. Ann. Reg. for 1809*, II. ii. 200–1. Peace followed, 15 Oct. For text of treaty, see ibid., II. i. xxv–xxix.

312 (d) To George Ellis] In *Lockhart*, iii. 195–8 and overlooked by Grierson when printing *SL* ii.

312 (e) while it is calld *today*] A reminiscence of *Bible, John* 9: 4.

312 (f) historiographer] Dutens did not die till 1812, when Southey was unsuccessful in his efforts to succeed him. See *SL* iii. 123–4, 125.

313 (a) Conqueror of Talavera] Brodrick and Fotheringham in their *History of England*, p. 99, say even Wellington's best friends began to lose heart by his retreat from Talavera. It is interesting to see Scott's despondency too, for Wellington was always his hero.

313 (d) Corsica] This should be Corisca.

313 *n.* 2] *Lockhart* (iii. 197) refers us to *ER* for Oct. 1802, but there is nothing in that review relevant to Scott's text. Scott is referring to *ER*, cited in this note, but the words 'high-souled' and 'contentus parvo' do not appear although the word 'independent' does.

314 (a) Miss Edgeworth] See my note to *SL* ii. 237 (d).

314 (a) article of Sir J. Moore] For 'of' read 'on.' The review in *QR* Vol. 2, No. 3, was by Ellis and Canning. (*Shine*, No. 46.)

314 (b) article on Insanity . . . & that on the Missionaries] In *QR* for Aug. 1809. The former was by Thomas Young (*Shine*, No. 43) and the latter by Robert Southey (*Shine*, No. 37).

314 (d) my late unfortunate relative] Scott's brother Daniel.

315 *n.* 1] For 'is printed here' read 'is now printed.'

316 (c) *totus teres & rotundus*] Horace, *Satires*, II. vii. 86.

318 (e) twenty royal copies] *Ruff*, No. 87.

319 (b) Pope] See my note to *SL* iii. 280 (c).

320 (a) my Senior in office] George Home.

320 (e) the Long Island] The comprehensive name given to the Islands of Lewis and Harris and other Islands of the Outer Hebrides.

320 (f) Mermaids] See my note to *SL* ii. 419 *n.*

321 (a) on Sir Fr. Burdetts liberation] See my note to *SL* ii. 355 (e).

321 (d) I wish you would trust him with us] i.e. if Cobbett tried to publish his *Weekly Register* in Scotland the Scottish criminal court would be more severe on him than the English.

322 (a) Gray] Charles Grey, 2nd Earl Grey.

322 (a) planting them on the Istmus] See Jeffrey's article, *The state of parties*, in the *ER*, Vol. 15 (Jan. 1810), pp. 504–21. He refers (p. 504) to 'the narrow isthmus upon which the adherents of the constitution are stationed.' Scott again referred to this isthmus nearly a year later (*SL* ii. 481).

322 (a) "hermit poor in pensive place"] Butler, *Hudibras*, Pt I, Canto II, line 1168.

323 (d) Poor Sir Peter] Sir Peter Parker.

325 (c) the O'Connors] The Irish rebels, Arthur (1763–1852) and his brother Roger (1762–1834).

325 (d) Arabian Magicians box of sand] *The story of Aladdin; or, the wonderful lamp* (Weber, *Tales of the East*, i. 368). 'Arabian Magician' should be 'African Magician.'

325 (d) sympathetic alphabet] The *Spectator*, No. 241, 6 Dec. 1711. By Addison.

325 (e) to march his ragged regiment] Shakespeare, *I Henry IV*, IV. 2.

325 *n.* 2] The Rev. Francis Hodgson, reviewing the poem in the *Monthly Review*, N.S. Vol. 62 (June 1810), p. 188, wrote of Douglas's capture and the rising of the mob: 'The mob rise to rescue him; and here, Oh! sad abuse of poetry! we have an allusion to recent tumults in the British metropolis.'

326 (c) Fabian system] Cf. *SL* vi. 483.

327 (a) Wellesly] Wellesley remained Foreign Secretary till Jan. 1812.

328 (b–c) Gaelic proverb] A Hebridean proverb, 'I'll never burn my harp for a woman.' It was the basis of Hector Macneill's poem, *The harp*. The editor of *The beauties of Scottish poets* (Glasgow, 1823), in a note to the poem, says the legend was communicated to Macneill

by Graham of Gartmore, who had it from Ramsay of Ochtertyre. Thomas Garnett, who heard the story in Mull, tells it in his *Observations on a tour through the Highlands*, 2 vols., 4to London, 1800, i. 197–202. A stanza from Macneill's *The harp* forms the motto to chap. 1 of *The Pirate*. Cf. *SL* ix. 195.

328 (f) he who runs may read] See *SL* xi. 443.

330 (b) "in good green-wood"] *Brown Adam*, st. III, line 3: 'And he's bigged a bour in gude green-wood.' (*Minstrelsy*, ed. Henderson, iii. 201.)

330 (d) black greyhound bitch] Lady Juliana Berners, presented to Scott by George Ellis. See above, pp. 320, 323–4 and *SL* ii. 362–3, 363 *n*.

331 (b) facturæ nepotibus umbram] Virgil, *Georgics*, II. 58.

331 (b) recumbent posture of Tityrus or Menalcas] Virgil, *Eclogues*, I. 1 and V. 5 respectively.

331 (d) former paymaster] William Hutchinson.

331 *n.* 1] Scott's letter to Heber of 17 Oct. 1811 is not in *SL* but it is in *Heber letters*, pp. 242–3.

332 *n.* 1] Delete 'Perhaps the.' He was Christopher Nixon.

333 (c–d) the chain of freindship] See *SL* ii. 535 and my note.

333 *n.* 3] Scott quotes 'sprag' from Shakespeare. See *SL* xi. 402.

334 (a) Genl. Malcolm has written] His letter to the *Bombay Courier* is printed in *Edin. Ann. Reg. for 1811*, IV. ii. lxiv–lxvi, and his *Verses to the memory of Dr John Leyden*, ibid., pp. xci–xcii.

334 (d) Sampsons foxes & firebrands] *Bible, Judges* 15: 4–5.

335 (b) This will be deliverd to you by Mr. Terry] See my note to *SL* iii. 127 (e).

335 (e) Masquerier] His portrait of Joanna Baillie is (or was) in Hampstead Parish Church.

335 (e) this great sale] Roxburghe Library sale.

336 (d–e) I will stand the Huon with delight] *Les prouesses et faictz merveilleux du noble Huon de Bordeaulx*, 4to Paris,

1516. This was Lot 6146 and Heber paid £20. 5s. 0d. In the list of buyers, Heber's name is given, not Scott's, as Heber presumably did not know if Scott would accept it. See also *SL* xii. 348 (d).

337 *n.*] For Jemmie Balfour (line 10) see my note to *SL* ii. 240 (a).

337 *n.* 2] For 'Ferrier' read 'Ferriar.' This note, however, is pointless, as Scott is quoting Dibdin, *not* Ferriar.

338 *n.* 1] Maturin's letter of 18 Dec. is in *Maturin Corr.*, pp. 6–7.

339 *n.* 1] A correction which itself needs correction. 'Lancelot' should be 'Launcelot' and 'Gibb' should be 'Gobbo.'

340 (c) When do we see Windham?] *A review of the life and genius of the late Right Hon. William Windham* appeared in the *Edin. Ann. Reg. for 1811*, (publ. 1813), IV. ii. i–xl. Scott's question seems to suggest that Ellis was the author. The *Biog. dict. of living authors* (1816), p. 427, stated that 'at the time of his decease he was engaged in a life of the late Mr. Windham.'

341 (f) "stuff o' the conscience"] Shakespeare, *Othello*, I. 2.

341 *n.* 1] Maturin's letter of 11 Jan. is in *Maturin Corr.*, pp. 8–10.

342 *n.* 2] Maturin's letter of 15 Feb. is in *Maturin Corr.*, pp. 13–15.

343 (a) publishd a novel] Scott may be referring either to Elizabeth Hamilton's *Cottagers of Glenburnie* or to Mrs Mary Brunton's *Self-control*, both of which had reached a third edition by this time.

343 (d) your Lord Lieut.] Duke of Richmond. The 'D. of R.' of two lines below.

343 (e) I am also at Drumlanrig] Scott means 'I am also to be at Drumlanrig.'

344 *n.* 2] Maturin's letter of 27 June is in *Maturin Corr.*, pp. 15–16.

345 (d) To C. R. Maturin] Maturin's letter which Scott is answering is not known to be extant.

345 (f) Fluellen says] Shakespeare, *Henry V*, IV. 8.

346 (d) Your favour of the 27 October] In *Maturin Corr.*, pp. 23–5.

346 (d) writing to Lady Abercorn] Scott had written on 6 Nov. (*SL* iii. 377–8).

347 (a) a man of high rank] The Duke of Buccleuch.

347 (f) stuff of the conscience] Shakespeare, *Othello*, I. 2.

348 (b) To Richard Heber] This letter should be dated 19 Dec. 1812: (1) Roxburghe sale was in 1812; (2) Scott was at Rokeby Park in 1812 but not in 1813; (3) The General Election was in 1812; (4) Reginald Heber's *Poems and translations* came out in 1812; (5) Scott is going to send a copy of *Rokeby*, nearly ready in Dec. 1812.

348 (b–c) Has your right hand] *Bible, Psalms* 137: 5.

348 (d) pleased with my purchase] In the list of buyers and prices at the Roxburghe sale Scott's name appears only once (Lot 6141, above, p. 336 *n.*). But see my note to *SL* xii. 336 (d–e).

349 (a) to heap coals of fire] *Bible, Proverbs* 25: 22, *Romans* 12: 20.

349 (c) To C. R. Maturin] The letter to which Scott is replying is not known to be extant.

349 (c) Your play] *Bertram.*

351 (c) De Montfort] The play was acted in Edinburgh in 1810 when the elder Mrs Siddons took the part of Jane. Scott is, therefore, presumably referring to her in this letter and not to Mrs Henry Siddons. Joanna Baillie recognized the fault pointed out by Scott and in printed editions added a note that, when acted, the play should end with Act V, sc. 4.

351 *n.* 1] Maturin's letter of 15 Oct. is in *Maturin Corr.*, pp. 33–5.

352 (c) To C. R. Maturin] The letter was not unsigned. The signature had been cut out before the letter was printed in *Maturin Corr.*, pp. 32–3.

353 *n.* 2] Maturin replied on 15 Oct. (*Maturin Corr.*, pp. 33–5). Scott then wrote about 1 Dec. (ibid., pp. 35–6). This letter is not 'undated and hurriedly finished'; it is mutilated, the signature, date, etc. having been cut off. 'Lord Bowling' should be 'Lieut. Bowling' [Smollett, *Roderick Random*, chap. 41]. Another letter from Scott followed on

10 Dec. as cited in this note. It is in *Maturin Corr.* pp. 36–7, but not in *SL*.

354 (b) mewling & puking in the nurses arms] Shakespeare, *As you like it*, II. 7.

354 (d) publishing your poems] Scott has misread Maturin's letter of 16 Mar. 1815 (*Maturin Corr.*, pp. 37–8) in which he says he hopes to print *Bertram* with a poem (Canto I of which he will send), together in one volume. See also below, p. 355 *n.* 1.

356 (a) my unfortunate scribe] This is presumably Henry Weber, but Scott's letter to Heber introducing him is not in *SL*.

356 (c) To C. R. Maturin] There is no reply in *Maturin Corr.* Scott's letter apparently did not reach him. See below, p. 358.

356 (d) Some family distress] Death of Scott's brother John.

356 (d) your splendid success] *Bertram* was performed at Drury Lane for the first time on 9 May.

357 (d) To C. R. Maturin] The letter was not unsigned. The signature has been cut off. It is in *Maturin Corr.*, pp. 62–3. The letter of 2 July to which Scott is replying is in ibid., pp. 58–61.

357 (e) *unlop'd* copy] Many passages in the MS. of *Bertram* were omitted in the printed version.

357 (f) cropping Sampsons hair] *Bible*, *Judges* 16: 17–19.

357 *n.* 1] This note does not apply to Scott's text, for Scott was asking for a loan of the MS. in order to make alterations in his *printed* copy.

358 (b) your new work] *Manuel*.

359 (a) *perditur inter haec*] Horace, *Satires*, II. vi. 59.

359 (c) To C. R. Maturin] This letter is in *Maturin Corr.*, pp. 73–5. It should be dated 10 Apr. 1817. Scott is answering Maturin's letters of 8 Jan. and 27 Mar., ibid., pp. 69–71.

360 (a) with most admired disorder] Shakespeare, *Macbeth*, III. 4.

360 (b) Non semel dicemus] Horace, *Odes*, IV. ii. 50.

360 *n.* 1] The letter of 19 Apr. (line 1) is in *Maturin Corr.*, pp. 76–7.

361 (a) profanum vulgus] Horace, *Odes*, III. i. 1.

361 (d–e) I am sure John Murray] See my note to *SL* iv. 481 (d).

362 (b) apt to overwork [?]] The reading in *Maturin Corr.*, p. 75, is 'apt to encroach.'

362 (c) I have . . . spoken to Constable] Presumably when he was at Abbotsford on 5 May (*SL* i. 514).

362 *n.* 1] Scott's letter of 25 Dec. 1816 and Maturin's letter of 8 Jan. 1817 are in *Maturin Corr.*, pp. 68–70.

363 (c) to bind up with that of Bertram] There is no evidence that the MS. of *Manuel* was retained by Scott.

364 (b) the poem on Paris] *Paris in 1815, a poem*, London, 1817.

364 (f) Solomon] *Bible*, *I Kings* 6: 7.

365 (a) a new drama and also of a romance] *Fredolfo* and *Melmoth the Wanderer*.

365 (d) your sermons] This work was published by Constable and printed by Thomas Davison, Whitefriars, London.

367 (a) To Mrs. Mathurin] For references to earlier correspondence on the same subject, see *Maturin Corr.*, pp. 102–7.

368 *n.* 1] Mrs Maturin's letter of 19 Apr. 1825 (line 5) is in *Maturin Corr.*, pp. 109–11.

369 (e) To Mrs. Mathurin] The year of this letter is 1827, as is shown by the reference to Lord Plunket.

370 *n.* 1] In line 3, for '26th' read '16th.' (NLS MS. 3901, ff. 204–5.)

375 (c) "Ed Io son pittore"] See *SL* ix. 216 *n.* 2.

375 (f) Sir James Stewart] He organized regiments of fencible cavalry in Scotland in 1795. He is Sir James Steuart Denham, Bart., of Coltness. In contemporary publications he is given as Sir James Stuart, Sir James Denham Stuart, or Sir James Stuart Denholme.

378 (c) Masquerier] See *Heber letters*, p. 189.

380 (b) 12vo.] Should be 12mo.

380 (f) Lord Lansdowne . . . Lord Henry Petty] The 1st Marquess, who

died the following month (7 May 1805), and his second son, who became 3rd Marquess in 1809.

381 (a) sold his birth-right for a mess of pottage] This is not in the Bible but is taken from the heading to Chap. 25 of Genesis in 'Matthew's Bible,' Antwerp, 1537, with notes by John Rogers, under the pseudonym of Thomas Matthew.

381 (d)–382 "but I would never trow him"] *Lucky Nansy*, burden, line 4: 'But ye wad never trow me.' In Ramsay, *Tea-table miscellany*.

384 (b) *ars est celare artem*] A proverb.

384 (d) repeatedly sat down to the task] For George Thomson. See *SL* i. 268, 268 n., 282–3, 310 n.

384 (f) To John Clerk] This letter is undated though 1805 appears at the head of the page with the running title. The address, Castle Street, does not fit May 1797, showing that Scott has borrowed the MS. a second time. The date must be 1801 as Scott refers to the MS. in his letter to Ellis of 8 Jan. 1802 (above, p. 215).

384 n. 1] In line 2, delete 'probably.' Scott gave a long extract from Clerk's MS. in the *Minstrelsy* (ed. Henderson, iii. 52–3) where he described Clerk as 'advocate.' The only John Clerk who was an advocate became Lord Eldin.

385 n.] Delete from 'Scott has apparently' down to the end of the note. There is nothing in this letter to Clerk or in the letter to Murray cited to link this MS. with Thomas Johnes and, incidentally, '1805' in line 4 on p. 385 should be '1809.' The words 'I think I have found a copy' in the letter to Ellis cited (above, p. 215) refer to Clerk's MS.

387 (d–e) like a beggar on horseback] Scott may be referring to the Scottish proverb: 'Set a beggar on horse-back, and he'll ride to the dee'l.' See *Kelly*, p. 298.

387 n. 1] There are obvious errors in Scott's quotation. The text as given by Leyden in his *Complaynt of Scotland* (1801), Introd., p. 59, is: 'The mode-warp is ane blind beist, haifand ane gronze in forme of ane porc, euir beand worseland in the eird; and signifeis, yat he yat bure it first, hes bene a theif and brigand, hydand him

daylie in woddis and cauernis, pilzend and reifand; for it is said comonly, he yat euill dois, hattis ye lyt.'

390 (c–d) obscure club in a country town] See the *Spectator*, No. 568. Scott may also have been thinking of Johnson's remark to Boswell that 'several of the characters in the Rambler were drawn so naturally that when it first circulated in numbers, a club in one of the towns in Essex imagined themselves to be severally exhibited in it' (Boswell's *Johnson*, ed. Hill-Powell, i. 215).

392 (d) Election 1806] Scott's only other references refer to the election of 1807 (above, pp. 95, 97).

392 n. 1] The *Paradyce of daynty devises* was compiled by Richard Edwards. Weber did not carry out his plan to publish an edition. There is a transcript by Brand from a transcript by Herbert in NLS (MS. 2754). See *Catalogue of manuscripts*, vol. 2, p. 112. Sir Samuel Brydges brought out an edition in 1810.

395 n. 1] The statement that 'the publishers did not fulfil this promise' (line 12) is wrong. Scott's name naturally appeared as the author of *The lay* but his name as author of the 'Anecdotes and descriptions' was omitted at Scott's request. The title-pages of the 1808 and 1810 eds. are the same.

396 (a) Schetky's title page] It was printed in London by J. M'Creery. The rest of the work was printed by Ballantyne.

397 (b) article of his gentry] Shakespeare, *Merry wives of Windsor*, II. 1.

398 (c–d) cancel the prefaces to the British Drama] William Miller published in 1804 *The British drama* (3 vols. in 5), printed by James Ballantyne. The reference to it here is the only one in *SL*; yet there would appear to be a link between it and the later work of 1810, also published by Miller, but not printed by Ballantyne as one would have expected. The format and general layout of both are the same and the engraving on the title-pages of both editions is the same. Some changes were made in the selection of plays.

399 (d) selling a pig in a poke] See *Kelly*, p. 221.

401 (b) *two* copies of Somers Vol. II]
So Surtees informed Scott on 5 Mar.
(Taylor's *Memoir of Robert Surtees*,
p. 96.)

403 (b) 1st Vol. of said translation]
Johnes's translation of Froissart's
Chronicles, 4 vols., Hafod, 1803–5,
reviewed by Scott in *ER*, Vol. 5, Jan.
1805 (*MPW* xix. 112–38).

403 (c) "Return my fees? . . ."] Said
by Dr Bulruddery in Bickerstaffe and
Foote, *Dr Last in his chariot*, I. 1.

404 (e) Polwhele . . . parcel] See *SL* ii.
388.

405 (c) about fifteen or sixteen years
ago] Scott's dating, often erratic, is
correct here. He visited Buchanan of
Cambusmore in Apr. 1796. See *SL* i.
45.

406 (d) Montroses Memoirs] *Memoirs
of . . . James Graham, Marquis of Montrose.
Translated from the Latin of the Rev.
Doctor George Wishart*, etc., 12mo Edinburgh, 1756, pp. 49–50.

407 (a) the present laird] William
Stewart of Ardvoirlich (1754–1838).

407 n. 1] Robert Stewart was 'Younger
of Ardvoirlich.' For '*The Legend*' read
'*A legend*'.

408 (c) "Yourself a Muse"] 'Himself a
Muse.' Dryden, *Absalom and Achitophel*,
line 878. (Scott's *Dryden*, ix. 243.)

409 (d) To Dr. Douglas] The complete
letter was printed in the *Scotsman*, 16
Feb. 1940, p. 9, c. 5.

409 n. 1] See also *SL* iii. 46.

410 n. 1] The original sketch by Bird is
no longer at Abbotsford.

411 (c) Patten] *The expedicion into Scot-
lāde*, in *Fragments of Scotish history* [ed.
by Sir John Graham Dalyell], 4to
Edinburgh, 1798, p. 69.

411 n. 1] Delete. The Patten at these
references is a different person.

413 (a) "His cloak . . ."] Earlier in 1811
Scott had quoted this stanza on costume.
See *SL* ii. 472.

415 (b) "giddy paced times"] Shakespeare, *Twelfth Night*, II. 4.

416 (c) gird up your loins] A common
Biblical expression; e.g. *II Kings* 4: 29.

416 (e) Dumfriesshire and in the North
of England] Drumlanrig and Keswick.

417 (a) the lives] See my note to *SL* iii.
403 (a).

417 (c) the Reviewer of Apollonius
Tyanius] See my note to *SL* ii. 322 *n*.

418 (a) A great sale of rare & curious
books] See *SL* iii. 376 *n*. 1 and my note.

418 (e) Political Memento] *The political
memento, or extracts from the speeches,
during the last six years, of near a hundred of
the most distinguished members of both
Houses of Parliament, on the policy and
probable results of the war*, 8vo London,
1814. The lines on the title-page are
from *The vision of Don Roderick*. (See *SL*
iii. 459.)

419 (a) "there would be a ram caught
in the thicket"] *Bible, Genesis* 22: 13.

419 (d) He who runs may read] See *SL*
xi. 443 (e).

419 n. 1] In line 4, delete 'Evidently.'

420 n. 2] In lines 2–3, delete 'to the
Hebrides.'

423 (e) "Waste not want not"] Scott
had these words carved on the stone
fireplace in the kitchen at Abbotsford.

424 (d) To Lord Byron] The correct
date is 7 Apr. 1815. Scott's words 'of
making your personal acquaintance'
show that the letter was written in Apr.,
not in Sept. The original ALS is in the
Huntington, not the Pierpont Morgan,
Library.

424 n. 2] With the redating of Scott's
letter this note is now inapplicable.

425 n. 1] As Scott is able to refer to
lines on p. 35, the work was already in
page-proof and there could be no
opportunity for any additions by Scott,
but Hogg may have been looking forward to a second ed. The page reference
is the same in the 2nd ed. The *Epistle to
Mr R. S***** was by Thomas Pringle
and was acknowledged by him when he
reprinted it under the title *The autumnal
excursion (addressed to a friend)* in his *The
autumnal excursion . . . with other poems*,
12mo Edinburgh, 1819, pp. 1–45. It
was in no sense an imitation of Scott.
Delete, therefore, the words 'Scott is
made to speak' and the three last lines.

426 (a) a ranting highlandman] An

allusion to John Hamilton's song, *The rantin Highlandman*. (Chambers, *Scottish songs*, i. 22.)

426 (a) A mons Briquet le fils] This is a son of Abraham Louis Briquet, famous watchmaker. The elder Briquet was a friend of the Boultons and Dumergues and often visited them in England. Charles F. Dumergue owned a number of very valuable watches made by Briquet.

426 (e) To J. W. Croker] See my note to *SL* iv. 364 *n*.

427 (d) To John Ballantyne] Ballantyne must have met Rees (p. 429) after he had been to Abbotsford on 23 or 24 Sept. Date of letter is likely to be late Sept. or Oct.

427 *n*. 1] Hugh Swinton Legaré is said to be descended from Sir John Swinton of Swinton. See *Swintons of that Ilk*, p. 86.

427 *n*. 2 [*rectius* 3]] 'Brother David' is David Hume.

430 *n*. 1] The work which Delarue sent was *Recherches sur les ouvrages des bardes de la Bretagne armoricaine dans le moyen âge*, 2e éd., 8vo Caen, 1817.

433 (b) To John Murray] Scott is answering Murray's letter of 6 June in Smiles, *John Murray*, ii. 12–13. Cf. Scott's letter here with his letter in *SL* v. 108–12.

433 (c) Elections] Parliament had been dissolved in June.

433 (c) I enclose the sheets] Scott's review of *Walpole's Letters . . . to G. Montagu* for *QR* (*Shine* No. 470). See Smiles, *John Murray*, ii. 12.

433 (d–e) Freres Whistlecraft] See *SL* v. 108 *n*., 110, 110 *n*., 168, and my note at the last reference.

433 (e) Evelyn] On 15 May Scott had suggested reviewing him. See *SL* v. 140. Scott made use of Evelyn in his review of Pepys in *QR* for Jan. 1826. Southey's review of Evelyn appeared in *QR* for Apr. 1818. (*Shine*, No. 467.)

433 (e) The article on the Poors laws] By Robert Southey in *QR* Vol. 18, No. 36, Jan. 1818, publ. June. (*Shine*, No. 454.)

434 (c) the Strange family] See my note to *SL* xi. 331 (d).

438 (d) Mr. Cooke] W. Cook, Postmaster, Melrose.

441 (f) Baron of Brackley] In Jamieson's *Popular ballads*, Edinburgh, 1806, i. 102–8. The text is from Mrs Brown of Falkland's collection collated with a version communicated to Jamieson by Scott.

441 *n*. 1] The 'Warder' articles have not been identified by Strout. From the wording of Scott's letter one might suspect that he is the author.

441 *n*. 2] The Marchioness was not Catherine Cope, whose husband did not succeed till 1836. The Marchioness here is Elizabeth Brodie, Marchioness of Huntly 1813 and Duchess of Gordon 1827. Her name is given correctly in *SL* ix. 26 *n*. 3.

442 (c) As I came down] *Willie Mackintosh*. In John Finlay, *Scottish historical and romantic ballads*, etc., 2 vols., 8vo Edinburgh, 1808, ii. 89–98. Finlay notes that the fragment was 'recollected by a lady of distinguished rank, and was communicated to the editor by Mr Scott.' From this letter the 'lady' is shown to be the Duchess of Gordon who died in 1812. By 1820 Scott has forgotten that he gave the ballad to Finlay and wrongly says he gave it to Jamieson.

443 (c–d) To Charles Joseph Harford] Harford's letter (NLS MS. 3895, f. 253) is undated but it is placed among the July–Dec. 1822 letters in the Walpole Coll. Scott's letter, therefore, is probably 27 Sept. 1822.

443 *n*. 2] This note is ambiguous and mixes references to different eds. of *Rokeby*. References to Harford's comments which apply to all eds. are: St Robert's Cave and Eugene Aram, Canto II, st. xix; Lidcote Hall, Canto V, st. xxvii; Mrs Leakey, Canto II, st. xi. The note is also a very garbled version of Harford's letter (NLS MS. 3895, f. 253). Harford says nothing about visiting Knaresborough. His visit was to Littlecote Hall and it was there that he saw a small Gothic door while sketching the house and asked General Popham about it. (The indefinite article before his name is absurd as Popham was the owner of Littlecote Hall.) Harford's reference to Eugene Aram concerned a similar case of detection of a murderer in 1772.

In line 1, delete 'Presumably' and in line 3, delete 'evidently.' They were second cousins, once removed.

444 n.] 'Lecky' should be 'Leaky' or 'Leakie.' The *Apparition-Evidence; or, a miraculous detection of the unnatural lewdness of Dr. John Atherton* is in Dunton's *Athenianism*, pp. 351–60. Mrs Leaky was related to Bishop Atherton by marriage.

445 (d) For lords and lairds] A parody of *Up and warn a' Willie*, st. [1] lines 5–8. In *Johnson*, Vol. 2 (1788), No. 188.

446 (a) To James Hogg] Hogg's letter of 3 Oct. is in *N. & Q.* Vol. 174 (2 Apr. 1938), pp. 243–4, and in Strout, *Hogg*, pp. 226–8. The first Saturday after this is 6 Oct. which, therefore, is the date of Scott's letter.

452 (a) the picture] See my note to *SL* vii. 245 n. 2.

453 (a) *Valeat . . . quantum valere potest*] See *SL* x. 102.

453 (c) gown of green] The proverb refers to a gown of gold and is so given in *SL* xi. 194, in *The Monastery*, chap. 17, and in *Redgauntlet*, Letter II. 'Gold' is here changed to 'green' to make the proverb fit Drumlanrig.

453 (d) first Duke's letters] Duke of Monmouth; he and Ann Scott his wife were created Duke and Duchess of Buccleuch.

453 (d) Duke of York] Afterwards King James II.

454 (a) tip her Goneril and abate her train] Shakespeare, *King Lear*, II. 4.

454 (a) Cantavit vacua] Adjusted from Juvenal, *Satires*, X. 22.

454 (b) make thread papers of bank notes] Sheridan, *The rivals*, I. 1.

454 (b) We nor breakfast] Scott quotes these lines (with 'Ratties' for 'Waspies') in his article on General Gourgaud in *Blackwood*, Vol. 4 (Nov. 1818), p. 221, where he says they are from the interlude of *Whittington and his cat*, where the Emperor of Monomotopa joins with the Vizier and Countess in singing this chorus.

456 (a–b) the proposed paper] *The Representative*.

456 (e) To James Ballantyne] Date can be confirmed from *SL* x. 74.

456 (e) Tasso] See *SL* x. 72 and my note.

458 (b) the staunchest Jacobite] This relates to Apr. 1815. See *SL* iv. 52.

458 (f) valiant Baron of Clackmannan] Bruce of Clackmannan was accused of shooting a hawk belonging to Sir John Shaw, and Lady Shaw, in her husband's absence, demanded an apology. Bruce wrote to her: 'I did not shoot the hawk. But sooner than have made such an apology as your ladyship has had the consideration to dictate, I would have shot the hawk, Sir John Schaw, and your ladyship.' (*Proceedings in the court-martial, held upon John, Master of Sinclair*, ed. by Scott for the Roxburghe Club, Edinburgh, 1828, p. xiii.) Scott told this story to Mrs Hughes. See her *Letters*, p. 281.

458 n. 1] Delete 'James's advice was taken, with unhappy effect, in *St. Ronan's Well*.' Such a comment is outwith the duties of an editor and would, in any case, be challenged by a Scott expert.

459 (d) To General Stuart of Garth] This letter was accompanied by a poem, *To General David Stewart of Garth*. The letter and poem were printed in *Life & Work*, Vol. 17 (Jan. 1895), pp. 4–5, and reprinted from that source in the *Scotsman*, 26 Dec. 1894, p. 10, c. 2, with omissions of portions of the letter. The poem was also printed in the *Poetry Review*, Vol. 40 (Aug.–Sept. 1949), p. 275 (and cf. ibid., Vol. 41 (Jan.–Feb. 1950), p. 49).

459 n. 1] Maxwell's MS. was quoted (with some errors in transcription) by Scott in his 1829 ed. of *Waverley* (note to chap. 58 of 1-vol. eds.).

460 (d) Subscriptions] In his letter of 6 Oct. (NLS MS. 3907, ff. 144–5) Stewart wrote: 'Several ladies friends of mine are most anxious to possess your signature—Will you favour us with a few lines and multiply your signature as often as the paper will hold.'

461 (a) To David Laing] The letter from William Yellowlees from London is dated 27 Oct. (Edin. Univ. Lib. La. IV Letter 17). Scott's letter to Laing is more likely to be Nov. than Dec.

461 (a) Provincial antiquities] Scott disposed of 21 copies to Heath. See *Journal*, 25 Apr. 1828.

461 (a) Mr Bell] Robert Bell and his brother William were both members of the Bannatyne Club at this time and both edited works for the Club in 1829. As William edited *Papers relative to the Regalia*, it was probably William who wanted the *Provincial antiquities* which contained a section on this subject.

462 (b) Durham on the Epistle to the Galatians] Scott, in giving this anecdote to Croker, had forgotten that Boswell had already recorded it in his *Journal of a tour to the Hebrides*, under 6 Nov.

463 (c) manuscript book of Travels] By James Skene. See *SL* xi. 164.

463 *n*. 3] There is no mention of an 'impudent fellow' in *SL* xi. 151, *n*. 2, unless Scott is referring to the '*intrepid lawyer*.'

464 (c) A title Dempster merits it] *Epistle to James Smith*, st. [23], lines 1–2. For 'gee' read 'gie.'

464 (c) Dempster a true blue Scott I warran'] *The author's earnest cry and prayer*, st. [13], line 1: 'Dempster, a true-blue Scot I'se warran'.'

464 (e) the scots Magazine] The obituary is in the *Scots Mag.*, Vol. 81, p. 296.

466 *n*. 1] Delete 'The threatened visit did not apparently come off.' The Duc de Chartres *did* visit Abbotsford while Mrs Hemans was there. See *Memoir of . . . Mrs Hemans*, by her sister, Edinburgh, 1840, p. 181. Scott could not be referring to Charles X, who was actually King at this time (1824–30). The Duc de Chartres was the son of Duc d'Orléans, who became King of France in 1830. The Duc de Chartres was his eldest son but was never King as he predeceased his father.

467 (a) Burns's Tam Samson] *Tam Samson's elegy*, st. [10], lines 1–2.

467 (a–b) Missie MacDonald] Margaret Macdonald Buchanan. See above, p. 466 *n*. 2.

467 (b) long promised £200] See *SL* xi. 269.

467 (f) Edinburgh] Scott means London. Lockhart left Abbotsford on 4 Oct. (*SL* xi. 398) to sail from Leith to London. By the date of this letter (10 Oct.) Lockhart would be in London.

468 (b) Doctor Forbes] Afterwards Sir John Forbes. See Index.

470 (a) Thomson Callendar] William Thomson Callender.

471 (d) To Charles Tilt] Tilt issued a facsimile which is sometimes offered for sale as the original; but it can easily be detected as it has a watermark dated 1831.

472 (a) To James Ballantyne] The suggested date is too early. As the apparition story comes at the end of *Demonology*, the date is probably July. Scott, on 22 July, told Murray that he had finished the work (*SL* xi. 376). The 'Tales' are *Tales of a grandfather*, 4th ser.

473 (e) I have considerd Beaumont & Fletcher] See *SL* i. 231 and my note.

474 (b) the pamphlet] *Examination of the charges maintained by Malone, Chambers, and others, of Ben Jonson's enmity towards Shakespeare*, London, 1808.

474 (c–d) Drummond . . . "Heads of his Conversation"] See *SL* xi. 279–80.

475 (a) To Robert Graham] This must have been written at Cartleyhole about the end of May 1812 when Scott was moving from Ashiestiel and, not having a settled address, he asked Graham to reply to him, care of Mr Erskine, Melrose.

477 (d) Duc de Chartres] See my note to *SL* xii. 466 *n*. 1.

479 (b) *par voie du fait* [*sic*]] No need for '*sic*.' This is the correct legal phrase and is so used in *The Heart of Mid-Lothian*, note to chap. 24; *Abbot*, chap. 35; *Nigel*, chap. 16; *Peveril*, chap. 32; and *My Aunt Margaret's mirror*.

480 (a) with a date so very melancholy] i.e. Canongate Jail, Scott using here, as he frequently does, 'date' in the sense of 'address.' See my note to *SL* i. 34 (a).

480 (b) a "pipe for fortunes finger"] Shakespeare, *Hamlet*, III. 2.

480 (e) to our exceeding refreshment] See my note to *SL* iii. 391 (a).

480 *n*. 1] This note repeats the error that Ardwall was Mrs Tom Scott's cousin. He was her brother.

493 List of correspondents] With the redating of letters and identification of correspondents it would be a very complicated task to indicate all the changes necessary to make this index accurate and I have let it stand as it is.

INDEX

PLAN OF THE INDEX

As the theme of this book is Sir Walter Scott, there is no entry for him in the index. Subjects relating to him are distributed throughout the index in their alphabetical order. Thus, references to Scott's relations with the Ballantynes, Constable, and others are indexed under their names. Scott's works are entered under their titles, e.g. *The Antiquary* and *Waverley* respectively under A and W. Projected, but abandoned, works, which have no definitive titles, are entered under the Heading 'Projected Works'. For authors, other than Scott, works are arranged alphabetically under their authors' names.

SUBJECT HEADINGS used are: Arboriculture; Archery; Armour and Weapons; Army; Ballads and Songs; Baronetcy; Bores; Breviaries; Brooch; Catholic Emancipation; Cats; Chancery; Chapbooks; Clan Badges; Clock; Coins; Continental Tours; Copyrights; Costume; Covenanters; Cryptography; Dogs; Drama; Drawing; Education; Episcopacy; Fables; Finance; Gas; German Literature; Gipsies; Greyhounds; Guisers; Hair; Handwriting; Harp; Health; Heraldry; Hieroglyphics; History; Horseracing; Horses; Hymns; Intemperance; Italian Language; Jacobites; Jugglers; Juries; Literature; Manuscripts; Music; Newspapers; Nicknames; Nursery Rhymes; Nursery Tales; Pens; Phrenology; Playing Cards; Plays; Poet Laureateship; Poetry; Politics, Domestic; Politics, Foreign; Poor Laws; Portraits; Projected Works; Proverbs; Publishers; Purses; Railways; Rings; Roads; Roman; Sagas; Seals; Snuff-boxes; Supernatural; Surnames; Tartan; Theatres; Thumbikins; Transport; Tunes; Unemployment; Volunteers; Walking-sticks; Wallpaper; Will.

PEERS. These are entered under the peerage titles, without references, unless Scott has used the family name or a lesser peerage title.

PERSONAL NAMES. It was very common in Scotland in Scott's day to address a landed proprietor by the name of his estate and even a tenant farmer by the name of his farm. I have, therefore, indicated in the Headings territorial titles, e.g.

Elliot-Lockhart (William) *of Borthwickbrae*
Rutherford (John) *of Edgerston*

Scott normally refers to these persons, not by surname, but as 'Borthwickbrae' and 'Edgerston'. References from the territorial titles are normally given.

PLACE-NAMES. With the exception of very well-known names, these are followed, in square brackets, by an indication of their locality with a 'q.v.' where such linkage seems justified. Many local names, mentioned by Scott, are difficult to find on small maps.

ARRANGEMENT. The arrangement of the Headings is strictly alphabetical by words, never by letters. Parts of the Heading in italics are ignored except where there is more than one person with the same surname and forenames. Untitled wives follow their husbands with the explanation 'Wife of preceding'; but wives of knights, baronets, and peers are arranged separately, firstly under the surname or peerage title and secondly under the maiden name which appears in the round brackets, thus:

Abercorn (Anne Jane Gore, *afterwards Marchioness of*)
Abercorn (John James Hamilton, *1st Marquess of*)
Scott (Jane Jobson, *afterwards Lady*)
Scott (*Sir* Walter) *2nd Bart.*

Hyphenated names are entered under the first part.
In German names, the umlaut is expanded. Thus, Bürger is alphabetized as if it were written Buerger.

INTERNAL ARRANGEMENT OF ENTRIES. Personal names are followed by brief biographies within square brackets. The term 'writer', frequently used, means a law agent or solicitor in Scotland, not an author. As family connections played a large part in patronage, relationships with other persons in the index are indicated by 'q.v.'. Where sources are given it is not to be assumed that I have taken the information from them. The inclusion, for example, of *DNB* merely means that that work contains a biography of the person. For contractions used for works cited, see p. ix.

References for most of the large entries are arranged chronologically and, in order to facilitate quick reference, dates are inserted. Actual dates, supplied by the indexer, are given in square brackets. Dates in round brackets are taken from the dates of the letters in which Scott records the events. The year only may be given, but where necessary the month may be added and when there is more than one reference to a month the day may also be given. Where there are a number of references to the same topic, only the first date is given unless there is a special reason for dating in detail. In order to follow the chronological arrangement, volume and page references are often out of numerical sequence.

SUB-HEADINGS. In the case of large entries Sub-Headings have been used to facilitate quick reference. In the case of Scott, for example, a reader who is not sure of the forename of the person wanted might have to read through the whole of the Scotts, but if he wants a Scott of Harden he has that section only to look through; and, furthermore, it is of great advantage to a reader to have in the smallest space possible a conspectus of the different branches such as the Scotts of Abbotsford or of Harden or of Raeburn. Sir Walter Scott's family are indexed under the Sub-Heading 'Abbotsford', but other relatives, without territorial distinctions, such as his father, mother, brothers, aunts, uncles, and cousins, are entered under section 'I. General'. This rule applies to junior members of other branches.

The references 'See above' and 'See below' mean that the reader should look above or below within the same Sub-Heading. The simple 'See' refers to a main Heading.

INDEX

Abbotsford (*cont.*)

Kaeside, S. contemplates buying (Oct. 1815) I. 487, 493; S. announces purchase of, IV. 97, 111–12, 116, 119–20, 121, XII. 153, IV. 122–3, 127, 131, 145, 165, 174, 184, 195, 214, 235, 442; bond on, 131 *n.*, 236 *n.*, IX. 359–60; S. suggests that the Fergusons might occupy the farmhouse (Mar. 1816) IV. 195–6; S. makes part-payment to Moss for (May 1816) 235–6, 236, 236 *n.*, 266; Moss has option to stay on as tenant (Mar. 1816) 196, (Feb. 1817) 392; Moss decides to leave at Whitsunday 1817, 427; Laidlaw to occupy the farmhouse (Apr. 1817) 427–8; S. planting trees at (Feb. 1818) V. 79–80; Laidlaw leaves (Aug. 1827) X. 273–4; S. would like farmhouse for Laidlaw's reoccupation (Nov. 1829) XI. 257; house suffers from damp (Feb. 1830) 299; Laidlaw returns to, at Whitsunday 1830, 299; quarry at, used for building Abbotsford House, IV. 398, 421, 433, 437, 515, 526

Mar's Lee, V. 80
Mary's Girdle, X. 350
Meg's Hill, X. 350
Moss's Stripe, V. 500
Mount Saint John, VII. 64
Rhymer's Glen (formerly Dick's Cleugh), S. wants to buy the glen from Usher (May 1816) IV. 237; S. makes agreement with Usher for (Dec. 1816) 324–5; S. announces his purchase of, 326, 328, 539; cascade being made in (Sept. 1817) 509, 539–40, (1818) V. 115, 186; blackcocks shot in (Sept. 1817) IV. 531–2; being planted (Feb. 1818) V. 80; stone steps being made in (May 1818) 151; S. describes, to Joanna Baillie (July 1818) 174; Mrs Terry makes sketch of rustic bridge in (Aug. 1820) VI. 262; S. tells Laing it is connected with Thomas the Rhymer (Apr. 1822) VII. 143, but qualifies this statement (Nov. 1822) 277; mentioned, V. 57

St. John's Well, V. 40
Sawmill. *See above under* Huntly-burn
Shearingflatts, VI. 305 (a)
Spy Law, III. 186
Stobs Meadow, V. 160, 255
Tinder-Coal Yards, VI. 305, 365, 368, 444
Toftfield, S. purchases (Sept. 1817) IV. 508, 512, 529, 531, I. 522, 523 *n.*,

Abbotsford (*cont.*)

IV. 534, 540, 541, 542, V. 132; to be occupied by Swanston and Leithead (May 1818) 152–3; parks at, to be top-dressed with marle (June 1818) 160; S. superintends dam and footpath at (Sept. 1818) 186; *see also above* Huntlyburn

Turnagain, IV. 146, 351, VI. 424
White Hill Park, IV. 541, V. 160
Whitehaugh, V. 16

III. *The House*

(1) New Cottage (proposed but not built)

Plans for (1811) II. 496, 501, 508, 509, 512, 513–14, 519, 521, 527, 535, 537, XII. 409, 439, III. 16, II. 435, (1812) III. 30, 50–1, 57, 151; Stark's plan (Oct. 1811) III. 10, 34, 65, 68–9, 71, 73, 79; all plans abandoned (Nov. 1814) 514

(2) Alterations to Old Cottage ('Mother Redford')

Description of, (Dec. 1811) III. 34, (1812) 153–4, 156, (1813) 263, (1814) 433, 441–2, 446, 448–9, 514–15, 521, (1815) IV. 8, 14; workmen at (1812) III. 115; building costs in 1812, I. 418; slates for, 419; proposed alterations to (1816) IV. 334–5, 345; further alterations to, abandoned (1817) 526–7, V. 4, (1818) 13, 63, 102; demolished [Jan. 1822] VII. 39, 56, 70, 73, 159, 193

Present House

For S.'s discussions with his architect on planning and furnishing, *see* Atkinson (William)

(3) First Portion, 1817–19

(a) General

Planning, furnishing, etc. (1816) IV. 285–6, 289–90, 296, 301–2, 306, 319, 328–9, 332, 333, 333–40, (1817) 346–7, 384, 388, 390–1, 391, 396–401, 415–16, 421, 422–3, 423–4, 425, 435–9, 441–2, 463–4, 493, 502, 509–10, 524–5, 525–7, 539, 542, V. 2–4, 32, (1818) 91, 100–1, 102–3, 117–18, 122, 133, 134, 147, 148–9, 163–4, 169–70, 171–2, 190–1, 199, 200, (1819) 421–2, (1820) VI. 186

Stone for, IV. 398, 421, 433, 437,

Abercorn (*cont.*)
1824) VIII. 196 *n.*, 260, 261; on *St Ronan's Well* (Feb. 1824) 196 *n.*; interrupted correspondence between S. and [1821–4] 196 *n.*, 196–8; S. denies authorship of Waverley Novels to (Mar. 1824) 196 *n.*, 198–9; invited to Abbotsford (Mar. 1824) 202, 260 *n.*, 261, 292; to be at Fulham Palace [June 1824] 197 *n.*; S. admits to, that he is writing another book [*Tales of the Crusaders*] (Aug. 1824) 339; *Tales of the Crusaders* presented to (July 1825) IX. 170; *Woodstock* presented to (Sept. 1826) X. 90

Abercorn (James Hamilton, *1st Duke of*) *1811–85* [*succ.* as 2nd Marquess 1818; *cr.* Duke 1868; *DNB*] II. 433

Abercorn (James Hamilton, *8th Earl of*) *1712–89* [*succ.* 1744; *DNB*] XI. 38

Abercorn (John James Hamilton, *1st Marquess of*) *1756–1818* [*succ.* as 9th Earl 1789; *m.* (1) Catherine, dau. of Sir Joseph Copley, (2) 1792 Cecil Hamilton and (3) 1800 Lady Anne Jane Gore, dau. of 2nd Earl of Arran and widow of Henry Hatton; *cr.* Marquess 1790; his dau. Katharine Elizabeth by first marriage *m.* 4th Earl of Aberdeen (q.v.)]
Calls Tom to London (1802) XII. 220; S. recommends to, John Thomson for Kirk of Duddingston (1805) 381 *n.* 1, 382; S. to visit, at The Priory (Mar. 1807) 97, 98; S. dines with, in London (Apr. 1807) 110; Tom misappropriates rents of Duddingston estates of (1807) I. 367–70, 373–4, 381; this trouble referred to (1817) VII. 485, 487, 489, 491; suggests additional lines on Fox in *Marmion* (1807) I. 385, II. 35, 35 *n.*, XII. 300; S. hopes to meet, at Dumfries (Nov. 1807) I. 395; his opinion of *Marmion* (Feb. 1808) II. 12, 16, 25; has 'best ear for English versification' (1808) 70; S. would like to dedicate *Swift* to (Oct. 1808) 95; S.'s reason for not dedicating *Marmion* to (1808) 110–11; *Lady of the Lake* dedicated to, 111, 240, 274, 286, 311, 324, 324 *n.*, 354, XII. 401; rumour that he is to be made Lord Chamberlain (Dec. 1810) II. 413–14; approves of *Rokeby* (Mar. 1813) III. 241; S.'s meeting with [Aug. 1813] III. 293, 294, 301, 303; portrait of, by Lawrence, obliquely alluded to (1815) IV. 7; death of,

Abercorn (*cont.*)
V. 105–6, VI. 26 *n.*; mentioned, I. 301 *n.*, III. 11 *n.*

Abercrombie (John) *1780–1844* [Scottish physician; *m.* Agnes, dau. of David Wardlaw of Netherbarns; *DNB, St. Cuthbert's*, No. 315]
Attends Lady Scott (1826) IX. 475, 490, X. 34; consulted by Dean of Chester (1828) 492; consulted by S. (1829–31) XI. 275, 317, 436, 436 *n.*, 484, XII. 13, 14; consulted by Anne (1830) XI. 420

Abercromby (James) *1st Baron Dunfermline. See* Dunfermline

Abercromby (Montagu Dundas, *afterwards Lady*) *1772–1837* [3rd dau. of 1st Viscount Melville (q.v.); *m.* 1799 2nd Baron Abercromby] VIII. 312, 312 *n.*

Abercromby (*Sir* Ralph) *1734–1801* [General; son of George Abercromby of Tullibody; *m.* 1767 Mary Anne Menzies (*cr.* Baroness Abercromby of Aboukir and Tullibody, 1801); knighted 1795; brother of Mrs Alexander Joass (q.v.) and father of Lord Dunfermline (q.v.); *DNB*] VII. 135, XII. 91

Abercromby (Thomas Sinclair) *of Glassaugh, d. 1823* [King's Limner for Scotland; *d.* Rome 9 Apr.] VIII. 30

Aberdeen, S. at (1796) I. 46; S. passes (1814) XII. 119–20; Terry going to (1818) V. 272; University, II. 52

Aberdeen (Catherine Elizabeth Hamilton, *afterwards Countess of*) *1784–1812* [2nd dau., by first marriage, of 1st Marquess of Abercorn (q.v.); *m.* 1805 4th Earl of Aberdeen (q.v.); *d.* 29 Feb.]
S. meets, at Bentley Priory (1807) XII. 100; illness of (1812) III. 89; death of, 110; mentioned (May 1807) XII. 116, (Nov. 1807) I. 395

Aberdeen (George Gordon, *4th Earl of*) *1784–1860* [*succ.* 1801; *m.* (1) 1805 Catherine Elizabeth Hamilton, 2nd dau. of 1st Marquess of Abercorn (q.v.); she *d.* 29 Feb. 1812 and he *m.* (2) 1815 Harriet, dau. of Hon. John Douglas and widow of James, Viscount Hamilton (q.v.); Foreign Secretary 1828–30; member of Bannatyne Club (q.v.) 31 Jan. 1827; *DNB*]
S. meets, at The Priory (1807) XII. 100; death of infant son (1808) II. 69; the Morritts visit, at

Antiquarian (The) Repository [Compiled by Francis Grose and others] II. 112

Antiquary (The) [Publ. May 1816] composition of (1815) I. 478, 480, 483, 489, 494, IV. 145, 147, (1816) 166, 186, 229; price of, I. 495, IV. 215; sales of, 233, 233 *n.*, 238; S.'s comments on, to Morritt, 233, and to Terry, 238; S. replies to Lady Abercorn on authorship of, 283; 2nd ed. (May 1816) 233, 235, 238; sales of, up to March 1817, 412; new ed. (1818) I. 528, V. 181; Terry's dramatization of (1820) VI. 10 *n.*, 11 *n.*; S. quotes Jonathan Oldbuck (1822) VII. 67, (1825) IX. 34; S. forecasts a better reception for (1822) VII. 278; S. quotes David Mailsetter (1828) X. 478; S. on allusion to Wilkie in (1829) XI. 105; S. relates his preference for, to Basil Hall (1831) XII. 36–7; editorial references to, I. 119 *n.*, XII. 336 *n.*; see also *Waverley Novels.* 3. 'Magnum Opus' ed.

Antiquitates Reekianæ. See Projected works

Antonius (Marcus) *83–30 B.C.* [Roman soldier and statesman] II. 174 *n.*, 175

Antrobus (*Sir* Edmund) *1st Bart.* of *Antrobus, Cheshire and Rutherford, Roxburghshire, d. 1826* [*cr.* Baronet 1815; *d. unm.* 6 Feb.] VIII. 74, 74 *n.*, 335, XII. 150

Antwerp, S. at (1815) IV. 78, XII. 136; mentioned, IV. 6

Apollonius, *of Tyana* [Greek philosopher, *b. c.* 4 B.C.]. For life of, *see* Philostratus

Appin [District or hamlet in W. Argyllshire] IV. 394 *n.*

Appleby [Town in Westmorland] III. 169, VIII. 259, 260, IX. 212, XI. 383

Apreece (Jane Kerr, *Mrs*) *afterwards* Lady Davy. See Davy

Apreece (*Sir* Thomas Hussey) *1st Bart. of Washingley, 1744–1833* [*cr.* Baronet 1782] I. 196 *n.*

Arabian Nights, Jonathan Scott's trans. of [1811] XII. 395, 395 *n.*; French ed. of (1829) XI. 270

General references to persons in: Abou Hassan, II. 528, VII. 241; Dinarzade, VI. 143; Haroun Alraschid, III. 398; Scheherazade, I. 311, VI. 143, IX. 27

Adventures of the Calif Haroun Alraschid. The story of Sidi Nonman, V. 333

Arabian Nights (*cont.*)
The story of Ali Baba and the forty thieves, VI. 293, IX. 431, XI. 428

Story of the fisherman, III. 164; *Story of the young King of the Black Isles,* I. 285

Story of the little hunchback. The story told by the tailor, VI. 39, XI. 9; *The story of the barber's fifth brother:* Alnaschar, VIII. 427, XI. 195, 206

The story of Prince Ahmed and the Fairy Peri Banou: the Fountain of Lions, IV. 500; Peri Banou's expanding tent, II. 527, IV. 497, VIII. 355; Prince Hussein's tapestry, I. 229, 311, 312 (twice), II. 220, IV. 251, VIII. 57, 67, 427, IX. 42, 317, 329, X. 67, 144, 284, 451, XI. 273, XII. 23

Story of Sindbad the sailor, I. 120 (error), 369, II. 214, 437, III. 59, 521

The story of the sleeper awakened, II. 528, VII. 241

The story of the three Calendars. The story of the third Calendar, I. 120

See also *Aladdin and the wonderful lamp*

Aram (Eugene) *1704–59* [Murderer; *DNB*] XII. 443 *n.*, 444, 444 *n.*

Arboriculture, neglected in the Borders (1804) XII. 249–50; S.'s delight in (1810) II. 402, (1814) III. 471, (1825) IX. 157–8; Duke of Atholl's plan for larches (1818–20) V. 73, 80, VI. 217, 224–5; S. on Sir Henry Steuart's plan for transplanting trees (1824) VIII. 138–40, 148–50; S. on profit in (1825) IX. 157–8; time for planting trees, VII. 163; *see also* Abbotsford. II. The Estate. (1) General; Planting

Arbroath [Coastal town of Angus] S. at (1796) I. 46

Arbruchill. See Aberuchill

Arbuthnot (Alexander) *d. 1585* [Scottish printer; *DNB*] I. 252

Arbuthnot (Anne Alves, *afterwards* Lady) *d. 1846* [Dau. of John Alves of Shipland; *m.* 1800 Sir William Arbuthnot, 1st Bart. (q.v.)] X. 41, XI. 243–4

Arbuthnot (Charles) *1767–1850* [Diplomatist; son of John Arbuthnot of Rockfleet Castle, co. Mayo; *m.* (2) Harriet, 3rd dau. of Hon. Henry Fane, 1739–1834, 2nd son of 8th Earl of Westmorland; *DNB*]

Biog. notes on, II. 444 *n.*, VI. 152 *n.*; Mrs Jackson becomes gover-

Ballads and Songs (*cont.*)

Balrinnes, (or *The Battle of Glenlivet*) I.
341; *The Battle of Bothwell Bridge*,
157, 161; *The Battle of Corrichie*,
103 *n.*; *The Battle of Glenlivet*. See
above *The Battle of Balrinnes*; *The
Battle of Loudon Hill*, 157, 161;
quoted, 400; *The Battle of Otterburn*,
109, 173, III. 208, XII. 377–8;
The Battle of Philiphaugh, I. 157, 161,
IV. 342; *Bessy Bell and Mary Gray*
[Traditional; completed by Allan
Ramsay] III. 28; *Bewick and Graham*,
I. 169, 169 *n.*, XII. 165 *n.*; *The
boatie rows*, 118; *Bonnie Dundee*,
quoted, IX. 356; see also below,
Jockey's escape from Dundee; *Bonny
Baby Livingston*, I. 172; *Bonny Barbara
Allan*, VIII. 255; *Bonny Lizie Baillie*,
I. 382, II. 412; VIII. 487, 491, 497,
IX. 22, XII. 78; *The boy and the
mantle*, quoted, II. 173, XII. 273;
The Braes of Yarrow, quoted, II. 531,
XII. 173; *The broom of Cowdenknows*,
I. 294; *Brown Adam*, XII. 163;
quoted, VI. 467; *The burning of
Frendraught*, VIII. 45 *n.*, 61; *Captain
Ward and the Rainbow*, 359 *n.*; *The
carle he came o'er the craft*, quoted,
VII. 267; *Carle now the Kings come*,
quoted, V. 278; *Charley fond of Popish
blessing*, IV. 191; *The Chevalier's
muster-roll*. See below, *Little wat ye
wha's coming*; *Chevy Chase* (or
Hunting of the Cheviot), I. 8, 18, 27,
229, 322, III. 82, VIII. 27–8, 28 *n.*;
Edward Bird's painting of, III. 227,
232, 232 *n.*, XII. 410–14; quoted,
III. 227, VI. 56, XI. 47; *Child Horn*,
II. 65; *Child Noryce* (or *Gil Morrice*),
IX. 100–2, 100 *n.*; *Christie's Will*, IV.
539; *Clerk Saunders*, I. 103 *n.*; *The
cobler*, quoted, IV. 346; *Come, come,
my Hearts of Gold*, quoted, IX. 329;
Cowdenknows. See above, *The broom of
Cowdenknows*; *The cruel brother*, I. 299;
The dæmon-lover, 170; *The death of
Featherstonhaugh* [Forgery by Surtees].
See Surtees (Robert); *The death of
Parcy Reed*, II. 65, XI. 292, 293,
426–7; *see also* Rokesby (George);
Dick of the Cow, IV. 104; quoted, IX.
45; *Donul and Evir*. *See* Jamieson
(Robert); *The Douglas tragedy*, I.
152 *n.*, 153; *Doune Shepherdess*, II.
65; *The dowie dens of Yarrow*, I. 294;
see also below, *Tushielaw's lines*;
The Dragon of Wantley, 161, 204
(XII. 240), VIII. 495, XI. 151,
XII. 241–2, 242 *n.*, 288; *The drinking

Ballads and Songs (*cont.*)

match [or *The luck of Eden-Hall* or
Parody on Chevy Chase]. *See* Lloyd
(Philip); *The drucken wife o' Gallowa*,
quoted, IX. 233; *The Duke of Gordon
has three daughters*, quoted, 61; *Earl
Richard*, quoted, XI. 129; *The Earle
of Westmorlande*, I. 108 *n.*, 109, XII.
169; *The Elfin Knight*, II. 65; *Factor's
garland*, I. 263; *The Fair Flower of
Northumberland*, VIII. 325, 325 *n.*;
Fair Helen of Kirconnell, I. 118 *n.*;
quoted, VII. 267; *Fair Janet*, I. 104 *n.*;
Fair 'Mabel' of Wallington, 238; *Fause
Foodrage*, quoted, VIII. 496; *The
felon sow of Rokeby and the Friars of
Richmond*, II. 98, 98 *n.*, 204–5,
204 *n.*, 306–7; *The fire of Frendraught*.
See above, *The burning of Frendraught*;
The flowers of the forest, I. 118 *n.*, 121,
IX. 243–4; *see also* Elliot (Jane) *and*
Cockburn (Alison Rutherford, *after-
wards Mrs*); *The fray of Suport*, I. 342;
quoted, XI. 139; *The gaberlunzie man*,
quoted, III. 10; *The gallant Grahams*,
XII. 209, 209 *n.*; *The gay goss hawk*,
I. 173, XII. 163; *Gentle river, gentle
river*, quoted, X. 426, XII. 113;
Geordie, I. 172; *George Ridler's oven*,
VIII. 367, 367 *n.*, 390–1, 390 *n.*,
421; *Gil Morrice*. See above, *Child
Noryce*; *Good night of Lord Derwentwater* [Forgery by Surtees]. *See*
Surtees (Robert). *Lord Derwentwater's
'good night'*; *The haggis o' Dunbar*,
quoted, VI. 445, X. 52; *The heir of
Linne*, quoted, IV. 470, X. 328;
Hobbie Noble, I. 174, 297; quoted,
371; *The hunting of the Cheviot*. See
above, *Chevy Chase*; *I am a jolly toper*,
quoted, XI. 272; *I have a horse, and
I have nae mair*, quoted, VI. 364;
I wish I were where Helen lies. See
above, *Fair Helen of Kirconnell*; *Jamie
Telfer o' the Fair Dodhead*, I. 29;
quoted, IV. 125; *Jock o' the Side*,
104; quoted, XI. 481, XII. 165;
Jock of Hazeldean, IV. 172, 177;
Jock of Milk, I. 140–1, 140 *n.*, 142–3,
160; *Jockey's escape from Dundee* [or
Bonnie Dundee], quoted, VI. 15, IX.
350; *Jocky fou, Jenny fain*, quoted, III.
187; *Johnie Armstrong*, X. 490; *Johnie
Faa, or the Gypsie laddie*, XI. 430;
Johnie of Breadislee, quoted, I. 56;
Johnie Scot, 238; *Joseph said to vex him*
[first line], V. 388–9; *Katharine
Janfarie*, I. 172, 172 *n.*; *see also
below*, *The Laird of Lamington*;
Kempion, XII. 242, 242 *n.*; *The King

Ballantyne (*cont.*)
to London [10 July–26 Aug. 1819]
401, 403 *n.*, 416, 419, 427; share by,
of *Tales of my Landlord*, 3rd ser. (July
1819) 422, 445; at Brighton (Aug.
1819) 403 *n.*, 441, 459; abandons
Continental trip (Aug. 1819) 439,
443; auctioning pictures (Jan. 1820)
VI. 121, 121 *n.*; biog. notes on (Mar.
1820) 161 *n.*, (May–July 1820) 197 *n.*;
in London and S. reads him a lecture
on his health (June 1820) 210–11;
going to Isle of Wight (June 1820)
211; ill health of [Aug. 1820] 459;
retires from business (Nov. 1820) 288,
288 *n.*; buys vote for Roxburghshire
(Jan. 1821) 330; S. objects to his
residing at Kelso (Apr. 1821) V.
368–70; S. and Terry to breakfast
with [at Kirklands, Melrose, 29 Apr.
1821] VI. 427; death of [16 June
1821] 477, 482, 483–4, 490, VII. 67,
127, 259

Miscellaneous references: of slim
build (1813) III. 327; good at
mimicry (1817) V. 8; bequeaths S.
money for his library (1821) VI.
482, 484, VII. 288; S. receives portrait of (1823) 381; Trustees of (1830)
XI. 398–9, 398 *n.*; *Widow's lodgings*
by, III. 241, VI. 478 *n.*; contributed
pieces to *Edin. Ann. Reg.* 478 *n.*

Ballantyne (*Mrs* John) *d. 1854* [Wife
of preceding; Hermione, dau. of
Charles Parker, London and Brooks-
bank, and step-dau. of Rev. William
Rutherford, assistant to Rev. Cornelius Lundie, minister of Kelso; *m.*
(2) 17 Sept. 1828 John Glover,
Kendal]
Left widow in straitened circum-
stances, VI. 484 *n.*, XI. 399, 399 *n.*,
XII. 26–7, 26 *n.*; S.'s payment to,
out of *Ballantyne's Novelist's Library*,
VII. 67, 79; sells MS. of *The Lady of
the Lake* to Cadell, XI. 399 *n.*; mentioned, VI. 210

Ballantyne (John) & Co. [Edinburgh
publishers]. *See under* Ballantyne
(John)

Ballantyne (John Alexander) *1816–
61* [Only son of James Ballantyne
(q.v.); *b.* 29 Nov.; *d.* 20 Jan.]
Birth of, IV. 339, 339 *n.*; unwell
(1819) V. 425, 427

Ballantyne (Mary Scott) *1818–21*
[Eldest dau. of James Ballantyne
(q.v.); *b.* 25 Mar.; *d.* 10 Jan.] VI.
334, 334 *n.*

Ballantyne's Novelist's Library,
VI. 288–9, 289 *n.*, 312, 481, 481 *n.*,
503, VII. 14–15, 14 *n.*, 67, IX.
224 *n.*, X. 95–6, 272
Vol. 4: VII. 41, 87, 88, 94–6, 109,
124
Vol. 5: 248–9, 248 *n.*
Vols. 6–8: VIII. 236
Vol. 9: 325, 325 *n.*
Vol. 10: 310, 310 *n.*

Ballingry [Hamlet in Fife] XI. 213

Ballinrobe [Town in co. Mayo,
Ireland] IX. 258, 432, 450 *n.*, 455

Balmain (*Count* Aleksandr Antonovich)
d. 1848 [Commissioner of Emperor
of Russia at St. Helena; *m.* 1820 at
St. Helena, Charlotte Johnson, step-
dau. of Sir Hudson Lowe (q.v.);
Burke, under Johnson of New York]
X. 270

Balmanno (Robert), X. 167, 167 *n.*,
169, 170

Balmuto (Claud Irvine Boswell,
Lord). *See* Boswell

Balthayock [or Balthavock; house
near Perth, Perthshire]. *See* Blair
(*Family of*) *of Balthayock*

Baltic (Battle of the) [1801] I. 129

Bamborough Castle [Northumber-
land] XII. 251 *n.*, 253

Bande (La) **Noire** [Society of building
speculators in France after the
Revolution] VIII. 13

Bandello (Matteo) *1480?–1562* [Italian
author] II. 540, 541 *n.*, III. 23–4,
179 *n.*

Bandon [Town SW. of Cork, Ireland]
VI. 55, 55 *n.*

Bangalore. *See* India

Bank of England, X. 58; *see also*
Banks

Bank of Scotland, I. 449, V. 311,
IX. 426; and Cadell's discharge
from bankruptcy, XI. 135–6, 135 *n.*,
167, 168 *n.*, 177

Bankes (Henry) *of Kingston Hall,
1757–1834* [succ. to Kingston Hall,
Dorset 1776; M.P. Corfe Castle
1780–1826 and of Dorset 1826–31;
m. 1784 Frances, dau. of William
Woodley, Governor of the Caribbee
Islands, and sister of Mrs P. L.
Fletcher (q.v.); *Burke LG* 1858, *DNB*]
III. 59, VII. 11

Bankhouse Inn [Formerly one of the
stages on the Edinburgh–London
road, on right bank of Gala Water,
south of Fountainhall, Midlothian] I.
372, II. 483, 533, III. 508, IV.
498

Berguer (*cont.*)
Maida's epitaph (1824) VIII. 412 *n.*,
417, 419
Berkeley (George) *1685–1753* [Bishop
of Cloyne; *DNB*] quoted, IV. 228
Berkeley (George Monck) *1763–93*
[Grandson of Bishop George
Berkeley (q.v.); miscellaneous writer;
member of Royal Company of
Scottish Archers 1789; *DNB*] II. 408,
408 *n.*
Berkeley (William Fitzhardinge) *after-
wards Earl Fitzhardinge*. *See* Fitz-
hardinge
Berlin, S. thinks of sending Walter to
(1821) VI. 389, 426, VII. 5, 5 *n.*;
Walter sets out for (Dec. 1821) 43;
Walter at (1822) 68, 70, 76–7, 85,
120, 140, 158, 199, (1823) 309, 376;
S. recalls Walter's good behaviour at,
VIII. 475–6, 492, X. 442
Bernadotte (Jean Baptiste Jules). *See*
Charles XIV, *King of Sweden and
Norway*
Berne [Switzerland] II. 399
Bernéaud (Arsenne Thiébaut de). *See*
Thiébaut de Bernéaud
Berners (John Bouchier, *2nd Baron*)
1467–1533 [English statesman and
translator of Froissart; *DNB*] II. 169,
XII. 402
Berners (*Lady* Juliana) [English
prioress and writer on hunting and
heraldry, early 15th cent.; *DNB*]
Caxton's original ed. of *Book of St.
Albans* attributed to, I. 115 (XII. 183),
115 *n.*, 138, 138 *n.*, XII. 179 *n.*, 183 *n.*,
184, 207, 217, 220; S. purchases
Haslewood's 1810 reprint, I. 481;
for dog named after, *see* Dogs.
Juliana
Berni (Francesco) *1490–1536*. For his
version of Boiardo's *Orlando innamorato*, *see* Boiardo
Berry (Charles Ferdinand d'Artois,
duc de) *1778–1820* [2nd son of
Charles X, King of France (q.v.)] VI.
138, 138 *n.*
Berry (Mary) *1763–1852* [English
author and diarist; *DNB*] II. 59
Bertolini (Joseph Philip) [A Pied-
montese; *m.* 30 Apr. 1821 Elizabeth
Johnston of Lathrisk] VIII. 460–1,
460 *n.*
Bertolini (*Mrs* Joseph Philip) [Wife of
preceding] VIII. 460–1, 460 *n.*
Bertrand (*Comte* Henri Gratien) *1773–
1844* [French general] X. 270, 277
Berwick. *See* Berwick-upon-Tweed
Berwick (Edward) *b. 1750* [Irish

Berwick (*cont.*)
clergyman; rector of Clongish;
domestic chaplain to Earl of Moira;
DNB]
S. receives assistance on Swift from
(1809) II. 199–202, 221–4, 232,
241–2, 252, 255, 256, (1810) 323–4,
385–6, 387, 408, (1811) 486, (1812)
III. 57–8, 162, (1813) XII. 417,
(1814) III. 402–4; S. presents to,
Lay, II. 323, *Marmion*, 323, *Lady
of the Lake*, 323, 387, *Rokeby*, XII.
418, *Swift*, III. 410, 429 (b), 449, *Lord
of the Isles*, IV. 10; owns portrait of
Stella, 317

Works

*Lives of Marcus Valerius Messala
Corvinus and Titus Pomponius Atticus*,
III. 58, 58 *n.*, 402 *n.*, 403, IV. 11, XII.
417
Life of Apollonius, by Philostratus.
See Philostratus
Berwick (Sophia Dubouchet, *afterwards
Lady*) *d. 1875* [Dau. of John James
Dubouchet and sister of Harriette
Wilson (q.v.); *m.* 1812 2nd Baron
Berwick] IX. 7
Berwick-upon-Tweed, I. 109, 285,
III. 111, 393, V. 185, 254, 363, VI.
54, 61, 71, XII. 251 *n.*, 253, 259 *n.*
Berwickshire, proposed railway in
(1812) III. 65; parliamentary can-
didate for (1812) 85–8; Scott of
Harden not to stand for (1820) VI.
137, 137 *n.*
Bessy Bell and Mary Gray. *See*
Ballads and Songs
Beton (Mary). *See* Beaton
Betrothed (The), VIII. 336, 416–17,
417 *n.*, IX. 156 *n.*, XI. 87; see also
Tales of the Crusaders and *Waverley
Novels*. 3. 'Magnum Opus' ed.
Betson. *See* Beatson
Betterton (Thomas) *1635?–1710* [Eng-
lish actor and dramatist; *DNB*] III.
443
Betty (William Henry West) *1791–
1874* [Actor; called the 'Young
Roscius'; *DNB*] I. 373 *n.*, 375, 380
Beverley (George Percy, *2nd Earl of*)
1778–1867 [Son of Algernon Percy
who was 2nd son of 1st Duke of
Northumberland; *succ.* as 2nd Earl
of Beverley 1830] *As Lord Lovaine*:
XI. 174
Bevis of Hampton [14th-cent. verse
romance] XII. 201
Bewick (William) *1795–1866* [English
artist; *DNB*] XII. 452

Bognor [Town on coast of Sussex; now Bognor Regis] Lady Abercorn at (10 Aug. 1820) VI. 253 n.

Bohemia, V. 408

Bohn (John) [London bookseller] V. 14

Bohte (J. H.) & Co. [Booksellers, York Street, London; John Henry Bohte, Foreign Bookseller to His Majesty, d. there Sept. 1824 aged 39] V. 457-8, VII. 304

Boiardo (Matteo Maria) *1430–95* [Italian poet] *Orlando innamorato* by, IX. 2, XII. 185, 196; W. S. Rose's trans. of Berni's version, VII. 286, 286 n., 374–5, 374 n.

Boileau-Despréaux (Nicolas) *1636– 1711* [French critic and poet] quoted, II. 27

Bold (The) dragoon. See *British Light Dragoons*

Boldero (*Messrs*). See Lushington, Boldero and Co.

Boleside [or Boldside; hamlet on River Tweed near Abbotsford] III. 431

Bolingbroke (Henry St. John, *1st Viscount*) *1678–1751* [English states-man; *DNB*] II. 201

Bolt (Andrew) [Merchant in Lerwick] VII. 12 n.

Bolt (Isabel) *afterwards Mrs Walter Scott.* See under Scott [of Scottshall]

Bolton. See also Boulton

Bolton (John) *of Storrs, 1756–1837* [West Indian merchant and slave trader; Sir Clement Jones, *John Bolton of Storrs*, Kendal, 1959] Meeting of Canning and Brougham at Storrs (1822) VII. 233, 234 n., 307 n.; S. visits (1825) IX. 207, 335

Bolton (Thomas Orde-Powlett, *1st Baron*) *1748–1807* [English politician; *DNB*] XII. 102, 102 n.

Bombay. See India

Bonaparte (Jerome) *1784–1860* [King of Westphalia; brother of Napoleon I; *m.* 1803 Elizabeth Patterson (q.v.)] XI. 169, 169 n., 173

Bonaparte (Louis) *1778–1846* [King of Holland; brother of Napoleon I] XI. 56–7, 56 n.

Bonaparte (Lucien) *1775–1840* [Brother of Napoleon I] XII. 404; epic on Charlemagne by, II. 543, 543 n., III. 3, 523–4, 531–2

Bond (Elizabeth) [Schoolmistress at Fortrose in Ross and Cromarty; author of *Letters of a village governess* (1814) with printed dedication to Scott] IV. 71, 71 n., XI. 278–9, 278 n.

Bonnets of Bonnie Dundee [This is a made-up title used on its first appearance in print—in *The Christmas Box*—but S. gave it no title and it appeared in *The doom of Devorgoil* simply as 'Song'] IX. 347, 350, 355–6, 372, 424, X. 323 n.

Bonnie Dundee. See *Bonnets of Bonnie Dundee*

Bonny Baby Livingston. See Ballads and Songs

Bonny Barbara Allan. See Ballads and Songs

Bonny Dundee. See Ballads and Songs. *Bonnie Dundee*

Bonny Heck. See Hamilton (William) *of Gilbertfield*

Bonny Lizie Baillie. See Ballads and Songs

Bonnymuir [A bleak moor in Falkirk Parish, Stirlingshire] skirmish with Radicals at (1820) VI. 209, 234

Boodle (Edward) [Marquess of North-ampton's solicitor] IV. 43, 45, 62, 63, 67

Book of St. Albans. See under Berners (*Lady* Juliana)

Book of Scotish pasquils. See Maidment (James)

Books, price of, I. 346, III. 121, XII. 310

Bookselling [i.e. publishing]. See Publishing

Boothby (*Sir* Brooke) *7th Bart., 1744–1824* [English poet and writer on politics; *d.* Boulogne 22 Jan.; *DNB*] III. 250, 250 n., V. 198

Bootle-Wilbraham (Anne Dorothea) *afterwards Lady Alvanley.* See Alvanley

Bootle-Wilbraham (Richard) *of Lathom House, 1724–96* [Richard Wilbraham; *m.* Mary Bootle, heiress of Lathom, and assumed additional name of Bootle; father of Lord Skermersdale, Randle Wilbraham (q.v.) and Lady Alvanley (q.v.); *Burke LG*] VII. 196

Borde or Boorde (Andrew) *1490–1549* [English physician; *DNB*] XI. 200

Bordeaux, V. 258, 268, 273, XI. 49, 184

Border (The) antiquities [Ed. by John Greig with an introd. by S.] S.'s comments on (1814) III. 449, (1815) IV. 16, (1817) I. 517; S.'s introd. and Appendixes to (1814–17) I. 501, III. 423–4, IV. 159 (a–b), 373 (d), 434 (a), (1827) X. 198, 199, 231

Border (The) Courier [Kelso news-paper, 1823] VII. 333

Boswell (*cont.*)
writes to, on archery (1818) V. 113, 126–30; death of, VII. 85, 114, 115, 140, 198, 259; S. says he was like his father, XI. 117

Boswell (*Sir* James) *2nd Bart. of Auchinleck, 1806–57,* IX. 26, 26 *n.,* XI. 117, 117 *n.,* XII. 470

Boswell (Janet Theresa) *afterwards Lady Eliott. See* Eliott

Boswell (Veronica) *1773–95* [Dau. of James Boswell (q.v.), biographer of Johnson] XII. 469, 469 *n.*

Boswell Fair. *See* St. Boswells. Fair

Botany, S. professes ignorance of, IV. 287, 335

Botany Bay, S. receives plants and seeds from (1822) VII. 99

Both (Jan) *1610–52* [Dutch artist] XI. 137

Bothwell (Francis Stewart, *5th Earl of*) *d. 1624* [*succ.* 1578; title and estates forfeited 1593; *DNB, under* Hepburn] IV. 341; for his grandson, *see* Stewart (Francis)

Bothwell Bridge (Battle of) [1679] IV. 321, 341; *see also* Ballads and Songs. *The Battle of Bothwell Bridge*

Bothwell Castle [Seat in Lanarkshire of Archibald, 1st Baron Douglas (q.v.) and Lady Frances Douglas (q.v.); now of the Earl of Home] S. visits (1799) I. 125 *n.*; poem on, by M. G. Lewis (1802) 151; S. visits (Sept. 1807) 377, 382, 393; S. proposes to visit (Dec. 1807) 391, 393; Lord and Lady Dalkeith go to (1808) II. 32; Lady Louisa Stuart going to (July 1809) 208 *n.,* 209; S. hopes to visit (1815) VII. 115; Henry Raeburn at (1821) VII. 3; S. hopes to visit (1825) IX. 154; S. passes, without visiting (1827) X. 309; *Young Lochinvar* written at, IX. 154

Bothwell lines. *See* Wilson (William) [Schoolmaster]

Bothwellhaugh [Lanarkshire]. *See* Hamilton (James) *of Bothwellhaugh*

Boughton House [Near Kettering, Northamptonshire] 4th Duke of Buccleuch buried at, V. 382, 386 *n.*; S. has never visited (1823) VIII. 1 *n.* 3

Boulton (*Family of*) [Of Soho, Staffordshire] S. says he will visit (Apr. 1807) XII. 111

Boulton (Anne) [Dau. of Matthew Boulton (q.v.)] probable reference to (1803) I. 184

Boulton (Matthew) *1728–1809* [Engineer, Soho Works, Stafford-

Boulton (*cont.*)
shire; *m.* 1760 Anne, dau. of Luke Robinson, Lichfield; F.R.S.E. 17 Aug. 1809; *DNB*]
Biog. note on, I. 183 *n.*; S. writes to (1803) 183–4

Bourmont (*Comte* Louis Auguste Victor) *1773–1846* [French marshal] expected at Abbotsford (1830) XI. 435, 435 *n.*

Bousquet (*Mons.* —) [Resident in Lyons, France, 1828] XI. 9

Boutourlin (*Count* Dmitry Petrovich) *1790–1850* [Russian soldier and author] IX. 232, 232 *n.*

Bowden [Village near St. Boswells, Roxburghshire] V. 401, X. 170

Bowden Moor [Moorland, SE. of Abbotsford] I. 94 *n.,* IV. 509, V. 18, 19, 42, 348, VIII. 4, 254

Bowdler (Henrietta Maria) *1754–1830* [Dau. of Thomas Bowdler, 1742–85 (q.v.); *DNB*] IX. 163 (d)

Bowdler (Thomas) *d. 1785* [*m.* Elizabeth Stuart (*d.* 1797), dau. of Sir John Cotton of Connington, 6th and last Bart. (*DNB*); father of Henrietta Maria Bowdler (q.v.) and Thomas Bowdler, 1754–1825 (q.v.)] IX. 163, 164 *n.*

Bowdler (Thomas) *1754–1825* [Editor of Shakespeare; *DNB*] V. 281, 281 *n.*

Bowdler (William) [Author of *Devil's cloven foot,* 1723] VIII. 408 *n.*

Bower [or Bowmaker] (Walter) *d. 1449* [Abbot of Inchcolm; *DNB*] VI. 269, XII. 222, 227, 227 *n.*

Bowerhope [A farm on E. side of St. Mary's Loch, Selkirkshire] I. 172 *n.*

Bowes (Matilda de Dalden, *afterwards Lady*) [14th/15th cent.; dau. of Robert de Dalden; *m.* Sir William Bowes; *Surtees Soc.* ii. 63–5] II. 174 *n.,* 175

Bowes Castle [Yorkshire] III. 169, VIII. 260

Bowhill [Seat of the Duke of Buccleuch near Selkirk] S.'s visits, or proposed visits, to (1811) III. 9, 10, 16, (1814) 508, 534, [Jan. 1815] 535, (Oct. 1815) I. 485, (Nov. 1815) XII. 154, (Dec. 1815) IV. 143, (1816) I. 505, IV. 311, 354, (Jan. 1817) 347, 348, [20–2 Oct. 1817] I. 524, IV. 535, 542, V. 6, 12, [14 Nov. 1817] 8–9, (Dec. 1817) 22, 36, [6 Nov. 1818] 195, 201, 213, [27–30 Nov. 1818] 224, 228, 230, 233, 234, 236, 236–8, (Nov. 1824) VIII. 417, 425, 429, (Oct. 1827) X. 300, (1830) XI. 311, 321

Bowhill (*cont.*)
Lady Dalkeith going to (Aug. 1809)
II. 233; alterations at (1812) III. 91;
rumour that Newark is to be added to
policies of (1812) 119; to be repaired
and enlarged (1813) 219; Carterhaugh
to be added to policies of (1814) 523;
ball at, after Carterhaugh football
match (Dec. 1815) IV. 143; improvements at (1817) 433, 542; Charlotte
and Anne at [14 Nov. 1817] V. 8–9;
Sophia at (Dec. 1817) 36; Hogg
going to (Jan. 1818) 45; cattle show
at [6 Nov. 1818] 195, 201, 213; Adam
Ferguson at (Oct. 1827) X. 300
Library, V. 351; Loch, IV. 463
Bowland House [S. of Stow, Mid-
lothian] VIII. 8
Bowles (William Lisle) *1762–1850*
[English clergyman and poet; *DNB*]
VI. 420 *n.*
Bowmaker (Walter). *See* Bower (Wal-
ter)
Bowring (*Sir* John) *1792–1872* [English
statesman, traveller and linguist;
DNB] at Abbotsford [Apr. 1830]
XI. 176, 339, 340
Boy (The) and the mantle. See
Ballads and Songs
Boyd (Henry) *d. 1832* [Irish clergyman,
poet and dramatist; translator of
Dante; *DNB*] XII. 398 400, 399 *n.*
Boyd (Robert) [Labourer at Fairnilee,
Selkirkshire] III. 422, 431–3
Boydell (John) *1719–1804* [Engraver
and publisher of engravings, London;
DNB] edition of Shakespeare by, I. 490
Boydell (Josiah) *1752–1817* [Engraver
and publisher with his uncle John
Boydell (q.v.); *DNB*] edition of
Shakespeare by, I. 490
Boyle (David) *of Shewalton, Lord Boyle,
1772–1853* [*succ.* his elder brother
1837; 2nd son of Rev. Patrick Boyle
who was 2nd son of 2nd Earl of
Glasgow; Advocate 1793; Lord
Justice Clerk 1811–41; Lord President 1841–52; father of Patrick
Boyle (q.v.); *Burke, DNB, Grant*]
S. reports to, on security measures
in Borders (1812) III. 111; S. dines
with Maconochie to meet (1818) V.
266; at Coronation (1821) VI. 499;
and Stuart–Boswell duel (1822) VII.
188 *n.*, 189; proposes S. should be
raised to the Bench (1826) IX. 441;
Anne attends ball given by (Feb.
1827) X. 160; S. recommends Pitcairn's *Criminal trials* to (July 1827)
248; mentioned, I. 26 *n.*

Boyle (Patrick) *of Shewalton, 1806–74*
[Eldest son of David Boyle (q.v.);
Oriel Coll. Oxford 1823, B.A. 1827,
M.A. 1832; Advocate 1829; father of
7th Earl of Glasgow; *Burke, Grant*]
VIII. 442 *n.*
Boyne (Battle of the) [1690] IX. 161
239
Boys and girls. See Nursery rhymes
Bracciolini (Poggio) *1380–1459*
[Florentine author]. *See under* Fables
Brackenridge (Hugh Henry) *1748–
1816* [American lawyer, son of a
Scottish emigrant; *DAB*] III. 454
Bradford [City in Yorkshire] X. 23
Bradford (*Sir* Thomas) *1777–1853*
[British general; *m.* at Fulham, 1
June 1818, Mary Anne, widow of
Lieut.-Col. Ainslie of 4th Dragoons;
Commander-in-Chief, Scotland,
1819–25; *DNB*] VI. 39, 174, 174 *n.*,
VII. 126 (c), VIII. 283, 285, XI.
395
Brady (John) *d. 1814* [Clerk in the
Victualling Office, London; *DNB*]
VI. 265, 265 *n.*
Brady (Nicholas) *1659–1726* [Irish
clergyman and poet; *DNB*]. For his
metrical version of the Psalms, *see*
Bible. Psalms: metrical versions
Braes (The) of Yarrow. See Ballads
and Songs
Bragge (Charles) *afterwards* Bathurst.
See Bathurst (Charles Bragge)
Braham (John) *1774?–1856* [English
operatic singer; *DNB*] II. 488, IV.
352, V. 62, 88, 88 *n.*
Brahan Castle [Seat of Lord Seaforth
near Dingwall, SE. Ross and
Cromarty] II. 339, VII. 386
Brain (Ephraim) [Engraver and
printer, London] XI. 88 (Bone)
Braine-l'Alleud [Town in Belgium]
IV. 79
Bramah (Joseph) *1748–1814* [English
inventor; *DNB*]. For pens invented
by, *see* Pens
Bran. *See* Dogs
Brandreth (John) [Dean of Armagh
1732; later Dean of Emly] II. 407
Branksome. *See* Branxholm
Brantôme (Pierre de Bourdeilles,
seigneur de) *1540–1614* [French
historian] quoted, VII. 246, XI. 59
Branxholm Castle [Ancient seat of
the Buccleuch family, SW. of Hawick,
Roxburghshire; in S.'s day the
residence of Charles Riddell of
Muselee (q.v.)] XII. 169
Brassa-head. *See* Bressay Head

Brougham (*cont.*)
Advocate 1800; English Bar 1808; M.P.; Lord Chancellor; *DNB*] And Jeffrey (1808) XII. 307, (1814) III. 417; and Queen Caroline (1820) VI. 138; Canning's alleged meeting with (1822) VII. 233; Morritt's interpretation of this, 234 *n.*, 307 *n.*; S.'s reply to Morritt, 309; and Society for the Diffusion of Useful Knowledge, X. 470 *n.*, 472; mentioned, II. 442, VI. 163, 364

Brougham (James) *1780–1833* [M.P.; brother of 1st Lord Brougham (q.v.) and of John Waugh Brougham (q.v.); *Burke*] VII. 112 *n.*, 137

Brougham (John Waugh) *1785–1829* [Wine merchant in Edinburgh; younger brother of 1st Lord Brougham (q.v.) and of James Brougham, M.P. (q.v.); *m.* 1809 Margaret, dau. of Patrick Rigg of Morton; *Burke*] I. 258

Brougham Castle [Near Penrith, Cumberland] III. 169

Broughton [Estate in parish of Whithorn, Wigtonshire]. *See* Murray (Alexander) *of Broughton*

Broughton (John Cam Hobhouse, *1st Baron*) *1786–1869* [British statesman; *succ.* as 2nd Bart. 1831; *cr.* Baron 1851; *m.* 28 July 1828 Lady Julia Hay, youngest dau. of 7th Marquess of Tweeddale; *DNB*] IV. 301 *n.*, VI. 213, VIII. 439 *n.*, IX. 388, 388 *n.*, X. 433, 433 *n.* 1–2

Brown (—), accused of stealing cow (1804) I. 226

Brown (—), examined by Scott as Sheriff (1814) III. 431

Brown (Alexander) *d. 1801* [Keeper of Advocates' Library, Edinburgh, 1766–1801; member of Royal Company of Scottish Archers 1771] IV. 140 *n.*

Brown (Andrew) *1763–1834* [Scottish clergyman and Prof. of Rhetoric, Edinburgh‚ Univ. 1801–34; *Fasti*, i. 72] IV. 200, 200 *n.*; probable reference to, III. 103

Brown (*Mrs* Andrew) *d. 1810* [*née* Anna Gordon; collector of Scottish ballads; known as 'Mrs Brown of Falkland'; youngest dau. of Prof. Thomas Gordon, King's College, Aberdeen; *m.* 1788 Rev. Andrew Brown, minister of Falkland 1784–1802 and of Tranent 1802–5; *d.* Old Aberdeen 11 July; *Fasti*, i. 397, v. 154] XII. 172, 172 *n.*

Brown (David) [Presumably son of David Brown, writer, Melrose, who *d.* 21 June 1800 and to whom William Scott, Younger of Raeburn, had been apprenticed] I. 218

Brown (David) *of Rawflat, 1800–69* [Son of Peter Brown of Rawflat (q.v.); *m.* 16 July 1829, as second wife, Margaret, dau. of Robert Shortreed (q.v.); Tancred, *Annals*, p. 75] XI. 214, 238, 245, 248

Brown (*Mrs* David) *b. 1806* [Wife of preceding] XI. 245, 245 *n.*

Brown (George) *of Elliston* [*m.* Dorothea (*d.* 25 Oct. 1810), dau. of James Dundas of Dundas; father of Margaret, Lady Wedderburn (q.v.); *Burke LG*, *under* Dundas] X. 332 *n.*

Brown (J.) [Minor canon of Carlisle Cathedral; *m.* 1789 Penelope Liddell, Carlisle] I. 67 *n.* 2

Brown (James) [Captain (Superintendent) of Edinburgh Police] VI. 300

Brown (Peter) *of Rawflat, d. 1822* [*m.* 10 Sept. 1799 Margaret, dau. of Elliot of Harwood; *d.* 15 Oct.; father of David Brown of Rawflat (q.v.); Tancred, *Annals*, p. 75] XI. 238 (e–f), 245 *n.*

Brown (Thomas) *1778–1820* [Scottish philosopher and poet; colleague to Dugald Stewart (q.v.), Prof. of Philosophy, Edinburgh Univ. 1810–20; *DNB*] I. 309

Brown (William) [Employee at Abbotsford] VIII. 485

Brown (William) *d. 1809* [Scottish journalist; *d.* 5 Mar.] IV. 432, V. 484 *n.*

Brown (William Henry) [Potter and Glass Manufacturer, 2 Waterloo Place, Edinburgh] IX. 230

Brown Adam. See Ballads and Songs

Brown Adam. *See* Horses

Brown Man of the Muirs. *See* Supernatural

Browne (George Adam) *1774–1843* [Fellow 1797 and Vice-Master 1842, Trinity Coll. Cambridge] X. 174 (d)

Browne (Harriett Mary) *afterwards Mrs Hughes. See* Hughes

Browne (James) *1793–1841* [Scottish clergyman, lawyer and journalist; Advocate 1826; ed. of the *Caledonian Mercury* (q.v.); *DNB*, *Grant*] duel with Maclaren of the *Scotsman* (1829) XI. 267, 267 *n.*

Browster (John). *See* Broster (John)

Brussels, S.'s visit to (1815) IV. 74, 75, 76, 78, 91, XII. 135, 136; bookshop at, IV. 306; John Ballantyne robbed at (1817) 487 *n.*

Brut. See Wace

Bryant (Jacob) *1715–1804* [English antiquary and classical author; *DNB*] II. 92, XII. 45

Bryden (George) *1786–1837* [Farmer; tenant in Crosslee 1799–1837; son of Walter Bryden (*d.* Newark 1799) and Agnes Ballantyne; *Tombstone in St. Mary's Churchyard, Yarrow*] VIII. 425, 429

Brydges (*Sir* Samuel Egerton) *1st Bart.*, *1762–1837* [English bibliographer; *DNB*] I. 270, II. 195, III. 108, 120, VIII. 27, XII. 389, 389 *n.*

Brydone (*Sir* Andrew) [Town Clerk of Selkirk who fought at Flodden, 1513] sword of, I. 102, II. 8

Brydone (George) [*of Crosslee*]. *See* Bryden

Buccleuch (*House of*), banner of, IV. 123, 124, 125, 127–8, 132, 135, 141, 146. *See also* Scott [Buccleuch]

Buccleuch (Anne Scott, *Duchess of*) *and Duchess of Monmouth. See* Monmouth

Buccleuch (Charles William Henry Scott, *4th Duke of*) *1772–1819* [*succ.* as 4th Duke of Buccleuch and 6th Duke of Queensberry 11 Jan. 1812; *m.* 1795 Harriet Katherine Townshend, dau. of 1st Viscount Sydney; *d.* 20 Apr.]

As Earl of Dalkeith: meets George Ellis at Naples (1802) I. 185 *n.*, XII. 219; insulted by Curver [Currie?] (1805) I. 258; and S.'s Clerkship (1806) 278, (1807) XII. 116, II. 519, 520; S. meets, in London (1807) XII. 94, 95, 97; goes to Bothwell (Mar. 1808) II. 32; and Laidlaw's agricultural plan (June 1808) 68–9; and Canning–Castlereagh duel (1809) 248; S. thanks him (Lord of Tyndale) for his assistance (1810) 331; at Ashiestiel (Aug. 1811) 54, 530, 532; mentioned, III. 63

As Duke: S. on his succession and on his character (Jan. 1812) III. 73, 90, 281, XII. 347; supports Don as M.P. for Roxburghshire (1812) III. 162, 185; S. asks, for financial guarantee from (Aug. 1813) I. 442, 445, 448, III. 322–5, 325–6, 326 *n.*, 329, 330, 333, 334, 348, 370, 371, 382–3, V. 138; discharge of the bond (1817–18) I. 516, IV. 508, 511, 514–15, V. 11,

Buccleuch (*cont.*)
13, 280, XII. 433, V. 17, 153–4; S. on political influence of (Nov. 1813) XII. 347; S.'s bet with (Dec. 1813) III. 48; gives gala at Dalkeith Palace (Jan. 1814) 398, 400; tells S. anecdote of Louis XVIII (July 1814) 456; death of his wife (1814) 495, 496–7, 500, IV. 28, XII. 132; and Hay Donaldson (Mar. 1815) IV. 40, 41; Waterloo armour for (Aug. 1815) XII. 140; gives silver cup to Selkirk (1816) IV. 150–1, 158–9, 160–1; Council threaten to melt it (1820) VI. 278; S. seeks his patronage for appointment to Court of Exchequer (Dec. 1816) IV. 311–14, (Jan. 1817) 367; *Tales of my Landlord* presented to (Dec. 1816) 319–20; head of Commission to search for Regalia (Jan. 1818) V. 50, 51, 54; unable to write with right hand (May 1818) 154; Wilkie makes sketch of, at Ditton (Jan. 1819) 350, 350 *n*; wants portrait of S. by Raeburn (Feb. 1819) 307 *n.*, 308

Health of (1816) IV. 295, 311, 314, (1817) 347, 433, 462, 479, (1818) V. 177, 213–15, 228–30, 234–43; S. wants him to go abroad (Nov. 1818) 214–15, 235, 237, 238, 240, 242, 243; Duke decides to go (Dec. 1818) 257–8, 262, 268; travels on Continent with Ferguson (1818–19) 268, 273, 276, 286, 302, 307 *n.*, 313–15, 326–7, 345, 346, 352–3, 353–4, 366, 371, 372, 374–5

Death of, V. 375–6, 378, 379, 382–3, 384, 385, 386 *n.*, 393, 409, 450, 472, 506, 509, VI. 26 *n.*, 29, 37, 49, 117, VII. 127, 259, XI. 62; buried at Boughton, V. 382, 386 *n.*

S. writes obituary of, for *Edinburgh Weekly Journal* (May 1819) V. 381; copy of newspaper sent to Montagu, 382; reprints of obituary presented to Montagu, 452, to Lady Louisa Stuart, 472, to Lady Abercorn, VI. 249; obituary to be included in *Prose Works* (1827) X. 156

Miscellaneous references: I. 99 *n.*, X. 506 *n.*; and Roxburgh politics, V. 470; and Waverley secret, X. 172 *n.*, 174

Buccleuch (*Lady* Charlotte Anne Thynne, *afterwards Duchess of*) *1811–95* [3rd dau. of 2nd Marquess of Bath; *m.* 13 Aug. 1829 5th Duke of Buccleuch (q.v.)]
Marriage of, XI. 220 *n.*, 221, 251;

Cadell (cont.)
167, 168 n., 177; has trouble with Ballantyne over printing charges (Sept. 1829) 236–7, 236 n.; introduced to Archdeacon Wrangham by letter from S. (Sept. 1829) 241–2; £50 required from, for Charles (Sept. 1829) 250; presents toddy ladles to S. (Dec. 1829) 277; sends £25 to Charles (Mar. 1830) 310, 311 n.; Ballantyne complains of his treatment (Apr. 1830) 325, 325–6, 328–9, 328 n., 330, 331–2, 339; to send £50 to Charles at Naples (Nov. 1830) 415; proposes to buy half of copyright of remaining novels (Dec. 1830) 449; S. stays with, in Edinburgh (Feb. 1831) 466–7, 468; engages Turner to illustrate *Poetical works* (Mar. 1831) 485–6, 485 n., 493–4, XII. 11, 13; might publish Stewart papers (Apr. 1831) 9; to escort Susan Ferrier to Abbotsford (May 1831) 15; in London (June 1831) 20, 21; and Miss Eccles (July 1831) 25, 25 n.; ready to help Mrs John Ballantyne (Aug. 1831) 27; to remit £200 per annum to Charles (Aug. 1831) 27–8; editorial note on his unfair conduct after the financial crash, IX. 401 n.
Cadell (*Mrs* Robert) *d. 1818* [First wife of preceding; *d.* 16 July]
S. presents Napoleon ring to (1815) IV. 89; invited to Abbotsford (1817) 502, 506, 519, 541; marriage of, V. 11 n., 13
Cadell & Davies (*Messrs*) [Thomas Cadell (*1773–1836*) and William Davies (*d.* 1819); London publishers; *Ann. Reg.* 1836, Chron., p. 222]
To supply S. with Polwhele's works (1808) II. 43, IV. 155; and proposed publication by Boyd (1809) XII. 400; *Lord of the Isles* to be offered to (June 1813) III. 289–90, (Oct. 1813) I. 450–1, 452; proposed sale of copyrights to (Aug.–Oct. 1813) I. 437, IV. 274, I. 448, III. 358–9, I. 449–50
Cadil gu lo. See Music
Cadiz, II. 171
Cadogan (*Hon.* Henry) *1780–1813* [8th son of 1st Earl Cadogan; Lieut.-Col. of 71st Foot; killed at Battle of Vitoria; *DNB*] III. 66, 66 n., 67, 76
Cadyow Castle, I. 149–51, 155, XII. 224, I. 185 n., XII. 228, I. 163–4, 174 n., 175, 180–1

Caerlaverock Castle [Ancient ruin in Dumfriesshire] III. 131
Caesar (Caius Julius) *102–44 B.C.* [Roman Emperor and author] II. 174 n., 533, VII. 449, XI. 134
Cahir [Town in co. Tipperary, Ireland] IX. 63
Cairns (—), causes trouble at Selkirk (1817) IV. 362, 371
Caithness, mermaid on coast of. *See* Mermaids
Calais, Walter at (1828) XI. 55
Calantha. *See* Lamb (*Lady* Caroline Ponsonby, *afterwards Lady* Caroline)
Calcutta. *See* India
Caldron Linns [Waterfall on River Devon, SE. Perthshire] VI. 466
Caledonia; or, the thistle and the rose [A play] III. 224, 224 n.
Caledonian Annual Register. See Projected works
Caledonian (The) Mercury [Edinburgh newspaper] I. 97, VI. 106
Callaghan (George) [6th son of Daniel Callaghan of Lotabeg, near Cork, Ireland; Paymaster 15th Hussars; *Burke LG*] VII. 362, IX. 89 n., X. 395
Callander [Town in SW. Perthshire] I. 45
Callander (William Burn) *of Preston Hall, 1792–1854* [*succ.* 1822; *m.* 9 May 1822, Jacquetta, dau. of Col. J. T. Hull of Marpool Hall, Devon; *Burke LG*] VIII. 308, 308 n.
Callender (William Thomson) [Messenger-at-Arms and Writer in Edinburgh; accused of sedition, failed to appear at his trial and outlawed 1793] XII. 470
Callot (Jacques) [French artist] I. 478, III. 122
Calonne (Charles Alexandre de) *1734–1802* [French statesman] quoted, V. 367
Cambrai [Town in N. of France] S. at (1815) IV. 78, 84, XII. 139 n.
Cambridge, S.'s songs sung at (1809) II. 147; S. visits (1815) XII. 134
University: S. offered honorary degree by (1820) VI. 194 n.; S. on merits of Oxford and (1824) VIII. 256, 300–1; King's College, IV. 453 n.; Magdalene College, 453; St. John's College, VIII. 300 n., IX. 28, 110, 154; Trinity College, VIII. 300 n.
Cambridge (Adolphus Frederick, *1st Duke of*) *1774–1850* [7th son of George III; *DNB*] VI. 389, X. 467

INDEX

Caravaggio (Michael Angelo Merigi, *called*) *1569–1609* [Italian artist] III. 222

Cardrona [Estate between Peebles and Innerleithen, Peeblesshire]. *See* Williamson (Walter) *of Cardrona*

Cardwell (Edward) *1787–1861* [Fellow of Brasenose Coll.; Prof. of Ancient History 1825–61; Principal of St. Alban Hall, 1831–61, Oxford; *DNB*] VIII. 442 *n.*

Carey (Henry) *1690?–1743* [English poet and dramatist; *DNB*] III. 17, 17 *n.*

Carey (Henry Charles) *1793–1879* [American publisher; partner in Messrs Carey & Lea, publishers, Philadelphia; *DAB*] X. 123, 123 *n.*

Carey (Patrick). *See* Cary

Carfrae [Farm N. of Oxton, Berwickshire; occupied by Robert Hogarth, 1741–1819 (q.v.)] IV. 104, VI. 481

Cargill (Donald) *1619–81* [Scottish Covenanter; *DNB*] V. 305

Carham (Battle of) [1018] XII. 256

Carisbrooke Castle [Isle of Wight] III. 400, XII. 102–3

Carle (The) he came o'er the craft. *See* Ballads and Songs

Carle now the Kings come [By S.], VII. 351 *n.*

Carle now the Kings come [Old song]. *See* Ballads and Songs

Carleton (George) [English soldier, 17th/18th cent.; *DNB*] Memoirs by, II. 38 *n.*, 229, XII. 304, 304 *n.*

Carlisle [City in Cumberland] Charlotte Carpenter at (1797) I. 65, 70, 78, 79, XII. 53, 61, 63, 64, 64 *n.*, 65; S.'s visits to (1797) I. 78, 79, 85–7, XII. 64, 65, (1812) III. 169, (1813) I. 436, (1818), V. 178; Walter at (1819) 418, 436; volunteers may be sent to (1819) VI. 54, 59, 62, 82, (1820) 106, 109, 113; references to, in early times, II. 493, XII. 192, 213, 255; David Hume's verses at, IV. 101; mentioned, I. 361, II. 150, 198, III. 82, V. 413, VIII. 259, XI. 247, 249, 383, XII. 192, 302

Castle, III. 318, XII. 13, 165

Carlisle (George Howard, *6th Earl of*) *1773–1848* [*succ.* 1825; *DNB*] as Lord *Morpeth*: VI. 285, XII. 159 *n.*

Carlisle (George William Frederick Howard, *7th Earl of*) *1802–64* [*succ.* 1848; *DNB*] as *Mr Howard*: IV. 469, VI. 285

Carlow [County and town, SE. Ireland] III. 13, IX. 211

Carlsbad. *See* Karlsbad

Carlton House. *See* London

Carlyle (Thomas) *1795–1881* [Scottish author; *DNB*] and Goethe medals, X. 249 *n.*

Carlyon (Clement) *1777–1864* [English physician, settled in Truro, and miscellaneous writer; *m.* Eliza, dau. of Thomas Carlyon of Tregrehan; *DNB*] I. 198, 212–13, II. 389, 424, III. 159, IV. 155, XII. 277 *n.*; biog. notes on, I. 207 *n.*, III. 159 *n.*

Carmichael (James Carmichael, *1st Baron*) *1579–1672* [*cr.* Baron Carmichael 1647; *GEC*] sons of, V. 319–20

Carmichael (Lewis) [Capt. 59th Foot] XI. 217

Carmichael (Mary) [One of the 'Queen's Maries' in the ballad *The Queen's Marie*, which relates to Mary of Guise and James V, not to Mary Queen of Scots] I. 162

Carmichael (William) [Writer in Edinburgh; appointed Extractor in office of James Ferrier and Walter Scott 1808] VII. 423, 425, 435, 453

Carnbroe [Estate in Lanarkshire] Lockhart at, V. 428

Carne (John) *1789–1844* [English author; *DNB*] VIII. 436, 436 *n.*

Carnegie (*Miss —*) [Dau. of Sir David Carnegie, 4th Bart. of Southesk; to which of the ten daughters S. refers not known] XI. 238

Carnwanolow (Battle of), I. 113, XII. 213, 213 *n.*

Caroline, *Queen Consort of George IV*, *1768–1821* [*DNB*]

As *Princess of Wales*: S. dines with, at Montague House (1806) I. 285, XII. 281; inquiry into charges of adultery made by Lady Douglas against (Aug. 1806) I. 313; S. visits, at Blackheath (Apr. 1807) XII. 111–12; S. recites Southey's *Queen Orraca* to, I. 387; S. hopes for patronage of (Nov. 1807) 395; S. presents copy of *Marmion* illustrated by Skene to (1807–8) 393, II. 11, 25, 30; presents cup to S. for compliments in *Marmion* (1808) I. 33, 35; spreads rumour that S. is editing Lady Louisa Stuart's *Ugly Meg*, III. 39–41, 39 *n.*, 42; S. several times sees (1809) II. 215, 240; supported by Whigs (1812–13) III. 112, 378–9; reunion of, with Prince (1812) 143; S. disapproves of her conduct but would obey her commands to wait on her (1813) 235–6, 242;

Caroline (*cont.*)

S.'s sympathy for (1813) 241-2; S. on need of reconciliation between Prince and (1813) 312; S. on (Nov. 1818) V. 224-5

As Queen: S.'s views on the struggle between King and (1820) VI. 138, 196-7, 200-1, 215, 216, 217-18, 235, 236-8, 279, 301, (1821) 335, 337, 337 *n.*, 369, 387, 503; trial of, and disturbances in her favour in Scotland (Nov. 1820), 301-2, 304, 307-8, 309-11; bonfire at Lampeter for, VIII. 216; allusion to a proposed visit by, to Scotland, VII. 194; behaviour of, at Coronation, VI. 494

Carolside [House near Earlston, Berwickshire] VIII. 235 *n.*

Carpenter. *See* 'Little (The) Carpenter'

Carpenter (Charles) [Capt. 15th Hussars 16 July 1812] VIII. 379

Carpenter (Charles) *1772-1818* [Brother of Lady Scott; christened Jean David Charpentier; appointed to East India Co. 17 Mar. 1789; Commercial Resident at Salem; *m.* 25 May 1805 Isabella Fraser; *d.* Salem 4 June]

On his first going to India, XI. 8, XII. 73, 74; and his sister's marriage to S. (1797), I. 69, 74, 75, 78, 81-2, XII. 76; sends packet to Downshire (1801) I. 122, 122 *n.*; marriage of, 270, 290, 290 *n.*, XII. 269 *n.*; may return from India (1805) 277; Leyden corresponds with, but has not met (Nov. 1805) 269 *n.*; Charles to be called after (Dec. 1805), I. 270; suffers pecuniary loss (1807) XII. 107, 107 (b), VI. 12; S. presents copy of *Marmion* to (1808) II. 1; may return from India (1813) III. 229; S. considers borrowing from (1813) I. 445; death of, V. 249, 253, 255, 259, 262, 268, 269, 297, VI. 117; certificate of birth sought (1828) X. 436, 437-8; found, XI. 19; for his estate left to S.'s children, *see under* Carpenter (*Mrs* Charles)

Carpenter (*Mrs* Charles) *1779-1862* [Wife of preceding; dau. of General Charles Fraser; sister of Mrs Josiah Marshall Heath (q.v.)]

Marmion presented to (1808) II. 13, 17; money left by husband to, with reversion to S.'s children, V. 256, 257, 260, 261, 263, 268, 269, 297, 441, VI. 12, 28, 28 *n.*, 107, 355,

Carpenter (*cont.*)

358, VII. 47-9, 181-2, 244, VIII. 445, 450-1, IX. 408, 437, 443, 443 *n.*, 452, 478, X. 90, XII. 434-8; S. writes to, on her arrival in Britain from India (Jan. 1821) VI. 339-41; S. goes to London to see (Feb. 1821) 351, 353; S. meets, in London, and reports on her health (Feb.-Mar. 1821) 357, 358, 364, 367, 372, 375, 380, 153-5, 383; her visit to Scotland postponed (Feb.-Apr. 1821) 365, 379, 381, 382, 396; expected in Scotland (May-June 1821) 436, 484; in Edinburgh (July 1821) 490, 492; at Abbotsford (Aug. 1821) VII. 1; returns south, 32-3, 32 *n.*; S. takes steps to safeguard his family's rights should she remarry (1821-4) 32 *n.*, 47-9, 48 *n.*, 49 *n.*, 51-3, 72-3, 343, VIII. 128, 161-2, 204-5; coming to Scotland (1824) 251; ill health due to carriage accident alluded to (1825) IX. 131; new trustees for (1826) 443, 443 *n.*, 452, 495; at Nice (1828-9) XI. 57, 92; copy of Magnum presented to (1829) 204; rumour that she is returning to India (1829) 208

Carpenter (*Mrs* Margaret Sarah) *1793-1872* [Portrait painter; *née* Margaret Sarah Geddes; *m.* 1817 William Hookham Carpenter; *DNB*] XI. 50(d), 67

Carpets. *See* Abbotsford. III (3) (b). Dining Room; III (4) (b). Drawing Room; V. Furniture

Carr (Arthur Morton) *1799-1852* [Solicitor of Excise, Scotland; eldest son of Thomas William Carr (*d.* 1829) and Frances, dau. of Andrew Morton of Ouzeburne, Northumberland; *m.* 12 July 1830 Caroline A. Mackay Graham, dau. of Robert Graham of Fintry (1749-1815)] X. 261, 262, 262 *n.*, XI. 174-5

Carr (Frances) [Sister of Arthur Morton Carr (q.v.)] probable references to XI. 171, 175

Carr (Isabella) *afterwards Lady Eardley.* *See* Eardley

Carr (*Sir* John) *1772-1832* [English barrister, traveller and author; *DNB*] II. 417 *n.*; his *Caledonian sketches* reviewed by S. in *QR*, 101 *n.*, 157, 158

Carr (Morton). *See* Carr (Arthur Morton)

Carre (Elizabeth) *Mrs William Riddell.* *See* Riddell

Carrick [District in Ayrshire] XII. 192

Constable (*cont.*)
that S. is writing novels without
sufficient intervals (June 1823) VIII.
17, 17 n., 21, 21 n., 417; wants
discussions on financial dealings between A.C. & Co. and James Ballantyne & Co. (Aug. 1823) 70–1, 70 n.,
76–80 and notes, 85 n.; S. sees signs
of insanity in [Sept. 1823 or 1824] 92;
S. presents terrier to (Mar. 1824) 232,
233, 235; in 'excellent spirits' (Apr.
1824) 259; S. proposes to visit, at
Polton with Charles and Lockhart
(June 1824) 295, 298; visits Abbotsford
(Sept. 1824) 371, 372; reference to an
'unhappy affair' of (Sept. 1824) 405;
and Maturin's works (Apr. 1825)
XII. 368; S. introduces Lemare to
(May 1825) IX. 111; his *Miscellany*
(Sept. 1825) 220, 220 n., 247 n.,
262–3, 294, 325, 325 n., 326–7, 339,
341, 351, XI. 28; thinks Lady de
Lancey's narrative of Waterloo
should be published (Oct. 1825) IX.
247 n., 248; S. on financial stability
of (Nov. 1825) 291–4 and notes;
references to financial crisis and
(Dec. 1825) 337, 341, 345, 358, (Jan.
1826) 360, 361–2, 363, 364, 369, 369–
72, 373, 374, 375, 376, 379–80, 382–4,
386, 391–2, (Feb. 1826) 401, 405,
411, 421–2, 436; appointment of
trustee for [6 Mar. 1826] 429, X. 70;
S. opposes claims of trustees for, to
publish *Woodstock* and *Napoleon* (Apr.
1826) 16–17, 48–9, 48 n., 51, 52, 53,
57–8, 65, 78–9, 94, 104; S. on other
claims by (July 1827) 265; death of,
263
Cadell's estimate of, VII. 78 n.; S.
accuses him of revealing authorship
of the novels, XI. 3; S.'s reflections
on, 28; S.'s copyrights, which had
been owned by, sold [19 Dec. 1827]
X. 314–15, 340, 343–4; *Lives of the
novelists* assigned to trustees for, by
Lord Newton (Apr. 1830) XI. 325;
S. says (Apr. 1830) that he 'lost a
very large sum of money' by bankruptcy of, 335
Constable (*Mrs* Archibald) [Charlotte
Neale, second wife of preceding]
VIII. 76, 76 n.; 85
Constable (David) *1795–1867* [Eldest
son of Archibald Constable (q.v.);
Advocate 1819; *Grant*]
Biog. note on, V. 341 n.; other
references to, IV. 480, 492, V. 325,
340, 341, 500, VI. 265, VII. 17,
322 n., 323, 369

Constable (Elizabeth) *afterwards Mrs
Robert Cadell. See* Cadell
Constable (George) *of Wallace-Craigie,
1719–1803* [Writer in Edinburgh;
prototype of Jonathan Oldbuck] VII.
302, 302 n., XI. 223, 223 n., XII.
37
Constable (*Sir* Robert) [Employed by
Queen Elizabeth as a spy on the
Scottish Borders] I. 365, II. 24, 87
Constable (Thomas) *1812–81* [Printer;
2nd surviving son of Archibald Constable (q.v.); *DNB*] VIII. 203
Constable & Co. [Publishers, Waterloo Place, Edinburgh] XI. 323 n.
**Constable, Hunter, Park and Hun-
ter** (*Messrs*) [10 Ludgate Street, London; Archibald Constable's short-
lived London branch] II. 44, 137
Constitution (The) [Suggested title
for London Tory newspaper which
became *The Guardian*]. See *Guardian
(The)*
Continental Tours

(a) Tours accomplished

1815: IV. 7, 74, 75, 76, 78–96,
108–9, 118, 188, VII. 483, XII.
134–52, 356; referred to, IX.
500
1826: *See* Paris
1831–2: XII. 28, 482, 29, 34–48

(b) Proposed but cancelled tours

1814: III. 389, 394, 395, 398, 406,
411, 456, IV. 6, VII. 474
1817: IV. 211, 224, 247, 263, 306
1818: IV. 477, V. 51, 58, 145
1819: V. 244, 256, 275–6, 291
1820: VI. 19, 41–2, 80
1823: VII. 167, 199, 228, 243, 273,
309, 327
Convention of Cintra. *See* Cintra
Convention of Jedburgh. *See* Jedburgh
Conyers (*Sir* Thomas) *Bart., 1731–
1810* [d. 15 Apr. when the baronetcy
became extinct] II. 317 (decayed
Aristocrat), 427 (your pensioner)
Conyngham (Elizabeth Denison, *afterwards Marchioness*) *1767–1861* [Dau.
of Joseph Denison; *m.* 1794 3rd
Baron Conyngham, cr. Marquess
1816 (q.v.)] VI. 200, 200 n. (Lady C.),
252 (Lady ——), 253 (Lady C——)
253 n. (Lady C.), VIII. 337 n. (Ldy
C——), 340 (unnamed)
Conyngham (Henry Conyngham, *1st
Marquess*) *1766–1832* [succ. as 3rd

Court of Session

General

S. suggests to Ballantyne session papers as work for his proposed Press in Edinburgh (1800) I. 97; reorganizing of (1807-10) 351, 370, II. 10, 32, 71, 179-80; S. declines judgeship in (1826) IX. 441-2; cases in, referred to by S., II. 358, III. 210, 295, 360, IV. 147, VII. 187, X. 70, XI. 261; *see also* Commission to Inquire into the Administration of Justice in Scotland; Parliament. Acts; Register of Entails; Register of Hornings

Extractors

See under Scott (Thomas) *1774-1823*

Principal Clerks

S. seeks appointment as (1806) I. 273-5; appointed (1806) 275-7, 278, 279, 291, II. 13-14, 18; takes up duties [Mar. 1806] I. 283-4, XII. 282, I. 302, 307, 328; S. seeks help in getting salary (July-Nov. 1807) 367-70, 394; S. wants to succeed Colin Mackenzie in event of his death or resignation (Dec. 1807) 404-6; hints that S. might have to resign his sheriffship (Dec. 1807) 405, 406, (1811) II. 452-3; S. refers to (1813) III. 336, 345; S. complains that Home has not been pensioned (Apr. 1810) II. 325-6; S. wants to succeed Pringle (Feb. 1811) 435-9; Home

INDEX

Defoe (*cont.*)
Works, publ. by John Ballantyne, I. 414

De Grey (Annabella Yorke, *afterwards Countess*) *1751–1833* [Dau. of 2nd Earl of Hardwicke; *m.* 1772 Viscount Polwarth who was *cr.* Baron Hume in 1776 but who predeceased his father, 3rd Earl of Marchmont; *succ.* as Baroness Lucas 1797; *cr.* Countess de Grey 1816] *as Lady Lucas*: I. 397

De Lancey (Magdalene Hall, *Lady*) *afterwards Mrs Henry Harvey*. *See* Harvey

De Lancey (*Sir* William Howe) *1781?–1815* [*b.* New York; Colonel in British Army; *m.* Magdalene Hall (q.v. under Harvey), dau. of Sir James Hall, 4th Bart. of Dunglass (q.v.); mortally wounded at Waterloo and *d.* 26 June; *DNB*] IX. 247, 247 *n.*

Delany (Mary Granville, *afterwards Mrs Patrick*) *1700–88* [Friend of Swift; *m.* (1) 1718 Alexander Pendarves (*d.* 1724) and (2) 1743 Dr Patrick Delany (q.v.); *DNB*] II. 72 *n.*, 270 *n.*

Delany (Patrick) *1685–1768* [Friend of Swift; *m.*, as second wife, 1743, Mrs Pendarves (*née* Mary Granville); Dean of Down; *DNB*] II. 72 *n.*, 201, 271, III. 121 *n.*

Delarue (Gervaise) *1751–1835* [French abbot and historian of the trouvères of north of France] XII. 430, 430 *n.*

Deliciae Galliae. *See* Ens (Gaspar)

Deloney (Thomas) *1543?–1600?* [English ballad writer; *DNB*] his *Thomas of Reading*, I. 495

Delrius (Martinus Antonius). *See* Rio (Martinus Antonius del)

Demerara [In British Guiana] Tom has prospects of post in (1810) VII. 399, 399 *n.*, 451–2, 453; but post not available, 399 *n.*, 455

Demonology. *See* Supernatural

Dempster (*Miss* —) [Sister of George Dempster of Dunnichen (q.v.)] and Dr Johnson, XI. 166

Dempster (*Miss* —) [Sister of George Dempster of Skibo (q.v.); could be Harriet, Charlotte or Rose] at Abbotsford (1829) XI. 155

Dempster (George) *of Dunnichen and Skibo, 1732–1818* [Son of John Dempster of Dunnichen, merchant, Dundee; Advocate 1755; M.P.; *d.* 13 Feb.; *DNB*, *Grant*, Chambers, *Biog. dict.* (1837), ii. 69–73, *Edin. Ann. Reg.* XI. i. 242–4] XI. 166, XII. 463–4; his verse epitaph on himself, 465

Dempster (George) *of Skibo, 1802–89* [Advocate 1826; *m.* 8 May 1827 Joanna Hamilton, 7th dau. of Robert Dundas of Arniston, 1758–1819 (q.v.); brother-in-law of Robert Dundas of Arniston, 1799–1838 (q.v.); *Grant*] XI. 155

Dempster (*Mrs* George) *of Skibo, d. 1891* [Wife of preceding] XI. 155, 166

Dempster (John Hamilton) *of Skibo* [Capt. H.E.I.C.S.; *m.* (1) Miss Thompson and (2) 1785 Jean, dau. of Charles Fergusson, London, and sister of Sir James Fergusson, 4th Bart. of Kilkerran; half-brother of George Dempster of Dunnichen (q.v.); *Burke LG*, Burke, *under* Fergusson] XI. 166

Dempster (Thomas) *1579–1625* [Scottish miscellaneous writer; *DNB*] I. 198

Denham (*Sir* James Steuart) *Bart. of Coltness, 1744–1839* [*succ.* 1780; M.P.; General 1803; *DNB*]
As *Sir James Steuart*: (1797) XII. 375; as *Sir James Steuart Denham*: (1822) VIII. 480

Denham (*Sir* John) *1615–69* [Poet; *b.* Dublin, but resided in England; *DNB*] III. 34

Denmark, II. 19, III. 231

'**Denmark** (*Prince* George of)'. *See* Leopold I, *King of the Belgians*

Dennis (Jehan) [Early French printer] I. 401

Dennistoun (Mary Ramsay Oswald, *afterwards Mrs* James) *of Colgrain* [Dau. of George Oswald of Auchencruive and Scotstoun] children of, being tutored by George Thomson (1820) VI. 292

Denon (Dominique Vivant, *Baron*) *1747–1825* [French engraver and traveller; Director-General of French Museums] X. 72, 72 *n.*, 86

Dent (John) *of Cockerham Hall, d. 1826* [M.P. who promoted the Act to license dogs; hence known as 'Dog-Dent'] II. 23

Depopulation. *See under* Scotland

Depping (Georges Bernard) *1784–1853* [French historian; *b.* Alsace] V. 339–40, 339 *n.*, 341, 500

De Quincey (Thomas) *1785–1859* [English author; *DNB*] X. 470 *n.*

Derby (Charlotte de la Trémouille, *afterwards Countess of*) *1599–1664* [Dau. of Claude de la Trémouille, duc de Thouars; *m.* 1626 7th Earl of Derby (q.v.); *DNB*] VII. 463

431

Articles in:

1808. Vol. 1, Pt 2 (1810)

View of the changes . . . in the administration of justice in Scotland. S. denies authorship of, II. 392

Of the living poets of Great Britain. [By S.] II. 283, 283 *n.*, 392

The alderman's funeral. By Robert Southey, II. 202 *n.*, 206, 206 *n.*

To discretion. [Spurious verses said to be by Swift] III. 255

1809. Vol. 2, Pt 2 (1811)

Cursory remarks upon the French order of battle. [By S., assisted by Patrick Murray] II. 482, 482 *n.*, 503 (c)

Original letters. [Contributed by C. K. Sharpe] II. 148, 156

The inferno of Altisidora. [By S.] I. 412, II. 525–6, 526 *n.*, III. 212 *n.*

The vision of Don Roderick. By S. II. 487, 495, 525, III. 185

The poet released from the law. By John Marriott, III. 4

1810. Vol. 3, Pt 1 (1812)

History of Europe. [By Robert Southey] III. 124

1810. Vol. 3, Pt. 2 (1812)

Account of the poems of Patrick Carey. [By S.] II. 426–7, III. 108

Verses. By Surtees, II. 425, 425 *n.*, III. 93 (?)

The trumpet and church-bell. By M. W. Hartstonge, IV. 104–5

INDEX

Forbes (cont.)
befriend Mrs Tom Scott (1813) III.
354 n., VII. 403, 468; S. receives
reply from, 469, 471; S. misses meet-
ing, in Edinburgh (Feb. 1814) 473;
helps Mrs Tom (Mar. 1814) 476;
fails to get in touch with S. in
Edinburgh (1824) VIII. 397-8,
397 n.
Forbes (James) [Tutor to 9th Earl of
Derby (1656-1702)] XII. 288, 288 n.
Forbes (James Ochoncar Forbes, 18th
Lord) 1765-1843 [Scottish soldier;
Lord High Commissioner to General
Assembly of Church of Scotland;
DNB] IX. 125, 133
Forbes (Jane) d. 1871 [Elder dau. of
Sir William Forbes, 7th Bart. of
Pitsligo (q.v.)] X. 41
Forbes (Sir John) 1787-1861 [Scottish
physician; M.D. Edinburgh 1817;
practised in Penzance, Chichester
and London; knighted 1853; DNB]
XII. 466 n., 468
Forbes (John Hay) Lord Medwyn,
1776-1854 [2nd son of Sir William
Forbes, 6th Bart. of Pitsligo (q.v.);
Advocate 1799; Sheriff of Perth
1807-24; Bench as Lord Medwyn
1825; DNB, Grant] VI. 25, 32, VII.
19, 19 n., X. 282
Forbes (Sir John Stuart) 8th Bart. of
Pitsligo, 1804-66 [2nd son of 7th
Bart.; Advocate 1826; succ. 1828;
Grant] XI. 227 n.
Forbes (Sir William) & Co. [Bankers,
Edinburgh] I. 219, 260, 261, 261 n.,
295, 421, 428, 429, 431, 432, 433,
435, 441, 442, 446, 455, 472, 474,
475, 476, 482, 486, 505, 511, 526,
III. 166, 167, 168, 309, 332, 333, 335,
395, IV. 236, V. 227, 345, 379, 381,
399, 422, VI. 223, 250, 256, 257, 258,
440, VII. 323, 417, 419, 421, 422,
425, VIII. 157-8, 276, 406, 428, X.
88
Forbes (William) d. 1826 [Eldest son of
Sir William Forbes, 7th Bart. of
Pitsligo (q.v.); captain in the army]
X. 57 n.
Forbes (Sir William) 6th Bart. of
Pitsligo, 1739-1806 [Scottish banker;
m. 1770 Elizabeth (d. 1802), dau. of
Sir James Hay, 4th Bart. of Haystoun;
father of John Hay Forbes, Lord
Medwyn (q.v.), Christian who m.
Sir Alexander Wood (q.v.), Rebecca
who m. Alexander Ranaldson Mac-
donell of Glengarry (q.v.), Elizabeth
who m. Colin Mackenzie of Portmore

Forbes (cont.)
(q.v.) and Jane who m. James Skene
of Rubislaw (q.v.); DNB] I. 56,
314 n.
Forbes (Sir William) 7th Bart. of
Pitsligo, 1773-1828 [Scottish banker;
succ. 1806; m. 19 Jan. 1797
Williamina Belsches (d. 1810) dau.
of Sir John Belsches, after 1798
Sir John Stuart, of Fettercairn (q.v.);
d. 24 Oct.]
At Fettercairn (1796) I. 54, 56;
S. sends letter to Ellis by (1808) II.
21; Rob Roy presented to (1817) V.
37; claims Pitsligo baronage (1824)
VIII. 170-1; presides at meeting of
S.'s trustees (1826) IX. 379, 385;
goes to Paris (1826) X. 57 n., 59;
serious illness of (Oct. 1828) XI. 20,
22; death of, 26-7, 26 n., 28
Forbes (Williamina Belsches, afterwards
Lady) 1776-1810 [Only child of Sir
John Belsches (later Stuart) of
Fettercairn and Lady Jane Leslie-
Melville, dau. of 6th Earl of Leven
and 5th Earl of Melville; m. 19 Jan.
1797 Sir William Forbes, 7th Bart. of
Pitsligo (q.v.); d. Lympstone, Devon-
shire, 5 Dec.]
S. as suitor, I. 25, 32, 40-2, 48-9,
54, 55 n., 56-7; later allusions to
(1797) 67, 69, (1808) 296, 296 n.,
(1810) II. 287, (1818) V. 145, 145 n.
Forbes-Mitchell (John) of Thainstone,
1785-1822 [Burke LG] and monument
to Burns (1819) V. 360
Ford (John) c. 1586-1639 [English
dramatist; DNB] I. 413, III. 32-3,
XII. 291 n.
Ford (William) 1771-1832 [English
bookseller and bibliographer; DNB]
XII. 457, 457 n.
Ford Castle [Northumberland] I. 18,
109
Fordun (John) [14th-cent. Scottish
historian; DNB] Scotichronicon by,
cited, I. 113, 160, VI. 269, VII. 446,
446 n., XII. 222, 234
Foreign Office. See London
Foreign Quarterly Review, X. 49-50,
50 n., 162, 184, 196, XI. 132, 132 n.
Foreigners, S. hates (1828) X. 510
Foreman (John). See Forman
Forest Club. See Selkirk
Forfar [Royal Burgh, Angus] I. 39
Forman (John) of Staffa, 1775-1841
[Scottish lawyer; W.S. 1801; W.S.
Soc.] VII. 420, 422, 429, X. 317,
317 n.
Forman: a tale. See Moysey (Abel)

466

Freke (*cont.*)
barrister and author; *DNB*] III.
154, 154 *n.*
French language, S.'s children learning, from their mother, I. 362; 'the
most unfit for poetry,' III. 523–4, 531
French Prisoners of War. *See*
France
French Revolution. *See* France
Frendraught [House near Huntly,
Aberdeenshire] *The burning of Frendraught. See* Ballads and Songs; *Satyr
against Frendraught,* VIII. 45, 45 *n.*
Frere (John Hookham) *of Roydon Hall,
1769–1846* [English diplomatist and
author; *DNB, Burke LG*]
Approves of S.'s conclusion of
Sir Tristrem (1805) XII. 270–1;
meets S. in London (1806) I. 285,
(1807) XII. 96, 97, 111 *n.*, 112; has
vol. of romances with *The Cid,* I.
272 *n.*, 387, II. 119, XII. 292, 293;
S. wants to go to Spain with (1808)
VII. 422; and *QR* (1808–9) II. 108,
138 *n.*, 142, 152; at Malta (1832) XII.
44–5; mentioned, I. 390, II. 203, IX.
499, XII. 288; *The loves of the
triangles* by, quoted, X. 420; *Ode on
Athelstane's victory,* XII. 186, 186 *n.*;
Whistlecraft by, John Murray sends
copy of, to S. (1818) V. 108 *n.*, 110,
110 *n.*, 168; S. thinks of reviewing,
XII. 433
Friday Club. *See* Edinburgh
Froissart (Jean) *c. 1338–1410* [French
historian] *Chronicles* by, S.'s proposed
ed. of (1809) II. 169, XII. 402;
Berner's trans. of, II. 169, XII. 402;
Johnes's trans. of, II. 169, III. 81–2,
XII. 402, 403, 412; James Ellis's
index to, IV. 219; general references
to, II. 493, IV. 214, 271, VI. 300,
VII. 253, XII. 253, 255
Froude (Robert Hurrell) *1768–1859*
[Educ. Oriel Coll. Oxford; Rector of
Denbury 1798, of Dartington 1799;
Archdeacon of Totnes 1820; *Ann.
Reg.* 1859, Chron., p. 425] I. 263 *n.*
Fuentes d'Oñoro [Town in
Salamanca, Spain] battle at [1811]
III. 66
Fugitive statesman, III. 27
Fulham Palace. *See* London
Fullarton's Legion. *See* Army. 3.
Foot Regiments. 101st.
Fullerton (John) *Lord Fullerton, 1775–
1853* [Advocate 1798; Bench 1829;
Grant] possible reference to, X. 289
Furniture. *See* Abbotsford. III (3) (b),
III (4) (b) and V.

Fushiebridge [Village in Midlothian]
X. 457
Fyffe (Archibald). *See* Fife

G. (M.), I. 25
Gabell (Henry Dison) *1764–1831*
[Headmaster of Winchester; *DNB*]
VIII. 184 *n.*, 205, 205 *n.*, 216, 229 *n.*,
305 *n.*, 313 *n.*, X. 460
Gaberlunzie (The) man. See Ballads
and Songs
Gaelic, S.'s ignorance of, I. 303; S.
would like to learn, II. 261, 263,
379, III. 116; its use in *Waverley,*
511 *n.*; S. on, XII. 470–1; words
used, VII. 226, IX. 230; proverb
quoted, XII. 328; for air in *Marmion,*
see under Music
Gaick [or Guiyock; district in
Inverness-shire]. *See* Cuming (Walter) *of Guiyock*
Gala Water [Runs south to meet
Tweed at Galashiels] VII. 243
Galafoot [Locality at junction of Gala
Water and River Tweed near
Abbotsford] VIII. 485
Galashan. See Galatian
Galashiels [Town in Selkirkshire]
Erskine to check weights and
measures in (1800) I. 102, 106;
constables at, to watch woman
giving trouble (1811) II. 476;
political disturbance at (1812) III.
124, 125–6, 152; men from, at
Carterhaugh football match (Dec.
1815) IV. 142; unrest at (1817) 363,
392; weavers in, loyal to government
(1819) V. 509–10, VI. 15, 18, 61, 65;
new road to Selkirk from (1830) XI.
416–17; 'sour plums' of, V. 495;
'Galashiels grey' cloth, VI. 61, 65,
113; 'an excellent market town,'
IX. 157

Leith Bank [Branch manager:
George Craig (q.v.)] V. 438, 439,
445, 448, VI. 88, 194, IX. 387, XII.
131
Galatian [*Galashan* or *Golaschin*; a
mummers' play] VIII. 144 *n.*, IX.
445–7, 446 *n.*, X. 98, XI. 282
Gale & Co. [London publishers; also
under names of Gale, Curtis and
Fenner, and Gale and Fenner] Gale
meets John Ballantyne in Edinburgh
(1813) I. 437, 442; negotiations with
(1816) 505; and Burt's *Letters* (1818)
V. 274–5
Gallant (The) Grahams. See Ballads
and Songs

Health (*cont.*)
report on (Dec. 1829) XI. 275; has
stroke (Feb. 1830) 297, 297 *n.*, 299,
300, 317, 321, 334, 336, 436; in-
creased infirmities (Oct.–Dec. 1830)
400, 413, 414, 436–7, 443, 445, 449,
(Jan.–Mar. 1831) 460, 462, 471,
479–80, 482–3, 489, (Apr. 1831) XII.
6; gets mechanical aid from Fortune
(Feb. 1831) XI. 466, 481
   Eyesight: (1801) XII. 177, (1802)
231, (1811) II. 515, (1817) XII. 360,
(1823) VII. 309, (1824) VIII. 157,
288–9, 386, 456, (1825) 494, IX. 130,
322, (1826) 369, 393, 488, 501, X. 13,
(1827) 159, 253, 331, (1828) 474, XI.
18, (1829) 120, 140, 277, (1830) 427
   For physicians consulted by S., see
Abercrombie (John), Clarkson
(Ebenezer), Clarkson (James Burnet),
Dick (William), Ross (Adolphus
Macdouall) and Scott (James) *of
Ellem*
Health to Lord Melville, I. 304, 305,
310, XII. 112, 285, 381 *n.*
Heart of Midlothian [Building]. *See*
Edinburgh. Tolbooth
Heart (The) of Mid-Lothian. See
Tales of my Landlord. Second Series
Heart (The) of Mid-Lothian [Terry's
dramatized version] V. 135, 148, 149,
169; produced at Covent Garden [17
Apr. 1819] 361 *n.*, 362, 364, 396 *n.*,
397
Heath (Charles) *1785–1848* [English
engraver; *DNB*] X. 374, 374 *n.*, 412,
478, XI. 75, 146 *n.*, XII. 461 (a)
Heath (Josiah Marshall) [Of Madras
Civil Service; Deputy to Charles
Carpenter at Salem 1813–18 and his
successor thereafter; *m. c.* Dec. 1816
at Madras Charlotte Catherine
Fraser, youngest dau. of General
Charles Fraser and sister of Mrs
Carpenter (q.v.)]
   And Mrs Carpenter's financial
affairs, V. 256, VII. 33 *n.*, XI. 51,
XII. 435–7; has had family distress,
VII. 74
Heath (*Mrs* Josiah Marshall) [Wife of
preceding] VII. 74
Heathfield (George Augustus Eliott,
1st Baron) *1717–90* [Younger son of Sir
Gilbert Eliott, 3rd Bart. of Stobs;
General; raised Eliott's Light Horse
in 1759, afterwards 15th Hussars
(q.v.); *DNB*] IX. 145
Heating. *See* Abbotsford. V
Heber (Reginald) *1783–1826* [Bishop
of Calcutta 1823–6; *m.* 1809 Amelia,

Heber (*cont.*)
dau. of William Davies Shipley, Dean
of St. Asaph; brother of Thomas
Cuthbert Heber (q.v.) and half-
brother of Richard Heber (q.v.);
DNB]
   S. hopes he will go to the Bar
(1805), XII. 268–9; tours Russia
etc. (1806) 282, 285, 286, 289; and
help with *QR* (1808) I. 108, 122, 143,
XII. 307; at Harrogate (1813)
[1812?] 349; reviews Milman's *Fall
of Jerusalem* for *QR* (1820) VI. 170 *n.*,
177; appointed Bishop of Calcutta,
VII. 339, 339 *n.*, 341 *n.*, VIII. 51;
James Gray wants introduction to
(1826) IX. 390; death of, X. 101

Works

Europe: lines on the present war, XII.
310, 310 *n.*
Palestine, XII. 237–8, 237 *n.*, 238;
quoted, 333
Poems and translations, XII. 337, 349
The sense of honour, XII. 282, 282 *n.*
Heber (*Mrs* Reginald) *1787–1870*
[Wife of preceding] X. 229
Heber (Richard) *of Hodnet*, *1774–1833*
[M.P. and book-collector; half-
brother of Reginald Heber and
Thomas Cuthbert Heber (qq.v.);
DNB]
   Present when S. wrote *The Fire
King*, VIII. 409; purchases in London
a phaeton for Mrs Scott (1800) XII.
159–61, 161–2, 164; writes to S.
(Oct. 1800) I. 100 *n.*; his handwriting (Nov. 1800) XII. 231–2,
232 *n.*; and John Leyden (1801) I.
114, 116, 124, (1802) 138 *n.*, (1806)
306, (1811) II. 442; visits France
(Dec. 1802) XII. 231; returns (Jan.
1803) 233; with S. at Oxford [Apr.
1803] I. 181, 185 (XII. 235), XII.
238; S. presents 2nd ed. of *Minstrelsy*
to (1803) 237; to receive uncastrated
copy of *Sir Tristrem* (1804) I. 214, XII.
245, 248, 260; copy of *The lay* to be
presented to (1805) 267; S. meets, in
London (Feb. 1806) I. 279, 308;
copy of Jamieson's *Ballads* to be sent
to [*c.* Sept. 1806] 336; visits Ashiestiel
(Oct. 1808) II. 99, 108, 120 (XII.
303); and *QR* (1808) 122, 143, XII.
307; to call on S. in London (Apr.
1809) II. 189; copy of *The Lady of the
Lake* presented to (1810) XII. 318;
copy of *Waterloo* presented to (Oct.
1815) I. 491; S. expects him to

INDEX

Loudon (Flora Mure Campbell, *Countess of*) *afterwards Marchioness of Hastings*. *See* Hastings

Loughborough [Town in Leicestershire] I. 361 (wrongly printed Liverpool), XII. 115

Louis XVIII, *King of France, 1814–24,* III. 452, 456, XII. 146; death of, VIII. 373, 374, 374 *n.,* 375, 376, 383, 391

Louviers [Town S. of Rouen, France] XII. 150 *n.*

Louvre [A dance] I. 141

Lovaine (George Percy, *Lord*). *See* Beverley (George Percy, *2nd Earl of*)

Lovat (Simon Fraser, *11th Baron*) *1668–1747* [Jacobite; *DNB*] VII. 98, X. 70

Love for love. *See* Congreve (William)

Love (A) song. *See* Ballads and Songs

Lovely Peggy [A ship] III. 118

Low Wood Inn [On Windermere, Westmorland] V. 491 *n:*, 498, 500, VI. 2

Lowe (*Sir* Hudson) *1769–1844* [*b*. Galway; General; Governor of St. Helena, 1815–21; *DNB*] V. 267 *n.,* VIII. 264, 264 *n.,* X. 281

Lowes (Thomas William) *of Ridley Hall, d. 1812* [*d*. Edinburgh 18 Sept.] II. 61–2, 61 *n.,* IV. 221

Lowood [House near Melrose, Roxburghshire]. *See* Somerville (Samuel Charters) *of Lowood*

Lowood Inn. *See* Low Wood Inn

Lowther Castle [Seat of Lord Lonsdale (q.v.), Penrith, Westmorland] II. 215, 215 *n.,* IX. 208, 212, 218

Loyal Foresters. *See* Volunteers

Lubnaig (Loch). *See* Loch Lubnaig

Lucan [Town near Dublin, Ireland] IX. 316

Lucas (Annabella Yorke, *afterwards Baroness*) *afterwards Countess De Grey*. *See* De Grey

Lucerne [Switzerland] XII. 202

Lucian, *c. 120–190* [Greek satirist] VI. 432 (c), XI. 393

Luck-in-a-Bag. *See* Armstrong (Thomas)

Lucretius Caro (Titus) *c. 99–55 B.C.* [Latin poet] quoted, V. 224; Dryden's trans. of, I. 284

Lucy (George) *of Charlecote, 1789–1845* [*succ.* 1823; *Burke LG, Ann. Reg.* 1845, Chron., p. 288] X. 463

Lukin (Robert), writes for Secretary at War (1811) III. 10 *n.*

Lullaby of an infant chief, IV. 217–18, 217 *n.,* 180, 238; for Gaelic air for, *see* Music

Lulworth Castle [Dorset; rented by Sir Robert Peel] VII. 238

Lumsden (Hugh) *of Pitcaple, 1783–1859* [Advocate 1806; Sheriff of Sutherland; *Grant*] IX. 148

Lundie (Robert) *1774–1832* [Minister of Gordon, Berwickshire 1801–7; of Kelso, Roxburghshire 1807–32; *Fasti,* ii. 72–3] V. 2, 487, VI. 472 (a)

Lundin (Richard) *of Auchtermairnie, d. 1832* [Capt. 73rd Foot; *d. unm.*; his father, Christopher Smith (who assumed name of Lundin), was brother of Margaret Smith who *m.* Lachlan Maclean of Torloisk (q.v.), whose dau. Marianne *m.* General Clephane of Carslogie; cousin, therefore, of Mrs Marianne Maclean Clephane of Torloisk (q.v.); *Burke LG*] X. 282 (c), XI. 359 *n.*

Lushington (R.) [Of the Treasury] VIII. 316 *n.,* 317

Lushington, Boldero and Co. [London bankers] III. 90

Lutherburg (Philippe Jacques) *1740–1812* [French painter] XII. 103

Luttrell (Narcissus) *1657–1732* [English annalist and bibliographer; *DNB*] XII. 298, 298 *n.*

Luxmoore (*Miss —*) [Dau. of John Luxmoore (1756–1830), Bishop of St. Asaph] X. 333 *n.*

Lybeaus Desconus [i.e. Le beau desconnu] XII. 275

Lycanthropy, works on, VIII. 67, 67 *n.*

Lyke-wake (A) dirge. *See* Ballads and Songs

Lymington [Town in Hampshire] IX. 343 *n.,* XII. 105

Lynedoch (Thomas Graham, *1st Baron*) *1750–1843* [British general; *cr.* Baron 1814; *DNB*]
    As *General Graham*: at Barrosa (1811) II. 474; given freedom of Edinburgh [Jan. 1814] III. 398; bombards Antwerp [Feb. 1814] XII. 136; as *Baron Lynedoch*: S. writes to (1827) 477

Lyon (George) [Lieut.-Col. 2nd Life Guards; son of George Lyon whose widow, Margaret Stewart, *m.* Sir Adam Ferguson (q.v.)] X. 140

Lyon (John) *b. 1804* [Son of George Lyon and Margaret Stewart, later Lady Ferguson (q.v.); stepson of Sir Adam Ferguson (q.v.)] VIII. 251, 342, IX. 229; X. 498 *n.*; possible reference to, IX. 92

Lyon (*Mrs* John) [Wife of preceding] X. 378, 498 *n.*

541

INDEX

Monteagle (*cont.*)
Earl of Derby; *cr.* Baron 1514; *DNB*] as *Sir Edward Stanley*: at Battle of Flodden [1513] I. 19

Monteath (Robert) [King's Forester; author of *The forester's guide*] X. 276, 276 *n.*

Montecuccoli (*Prince* Raimondo) *1609–80* [Austrian general] IX. 492 (a)

Monteith (Henry) *of Carstairs, 1765–1848* [Lord Provost of Glasgow and M.P. for Selkirk Burghs; *Burke LG*] Candidate for Selkirk Burghs (1819–20) V. 375, VI. 37–8, 69–70, 72, 133, 136, 303; not likely to seek re-election (1824) VIII. 428 *n.*, 429

Monteith (James) [17th-cent. Scottish metal founder] XI. 217

Montemayor (Jorge de) *1520–61* [Spanish poet] VIII. 324 *n.*, 325

Montfauçon (Bernard de) *1655–1741* [French Benedictine scholar] *Antiquité expliquée* by, I. 478, 478 *n.*, 479, VIII. 148 *n.*

Montfort (Simon de) *Earl of Leicester.* See Leicester

Montgomerie (Mathew) *d. 1811* [Writer in Edinburgh; *d.* 8 Aug.] II. 532

Montgomery [or Montgomerie] (Alexander) [Scottish poet, 16th cent.; *DNB*] VIII. 406, 406 *n.*

Montgomery (James) *1771–1854* [Scottish poet and journalist; *DNB*] II. 530, VIII. 147, 147 *n.*, 177, 177 *n.*

Monthly Magazine, I. 294

Monthly Mirror, II. 416, 417 *n.*

Montmorency [Château N. of Paris] IV. 94

Montolieu (Jeanne Isabelle Pauline de Bottens, *baronne de*) *1751–1832* [Swiss author] VI. 12, 12 *n.*, 285, 285 *n.*

Montrose [Royal Burgh NE. Angus] I. 46

Montrose (James Graham, *1st Duke of*) *d. 1742* [Scottish statesman; *succ.* as 4th Marquess 1684; *cr.* Duke 1707; *DNB*] letters of, relating to Rob Roy, XI. 266–7, 266 *n.*

Montrose (James Graham, *3rd Duke of*) *1755–1836* [*succ.* 1790; statesman; *DNB*]
As Lord Justice General, II. 10; S. stays at Buchanan Castle [the Duke's seat near Loch Lomond] (1809) 241; to support Tom's extractorship (1810) 353; S. receives

Montrose (*cont.*)
letters relating to Rob Roy from (1829) XI. 267; mentioned, XII. 8

Montrose (James Graham, *1st Marquess of*) *1612–50* [*succ.* as 5th Earl 1626; *cr.* Marquess 1644; Covenanter but later fought for King Charles; hanged at Edinburgh; *DNB*]
Montrose's Lines, II. 227, 239, 261, 262; his sword, III. 69, 100, 312, VII. 215, 260; at Tippermuir, XII. 406; mentioned, II. 75, III. 28

Montrose (William Graham, *2nd Duke of*) *d. 1790* [*succ.* 1742] XII. 8

Monypenny (Alexander) *1778–1844* [4th son of Lieut.-Col. Alexander Monypenny of Pitmilly, Fife; brother of David Monypenny, Lord Pitmilly (q.v.); W.S. 1801; one of Scott's trustees 1826; *W.S. Soc., Burke LG*] IX. 428, 506, X. 56, 78, 115, 265, 325, 342

Monypenny (David) *of Pitmilly, Lord Pitmilly, 1769–1850* [Eldest son of Lieut.-Col. Alexander Monypenny of Pitmilly, Fife; brother of Alexander Monypenny, W.S. (q.v.); Advocate 1791; Solicitor-General 1811; Bench as Lord Pitmilly 1813–30; *Grant, Burke LG*]
As Solicitor-General, III. 15, 19; as Lord Pitmilly, IV. 271, 271 *n.*, VI. 282

Moody (John) [Character in Vanbrugh's *The provoked husband*]. See Vanbrugh (*Sir John*)

Moore (*Lady* Harriet Janet Sarah Montagu Douglas Scott, *afterwards Lady* Harriet) *1814–70* [6th dau. of Charles, 4th Duke of Buccleuch; *b.* 13 Aug. 1814; *m.* 1842 Rev. Edward Moore, Rector of Frittenden, Kent] ill health of (1822) VII. 46

Moore (James Carrick) *1763–1834* [James Moore, younger brother of Sir John Moore (q.v.); adopted name Carrick on inheriting fortune from a second cousin; surgeon and author; *DNB*] letters from, and S.'s replies to, on article in *QR* on Sir John Moore (1809) II. 249 *n.*, 249–50, 256

Moore (*Sir* John) *1761–1809* [Scottish soldier; Lieut.-General 1805; killed at Corunna; *DNB*]
S. on his conduct in the Peninsula, II. 138, 140, 159, 543, XII. 309; defended by his brother against review in *QR*, II. 249–50, 249 *n.*, 256

Moore (Thomas) *1779–1852* [Irish

Murray (*cont.*)
(July 1819) 427, 401–2; S. introduces
Walter to, by letter [mid-July 1819]
414; Walter visits [late July 1819]
402; S. writes to, on Byron's *Cain*
(Dec. 1821) VII. 37; transmits to
S. mourning ring from Byron (Sept.
1824) VIII. 360; S.'s views on
Lockhart's appointment to editor-
ship of *QR* by (Oct.–Dec. 1825) IX.
249–50, 251–4, XII. 454–6, IX.
284–9, 289–91, 295–6, 297–9, 302–3,
303–4, 307, 309–12, 322, 332, 334,
335–6; on Constable's financial
stability (Nov. 1825) 293 *n.*, 294;
possible sale of *Woodstock* to (Mar.
1826) 475–6, 487, 489, 492, 494, 495,
496; Lockhart complains of inter-
ference with *QR* by (June 1826) X.
67, 67 *n.*; wants to be S.'s publisher
(Nov. 1827) 318, 318 *n.*, 319–20,
343; *The Family Library* published by
(July 1828–June 1830) 470–1, 470 *n.*,
472, 497, XI. 9, 28, 140, 140 *n.*, 164,
364–5; returns to S. his fourth share
of *Marmion* (June 1829) 197, 197 *n.*,
203, 205; sends S. review money
(Oct. 1829) 253, 255; publishes
Letters on demonology (Apr. 1830) 313,
345, 376; wants to purchase *Lives of
the novelists* (Apr. 1830) 324, 324 *n.*,
325; S. due payment from, for a
review (Dec. 1830) 446, 453; might
publish Stewart papers (1831) XII. 9;
called by Byron 'the most timorous of
God's booksellers,' IX. 336; see also
Quarterly (The) Review and *Representa-
tive (The)*
Murray (John) *of Philiphaugh, d. 1830*
[*succ.* 1800; *d. unm.*; elder brother of
James (q.v.; *Burke LG*] XI. 429
Murray (*Sir* John) *8th Bart. of Clermont,
1768?–1827* [*succ.* 1811; Major-
General 1805; General 1825; com-
manded in Red Sea 1798–1800;
Quarter-Master-General of Indian
Army 1801–5; *m.* 1807 Anne Eliza-
beth Cholmondeley, dau. of 2nd
Lord Mulgrave; *DNB*; *Burke, under
Murray of Dunerne*] II. 237
Murray (*Sir* John Archibald) *Lord
Murray, 1778–1859* [2nd son of
Alexander Murray, Lord Hender-
land; Advocate 1800; *m.* 23 Dec.
1826 Mary, dau. of William Rigby of
Oldfield Hall, Cheshire; M.P. Leith
1832–8; knighted 1839; Bench as
Lord Murray 1839; original member
of the Bannatyne Club (q.v.) Feb.
1823; *DNB, Grant*]

Murray (*cont.*)
Probable reference to (1808) II.
111; joint-editor of *ER* while Jeffrey
is in U.S.A. (1813) III. 301; invited
to Abbotsford (1817) IV. 486;
marriage of [1826] X. 160; visits
Abbotsford (1828) 494; and Catholic
emancipation bill (1829) XI. 144
Murray (Mary Rigby, *afterwards Lady*)
1778–1861 [Wife of preceding] X. 160
Murray (Patrick) *of Simprim* [Natural
son of 5th Lord Elibank (q.v.) who
in 1776 entailed on him estate of
Simprim in Berwickshire; Capt. in
Perthshire Regt of Scots Fencible
Cavalry; *m.* 24 May 1802 Susan,
dau. of Sir Robert Murray of Hill-
head, Bart.]
S. and he dig up sculptures at
Meigle [*c.* 1793] XII. 180; to procure
sketches of them (1801) 208; S. hopes
he will come to Kelso (1793) I. 26–8;
S. writes to, about row in Edinburgh
theatre (1794) 30; S. visits Bannockburn with (Apr. 1796) 45; expected
at Rosebank (Mar. 1797) 63; at
Carlisle (Nov. 1797) XII. 60–1; S.
announces his marriage to (Dec.
1797) I. 85–7; S. recalls (June 1799)
meeting, at Newcastle, 92; S. asks
him for contributions to *Edin. Ann.
Reg.* (Feb. 1809) II. 165; collaborates
with S. on subject of Napoleon's
tactics (1811) 482 *n.*, 503, III. 232; S.
presents *Don Roderick* to [July 1811]
II. 503, 509; witnesses Blackwood's
assault on Douglas (May 1818) V.
155; may be one of the sureties for
Adam Ferguson as Deputy Keeper of
the Regalia (Dec. 1818) 251; S.
proposes to meet, at Bath (Mar. 1821)
VI. 376; Adam Ferguson visits, at
Meigle (Nov. 1825) IX. 315
Murray (*Mrs* Patrick) *of Simprim* [Wife
of preceding] receives fine paper copy
of *Minstrelsy* (1803) I. 187
Murray (*Sir* Patrick) *6th Bart. of
Ochtertyre, 1771–1837* [*succ.* 1800;
Advocate 1793; *m.* 1794 Lady Mary
Anne Hope, dau. of 2nd Earl of
Hopetoun (q.v.); M.P. Edinburgh
1806–12; Baron of Exchequer 1820;
elder brother of Sir George Murray
(q.v.); *Grant*] II. 46 *n.*, IX. 441
Murray (William Henry) *1790–1852*
[Son of Charles Murray, actor, and
grandson of Sir John Murray of
Broughton; manager of Theatre
Royal, Edinburgh; *m.* 1819 Anne
Dyke, actress, sister of Elizabeth

INDEX

Paris (Matthew) *1200?–59* [Chronicler; · *DNB*] VII. 449
Parish (Richard) [Edinburgh merchant in Hamburg] VII. 327
Parish (Woodbine) *d. 1848* [Chairman of Board of Excise, Scotland; *d.* 13 May, aged 79; *Ann. Reg.* 1848, Chron., p. 229] VI. 314
Park (Alexander) *1774–1814* [Writer in Selkirk; brother of Archibald and Mungo Park (qq.v.); *d.* Selkirk 1 June; *Tombstone at Selkirk*] IV. 129, 330
Park (Archibald) *1770–1820* [Farmer in Hartwoodmyres, SW. of Selkirk; Comptroller, later Collector, of Customs, Tobermory, Mull; *m.* Margaret, eldest dau. of John Lang, Sheriff Clerk of Selkirkshire (q.v.); *d.* 1 May; brother of Alexander and Mungo Park (qq.v.)]
  Suffers financially (1815) IV. 128–9, 130–1; S. secures pension for (Jan. 1816) 167; goes to Tobermory as Comptroller of Customs (Dec. 1816) 329, (Jan. 1817) 368–9; has trouble with Collector there (Mar. 1817) 418 *n.*, 419; S. refers to appointment (Feb. 1818) V. 94; death of, VI. 187
Park (*Mrs* Archibald) *d. 1818* [Wife of preceding] IV. 129
Park (George) [Tenant in farm of Carterhaugh down to 1814; thereafter tenant in Oakwoodmill] I. 254, 268, 272, III. 523
Park (John) *1783–1809* [Bookseller, London; *d.* London 13 Nov.] II. 44
Park (Mungo) *1771–1806* [Scottish surgeon and African explorer; *b.* Foulshiels, Yarrow; *m.* 2 Aug. 1799 Alice (1780–1840), dau. of Thomas Anderson, surgeon, Selkirk; *DNB*] I. 111 *n.*, IV. 52–5, 129
Park (Mungo) *1801–34* [Son of Archibald Park (q.v.) and Margaret Lang (q.v.), dau. of Andrew Lang (q.v.); nephew of Mungo Park the explorer (q.v.); *d.* Liverpool 23 Jan.; *Ann. Reg.* 1834, Chron., p. 207] VI. 187, 187 *n.*
Park (Thomas) *1759–1834* [English antiquary and bibliographer; *DNB*] III. 93, 93 *n.*, 136, XII. 189, 189 *n.*, 239, 248, 248 *n.*, 260, 403
Parker (—) [Prebendary of Kilroot, *c.* 1785] III. 12
Parker (Christopher) *1761–1804* [Son of Sir Peter Parker (q.v.); brother of Anne Parker, wife of George Ellis

Parker (*cont.*)
  (qq.v.); Vice-Admiral 1804; *d.* 26 May; *DNB*]
  Illness of, I. 215 *n.*, 222 *n.*, XII. 250, 250 *n.*; death of, I. 222 *n.*, XII. 258 *n.*
Parker (Juliana). See Ellis (*Mrs* Charles Parker)
Parker (Margaret Nugent, *afterwards* Lady) *d. 1803* [Dau. of Walter Nugent, Esq.; *m.* Sir Peter Parker, 1st Bart. (q.v.); *d.* 18 Jan.] I. 185 *n.*, XII. 230, 232, 232 *n.*
Parker (*Sir* Peter) *1st Bart. of Basingbourn, 1721–1811* [Baronet 1782; Admiral 1799; *m.* Margaret Nugent; *d.* 21 Dec.; father of Anne, wife of George Ellis (qq.v.), Christopher (q.v.) and Antoinette, wife of John Ellis (q.v.); *DNB*] I. 215 *n.*, II. 21, XII. 225 *n.*, 235, 244, 259, 264, 323
Parliament, general election [1802] I. 150; dissolution of [27 Apr. 1807] XII. 101, 104, I. 364; general election [1807] 361, [1818] V. 167, 168; not to be dissolved till 1826 (Oct. 1825) IX. 235; *see also* Jedburgh Burghs, Roxburghshire, Selkirk Burghs *and* Selkirkshire
  Election of Scottish Peers to, III. 193, 199, 217, 382–3, X. 479–80

Acts:
  Bail [1799] I. 105; Brokerage and reversion Acts, II. 437, 443, 466; Court of Session [1808] I. 351, 358–9, 370, II. 10, 32, 71, 179, XII. 99, 105, 109, 115, 285; [1810] VII. 443; [1821] VI. 342, 357, 382, VII. 43; [1830] XI. 276, 298, 302, 310, 329, 332, 345, 348, 357; Juries [1825] XI. 347; Population census [1811] II. 477; Representation of People, England [1832] XI. 487–8, 487 *n.*; Roads, X. 407, XI. 412; Superannuation, II. 448, 450, 454, 455, 456, 465–6, III. 59; Theatre, XI. 305, 311; Tweed Fisheries [1830], 444, 444 (a); Volunteers, I. 64

Bills:
  Gas bill proposed (1827) X. 159, but dropped (1828) 401; Reform (1831) XI. 487
Parnell (Thomas) *1679–1718* [Irish poet; *DNB*]
  A fairy tale by, quoted, II. 42, VI. 242, IX. 494, XI. 100; *The hermit* by, quoted, IX. 385, 409; *Verses on the Peace* by, quoted, II. 507

Quarterly (The) Review (cont.)
  Art. 6. Tracts on saving banks.
[By W. S. Walker or R. Lundie]
IV. 414–15
  Art. 9. Byron's Childe Harold III.
[By S.] IV. 296 n., 363–5, 363 n.,
366, 377–8, I. 527, XII. 426, IV.
409, VII. 116 n.

  Vol. 16, No. 32, Jan. 1817 [Publ.
Apr.]
  Art. 8. Tales of my Landlord.
[By S.] IV. 318, 356, 365, 378, 379,
388–9, 544, VII. 360

  Vol. 18, No. 36, Jan. 1818 [Publ.
June]
  Art. 1. Poor laws. [By Southey]
XII. 433
  Art. 7. Douglas on military
bridges. [By S.] V. 109, 112, 113,
139
  Art. 13. Kirkton's history. [By S.]
IV. 485, 487, V. 35, 108, 135, 140,
141

  Vol. 19, No. 37, Apr. 1818 [Publ.
Sept.]
  Art. 1. Evelyn's Memoirs. [By
Southey] XII. 433
  Art. 4. Walpole's letters to Mon-
tagu. [By S.] V. 109, 113, 130, 136,
140
  Art. 9. Byron's Childe Harold IV.
[By S.] V. 136, 140, 168, 169 n.,
223, XII. 433

  Vol. 30, No. 60, Jan. 1824 [Publ.
Aug.]
  Art. 12. Correspondence of Lady
Suffolk. [By S.] VII. 390 n. (e), VIII.
258

  Vol. 33, No. 66, Mar. 1826
  Art. 1. Pepys's Memoirs. [By S.]
IX. 349 n., 350, 367, 509, 509 n.

  Vol. 34, No. 67, Sept. 1826
  Art. 10. Life of John Philip
Kemble. [By S.] IX. 509 n., 510, X.
18–19, 18 n., 19 n., 23, 27, 28–9, 30,
32, 47, 92

  Vol. 36, No. 71, June 1827
  Art. 7. Works of John Home. [By
S.] X. 142, 160, 185, 196, 206, 208

  Vol. 36, No. 72, Oct. 1827
  Art. 8. On planting waste lands.
[By S.] X. 274, 298–9, 298 n.

Quarterly (The) Review (cont.)
  Vol. 37, No. 74, Mar. 1828
  Art. 1. On ornamental and landscape gardening. [By S.] X. 299,
315, 317

  Vol. 38, No. 76, Oct. 1828
  Art. 9. Davy's Salmonia. [By S.]
X. 481, 496, XI. 43 n.
  Art. 10. The Roman Catholic
question—Ireland. [By R. Southey]
XI. 24 n., 25–6, 34, 140

  Vol. 39, No. 77, Jan. 1829
  Art. 3. Morier's Hajji Baba in
England. [By S.] X. 435 n., 436,
481, 492, 496, XI. 8, 18

  Vol. 41, No. 81, July 1829
  Art. 5. Ancient history of Scotland.
[Ritson's Annals.] [By S.] XI. 155,
160, 163, 168, 168 n., 177

  Vol. 41, No. 82, Nov. 1829
  Art. 3. Tytler's History of Scotland. [By S.] XI. 155, 156, 160, 168,
170, 178, 270

  Vol. 43, No. 86, Oct. 1830
  Art. 5. Southey's Life of John
Bunyan. [By S.] XI. 392–3

  Vol. 44, No. 88, Feb. 1831
  Art. 5. Pitcairn's Ancient criminal
trials of Scotland. [By S.] XI. 413,
413 n.
Quebec, VI. 236 n., VII. 497
Queen [East Indiaman, destroyed by
fire, 9 July 1800] I. 106, VI. 212
Queen Mab. See Horses
Queen Orraca. See Southey (Robert)
Queen's (The) Marie. See Ballads and
Songs
Queensberry (House of), C. K.
Sharpe's interest in correspondence
of, IV. 316, 354, 354 n., 539
Queensberry (Caroline Montagu
Douglas Scott, afterwards Marchioness
of) 1774–1854 [3rd dau. of 3rd Duke
of Buccleuch (q.v.); m. 1803 Charles
Douglas who succ. as 5th Marquess
of Queensberry (q.v.) in 1810] III.
347
Queensberry (Catherine Hyde, after-
wards Duchess of) 1701–77 [Dau. of
Henry Hyde, Earl of Clarendon; m.
1720 3rd Duke of Queensberry (q.v.);
Prior's 'Kitty'; DNB] III. 318, 356
Queensberry (Charles Douglas, 3rd
Duke of) 1698–1778 [succ. 1711;
DNB] III. 356

INDEX

Roxburghe Peerage Case, I. 358, II. 7–8

Roxburghshire, Scott of Harden's account of, I. 331; S. creates vote for (1811) VII. 460; Collectorship of Taxes for (1821) VI. 409, 411–12, 413–14, 420, 421–2, 421 *n.*, 427, 428–30, 431–2, 434, 436, 455–6, 460–1, 475–7, VII. 9–10, 9 *n.*, (1822) 127, 129, 131–2, 165; Lieutenancy of, VIII. 280–1, 280 *n.*; Parliamentary election for [2 Nov. 1812] (1811) II. 439, 441, VII. 460, (1812) III. 75, 131, 132, 162, 169, 174, 184–5, 186, 192, 197; referred to (1820) VI. 205; Politics in (1817) IV. 482, 500–1, 513, 536, (1818) V. 194, (1819) 470; Roll of Electors, IX. 482, 513; Sheriff Clerk, III. 347; Yeomanry. *See* Volunteers. Roxburghshire, Yeomanry Cavalry. For proposed volunteers in (1819–20), *see* Volunteers. Loyal Foresters

Roxby (Robert). *See* Rokesby (George)

Roy (William) [16th-cent. Franciscan friar; *DNB*] III. 149

Royal Bank of Scotland, I. 435, 436, 457, 502; James Ballantyne's loan from, VI. 472; and Cadell's discharge as bankrupt, XI. 76–8

Royal Celtic Society [Founded Jan. 1820 as Celtic Society; now the Royal Celtic Society] S. presides over meeting of [19 Jan. 1821] VI. 338, 343; S. presides at dinner of [25 May 1821] 452, 454; George Pitt Rose wants to become member of (May 1822) VII. 166; takes part in King's visit [Aug. 1822] 213, 226; has row with Glengarry (1822) 237; S. dines with (1829) XI. 148, 150; mentioned, VIII. 201

Royal Cinque Ports Light Dragoons. *See* Army. 2. Cavalry

Royal Company of Archers, V. 128

Royal Edinburgh Volunteer Light Dragoons. *See* Volunteers

Royal Edinburgh Volunteers. *See* Volunteers

Royal Literary Fund [Founded 1790; incorporated 1818] IV. 275, 325, XI. 269 *n.*, 496; *see also* Royal Society of Literature

Royal Medical Society. *See* Edinburgh. Royal Medical Society

Royal Military College. *See* Sandhurst. For Senior Department, *see* High Wycombe

Royal Society of Edinburgh. *See* Edinburgh

Royal Society of Literature [Founded 1823] VI. 397–405, 397 *n.*, 417–19, 417 *n.*, 488–9, 488 *n.*, VIII. 217 *n.*, X. 184–5, 208; *see also* Royal Literary Fund

Roye [Town in Dept. of Somme, NE. France] IV. 83, XII. 139 *n.*, 141

Rubens (Peter Paul) *1577–1640* [Flemish artist] IV. 226, XII. 136

Rullion Green [Locality near Penicuik, Midlothian] VIII. 146

Rumbling Bridge [Place on borders of Kinross and Perthshire] VII. 466

Rundell, Bridge & Co. (*Messrs*) [Afterwards Rundell, Bridge, and Rundell; goldsmiths and jewellers, 32 Ludgate Hill, London] I. 517, IV. 390

Runnington (*Miss* —) [Dau. of Charles Runnington (q.v.)] XII. 5 *n.*, 6

Runnington (Charles) *1751–1821* [English lawyer; *m.* 1777 Anna Maria Shepherd, sister of Sir Samuel Shepherd (q.v.); *DNB*] XII. 5 *n.*

Rupert, *Prince, 1619–82* [Son of Elizabeth, Queen of Bohemia and Frederick V, Count Palatine; hero of the Civil War in England; *DNB*] VII. 34

Rush. *See* Bushe

Rushyford [Hamlet near Bishop Auckland, Durham] I. 356, II. 298

Russell (—) *d. 1825 or earlier*, IX. 226

Russell (*Misses*) *of Ashiestiel,* XII. 127, 129, 131, 132, 133

Russell (Alexander Pringle) *1792–1818* [5th son of Col. William Russell of Ashiestiel (q.v.); *b.* Ashiestiel 28 Nov.; *d. unm.* at Madras 28 Jan.]

Sets out for Madras (1808) II. 13, 13 *n.*, 19; death of, V. 191, VI. 117

Russell (Anne) *1780–1849* [3rd dau. of Col. William Russell of Ashiestiel (q.v.); *b.* Cuddalore, India, 1 Feb.; *d. unm.* at Ashiestiel 29 May; S.'s first cousin] I. 36, V. 192, 453, VI. 182, 234, 234 *n.*, IX. 234, 415, X. 43, 47

Russell (Catherine). *See* Rutherford (Catherine Russell, *afterwards Mrs*)

Russell (Claud) *1769–1846* [Accountant in Edinburgh; 5th son of John Russell of Roseburne, W.S.; *m.* (1) Euphemia (*d.* 1836) dau. of Rev. Dr. James Gillespie, Principal of St. Mary's Coll., St. Andrews, and (2) Cecelia Margaret, dau. of Sir John Leslie, 4th Bart. of Wardis, and

INDEX

Saltoun (cont.)
Fraser, 15th Lord Saltoun; dowager in 1826, her son having become 16th Lord in 1815] XI. 41
Salvo (Carlo, marchese di) [Author of work on Byron, 1825] IX. 236-7, 236 n.
Samieston [Estate between Jedburgh and Cessford, Roxburghshire]. See Robson (Charles) of Samieston
Sanderson (—) [Litigant in Selkirk Sheriff Court 1801] I. 116-17
Sanderson (—), wants appointment in India (1821) VI. 391
Sanderson (John) [Joiner, Galashiels] V. 65, 254; see also Sanderson & Paterson
Sanderson (John) [Lapidary, Edinburgh; Burgess and Guild Brother 1805] II. 379, 398
Sanderson & Paterson (Messrs) [Building Contractors and Carriers, Galashiels; firm founded in 1806 by John Sanderson, joiner, and William Paterson, mason; employed at Abbotsford 1812-19 and continued to supply goods to S. thereafter] paid for work at Abbotsford (Sept. 1812) III. 178; debt to, due by Robert Boyd (Apr. 1814) 432; S. accepts estimates of, for first portion of present building (Dec. 1816) IV. 333; references to, while building is in progress (1817) 396, 399, 424; plans for first study sent to (Jan. 1818) V. 65-6; employed as carriers by S. (May 1818) 158; to finish dining-room [late 1818] 254; S. pays account to, for work done at Abbotsford (Feb. 1820) VI. 131, (July 1820) 219
Sandford (Daniel) 1766-1830 [2nd son of Daniel Sandford of Sandford Hall, Shropshire, and Sarah Chapone; Bishop of Edinburgh; Burke LG, DNB] V. 60, 60 n.
Sandhurst. Royal Military College. S. wants Walter to go to (1820) VI. 271, (1821) 370; negotiations for Walter's attendance at (1821) 388, 406, 423-4, 423 n., 426, 435-6, 453, (1823) VII. 361-2, 377, VIII. 3-4, 25, 57; Walter at (1823) 73-4, 75, 100, 106, 110, (1824) 159, 196, 199
Sandwich Islands, VII. 4, VIII. 340
Sandyknowe [S.'s grandfather's farm N. of Kelso, Roxburghshire] S. visits (1788) I. 9-10; mentioned (1809) II. 259; S. recalls (1826) childhood incident at, X. 27, 27 n.; see also Smailholm

Sang (The) of the Outlaw Murray. See Ballads and Songs
Sangster (—) [Litigant in Selkirk Sheriff Court 1800] I. 101
Sanquhar [Royal Burgh in Dumfriesshire] I. 431, IV. 472, VI. 279
Santo Domingo. See Haiti
Sappho [Greek poetess, 7th cent. B.C. II. 412, III. 143
Saragossa [Town in N. Spain] siege of [1809] alluded to, V. 328, VIII. 70
Sass (Richard) 1774-1849 [Landscape painter; DNB] I. 489, III. 179
Satyre on the familie of Stairs. See Hamilton (Sir William) of Whitelaw
Savage (Richard) 1697-1743 [English poet and dramatist; DNB] Works, I. 33; The wanderer, quoted, VII. 146
Saville (John) d. 1803 [Vicar-choral of Lichfield Cathedral; friend of Anna Seward; d. 2 Aug., aged 67] III. 29
Sawmill. See Abbotsford. II. Estate. (2) Separate Parts. Huntlyburn
Scalloway [Near Lerwick, Shetland] XII. 124; see also [Scott II] Scott of Scalloway
Scarborough [Coastal town, Yorkshire] IV. 265
Scarlett (Sir James) 1st Baron Abinger. See Abinger
Schetky (John Christian) 1778-1874 [Artist; b. Edinburgh; DNB] Illustrations of Walter Scott's Lay by, I. 527, II. 66, XII. 395 n., 396
Schiller (Johann Christoph Friedrich von) 1759-1805 [German poet] II. 495, VIII. 54, X. 440; S.'s trans. of Fiesco by, I. 57, 57 n., 130 n., X. 283, 331, 348; Die Räuber, V. 67
Schlegel (August Wilhelm von) 1767-1845 [German author and literary critic] IV. 437-8, VII. 270
Schneiders (Frans). See Snyders
Scholey (Robert) [London publisher; one of the publishers of Weber's Tales of the East and Edin. Ann. Reg., Vol. 1] I. 421, 427
Schopenhauer (Arthur) 1788-1860 [German philosopher] S. writes to (1832) XII. 47-8, 47 n.
Schubart (Henriette von) [German musical composer] V. 14, 14 n.
Scornfu' Nansy. See Ballads and Songs
Scotland, S. on climate of (1824) VIII. 261; S. appointed to serve on Commission on universities of (1826) X. 92, 106, 106 n.; S. on early languages of (1828) 365-7; declining

622

Scott (*cont.*)

newspaper in Isle of Man (May–June 1810) 440–1, 442, 444; birth of his daughter Eliza (Sept. 1810) 447, 447 *n.*; Charlotte stands godmother to Eliza, 447, 451, 454, 458; has prospect of post in Demerara (Nov. 1810) 399, 399 *n.*, 451–2, 453; but appointment not available, 399 *n.*, 455; S. opposes his being a clergyman (Nov. 1810) 452; S. suggests he should write biographies for *Edin. Ann. Reg.* (Dec. 1810) 453; S. on prospects of (Aug. 1811) II. 532–3; his appointment to Paymastership of 70th Foot (Sept. 1811) III. 5, 5 *n.*, 6–7, 7 *n.*, 8, 9–10, 9 *n.*, XII. 331–2, III. 13–15, VII. 464, III. 18, 20, VII. 400; unable to visit Ellis at Sunninghill (Jan. 1813) XII. 340, 340 *n.*; introduced by letter to Terry at Perth (July 1813) III. 296, 297, VII. 401, 466; would like to be a District Paymaster (July 1813) 401, 466; ordered to leave Perth and passes through Ayr and Belfast [July–Aug. 1813] 401; and passes through Donahadee, III. 352, VII. 401; writes from Dublin (8 Aug. 1813) 401–2; Regiment ordered to Canada (Sept. 1813) 466–7, III. 349, 353–4, 354 *n.*; rumour that he is author of *Waverley* (1814–24) 502, IV. 283–4, 294, 340, 340 *n.*, 367, 417, VI. 311, VIII. 337 *n.*; S. urges him to write a novel (Dec. 1814) III. 502–3; draws bills on S. [*c.* Oct. 1815] I. 491, 494; mentioned as being permanently in Canada (May 1816) IV. 232; S. gives financial statement to, following John's death (May 1816) VII. 478–81, 483; sends deer's foot knocker from Canada (Dec. 1816) IV. 337, V. 32; his share of John's estate (Dec. 1816) IV. 340; S. tries to get a post for, in Canada (Jan. 1817) 366–8, 417; inquiries into moral character of, and S.'s defence of (1817) 406–7, VII. 484–93, 496; S. on his failings (Mar. 1817) IV. 417; draws on S. for £500 (Sept. 1817) 504; bill of, and Dr Tobin (Sept. 1817) 530–1, 530 *n.*; wants tutor for his son (Dec. 1817) V. 30–1; S. advises him to return to Scotland (Dec. 1817) 31; note of his cash in S.'s hands (Dec. 1817) VII. 494–6; draws on S. for £65. 5*s.* o*d.* (Apr. 1818) I. 526; marriage of his daughter Jessie [1 Nov. 1819] V. 510, VI. 1–2;

Scott (*cont.*)

draws on S. for £800 (Dec. 1819) 7, 48; S. gives financial statement to, following death of their mother (Jan. 1820) 107–9; S. outlines plans for his son Walter (1820) 229–33, (1821) 393–4, 396; S. gives financial statement to (July 1820) 233–4; seeks posts in Quebec and then in Bahamas (Sept. 1820) 236 *n.*; in financial difficulties (Feb. 1822) VII. 498–500, (Nov. 1822) 274; text of letter to S. from [27 May 1822] 498 *n.*; S. on his ill health and bad habits (Oct. 1822) 266, (Nov. 1822) 275, (Dec. 1822) 285, (Mar. 1823) 350–1; death of, 350 *n.*, 356, 357, 366, VIII. 6, 200, 261 *n.*; sole assets of, at death, VII. 511 *n.*; bills drawn by, honoured by S. (Apr. 1823) 501; claim by War Office against, for Irish funds (1823) VIII. 130, (1824) VII. 504–5, 511 *n.*, VIII. 274–5, 414, 445, 446–7, 447 *n.*, (1825) IX. 305–6, (1829) XI. 211; S. says (1824) he has suffered financial loss by, VIII. 288; Robert Shortreed on, III. 429 *n.*

Scott (*Mrs* Thomas) *1776–1848* [S.'s sister-in-law; wife of preceding; *d.* Canterbury 13 Apr.]

Private income of (Sept. 1809) VII. 432, (Oct. 1811) III. 15, (Dec. 1823) VII. 502; S. advises, to delay following Tom to Canada (14 Sept. 1813) 468–9; approaching confinement of (Sept. 1813) III. 350, VII. 469, (Oct. 1813) 470–1; in Cork (1813) III. 350, 354 *n.*, VII. 472, (1814) III. 249 *n.*; S. sends Bank bill to (Mar. 1814) 415, VII. 475; S. advises, not to go to Canada but to go to Dumfries (Mar. 1814) 474–6; sails for Halifax [28 Mar. 1814] III. 429, 429 *n.*; returns from Canada to Dumfries (1816) VIII. 484, IV. 340, 366; in Edinburgh (Mar. 1817) 408; S. sends money to (Mar. 1817) 422, 426; sails from Greenock for Canada (21 Apr. 1817] 426 *n.*, VII. 492 *n.*; returns to Scotland from Canada (Sept. 1823) VIII. 93, 107, 200; has been at Abbotsford (Nov. 1823) 126; S. arranges income of (Dec. 1823) VII. 501–4; has trouble with War Office over her pension (Dec. 1823) 503, (Mar. 1824) 504–5, 506, (May 1824) 507, VIII. 275; at Abbotsford (Jan. 1824) 143; S.'s efforts to help, financially (Mar.

Scott (*cont.*)

464; S. proposes to present gold watch to (May 1816) 480; S. considers future of (May 1816) 481, (Dec. 1817) V. 30–1, (Oct. 1819) VI. 3, (Dec. 1819) 50, (Jan. 1820) 109, (July 1820) 229–33; to come from Canada to S. (Feb. 1821) 347; S. secures cadetship in India for [Mar. 1821] 393–4, 393 *n.*, 396, VII. 285; outfit for (Aug. 1821) 3, (May 1822) 179; S.'s opinion of (Feb. 1822) 64–5, 499, 92; mentioned (June 1822) 207; acts as page during George IV's visit to Edinburgh [Aug. 1822] 226; Constable's good opinion of (Oct. 1822) 254 *n.*; leaves Edinburgh with Huxley (Feb. 1823) 327, 329; is settled at Addiscombe Academy (Feb. 1823) 329, 337, 351, VIII. 107, 130, (1824) 143, 200–1, VII. 507–8, VIII. 275–6, 344; and studying for the Engineers, VII. 329, VIII. 130, 200; but may have to transfer to the Artillery (May 1824) VII. 507–8, VIII. 275–6; S. expects him at Midsummer 1823, 6, 11; S.'s good opinion of (Sept. 1823) 93; expected at Christmas 1823, 126, 130, 167; does not share with his sisters in S.'s mother's legacy (Dec. 1823) VII. 502; S. has remonstrated with him on his handwriting (Dec. 1823) 503; gains prize at Addiscombe (Jan. 1824) VIII. 143; S. has no letters from (Mar.–Apr. 1824) VII. 506, VIII. 224, 270; at Edinburgh and going to Ayr (June 1824) 316; S.'s opinion of (July 1824) 331; mentioned (Oct. 1824) 414, 415; hopes to be appointed to Engineers (Dec. 1824) 451; S.'s good reports of (May 1825) IX. 104, 112, 123–4; given temporary rank of Lieutenant, 121, 121 (a); appointed to Engineers, Bombay Presidency (1825) 104 *n.*; S. makes arrangements for his equipment (1825–6) 106–7, 120, 384–5, 414, 415–16, 426, X. 30; loan to S. from John Gibson for equipment (1826–7) 31, 81, 86–8, 334–5; Brewster assists (Nov. 1825) IX. 270, 283, 305; S. on his studies (Oct. 1825) 241, 242, (Nov. 1825) 305; going to India (Feb. 1826) 414, 422, 430, X. 10; good report of, from India (Jan. 1827) 154, (Apr. 1827) 188, 191; S. has letter from (Oct. 1827) 288; Sir John Malcolm's approval of (May 1830) XI. 409;

Scott (*cont.*)

proposes to return to Britain to study engineering (Sept. 1830) 393–6, 393 *n.*, (Feb. 1831) 478

Scott (William) [Banker at Ayr] VII. 417, 417 *n.*, 419, 420, 421, 422, 457, 468, 471, 473, 483, 489, 490

Scott (William) *d. 1800* [S.'s cousin; son of Thomas Scott, 1731–1823 (q.v.) and brother of Charles Scott of Knowesouth (q.v.); lost when *Queen* East Indiaman was destroyed by fire at St. Salvadore 9 July] I. 106, VI. 212

Scott (William) *d. 1835* [Son of Sir William Scott, afterwards Lord Stowell (q.v.), and nephew of Lord Eldon (q.v.)] VI. 167, 306, 306 *n.*

Scott (William) *1800?–69* [Natural son of S.'s brother Daniel (q.v.) and Carrie Lamb, afterwards Mrs Thomas Mitchell (q.v.); brought up by his mother with S.'s help; apprenticed in 1821 to David Bridges, clothier, High Street, Edinburgh; went to Canada 1828 where he *d.* in poor circumstances]

Biog. note on, II. 234 *n.*; S. comes to terms with William's mother at Selkirk regarding (1806) I. 295; annuity to, VII. 418, 434, IV. 379, V. 42; S. considers his future (1809), II. 234; references to (1811) III. 19, (1826) IX. 454; goes to Canada (1828) X. 412, 487–8, 489 *n.*, XI. 13

Scott (*Sir* William) *afterwards 1st Baron Stowell. See* Stowell

II. *With Territorial Designations*

Abbotsford

Scott (Anne) *1803–33* [Younger dau.; *b.* 2 Feb.; *d. unm.* 25 June; buried in Kensal Green Cemetery, London]

Birth of, I. 176; has had face trouble (Apr. 1805) XII. 382; is like her mother (1806) I. 307; has cough (Apr. 1807) XII. 108; ill with inflammatory fever (Apr. 1810) II. 325, 327; at Mertoun (Dec. 1810) VII. 454; at Bowhill [14 Nov. 1817] V. 9; tires of visit of the Misses MacAllister (Sept. 1819) 483; S. proposes to take her on a Continental tour about July 1820 (Dec. 1819) VI. 42; afraid of Radicals (Dec. 1819) 42; S. on her prospects of marriage (1820) 183, 201, 247, (1824) VIII.

INDEX